SAM FAY
1-401-624-6491
K-202 8AM.
T-Th-FRI
INST
P. GROGER

Teach Yourself Visual dBASE 5.5 Programming in 21 Days

Teach Yourself Visual dBASE 5.5 Programming in 21 Days

Ori Gurewich
Nathan Gurewich

SAMS PUBLISHING

201 West 103rd Street
Indianapolis, Indiana 46290

International Standard Book Number: 0-672-30673-5

Library of Congress Catalog Card Number: 95-71946

98 97 96 95 4 3 2 1

Interpretation of the printing code: the rightmost double-digit number is the year of the book's printing; the rightmost single-digit, the number of the book's printing. For example, a printing code of 95-1 shows that the first printing of the book occurred in 1995.

Composed in AGaramond and MCPdigital by Macmillan Computer Publishing

Printed in the United States of America

Publisher and President *Richard K. Swadley*
Acquisitions Manager *Greg Wiegand*
Development Manager *Dean Miller*
Managing Editor *Cindy Morrow*
Marketing Manager *Gregg Bushyeager*

Acquisitions Editor
Christopher Denny

Development Editor
L. Angelique Brittingham

Production Editor
Kitty Wilson

Copy Editors
Cheri Clark
Lisa Lord

Technical Reviewer
Sundar Rajan

Borland International, Inc., Technical Reviewers
Michael Martinelli
Chad Raynal

Editorial Coordinator
Bill Whitmer

Technical Edit Coordinator
Lynette Quinn

Formatter
Frank Sinclair

Editorial Assistants
Sharon Cox
Andi Richter
Rhonda Tinch-Mize

Cover Designer
Tim Amrhein

Book Designer
Alyssa Yesh

Production Team Supervisor
Brad Chinn

Production
Angela Bannan, Carol Bowers, Mona Brown, Michael Brummitt, Charlotte Clapp, Michael Dietsch, Jason Hand, Michael Henry, Damon Jordan, Ayanna Lacey, Paula Lowell, Steph Mineart, Brian-Kent Proffitt, Bobbi Satterfield, SA Springer, Susan Van Ness, Mark Walchle, Colleen Williams

Indexer
Jeanne Clark

Overview

Contents

Acknowledgments

We would like to thank Chris Denny, the acquisition editor for this book; Angelique Brittingham, the development editor; Kitty Wilson, the production editor; and all the other people at Sams Publishing who contributed to this book.

Thanks also to Borland International, who supplied us with technical information and various betas and upgrades of the software product. In particular, thanks to Nan Borreson from Borland International.

About the Authors

Ori Gurewich and **Nathan Gurewich** are well-known authors of several best-selling books in the areas of Visual Basic for Windows, Visual C++ programming, multimedia programming, database design and programming, and other topics.

Ori Gurewich

Ori Gurewich holds a bachelor's degree in electrical engineering from Stony Brook University, New York. His background includes working as a senior software engineer and as a software consultant engineer for software companies, and developing professional multimedia and Windows applications. He is an expert in the field of PC programming and network communications, and he has developed various multimedia algorithms for the PC. Ori can be contacted via the following e-mail addresses:

CompuServe: CompuServe ID `72072,312`
Microsoft Network: `Ori_Gurewich`
Internet: `Ori_Gurewich@msn.com`

Nathan Gurewich

Nathan Gurewich holds a master's degree in electrical engineering from Columbia University, New York, and a bachelor's degree in electrical engineering from Hofstra University, Long Island, New York. Since the introduction of the PC, Nathan has been involved in the design and implementation of commercial software packages for the PC. He is an expert in the field of PC programming and in providing consulting services in the areas of local area networks, wide area networks, database management and design, and software marketing. Nathan can be contacted via the following e-mail addresses:

CompuServe: CompuServe ID `75277,2254`
Microsoft Network: `Nathan_Gurewich`
Internet: `Nathan_Gurewich@msn.com`

Introduction

Welcome to the fascinating world of Visual dBASE!

As the word *Visual* implies, you perform the dBASE programming visually. This means that you use the mouse and the keyboard to design your Windows applications. So as you can imagine, designing and implementing Visual dBASE programs amounts to a lot of clicking and dragging with your mouse.

Applications You Can Design with dBASE

Basically, you can use dBASE for implementing any Windows program that you can think of. The word dBASE implies that the dBASE programming language has to do with database programming. In fact, this is the case. With Visual dBASE you can design very sophisticated database-related applications. This means that the designers of dBASE incorporated into the dBASE programming language statements and functions that are typically needed when designing database-related projects. Therefore, as you'll see during the course of this book, you'll be able to easily open databases, search for data in databases, perform relational database operations, and perform other common database operations.

No previous database programming is assumed in this book. So all the database know-how that you'll need is covered in this book. That is, you'll learn about databases, tables, fields, linking tables, relations, and so on.

But as stated, dBASE is useful even if your project has nothing to do with databases.

The dBASE Programming Language

Once you visually design the windows of your applications, you'll have to write code. The code-writing process is no different from writing code with other programming languages. Therefore, you'll use various decision-making statements such as `IF` and `FOR` loops. This book assumes no previous programming experience, so all the programming topics you'll need are covered in this book.

Practice and Experiment

There is only one way to learn a programming language: to practice and to experiment by actually writing programs. During the course of this book you'll be instructed to design and implement many programs. Each program demonstrates several features and capabilities of Visual dBASE. It is very important that you implement the programs of this book, because that's the only way you can master the art of programming. In addition, it is recommended that you further explore the programs you are designing by modifying them. Instead of just asking yourself what would happen if I do this instead of this, actually perform the experiment and observe the results.

Q&A, Quiz, and Exercise Sections

Another important component in the study of this book is the sections that appear at the end of each chapter. Each chapter ends with a section of questions and answers, a quiz, and exercises. Make sure to read these sections, and try to solve the quizzes and the exercises in each chapter. The answers to the questions, quizzes, and exercises are provided in the chapters, but it is recommended that you try to solve them by yourself before looking at the answers.

VBX Controls

Visual dBASE for Windows is a highly modular programming language. One of the main advantages of a modular programming language is the fact that you can design projects by "plugging in" external software modules. Suppose you need to implement a certain feature in your program, and this particular feature is not included in the out-of-the-box Visual dBASE package. One solution is to implement the feature by writing dBASE code. That is, you'll implement the feature by yourself. However, this process may take you a long time. The advantage of a modular programming language is that you can utilize third-party software modules called *VBX controls*. These VBX controls enable you to incorporate the particular feature that you are looking for.

So instead of sitting down and spending a huge amount of time designing a certain feature, you can spend your time searching for a VBX control that is readily available at a reasonable price. This is the trend used by programmers who are using modern modular programming languages such as Visual dBASE, Delphi, Visual Basic, and Visual FoxPro. In this book you'll have a chance to learn about various VBX controls.

Multimedia and 3D Virtual Reality

Nowadays, PC vendors ship their PCs with multimedia equipment already installed in the PC. In this book you'll also learn how to incorporate advanced multimedia technology into your dBASE projects. Therefore, you can use dBASE for implementing encyclopedia-type applications, animation programs, programs that play sound WAV files, MIDI sound files, CD audio, and movie AVI files.

Although the majority of this book concentrates on "classic" dBASE programs such as database operations, in this book you'll also learn how you can use dBASE for performing some very sophisticated 3D virtual reality programs with dBASE. In particular, you'll learn how to do two-dimensional drawing with a text editor, and then you'll learn how you can use an external VBX control that converts your 2D drawing to a 3D picture. You'll then learn how to implement code that lets you use the keyboard and the mouse for "traveling" inside the 3D picture. You'll be able to travel from one room to another, run across the halls, and so on. And as you use the keyboard or the mouse, the 3D picture will change according to your movements! Furthermore, you'll be able to incorporate all types of moving objects into your 3D pictures! As you will see, dBASE can also be used for fun. The 3D virtual reality program is presented only at the end of the book (Chapters 20 and 21) because first you have to know the dBASE fundamentals that are covered in the earlier parts of this book.

The Disk You Can Order to Accompany This Book

As stated, some of the programs that you'll write in this book are very powerful, state-of-the-art technology Windows applications. These programs require external software modules that extend the capability of the Visual dBASE package. It is highly recommended that even if you do not have the external VBX files, you read the material. This way, you'll be able to understand how dBASE can be extended without limits and how you can incorporate external VBX modules into your dBASE projects.

An offer for the book's companion disk is included at the end of this book. This disk includes all the external VBX modules that some of the book's programs utilize, as well as all the source code of all the programs that are covered in this book.

Teach Yourself Visual dBASE 5.5 Programming in 21 Days

The title of this book is *Teach Yourself Visual dBASE 5.5 Programming in 21 Days.* There are 21 chapters in this book, and this means that you are expected to complete a chapter each day. However, you should work at your own pace. That is, if you feel comfortable completing 2 (or more) chapters a day, then go for it. Likewise, if you feel that you want to stay with some chapters for more than a day, do it.

As you'll soon see, Visual Basic is an easy programming language, and is actually fun to work with. So relax, and prepare yourself for a very pleasant journey.

WEEK 1

AT A GLANCE

1

2

3

4

5

6

7

This is your first week! In Chapter 1 you'll immediately dive into the dBASE water! As you'll see, you'll implement a dBASE program using the visual tools of Visual dBASE. You'll also learn how to create standalone EXE programs, so your user who does not own dBASE will be able to execute your dBASE programs just like any other Windows application.

During the course of this book you'll design programs that deal with databases. This means that you will need some databases that your dBASE program will utilize. How will you generate the dBASE database? You'll use some of the database tools of dBASE.

In Chapter 2 you'll learn how to use dBASE for creating tables, saving the structures of the tables, navigating among the records of a table, entering records, deleting records, indexing, and other important database-related topics you'll need to understand during the course of this book.

Week 1 at a Glance

In Chapter 3 you will write a dBASE program that uses a table. You'll design a table and then write a program that uses this table.

Like any programming language, dBASE includes basic programming building blocks that enable you to write programs with decision-making statements such as `IF` statement, `For` loops, and `Case` statements. In Chapter 4 you'll practice with the programming building blocks of dBASE. You'll also learn how to add procedures and methods to your programs.

In Chapter 5 you'll learn how to implement dialog boxes. You'll implement a dBASE program that uses the built-in dialog boxes, and you'll also implement a dBASE program that uses a custom-made dialog box. You'll learn about the important topic of multiple-form dBASE programs.

In Chapter 6 you'll learn about important menu topics: You'll learn how to design a cascading menu (a submenu), how to assign shortcut keys to menu items, how to include a separator bar in a menu, how to write code that disables and enables menu items, and how to write code that places a check mark next to a menu item.

In Chapter 7 you'll write a program that utilizes three popular Windows controls: a scroll bar, radio buttons, and check boxes.

1

WEEK
1

Writing Your First dBASE Program

In this chapter you will write your first Windows program using the Visual dBASE for Windows programming language. Writing a true Windows program with Visual dBASE for Windows is easy because it includes many useful visual tools.

You'll learn three things in this chapter:

- How to write a dBASE program
- How to execute a dBASE program
- How to make a "standalone" version of your program so that other people who don't own the dBASE package can execute your program

Visual Programming

You'll use the following two steps when you write a dBASE Windows program:

- The visual programming step
- The code programming step

During the *visual programming step*, you design your program by using software tools that come with the dBASE package. With these tools, you design your application using the mouse and the keyboard. You don't have to write any code in this step! You just have to know how to use the tools to place objects (for example, menus, pushbuttons, scroll bars, and so on) in your application's windows.

In the *code programming step*, you write code using the text editor that comes with the dBASE package. The code statements are written in the dBASE programming language.

The SAY Program

Later in this chapter you will implement a simple dBASE program called SAY. Before you start writing the SAY program, specify how the program should look and what it should do.

When you execute the SAY program, its main window should look like the one shown in Figure 1.1.

The main window of the SAY program has two buttons (Say Hello and Clear) and one blank entry field (an edit box). When you click the Say Hello button, the SAY program should display the text `Hello! This is my first program.` in the entry field. (See Figure 1.2.)

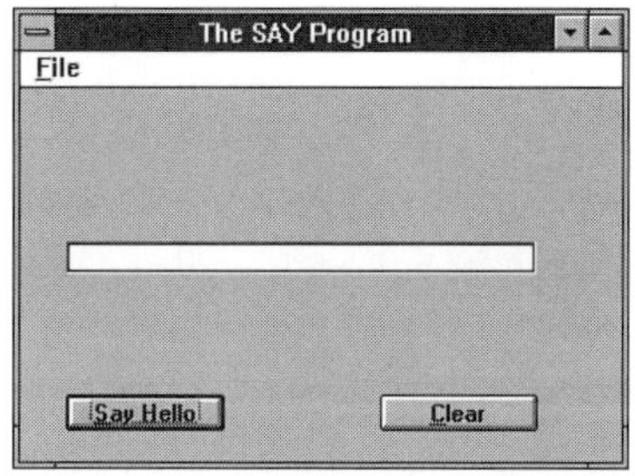

Figure 1.1.
The main window of the SAY program.

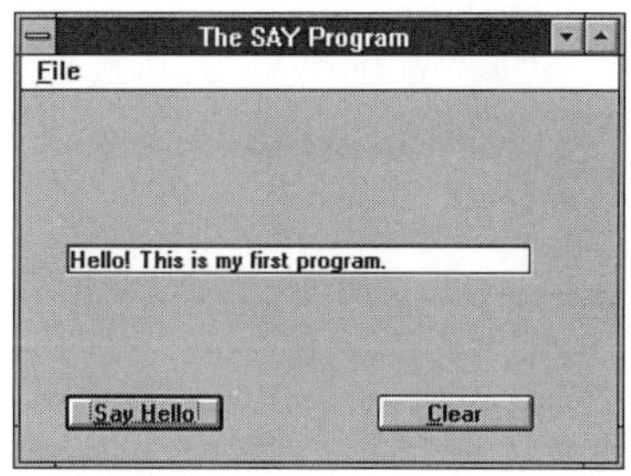

Figure 1.2.
The SAY program after you click the Say Hello button.

When you click the Clear button, the SAY program should clear the entry field (that is, erase the text in the edit box).

The main window of the SAY program also has a File menu, shown in Figure 1.3. It has only one item: Exit. When you select Exit from the File menu, the program should terminate.

Figure 1.3.
The File menu of the SAY program.

Now that you know what the SAY program is supposed to do, it's time to write it on your own. Follow the step-by-step instructions in the following sections to write the SAY program.

Creating the Program File of the SAY Program

The *program file* is the file your user has to execute in order to see your program in action. For example, if you write a program called MyProg.WFM, whoever wants to see your program in action will have to execute the file MyProg.WFM.

In this section you'll create the program file of the SAY program: SAY.WFM. In the next sections of this chapter you'll customize the SAY.WFM program file until it finally behaves and looks as it should.

Start the dBASE for Windows program as follows:

☐ Double-click the icon of the dBASE for Windows program in the dBASE for Windows program group.

Windows responds by running the dBASE for Windows program. Figure 1.4 shows the desktop of dBASE for Windows.

Figure 1.4.
The desktop of dBASE for Windows.

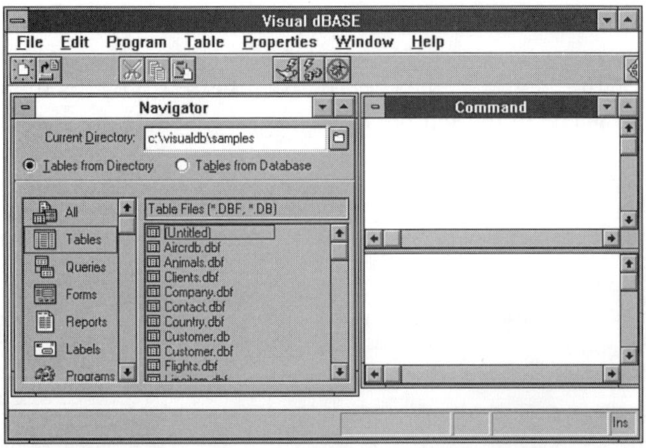

> **Note:** Depending on your desktop setting, your dBASE program may look different from the one shown in Figure 1.4.

The dBASE desktop currently has two windows: Command and Navigator. You type dBASE commands in the *Command window* to create files, open files, modify files, and perform hundreds of other operations. The dBASE *Navigator window* and the menu bar also let you perform dBASE operations. However, in this and most other chapters in this book, you'll be instructed to perform dBASE operations using the Command window. Why? The commands you type in the Command window are regular dBASE statements—so it's a good way to practice with the dBASE programming language.

Since you're going to use only the Command window in this chapter, you can minimize the Navigator window and maximize the Command window:

- ☐ Click the icon at the upper-left corner of the Navigator window and select Minimize from the system menu that pops up.
- ☐ Click the icon at the upper-left corner of the Command window and select Maximize from the system menu that pops up.

Your dBASE desktop should now look like the one shown in Figure 1.5.

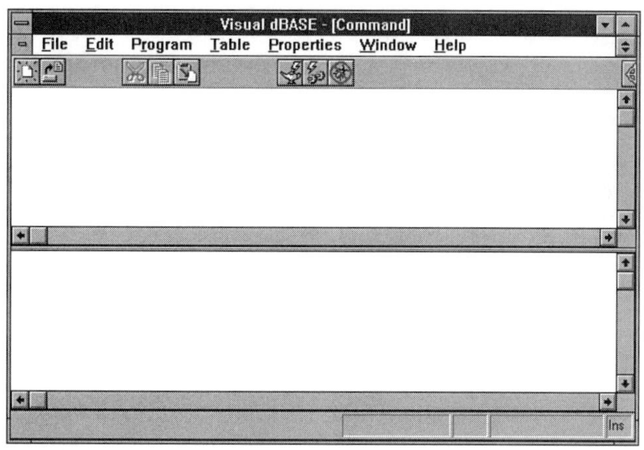

Figure 1.5.
The dBASE desktop with the Command window maximized.

When maximized, the Command window occupies the entire desktop of dBASE. Also, the title of the dBASE window contains the text `[Command]`, which means that the Command window is the currently active window.

Soon you'll be instructed to use the Command window to create the SAY program file. However, before you do that, first get familiar with the Command window. As shown in Figure 1.5, the Command window has two parts. The upper part of the window (where the cursor is located) is the input pane and the bottom part is the results pane. The *input pane* is where you type dBASE commands and the *results pane* is where the results of the commands are displayed.

Note: If your Command window looks different from the one in Figure 1.5 (for example, the input pane is at the right side of the window and the results pane is at the left side of the window), then do the following:

- ☐ Select Command Window Properties from the Properties menu of dBASE.

  dBASE responds by displaying the Command window properties window.

- ☐ Select the Top option in the Input Pane Position options box and then click the OK button.

Note: Your Command window should now look like the one shown in Figure 1.5, with the input pane (where the cursor is located) at the top of the window and the results pane at the bottom of the window.

You can change the size of the panes by dragging the horizontal center divider between them. If you drag the center divider upward, then the results pane increases and the input pane decreases. If you drag the center divider downward, then the results pane decreases and the input pane increases.

To see the Command window in action, practice by typing the `DIR` command to display all the files in the root directory of your C: hard drive:

- ☐ Type `DIR C:\*.*` in the Command window, then press Enter on your keyboard.

  dBASE responds by listing all the files of your C:\ directory in the results pane of your Command window. Figure 1.6 shows a typical directory listing.

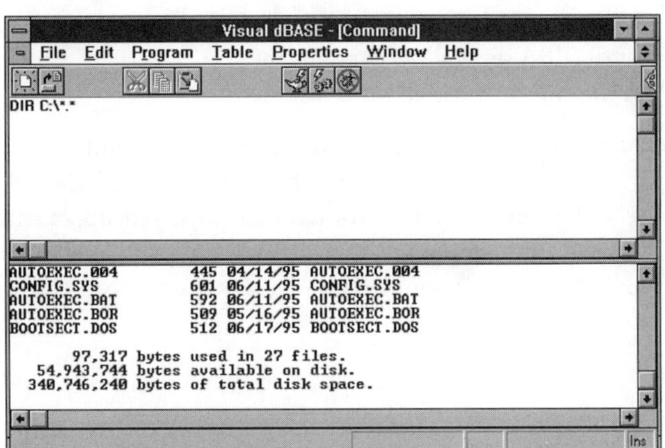

Figure 1.6.
The Command window after you execute the command `DIR C:\*.*`.

If the list of files in your C:\ directory requires more space than the size of the results pane, dBASE will list the files one screen at a time and display a More dialog box between screens. (See Figure 1.7.) To see the next screen, click the OK button in the More dialog box.

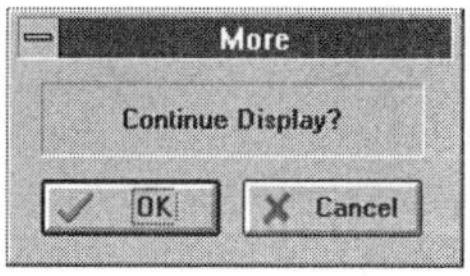

Figure 1.7.
The More dialog box displayed between screens.

The dBASE `DIR` command is similar to the DOS `DIR` command. By typing `DIR C:\*.*` you are asking dBASE to list all the files in the root directory of your hard drive.

Note that statements in dBASE are not case sensitive. Therefore, the statement `DIR C:\MYDIR\*.*` and the statement `dir C:\MYDIR\*.*` will produce the same result—listing all the files in the C:\MYDIR directory.

The cursor in the input pane has moved to the next line because dBASE is waiting for you to enter another command. Try the dBASE `CLEAR` command as follows:

☐ Type `CLEAR` in the Command window and press Enter.

dBASE responds by clearing the results pane of the Command window. Your Command window should now look like the one shown in Figure 1.8.

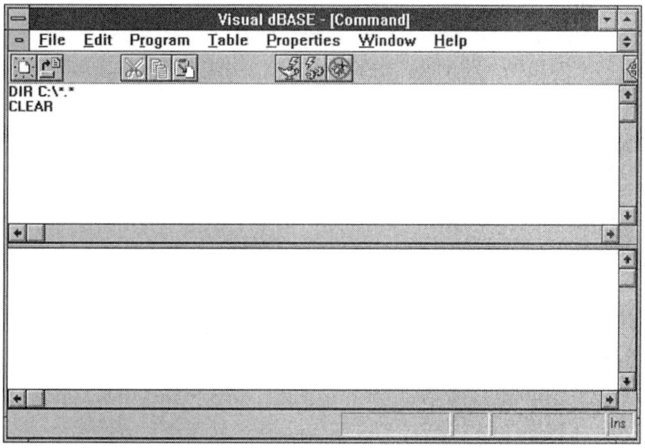

Figure 1.8.
The Command window after you execute the `CLEAR` *command.*

Say you want to execute the `DIR C:\*.*` command again. You can type `DIR C:\*.*` in the Command window again, or you can use the following steps:

☐ Press the up-arrow key of your keyboard two times.

dBASE responds by moving the cursor to the line with the `DIR C:\*.*` *command you typed earlier.*

☐ Press the Enter key of your keyboard.

dBASE responds by executing the `DIR C:\*.*` *command again.*

As you can imagine, this feature of the Command window will save you a lot of time—whenever you want to use the Command window to execute a command you have already executed, simply use the up-arrow key (or the mouse) to move the cursor to the command line and press the Enter key on your keyboard.

Now that you are familiar with how the Command window works, use it to create the program file of the SAY program, SAY.WFM, in the directory C:\DBPROG\CH01. First create this directory:

☐ Type `MD C:\DBPROG` in the Command window and then press Enter.

dBASE responds by creating the directory C:\DBPROG. (If this directory already exists, dBASE will display a message box telling you the directory cannot be created.)

☐ Type `MD C:\DBPROG\CH01` in the Command window and then press Enter.

dBASE responds by creating the directory C:\DBPROG\CH01. (If this directory already exists, dBASE will display a message box telling you the directory cannot be created.)

> **Note:** The dBASE `MD` command is like the DOS `MD` command—it lets you create new directories.

You can now create the program file of the SAY program in the C:\DBPROG\CH01 directory. Here is how you do that:

☐ Type `CREATE FORM C:\DBPROG\CH01\SAY` in the Command window and press Enter.

dBASE responds by creating the SAY.WFM form and displaying it in design mode. (See Figure 1.9.) You can tell that you are now in design mode because there is a ruler in the left margin of the form.

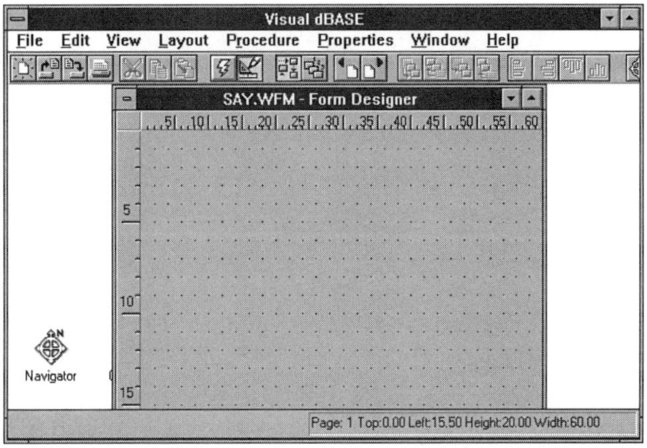

Figure 1.9.
The SAY.WFM form in design mode.

The `CREATE FORM` command creates a new form, which is a program file with a .WFM file extension that users can execute. Designing a form file with dBASE is very easy because you use the visual tools of dBASE. You simply use your mouse to place various controls (for example, pushbuttons) in the form.

The Visual Implementation of the SAY.WFM Form

As shown in Figure 1.9, the SAY.WFM form is currently blank (it doesn't have any controls in it). You'll now visually design the SAY.WFM form until it looks like the one shown in Figure 1.1.

> **Note:** The desktop of dBASE is an MDI (multiple-document interface) window. This means that the desktop window can have several windows in it.
>
> The menu that appears on the menu bar of the dBASE desktop depends on which window is currently selected. For example, when the Command window is the selected window, there is no View menu on the dBASE desktop. The View menu appears when the form window is the currently selected window.

☐ Make sure that the blank form window is currently selected (that is, click the frame of the blank form window).

☐ Select Control Palette from the View menu.

Visual dBase responds by making the Control Palette window the active window. Figure 1.10 shows the Control Palette window as the active window. You will use this window to place a control in the SAY.WFM form.

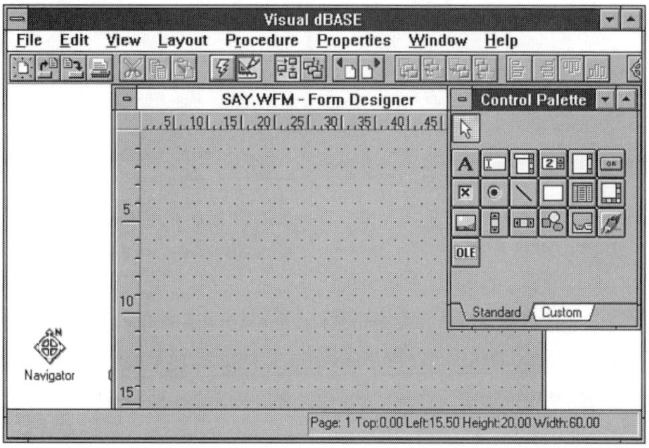

Figure 1.10.
The Control Palette window.

Figure 1.11 shows a magnified view of the Control Palette window with the pushbutton control and Standard/Custom tabs enlarged. As you can see, the Control Palette window has icons of various controls you can place in the form. The SAY.WFM form should have three controls—two pushbuttons (Say Hello and Clear) and an entry field. You'll now use the Control Palette window to place these controls in the SAY.WFM form.

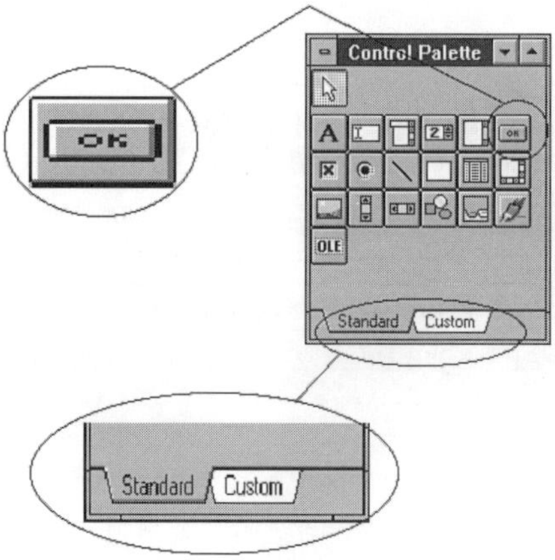

Figure 1.11.
A magnified view of the Control Palette window.

Note: As shown in Figure 1.11, the Controls window has two tabs at its bottom: Standard and Custom.

When you want to place a standard control in the form, select the Standard tab. When you want to place a custom control in the form, select the Custom tab.

All the controls you'll place in the SAY.WFM form are standard, so select the Standard tab.

Place a pushbutton control in the SAY.WFM form:

☐ Make sure the Standard tab is selected at the bottom of the Controls window.

☐ Double-click the pushbutton control in the Controls window. As shown in Figure 1.11, the pushbutton control in the Controls window is the control with the letters OK on it.

dBASE responds by placing a pushbutton control at the upper-left corner of the SAY.WFM form. (See Figure 1.12.)

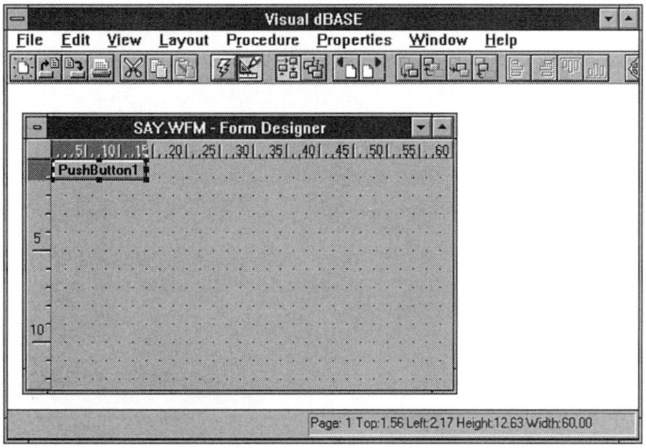

Figure 1.12.
The SAY.WFM form after you place a pushbutton control.

You can now move the pushbutton you placed in the form to any desired location by dragging it:

☐ Drag the pushbutton control you placed in the SAY.WFM form to the location shown in Figure 1.13. (You don't have to be 100 percent accurate—just move the pushbutton close to the location shown in Figure 1.13.)

Note: To drag the pushbutton control, place the mouse cursor over the pushbutton, click and hold the left mouse button, and move the mouse cursor to the desired location.

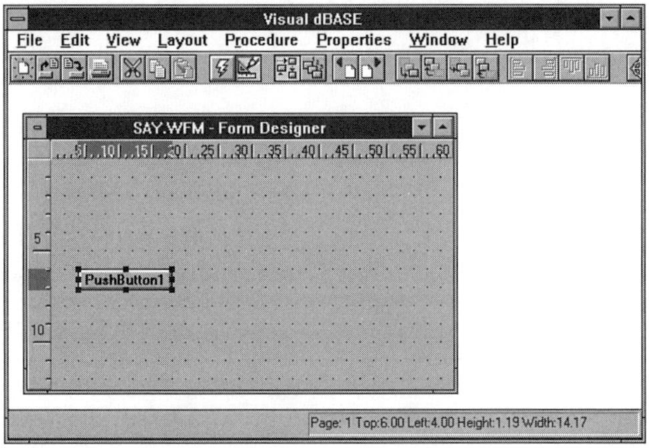

Figure 1.13.
The SAY.WFM form after you move (drag) the pushbutton to a new location.

As you can see, the text on the pushbutton is currently PushButton1. You'll now change the button's text to Say Hello by using the Inspector window:

☐ Make sure the PushButton1 pushbutton is currently selected by clicking on it.

☐ Select Inspector from the View menu.

dBASE responds by making the Inspector window, shown in Figure 1.14, the active window.

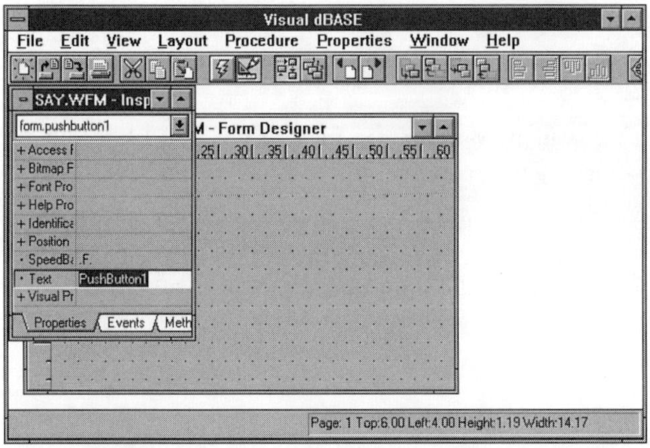

Figure 1.14.
The Inspector window.

As its name implies, the Inspector window lets you inspect and change a control's properties. You'll now use the Inspector window to change the Text property of the PushButton1 pushbutton from PushButton1 to Say Hello. The Inspector window has three tabs at its bottom: Properties, Events, and Methods. Right now you want to change a property, so you have to select the Properties tab:

☐ Make sure that the Properties tab is selected at the bottom of the Inspector window.

At the top of the Inspector window a pull-down list box specifies the control whose properties are currently listed. As shown in Figure 1.14, the pull-down list box is set to form.pushbutton1. This means that the properties listed in the Inspector window are the properties of the pushbutton1 control.

☐ Make sure that the pull-down list box at the top of the Inspector window is set to form.pushbutton1.

You can now change the Text property of the PushButton1 pushbutton:

☐ Look for the Text property in the Inspector window and click on it.

As you can see, the current value of the Text property is PushButton1. You want to change it to Say Hello:

☐ Set the Text property to &Say Hello.

Note: The & character that prefixes the *S* in &Say Hello underlines the character *S*. This means that during the execution of the SAY.WFM form, pressing Alt+S produces the same results as clicking the Say Hello button. (The character & is on the 7 key of your keyboard.) The underlined character in the caption is called a mnemonic.

Your SAY.WFM form should now look like the one shown in Figure 1.15.

There is one more property of the pushbutton that you have to change—the Name property. Currently, the Name property of the control is set to PUSHBUTTON1, the default name dBASE assigned to the pushbutton. Although there is nothing wrong with the name that dBASE assigned to the control, you'll now change the control name to a more friendly name. This will help you identify the button later when you write the program code.

Change the Name property of the pushbutton to SAYHELLOBUTTON as follows:

☐ Select the Identification Properties item in the Inspector window.

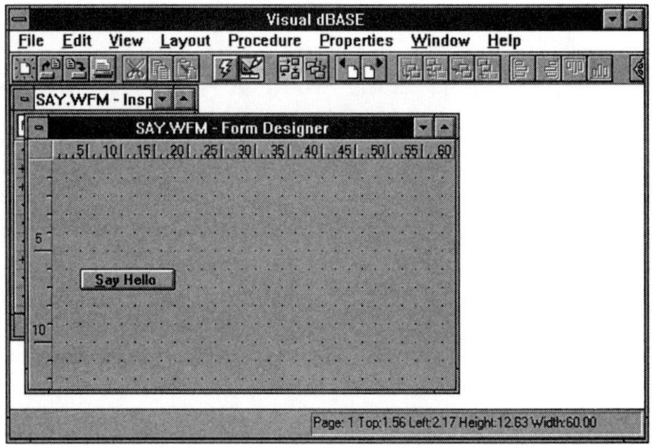

Figure 1.15.
Changing the text on the pushbutton to Say Hello.

The properties listed under the Identification Properties item are ClassName, hWnd, ID, Name, and Parent. (See Figure 1.16.)

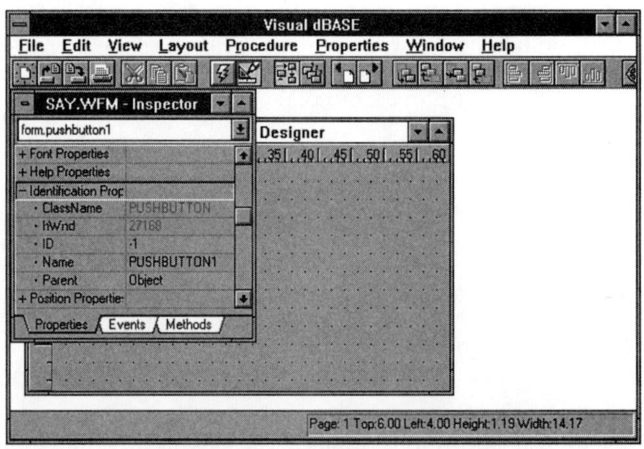

Figure 1.16.
The Identification Properties item in the Inspector window.

Note: If you don't see the ClassName, hWnd, ID, Name, and Parent properties under the Identification Properties item, then you need to expand the Identification Properties item by double-clicking it.

Note: As you develop your dBASE programs, you'll frequently use the Inspector window, so you may want to enlarge it by dragging its right side to the right. You can also drag the vertical divider line between the left and right sides of the Inspector window.

- ☐ Select the Name property under the Identification Properties item and change it to SAYHELLOBUTTON.
- ☐ Press Enter on your keyboard to make the change to the Name property effective.

Your Inspector window should now look like the one shown in Figure 1.17. The pull-down list box at the top of the Inspector window is set to form.sayhellobutton. From now on, dBASE will refer to the pushbutton you placed in the form as the SAYHELLOBUTTON pushbutton.

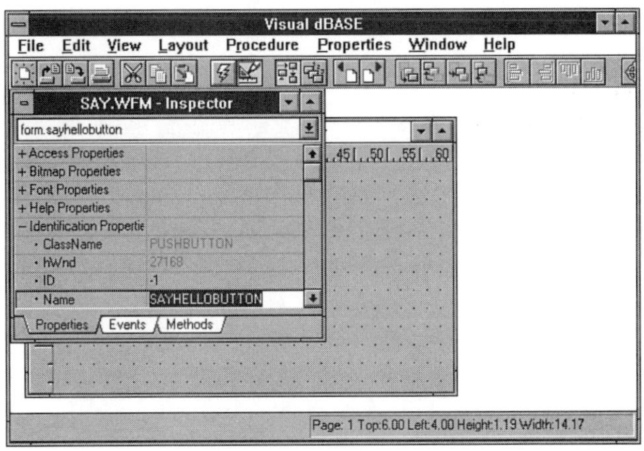

Figure 1.17.
The Inspector window after you change the Name property of the pushbutton to SAYHELLOBUTTON.

You have finished placing a pushbutton in the SAY.WFM form. You set its Text property to Say Hello and its Name property to SAYHELLOBUTTON. Now you need to place two more controls in the form: another pushbutton and an entry field. Start by placing another pushbutton in the SAY.WFM form as follows:

- ☐ Make the Control Palette window the active window by selecting Control Palette from the dBASE View menu.
- ☐ Double-click the pushbutton control in the Controls window.

dBASE responds by placing a new pushbutton control in the form. (See Figure 1.18.)

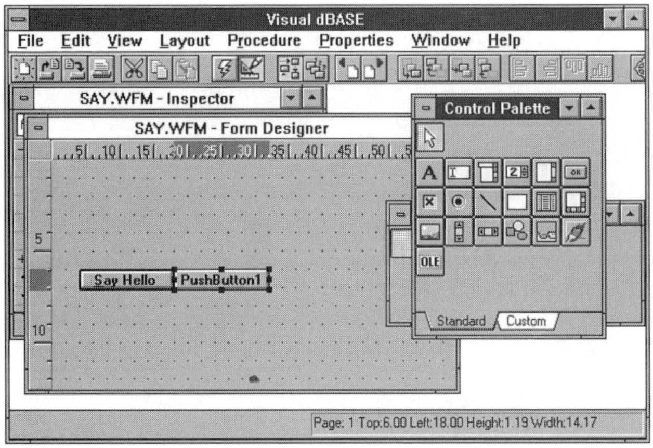

Figure 1.18.
The SAY.WFM form after you've placed a second pushbutton control.

☐ Move the new pushbutton control (by dragging it) to put some space between it and the Say Hello pushbutton, as shown in Figure 1.19.

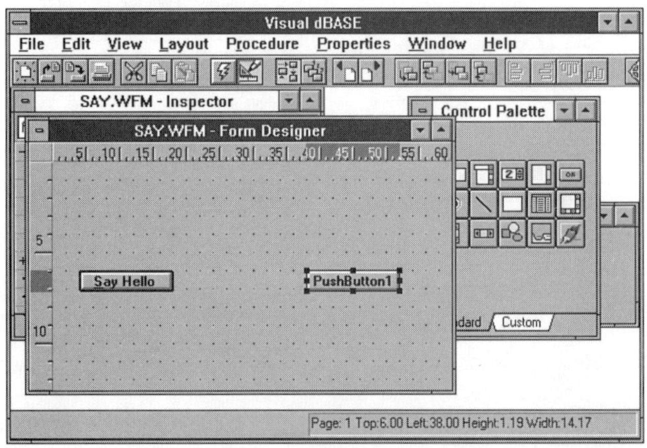

Figure 1.19.
The SAY.WFM form after you move the new pushbutton.

Change the Text property and Name property of the new pushbutton as follows:

☐ Make sure the new pushbutton is selected by clicking on it. (When the pushbutton is selected, dBASE encloses it with a rectangle that has small black squares, called *handles*, on the sides of the rectangle.)

☐ Make the Inspector window the active window by selecting Inspector from the dBASE View menu.

☐ Make sure the pull-down list box at the top of the Inspector window is set to form.pushbutton1 (the default name).

- ☐ Change the Name property (under the Identification Properties item) to CLEARBUTTON.
- ☐ Change the Text property to &Clear.

Your SAY.WFM form should now look like the one shown in Figure 1.20.

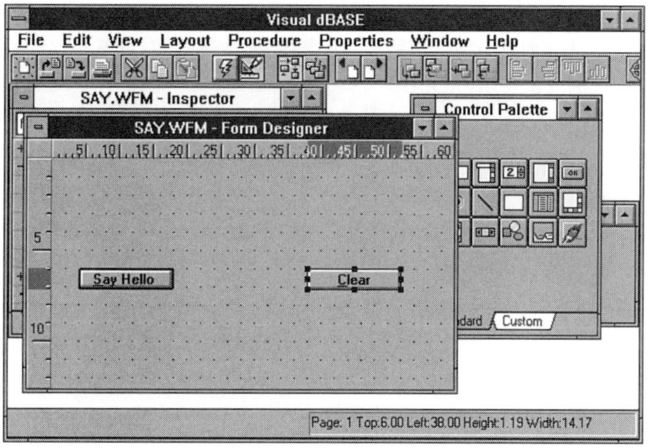

Figure 1.20.
The SAY.WFM form after you set the properties of the Clear pushbutton.

You are almost done with the visual implementation of the SAY.WFM form. The last control you have to place in the form is an EntryField control. Follow these steps to place it in the SAY.WFM form:

- ☐ Make the Control Palette window active by selecting Control Palette from the dBASE View menu.
- ☐ Double-click the EntryField control in the Control Palette window. In Figure 1.18, the EntryField icon is to the right of the icon with the character *A* on it.

> **Note:** If you are not sure about the name of a particular control inside the Control Palette window, then you can place the mouse cursor (without clicking) on the control and dBASE will display a small caption with the name of the control.

dBASE responds by placing an EntryField control in the SAY.WFM form. (See Figure 1.21.)

Note: Although Figure 1.21 shows that dBASE placed the EntryField control to the right of the Say Hello button, sometimes dBASE places the control in another location in the form.

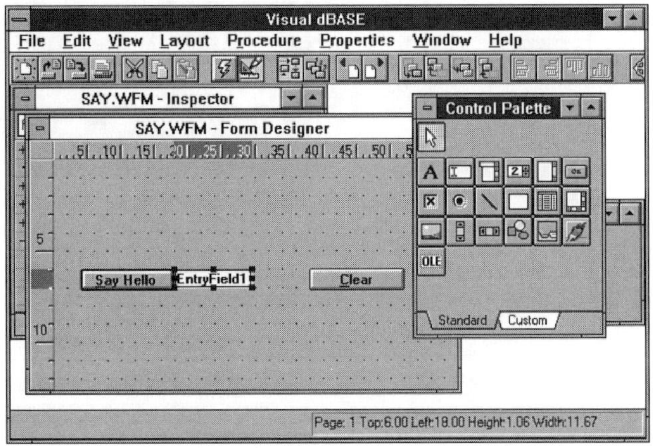

Figure 1.21.
The SAY.WFM form after you place an EntryField control.

□ Move the EntryField control (by dragging it) above the Say Hello pushbutton, as shown in Figure 1.22.

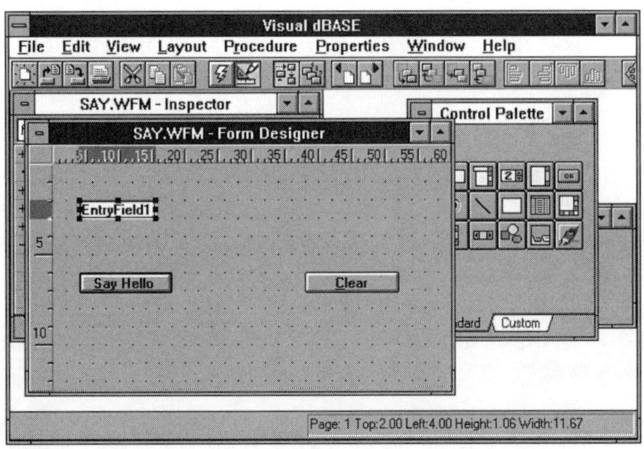

Figure 1.22.
The SAY.WFM form after you move the EntryField control.

The default size of the EntryField control is not large enough. You should enlarge its width so that it looks like the one shown back in Figure 1.1. Here is how you do that:

☐ Select the EntryField control by clicking on it, then drag the handle on its right edge until the control is the desired size. The enlarged EntryField control is shown in Figure 1.23.

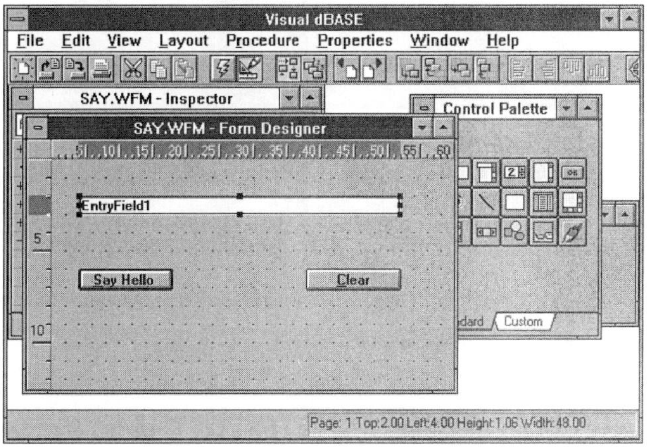

Figure 1.23.
The SAY.WFM after you enlarge the EntryField control.

Change the Name property of the EntryField control as follows:

☐ Make sure the EntryField control is selected by clicking on it.

☐ Make the Inspector window active by selecting Inspector from the dBASE View menu.

☐ Make sure the pull-down list box at the top of the Inspector window is set to form.entryfield1. (EntryField1 is the default name that dBASE assigned to the entry field).

☐ Change the Name property (under the Identification Properties item) to MYFIELD.

Now you need to change the Value property, which is the text displayed in the entry field control. As you can see from Figure 1.23, `EntryField1` is currently the text in the MYFIELD entry field. You'll now change the Value property of the MYFIELD entry field to blank:

☐ Select the Value property in the Inspector window, and use the Delete key to delete the text `EntryField1`.

☐ Make your changes effective by pressing Enter.

Your SAY.WFM dialog box should now look like the one shown in Figure 1.24—the MYFIELD entry field is blank.

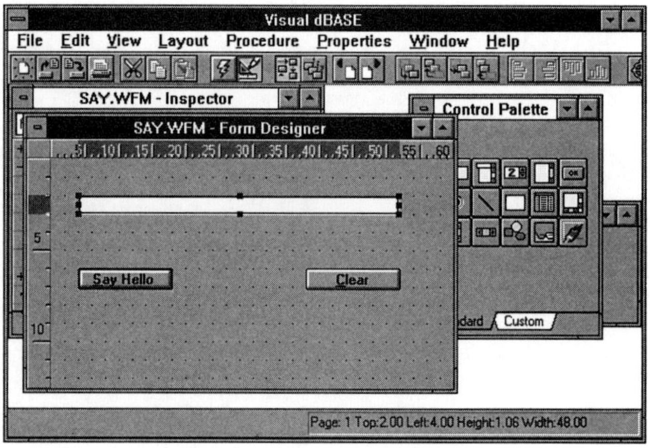

Figure 1.24.
The SAY.WFM form after you set the Value property of the MYFIELD entry field to blank.

You have finished the visual implementation of the SAY.WFM form!

Perform the following steps to save your work:

☐ Make the SAY.WFM window the active window by clicking the caption of the SAY.WFM form.

☐ Select Save from the File menu of dBASE.

dBASE responds by saving all your visual design work in the file SAY.WFM.

In the following section you'll execute the SAY program to see your visual design in action.

Executing the SAY Program

Although you haven't written a single line of code, you have finished the visual implementation of the SAY program, so you can now execute the program and test it. Before you execute the SAY program, close the SAY.WFM form:

☐ Click the icon on the upper-left corner of the SAY.WFM window, and then select Close from the system menu that pops up.

dBASE responds by closing the SAY.WFM form.

To execute the SAY program do the following:

☐ Type `DO C:\DBPROG\CH01\SAY.WFM` in the Command window and then press Enter.

dBASE responds by executing the SAY program. The window of the SAY program looks like the one as shown in Figure 1.25.

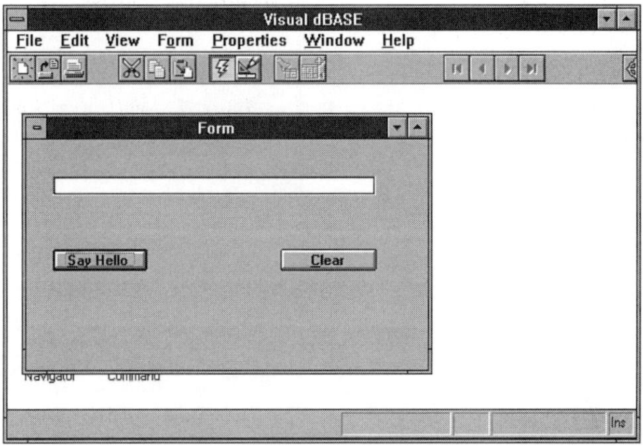

Figure 1.25.
The window of the SAY program.

The window of the SAY program appears just as you designed it—it has two pushbuttons (Say Hello and Clear) and one entry field. Experiment with the SAY program as follows:

☐ Click the Say Hello button.

Nothing happens! Why? You haven't attached any code to the Say Hello button. If you click the Clear button, nothing will happen. You'll attach code to the Say Hello and Clear buttons later in this chapter.

☐ Try to type something in the entry field of the SAY program.

As you can see, SAY.WFM allows you to type in the entry field, which is a standard feature of the entry field. You don't have to write any code to accomplish this feature.

Notice that the SAY.WFM doesn't have a File menu, as shown back in Figure 1.3. You'll create the menu of the SAY program later in this chapter.

The title of the SAY program is Form, but in Figure 1.1 the title was The SAY Program. In the next section you'll enhance the SAY program so that its title will be The SAY Program.

Terminate the SAY program:

☐ Click the icon at the upper-left corner of the SAY.WFM window.

The SAY program responds by opening a system menu. (See Figure 1.26.) You don't have to write any code to display the system menu.

☐ Select Close from the system menu.

dBASE responds by terminating the SAY program.

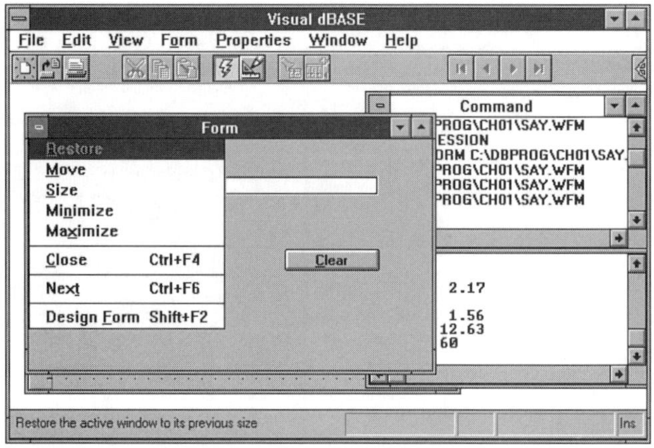

Figure 1.26.
The system menu of the SAY program.

Note: In the previous steps, you executed the SAY program by typing the `DO` command in the Command window of dBASE. Executing a program this way is easy enough. However, if you want users who aren't familiar with the dBASE package to execute your program, you can't expect these users to know how to type commands in the Command window to execute your program. Some users may not even own the dBASE package.

At the end of this chapter you'll learn how to create a "standalone" version of your program. After you do this, users can execute your program directly from Windows without having to start dBASE.

Changing the SAY Program's Window Title

As you have just seen, the title of the SAY program window is Form. (Refer to Figure 1.25.) You'll now enhance the SAY program so that its window title will be The SAY Program.

☐ Type `MODIFY FORM ?` in the Command window and press Enter.

dBASE responds by displaying the Open Form dialog box. (See Figure 1.27.)

☐ Use the Open Form dialog box to select the file C:\DBPROG\CH01\SAY.WFM.

dBASE responds by opening the SAY.WFM form in design mode. (See Figure 1.28.)

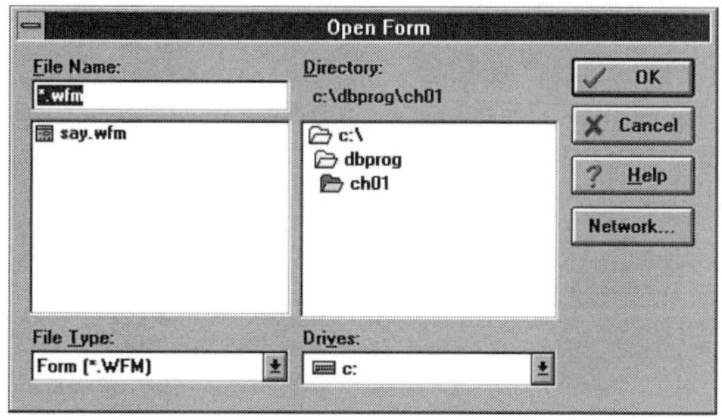

Figure 1.27.
The Open Form dialog box.

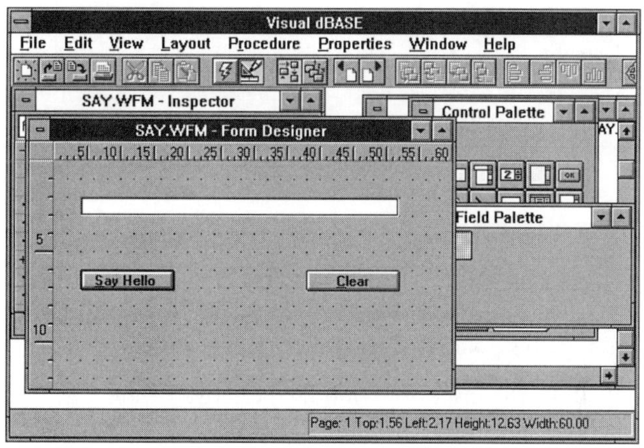

Figure 1.28.
The SAY.WFM form in design mode.

Note: In the previous step you opened the SAY.WFM form in design mode by typing `MODIFY FORM ?` in the Command window, then selecting SAY.WFM from the Open Form dialog box. Since you used the `MODIFY FORM` command followed by the `?` character, dBASE displayed an Open Form dialog box so you could select the form file you wanted to modify.

Alternatively, you could have used the `MODIFY FORM` command as follows:

```
MODIFY FORM C:\DBPROG\CH01\SAY.WFM
```

If you use the `MODIFY FORM` command this way, dBASE will open the form file immediately without opening a dialog box to select a file. However, it's preferable to use the `MODIFY FORM` command with the `?` character. Why? If you specify the filename on the command line, you could make a typing mistake, in which case dBASE would open a new form.

For example, if you typed the following command by mistake:

```
MODIFY FORM C:\DBPROG\CH01\SAYY.WFM
```

(that is, you typed `SAYY` instead of `SAY`) dBASE would think you wanted to create a new form called SAYY.WFM. But if you used the `MODIFY FORM` command with the `?` character, then you couldn't make a mistake because you selected the form file using the Open Form dialog box—the Open Form dialog box lists only files that exist.

Note: So far you have used the Inspector window to change properties of controls in the form. In the following steps, you'll use the Inspector window to change a property of the form itself.

Your objective now is to modify the title of the SAY.WFM form. To do that you have to change the Text property of the SAY.WFM form:

- ☐ Click in a free area of the SAY.WFM form that isn't occupied by a control, because you are now going to change a property of the form.
- ☐ Make the Inspector window the active window by selecting Inspector from the dBASE View menu.
- ☐ Make sure that the pull-down list box at the top of the Inspector window is set to form (because you are now going to change a property of the form).
- ☐ Locate the Text property in the Inspector window.

As you can see, the current value of the Text property is form.

- ☐ Change the Text property to The SAY Program.
- ☐ Save your work by selecting Save from the File menu.

To see your work in action, execute the SAY program as follows:

- ☐ Close the SAY.WFM form by clicking the icon on the upper-left corner of the SAY.WFM window, then selecting Close from the system menu that pops up.
- ☐ Type `DO C:\DBPROG\CH01\SAY.WFM` in the Command window and press Enter.

  dBASE responds by executing the SAY program. The window of the SAY program appears with the title The SAY Program, as shown in Figure 1.29.

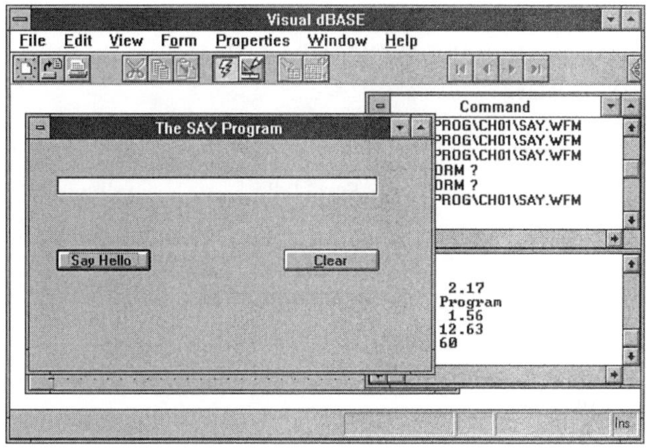

Figure 1.29.
The window of the SAY program.

Terminate the SAY program:

□ Click the minus icon at the upper-left corner of the SAY.WFM window, then select Close from the system menu that pops up.

dBASE responds by terminating the SAY program.

Enhancing the SAY Program

The window of the SAY program has three controls: a Say Hello pushbutton, a Clear pushbutton, and an entry field. In the following sections you'll enhance the SAY program as follows:

- You'll attach code to the Say Hello pushbutton.
- You'll attach code to the Clear pushbutton.
- You'll design the menu bar of the SAY program.
- You'll create a standalone version for the SAY program.

Attaching Code to the Say Hello Button

As you have seen, when you click the Say Hello and Clear buttons, nothing happens at this point. In this section you'll attach code to the Say Hello button so that when you click this button the application will do what it's supposed to do. In the next section you'll attach code to the Clear button.

When you click the Say Hello button, the SAY program should display a Hello message in the entry field, shown in Figure 1.2. To accomplish that, you'll now attach dBASE code to the Say Hello button.

- ☐ Type `MODIFY FORM ?` in the Command window, press the Enter key, and then select the file C:\DBPROG\CH01\SAY.WFM from the Open Form dialog box that dBASE displays.

    dBASE responds by displaying the SAY.WFM form in design mode.

Now attach code to the Say Hello button as follows:

- ☐ Select the Say Hello button in the SAY.WFM form by clicking it.
- ☐ Make the Inspector window the active window by selecting Inspector from the dBASE View menu.

    dBASE responds by making the Inspector window the active window.

- ☐ Make sure that the pull-down list box at the top of the Inspector window is set to form.sayhellobutton. (See Figure 1.30.) Recall that SAYHELLOBUTTON is the name you gave the Say Hello button.

Figure 1.30.
The Inspector window showing the properties of SAYHELLOBUTTON.

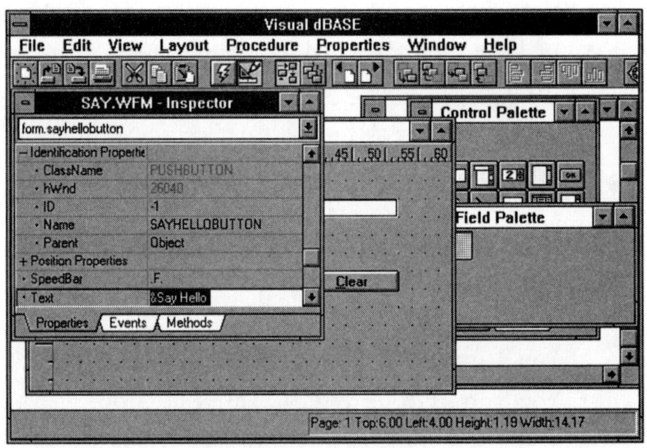

The Inspector window has three tabs at its bottom: Properties, Events, and Methods. So far you've used only the Properties tab. Now you'll use the Events tab:

- ☐ Select the Events tab of the Inspector window by clicking it.

Figure 1.31 shows the Inspector window after you select the Events tab.

As its name implies, the Events tab lists various events. Right now, you want to attach code to this event:

```
User clicked the Say Hello button
```

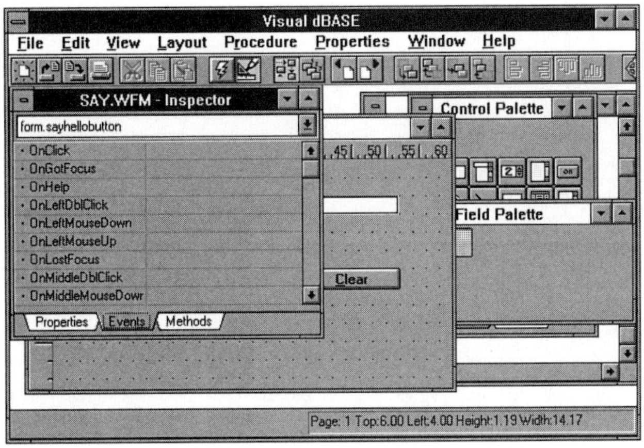

Figure 1.31.
The Inspector window after you select the Events tab.

That is, you want to write dBASE code that is automatically executed when the user clicks the Say Hello button.

As shown in Figure 1.31, the pull-down list box at the top of the Inspector window is currently set to form.sayhellobutton. This means that all the events currently listed in the Inspector window are events associated with the Say Hello button. The event that you need right now is the `OnClick` event, which occurs when the user clicks the Say Hello button.

☐ Select the `OnClick` event by clicking it.

Your Inspector window should now look like the one shown in Figure 1.32.

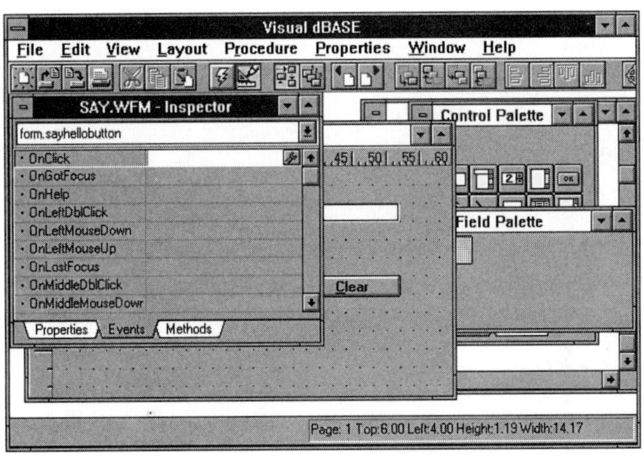

Figure 1.32.
The Inspector window after you select the `OnClick` *event.*

As shown in Figure 1.32, the `OnClick` entry in the Inspector window now has a small Tool button on the right.

☐ Click the Tool button of the `OnClick` event.

dBASE responds by opening the Procedure Editor to let you write code. (See Figure 1.33.) The code that you'll write will be executed automatically whenever the user clicks the Say Hello pushbutton.

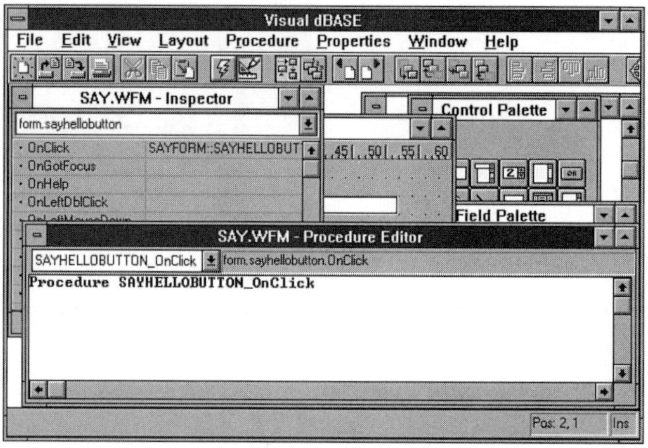

Figure 1.33.
The Procedure Editor.

As shown in Figure 1.33, the pull-down list box at the top of the Procedure Editor is set to `SAYHELLOBUTTON_OnClick`. This means you are currently writing code in a procedure called `SAYHELLOBUTTON_OnClick`.

What is a procedure? A *procedure* is a place where you write dBASE code. As shown in Figure 1.33, dBASE already wrote the first line of the `SAYHELLOBUTTON_OnClick` procedure for you:

```
Procedure SAYHELLOBUTTON_OnClick
```

This line identifies the procedure as `SAYHELLOBUTTON_OnClick`. It is your job to write the rest of the lines of the procedure.

☐ Write the rest of the lines of the procedure so that it will look as follows:

```
Procedure SAYHELLOBUTTON_OnClick

  * Fill the entry field with a Hello message.
  form.MyField.Value = "Hello! This is my first program."

Return
```

Your Procedure Editor window should now look like the one shown in Figure 1.34.

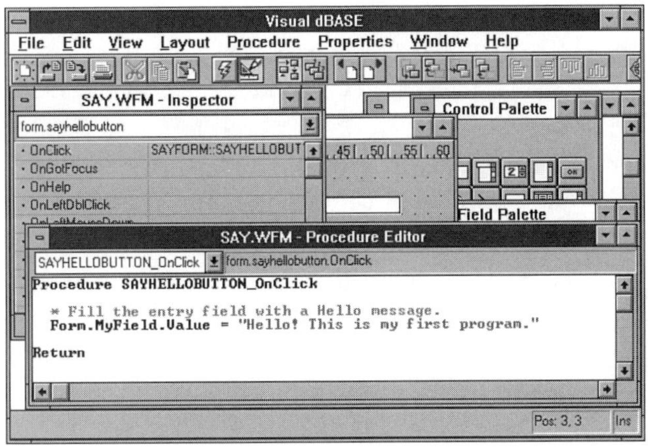

Figure 1.34.
Entering code in the `SAYHELLOBUTTON_OnClick` *procedure.*

Review the code you just typed in the `SAYHELLOBUTTON_OnClick` procedure. This is the first line you typed:

```
* Fill the entry field with a Hello message.
```

Because this line starts with the `*` character, dBASE considers it a comment line. In dBASE, all lines of code that start with the `*` character have no effect on the program—they serve as comments. Whoever reads your program code (including you) can better understand it by reading the comment lines.

This is the second line you typed in the `SAYHELLOBUTTON_OnClick` procedure:

```
form.MyField.Value = "Hello! This is my first program."
```

Can you guess what this line of code does? It fills the MYFIELD entry field with this text:

```
Hello! This is my first program.
```

Recall that MYFIELD is the name you gave the entry field control you placed in the SAY.WFM form. Therefore, this statement:

```
form.MyField.Value = "Hello! This is my first program."
```

is telling dBASE to fill the Value property of the MYFIELD entry field in the Form form with the text `Hello! This is my first program.`

Note: The `form` keyword refers to a form. Which form? Well, it depends where the `form` keyword is mentioned. For example, in the preceding code, the keyword `form` is written in the `SAYHELLOBUTTON_OnClick()` procedure of the SAYHELLOBUTTON control. The SAYHELLOBUTTON control is in the SAY.WFM form. Therefore, when you say `Form` in the above code, dBASE knows you are referring to the SAY.WFM form. So this statement:

```
form.MyField.Value = "Hello! This is my first program."
```

literally means fill the Value property of the entry field MYFIELD in the SAY.WFM form with the text `Hello! This is my first program.`

When you (or your users) run the SAY program and click the Say Hello button, the `SAYHELLOBUTTON_OnClick` event will occur and the code you attached to that event will fill the Value property of MYFIELD entry field with the text `Hello! This is my first program.` As a result, you will see the MYFIELD entry field filled with the text `Hello! This is my first program.`

The last line of code you typed in the `SAYHELLOBUTTON_OnClick` procedure is this:

```
Return
```

The `Return` statement terminates the procedure.

Don't forget to save your work:

☐ Select Save from the File menu of dBASE.

Review what you did to attach code to the `OnClick` event of the Say Hello button:

1. You opened the SAY.WFM form in design mode by using the `MODIFY FORM` command.
2. You selected the Say Hello button by clicking on it in the SAY.WFM form.
3. You made the Inspector window the active window.

   dBASE responded by displaying the Inspector window with the pull-down list box at the top set to form.sayhellobutton. (SAYHELLOBUTTON is the name you gave to the Say Hello button.)

4. You selected the Events tab of the Inspector window.
5. You selected the `OnClick` event.
6. You clicked the Tool button of the `OnClick` event.

   dBASE responded by displaying the Procedure Editor, with the procedure `SAYHELLOBUTTON_OnClick` ready to be edited by you.

7. You typed code in the `SAYHELLOBUTTON_OnClick` procedure to display a Hello message in the MYFIELD entry field. When you run the SAY program, the `SAYHELLOBUTTON_OnClick` procedure will be executed automatically when you click the Say Hello button.

Execute the SAY program and check that the code you attached to the `OnClick` event of the Say Hello button is working:

- ☐ Close the SAY.WFM window by clicking the icon on the upper-left corner of the SAY.WFM window, then selecting Close from the system menu that pops up.
- ☐ Type `DO C:\DBPROG\CH01\SAY.WFM` in the Command window and press Enter.

  dBASE responds by executing the SAY program. The window of the SAY program appears, as shown back in Figure 1.29.

- ☐ Click the Say Hello button.

  The SAY program responds by displaying the text `Hello! This is my first program.` *in the entry field. (See Figure 1.35.)*

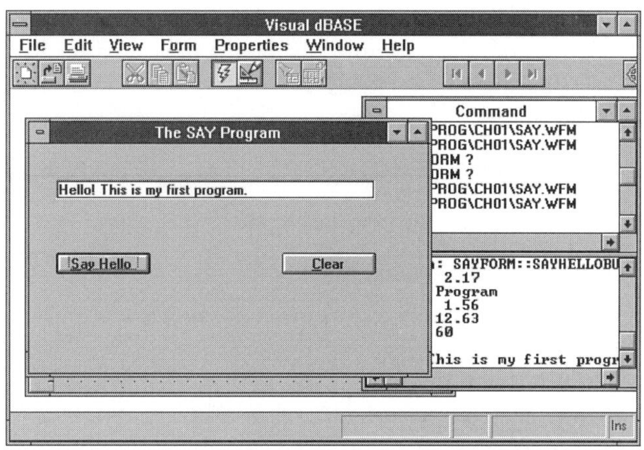

Figure 1.35.
The window of the SAY program after you click the Say Hello pushbutton.

So as you have just seen, the code you attached to the `OnClick` event of the Say Hello button is working! When you click the Say Hello button, the `OnClick` event of the Say Hello button occurs, and the `SAYHELLOBUTTON_OnClick` procedure is executed automatically.

- ☐ Now click the Clear button.

Of course, nothing happens when you click the Clear button because you haven't attached any code to the `OnClick` event of the Clear button. In the next section you'll attach code to the `OnClick` event of the Clear button so that the Clear button will do what it's supposed to do.

Terminate the SAY program:

- ☐ Click the icon at the upper-left corner of the SAY.WFM window, then select Close from the system menu that pops up.

  dBASE responds by terminating the program.

Attaching Code to the Clear Button

As you have seen, when you click the Clear button at this point nothing happens. In this section you'll attach code to the `OnClick` event of the Clear button so that when the user clicks it, the SAY program will clear the text in the entry field.

☐ Type `MODIFY FORM ?` in the Command window, press Enter, and then select the file C:\DBPROG\CH01\SAY.WFM from the Open Form dialog box.

dBASE responds by displaying the SAY.WFM form in design mode.

Now attach code to the `OnClick` event of the Clear button as follows:

☐ Select the Clear button in the SAY.WFM form by clicking it.

☐ Make the Inspector window the active window by selecting Inspector from the dBASE View menu.

☐ Make sure the pull-down list box at the top of the Inspector window is set to form.clearbutton. (Recall that CLEARBUTTON is the name that you gave to the Clear button.)

☐ Make sure the Events tab at the bottom of the Inspector window is selected by clicking it.

Right now, you want to attach code to this event:

```
User clicked the Clear button
```

That is, you want to write dBASE code that is executed automatically when you click the Clear button.

Because the pull-down list box at the top of the Inspector window is currently set to form.clearbutton, it means that all the events currently listed in the Inspector window are events associated with the Clear button. The event that you need right now is the `OnClick` event, which occurs when the user clicks the Clear button.

☐ Select the `OnClick` event by clicking it.

☐ Click the Tool button of the `OnClick` event.

dBASE responds by opening the Procedure Editor to let you write code in the `CLEARBUTTON_OnClick` procedure. (See Figure 1.36.) The code you'll write in this procedure will be executed automatically when the user clicks the Clear pushbutton.

☐ Enter the following code in the `CLEARBUTTON_OnClick` procedure:

```
Procedure CLEARBUTTON_OnClick

  * Clear the entry field.
  form.MyField.Value = ""

Return
```

Figure 1.36.
The Procedure Editor with the `CLEARBUTTON_OnClick` *procedure ready for editing.*

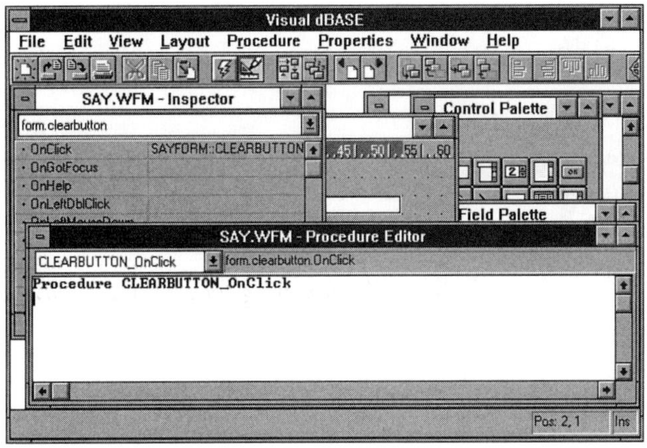

Your Procedure Editor window should now look like the one shown in Figure 1.37.

Figure 1.37.
The Procedure Editor after you enter code in the `CLEARBUTTON_OnClick` *procedure.*

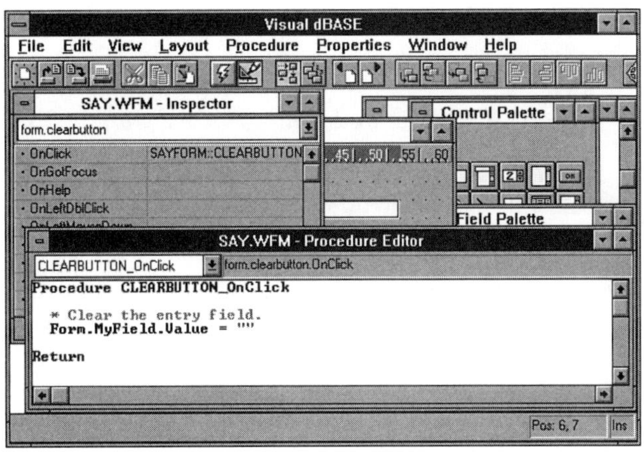

Review the code you just typed in the `CLEARBUTTON_OnClick` procedure. This is the first line you typed:

```
* Clear the entry field.
```

As you know, because this line starts with the `*` character, dBASE considers it a comment line. In other words, this line has no effect on the program.

This is the second line you typed in the `CLEARBUTTON_OnClick` procedure:

```
form.MyField.Value = ""
```

Can you guess what this line of code does? This line of code fills the MYFIELD entry field with a null string (that is, blank text). Therefore, this statement:

```
form.MyField.Value = ""
```

is telling dBASE to set the Value property of the MYFIELD entry field in the Form form with the text `""` (that is, blank text). As discussed earlier, the `Form` keyword refers to the SAY.WFM form.

The last line of code you typed in the `CLEARBUTTON_OnClick` procedure terminates the procedure:

```
Return
```

Don't forget to save your work:

☐ Select Save from the File menu of dBASE.

Now run the SAY program and check that the code you attached to the `OnClick` event of the Clear button is working:

☐ Close the SAY.WFM window.

☐ Type `DO C:\DBPROG\CH01\SAY.WFM` in the Command window and press the Enter key.

dBASE responds by executing the SAY program. The window of the SAY program appears, as shown back in Figure 1.29.

☐ Click the Say Hello button.

The SAY program responds by displaying the text `Hello! This is my first program.` *in the entry field. (Refer to Figure 1.35.)*

☐ Now click the Clear button.

The SAY program responds by clearing the text in the entry field.

The code you attached to the `OnClick` event of the Clear button is working! When you click the Clear button, the `OnClick` event of the Clear button occurs, and the `CLEARBUTTON_OnClick` procedure is automatically executed.

To terminate the SAY program:

☐ Click the icon at the upper-left corner of the SAY.WFM window, then select Close from the system menu that pops up.

dBASE responds by terminating the SAY program.

You have finished attaching code to the Say Hello and Clear buttons. In the next section you'll design the menu of the SAY program.

Designing the Menu Bar of the SAY Program

As shown back in Figure 1.3, the SAY program should have a menu bar with one menu, the File menu. You'll now follow these steps to design the menu bar of the SAY program:

☐ Type `CREATE MENU C:\DBPROG\CH01\SAY` in the Command window and press Enter.

dBASE responds by creating the SAY.MNU menu in the C:\DBPROG\CH01 directory and displaying it in design mode. (See Figure 1.38.)

Figure 1.38.
The SAY.MNU menu in design mode.

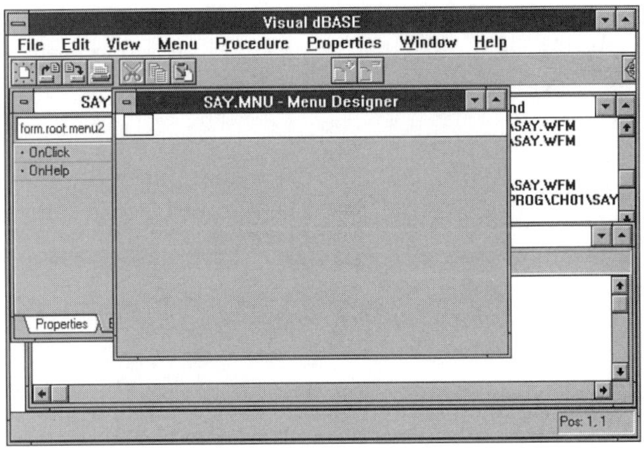

As its name implies, the `CREATE MENU` command creates a menu. In dBASE a menu is a file with an .MNU file extension that your programs can use. Designing a menu with dBASE is very easy because you use its visual tools. You simply use your mouse and keyboard to set the menu titles and menu items.

> **Note:** In the preceding step you used the `CREATE MENU` command to create a menu file called SAY.MNU. Of course, you could have given the menu any other name you wished (for example, MyMenu.MNU). However, you were instructed to name the menu SAY.MNU because it will serve as the menu of the SAY program—the name SAY.MNU will help you identify this menu as the SAY program's menu.

As shown in Figure 1.38, the SAY.MNU menu is currently blank (that is, it doesn't have any menus). You'll now design the SAY.MNU form so it looks like the one shown back in Figure 1.3. It should have a File menu with one menu item, Exit.

Notice the small blank rectangle on the left side of the SAY.MNU menu bar. It represents the title of the menu bar's leftmost menu. Since you want the title to be File, you have to type `File` in this rectangle:

☐ Type `&File` in the small rectangle at the upper-left corner of the SAY.MNU window.

Your SAY.MNU menu should now look like the one shown in Figure 1.39.

> **Note:** The & character that prefixes the *F* in &File underlines the character *F*. When the SAY.MNU menu is displayed, pressing Alt+F will produce the same results as clicking the File menu title—opening the File menu.

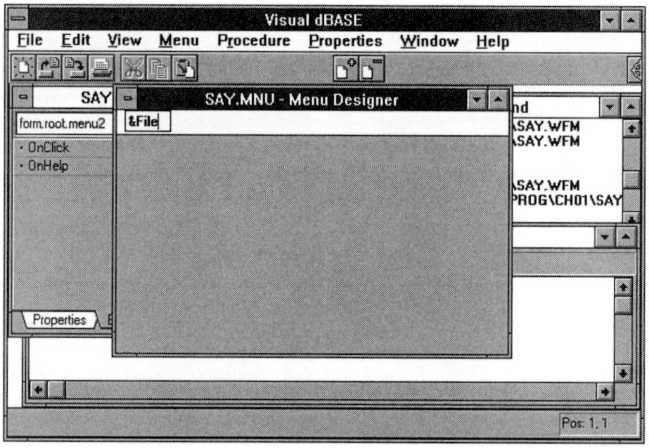

Figure 1.39.
The SAY.MNU menu after you set the title of the leftmost menu to File.

Now add the Exit menu item to the File menu as follows:

☐ Press the down-arrow key on your keyboard.

dBASE responds by placing a small rectangle below the File menu title. (See Figure 1.40.)

☐ Type `E&xit` in the rectangle.

Your SAY.MNU menu should now look like the one shown in Figure 1.41.

> **Note:** The & character that prefixes the *x* in E&xit underlines the character *x*. This means that when the File menu is opened, pressing x will produce the same results as selecting the Exit menu item.

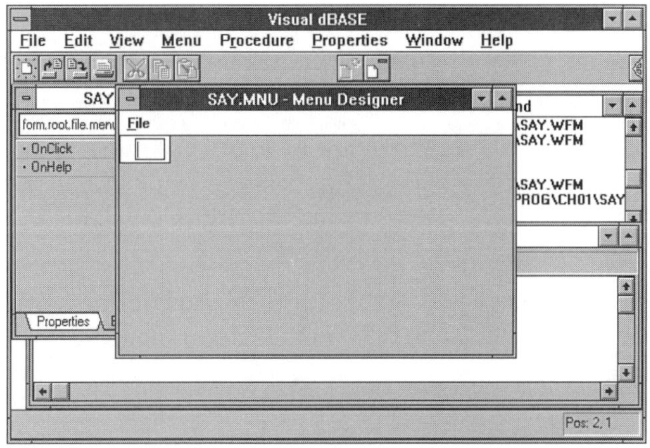

Figure 1.40.
Pressing the down-arrow key to add a menu item to the File menu.

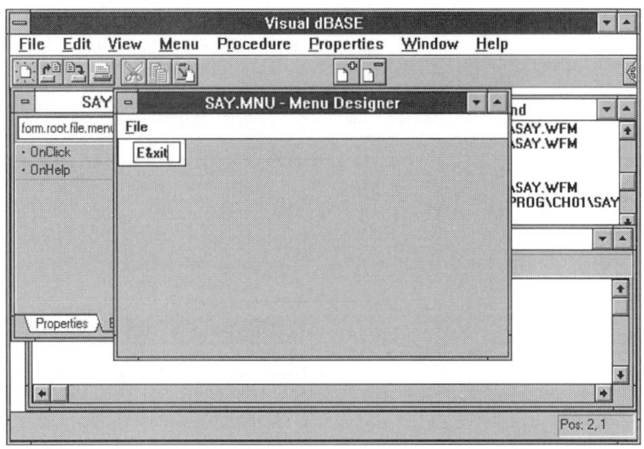

Figure 1.41.
The SAY.MNU menu after you add the Exit menu item.

You have finished the visual implementation of the SAY.MNU menu!

Save your work:

☐ Select Save from the File menu of dBASE.

In the next section you'll attach the SAY.MNU menu to the SAY program, but first close the SAY.MNU menu:

☐ Click the icon on the upper-left corner of the SAY.MNU window, then select Close from the system menu that pops up.

dBASE responds by closing the SAY.MNU menu.

Attaching the SAY.MNU Menu to the SAY Program

In the previous section you created the SAY.MNU menu. You'll now attach the SAY.MNU menu to the SAY.WFM form by performing the following steps:

- ☐ If the SAY.WFM window isn't currently displayed on the dBASE desktop, open the SAY.WFM window. (Type `MODIFY FORM ?` in the Command window, press the Enter key, and then select the file C:\DBPROG\CH01\SAY.WFM from the Open Form dialog box that dBASE displays.)

Now you have to set the MenuFile property of the SAY.WFM form to C:\DBPROG\CH01\SAY.MNU. Here is how you do that:

- ☐ Click in a free area of the SAY.WFM form that isn't occupied by a control (because you are now going to change a property of the form).
- ☐ Make the Inspector window the active window by selecting Inspector from the dBASE View menu.
- ☐ Make sure the pull-down list box at the top of the Inspector window is set to Form (because you are now going to change a property of the form).
- ☐ Select the Properties tab at the bottom of the Inspector window.
- ☐ Locate the MenuFile property in the Inspector window and select it by clicking on it.

Your Inspector window should now look like the one shown in Figure 1.42.

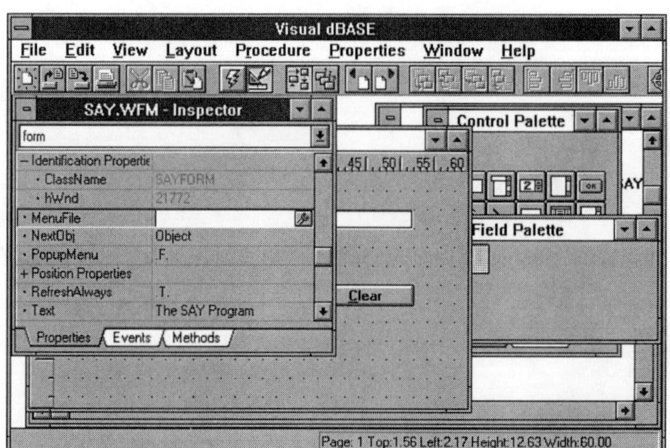

Figure 1.42.
The MenuFile property of the SAY.WFM form.

As you can see, the current value of the MenuFile property is blank because SAY.WFM isn't associated with any menu. As shown in Figure 1.42, the MenuFile property has a small Tool button. You'll now use this Tool button to select the menu file C:\DBPROG\CH01\SAY.MNU:

☐ Click the Tool button of the MenuFile property.

dBASE responds by displaying the Choose MenuFile Property Builder dialog box. (See Figure 1.43.)

Figure 1.43.
The MenuFile Property Builder dialog box.

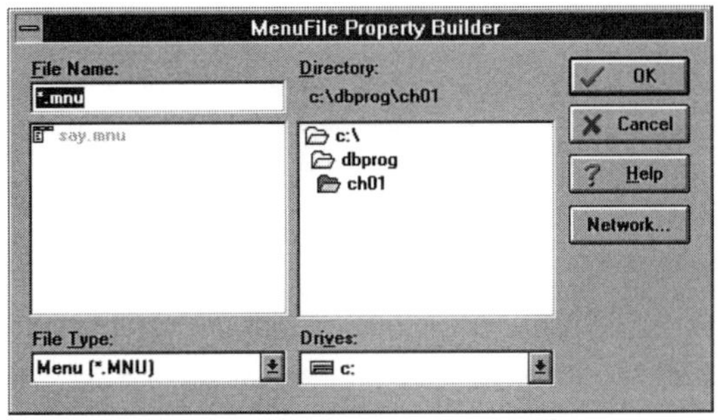

☐ Use the MenuFile Property Builder dialog box to select the file C:\DBPROG\CH01\SAY.MNU and then click the OK button.

The SAY.MNU is now attached to the SAY.WFM form!

☐ Save your work by selecting Save from the File menu.

To see your work in action, run the SAY program as follows:

☐ Close the SAY.WFM window.

☐ Type `DO C:\DBPROG\CH01\SAY.WFM` in the Command window and press Enter.

dBASE responds by executing the SAY program. (See Figure 1.44.)

Figure 1.44.
The SAY program with the SAY.MNU menu attached.

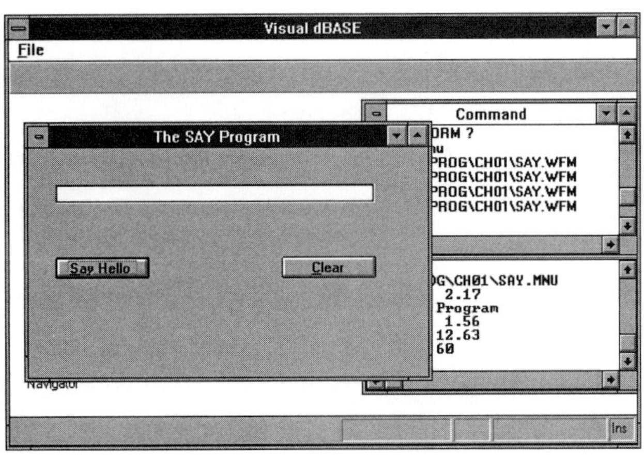

As shown in Figure 1.44, the dBASE desktop menu bar has been replaced with the menu bar SAY.MNU that you designed. That is, the dBASE menu bar now has only one menu: the File menu that you designed.

You've attached the SAY.MNU menu to the SAY program, but it isn't part of the SAY program's window. It has become the menu bar of the dBASE main window, and the window of the SAY program doesn't have a menu bar. Take a look back at Figure 1.3. As you can see, the SAY.MNU menu is part of the window of the SAY program. In the next section, you'll enhance the SAY program so that its menu bar will be part of its main window, as shown back in Figure 1.3.

To see the menu of the SAY program in action, do the following:

☐ Open the File menu by clicking File or by pressing Alt+F on your keyboard.

The SAY program responds by opening the File menu you designed. (See Figure 1.45.)

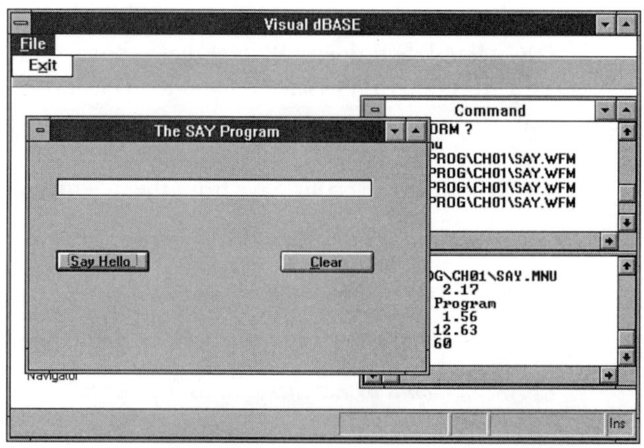

Figure 1.45.
The File menu of the SAY program.

☐ Select Exit from the File menu.

Nothing happens because you haven't attached any code to the Exit menu item. You'll attach code to the Exit menu item later in this chapter.

Before you continue with the next section, perform the following experiment while the SAY program is running:

☐ Move the window of the SAY program and the Command window so that both will be displayed on the dBASE desktop without overlapping each other. (See Figure 1.46.) You move a window by dragging its title.

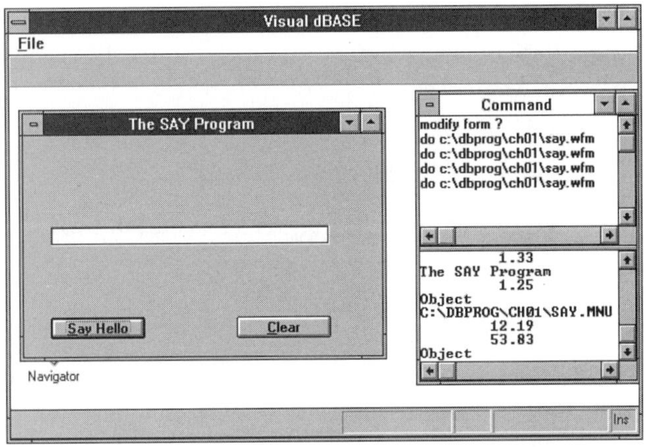

Figure 1.46.
Moving the window of the SAY program and the Command window.

- Select the window of the SAY program by clicking on its title.

  Because the window of the SAY program is currently selected, the SAY.MNU menu bar is on the dBASE main window's menu bar. (Refer to Figure 1.46.)

- Now select the Command window by clicking on its title.

As you can see, now the SAY.MNU menu bar has been replaced with a new menu bar. (See Figure 1.47.)

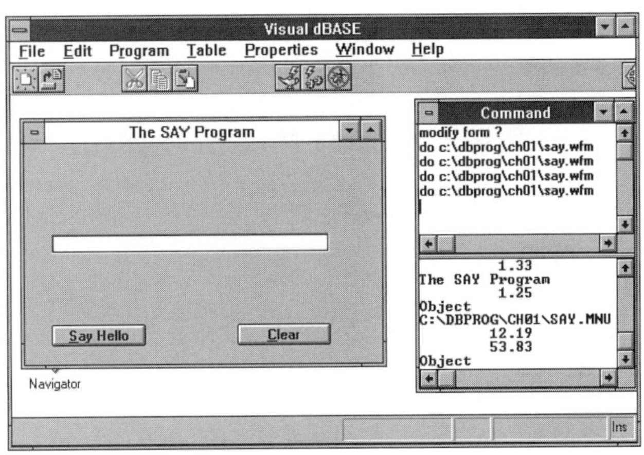

Figure 1.47.
The menu bar of the dBASE main window when the Command window is selected.

- Keep changing the active window—alternate between the SAY program window and the Command window—and notice how the menu bar displayed in the dBASE main window changes accordingly.

Note also that the SAY program window is a *child window* of the dBASE main window. That is, the SAY program window is always inside the dBASE main window. You can't move the SAY program window outside the dBASE main window. For example, if you minimize the dBASE main window, the SAY program window will also be minimized:

☐ Minimize the dBASE main window.

As expected, the SAY program window disappears.

☐ Maximize the dBASE main window.

The SAY program window reappears.

The features you just experimented with— the menu bar of the dBASE main window changing according to the currently active window and the SAY program window being a child window of the dBASE main window—are called MDI features.

In the following section you'll enhance the SAY program so that its window won't conform to the MDI standard. The SAY program menu will always be displayed on the window of the SAY program (not on the window of the dBASE program). And the SAY program window won't be a child window of the dBASE main window.

Terminate the SAY program:

☐ Make the window of the SAY program the active window by clicking on its title.

☐ Click the icon at the upper-left corner of the SAY.WFM window and then select Close from the system menu.

dBASE responds by terminating the SAY program.

Disabling the MDI Feature of the SAY Program

As you have just seen, the SAY program window currently conforms to the Windows MDI standard. You'll now disable the MDI feature of the SAY program so that its menu will always be displayed on its own window, no matter which window is currently active.

☐ Type `MODIFY FORM ?` in the Command window, press the Enter key, and then select the file C:\DBPROG\CH01\SAY.WFM from the Open Form dialog box that dBASE displays.

dBASE responds by displaying the SAY.WFM form in design mode.

To disable the MDI feature of the SAY program, you have to change the current value of the MDI property of the SAY.WFM form. Here is how you do that:

☐ Click in a free area of the SAY.WFM form that isn't occupied by a control.

☐ Make the Inspector window the active window by selecting Inspector from the dBASE View menu.

- ☐ Make sure the pull-down list box at the top of the Inspector window is set to Form (because you are now going to change a property of the form).
- ☐ Make sure the Properties tab at the bottom of the Inspector window is selected.
- ☐ Locate the MDI property (under the Windows Properties item) and select it by clicking on it.

Your Inspector window should now look like the one shown in Figure 1.48.

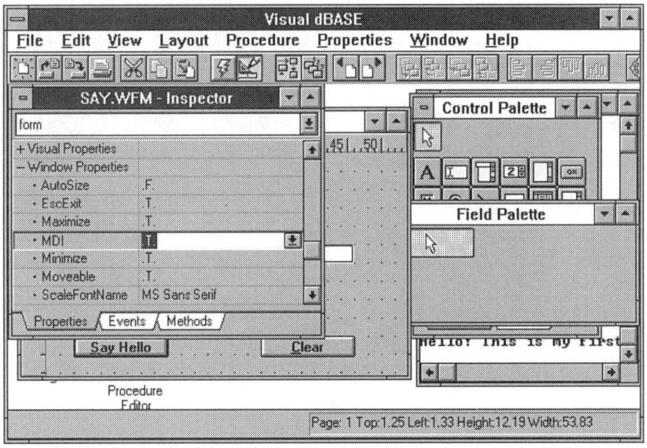

Figure 1.48.
The MDI property of the SAY.WFM form.

Note: The MDI property is listed in the Inspector window under the Windows Properties item. If you don't see it, then expand the Windows Properties item by double-clicking it. Once you expand the Window Properties item, you'll see several properties under it. As shown in Figure 1.48, one of these properties is the MDI property.

As you can see, the current value of the MDI property is .T., which means TRUE in dBASE. That is, the MDI property of the SAY.WFM form is set to TRUE, so the MDI feature of the SAY.WFM is currently active. To disable the MDI feature, set the MDI property to .F. (that is, FALSE):

- ☐ Click the down-arrow icon to the right of the MDI property.

  dBASE responds by displaying a pull-down list with two items: .T. and .F..

- ☐ Select the .F. item.

Your Inspector window should now look like the one shown in Figure 1.49.

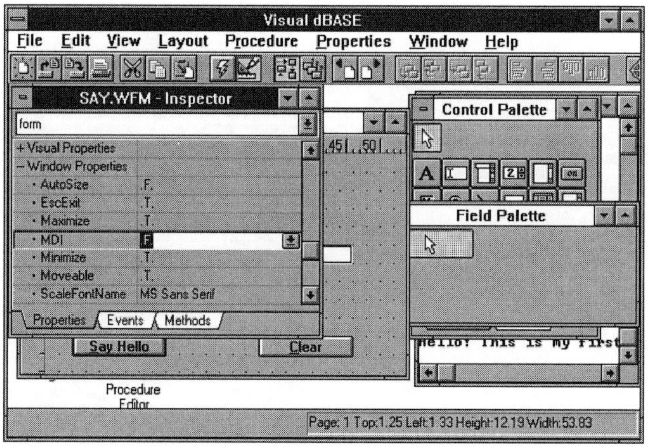

Figure 1.49.
Setting the MDI property of the SAY.WFM form to FALSE.

☐ Save your work by selecting Save from the File menu.

To see your work in action, run the SAY program as follows:

☐ Close the SAY.WFM window.

☐ Type `DO C:\DBPROG\CH01\SAY.WFM` in the Command window and press Enter.

dBASE responds by executing the SAY program. (See Figure 1.50.)

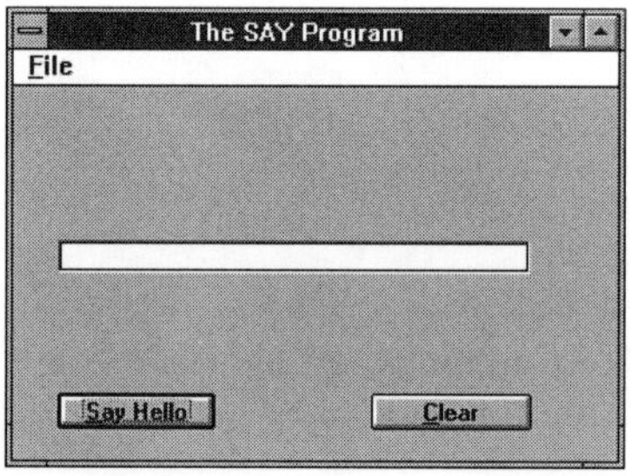

Figure 1.50.
The SAY program with the SAY.MNU menu attached.

As shown in Figure 1.50, now the SAY.MNU menu you designed appears on the window of the SAY program (not on the main window of dBASE). Also, the SAY program window is no longer a child window of the dBASE main window. Check that the window of SAY.WFM is not a child of the dBASE main window:

☐ Minimize the main window of dBASE.

As you can see, the SAY program window remains on the desktop! This proves that the SAY program window isn't a child window of the dBASE main window.

- Select Exit from the File menu of the SAY program. (See Figure 1.51.)

  Of course, nothing happens because you haven't attached any code to the Exit menu item. You'll do that in the next section.

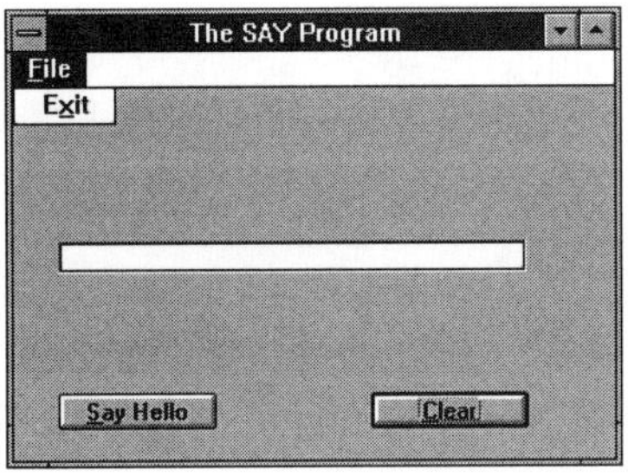

Figure 1.51.
Selecting Exit from the File menu of the SAY program.

- Terminate the SAY program by clicking the minus icon at the upper-left corner of the SAY.WFM window and selecting Close from the system menu.
- Maximize the dBASE main window.

Attaching Code to the Exit Menu Item

Now the SAY.MNU menu you designed is attached to the SAY program window. However, when you select Exit from the File menu, nothing happens. In this section you'll attach code to the `OnClick` event of the Exit menu item so that when you select this menu item the program will do what it's supposed to do—terminate itself.

Open the SAY.MNU menu in design mode as follows:

- Type `MODIFY MENU ?` in the Command window, press the Enter key, then select the menu file C:\DBPROG\CH01\SAY.MNU from the Open Form dialog box that dBASE displays.

  dBASE responds by displaying the SAY.MNU menu in design mode.

Now attach code to the `OnClick` event of the Exit menu item as follows:

- Select the `E&xit` menu item of the SAY.MNU menu by clicking it.
- Make the Inspector window the active window by selecting Inspector from the dBASE View menu.
- Make sure the pull-down list box at the top of the Inspector window is set to form.root.file.exit (because you're attaching code to an event associated with the Exit menu item of the File menu).
- Select the Events tab at the bottom of the Inspector window by clicking it.

You want to attach code to this event:

```
User selected the Exit menu item
```

That is, you want to write dBASE code that is executed automatically when the user selects Exit from the File menu. The pull-down list box at the top of the Inspector window is currently set to form.root.file.exit, so all the events currently listed in the Inspector window are events associated with the Exit menu item of the File menu. The event you need right now is the `OnClick` event—the `OnClick` event of a menu item occurs when the user selects this menu item (with either the mouse or the keyboard).

☐ Select the `OnClick` event by clicking it.

☐ Click the Tool button of the `OnClick` event.

dBASE responds by opening the Procedure Editor to let you write code in the `EXIT_OnClick` *procedure. (See Figure 1.52.) The code you'll write in this procedure will be executed automatically when the user selects the Exit menu item.*

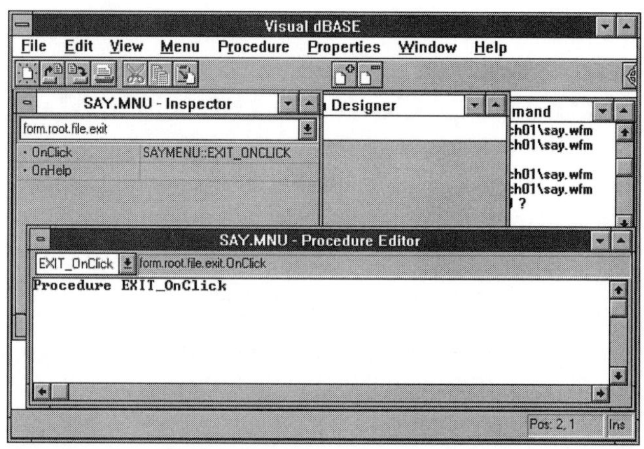

Figure 1.52.
The Procedure Editor with the `EXIT_OnClick` *procedure ready for editing.*

☐ Enter the following code in the `EXIT_OnClick` procedure:

```
Procedure EXIT_OnClick

  * Terminate the program by closing the form.
  form.Close()

Return
```

Your Procedure Editor window should now look like the one shown in Figure 1.53.

> **Note:** When you type the preceding code, don't forget to type the parentheses that follow the word `Close`.

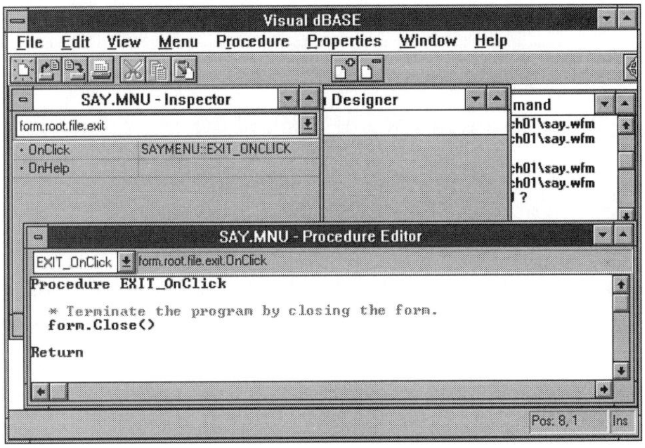

Figure 1.53.
The Procedure Editor after you enter code in the `EXIT_OnClick()` procedure.

Review the code you just typed in the `EXIT_OnClick()` procedure.

This is the first statement you typed in the `EXIT_OnClick()` procedure:

```
form.Close()
```

This statement executes the `Close()` method on form. What does the `Close()` method do? As implied by its name, the `Close()` method closes something. So this statement:

```
form.Close()
```

is telling dBASE to close `form`. The `form` keyword refers to the SAY.WFM form because you're attaching code to the SAY.MNU menu, which is attached to the SAY.WFM form. Therefore, the `form.Close()` statement closes the SAY.WFM form. And because the SAY.WFM form is the main window of the program, closing the SAY program terminates the program. The statement `form.Close()` has the same effect as selecting Close from the system menu of the SAY program. (Refer to Figure 1.26.)

The last statement you typed in the `EXIT_OnClick` procedure is `Return`, which terminates the procedure.

Don't forget to save your work:

- ☐ Select Save from the file menu of dBASE.

Run the SAY program and check whether the code you attached to the `OnClick` event of the Exit menu item is working:

- ☐ Close the SAY.MNU window.
- ☐ Type `DO C:\DBPROG\CH01\SAY.WFM` in the Command window and press Enter.

  dBASE responds by executing the SAY program. The window of the SAY program appears, as shown back in Figure 1.50.

- ☐ Select Exit from the File menu of the SAY program.

  The SAY program responds by terminating itself. The code you attached to the `OnClick` *event of the Exit menu item is working!*

A Shortcut for Testing Your Forms

In the preceding sections, you executed the SAY.WFM form by typing the statement `DO C:\DBPROG\CH01\SAY.WFM` in the Command window of dBASE. You were instructed to execute the SAY.WFM form this way so you would realize that SAY.WFM isn't just a form, but actually a dBASE program that can be executed.

However, while you develop your form, using the `DO` statement isn't very convenient for testing your form. A shorter and more convenient way to test your form while you develop it is using the Run tool in the dBASE toolbar. To see the Run tool in action, follow these steps:

- ☐ Type `MODIFY FORM ?` in the Command window, press the Enter key, and then select the file C:\DBPROG\CH01\SAY.WFM from the Open Form dialog box that dBASE displays.

  dBASE responds by displaying the SAY.WFM form in design mode.

- ☐ Now execute the SAY.WFM form by clicking the Run tool in the dBASE toolbar. (See the left icon shown in Figure 1.54.)

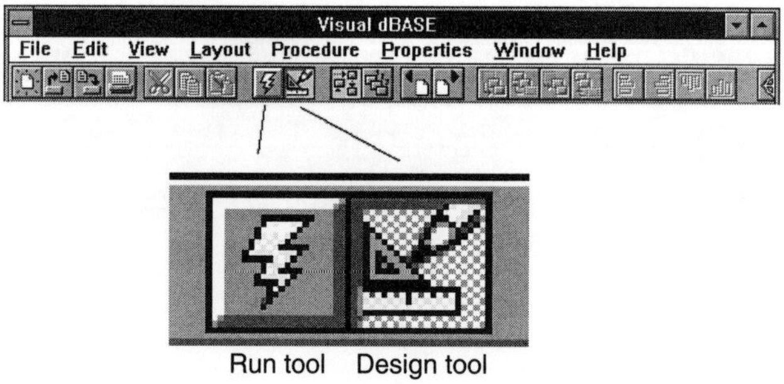

Figure 1.54.
The Run tool and the Design tool in the dBASE toolbar.

As you have just seen, you managed to execute the SAY.WFM form by simply clicking the Run tool. This is much more convenient than the two-step process of first closing the form and then executing the `DO` statement in the Command window.

As shown in Figure 1.54, the dBASE toolbar also has a Design tool. Clicking the Design tool brings the form back to design mode. However, in the case of the SAY.WFM form, after you click the Run tool, the dBASE toolbar disappears and you cannot click the Design tool.

When you design a form without a menu (the MenuFile property is set to blank) and with the MDI property set to .T. (the form conforms to the MDI standard), after you click the Run tool, the dBASE toolbar remains on the screen and you can bring the form back to design mode by clicking the Design tool.

☐ Terminate the SAY program by selecting Exit from its File menu.

Making a Standalone Version of the SAY Program

So far you have executed the SAY program by typing the `DO` command in the dBASE Command window. Running a program this way is easy enough. However, if you want users who aren't familiar with the dBASE package to execute your program, you can't expect these users to know how to type commands in the Command window to execute your program. Some users may not even own the dBASE package. Typically, Windows users expect to run a program directly from Windows or the File Manager program of Windows without first having to run another program.

In this section, you'll enhance the SAY program so that the user will be able to run it directly from Windows or the File Manager of Windows. To create a standalone EXE program, you must first install the dBASE compiler.

Take a look at the dBASE menu bar when the Command window is the active window. One of the menus is the Program menu. (See Figure 1.55.) If you installed the dBASE compiler, you'll see the Build Executable item in the Program menu.

True standalone programs usually have an EXE file extension (for example, MyProg.EXE). A true standalone EXE program can be executed directly from Windows (even on a PC that doesn't have the dBASE package installed).

You'll now create the SAY program:

☐ Select Build Executable from the dBASE Program menu, which appears when the Command window is the active window. The Build Executable item of the Program menu appears if you installed the dBASE compiler.

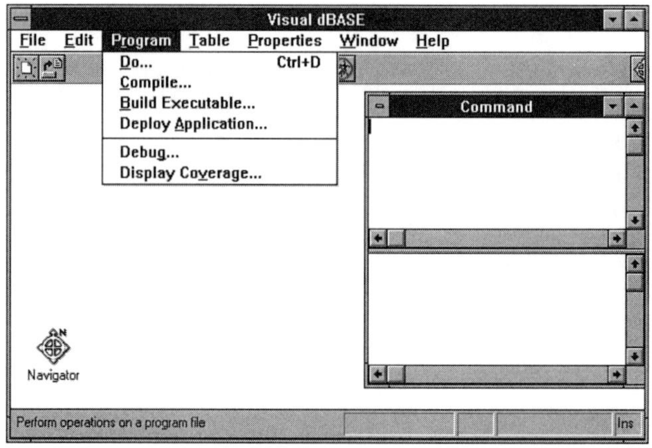

Figure 1.55.
The Program menu (while the Command window is the active window).

Note: The Build Executable menu item will appear in the Program menu of your Visual dBASE only if you installed the Visual dBASE compiler. The Visual dBASE compiler is available from Borland as an add-on to Visual dBASE (at extra cost).

You can perform the preceding step only if you have installed the Visual dBASE compiler. However, even if you do not have the Visual dBASE compiler, we recommend that you read through the steps of this section (without performing them) so that you'll see how easy it is to create an EXE file from your dBASE programs.

dBASE responds by displaying the Build Executable window, as shown in Figure 1.56.

☐ Click the Tool icon to the right of the Directory box.

dBASE responds by displaying the Choose Directory window.

☐ Select the \DBPROG\CH01 directory, as shown in Figure 1.57, and then click the OK button.

dBASE responds by displaying the Build Executable window again. However, now it contains two files: say.mno and say.wfo. (See Figure 1.58.)

☐ Select the say.wfo file from the Available Files list and click the right-arrow button.

dBASE responds by listing the say.wfo file in the Files to Build list.

☐ Select the say.mno file from the Available Files list and click the right-arrow button.

dBASE responds by listing the say.mno file in the Files to Build list. Your Build Executable window should now look like the one shown in Figure 1.59.

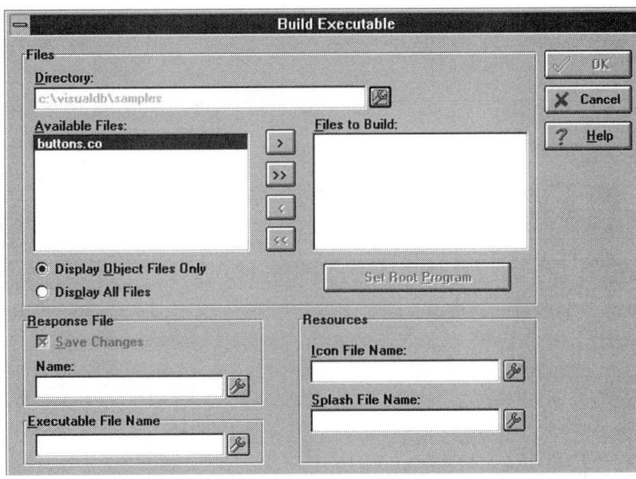

Figure 1.56.
The Build Executable window for creating EXE programs.

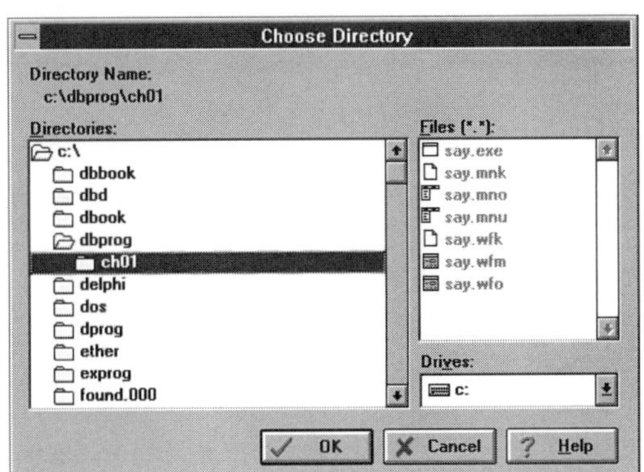

Figure 1.57.
Selecting the C:\DBPROG\CH01 directory.

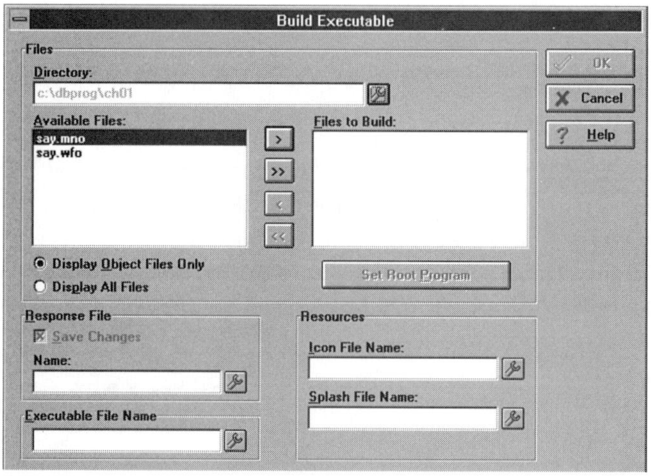

Figure 1.58.
The Build Executable window with the files ready to be linked.

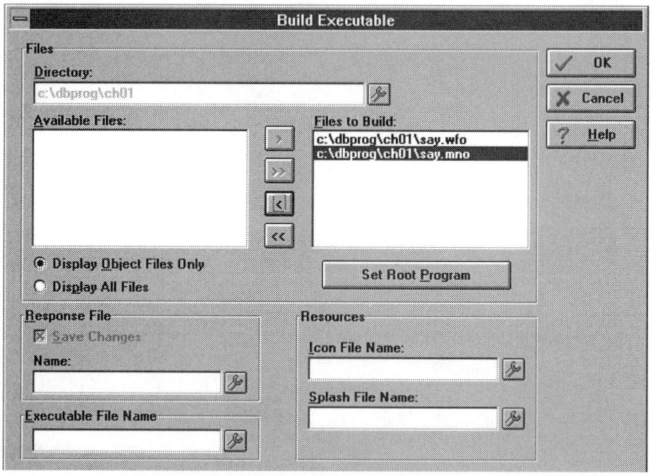

Figure 1.59.
The Build Executable window ready to generate the SAY.EXE file.

- ☐ Click the OK button in the Build Executable window.

  dBASE generates the C:\DBPROG\CH01\SAY.EXE file and then displays the Build Completed dialog box shown in Figure 1.60.

- ☐ Click the OK button of the Build Completed dialog box.

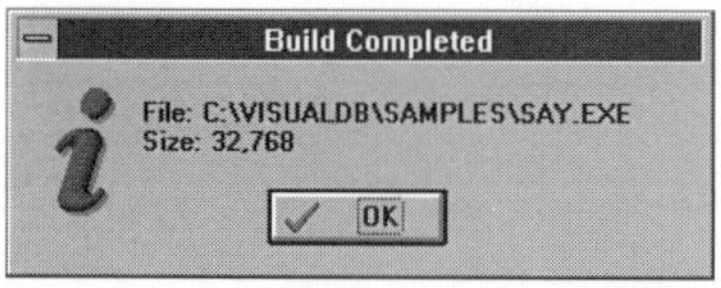

Figure 1.60.
The Build Completed dialog box.

☐ Terminate the dBASE program.

☐ Use the Windows File Manager program to execute the C:\DBPROG\CH01\SAY.EXE program.

As you can see, the SAY.EXE program is executed like any other standalone EXE program.

Summary

In this chapter you have learned the following:

- How to design a dBASE form (a WFM program)—creating the form, placing controls in it, and executing the form
- How to attach dBASE code to the events of the controls you place in the form
- How to design a menu and attach it to a form
- How to attach code to the menu
- How to create a standalone version of your dBASE program so that users who are not familiar with the dBASE package and users who don't own the dBASE package will be able to execute your program directly from Windows

Q&A

Q The title of this book is *Teach Yourself Visual dBASE 5.5 Programming in 21 Days.* Can I read and learn the book in fewer (or more) days?

A Yes. Some people work through a couple of chapters each day. You should learn at your own pace.

Q Can I write professional programs using dBASE for Windows?

A Yes. dBASE for Windows is designed so you can write fancy, professional Windows applications in a very short time.

Q The word *dBASE* in dBASE for Windows implies that it's designed specifically to write programs that work with databases. But in this chapter the SAY program I wrote didn't use any databases. How come?

A You can use the dBASE for Windows package to write any type of program—with databases or without. Although dBASE for Windows programs typically use databases, you can use dBASE for Windows to write a "regular" program that doesn't use any database, as you have seen in this chapter.

However, the database feature of dBASE for Windows is a great advantage over other programming languages. For example, if you write a game program using dBASE for Windows, you can use a database to keep the players' scores.

Q I get confused! The SAY.WFM file I created in this chapter is sometimes referred to as a form and other times as a program. Which is it? Is SAY.WFM a program or a form?

A The SAY.WFM file you created in this chapter is both a form and a program. The SAY.WFM file is a form because you can place controls in it by using the visual tools of dBASE for Windows. The SAY.WFM file is also a program because after you complete the visual design of the form and attach code to its controls, you can execute the SAY.WFM file.

Quiz

1. What are the two steps in the design process of a dBASE for Windows program?
2. What is the command you type in the dBASE Command window to create a new form (WFM file) called MyForm.WFM in the directory C:\TRY?
3. Suppose you created the form C:\TRY\MyForm.WFM, you customized this form, and then you closed it. What is the command you type in the dBASE Command window to modify the form C:\TRY\MyForm.WFM?
4. Give several examples of controls you can place in a form. (Hint: Use Figure 1.11 to answer this question.)
5. How do you place a pushbutton control in a form?
6. After placing a control in a form, how can you move it to any location in the form?
7. After placing a control in a form, how do you size the control?
8. Describe how you change the Text property of a pushbutton control.
9. What is the `OnClick` event of a pushbutton control?
10. Describe how you attach code to the `OnClick` event of a pushbutton control.
11. If MYFIELD is the name of an entry field control, what does the following statement do?

    ```
    form.MyField.Value = "This is a test."
    ```

12. Bug buster: What's wrong with the following statement?

    ```
    form.MyField.Value = Hi there!
    ```

13. What is the command you type in the dBASE Command window to create a menu called C:\TRY\MyMenu.MNU?
14. What is the command you type in the dBASE Command window to modify the menu C:\TRY\MyMenu.MNU?

15. Suppose you have designed a form called MyForm.WFM and a menu called MyMenu.MNU. How do you attach the MyMenu.MNU menu to the MyForm.WFM form?
16. What is the MDI property of a form?

Exercise

Write a program called BEEP.WFM that has the following characteristics:

- The title of the main window of the BEEP program is The BEEP Program.
- The main window of the program has one pushbutton in it with the caption Beep.
- When you click the Beep button, the PC beeps. (See note below.)
- The window of the BEEP program has a menu bar attached to it. This menu bar has one menu with the title File. The File menu has one menu item, Exit. When you select Exit from the File menu, the program terminates.

Note: The dBASE statement that causes the PC to beep is `??CHR(7)`. You can check this by typing `??CHR(7)` in the dBASE Command window and pressing the Enter key. After you execute this statement, the PC will beep.

Quiz Answers

1. The two steps are the visual programming step (placing objects in the form and setting their properties) and the code programming step (writing and attaching code to objects and events).
2. To create a form called MyForm.WFM in the directory C:\TRY, type the command `CREATE FORM C:\TRY\MyForm` in the Command window.

   After executing this command, dBASE will create the file C:\TRY\MyForm.WFM and let you design this form (place controls in the form, set their properties, attach code to them, and so on.)
3. To modify the form C:\TRY\MyForm.WFM, enter the command `MODIFY FORM ?` in the Command window, then select the C:\TRY\MyForm.WFM file from the Open Form dialog box that dBASE displays.

   After selecting the C:\TRY\MYFORM.WFM file, dBASE will open the MyForm.WFM form in design mode and let you design this form.

Or you can type the command `MODIFY FORM C:\TRY\MyForm`. However, using the `MODIFY FORM ?` command is safer because you avoid typing errors that may result in the creation of a new form.

4. You can place any of the controls in the dBASE Control Palette in a form (for example, Text, EntryField, PushButton). (Refer to Figure 1.11.)
5. To place a pushbutton control in a form, simply double-click the pushbutton control in the Control Palette. Similarly, to place any other control in the form, click the control in the Control Palette.
6. After placing a control in a form, you can move it to any location in the form by dragging the control with the mouse.
7. After placing a control in a form, you can change the control to any size by dragging its handles.
8. To change the Text property of a pushbutton control, select the pushbutton control by clicking it, then display the Inspector window, then select the Properties tab of the Inspector window, and finally change the Text property to the desired text.
9. The `OnClick` event of a pushbutton control occurs when you click the pushbutton control.
10. To attach code to the `OnClick` event of a pushbutton control, select the pushbutton control by clicking it, then display the Inspector window, then select the Events tab of the Inspector window, then select the `OnClick` event, and finally click the Tool button of the `OnClick` event. dBASE will respond by opening the Procedure Editor to let you write code in the procedure of the `OnClick` event.
11. The following statement:

    ```
    form.MyField.Value = "This is a test."
    ```

    sets the Value property of the MYFIELD entry field control to the string `"This is a test."`. As a result, the MYFIELD entry field is filled with the text `This is a test.`
12. This is the correct syntax:

    ```
    form.MyField.Value = "Hi there!"
    ```

    That is, you must enclose the text within double quotes.
13. To create the menu C:\TRY\MyMenu.MNU, type `CREATE MENU C:\TRY\MyMenu` in the Command window.

    After executing this command, dBASE will create the file C:\TRY\MyMenu.MNU and let you design this menu.
14. To modify the menu C:\TRY\MyMenu.MNU, type `MODIFY MENU ?` in the Command window, press Enter, and then select the C:\TRY\MyMenu.MNU file from the Open Form dialog box that dBASE displays.

After you select the C:\TRY\MyMenu.MNU file, dBASE will open the MyMenu.MNU menu in design mode and let you design this menu.

Or you can type the command `MODIFY MENU C:\TRY\MyMenu`. However, using the `MODIFY MENU ?` command is safer because you avoid typing errors that may result in the creation of a new menu.

15. To attach the MyMenu.MNU menu to the MyForm.WFM form, you have to set the MenuFile property of the MyForm.WFM form to the full pathname of the MyMenu.MNU menu. For example, if the MyMenu.MNU file is in the C:\TRY directory, then you have to set the MenuFile property of the MyForm.WFM form to C:\TRY\MyMenu.MNU.
16. The MDI property of a form determines whether the form conforms to the Windows MDI standard. If you set the MDI property of a form to .T. (that is, TRUE), then the form will conform to the MDI standard. If, however, you set the MDI property of a form to .F. (that is, FALSE), then the form will not conform to the MDI standard.

    When a form conforms to the MDI standard, its menu is not displayed on its own window, but rather on the dBASE main window (whenever the form's window is active). Also, the form's window is a child window of the dBASE main window.

    When a form does not conform to the MDI standard (the MDI property is set to .F.), its menu is displayed on its own window, which is independent of the dBASE main window. That is, the form's window isn't a child window of the dBASE main window.

Exercise Answer

The steps for writing the BEEP program are similar to the steps you took when you wrote the SAY program. These are the main differences:

- When you set the Text property of the pushbutton control, you should set it to &Beep.
- When you set the Name property of the pushbutton control, you should set it to BEEPBUTTON.
- When you attach code to the `OnClick` event of the BEEP pushbutton, this is the code you write in the procedure of this event:

```
Procedure BEEPBUTTON_OnClick

   * Beep
   ??Chr(7)

Return
```

WEEK 1

2

Designing Your First Table

In this chapter you will design your first dBASE table. You'll learn what a table is, how to design a table, how to enter data into a table, and how to manipulate the data.

Note: In Chapter 1, "Writing Your First dBASE Program," you learn how to write a dBASE program. In this chapter, you learn how to design and use a dBASE table. In Chapter 3, "Using a Table from Within Your Program," you use the knowledge you gain in Chapter 1 and this chapter to write a dBASE program that uses a table.

Creating a dBASE Table

A *dBASE table* is a file with a .DBF extension (for example, MyTable.DBF) that stores data. Creating a dBASE table is not much different from creating a table on a piece of paper. Just like a table you draw on a piece of paper, a dBASE table has vertical columns and horizontal rows. To design the table, you simply have to define the column headings and sizes. Once the structure of the table is ready, you can enter data into the table. For practice, in this chapter you'll use dBASE to create a table that looks like the one shown in Figure 2.1.

Figure 2.1.
A table for storing information about people.

First Name	Last Name	Age	Phone Number

As you can see, the table shown in Figure 2.1 is used for storing information about people. Each horizontal row in the table stores information about a particular person: the person's first name, last name, age, and phone number. In the following steps you'll create a dBASE table, called PERSONS.DBF, with the same structure as the table shown in Figure 2.1.

> **Note:** Just as a table you draw manually has columns and rows, so does a dBASE table. However, in dBASE terminology, the columns are called *fields* and the rows are called *records*. For example, the PERSONS.DBF table you create in the following steps will have four fields: FirstName, LastName, Age, and Phone.
>
> After you finish creating the structure of the PERSONS.DBF table, you'll use dBASE commands to add records to the table. Each record will store information about a particular person (just as each row in the "paper" table shown in Figure 2.1 can store information about a particular person).

Before you create the PERSONS.DBF table, first create the directory where the table will reside:

☐ Start dBASE for Windows.

☐ Type `MD C:\DBPROG` in the Command window and then press Enter.

dBASE responds by creating the directory C:\DBPROG. (If this directory already exists, dBASE will display a message box telling you that it can't be created.)

☐ Type `MD C:\DBPROG\CH02` in the Command window and then press Enter.

dBASE responds by creating the directory C:\DBPROG\CH02.

Now create the PERSONS.DBF table as follows:

☐ Type `CREATE C:\DBPROG\CH02\PERSONS` in the Command window and press Enter.

dBASE responds by displaying the empty Table Structure window for the PERSONS.DBF table. (See Figure 2.2.)

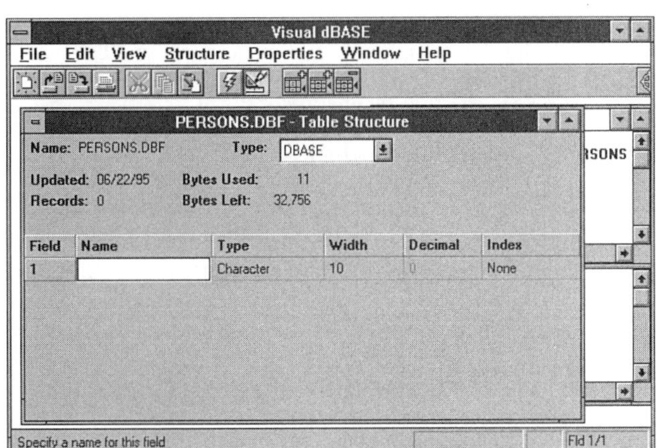

Figure 2.2.
The empty Table Structure window for the PERSONS.DBF table.

You'll now use the Table Structure window to set the names and sizes of the PERSONS.DBF table fields. As you can see, the mouse cursor is currently in the cell under the Name heading. dBASE is waiting for you to specify the name of the first field of the PERSONS.DBF table.

☐ Type `FIRSTNAME`.

Your Table Structure window should now look like the one shown in Figure 2.3.

Figure 2.3.
Setting the first field name to FIRSTNAME.

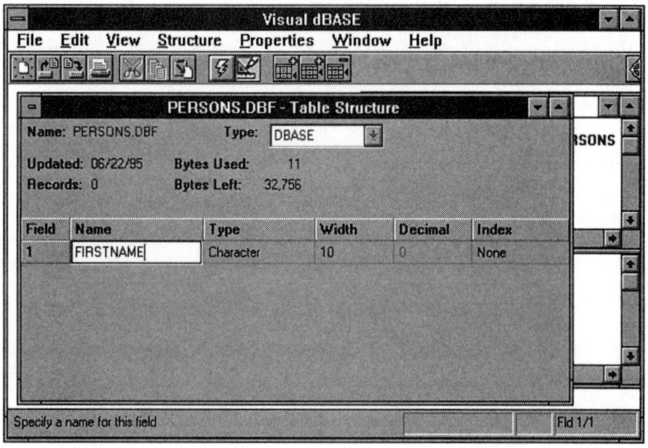

Next you have to specify the type of the FIRSTNAME field. That is, you have to specify what type of data will be stored in the FIRSTNAME field (for example, character, numeric, date).

☐ Click the mouse in the Type cell (under the Type heading).

As you can see, the Type cell becomes highlighted and a small down-arrow icon appears to the right of the Type cell.

☐ Click the down-arrow icon next to the Type cell.

dBASE responds by opening a list of field types. (See Figure 2.4.)

☐ Select Character from the list.

You set the type of the FIRSTNAME field to character because it will be used for storing the first names of people in characters. Next you have to specify the width of the FIRSTNAME field—how many characters it will hold.

☐ Click the mouse in the Width cell (under the Width heading), type `20` in the Width cell, and press Enter.

You have finished setting the specifications for the first field of the PERSONS.DBF table! Your Table Structure window should now look like the one shown in Figure 2.5.

Figure 2.4.
Selecting the type of the first field.

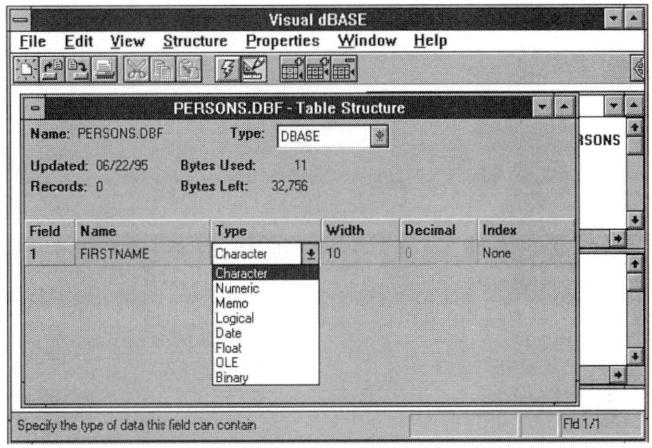

Figure 2.5.
The Table Structure window after you finish adding the FIRSTNAME field.

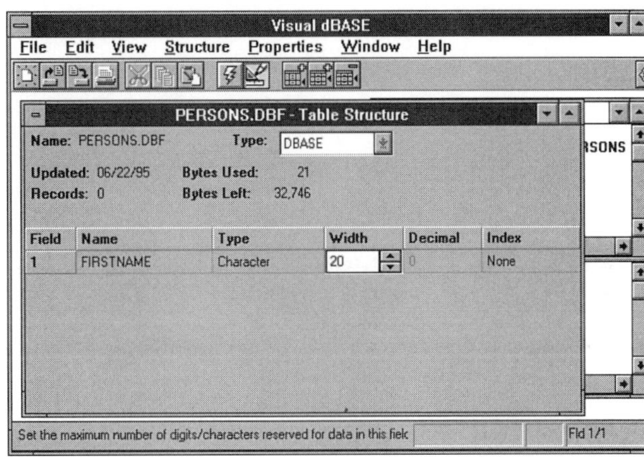

As shown in Figure 2.5, you defined the first field of the PERSONS.DBF table as follows:

Field Name	*Type*	*Width*	*Decimal*	*Index*
FIRSTNAME	Character	20	0	None

The Decimal cell specifies the number of decimal places for numeric fields. Because the FIRSTNAME field's type is character, dBASE sets the Decimal cell to 0, and you can't change this value. The Index cell is set to None by default. Later in this chapter, you'll learn what the Index is used for and how to set it.

Now add a second field to the PERSONS.DBF table:

☐ Select Add Field from the Structure menu of dBASE (or press Ctrl+A on your keyboard).

dBASE responds by adding a new field to the PERSONS.DBF table.

☐ Define the new field as follows:

Field Name	*Type*	*Width*	*Decimal*	*Index*
LASTNAME	Character	20	0	None

Your Table Structure window should now look like the one shown in Figure 2.6.

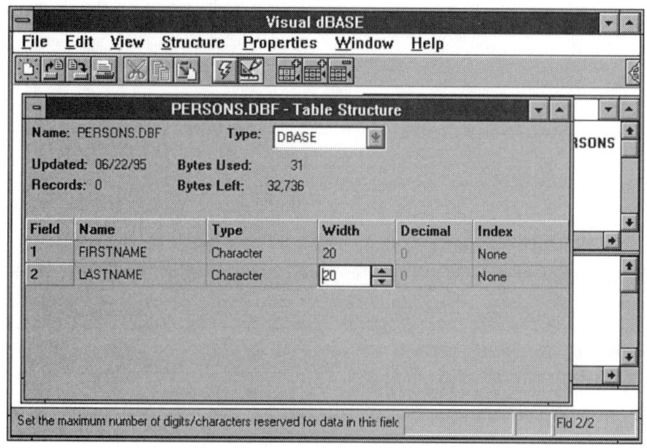

Figure 2.6.
The Table Structure window after you finish adding the LASTNAME field.

☐ Repeat the preceding steps to add two additional fields to the PERSONS.DBF table. Define the two new fields as follows:

Field Name	*Type*	*Width*	*Decimal*	*Index*
BIRTHDATE	Date	8	0	None
PHONE	Character	13	0	None

You have finished defining the structure of the PERSONS.DBF table! Your Table Structure window should now look like the one shown in Figure 2.7.

☐ Save your work by selecting Save from the File menu.

☐ Close the Table Structure window by selecting Close from the File menu.

Although you have finished building the structure of the PERSONS.DBF table, later you can change the table's structure. dBASE allows you to change the sizes of the fields or remove and add fields to the table. Later in this chapter you'll learn how to modify a table's structure.

Figure 2.7.
The complete Table Structure window for the PERSONS.DBF table.

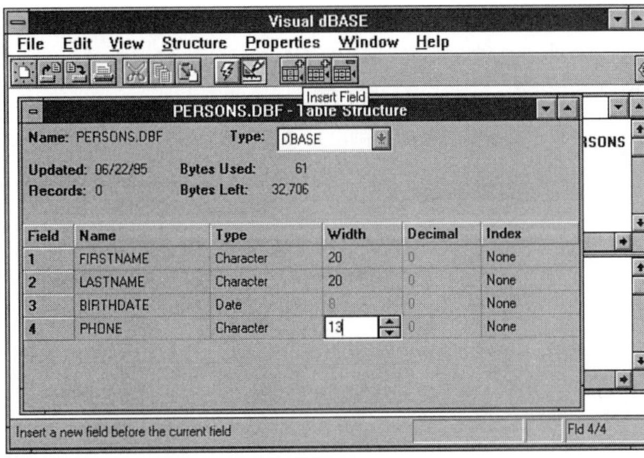

Opening and Closing a dBASE Table

Before you can perform operations on a dBASE table, first you must open the table. The PERSONS.DBF table is currently open because in the preceding steps you created it. After you create a new table, dBASE opens it for you automatically. You can check that the PERSONS.DBF table is currently open as follows:

☐ Type `?DBF()` in the Command window and press Enter.

dBASE responds by displaying the name of the PERSONS.DBF table in the results pane of the Command window. This means that the PERSONS.DBF table is currently open.

Note: The `?` statement displays whatever expression you tell it to display in the results pane of the Command window. For example, if you execute this statement:

```
?"This is a test"
```

dBASE will display the text `This is a test` in the results pane of the Command window.

In the preceding step, you executed the statement `?DBF()` in the Command window. As a result, dBASE displayed the name of the currently open table (PERSONS.DBF) in the results pane of the Command window. The `DBF()` function returns the name of the currently open table.

To close the PERSONS.DBF table, do the following:

☐ Type `CLOSE DATABASES` in the Command window and press Enter.

dBASE responds by closing the PERSONS.DBF table.

The `CLOSE DATABASES` command closes all the currently open tables. As you'll learn later in this book, it is possible to open several tables at the same time. Ensure that the PERSONS.DBF table isn't open:

☐ Type `CLEAR` in the Command window and press Enter.

dBASE responds by clearing the results pane of the Command window.

☐ Type `?DBF()` in the Command window and then press the Enter key.

dBASE responds by printing a blank line in the results pane of the Command window—the PERSONS.DBF table isn't open.

To open the PERSONS.DBF table, do the following:

☐ Type `USE C:\DBPROG\CH02\PERSONS` and press Enter.

dBASE responds by opening the PERSONS.DBF table.

Now check again whether the PERSONS.DBF table is open:

☐ Type `?DBF()` in the Command window and press Enter.

dBASE responds by displaying the name of the PERSONS.DBF table in the results pane of the Command window, so it is currently open.

Note: To open a table, use the `USE` command. For example, the statement `USE C:\TRY\MyTable` opens the C:\TRY\MyTable.DBF table.

To close all the currently open tables, use the `CLOSE DATABASES` command.

The topic of opening several tables at one time is covered in later chapters in the book.

Using the *BROWSE* Command

The `BROWSE` command enables you to manipulate the records of a table very easily. For example, you can use the `BROWSE` command to add records to a table, to view a table's records, and to edit a table's records. To see the `BROWSE` command in action, do the following:

☐ Type `BROWSE` in the Command window and press Enter.

dBASE responds by displaying the PERSONS.DBF table for you to browse through. (See Figure 2.8.)

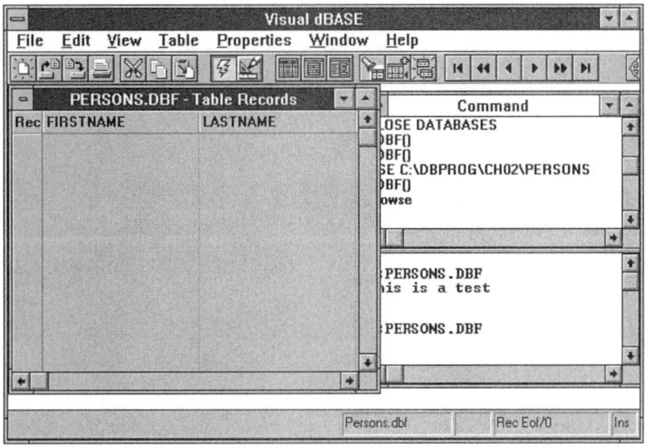

Figure 2.8.
Browsing through the PERSONS.DBF table.

Note: When you executed the `BROWSE` command in the preceding step, dBASE displayed the PERSONS.DBF table because it's the table that's currently open. Before you issued the `BROWSE` command you opened the PERSONS.DBF table, so dBASE knows you want to browse the PERSONS.DBF table.

As you can see, the browse window isn't wide enough; you can't see all the fields in the PERSONS.DBF table. Here's how you enlarge the width of the browse window:

- ☐ Enlarge the width of the PERSONS.DBF browse window by dragging the right edge of the window to the right.

The enlarged browse window of the PERSONS.DBF table is shown in Figure 2.9.

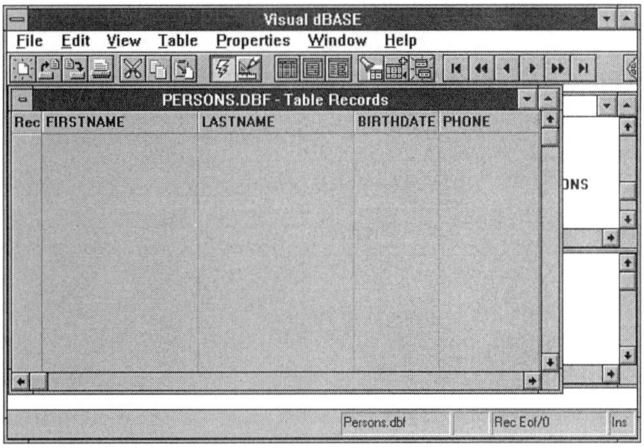

Figure 2.9.
The enlarged browse window of the PERSONS.DBF table.

The PERSONS.DBF table is currently empty—it has no records. To add a new record to the PERSONS.DBF table, do the following:

- ☐ Select Add Records from the Table menu.

  dBASE responds by adding a blank record to the PERSONS.DBF table. This new blank record appears as a new row in the browse window. (See Figure 2.10.)

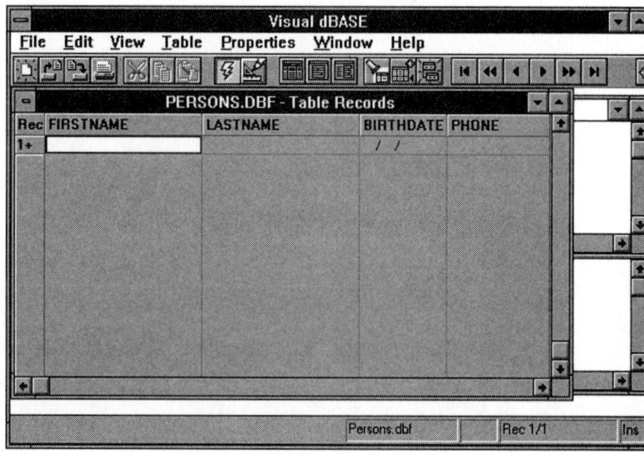

Figure 2.10.
Adding a new record to the PERSONS.DBF table.

- ☐ Fill the blank record as follows:

Rec	*FIRSTNAME*	*LASTNAME*	*BIRTHDATE*	*PHONE*
1	Jane	Smart	02/14/70	(212)555-2222

As you enter the data, note that you can move from one field to another by using the Tab key. To move to the next field, press the Tab key. To move back to the previous field, press Shift+Tab. The PERSONS.DBF table should now look like the one shown in Figure 2.11.

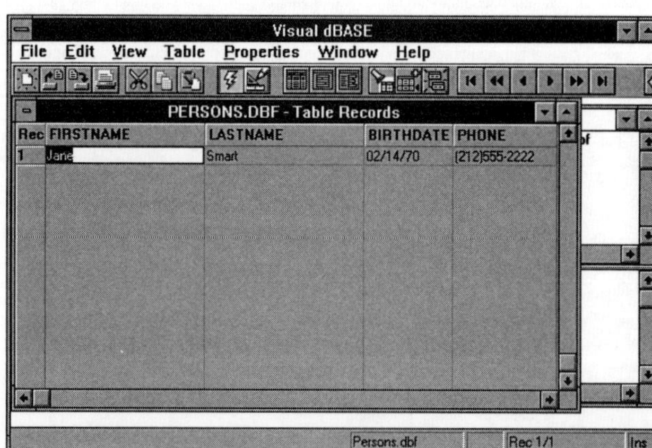

Figure 2.11.
Filling the first record of the PERSONS.DBF table.

Note: The leftmost column in the table is the Rec column, which represents the record number. dBASE automatically fills this column with the record number of the record you're entering. For example, in the preceding step you entered data into record number 1 of the table. Therefore, the Rec column is filled with 1.

When you finish typing the data of the last field (the PHONE field), dBASE is ready to enter a new record in the PERSONS.DBF table.

☐ Use the down-arrow key on your keyboard to move to the next row of the PERSONS.DBF table.

dBASE responds by displaying a blank row. (See Figure 2.12.)

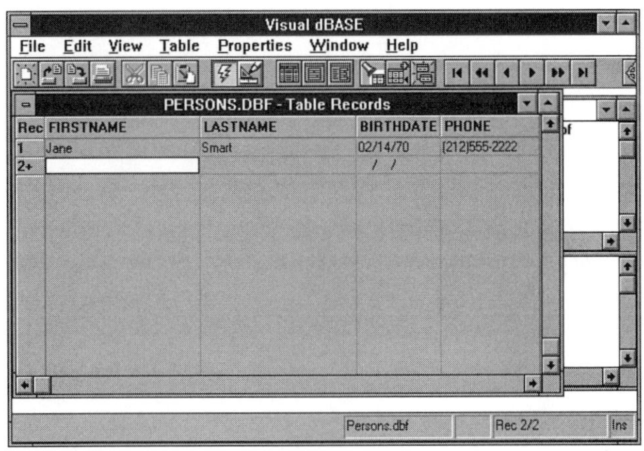

Figure 2.12.
Adding a second record to the PERSONS.DBF table.

☐ Enter data in four more records so the table looks like this (you already entered the data for the first record):

Rec	*FIRSTNAME*	*LASTNAME*	*BIRTHDATE*	*PHONE*
1	Jane	Smart	02/14/70	(212)555-2222
2	Al	Smith	06/21/55	(212)555-4444
3	Julie	Eden	02/14/81	(212)555-5555
4	Mark	Gold	01/01/81	(212)555-1111
5	Bill	Smart	05/10/65	(212)555-3333

Since you don't want to enter a sixth record in the PERSONS.DBF table, do the following:

☐ Press the up-arrow key on your keyboard.

dBASE responds by moving to the previous field. The browse window of the PERSONS.DBF table now looks like the one shown in Figure 2.13.

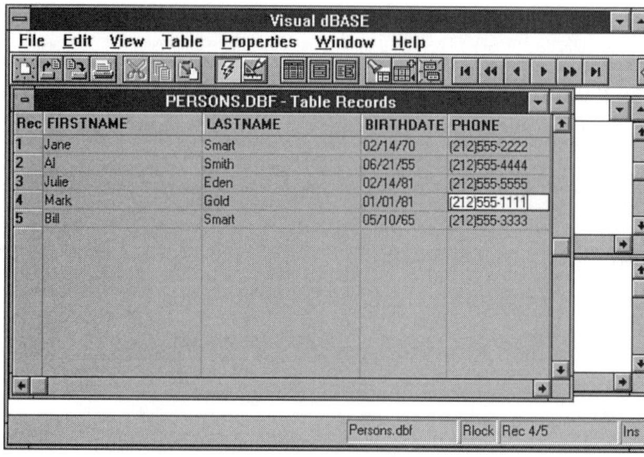

Figure 2.13.
The browse window of the PERSONS.DBF table with all five records entered.

You can now navigate around the records by using the up-arrow and down-arrow keys, and you can navigate around the fields by using Tab and Shift+Tab.

- ☐ Make sure the data for the five records you added to the table is the same as shown in Figure 2.13. If it's not, use the up-arrow, down-arrow, Tab, and Shift+Tab keys to navigate to the desired record and field and type the correct data.

It's important that the data you entered into the table is exactly as shown in Figure 2.13, so that later in this chapter you can follow the steps that manipulate these records.

Now close the browse window:

- ☐ While the browse window is the active window, select Close from the File menu.

  dBASE responds by closing the browse window.

> **Note:** In the preceding step you closed the browse window of the PERSONS.DBF table. You did *not* close the PERSONS.DBF table itself. Closing the browse window doesn't close the table.
>
> You can tell that the PERSONS.DBF table is still open by observing the status bar at the bottom of the dBASE window (the status bar displays the text PERSONS.DBF). As mentioned earlier, another way of telling that PERSONS.DBF is currently open is by typing `?DBF()` inside the Command window.
>
> To close the table itself you can use the `CLOSE DATABASES` statement. However, in the following sections you'll perform various operations on the PERSONS.DBF table, so don't close the table now.

The Record Pointer

When you work with a dBASE table, dBASE stores the current record number in the record pointer. For example, if the current record is record number 1, then the record pointer is equal to 1; if the current record is record number 2, then the record pointer is equal to 2; and so on. To understand how the record pointer works, do the following:

☐ Type `BROWSE` in the Command window and press Enter.

dBASE responds by displaying the browse window of the PERSONS.DBF table.

☐ If necessary, enlarge the width of the PERSONS.DBF browse window so you'll be able to see all the fields in the table.

☐ Use the up-arrow and down-arrow keys to navigate to record number 3 of the PERSONS.DBF table.

Since you selected record number 3 in the browse window, the current value of the record pointer is 3. To check this, do the following:

☐ Make the Command window the active window by clicking in it.

☐ Type `?RECNO()` in the Command window and press Enter.

dBASE responds by displaying the number 3 in the results pane of the Command window.

As you may have guessed, the `RECNO()` function returns the current value of the record pointer—the number of the current record. Because record number 3 is currently selected in the browse window, the record pointer is equal to 3 and the `RECNO()` function returns the number 3.

☐ Make the browse window the active window and use the down-arrow key to select record number 4.

☐ Make the Command window the active window, type `?RECNO()` in the Command window, and press Enter.

As expected, this time dBASE responds by displaying the number 4 in the results pane of the Command window—the record pointer is currently equal to 4.

Now close the browse window:

☐ Make the browse window the active window and select Close from the File menu.

dBASE responds by closing the browse window.

The *GOTO* Command and the *SKIP* Command

In the preceding section you moved the record pointer of the PERSONS.DBF table by selecting a record in the table's browse window. For example, you moved the record pointer to record number 4 by selecting record number 4 in the browse window. Another way to move the record pointer of a table is to use the `GOTO` and `SKIP` commands.

To see the `GOTO` command in action, do the following:

☐ Type `BROWSE` in the Command window and press Enter.

dBASE responds by displaying the browse window for the PERSONS.DBF table.

☐ If necessary, enlarge the width of the PERSONS.DBF browse window so you'll be able to see all the fields in the table.

☐ Make the Command window the active window.

☐ Type `GOTO 2` in the Command window and press Enter.

dBASE responds by moving the record pointer of the PERSONS.DBF table to record number 2. As you can see, the current record selected in the browse window is record number 2.

☐ Type `GOTO 4` in the Command window and press Enter.

dBASE responds by moving the record pointer of the PERSONS.DBF table to record number 4. As you can see, the current record selected in the browse window is record number 4.

To move the record pointer to the first record in the table you can use the `GOTO TOP` statement. To see the `GOTO TOP` statement in action, do the following:

☐ Type `GOTO TOP` in the Command window and press Enter.

dBASE responds by moving the record pointer of the PERSONS.DBF table to the first record in the table. As you can see, the current record selected in the browse window is record number 1.

To move the record pointer to the last record in the table you can use the `GOTO BOTTOM` statement. To see the `GOTO BOTTOM` statement in action, do the following:

☐ Type `GOTO BOTTOM` in the Command window and press Enter.

dBASE responds by moving the record pointer of the PERSONS.DBF table to the last record in the table. As you can see, the current record selected in the browse window is record number 5.

Another command that lets you move the record pointer is the `SKIP` command. To see the `SKIP` command in action, use the following steps:

☐ Type `GOTO TOP` in the Command window and press Enter.

dBASE responds by moving the record pointer of the PERSONS.DBF table to the first record in the table.

☐ Type `SKIP 1` in the Command window and press Enter.

dBASE responds by moving the record pointer to the next record. As you can see, the current record selected in the browse window is record number 2.

☐ Type `SKIP 1` in the Command window and press Enter.

dBASE responds by moving the record pointer to the next record. Now the current record selected in the browse window is record number 3.

☐ Type `SKIP -1` in the Command window and press Enter.

dBASE responds by moving the record pointer to the previous record. Now the current record selected in the browse window is record number 2.

As you have just seen, the `SKIP 1` statement moves the record pointer one record forward and the `SKIP -1` statement moves the record pointer one record backward.

You can also use the `SKIP` command to move the record pointer several records forward or backward. For example, the statement `SKIP 2` will move the record pointer two records forward, and the statement `SKIP -2` will move the record pointer two records backward.

In the preceding steps, the browse window of the PERSONS.DBF table was open while you used the `GOTO` command and `SKIP` command so you could see that the new record was selected. Of course, it isn't necessary to leave the browse window open when you use the `GOTO` and `SKIP` commands. To see the `GOTO` and `SKIP` commands in action without the browse window on the desktop, do the following:

☐ Make the browse window the active window, and select Close from the File menu.

dBASE responds by closing the browse window.

☐ Type `GOTO 1` in the Command window and press Enter.

dBASE responds by moving the record pointer to record number 1. To check that the record pointer is at record number 1, do the following:

☐ Type `?RECNO()` in the Command window and press Enter.

As expected, dBASE responds by displaying the number 1 in the results pane of the Command window. (Remember that the `RECNO()` function returns the current value of the record pointer.)

☐ Type `?FIRSTNAME` in the Command window and press Enter.

dBASE responds by displaying the text `Jane` *in the results pane of the Command window.*

The statement `?FIRSTNAME` tells dBASE to display the value of the FIRSTNAME field of the current record. Because the current record is record number 1, dBASE displayed the text `Jane`, the contents in the FIRSTNAME field of record number 1.

☐ Type `SKIP 1` in the Command window and press Enter.

dBASE responds by moving the record pointer to the next record (record number 2).

To check that the record pointer is at record number 2, do the following:

☐ Type `?RECNO()` in the Command window and press Enter.

As expected, dBASE responds by displaying the number `2` *in the results pane of the Command window.*

☐ Type `?FIRSTNAME` in the Command window and press Enter.

dBASE responds by displaying the text `Al` in the results pane of the Command window (the contents of the FIRSTNAME field of record number 2).

The End of File

When you move the record pointer past the last record of the table, the record pointer is at the *end of file.* You can think of the end of file as an imaginary record that follows the last record in the table.

dBASE includes a function called `EOF()` that enables you to detect when the record pointer has reached the end of file. Almost all dBASE programs with tables use the `EOF()` function. (You will learn how to use the `EOF()` function in a dBASE program in Chapter 3.)

The `EOF()` function returns either .T. (TRUE) or .F. (FALSE). If the record pointer is currently at the end of file, the `EOF()` function returns .T.. Otherwise, the `EOF()` function returns .F..

To see the `EOF()` function in action, follow these steps:

☐ Type `GOTO 4` in the Command window and press Enter.

dBASE responds by moving the record pointer to record number 4.

☐ Type `?EOF()` in the Command window and press Enter.

dBASE responds by displaying .F. in the results pane of the Command window. The `EOF()` *function returned .F. because record number 4 is not the end of file.*

☐ Type `SKIP 1` in the Command window and press Enter.

dBASE responds by moving the record pointer to record number 5 (the last record in the PERSONS.DBF table).

☐ Type `?EOF()` in the Command window and press Enter.

dBASE responds by displaying .F. in the results pane of the Command window. The `EOF()` *function returned .F., because record number 5 (the last record in the table) is not the end of file.*

☐ Type `SKIP 1` in the Command window and press Enter.

dBASE responds by moving the record pointer past the last record—to the end of file.

☐ Type `?EOF()` in the Command window and press Enter.

This time, dBASE displays .T. in the results pane of the Command window. The `EOF()` *function returned .T. because now the record pointer is at the end of file.*

The Beginning of File

When you move the record pointer to a record before the first record of the table, the record pointer is at the *beginning of file*. You can think of the beginning of file as an imaginary record that precedes the first record in the table.

dBASE includes a function called `BOF()` that enables you to detect when the record pointer has reached the beginning of file. Almost all dBASE programs with tables use the `BOF()` function. (You will learn how to use the `BOF()` function in a dBASE program in Chapter 3.)

The `BOF()` function returns either .T. or .F.. If the record pointer is at the beginning of file, the `BOF()` function returns .T.. Otherwise, the `BOF()` function returns .F..

To see the `BOF()` function in action, follow these steps:

☐ Type `GOTO 2` in the Command window and press Enter.

dBASE responds by moving the record pointer to record number 2.

☐ Type `?BOF()` in the Command window and press Enter.

dBASE responds by displaying .F. in the results pane of the Command window. The `BOF()` *function returned .F. because record number 2 is not the beginning of file.*

☐ Type `SKIP -1` in the Command window and press Enter.

dBASE responds by moving the record pointer to record number 1 (the first record in the table).

☐ Type `?BOF()` in the Command window and press Enter.

dBASE responds by displaying .F. in the results pane of the Command window. The `BOF()` *function returned .F. because record number 1 (the first record in the table) is not the beginning of file.*

☐ Type `SKIP -1` in the Command window and press Enter.

dBASE responds by moving the record pointer to the beginning of file.

☐ Type `?BOF()` in the Command window and press Enter.

This time, dBASE displays .T. in the results pane of the Command window. The `BOF()` *function returned .T. because now the record pointer is at the beginning of file.*

Deleting a Record

In this section you'll learn how to delete a record from a table. Before you begin practicing deleting records, you'll add two new records to the PERSONS.DBF table. This way you'll be able to practice deleting these records, without "hurting" the original records you added to the table (you'll need to use these original records later in this tutorial).

Follow these steps to add a new record to the PERSONS.DBF table:

☐ Type `BROWSE` in the Command window and press Enter.

dBASE responds by displaying the browse window of the PERSONS.DBF table.

☐ If necessary, enlarge the width of the PERSONS.DBF browse window so you'll be able to see all the fields in the table.

☐ Type `GOTO BOTTOM` in the Command window and press Enter.

dBASE responds by moving the record pointer to the last record in the table.

☐ Make the browse window the active window.

☐ Press the down-arrow key.

dBASE responds by adding a new blank record to the table.

☐ Fill the FIRSTNAME field of the new blank record with the text `TEST1`. (There's no reason to fill in the rest of the fields because you'll be deleting this record soon.)

☐ Press the down-arrow key again.

dBASE responds by adding another new blank record to the table.

☐ Fill the FIRSTNAME field of the new blank record with the text `TEST2`.

Figure 2.14 shows the browse window of the PERSONS.DBF table with the two new records.

Figure 2.14.
The browse window of the PERSONS.DBF table with two new records.

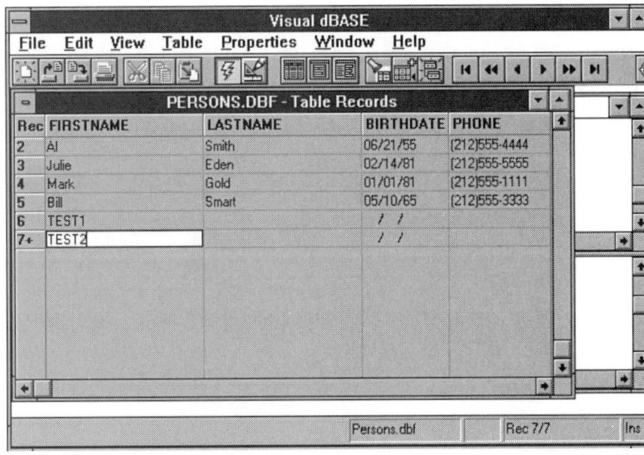

Now that you have two new records (record number 6 and record number 7), practice deleting a record. You'll move the record pointer to the record you want to delete and then issue the `DELETE` command. Follow these steps to delete record number 6:

- ☐ Make the Command window the active window.
- ☐ Type `GOTO 6` in the Command window and press Enter.

  dBASE responds by moving the record pointer to record number 6.

- ☐ Type `DELETE` in the Command window and press Enter.

  dBASE responds by deleting record number 6.

The browse window of the PERSONS.DBF table now looks like the one shown in Figure 2.15. It lists records numbers 1, 2, 3, 4, 5, and 7. Record number 6 has disappeared!

Figure 2.15.
Deleting record number 6 from the PERSONS.DBF table.

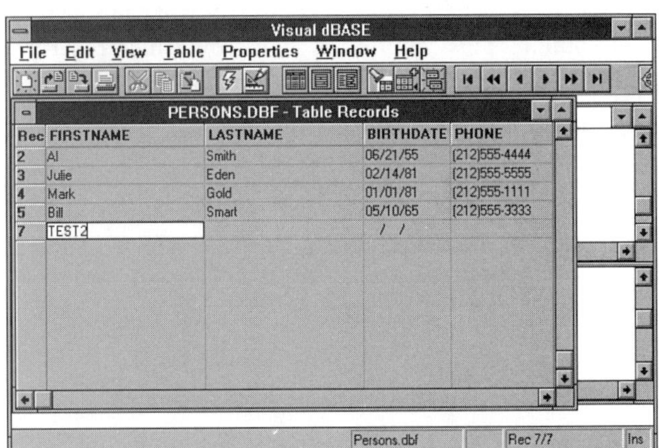

Although record number 6 isn't displayed in the browse window, it still exists in the table. When you issue a `DELETE` command, the deleted record isn't removed from the table—it is merely marked for deletion so commands like `BROWSE` and `SKIP` will ignore this record. The record you deleted still exists in the table, but it is hidden.

To check that the record you deleted (record number 6) still exists in the PERSONS.DBF table, follow these steps:

☐ Type `SET DELETED OFF` in the Command window and press Enter.

dBASE responds by showing the deleted record (record number 6). The browse window of the PERSONS.DBF table now looks like the one shown in Figure 2.16—record number 6 is visible.

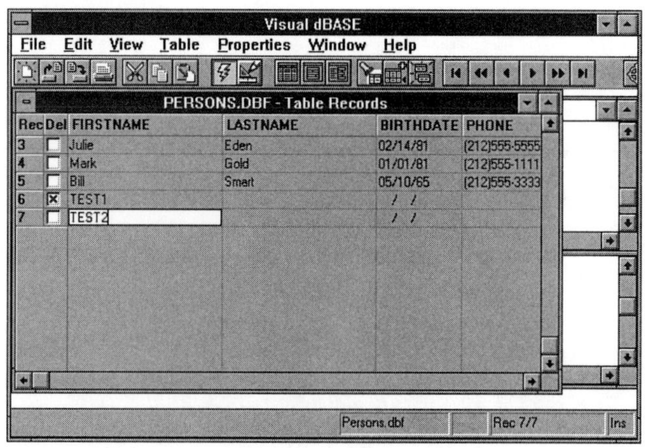

Figure 2.16.
The browse window of the PERSONS.DBF table after you execute the `SET DELETED OFF` statement.

By executing the `SET DELETED OFF` statement, you told dBASE to make all the deleted records visible. As shown in Figure 2.16, the browse window now includes an additional column: the `Del` column. This column lets you know which records are deleted. You can tell that record number 6 is deleted because it has an X in its Del column.

To tell dBASE to hide all the deleted records, you have to execute the `SET DELETED ON` statement:

☐ Type `SET DELETED ON` in the Command window and press Enter.

dBASE responds by hiding the deleted records. Now the browse window looks as it did back in Figure 2.15—the deleted record (record number 6) is hidden.

Suppose that after deleting a record, you change your mind and want to undelete the record. Just use the RECALL command. To undelete a record, move the record pointer to the record you want to undelete, then issue the RECALL command. To see the RECALL command in action, do the following:

☐ Close the browse window of the PERSONS.DBF table. (Make the browse window the active window, then select Close from the File menu.)

Note: In the preceding step you were instructed to close the browse window because in the next step you'll have to move the record pointer to record number 6. When SET DELETED is OFF (as it is now), dBASE won't let you move the record pointer to a deleted record while the browse window is open.

☐ Type GOTO 6 in the Command window and press Enter.

dBASE responds by moving the record pointer to record number 6.

☐ Type RECALL in the Command window and press Enter.

dBASE responds by recalling (undeleting) record number 6.

Now make sure record number 6 isn't deleted:

☐ Type BROWSE in the Command window and press Enter.

dBASE responds by displaying the browse window of the PERSONS.DBF table. As you can see, record number 6 is listed in the table.

As you have seen in the preceding steps, when you delete a record, it isn't removed from the table. You can still restore this record by using the RECALL command. To remove the deleted records from the table, you have to issue the PACK command. To see the PACK command in action, follow these steps:

☐ Type GOTO 6 in the Command window and press Enter.

dBASE responds by moving the record pointer to record number 6.

☐ Type DELETE in the Command window and press Enter.

dBASE responds by deleting record number 6.

☐ Type GOTO 7 in the Command window and press Enter.

dBASE responds by moving the record pointer to record number 7.

- ☐ Type `DELETE` in the Command window and press Enter.

  dBASE responds by deleting record number 7.

- ☐ Type `PACK` in the Command window and press Enter.

  dBASE responds by displaying an error message box, telling you it can't execute the `PACK` *command because the table is not used exclusively. (See Figure 2.17.)*

Figure 2.17.
The error message box that dBASE displays when you try to pack a table that isn't used exclusively.

dBASE will let you execute the `PACK` command only if the table was opened exclusively, which means that no one else can use the table. As you'll learn later in this book, several programs can use the same table simultaneously. However, if you open a table exclusively, other programs can't use it.

Since the `PACK` command requires that the table be opened exclusively, use the following step to do that:

- ☐ Type `USE C:\DBPROG\CH02\PERSONS EXCLUSIVE` in the Command window and press Enter.

  dBASE responds by opening the PERSONS.DBF table exclusively.

Now you can issue the `PACK` command:

- ☐ Type `PACK` in the Command window and press Enter.

  dBASE responds by packing the PERSONS.DBF table. This means that all the records you deleted (records 6 and 7) have been removed from the table. You cannot restore these records anymore!

> **Note:** To delete a record, move the record pointer to the record you want to delete and then execute the `DELETE` command.
>
> To make the deleted records visible, use the `SET DELETED OFF` statement. After executing this statement, dBASE will display deleted records in the browse window.

> To make deleted records invisible, use the `SET DELETED ON` statement. After executing this statement, dBASE ignores deleted records—they won't be displayed in the browse window.
>
> To restore a deleted record, move the record pointer to the record you want to restore and then execute the `RECALL` command.
>
> To remove all the deleted records, issue the `PACK` command.

2

Using the *APPEND BLANK* Command

So far you've added records to the PERSONS.DBF table by using the browse window. Another way to add a new record to a table is by using the `APPEND BLANK` statement. As its name implies, the `APPEND BLANK` statement adds a blank record to the table.

To see the `APPEND BLANK` statement in action, follow these steps:

☐ Type `APPEND BLANK` in the Command window and press Enter.

dBASE responds by appending a new blank record to the PERSONS.DBF table.

Ensure that the PERSONS.DBF table has a new blank record:

☐ Type `GOTO TOP` in the Command window and press Enter.

dBASE responds by moving the record pointer to the first record in the table.

☐ Type `BROWSE` in the Command window and press Enter.

dBASE responds by displaying the browse window of the PERSONS.DBF table.

☐ If necessary, enlarge the width of the PERSONS.DBF browse window so you'll be able to see all the fields in the PERSONS.DBF table.

As you can see, the PERSONS.DBF table has a new blank record (record number 6).

Using the *REPLACE* Command

So far you've filled the PERSONS.DBF table with data by using the browse window, but you can also use the `REPLACE` command. To see the `REPLACE` command in action, follow these steps:

☐ Type `GOTO 6` in the Command window and press Enter.

dBASE responds by moving the record pointer to record number 6.

☐ Type `REPLACE FIRSTNAME WITH "Jennifer"` in the Command window and press Enter.

dBASE responds by filling the FIRSTNAME field of the current record (record number 6) with the text `Jennifer`.

☐ Type `REPLACE LASTNAME WITH "Gold"` in the Command window and press Enter.

dBASE responds by filling the LASTNAME field of record number 6 with the text `Gold`.

☐ Type `REPLACE BIRTHDATE WITH CTOD("01/01/81")` in the Command window and press Enter.

dBASE responds by filling the BIRTHDATE field of record number 6 with the date `01/01/81`.

Note: In the preceding step, you executed this statement:

```
REPLACE BIRTHDATE WITH CTOD("01/01/81")
```

This statement fills the BIRTHDATE field of the current record with the expression `CTOD("01/01/81")`.

`CTOD()` is a dBASE function that converts a character string to a date. Therefore, the expression `CTOD("01/01/81")` converts the character string `"01/01/81"` to the date 01/01/81.

An alternate way of filling the BIRTHDATE field with the date 01/01/81 is to use the `REPLACE` command as follows:

```
REPLACE BIRTHDATE WITH {01/01/81}
```

That is, you can specify a date in dBASE by enclosing the date with the curly parentheses (`{}`).

☐ Type `REPLACE PHONE WITH "(212)555-0000"` in the Command window and press Enter.

dBASE responds by filling the PHONE field of record number 6 with the text `(212)555-0000`.

Record number 6 now contains the data you entered by using the `REPLACE` statements.

Ordering the Records of the Table

Suppose you want to view the records of the PERSONS.DBF table in alphabetical order by the LASTNAME field. To do that, you have to use the `SET ORDER TO` statement, as follows:

```
SET ORDER TO LASTNAME
```

However, before you can use this statement, you must first add an index to the LASTNAME field. After you do this, you'll be able to order the records of the table by the LASTNAME field using the `SET ORDER TO` statement. To add an index to the LASTNAME field, you have to modify the structure of the PERSONS.DBF table. Follow these steps to add an index to the LASTNAME field:

☐ Type `MODIFY STRUCTURE` in the Command window and press Enter.

dBASE responds by displaying the Table Structure window of the PERSONS.DBF table. (See Figure 2.18.)

> **Note:** Just like the `PACK` command, the `MODIFY STRUCTURE` command requires that the table be opened exclusively. Earlier you opened the PERSONS.DBF table exclusively so you could use the `PACK` command. This is why dBASE lets you execute the `MODIFY STRUCTURE` command without displaying an error message.

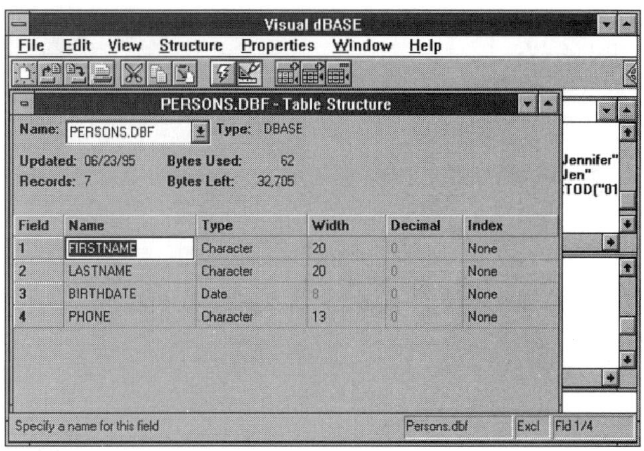

Figure 2.18.
The Table Structure window of the PERSONS.DBF table.

As shown in Figure 2.18, the last column in the Table Structure window is the Index column. It is currently set to NONE for all the fields.

Now add an index to the LASTNAME field:

☐ Click the mouse in the Index cell of the LASTNAME field.

The Index cell becomes highlighted and a small down-arrow icon appears to the right of the Index cell.

☐ Click the down-arrow icon next to the Index cell.

dBASE responds by opening a list of Index types. (See Figure 2.19.)

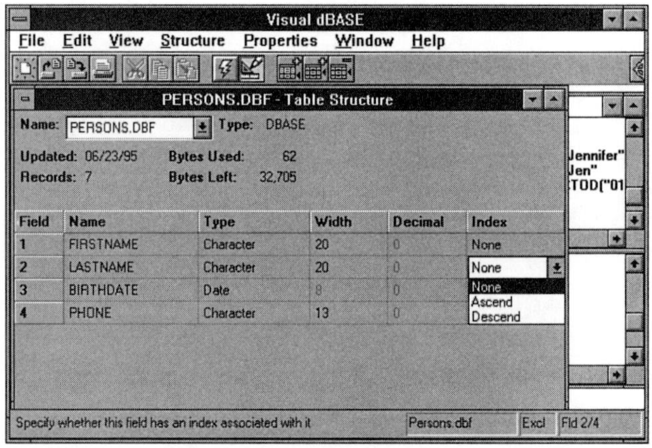

Figure 2.19.
Selecting an index type for the LASTNAME field.

☐ Select Ascend from the list.

Your Table Structure window should now look like the one shown in Figure 2.20.

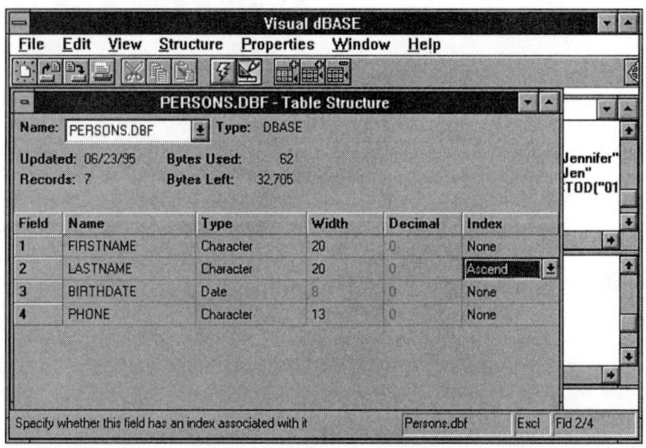

Figure 2.20.
Adding an ascending index to the LASTNAME field.

You set the Index type of the LASTNAME field to Ascend because you want the index of the LASTNAME field to organize the records in ascending order. If you want the index to organize the records in descending order, then select Descend from the Index list.

☐ Save your work by selecting Save from the File menu.

☐ Close the Table Structure window by selecting Close from the File menu.

Now that you've added an index to the LASTNAME field, you can use the `SET ORDER TO` statement to order the records in the table by the LASTNAME field. Here is how you do that:

☐ Type `SET ORDER TO LASTNAME` in the Command window and press Enter.

dBASE responds by organizing the records in the PERSONS.DBF table by the LASTNAME field in ascending order.

☐ Type `GOTO TOP` in the Command window and press Enter.

dBASE responds by moving the record pointer to the first record of the table.

☐ Type `BROWSE` in the Command window and press Enter.

dBASE responds by displaying the browse window of the PERSONS.DBF table.

The PERSONS.DBF table is now ordered by the LASTNAME field in ascending order.

To organize the records of the PERSONS.DBF table by their natural order (that is, first record 1, then record 2, then record 3, and so on), use the `SET ORDER TO` statement without specifying an index name:

☐ Type `SET ORDER TO` in the Command window and press Enter.

dBASE responds by ordering the records of the PERSONS.DBF table in their natural order.

Adding Another Index to the PERSONS.DBF Table

Now you can order the PERSONS.DBF table by the LASTNAME field because you added an index to the LASTNAME field. Suppose you also want to order the records in the PERSONS.DBF table by the PHONE field. To do that, you simply add an index to the PHONE field, just as you added an index to the LASTNAME field.

Follow these steps to add an index to the PHONE field:

☐ Type `MODIFY STRUCTURE` in the Command window and press Enter.

dBASE responds by displaying the Table Structure window of the PERSONS.DBF table.

☐ Set the Index of the Phone field to Ascend.

Your Table Structure window should now look like the one shown in Figure 2.21.

You set the type of the PHONE field to Ascend because you want the index of the PHONE field to organize the records in ascending order. If you want the index to organize the records in descending order, then select Descend.

☐ Save your work by selecting Save from the File menu.

☐ Close the Table Structure window by selecting Close from the File menu.

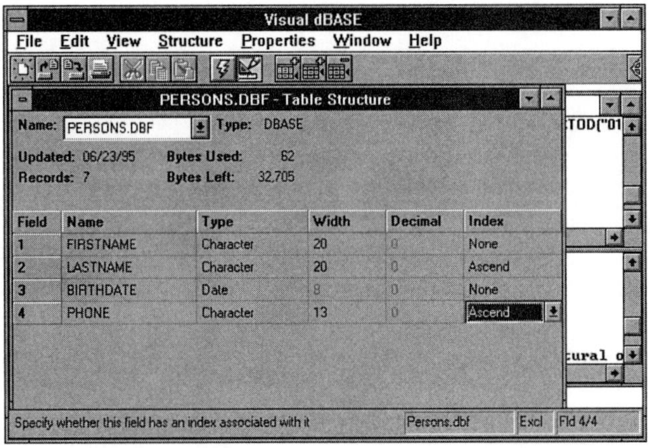

Figure 2.21.
Adding an ascending index to the PHONE field.

Now that you've added an index to the PHONE field, you can use the `SET ORDER TO` statement to order the records of the table by the PHONE field:

☐ Type `SET ORDER TO PHONE` in the Command window and press Enter.

dBASE responds by ordering the records in the PERSONS.DBF table by the PHONE field in ascending order.

☐ Type `GOTO TOP` in the Command window and press Enter.

dBASE responds by moving the record pointer to the first record of the table.

☐ Type `BROWSE` in the Command window and press Enter.

dBASE responds by displaying the browse window of the PERSONS.DBF table.

☐ If necessary, enlarge the width of the PERSONS.DBF browse window so you'll be able to see all the fields in the PERSONS.DBF table.

The PERSONS.DBF table is now ordered by the PHONE field in ascending order.

The PERSONS.DBF table now has two indexes: LASTNAME and PHONE. This means you can do the following:

- Order the records of the PERSONS.DBF table by the PHONE field (by executing the statement `SET ORDER TO PHONE`).
- Order the records of the PERSONS.DBF table by the LASTNAME field (by executing the statement `SET ORDER TO LASTNAME`).
- Order the records of the PERSONS.DBF table by their natural order (by executing the statement `SET ORDER TO` without specifying an index name).

Indexing on Multiple Fields

Sometimes you'll find it useful to index a table on a combination of several fields (that is, add an index to the table that is based on a combination of several fields). To see how you can index a table on a combination of several fields, add an index to the table that will organize the table's records by the combination of these two fields:

```
LASTNAME + FIRSTNAME
```

To add a new index to the table that will order the table's records by the combination LASTNAME + FIRSTNAME, follow these steps:

☐ Type `MODIFY STRUCTURE` in the Command window and press Enter.

dBASE responds by displaying the Table Structure window of the PERSONS.DBF table.

☐ Select Manage Indexes from the Structure menu.

dBASE responds by displaying the Manage Indexes dialog box for the PERSONS.DBF table. (See Figure 2.22.)

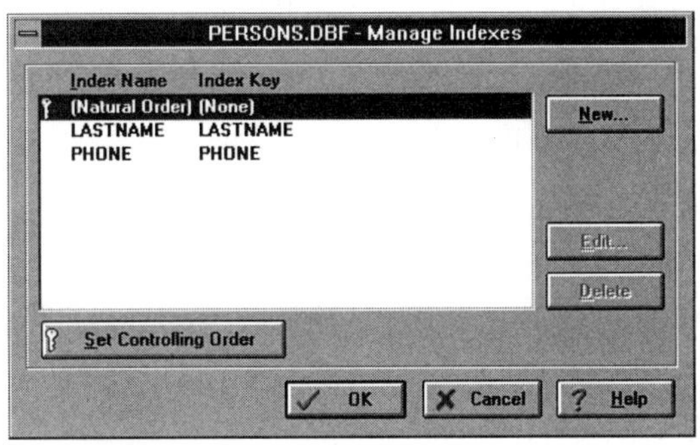

Figure 2.22.
The Manage Indexes dialog box.

As shown in Figure 2.22, the PERSONS.DBF table currently has two indexes: LASTNAME and PHONE. You added these indexes to the table earlier by setting the Index column of the LASTNAME and PHONE fields to Ascend.

Now add a third index to the table:

☐ Click the New button in the Manage Indexes dialog box.

dBASE responds by displaying the Define Index dialog box. (See Figure 2.23.)

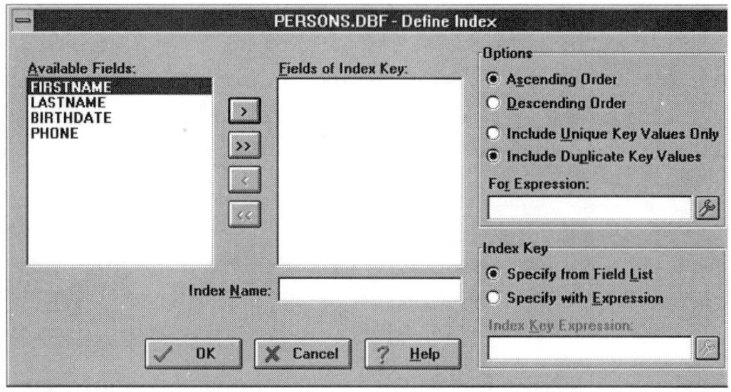

Figure 2.23.
The Define Index dialog box.

☐ Type `LAST_FIRST` in the Index Name entry field.

By typing `LAST_FIRST` in the Index Name entry field, you are specifying that the name of the index you are now creating will be `LAST_FIRST`.

☐ Select the LASTNAME field from the Available Fields list, then click the right-arrow button.

dBASE responds by moving the LASTNAME field to the Fields of Index Key list.

☐ Select the FIRSTNAME field from the Available Fields list, then click the right-arrow button.

dBASE responds by moving the FIRSTNAME field to the Fields of Index Key list.

Your Define Index dialog box should now look like the one shown in Figure 2.24.

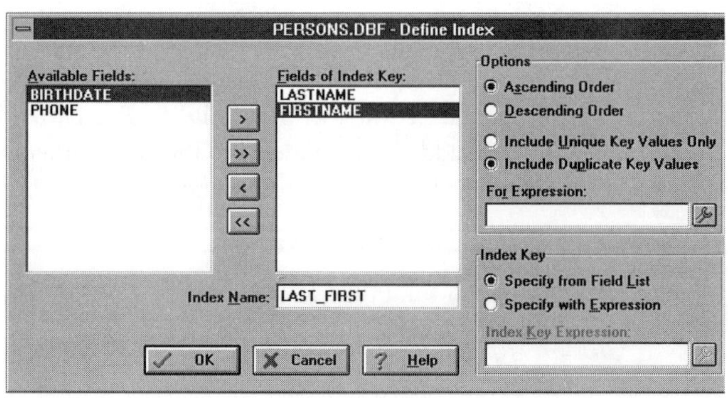

Figure 2.24.
Adding a new index to the PERSONS.DBF table.

In the preceding steps you instructed dBASE to create an index based on the LASTNAME and FIRSTNAME fields. You named the index LAST_FIRST.

☐ Click the OK button of the Define Index dialog box.

Your Manage Indexes dialog box appears, as shown in Figure 2.25. As shown in Figure 2.25, the last index listed in the Manage Indexes dialog box is the index that you just created—the LAST_FIRST index.

Figure 2.25.
The Manage Indexes dialog box (with the LAST_FIRST index).

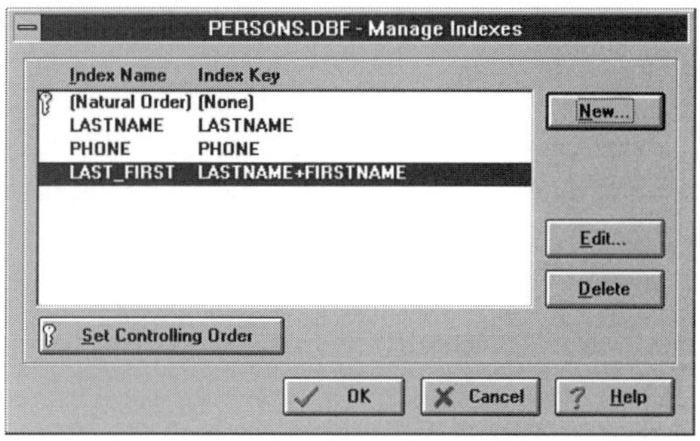

☐ Click the OK button of the Manage Indexes dialog box.

☐ Save your work by selecting Save from the File menu.

☐ Close the Table Structure window by selecting Close from the File menu.

Now that you've added the LAST_FIRST index to the PERSONS.DBF table, you can use the `SET ORDER TO` statement to order the table's records by the combination of the fields LASTNAME + FIRSTNAME:

☐ Type `SET ORDER TO LAST_FIRST` in the Command window and press Enter.

dBASE responds by ordering the records of the PERSONS.DBF table by the combination of fields LASTNAME + FIRSTNAME.

☐ Type `GOTO TOP` in the Command window and press Enter.

dBASE responds by moving the record pointer to the first record of the table.

☐ Type `BROWSE` in the Command window and press Enter.

dBASE responds by displaying the browse window of the PERSONS.DBF table.

☐ If necessary, enlarge the width of the PERSONS.DBF browse window so you'll be able to see all the fields in the PERSONS.DBF table.

The PERSONS.DBF table is now ordered by the combination of fields LASTNAME + FIRSTNAME:

Rec	*FIRSTNAME*	*LASTNAME*
3	Julie	Eden
6	Jennifer	Gold
4	Mark	Gold
5	Bill	Smart
1	Jane	Smart
2	Al	Smith

As you can see, when two records have the same LASTNAME, these records are ordered by the FIRSTNAME field. For example, the following record:

```
LASTNAME      = Gold
FIRSTNAME     = Jennifer
```

is listed before this record:

```
LASTNAME      = Gold
FIRSTNAME     = Mark
```

Where Are the Indexes of the Table Stored?

In the preceding sections you added three indexes to the PERSONS.DBF table: LASTNAME, PHONE, and LAST_FIRST, so you can now use the `SET ORDER TO` statement to order the table's records with any of these indexes.

Where are these indexes stored? dBASE saved them in the file PERSONS.MDX, but you don't have to worry about this file. When you open the PERSONS.DBF table, dBASE will open the PERSONS.MDX file automatically. However, you should know that the PERSONS.MDX file exists because when you distribute the PERSONS.DBF table to other people, you should distribute it with the PERSONS.MDX file.

Summary

In this chapter you have learned how to create and manipulate a dBASE table. In the next chapter you'll learn how to use a dBASE table from within a dBASE program. As you have seen, manipulating a dBASE table amounts to knowing how to use dBASE commands. In this chapter you used dBASE commands in the Command window of dBASE. In the next chapter you'll write a dBASE program that makes use of dBASE commands.

Q&A

Q In this chapter I executed dBASE commands like `SKIP`, `SET ORDER TO`, and `GOTO` from the Command window of dBASE. Can I execute the same commands when I write dBASE programs?

A Yes. As you will see in the next chapter, you will use the same commands when you write dBASE programs.

Q When I design a new table, how can I decide which fields to add an index to?

A Add indexes to fields you want the table ordered by. For example, in the PERSONS.DBF table you added an index to the PHONE field so you could use the `SET ORDER TO PHONE` statement to order the table by the PHONE field.

Quiz

1. What file extension do dBASE tables have?
2. What will happen after you execute the following statement in the Command window of dBASE?

   ```
   CREATE C:\TRY\MyTable
   ```

3. What does the `?` statement do?
4. What does the following statement do?

   ```
   USE C:\TRY\MyTable
   ```

5. What does the `CLOSE DATABASES` command do?
6. What is the `BROWSE` command used for?
7. What does the `RECNO()` function return?
8. What does the statement `GOTO 5` do?
9. What does the statement `GOTO TOP` do?
10. What does the statement `GOTO BOTTOM` do?
11. What does the statement `SKIP 1` do?
12. What does the statement `SKIP -1` do?
13. What is the end of file?
14. What does the `EOF()` function return?
15. What is the beginning of file?
16. What does the `BOF()` function return?
17. What do the following two statements do?

   ```
   GOTO 5
   DELETE
   ```

18. When you delete a record using the `DELETE` command, is the record removed from the table?
19. What does the statement `SET DELETED OFF` do?
20. What does the statement `SET DELETED ON` do?
21. What do the following two statements do?

```
GOTO 5
RECALL
```

22. What does the `PACK` command do?
23. dBASE will let you execute the `PACK` command only if the table was opened exclusively.

    a. True
    b. False
24. What does the following statement do?

```
USE C:\TRY\MyTable EXCLUSIVE
```

25. What does the statement `APPEND BLANK` do?
26. What do the following two statements do?

```
GOTO 4
REPLACE FIRSTNAME WITH "Jennifer"
```

27. Suppose you added an index to the PHONE field of the table. What does the following statement do?

```
SET ORDER TO PHONE
```

28. What does the following statement do?

```
SET ORDER TO
```

Exercise

Design a dBASE table called CLIENTS.DBF with the following structure:

Field Name	*Type*	*Width*	*Decimal*	*Index*
NAME	Character	20	0	Ascend
STREET	Character	30	0	None
CITY	Character	20	0	None
STATE	Character	2	0	None
ZIP	Character	5	0	None
PHONE	Character	13	0	Ascend

- ☐ Use the `BROWSE` statement to add several records to the CLIENTS.DBF table.
- ☐ Use the `SET ORDER TO` statement in the Command window to order the records of the CLIENTS.DBF table by the NAME field.

- ☐ Use the `SET ORDER TO` statement in the Command window to order the records of the CLIENTS.DBF table by the PHONE field.
- ☐ Use the `SET ORDER TO` statement in the Command window to order the records of the CLIENTS.DBF table by their natural order.

Quiz Answers

1. dBASE tables have a .DBF file extension (for example, MyTable.DBF).
2. After you execute the statement `CREATE C:\TRY\MyTable`, dBASE will display the Table Structure window to let you create a new table called MyTable.DBF in the C:\TRY directory.
3. The `?` statement displays whatever expression you tell it to display in the results pane of the Command window. For example, if you execute this statement:

   ```
   ?"This is a test"
   ```

   dBASE will display the text `This is a test` in the results pane of the Command window.
4. The statement `USE C:\TRY\MyTable` opens the C:\TRY\MyTable.DBF table.
5. The `CLOSE DATABASES` command closes all the currently open tables.
6. The `BROWSE` command enables you to manipulate a table's records very easily. It lets you view and edit a table's records.
7. The `RECNO()` function returns the current value of the record pointer.
8. The statement `GOTO 5` moves the record pointer to record number 5.
9. The statement `GOTO TOP` moves the record pointer to the first record in the table.
10. The statement `GOTO BOTTOM` moves the record pointer to the last record in the table.
11. The statement `SKIP 1` moves the record pointer to the next record in the table.
12. The statement `SKIP -1` moves the record pointer to the previous record in the table.
13. When you move the record pointer past the last record of the table, the record pointer is at the end of file.
14. The `EOF()` function returns either .T. or .F.. It returns .T. if the record pointer is currently at the end of file. Otherwise, it returns .F..
15. When you move the record pointer to a record before the first record of the table, the record pointer is at the beginning of file.
16. The `BOF()` function returns either .T. or .F.. It returns .T. if the record pointer is currently at the beginning of file. Otherwise, it returns .F..
17. The following two statements delete record number 5:

   ```
   GOTO 5
   DELETE
   ```

18. When you delete a record using the `DELETE` command, the deleted record is not removed from the table. It is only marked for deletion.
19. The statement `SET DELETED OFF` shows all the deleted records. After you execute this statement, commands such as `BROWSE` and `SKIP` will not ignore deleted records.
20. The statement `SET DELETED ON` hides all the deleted records. After you execute this statement, commands such as `BROWSE` and `SKIP` will ignore deleted records as if they don't exist.
21. The following two statements restore record number 5:

    ```
    GOTO 5
    RECALL
    ```
22. The `PACK` command removes all the deleted records from the table.
23. a (True). dBASE will let you execute the `PACK` command only if the table was opened exclusively.
24. The statement `USE C:\TRY\MyTable EXCLUSIVE` opens the C:\TRY\MyTable.DBF table exclusively.
25. The statement `APPEND BLANK` adds a new blank record to the table.
26. These two statements fill the FIRSTNAME field of record number 4 with the text `Jennifer`:

    ```
    GOTO 4
    REPLACE FIRSTNAME WITH "Jennifer"
    ```
27. The statement `SET ORDER TO PHONE` will order the table's records by the PHONE field.
28. The statement `SET ORDER TO` will order the table's records by their natural order (first record 1, then record 2, then record 3, and so on).

Exercise Answer

To create the CLIENTS.DBF table use similar steps to the ones you took when you created the PERSONS.DBF table.

WEEK 1

3

Using a Table from Within dBASE

In this chapter you will write a dBASE program called PHONE that uses a table. You'll design the table first, and then write a program that uses it. You'll use the programming skills you learned in Chapter 1, "Writing Your First dBASE Program": placing controls in a form, setting the form's properties, setting the controls' properties, and attaching code to events.

The PHONE Program

In the following sections you will write a dBASE program called PHONE that uses a table. Before you start writing the PHONE program, specify how the program should look and what it should do. When you run the PHONE program, the main window of the PHONE program should look like the one shown in Figure 3.1.

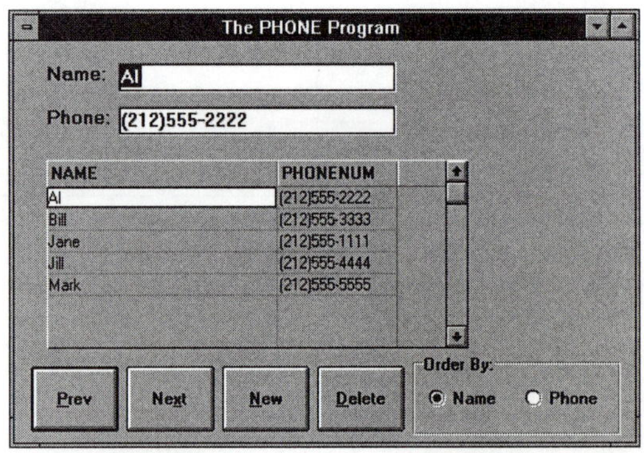

Figure 3.1.
The main window of the PHONE program.

The PHONE program enables you to maintain a table that keeps records of names and phone numbers. As shown in Figure 3.1, the main window of the PHONE program has two entry fields (NAME and PHONENUM), four buttons (Prev, Next, New, and Delete), a tabular list that displays all the names and phone numbers, and two Order By radio buttons (Name and Phone).

You can navigate among the records of the table by using the Prev and Next buttons or by selecting the desired record in the tabular list. You can add a new record to the table by clicking the New button and delete the currently displayed record by clicking the Delete button. You can also order the records of the table by clicking the Order By radio buttons. When you select the Name radio button, the records are ordered by Name, as shown in Figure 3.1, and when you select the Phone radio button, the records are ordered by Phone number. (See Figure 3.2.)

You might think that writing a program with so many powerful features requires a lot of code writing, but writing the PHONE program is very easy! Very little code writing is required to build a program like the PHONE program.

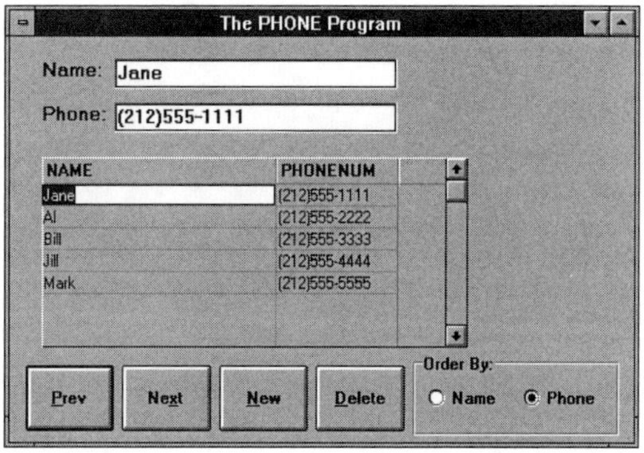

Figure 3.2.
The main window of the PHONE program, listing the records ordered by phone number.

Now you know what the PHONE program is supposed to do. In the following sections you'll write the PHONE program from the beginning.

Creating a Table for the PHONE Program

The PHONE program will use a simple table called PHONE.DBF that has two fields: NAME and PHONENUM. Before creating the PHONE.DBF table, first create the directory C:\DBPROG\CH03 for both the PHONE.DBF table and the PHONE program. Create the C:\DBPROG\CH03 directory as follows:

☐ Start Visual dBASE.

☐ Type `MD C:\DBPROG` in the Command window, and then press Enter.

dBASE responds by creating the directory C:\DBPROG. (If this directory already exists, dBASE will display a message box telling you the directory can't be created.)

☐ Type `MD C:\DBPROG\CH03` in the Command window, and then press Enter.

dBASE responds by creating the directory C:\DBPROG\CH03.

Now create the PHONE.DBF table as follows:

☐ Type `CREATE C:\DBPROG\CH03\PHONE` in the Command window, and then press Enter.

dBASE responds by displaying the Table Structure window for the PHONE.DBF table.

☐ Set the structure of the PHONE.DBF table, which is shown in Table 3.1.

☐ Save your work by selecting Save from the File menu.

☐ Close the Table Structure window by selecting Close from the File menu.

Table 3.1. The structure of the PHONE.DBF table.

Name	Type	Width	Decimal	Index
NAME	Character	25	0	Ascend
PHONENUM	Character	13	0	Ascend

As you can see, the PHONE.DBF has two fields—NAME and PHONENUM. The NAME field will be used for storing names of people, and the PHONENUM field will be used for storing phone numbers. An ascending index is set for both the NAME and PHONENUM fields so that later the PHONE program will enable you to order the records of the PHONE.DBF table by either the NAME field or the PHONENUM field (in ascending order).

Filling the PHONE.DBF Table with Test Data

Soon you'll write the code of the PHONE program so you can view, edit, and order the records of the PHONE.DBF table. But before you write the code, first add some test data to the PHONE.DBF table to test your code.

- ☐ Type `BROWSE` in the Command window, and then press Enter.
- ☐ Press the down-arrow key of your keyboard and add five records to the PHONE.DBF, as specified in Table 3.2.
- ☐ Close the Browse window by selecting Close from the File menu.

Table 3.2. The five test records in the PHONE.DBF table.

Record Number	NAME Field	PHONENUM Field
1	Mark	(212)555-5555
2	Bill	(212)555-3333
3	Jill	(212)555-4444
4	Jane	(212)555-1111
5	Al	(212)555-2222

Note: When you add these test records to the PHONE.DBF table, make sure to type the names and phone numbers exactly as specified in Table 3.2 so that later you'll be able to test the code that orders the records.

The Visual Implementation of the PHONE Program

Create the PHONE.WFM form as follows:

☐ Type `CREATE FORM C:\DBPROG\CH03\PHONE` in the Command window and press Enter.

dBASE responds by creating the PHONE.WFM form and displaying it in design mode.

☐ Customize the PHONE.WFM form according to the specifications in Table 3.3. When you finish customizing the form, it should look like the one shown in Figure 3.3.

Note: The preceding step instructs you to customize the PHONE.WFM form by following a properties table. (See Table 3.3.) Following a properties table is very easy. Simply place the listed objects in the form and set their properties as specified. (Recall that in Chapter 1 you learned how to place an object in the form and how to set the properties of the object.)

For example, the first group of lines in Table 3.3 lists the properties you should set for the form:

Object	*Property*	*Setting*
Form	**Text**	**The PHONE Program**
	Height	18.47
	Left	1.00
	Top	0.00
	Width	77.83

These lines instruct you to set the Text property to The PHONE Program, the Height property to 18.47, the Left property to 1.00, the Top property to 0.00, and the Width property to 77.83.

Similarly, the next group of lines in the table instructs you to place a Text control in the form and set its Name, Height, Left, Top, Width, Text, and FontSize properties:

Object	*Property*	*Setting*
Text	**Name**	**NameText**
	Height	1.35
	Left	4.00
	Top	1.00
	Width	8.00

Object	*Property*	*Setting*
Text	**Name**	**NameText**
	Text	Name:
	FontSize	11

Note that the Height, Left, Top, and Width properties are listed under the Position Properties entry in the Inspector window. They determine the position and size of the object. The FontSize property is listed under the Font Properties entry in the Inspector window.

Note: If you have trouble locating any of the icons for the controls mentioned in Table 3.3, use Figure 3.4, which shows the icons of all the standard controls in the Control Palette window.

Table 3.3. The properties table of the PHONE.WFM form.

Object	Property	Setting
Form	**Text**	**The PHONE Program**
	Height	18.47
	Left	1.00
	Top	0.00
	Width	77.83
Text	**Name**	**NameText**
	Height	1.35
	Left	4.00
	Top	1.00
	Width	8.00
	Text	Name:
	FontSize	11
Entry Field	**Name**	**NameEntry**
	Height	1.35
	Left	13.00
	Top	1.00

Object	Property	Setting
	Width	35.00
	FontSize	11
	Value	(empty)
Text	**Name**	**PhoneText**
	Height	1.35
	Left	4.00
	Top	3.00
	Width	9.00
	Text	Phone:
	FontSize	11
Entry Field	**Name**	**PhoneEntry**
	Height	1.35
	Left	13.00
	Top	3.00
	Width	35.00
	FontSize	11
	Value	(empty)
PushButton	**Name**	**PrevButton**
	Height	3.00
	Left	2.00
	Top	15.00
	Width	11.00
	Text	&Prev
PushButton	**Name**	**NextButton**
	Height	3.00
	Left	14.00
	Top	15.00
	Width	11.00
	Text	Ne&xt
PushButton	**Name**	**NewButton**
	Height	3.00

continues

Table 3.3. continued

Object	Property	Setting
	Left	26.00
	Top	15.00
	Width	11.00
	Text	&New
PushButton	**Name**	**DeleteButton**
	Height	3.00
	Left	38.00
	Top	15.00
	Width	11.00
	Text	&Delete
Rectangle	**Name**	**OrderRect**
	Height	3.53
	Left	50.00
	Top	14.47
	Width	26.00
	Text	Order By:
Radio Button	**Name**	**NameRadio**
	Height	1.00
	Left	52.00
	Top	16.00
	Width	9.00
	Text	Name
	Value	.T.
Radio Button	**Name**	**PhoneRadio**
	Height	1.00
	Left	64.00
	Top	16.00
	Width	10.00
	Text	Phone
	Value	.F.

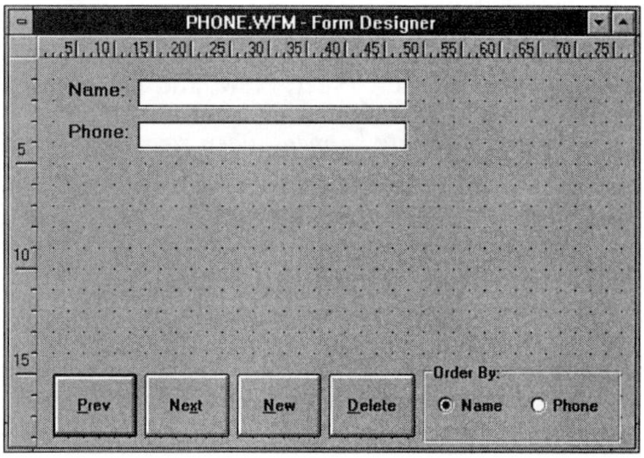

Figure 3.3.
The PHONE.WFM form in design mode (after customization).

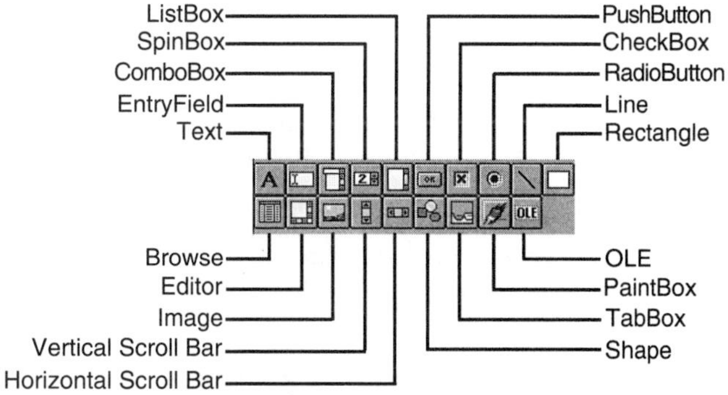

Figure 3.4.
The icons of the standard controls in the Control Palette.

> **Note:** As specified in Table 3.3, you have to place a Rectangle control in the form and then place two radio buttons in it. The Rectangle control encloses the two radio buttons.

Table 3.3 specifies that the Value property of the NameRadio radio button should be set to .T. (TRUE) and the PhoneRadio radio button should be set to .F. (FALSE). When the Value property of a radio button is set to .T., the radio button is selected (that is, it has a dot in it). This is why the NameRadio radio button has a dot in it and the PhoneRadio radio button doesn't in Figure 3.3.

To see your visual implementation in action, follow these steps:

☐ Execute the form by clicking the Run tool on the dBASE toolbar. (If you have forgotten which tool is the Run tool, refer to Figure 1.54 in Chapter 1.)

dBASE responds by executing the PHONE.WFM form.

Experiment with the PHONE.WFM form as follows:

- ☐ Try clicking the Prev, Next, New, and Delete buttons.

  Of course, nothing happens when you click these buttons because you haven't attached any code to their `OnClick` *events.*

- ☐ Type something in the NAME field.
- ☐ Type something in the PHONENUM field.
- ☐ Try to select a radio button in the Order By rectangle, and notice that only one radio button can be selected at a time. You can select either Name or Phone, but you can't select both.
- ☐ Change the mode of the PHONE.WFM back to design mode by clicking the Design tool on the dBASE toolbar. (If you have forgotten which tool is the Design tool, refer to Figure 1.54 in Chapter 1.)

The PHONE.WFM form is operational. However, it isn't doing what it's supposed to do—let you view and edit the records of the PHONE.DBF table. The PHONE.WFM form accepts your input but it doesn't store your input.

In the following section you'll associate the PHONE.WFM form with the PHONE.DBF table so the two entry fields in the form will display the fields in the PHONE.DBF table.

Associating the PHONE.WFM Form with the PHONE.DBF Table

To associate the PHONE.WFM form with the PHONE.DBF table, you have to set the View property of the PHONE.WFM form to the name of the PHONE.DBF table. Here is how you do that:

- ☐ Click any free area of the form.
- ☐ Select the Inspector window and click the View property.
- ☐ Click the Tool button of the View property.

  dBASE responds by displaying the View Property Builder dialog box. (See Figure 3.5.)

- ☐ Use the View Property Builder dialog box to select the table C:\DBPROG\CH03\PHONE.DBF, then click the OK button.

The PHONE.WFM form is now associated with the PHONE.DBF table. When PHONE.WFM is opened, the PHONE.DBF table will be automatically opened.

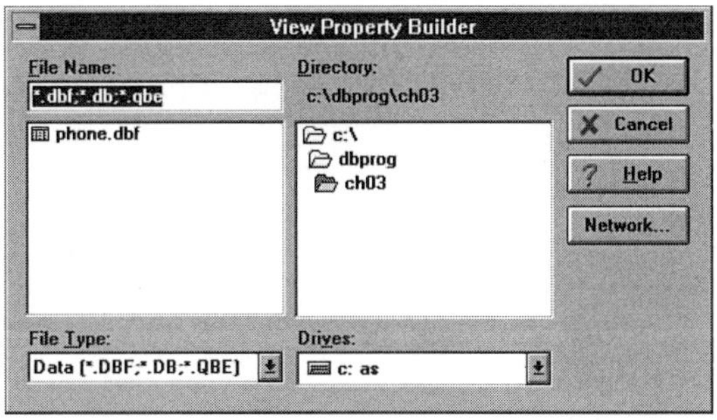

Figure 3.5.
The View Property Builder dialog box.

Next you have to link the two entry fields in the PHONE.WFM form (NameEntry and PhoneEntry) to the two fields in the PHONE.DBF table (NAME and PHONENUM). To link the NameEntry entry field to the NAME field of the PHONE.DBF table, do the following: 3

- ☐ Click the NameEntry entry field in the form.
- ☐ Select the Inspector window and click the DataLink property in the Inspector window.
- ☐ Click the Tool button of the DataLink property.

dBASE responds by displaying the Choose Field dialog box. (See Figure 3.6.)

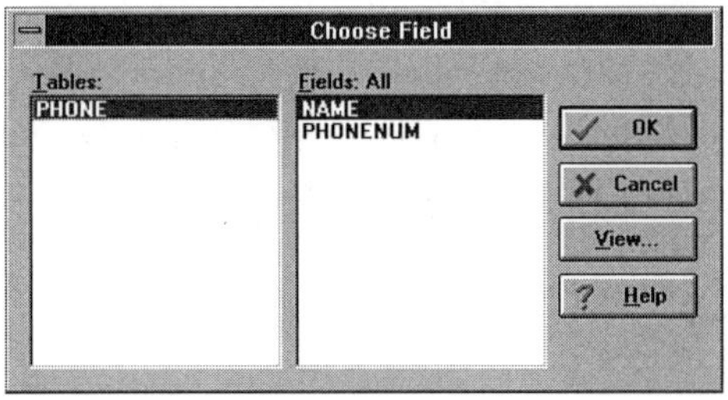

Figure 3.6.
The Choose Field dialog box.

As you can see, the Choose Field dialog box lists the fields of the PHONE.DBF table because you associated it with the PHONE.WFM form.

- ☐ Click the NAME field in the Fields list box, then click the OK button.

The NameEntry entry field is now linked to the NAME field of the PHONE.DBF table and will display the data of the NAME field.

- ☐ Repeat the previous steps to link the PhoneEntry entry field to the PHONENUM field of the PHONE.DBF table.

Notice that even now (while the form is in design mode), you can see the data from the table in the entry fields that you linked to the table.

To see the form in run mode do the following:

☐ Execute the PHONE.WFM form by clicking the Run tool on the dBASE toolbar.

The PHONE.WFM form appears, as shown in Figure 3.7.

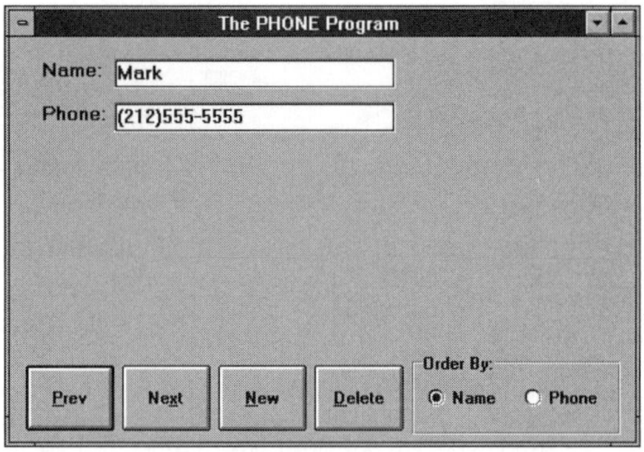

Figure 3.7.
The PHONE.WFM form in run mode (the NameEntry and PhoneEntry entry fields are linked to the NAME and PHONENUM fields of the PHONE.DBF table).

As shown in Figure 3.7, the NameEntry and PhoneEntry entry fields display the following data:

Name: Mark
Phone: (212)555-5555

This is the data you entered in the first record of the PHONE.DBF table, so the PHONE.WFM form is displaying the first record of the PHONE.DBF table.

☐ Change back to design mode by clicking the Design tool on the dBASE toolbar.

Notice that the NameEntry and PhoneEntry entry fields display the data of the first record of the PHONE.DBF table even though the PHONE.WFM form is in design mode and no code has been written yet.

Entering the Code of the PHONE Program

In the following sections, you'll attach code to the Prev and Next pushbuttons so you can navigate from one record to another.

Attaching Code to the *OnClick* Event of the Next Pushbutton

When you click the Next button, the PHONE.WFM form should display the data of the next record in the PHONE.DBF table. You'll now write the code that accomplishes this.

☐ Attach the following code to the `OnClick` event of the Next pushbutton (if you have forgotten how to attach code to an event, review the section "Attaching Code to the Say Hello Button" in Chapter 1). After you enter the code, the `NEXTBUTTON_OnClick` procedure should look like this:

```
Procedure NEXTBUTTON_OnClick

* Skip to the next record.
SKIP 1

* If at end of file, beep and go to the last record.
IF EOF()
   ??CHR(7)
   GOTO BOTTOM
ENDIF

Return
```

☐ Save your work by selecting Save from the File menu.

The first statement you typed in the `NEXTBUTTON_OnClick` procedure uses the `SKIP` command to move the record pointer to the next record in the table:

```
SKIP 1
```

The next statement is an `IF` statement:

```
IF EOF()
   ??CHR(7)
   GOTO BOTTOM
ENDIF
```

This `IF` statement uses the `EOF()` function to ensure that the record pointer doesn't point to the end of file. If the record pointer points to the end of file, the `IF` condition, `IF EOF()`, is satisfied and the two statements under the `IF` statement are executed:

```
??CHR(7)
GOTO BOTTOM
```

The first statement causes the PC to beep:

```
??CHR(7)
```

The second statement moves the record pointer to the last record in the table:

```
GOTO BOTTOM
```

To see in action the code you attached to the `OnClick` event of the Next pushbutton, follow these steps:

☐ Execute the PHONE.WFM form by clicking the Run tool on the dBASE toolbar.

☐ Experiment with the Next button.

Every time you click the Next button, the PHONE.WFM form displays the next record in the table. Once the end of file is reached, the PC beeps.

☐ Change back to design mode by clicking the Design tool on the dBASE toolbar.

Attaching Code to the *OnClick* Event of the Prev Pushbutton

When you click the Prev button, the PHONE.WFM form should display the data of the previous record in the PHONE.DBF table. You'll now write the code that accomplishes this.

☐ Attach the following code to the `OnClick` event of the Prev pushbutton. After you enter the code, the `PREVBUTTON_OnClick` procedure should look like this:

```
Procedure PREVBUTTON_OnClick

* Skip to the previous record.
SKIP -1

* If at the beginning of file, beep and go to the
* first record.
IF BOF()
   ??CHR(7)
   GOTO TOP
ENDIF

Return
```

☐ Save your work by selecting Save from the File menu.

The first statement you typed in the `PREVBUTTON_OnClick` procedure uses the `SKIP` command to move the record pointer to the previous record in the table:

```
SKIP -1
```

That is, skipping minus 1 (-1) records moves the record pointer to the previous record.

The next statement is an `IF` statement:

```
IF BOF()
   ??CHR(7)
   GOTO TOP
ENDIF
```

This `IF` statement uses the `BOF()` function to ensure that the record pointer isn't at the beginning of file. If the record pointer points to the beginning of file, the `IF` condition, `IF BOF()`, is satisfied and the two statements under the `IF` statement are executed:

```
??CHR(7)
GOTO TOP
```

The first statement causes the PC to beep:

```
??CHR(7)
```

The second statement moves the record pointer to the first record in the table:

```
GOTO TOP
```

To see in action the code you attached to the `OnClick` event of the Prev pushbutton, follow these steps:

☐ Execute the PHONE.WFM form by clicking the Run tool on the dBASE toolbar.

☐ Click the Next button several times, then experiment with the Prev button.

Every time you click the Prev button, the PHONE.WFM form displays the previous record in the table. Once the beginning of file is reached, the PC beeps.

☐ Change back to design mode by clicking the Design tool on the dBASE toolbar.

3

Attaching Code to the *OnOpen* Event of the PHONE.WFM Form

You'll now attach code to the `OnOpen` event of the PHONE.WFM form. As its name implies, the `OnOpen` event of a form occurs when the form is first opened, so it's a good place to write initialization code for the form.

☐ Attach the following code to the `OnOpen` event of the PHONE.WFM form. After you enter the code, the `Form_OnOpen` procedure should look like this:

```
Procedure Form_OnOpen

  * Deleted records should not be displayed.
  SET DELETED ON

  * Order the PHONE.DBF table by the NAME field.
  SET ORDER TO TAG NAME

  * Move the record pointer to the first record.
  GOTO TOP

  * Make sure that the table has at least one record.
  IF EOF()
     APPEND BLANK
  ENDIF

Return
```

☐ Save your work by selecting Save from the File menu.

The first statement you typed in the `Form_OnOpen` procedure tells dBASE not to process records that are marked for deletion:

```
SET DELETED ON
```

Later in this chapter you'll write code that enables you to delete records. By setting the `SET DELETED` to `ON`, you are specifying that all the records you delete will be hidden.

The next statement orders the PHONE.DBF table by the NAME field in ascending order:

```
SET ORDER TO NAME
```

(When you created the PHONE.DBF table, you specified that the NAME field would have an ascending index.)

The next statement moves the record pointer to the first record of the table:

```
GOTO TOP
```

Because the preceding command moved the record pointer to the beginning of file, the record pointer should now point to the first record in the table. However, if the table has no records in it, then the record pointer will point to the end of file. To make sure the table has at least one record in it, an `IF` statement is used:

```
IF EOF()
   APPEND BLANK
ENDIF
```

If the `IF` condition `IF EOF()` is satisfied, the record pointer is pointing to the end of file, which means that the table has no records in it. If this is the case, the command `APPEND BLANK` will add a blank record to the table.

You use the preceding `IF` statement to make sure the table has at least one record in it because when you type something in the form's entry fields, you want what you type to always go to the table. If the table has no records, you can type data in the entry fields but it won't be stored in the table.

When you start the PHONE.WFM program, the `OnOpen` event of the form occurs and the code you attached to this event performs four tasks:

- Sets the DELETED flag to ON (so deleted records will be hidden).
- Orders the table by the NAME field.
- Moves the record pointer to the first record in the table.
- Makes sure the table has at least one record. If it doesn't, a blank record is added to the table.

To see in action the code you attached to the `OnOpen` event, do the following:

- ☐ Execute the PHONE.WFM form by clicking the Run tool on the dBASE toolbar.
- ☐ Navigate among the records of the PHONE.DBF table (using the Next and Prev buttons) and check that the records are now organized in ascending order by the NAME field.
- ☐ Change back to design mode by clicking the Design tool on the dBASE toolbar.

Attaching Code to the *OnChange* Event of the Phone Radio Button

When you select the Phone radio button, the PHONE.WFM form should order the records of the PHONE.DBF table by the PHONE field. You'll now attach code to the `OnChange` event of the Phone radio button. As its name implies, the `OnChange` event of a radio button occurs when you change the value of the radio button.

3

- ☐ Attach the following code to the `OnChange` event of the Phone radio button. After you enter the code, the `PHONERADIO_OnChange` procedure should look like this:

```
Procedure PHONERADIO_OnChange

  * If you selected the Phone radio button, order
  * the PHONE.DBF table by the PHONENUM field.
  IF form.PhoneRadio.Value = .T.
     SET ORDER TO PHONENUM
  ENDIF

Return
```

- ☐ Save your work by selecting Save from the File menu.

The code you typed in `PHONERADIO_OnChange` begins with an `IF` statement:

```
IF form.PhoneRadio.Value = .T.
   SET ORDER TO PHONENUM
ENDIF
```

This `IF` statement determines whether the Phone radio button has been selected by examining its Value property. If the Value property is equal to .T., it means the Phone radio button is selected. If this is the case, the statement under the `IF` statement organizes the PHONE.DBF table by the PHONENUM field in ascending order:

```
SET ORDER TO PHONENUM
```

(When you created the PHONE.DBF table, you specified that the PHONENUM field would have an ascending index.)

When the Phone radio button's selection is changed, the code you attached to the `OnChange` event of the Phone radio button will be executed automatically; this code will order the PHONE.DBF table by the PHONE field if the Phone radio button is selected.

To see in action the code you attached to the `OnChange` event of the Phone radio button, follow these steps:

- ☐ Execute the PHONE.WFM form by clicking the Run tool on the dBASE toolbar.
- ☐ Select the Phone radio button.
- ☐ Use the Prev and Next buttons to check that the records of the PHONE.DBF table are organized by the PHONE field in ascending order.
- ☐ Change back to design mode by clicking the Design tool on the dBASE toolbar.

Attaching Code to the *OnChange* Event of the Name Radio Button

When you select the Name radio button, the PHONE.WFM form should order the records of the PHONE.DBF table by the NAME field. You'll now write the code that accomplishes this.

- ☐ Attach the following code to the `OnChange` event of the Name radio button. After you enter the code, the `NAMERADIO_OnChange` procedure should look like this:

```
Procedure NAMERADIO_OnChange

  * If you selected the Name radio button, order
  * the PHONE.DBF table by the NAME field.
  IF form.NameRadio.Value = .T.
     SET ORDER TO NAME
  ENDIF

Return
```

- ☐ Save your work by selecting Save from the File menu.

The code you typed in the `NAMERADIO_OnChange` begins with an `IF` statement:

```
IF form.NameRadio.Value = .T.
     SET ORDER TO NAME
ENDIF
```

This `IF` statement determines whether the Name radio button has been selected by examining its Value property. If the Value property is equal to .T., it means that the Name radio button is selected. If this is the case, the statement under the `IF` statement organizes the PHONE.DBF table by the NAME field in ascending order:

```
SET ORDER TO NAME
```

(When you created the PHONE.DBF table, you specified that the NAME field would have an ascending index.)

To see in action the code you attached to the `OnChange` event of the Name radio button, follow these steps:

- ☐ Execute the PHONE.WFM form by clicking the Run tool on the dBASE toolbar.
- ☐ Select the Phone radio button.
- ☐ Use the Prev and Next buttons to check that the records of the PHONE.DBF table are organized by the PHONE field in ascending order.
- ☐ Select the Name radio button.
- ☐ Use the Prev and Next buttons to check that the records of the PHONE.DBF table are organized by the NAME field in ascending order.
- ☐ Change back to design mode by clicking the Design tool on the dBASE toolbar.

3

Attaching Code to the *OnClick* Event of the New Pushbutton

When you click the New button, the PHONE.WFM program should add, or *append*, a new record to the PHONE.DBF table and let you edit this record. You'll now write the code that accomplishes this task.

- ☐ Attach the following code to the `OnClick` event of the New pushbutton. After you enter the code, the `NEWBUTTON_OnClick` procedure should look like this:

```
Procedure NEWBUTTON_OnClick

* Append a blank record to the PHONE.DBF table.
APPEND BLANK

* Place the keyboard cursor in the NameEntry
* entry field.
form.NameEntry.SetFocus()

Return
```

- ☐ Save your work by selecting Save from the File menu.

The first statement you typed in the `NEWBUTTON_OnClick` procedure appends a new blank record to the PHONE.DBF table:

```
APPEND BLANK
```

The second statement you typed uses the `SetFocus()` method to give the keyboard focus to the NameEntry entry field:

```
form.NameEntry.SetFocus()
```

When an entry field has the *keyboard focus*, the keyboard cursor appears in the entry field and whatever you type appears in the entry field.

To see the code you attached to the `OnClick` event of the New pushbutton in action, follow these steps:

- ☐ Execute the PHONE.WFM form by clicking the Run tool on the dBASE toolbar.
- ☐ Click the New button.

  The PHONE.WFM program responds by adding a new blank record to the PHONE.DBF table, and the blank Name and Phone fields are displayed. (See Figure 3.8.) Note that the keyboard cursor appears in the Name field, so you can type in it immediately.

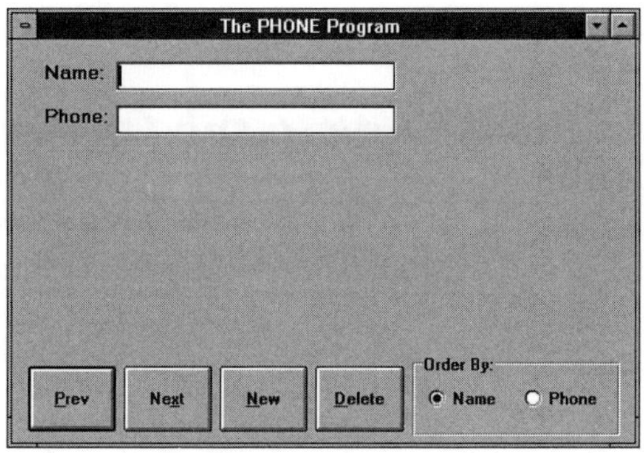

Figure 3.8.
After you click the New button, a new blank record is appended to the PHONE.DBF table.

- ☐ Type any name in the Name field.
- ☐ Type any phone number in the Phone field.
- ☐ Experiment with the Prev and Next buttons and check that when you order the table (by selecting the Name or Phone radio button), the records of the PHONE.DBF table (including the new record you added) are ordered properly.
- ☐ Change back to design mode by clicking the Design tool on the dBASE toolbar.

Attaching Code to the *OnClick* Event of the Delete Pushbutton

When you click the Delete button, the PHONE.WFM program should delete the currently displayed record from the PHONE.DBF table. You'll now write the code that accomplishes this task.

- [ ] Attach the following code to the OnClick event of the Delete pushbutton. After you enter the code, the DELETEBUTTON_OnClick procedure should look like this:

```
Procedure DELETEBUTTON_OnClick

* Delete the current record.
DELETE

* Skip back to the previous record.
SKIP -1

* If at the beginning of file, go to the first record.
IF BOF()
   GOTO TOP
ENDIF

* Make sure that the table has at least one record.
IF EOF()
   APPEND BLANK
ENDIF

Return
```

- [ ] Save your work by selecting Save from the File menu.

The first statement you typed in the DELETEBUTTON_OnClick procedure deletes the current record from the PHONE.DBF table:

```
DELETE
```

The second statement uses the SKIP command to move the record pointer to the previous record in the table so the record pointer will point to a record that isn't deleted:

```
SKIP -1
```

The next statement is an IF statement:

```
IF BOF()
   GOTO TOP
ENDIF
```

This IF statement uses the BOF() function to ensure that the record pointer isn't at the beginning of file. If the record pointer points to the beginning of file, this statement:

```
GOTO TOP
```

is executed so the record pointer will point to the first record in the table.

The record pointer should now point to a valid record after executing the preceding statements. However, if the table has no records in it, then the record pointer will point to the end of file. To make sure the table has at least one record in it, an `IF` statement is used:

```
IF EOF()
   APPEND BLANK
ENDIF
```

If the condition `IF EOF()` is satisfied, the record pointer is pointing to the end of file, which means that the table has no records in it. If this is the case, the command `APPEND BLANK` will add a blank record to the table.

As discussed earlier, you have to make sure the table has at least one record in it because when you type something in the form's entry fields, you want what you type to always go to the table. If the table has no records, you can type data in the entry fields but it won't be stored in the table.

To see in action the code you attached to the `OnClick` event of the Delete pushbutton, follow these steps:

☐ Execute the PHONE.WFM form by clicking the Run tool on the dBASE toolbar.

☐ Use the Prev and Next buttons to display any record of the table.

☐ Click the Delete button.

The PHONE.WFM program responds by deleting the displayed record.

☐ Change back to design mode by clicking the Design tool on the dBASE toolbar.

Adding a Browse Control to the PHONE.WFM Form

As shown back in Figure 3.1, the PHONE.WFM program should also display the records of the PHONE.DBF table in a tabular format (in rows and columns). Displaying the records of the table in tabular format is very easy because dBASE includes a very useful tool called a browse control.

To see the browse control in action, follow these steps:

☐ Use the Control Palette window to place a browse control in the PHONE.WFM form. (The browse control's icon in the Control Palette window is shown in Figure 3.9.)

☐ Move and size the browse control in the PHONE.WFM form so that it will be in the same position and same size as the browse control shown in Figure 3.10.

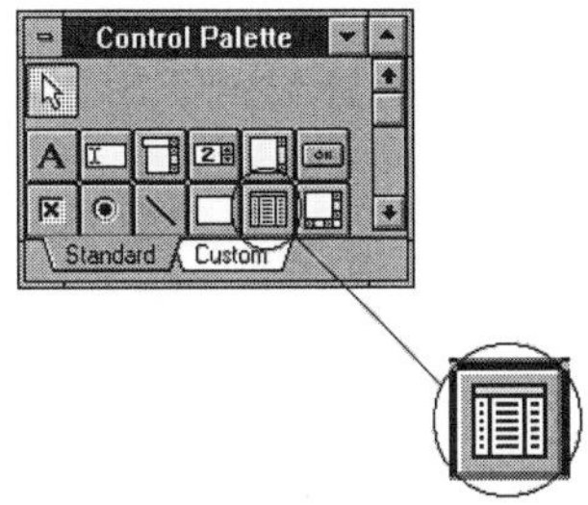

Figure 3.9.
The browse control's icon in the Control Palette window.

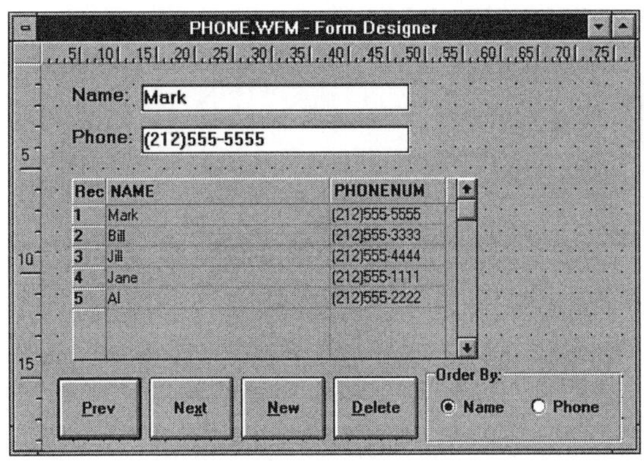

Figure 3.10.
The PHONE.WFM form in design mode with a browse control added.

☐ Execute the PHONE.WFM form by clicking the Run tool on the dBASE toolbar.

The main window of the PHONE.WFM program appears with a browse control in it. (See Figure 3.11.)

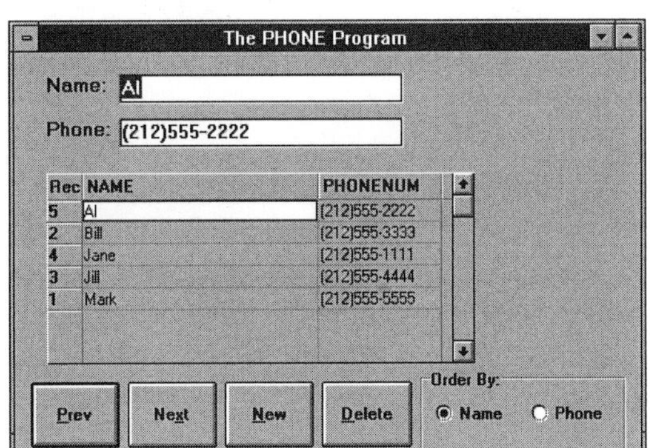

Figure 3.11.
The PHONE.WFM form in runtime mode with a browse control added.

☐ Experiment with the Next and Prev buttons and notice how the browse control highlights the appropriate record as you move from one record to another.

☐ Click any record in the browse control and notice how the Name and Phone entry fields at the top of the PHONE.WFM form are updated automatically.

☐ Change back to design mode by clicking the Design tool on the dBASE toolbar.

Experimenting with the Properties of the Browse Control

The browse control is a very powerful tool with many properties. Experiment with two properties of the browse control—Modify and ShowRecNo.

The current value of the browse control's Modify property is .T., which means you can use the browse control to modify the PHONE.DBF table.

☐ Change the browse control's Modify property to .F. (the Modify property is listed under the Edit Properties entry in the Inspector window).

The current value of the ShowRecNo property of the browse control is .T., which means that the leftmost column of the browse control currently displays record numbers. (See Figure 3.11.)

☐ Change the ShowRecNo property of the browse control to .F. (the ShowRecNo property is listed under the Visual Properties entry in the Inspector window).

To see in action the changes you made in the browse control's Modify and ShowRecNo properties do the following:

☐ Execute the PHONE.WFM form by clicking the Run tool on the dBASE toolbar.

As you can see, now the browse control doesn't include the Rec column. (See Figure 3.12.)

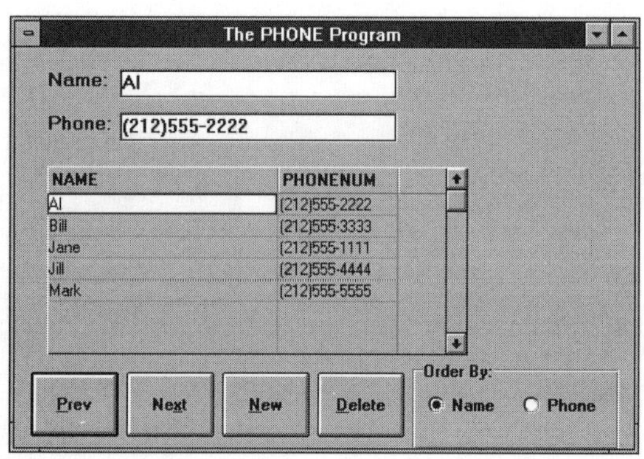

Figure 3.12.
The browse control without the Rec column.

☐ Try to type something in the fields of the browse control.

As you can see, dBASE won't let you modify the table's fields in the browse control.

Summary

In this chapter you have written a dBASE program that uses a table. You have learned the following:

- How to associate a form with a table
- How to link the form's entry fields to the table's fields
- How to set up buttons (Prev and Next) that enable you to navigate between the records of the table
- How to order the records of the table
- How to delete records from the table
- How to add a browse control to a form

3

Q&A

Q In the previous chapter I learned that to open a table I have to use the `USE` statement. Yet in this chapter I wrote a program that uses a table and the `USE` statement wasn't used. Why?

A You don't have to use the `USE` statement in the PHONE.WFM program's code because you set the form's View property to the name of the table you want to use (the PHONE.DBF table) during the visual implementation step. This means that when the PHONE.WFM is opened, the PHONE.DBF table will be opened automatically.

Q When I designed the PHONE.DBF table, the tutorial of this chapter instructed me to set one index for the NAME field and one index for the PHONENUM field. Why was this necessary?

A The reason for setting an index for both the NAME and PHONENUM fields is so the PHONE.WFM program's code would enable you to order the records of the PHONE.DBF table by either the NAME field or the PHONENUM field.

The statement that orders the table by the NAME field is `SET ORDER TO NAME`. You attached this statement to the `OnChange` event of the Name radio button.

The statement that orders the table by the PHONENUM field is `SET ORDER TO PHONENUM`. You attached this statement to the `OnChange` event of the Phone radio button.

Quiz

1. Suppose you have a form called MyForm.WFM and a table called MyTable.DBF. How would you associate the MyTable.DBF table with the MyForm.WFM form?

2. Which property of an entry field do you have to set to link the entry field to a table's field?
3. What does the following code do?

```
SKIP 1
IF EOF()
   ??CHR(7)
   GOTO BOTTOM
ENDIF
```

4. What does the following code do?

```
SKIP -1
IF BOF()
   ??CHR(7)
   GOTO TOP
ENDIF
```

5. What does the following statement do?

```
APPEND BLANK
```

6. Suppose a form has an entry field called MyEntryField. What does the following statement do?

```
form.MyEntryField.SetFocus()
```

7. What does the following code do?

```
DELETE
SKIP -1
IF BOF()
   GOTO TOP
ENDIF
```

Exercise

Enhance the PHONE.WFM program as follows:

☐ Add a pushbutton control to the PHONE.WFM form and set its properties as follows:

Property	*Setting*
Name	TopButton
Text	Top

☐ Attach code to the `OnClick` event of the Top button so that when the user clicks the Top button, the record pointer of the PHONE.DBF table will move to the first record in the table.

Quiz Answers

1. To associate the MyForm.WFM form with the MyTable.DBF table, set the View property of the MyForm.WFM form to the name of the MyTable.DBF file.
2. To link an entry field to a table's field, set the DataLink property of the entry field to the name of the table field.
3. The first statement moves the record pointer to the next record in the table:

   ```
   SKIP 1
   ```

   Then the `IF` statement determines whether the end of file was reached:

   ```
   IF EOF()
      ??CHR(7)
      GOTO BOTTOM
   ENDIF
   ```

   If so, this statement causes the PC to beep:

   ```
   ??CHR(7)
   ```

   This statement moves the record pointer to the last record in the table:

   ```
   GOTO BOTTOM
   ```

4. The first statement moves the record pointer to the previous record in the table:

   ```
   SKIP -1
   ```

   Then the `IF` statement determines whether the beginning of file was reached:

   ```
   IF BOF()
      ??CHR(7)
      GOTO TOP
   ENDIF
   ```

   If it was, this statement causes the PC to beep:

   ```
   ??CHR(7)
   ```

   This statement moves the record pointer to the first record in the table:

   ```
   GOTO TOP
   ```

5. The statement `APPEND BLANK` appends a new blank record to the table.
6. The statement `form.MyEntryField.SetFocus()` sets the keyboard focus to the MyEntryField entry field. After this statement is executed, the keyboard cursor will appear in the MyEntryField entry field and whatever you type will be entered in the MyEntryField entry field.
7. The first statement deletes the current record:

   ```
   DELETE
   ```

The next statement moves the record pointer to the previous record:

```
SKIP -1
```

Then the `IF` statement determines whether the beginning of file was reached:

```
IF BOF()
   GOTO TOP
ENDIF
```

If it was, this statement moves the record pointer to the first record in the table:

```
GOTO TOP
```

Exercise Answer

The code you have to attach to the `OnClick` event of the Top pushbutton is a single statement:

```
GOTO TOP
```

After the user clicks the Top button, the preceding statement will move the record pointer to the first record in the table.

WEEK 1

4

dBASE Programming Building Blocks

Like any programming language, dBASE includes basic programming building blocks that enable you to write programs with decision-making statements such as the `If` statement, `For` loops, and `Case` statements.

In this chapter you'll practice with the programming building blocks of dBASE and learn how to add procedures and methods to your programs.

The Decide Program

The Decide program is a simple program that demonstrates how to use the decision-making statements of dBASE. During the course of this book, you'll use dBASE decision-making statements extensively.

Use the following steps to create the directory and form for the Decide program:

- ☐ Type `MD C:\DBPROG\CH04` in the dBASE Command window, and then press Enter.

  dBASE responds by creating the C:\DBPROG\CH04 directory.

- ☐ Type `Create Form C:\DBPROG\CH04\Decide` in the dBASE Command window, and then press Enter.

  dBASE responds by displaying the Decide.WFM form in design mode.

- ☐ Set the Text property of the form to The Decide Program.
- ☐ Set the MDI property of the form to .F..
- ☐ Select Save from the File menu.

Setting Up the Exit Button

Use the following steps to set up the Exit button:

- ☐ Double-click the PushButton control in the Control Palette window.

  dBASE responds by placing a pushbutton on the form.

- ☐ Set the Text property of the pushbutton to E&xit.
- ☐ Set the Name property of the pushbutton to EXITBUTTON.
- ☐ Attach code to the `OnClick` event of the Exit button. After you attach the code, the `EXITBUTTON_OnClick()` procedure should look like this:

```
Procedure EXITBUTTON_OnClick

form.Close()

Return
```

The code you typed closes the form, which terminates the program.

☐ Drag the Exit button to the lower-left corner of the form and enlarge it.

The form should now look like the one shown in Figure 4.1.

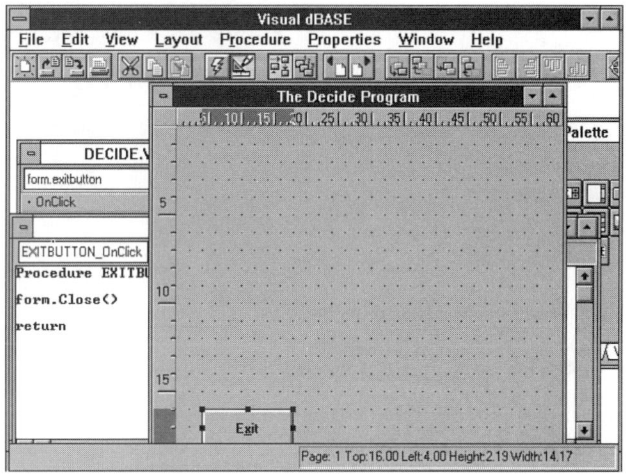

Figure 4.1.
The form of the Decide program in design mode.

☐ Select Save from the File menu to save your work.

Placing Two Check Boxes in the Form

Use the following steps to place two check boxes in the form:

☐ Double-click the CheckBox control in the Control Palette window.

dBASE responds by placing a check box control in the form.

☐ Set the Name property of the check box to SOUNDCHECKBOX.

☐ Set the Text property of the check box to &Sound.

☐ Double-click the CheckBox control in the Control Palette window.

dBASE responds by placing a second check box control in the form.

☐ Set the Name property of the check box to COLORSCHECKBOX.

☐ Set the Text property of the check box to &Colors.

The form should now look like the one shown in Figure 4.2.

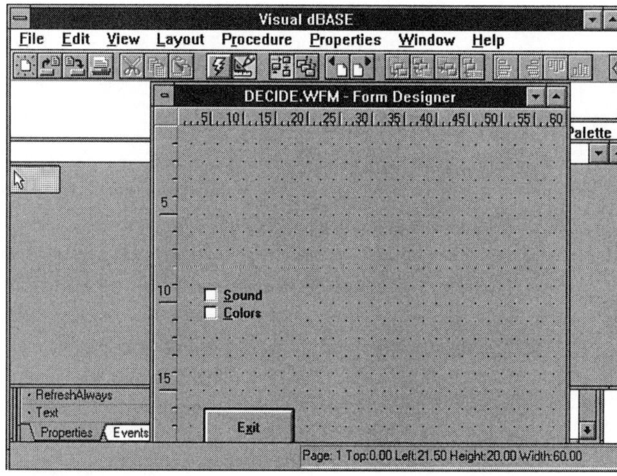

Figure 4.2.
Placing two check boxes in the form.

☐ Select Save from the File menu to save your work.

Even though you haven't finished designing the Decide program, try executing it:

☐ Press F2 to execute the Decide program.

The window of the Decide program appears, as shown in Figure 4.3.

Figure 4.3.
The Decide program with the two check boxes and an Exit button.

☐ Click the check boxes.

As you can see, the state of the check box toggles—when you click a check box, an × is either placed in or removed from the check box. You don't have to write any code to place or remove the × from the check box.

☐ Click the Exit button to terminate the program.

Examining the State of the Check Boxes

You'll now write code that checks the status of the check boxes and displays a message box.

☐ Type `Modify Form ?` in the Command window, and then press Enter.

☐ Select the C:\DBPROG\CH04\Decide.WFM form.

dBASE responds by displaying the Decide.WFM form in design mode.

You'll now attach code to the `OnChange` event of the SOUNDCHECKBOX check box. When you click the SOUNDCHECKBOX (which changes the state of the check box), the `SOUNDCHECKBOX_OnChange` procedure will be executed automatically.

☐ Attach code to the `OnChange` event of the SOUNDCHECKBOX. After you attach the code, the `SOUNDCHECKBOX_OnChange` procedure should look as follows:

```
Procedure SOUNDCHECKBOX_OnChange

?chr(7)

Return
```

This statement causes the PC to beep:

```
?chr(7)
```

Now when you change the state of the Sound check box, the PC beeps. Run the Decide program to see this in action:

☐ Press F2 to execute the Decide program.

☐ Click the Sound check box several time to place and remove an × in the Sound check box.

When the state of the Sound check box is changed, the PC beeps because the `SOUNDCHECKBOX_OnChange` procedure executes the `?chr(7)` statement.

☐ Press Shift+F2 to return to design mode.

Note: In the previous steps you were instructed to place the statement `?chr(7)` in the `SOUNDCHECKBOX_OnChange` procedure to check whether the `OnChange` event occurs when the state of the check box changes. In the following sections you'll enter new code in the `SOUNDCHECKBOX_OnChange` procedure.

When you want to check for yourself that a certain event occurs, you can use the technique of making the PC beep.

☐ Modify the code of the SOUNDCHECKBOX_OnChange procedure. After you modify the code, the SOUNDCHECKBOX_OnChange procedure should look like this:

```
Procedure SOUNDCHECKBOX_OnChange

*** ?chr(7)

If form.SOUNDCHECKBOX.Value = .T.

   MSGBOX("The Sound Check box has an X in it","Message",0)

EndIf

Return
```

The code you typed comments out the statement that causes the PC to beep:

```
*** ?chr(7)
```

Then an If…EndIf block is executed with these statements:

```
If form.SOUNDCHECKBOX.Value = .T.

   MSGBOX("The Sound Check box has an X in it","Message",0)

EndIf
```

The code under the If statement is executed if the If condition is satisfied. The If condition is satisfied if form.SOUNDCHECKBOX.Value is equal to .T.. The Value property of a check box is equal to .T. if an × is in the check box; it's equal to .F. if there's no × in the check box.

If there's an × in the SOUNDCHECKBOX check box, the code under the If statement displays a message box using the MSGBOX() function:

```
MSGBOX("The Sound Check box has an X in it","Message",0)
```

The title of the message box that will be displayed is Message (because this is the second parameter of the MSGBOX() function). The message box contains this text:

```
The Sound Check box has an X in it
```

because this is the first parameter supplied to the MSGBOX() function. The third parameter of the MSGBOX() function is 0, which means the message box has an OK button in it.

Note: The If statement has the following structure:

```
If ...Condition....

  ..................................
  ... This code is executed provided
  ... that the condition is satisfied.
  ..................................
```

```
EndIf
```

Remember to terminate the `If` block with the `EndIf` keyword.

To see your code in action do the following:

- ☐ Press F2 to execute the Decide program.
- ☐ Click the Sound check box several times. When you click the Sound check box to place an × in the check box, the message box shown in Figure 4.4 is displayed.

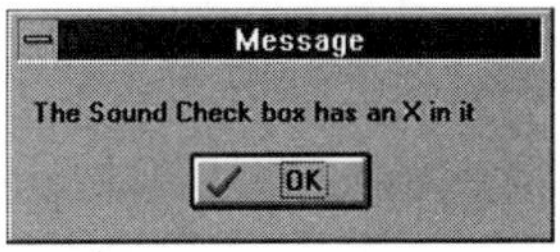

Figure 4.4.
The message box displayed when you click the Sound check box to place an × in the check box.

- ☐ Experiment with the Decide program, then press Shift+F2 to terminate the program and return to design mode.

In the previous steps you executed an `If...EndIf` block to determine whether the Sound check box has an × in it. You can add another `If` statement to determine when there's no × in the check box.

- ☐ Add code to the `SOUNDCHECKBOX_OnChange` procedure. After you add the code, the `SOUNDCHECKBOX_OnChange` procedure should look like this:

```
Procedure SOUNDCHECKBOX_OnChange

*** ?chr(7)

If form.SOUNDCHECKBOX.Value = .T.

   MSGBOX("The Sound Check box has an X in it","Message",0)

EndIf


If form.SOUNDCHECKBOX.Value = .F.

   MSGBOX("The Sound Check box does not have an X in it",;
          "Message",0)

EndIf

Return
```

The code you added executes a second `If` statement:

```
If form.SOUNDCHECKBOX.Value = .F.
   MSGBOX("The Sound Check box does not have an X in it",;
          "Message",0)
EndIf
```

The second `If` statement checks whether there's no × in the Sound check box. If there isn't, a message box is displayed:

```
MSGBOX("The Sound Check box does not have an X in it",;
          "Message",0)
```

Note that a semicolon character (;) is used so the second and third parameter of the `MSGBOX()` function could be typed on the next line.

☐ Select Save from the File menu to save your work.

☐ Press F2 to execute the Decide program.

☐ Click the Sound check box several times.

The Decide program displays the message box shown in Figure 4.4 when you place an × in the check box. When you remove the × from the Sound check box, the message box shown in Figure 4.5. is displayed.

Figure 4.5.
The message box displayed when you remove the × from the Sound check box.

Using *If...Else* Statements

In the preceding steps you executed two `If` statements in the `SOUNDCHECKBOX_OnChange` procedure. There is nothing wrong with executing two `If` statements, but there's a better way to accomplish the same task. You can use an `If...Else` statement rather than two separate `If` statements.

☐ Modify the code in the `SOUNDCHECKBOX_OnChange` procedure. After you modify the code, the `SOUNDCHECKBOX_OnChange` procedure should look like this:

```
Procedure SOUNDCHECKBOX_OnChange

*** ?chr(7)

If form.SOUNDCHECKBOX.Value = .T.

   MSGBOX("The Sound Check box has an X in it","Message",0)

Else
```

```
    MSGBOX("The Sound Check box does not have an X in it",;
           "Message",0)

EndIf

Return
```

In the preceding code the `If` condition is examined. If the condition is satisfied, the code between the `If` and `Else` statements is executed, then the program continues with the execution of the statement following the `EndIf` statement.

If the `If` condition is not satisfied, the code between the `If` and `Else` statements is not executed. Rather, the code between the `Else` and `EndIf` statements is executed.

- ☐ Select Save from the File menu to save your work.
- ☐ Press F2 to execute the Decide program.
- ☐ Click the Sound check box several times and check that the Decide program works as expected.
- ☐ Press Shift+F2 to return to design mode.

4

Using *DO CASE* Statements

In the preceding statement you saw that your dBASE program can make a decision by using `If…EndIf` and `If…Else…EndIf` statements. Theoretically, the `If` statement is the only decision-making statement you need; you can write the most sophisticated Windows program using only the `If` statement. However, sometimes you'll write code requiring many `If` statements, so it's more convenient to use the `DO CASE` statement. You can think of the `DO CASE` statement as another syntax of the `If` statement.

- ☐ Modify the code in the `SOUNDCHECKBOX_OnChange` procedure to see how the `DO CASE` statement is used. After you modify the code, the `SOUNDCHECKBOX_OnChange` procedure should look like this:

```
Procedure SOUNDCHECKBOX_OnChange

*** ?chr(7)

DO CASE

   CASE form.SOUNDCHECKBOX.Value = .T.

   MSGBOX("The Sound Check box has an X in it","Message",0)

   CASE form.SOUNDCHECKBOX.Value = .F.
```

```
    MSGBOX("The Sound Check box does not have an X in it",;
        "Message",0)

ENDCASE

Return
```

The code you typed uses a `DO CASE` statement. During the execution of the procedure, the first `CASE` statement is examined:

```
CASE form.SOUNDCHECKBOX.Value = .T.
```

If the `CASE` condition is satisfied, the code under the `CASE` statement is executed; if it isn't, the code under the `CASE` statement is ignored. The procedure then continues with the next `CASE` statement—examining the `CASE` condition and either executing or ignoring the code under the `CASE` statement.

The `DO CASE` statement can have as many `CASE` statements as you want. For example, suppose you have a variable called `MyVariable`. The following `DO CASE` statement examines the value of `MyVariable`:

```
DO CASE

   CASE MyVariable = 1

        .........................................
        ... This code is executed when MyVariable
        ... is equal to 1
        .........................................

   CASE MyVariable = 2

        .........................................
        ... This code is executed when MyVariable
        ... is equal to 1
        .........................................

CASE MyVariable = 3

        .........................................
        ... This code is executed when MyVariable
        ... is equal to 3
        .........................................


   OTHERWISE

        .........................................
        ... This code is executed when MyVariable
        ... is not equal to 1 and not equal to 2
        ... and not equal to 3
        .........................................

ENDCASE
```

If `MyVariable` is equal to 1, the code under the first `CASE` statement is executed. If it's equal to 2, the second `CASE` statement is satisfied, and if it's equal to 3, the third `CASE` statement is satisfied.

In the preceding code the `OTHERWISE` keyword is used. If none of the `CASE` statements were satisfied, the code under the `OTHERWISE` keyword is executed. For example, if `MyVariable` is equal to 4, none of the `CASE` statements will be satisfied and the code under the `OTHERWISE` keyword will be executed. You don't have to include the `OTHERWISE` keyword when you use a `DO CASE` statement; `OTHERWISE` is optional.

Loops

The loop statement is another important statement in every programming language. *Loop statements* continue to execute the same code until a certain condition occurs. Enhance the Decide program as follows to see how this method works:

☐ Add a pushbutton to the form of the Decide program by double-clicking the PushButton icon in the Control Palette window.

☐ Set the Name property of the pushbutton to LOOPBUTTON.

☐ Set the Text property of the pushbutton to &Loop.

☐ Add a Text control to the form of the Decide program by double-clicking the Text icon in the Control Palette window.

☐ Set the Name property of the Text control to RESULTTEXT.

☐ Set the Text property of the Text control to blank (that is, delete the text inside the Text property of the Text control).

The form of the Decide program should now look like the one shown in Figure 4.6.

☐ Attach code to the `OnClick` event of the Loop button. After you attach the code, the `LOOPBUTTON_OnClick` procedure should look like this:

```
Procedure LOOPBUTTON_OnClick

   For i=1 to 1000

      form.ResultText.Text = Str(i,6,0) && Update Text

   Next

Return
```

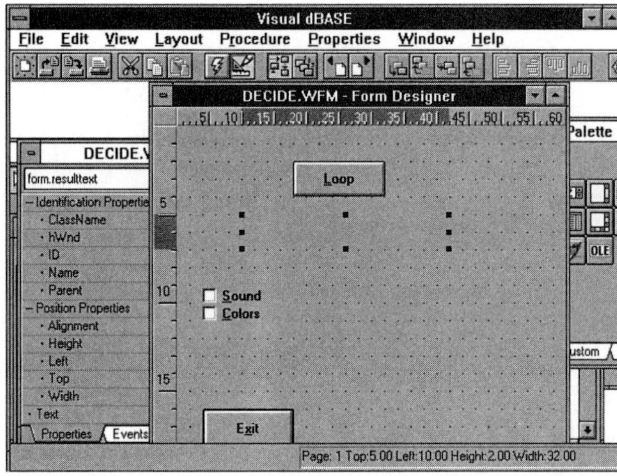

Figure 4.6.
Adding a Loop button and Text control to the form of the Decide program.

The code you typed uses a `For` loop from i=0 to i=1000. This means that the code between the `For` line and the `Next` line is executed as follows:

First, i is equal to 1, so the Text property of the ResultText control is updated as follows:

```
form.ResultText.Text = Str(i,6,0) && Update Text
```

The `Str()` function returns a string. The first parameter of the `Str()` function is numeric, which you want to convert to a string. The second parameter of the `Str()` function is the maximum number of characters in the string. The third parameter is the number of decimal digits. So in the first iteration of the `For` loop, the Text property of the ResultText control is assigned the string 1 (because currently i is equal to 1). Note that the preceding conversion (from numeric to string) is needed because the Text property cannot be assigned with a numeric value. It must be assigned with a string value.

Then the `Next` statement is executed. `Next` causes the program to increase the value of i and then return to the `For` line. Since i was increased by 1, now it's equal to 2 (1+1=2). The `For` statement checks whether i is equal to 1000. Since it's currently equal to 2, the body of the `For` loop is executed again. Now the Text property of the ResultText control is updated with the string `2`.

This process continues until eventually i is equal to 1001. Now the program continues with the execution of the statement after the `Next` statement.

Therefore, the Text control will display the following numbers:

```
1
2
3
...
```

```
...
...
1000
```

To see your code in action do the following:

- ☐ Select Save from the File menu.
- ☐ Press F2 to execute the Decide program.
- ☐ Click the Loop button.

  The Decide program starts counting from 1 to 1000, and the ResultText control displays the numbers during the counting.

- ☐ Experiment with the Decide program, then press Shift+F2 to terminate the program.

Note: The `&&` characters that appear in the statement updating the Text control are used for comments:

```
form.ResultText.Text = Str(i,6,0) && Update Text
```

When a comment starts on a new line, it starts with the * character:

```
* This is my comment
```

However, you can use the `&&` characters for including a comment on the same line as a statement:

```
MyVariable = 3 && This is my comment
```

- ☐ Modify the code of the `LOOPBUTTON_OnClick` procedure so that it looks like this:

```
Procedure LOOPBUTTON_OnClick

   For i=1 to 1000 Step 10

      form.ResultText.Text = Str(i,6,0) && Update Text

   Next

Return
```

As you can see, you added the text `Step 10` in the first line of the `For` loop to increase i by 10 in each iteration. So in the first iteration, i is equal to 1; in the next iteration, i is equal to 1+10=11; in the next iteration, i is equal to 11+10=21; and so on.

Eventually i is equal to 991, then it's increased by 10 to 991+10=1001. But the `For` statement is for i=1 to i=1000, so when you execute the program you'll see the following values:

```
i=1
i=11
i=21
...
...
...
i=991
```

- ☐ Select Save from the File menu.
- ☐ Press F2 to execute the Decide program.
- ☐ Click the Loop button.

  The Text control keeps displaying the numbers from i=1 to i=991 in increments of 10. The last number you'll see is i=991.

- ☐ Experiment with the Decide program, then press Shift+F2 to return to design mode.

You can include the `EXIT` keyword in the `For` loop. This will cause the `For` loop to immediately exit the loop, as shown in the following steps.

- ☐ Modify the code of the `LOOPBUTTON_OnClick` procedure so that it looks like this:

```
Procedure LOOPBUTTON_OnClick

   For i=1 to 1000 Step 1


      form.ResultText.Text = Str(i,6,0) && Update Text

      if i = 800
EXIT
      endif

   Next

Return
```

The code you typed sets the Step to 1 so the `For` loop will increment i by 1 in each iteration. If you omit Step 1, the `For` loop will behave as if Step 1 is included.

An `If` statement is included in the `For` loop. The `If` statement "catches" the point in the program when i is equal to 800. So the loop will display the following values of i:

```
1
2
3
...
...
...
800
```

That is, the `If` statement “catches” when i is equal to 800, and the `EXIT` keyword in the `If` statement causes the immediate premature termination of the `For` loop.

- ☐ Select Save from the File menu to save your work.
- ☐ Press F2 to execute the Decide program.
- ☐ Click the Loop button and check that the counter counts from 1 to 800.
- ☐ Press Shift+F2 to terminate the program.

The *Do While* Statement

In the preceding section you learned about the `For` loop. dBASE is also equipped with other loop statements such as the `Do While` statement, which is similar to the `For` loop.

- ☐ Modify the code of the `LOOPBUTTON_OnClick` procedure so that it looks like this:

```
Procedure LOOPBUTTON_OnClick

i = 1

Do While i<1000

   i = i + 1
   form.ResultText.Text = Str(i,5,0)

EndDo

Return
```

The code you typed initializes the variable i to 1:

```
i = 1
```

Then a `Do While` statement is executed:

```
Do While i<1000

   i = i + 1
   form.ResultText.Text = Str(i,5,0)

EndDo
```

The code between the `Do While` and the `EndDo` statement is executed. So because i is equal to 1 in the first iteration, the code increases i to 2 (1+1=2), and the Text property of the Text control is updated with the value of i.

Then the `EndDo` statement is encountered, which causes the program to return to the `Do While` statement. Because i is now equal to 2, which is still less than 1000, the body of the loop is executed again.

4

Eventually i will be equal to 1001, and the program will continue with the execution of the statement following the EndDo statement.

Therefore, the Text control displays the following values:

```
i = 1
i = 2
i = 3
...
...
...
i = 1000
```

☐ Select Save from the File menu to save your work.

☐ Press F2 to execute the Decide program.

☐ Click the Loop button.

The program counts from 1 to 1000.

☐ Experiment with the Decide program, then press Shift+F2 to terminate the program.

Adding a Procedure to the General Area

You'll now learn how to add a procedure. Suppose you want your PC to beep twice after the counter finishes counting. You'll have to add code to the LOOPBUTTON_OnClick procedure. For example, you can add code to the LOOPBUTTON_OnClick procedure so that it will look like this:

```
Procedure LOOPBUTTON_OnClick

i = 1

Do While i<1000

   i = i + 1
   form.ResultText.Text = Str(i,5,0)

EndDo

?chr(7)
?chr(7)

Return
```

To illustrate how a procedure works, you'll add the beeping in a different way.

☐ Modify the code of the LOOPBUTTON_OnClick procedure so that it looks like this:

```
Procedure LOOPBUTTON_OnClick

i = 1

Do While i<1000

   i = i + 1
   form.ResultText.Text = Str(i,5,0)

EndDo


BeepNTimes(2)

Return
```

After the counter finishes counting, the following statement is executed:

```
BeepNTimes(2)
```

`BeepNTimes()` is a procedure that causes the PC to beep. How many times will the PC beep? That depends on the number you supply as the parameter of the `BeepNTimes()` procedure. `BeepNTimes()` is a custom-made procedure, so you have to write the code yourself. Here's how you do that:

- ☐ Double-click the Loop button.

  dBASE responds by displaying the Procedure Editor window.

- ☐ Select the (General) item, as shown in Figure 4.7.

  dBASE responds by displaying an empty area, called the General area, where you'll type code.

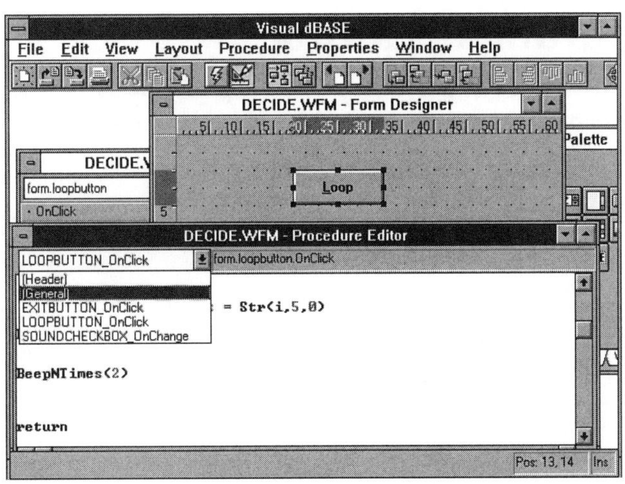

Figure 4.7.
Selecting the (General) item.

☐ Type the following code in the General area:

```
Procedure BeepNTimes(N)

For i=1 to N

  ?chr(7)

Next

Return
```

The code you typed is the code for the `BeepNTimes()` procedure. The procedure has one parameter, `N`, which determines the number of beeps. In this procedure you execute a `For` loop that causes your PC to beep `N` times:

```
For i=1 to N

  ?chr(7)

Next
```

☐ Select Save from the File menu.

☐ Press F2 to execute the Decide program.

☐ Click the Loop button.

The program counts from 1 to 1000, then the PC beeps twice (because the `BeepNTimes()` procedure is executed with 2 as the parameter).

☐ Experiment with the Decide program, then press Shift+F2 to terminate the program.

Adding a Method

In the preceding section you added a procedure. However, this procedure is not considered part of the form. For example, you can't use the following statement in the `BeepNTimes()` procedure:

```
form.ResultText.Text = "Beeping"
```

To use the form's objects from within the procedure you write, you have to write a method. To do this, use the following steps:

☐ Select New Method from the Procedure menu.

dBASE responds by displaying an area in the Procedure Editor window, where you'll write your method. (See Figure 4.8.)

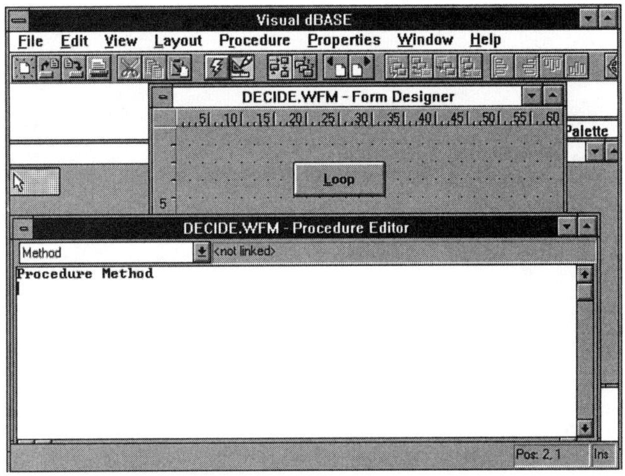

Figure 4.8.
dBASE prepares the area where you'll write the code for the new method.

The default name of the new method is `Method`, but you'll change it to `MyMethod`.

☐ Change the name of the method to `MyMethod` by replacing the text `Method` with `MyMethod`.

So now the Procedure Editor window should look like this:

```
Procedure MyMethod
```

☐ Add code to the `MyMethod` method.

After adding the code, the `MyMethod` method should look like this:

```
Procedure MyMethod
form.ResultText.Text = "Beeping"

Return
```

☐ In the `LOOPBUTTON_OnClick` procedure add code that executes the `MyMethod` method. After you add the code, the `LOOPBUTTON_OnClick` procedure should look like this:

```
Procedure LOOPBUTTON_OnClick

i = 1

Do While i<1000

   i = i + 1
   form.ResultText.Text = Str(i,5,0)

EndDo

form.MyMethod()

BeepNTimes(2)

Return
```

In the preceding code, you executed the `MyMethod()` procedure as follows:

```
form.MyMethod()
```

So once the counter finishes counting, the ResultText Text control will display the text `Beeping` and the PC will beep twice.

- ☐ Select Save from the File menu.
- ☐ Press F2 to execute the Decide program.
- ☐ Click the Loop button.

The Decide program responds by counting from 1 to 1000, then the text `Beeping` *is displayed and the PC beeps twice.*

- ☐ Press Shift+F2 to terminate the program.

Summary

In this chapter you have learned about several programming building blocks in dBASE. These programming building blocks are used in almost every program you'll write. You'll have a chance to experiment with these statements in subsequent chapters of this book.

In this chapter you have also learned how to add a procedure in the General area of the program and how to add a method to the form.

Q&A

Q Are the statements discussed in this chapter the only decision statements in dBASE?

A There are several other decision-making statements you can use in dBASE, which you'll learn about during the course of this book. The statements you learned in this chapter are the fundamental and most important statements.

Q Should I use a series of `If` statements or a `DO CASE` statement?

A The reason dBASE gives you the option of writing code with an `If` statement or a `DO CASE` statement is so your code will be easier to understand. Suppose you are checking the value of a variable called `MyVariable`. Depending on its value, a different code is executed. As you have learned in this chapter, you can do this by writing a series of `If` statements or a `DO CASE` statement. Typically, if you use a `DO CASE` with several `CASE` statements in it, the code will be easier to understand than if you type a series of several `If` statements.

Quiz

1. What is wrong with the following code?

```
If MyVariable = 2
  MyVariable = MyVariable + 2
```

2. What is the value of MyVariable after you execute the following statements?

```
MyVariable = 2
If MyVariable = 2

  MyVariable = MyVariable + 2

EndIf
```

Exercises

1. Modify the Decide program as follows: Write code that causes the PC to beep once when you remove the × from the Colors check box and beep again when you place an × in the Colors check box.
2. Write the code for Exercise 1 by using the `BeepNTimes()` procedure.

Quiz Answers

1. The `If` statement must be terminated with an `EndIf` statement as follows:

```
If MyVariable = 2

  MyVariable = MyVariable + 2

EndIf
```

2. `MyVariable` is first set to 2:

```
MyVariable = 2
```

Then an `If` statement is executed:

```
If MyVariable = 2

  MyVariable = MyVariable + 2

EndIf
```

The `If` condition is satisfied because `MyVariable` is equal to 2. So `MyVariable` is increased by 2:

```
MyVariable = MyVariable + 2
```

At the end of the execution, `MyVariable` is equal to 4 (2+2=4)

Exercise Answers

1. These are the steps you use to modify the Decide program:

   - Attach code to the `OnChange` event of the `COLORSCHECKBOX`. After you attach the code, the `COLORSCHECKBOX_OnChange` procedure should look like this:

```
Procedure COLORSCHECKBOX_OnChange

if form.COLORSCHECKBOX.Value = .T.

   ?chr(7)

endif

if form.COLORSCHECKBOX.Value = .F.

   ?chr(7)
   ?chr(7)

EndIf

Return
```

   The code you typed uses two `If` statements to check the status of the Colors check box, and accordingly, the PC will beep once or twice.

2. Here's how you use the `BeepNTimes()` procedure to write the code for Exercise 1:

   - Modify the code of the `COLORSCHECKBOX_OnChange` procedure so that it looks like this:

```
Procedure COLORSCHECKBOX_OnChange

if form.COLORSCHECKBOX.Value = .T.

   * ?chr(7)
   BeepNTimes(1)

endif

if form.COLORSCHECKBOX.Value = .F.

   * ?chr(7)
   * ?chr(7)
   BeepNTimes(2)

EndIf

Return
```

   The code you added comments out the `?chr(7)` statements and uses the `BeepNTimes()` procedure instead.

To make the PC beep once, you execute the following statement:

```
BeepNTimes(1)
```

To make it beep twice, use the following statement:

```
BeepNTimes(2)
```

5

WEEK 1

Dialog Boxes

Dialog boxes serve an important role in Windows applications. In this chapter you'll learn how to incorporate dialog boxes into your dBASE applications.

Dialog Boxes—What For?

While your application is running, it might need some information from your user. Typically, your application gets information from the user by displaying a dialog box. The user provides information by typing text into the dialog box's entry fields, placing ×s in or removing them from check boxes, and so on. Dialog boxes are also used to give information to the user. For example, if the user performs an illegal operation, your dBASE application can prompt the user that he or she did something wrong by displaying a dialog box with a message.

The DIALOGS Program

In the following sections you'll write a program called DIALOGS that demonstrates how to incorporate simple dialog boxes into your dBASE application. Before you start writing the DIALOGS program, you need to know what it should do. Figure 5.1 shows the main window of the DIALOGS program. As you can see, the main window of the DIALOGS program contains two pushbuttons: Exit and Display Message.

Figure 5.1.
The main window of the DIALOGS program.

When you click the Exit button, the DIALOGS program terminates; when you click the Display Message pushbutton, the DIALOGS program displays a dialog box with a message. (See Figure 5.2.)

The dialog box shown in Figure 5.2 is a simple, standard dialog box that dBASE designed for you already. This dialog box has been incorporated into the dBASE language, so you don't have to design it. Sometimes, however, you'll need more complex dialog boxes. In this case, you'll need to design your own custom dialog box. The DIALOGS2 program (discussed later in this chapter) illustrates how to design custom-made dialog boxes.

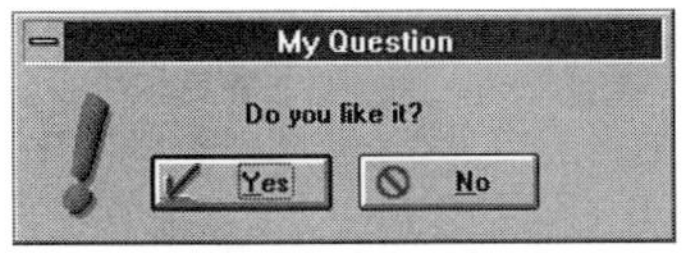

Figure 5.2.
The dialog box that displays when you click the Display Message pushbutton.

The Visual Implementation of the DIALOGS Program

You'll now design the main window of the DIALOGS program.

- ☐ If the dBASE desktop contains any WFM forms, close these forms (that is, make the WFM form you want to close the active form, then select Close from the File menu).

You'll now create the directory for the DIALOGS program files.

- ☐ If you don't have the C:\DBPROG directory, create it by typing `MD C:\DBPROG` in the dBASE Command window.
- ☐ Type `MD C:\DBPROG\CH05` in the dBASE Command window, then press the Enter key.

  dBASE responds by creating the C:\DBPROG\CH05 directory.

- ☐ Type `MD CH05` in the Command window, and then press Enter.

  dBASE responds by creating the C:\DBPROG\CH05 directory.

- ☐ Type `CD C:\DBPROG\CH05` in the Command window, and then press Enter.

  dBASE responds by changing the current directory to the C:\DBPROG\CH05 directory.

- ☐ Type `CREATE FORM C:\DBPROG\CH05\DIALOGS` in the Command window, and then press Enter.

  dBASE responds by creating the DIALOGS.WFM form in the C:\DBPROG\CH05 directory and displaying the empty DIALOGS form.

- ☐ Build the DIALOGS.WFM form according to the specifications in Table 5.1. When you finish building the form, it should look like the one shown in Figure 5.3.

Table 5.1. The properties table of the DIALOGS.WMF form.

Object	Property	Setting
Form	**Text**	**The DIALOGS Program**
	Height	18
	Left	1

continues

Table 5.1. continued

Object	Property	Setting
	Top	0
	Width	63
	MDI	.F.
Image	**Name**	**FaceImage**
	DataSource	MyPic.BMP
	Alignment	0 (Stretch)
	Height	13
	Left	26
	Top	1
	Width	37
PushButton	**Name**	**DisplayMessagePushButton**
	Text	&Display Message
	Height	2
	Left	11
	Top	15
	Width	40
PushButton	**Name**	**ExitPushButton**
	Text	E&xit
	Height	5
	Left	2
	Top	3
	Width	22

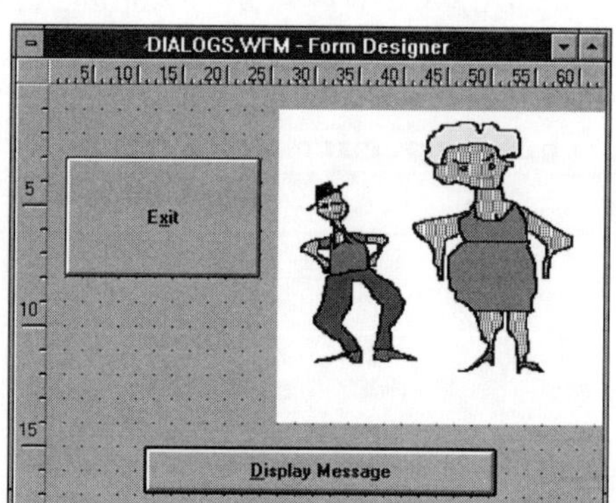

Figure 5.3.
The DIALOGS.WMF form in design mode.

Note: Table 5.1 instructs you to set the DataSource property of the FACEIMAGE image control to MyPic.BMP. This image control is placed on the form to show how you can make your forms more attractive by using BMP pictures.

You can draw your own BMP pictures using a drawing program such as Paintbrush, or you can purchase professional clip art. When you buy clip art, make sure you read the software licensing agreement to find out whether you're allowed to distribute this clip art with your programs.

In addition to BMP files, dBASE also supports the following graphics files: PCX files, WMF files, EPS files, TIF files, and ICO files.

For this exercise, draw the BMP picture yourself:

☐ Start Paintbrush.

☐ Select Image Attributes from the Options menu.

☐ Select the Pels option for the units (that is, set the units to pixels).

☐ Set Width to 250 and Height to 390.

☐ Click the OK button of the Image Attributes dialog box.

Paintbrush responds by displaying a new picture with its width equal to 250 pixels and height equal to 390 pixels.

☐ Draw something with Paintbrush.

☐ Save your drawing as MyPic.BMP in the C:\DBPROG\CH05 directory.

When you design the form using Table 5.1, set the DataSource property of the FaceImage image to MyPic.BMP as follows:

☐ Click the tool icon on the right side of the DataSource property.

dBASE responds by displaying the DataSource Property Builder dialog box.

☐ Set the Location combo box to Filename.

☐ Click the tool icon to the right of the Bitmap box.

dBASE responds by displaying the Choose Image dialog box.

☐ Select the MyPic.BMP file you drew with Paintbrush, and then click the OK button.

Entering the Code of the DIALOGS Program

In the following sections you'll enter the code of the DIALOGS program.

Attaching Code to the *OnClick* Event of the Exit Button

You'll now attach code to the `OnClick` event of the Exit button.

- ☐ Attach the following code to the `OnClick` event of the EXITPUSHBUTTON button. When you finish typing the code, the `EXITPUSHBUTTON_OnClick` procedure should look like this:

```
Procedure EXITPUSHBUTTON_OnClick

        form.Close()

Return
```

- ☐ Save your work by selecting Save from the File menu.

The code you typed executes the `Close()` method on the form. Therefore, clicking the Exit button closes the form and terminates the DIALOGS program.

Attaching Code to the *OnClick* Event of the Display Message Button

You'll now attach code to the `OnClick` event of the Display Message button.

- ☐ Attach the following code to the `OnClick` event of the DISPLAYMESSAGEPUSHBUTTON button. When you finish typing the code, the `DISPLAYMESSAGEPUSHBUTTON_OnClick` procedure should look like this:

```
Procedure DISPLAYMESSAGEPUSHBUTTON_OnClick

Result = MSGBOX("Do you like it?",;
                "My Question",;
                 4+16)

DO CASE
   Case Result = 6
         MSGBOX("You said that you like it!",;
                "Your Answer",;
                 0+16)

   Case Result = 7
         MSGBOX("You said that you don't like it!",;
                "Your Answer",;
                 0+64)

ENDCASE

Return
```

- ☐ Save your work by selecting Save from the File menu.

The code you typed executes the `MSGBOX()` function:

```
Result = MSGBOX("Do you like it?",;
                "My Question",;
                 4+16)
```

The `MSGBOX()` function has three parameters. The first parameter is equal to the string `"Do you like it?"`. This means that when you click the Display Message button, a message box will appear with the message `Do you like it?`.

The second parameter of the `MSGBOX()` function sets the title of the message box to `My Question`.

The third parameter of the `MSGBOX()` function is 4+16. You can type 20 instead of 4+16, but typing 4+16 makes the program easier to read. The third parameter is composed of two integers (4+16). The first integer (4) indicates which pushbuttons will appear in the message box. Take a look at Table 5.2, which displays the six possible values for the first integer.

Table 5.2. The six possible values of the first integer.

Value	Button
0	OK
1	OK and Cancel
2	Abort and Retry and Ignore
3	Yes and No and Cancel
4	Yes and No
5	Retry and Cancel

Since the first integer you typed is 4, the message box will appear with two buttons—Yes and No. The second integer determines which icon will appear in the message box. The four possible values for the second integer are 16 (an exclamation icon), 32 (a question mark icon), 48 (another exclamation icon), and 64 (the information icon). Since the second integer you typed is 16, the message box will contain the exclamation icon as well as the Yes and No buttons.

Note that the returned value of `MSGBOX()` is assigned to the `Result` variable:

```
Result = MSGBOX("Do you like it?",;
                "My Question",;
                 4+16)
```

Once the message box is displayed, you can click either the Yes button or the No button. If you click the Yes button, `Result` is updated with the number 6; if you click the No button, `Result` is updated with the number 7. Of course, if you have other buttons in the message box, `MSGBOX()` will be able to return other values that correspond to the clicked button. Table 5.3 shows the seven possible values that `MSGBOX()` can return.

Table 5.3. The seven possible values that `MSGBOX()` can return.

Clicked Button	Returned Value
OK	1
Cancel	2
Abort	3
Retry	4
Ignore	5
Yes	6
No	7

You then typed a `DO CASE` block of statements:

```
DO CASE
   Case Result = 6
        MSGBOX("You said that you like it!",;
                "Your Answer",;
                 0+16)

   Case Result = 7
        MSGBOX("You said that you don't like it!",;
                "Your Answer",;
                 0+64)

ENDCASE
```

The `DO CASE` analyzes the returned value of `Result`. If `Result` is equal to 6, you clicked the Yes button in the message box (see Table 5.3) and the following case is satisfied:

```
Case Result = 6
     MSGBOX("You said that you like it!",;
             "Your Answer",;
              0+16)
```

That is, if you clicked the Yes button, `Result` is equal to 6 and the code you typed displays another message box with the message `You said that you like it!`. The title of the message box is `Your Answer`, and the message box has an OK button and an exclamation icon (0+16).

If you clicked the No button, the following case is satisfied (because `MSGBOX()` returns 7):

```
Case Result = 7
     MSGBOX("You said that you don't like it!",;
             "Your Answer",;
              0+64)
```

This code displays another message box with the message `You said that you don't like it!`.

To see your code in action do the following:

☐ Execute the DIALOGS program.

The window of the DIALOGS program appears, as shown in Figure 5.1.

☐ Click the Display Message button.

DIALOGS responds by displaying the message box shown in Figure 5.2.

☐ Click the Yes button.

DIALOGS responds by displaying the message box shown in Figure 5.4.

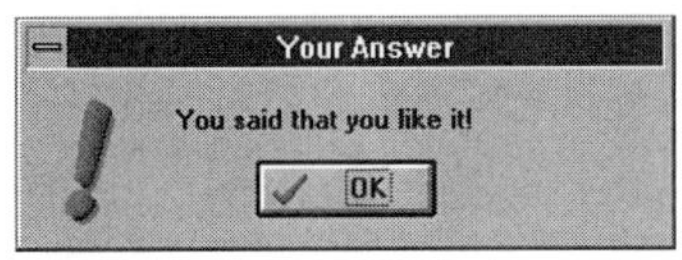

Figure 5.4.
The message box that displays after you click the Yes button.

☐ Click the OK button to close the dialog box.

☐ Click the Display Message button again.

DIALOGS responds by displaying the message box shown in Figure 5.2.

☐ Click the No button.

DIALOGS responds by displaying the message box shown in Figure 5.5.

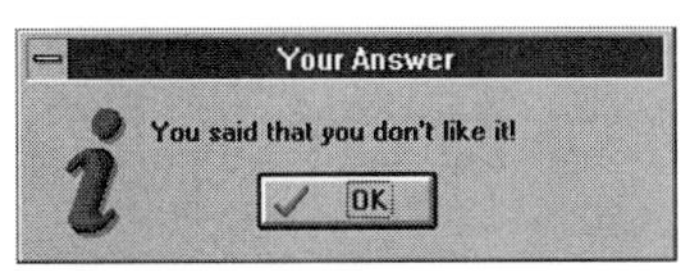

Figure 5.5.
The message box that displays after you click the No button.

☐ Click the OK button to close the dialog box.

☐ Click the Exit button to terminate the DIALOGS program.

As you just saw, you can use the `MSGBOX()` function to set up dialog boxes that ask you simple questions. Your code can then analyze the answer you give.

The DIALOGS2 Program

You'll now design the DIALOGS2 program, which demonstrates how to design and display a custom-made dialog box. Before starting the design of the DIALOGS2 program, a word of caution: The DIALOGS2 program uses two different forms, the DIALOGS2.WFM form and the MyDlg.WFM form, so it's a little more complicated than the single-form–based programs presented in this book so far. However, using multiple forms is an important feature of dBASE; you will find this feature invaluable in your future dBASE projects.

Before you begin writing the DIALOGS2 program, review what it should do. When you start the DIALOGS2 program, the DIALOGS2.WFM form is displayed, as shown in Figure 5.6.

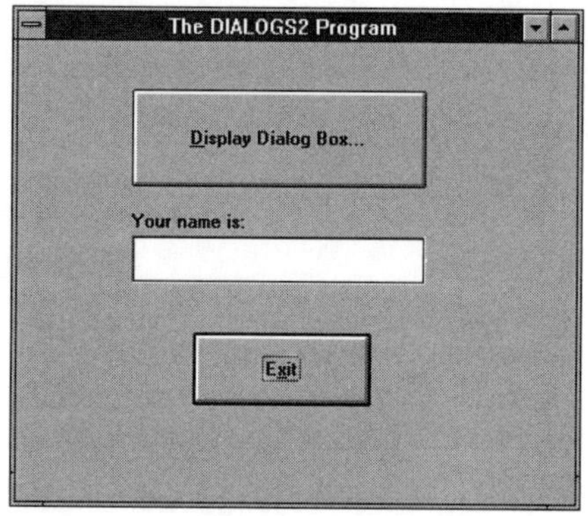

Figure 5.6.
The DIALOGS2.WFM form (the main window of the DIALOGS2 program).

As you can see in Figure 5.6, the DIALOGS2 form contains the Exit button, the Display Dialog Box... button, and an entry field. The entry field is used to display your name. However, this entry field is disabled—you can't type text in it. Why? It demonstrates how a dialog box is used to get input from you.

To set the name, click the Display Dialog Box... button. The dialog box shown in Figure 5.7 is displayed.

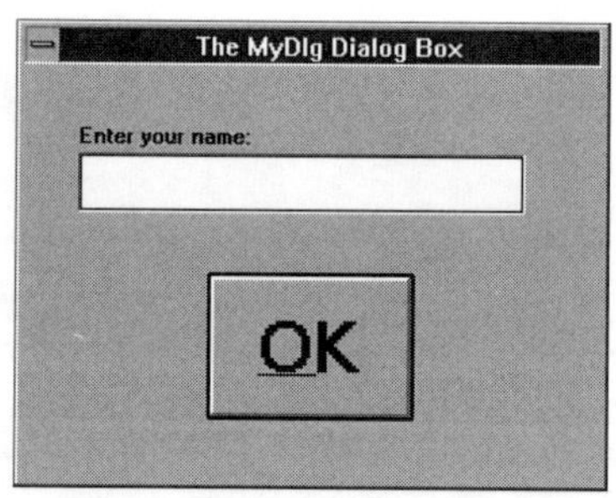

Figure 5.7.
The MyDlg.WFM dialog box that displays after you click the Display Dialog Box... button.

Type your name in the entry field of the MyDlg.WFM form, then click the OK button. The MyDlg dialog box closes and the DIALOGS2.WFM form is displayed. However, now the entry field in the DIALOGS2.WFM form displays the name typed in the MyDlg dialog box.

The Visual Implementation of the DIALOGS2 Program

The DIALOGS2 program has two forms: DIALOGS2.WFM, the main window, and MyDlg.WFM, the custom-made dialog box. Start by designing the DIALOGS2.WFM form:

☐ Type `CREATE FORM C:\DBPROG\CH05\DIALOGS2` in the Command window, and then press Enter.

dBASE responds by creating the DIALOGS2.WFM in the C:\DBPROG\CH05 directory and displaying the empty DIALOGS2.WFM form.

☐ Design the DIALOGS2.WFM form according to the specifications in Table 5.4. When you finish designing the form, it should look like the one shown in Figure 5.8.

Table 5.4. The properties table of the DIALOGS2.WFM form.

Object	Property	Setting
Form	**Text**	**The DIALOGS2 Program**
	Top	0
	Width	63
	MDI	.F.
	Height	19
	Left	5
PushButton	**Name**	**ExitPushButton**
	Top	12
	Width	20
	Text	E&xit
	Height	3
	Left	20
PushButton	**Name**	**DisplayDlgBoxPushButton**
	Top	2
	Width	33
	Text	&Display Dialog Box...
	Height	4
	Left	13

continues

Table 5.4. continued

Object	Property	Setting
Text	**Name**	**Text1**
	Top	7
	Width	24
	Text	Your name is:
	Height	1
	Left	13
Entry Field	**Name**	**NameEntryField**
	Value	(empty)
	Top	8
	Width	33
	Height	2
	Enabled	.F.
	Left	13

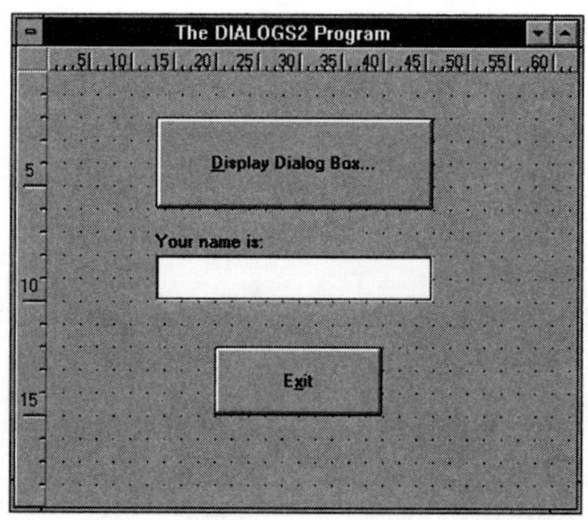

Figure 5.8.
The DIALOGS2.WFM form in design mode.

Note that Table 5.4 instructs you to set the Enabled property of the NameEntryField entry field to .F.. This means that during the execution of the DIALOGS2 program, you can't enter text in this entry field. As you'll soon see, this entry field is filled by the DIALOGS.WFM program's code.

Entering the Code of the DIALOGS2 Program

In the following section, you'll enter the code of DIALOGS2 program.

Attaching Code to the *OnClick* Event of the Exit Button

☐ Attach the following code to the `OnClick` event of the Exit button of the DIALOGS2.WFM form. After you type this code, the `ExitPushButton_OnClick()` procedure should look like this:

```
Procedure EXITPUSHBUTTON_OnClick

        form.Close()

Return
```

☐ Save your work by selecting Save from the File menu.

The code you typed executes the `Close()` method on the form. Therefore, clicking the Exit button closes the form and terminates the DIALOGS2 program.

Attaching Code to the *OnOpen* Event

☐ Attach the following code to the `OnOpen` event of the DIALOGS2.WFM form. After you type this code, the `Form_OnOpen` procedure of the DIALOGS2.WFM form should look like this:

```
Procedure Form_OnOpen


* Set the path to the directory
* where the program resides.
ProgramPath = Left (Program(0),Rat("\",Program(0)))
SET PATH TO &ProgramPath


* Load the MyDlg.WFM form.
* (From now on, form.MyDlgForm is the MyDlg.WFM form.)
set procedure to MyDlg.wfm additive
form.MyDlgForm=new MYDLGFORM()


Return
```

5

☐ Save your work by selecting Save from the File menu.

The code you typed extracts the path of the directory from which the DIALOGS2.WFM program is executed:

```
ProgramPath = Left (Program(0),Rat("\",Program(0)))
```

For example, if the DIALOGS2.WFM program is in the C:\DBPROG\CH05 directory, then after executing the preceding statement, `ProgramPath` is equal to C:\DBPROG\CH05.

The next statement sets the PATH of the program:

```
SET PATH TO &ProgramPath
```

Don't confuse the DOS PATH and the dBASE PATH. For example, if the DOS PATH includes the directory C:\MyDIR, and you try to execute a program called MyProg.EXE in the C:\MyDir directory from the DOS prompt, then DOS will find the MyProg.EXE file no matter what the current directory is.

The dBASE PATH is similar to the DOS PATH when your code refers to a file. For example, your program may load a BMP file during runtime. If the BMP file is called MyPic.BMP and is in the C:\Pictures directory, then your program will load MyPic.BMP from the C:\Pictures directory. Just like the DOS PATH, you can set the dBASE PATH to various directories. When your program is executed, the statement that loads the MyPic.BMP file searches for the file in the current directory. If the MyPic.BMP file isn't found in the current directory, then dBASE searches all the directories within the dBASE PATH.

> **Note:** You can set the dBASE PATH as follows:
>
> ```
> Dir1 = "C:\MyDir"
> Dir2 = "C:\HerDir"
> SET PATH TO &Dir1, &Dir2, C:\OurDir
> ```
>
> The preceding statement sets the dBASE PATH to three directories. When you use variables containing the name of directories (such as Dir1 and Dir2), you must precede the name of the variable with the & character.

The next statements load the MyDlg.WFM form, which will serve as the custom-made dialog box:

```
set procedure to MyDlg.wfm additive
form.MyDlgForm=new MYDLGFORM()
```

This statement causes the program to load the MyDlg.WFM file:

```
set procedure to MyDlg.wfm additive
```

But what directory is the MyDlg.WFM file in? Later, you will save the MyDlg.WFM file in the same directory as the DIALOGS2.WFM file (the C:\DBPROG\CH05 directory).

Now suppose you're currently logged into the C:\ directory and you execute the DIALOGS2 program. Will the set procedure statement be able to find the MyDlg.WFM file? The answer is yes, because you set the dBASE PATH to the directory from which the DIALOGS2.WFM program is executed. The DIALOGS2 program will search for the MyDlg.WFM file in the

C:\DBPROG\CH05 directory, then in the directory mentioned in the dBASE PATH. Since you'll save the MyDlg.WFM file in the C:\DBPROG\CH05 directory, the `set procedure` statement will find the MyDlg.WFM file.

> **Note:** Instead of dealing with this business of the dBASE PATH, you can simply use the `set procedure` statement as follows:
>
> ```
> set procedure to c:\dbprog\ch05\MyDlg.wfm additive
> ```
>
> However, the preceding statement assumes that the MyDlg.WFM file is in the C:\DBPROG\CH05 directory.
>
> On the other hand, when you use the dBASE PATH feature, the program doesn't assume that the MyDlg.WFM file is in any particular directory. Therefore, as long as the DIALOGS2.WFM file and the MyDlg.WFM file are in the same directory (any directory), the program will work fine.

You also typed this statement:

```
form.MyDlgForm=new MYDLGFORM()
```

This statement declares the MyDlgForm form. From now on, the statements in the DIALOGS2.WFM form will refer to the MyDlg.WFM form as `form.MyDlgForm`.

5

> **Note:** If you are new to dBASE, the preceding statements may confuse you. However, you can look at the process of using more than one form in your program as follows: The main program is the DIALOGS2.WFM file. This file uses another WFM file, the MyDlg.WFM file. During the execution of the program, the MyDlg.WFM form will be referred to as form.MyDlgForm.
>
> These statements load the MyDlg.WFM form:
>
> ```
> set procedure to MyDlg.wfm additive
> form.MyDlgForm=new MYDLGFORM()
> ```
>
> If you want to load another form called HerDlg.WFM, use these statements:
>
> ```
> set procedure to HerDlg.wfm additive
> form.HerDlgForm=new HERDLGFORM()
> ```

To summarize, the procedure of the `OnOpen` event includes some overhead code that enables the DIALOGS2.WFM form to use another form called MyDlg.WFM, which will be referred to as `form.MyDlgForm` in the code you enter.

Attaching Code to the *OnClose* Event

The DIALOGS2.WFM form loads the MyDlg.WFM form. But what will happen to the MyDlg.WFM form when you terminate the DIALOGS2.WFM program? You need to unload the MyDlg.WFM form when the DIALOGS2.WFM terminates. To do this, enter code in the `Form_OnClose` procedure of the DIALOGS2.WFM form.

☐ Attach the following code to the `OnClose` event of the DIALOGS2.WFM form. After you enter this code, the `Form_OnClose` procedure of the DIALOGS2.WFM form should look like this:

```
Procedure Form_OnClose

   * Unload the MyDlg.WFM form.
   Close Procedure MyDlg.WFM

Return
```

☐ Save your work by selecting Save from the File menu.

The code you typed unloads the MyDlg.WFM form.

Attaching Code to the *OnClick* Event of the Display Dialog Box... Button

☐ Attach the following code to the `OnClick` event of the Display Dialog Box... button of the DIALOGS2.WFM form. After you enter this code, the `DisplayDlgBoxPushButton_OnClick` procedure of the DIALOGS2.WFM form should look like this:

```
Procedure DISPLAYDLGBOXPUSHBUTTON_OnClick

* Display the MyDlg.WFM form as a Modal dialog box.
form.MyDlgForm.ReadModal()

* Fill the NameEntryField with the value that
* the user entered in the MyDlgForm dialog box.
form.NameEntryField.Value = ;
             form.MyDlgForm.NameEntryField.Value

Return
```

☐ Save your work by selecting Save from the File menu.

The code you typed displays the MyDlgForm form as a modal dialog box:

```
form.MyDlgForm.ReadModal()
```

Remember that the MyDlg.WFM form serves as a dialog box. In the `Form_OnOpen` procedure of the DIALOGS2.WFM form you loaded the MyDlg.WFM form, referred to as form.MyDlgForm. The preceding statement displays the MyDlg.WFM form as a modal dialog box. A *modal dialog box* doesn't let you return to the form that generated the dialog box until the dialog box is closed. In this program, you click the Display Dialog Box... button in the DIALOGS2.WFM form, which displays the MyDlg.WFM form. Because the MyDlg.WFM form is displayed with the `ReadModal()` method, the MyDlg.WFM form is a modal dialog box. This means you can't return to the DIALOGS2.WFM form until the MyDlg.WFM form is closed.

Note: A modal dialog box doesn't let you return to the form that generated it until the dialog box is closed. You should know, however, that while the modal dialog box is displayed, you can switch to other windows. For example, while the MyDlg.WFM dialog box is displayed, you can switch to Paintbrush, but you can't switch back to the DIALOGS2.WFM form until you close the dialog box.

The next statement you typed updates the Value property of the NameEntryField entry field of the DIALOGS2 form:

```
form.NameEntryField.Value = ;
           form.MyDlgForm.NameEntryField.Value
```

As you'll see when you design the MyDlg.WFM form, it has an entry field called NameEntryField. You type text in the NameEntryField of the MyDlg form, then click the OK button.

You displayed the MyDlg form as a modal dialog box, so the statement that follows `form.MyDlgForm.ReadModal()` is executed once you close the MyDlg dialog box.

Since the entry field of the MyDlg form is called NameEntryField, this is the text you type in the entry field:

```
form.MyDlgForm.NameEntryField.Value
```

During the visual design of the DIALOGS2.WFM form you set the Name property of the entry field to NameEntryField. So this statement:

```
form.NameEntryField.Value = ;
           form.MyDlgForm.NameEntryField.Value
```

assigns the text you typed in the NameEntryField of the MyDlg.WFM form to the NameEntryField of the DIALOGS2 form.

☐ Close the DIALOGS2.WFM form (that is, make the DIALOGS2.WFM window the active window, then select Close from the File menu).

The Visual Implementation of the MyDlg.WFM Form

You'll now visually design the MyDlg.WFM form:

☐ Type `CREATE FORM C:\DBPROG\CH05\MyDlg` in the Command window, and then press Enter.

dBASE responds by creating the MyDlg.WFM form in the C:\DBPROG\CH05 directory and displaying the empty MyDlg.WFM form.

☐ Design the MyDlg.WFM form according to the specifications in Table 5.5. When you finish designing the form, it should look like the one shown in Figure 5.9.

Table 5.5. The properties table of the MyDlg.WFM form.

Object	Property	Setting
Form	**Text**	**The MyDlg Dialog Box**
	Top	0
	Width	53
	Maximize	.F.
	Minimize	.F.
	MDI	.F.
	Height	142
	Left	1
Entry Field	**Name**	**NameEntryField**
	Value	(empty)
	Top	3
	Width	41
	Height	2
	Left	5
Text	**Name**	**Text1**
	Top	2
	Width	23
	Text	Enter your name:
	Height	1
	Left	5

Object	Property	Setting
PushButton	**Name**	**OKPushButton**
	Top	7
	Width	19
	Text	&OK
	Height	5
	FontSize	27
	Left	17

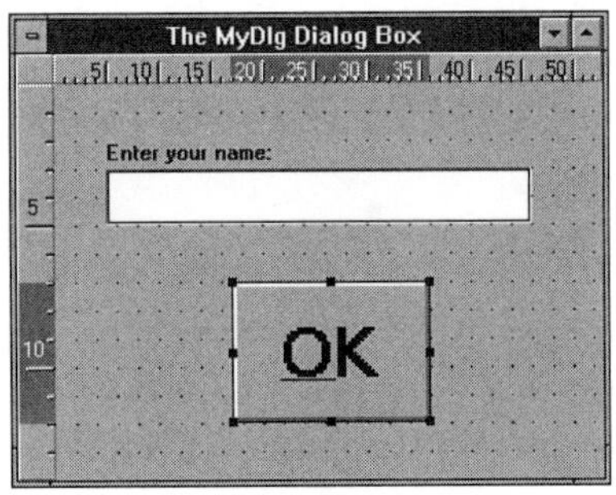

Figure 5.9.
The MyDlg.WFM form in design mode.

Note that Table 5.5 instructed you to set the Maximize and Minimize properties of the MyDlg.WFM form to .F.. This means that during runtime, you can't maximize or minimize the MyDlg.WFM form. This is a standard design for a dialog box.

Attaching Code to the *OnClick* Event of the OK Button

You'll now attach code to the `OnClick` event of the OK button of the MyDlg.WFM form.

☐ Type the following code in the `OKPushButton_OnClick` procedure of the MyDlg.WFM form:

```
Procedure OKBUTTON_OnClick

        form.Close()

Return
```

This code closes the MyDlg.WFM form.

☐ Select Save from the File menu to save your work.

- Select Close from the File menu to close the MyDlg.WFM form.
- Execute the DIALOGS2 program and make sure it's working properly by typing `DO C:\DBPROG\CH05\DIALOGS2.WFM` in the Command window.

The Modularity Feature of dBASE

The MyDlg.WFM form is completely independent of the DIALOGS2.WFM form. Nothing in the MyDlg.WFM form makes it belong to, or be associated exclusively with, the DIALOGS2.WFM form. Suppose that the MyDlg.WFM form is a very complex form that takes a substantial amount of time to develop. Once you finish developing the MyDlg.WFM form, you can use it with the DIALOGS2.WFM form or any other form that can use such a dialog box. In other words, you can "plug in" the MyDlg.WFM form to any program that uses such a form, and you don't have to change a single line of code in the MyDlg.WFM form.

Summary

In this chapter you have learned how to display dialog boxes. You can display simple dialog boxes by using the `MSGBOX()` function, and you can also display custom-made dialog boxes by incorporating additional forms into your program.

Q&A

Q In the DIALOGS2 program, I used the DIALOGS2.WFM form as the main window of the application and the MyDlg.WFM form as a custom-made dialog box. Can I incorporate additional forms?

A Yes. As you'll see in the exercise at the end of this chapter, you can incorporate additional forms into your program.

Q I want to design an About... dialog box. Should I use the `MSGBOX()` function for this purpose, or should I use a custom-made dialog box?

A If you are in a rush, use the `MSGBOX()` function. However, if you have the time, you can design a custom-made dialog box to serve as your About... dialog box. For example, you can place an image control in the form to make the About... dialog box more attractive.

Quiz

1. You can design the custom-made dialog box so that you can't maximize it during runtime.
   a. True
   b. False
2. You can place an entry field control that is disabled, so you can't type text in the entry field.
   a. True
   b. False
3. You can use the `MSGBOX()` function to display a message with a question mark icon.
   a. True
   b. False
4. You can use the `MSGBOX()` function to display a message with a picture of President Kennedy.
   a. True
   b. False

Exercise

Outline the steps needed to incorporate a custom-made About... dialog box into the DIALOGS2 program.

5

Quiz Answers

1. a (simply set the Maximize property of the form to .F.)
2. a (simply set the Enabled property of the entry field control to .F.)
3. a
4. b

Exercise Answer

You have to design a new form to serve as the About... custom-made dialog box. For example, you can create the ABOUT.WFM form.

In the `Form_OnOpen` procedure of the DIALOGS2.WFM form, add code that loads the ABOUT.WFM form. After you add this code, the `Form_OnOpen` procedure of the DIALOGS2.WFM form should look like this:

```
Procedure Form_OnOpen


* Set the path to the directory
* where the program resides.
ProgramPath = Left (Program(0),Rat("\",Program(0)))
SET PATH TO &ProgramPath


* Load the MyDlg.WFM form.
* (From now on, form.MyDlgForm is the MyDlg.WFM form.)
set procedure to MyDlg.wfm additive
form.MyDlgForm=new MYDLGFORM()

* Load the About.WFM form.
* (From now on, form.AboutForm is the About.WFM form.)
set procedure to About.wfm additive
form.AboutForm=new ABOUTFORM()

Return
```

Add code to the `Form_OnClose` procedure of the DIALOGS2.WFM form that unloads the ABOUT.WFM dialog box. After you add the code, the `Form_OnClose` procedure of the DIALOGS2.WFM form should look like this:

```
Procedure Form_OnClose

   * Unload the MyDlg.WFM form.
   Close Procedure MyDlg.WFM

   * Unload the About.WFM form.
   Close Procedure About.WFM


Return
```

- ☐ Place a pushbutton in the DIALOGS2.WFM form.
- ☐ Set the Name property of the new pushbutton to AboutButton.
- ☐ Set the Text property to About....
- ☐ Attach code to the `OnClick` event of the AboutButton pushbutton as follows:

```
Procedure ABOUTBUTTON_OnClick

* Display the About.WFM form as a Modal dialog box.
form.AboutForm.ReadModal()

Return
```

The ABOUT.WFM form should contain text with information such as copyrights and the program's version number. You can also place an image control in the ABOUT.WFM form to make the About... dialog box more attractive.

The Maximize and Minimize properties of the ABOUT.WFM form should be set to .F. (because your user shouldn't be able to maximize or minimize the About... dialog box).

The About... dialog box should also contain a pushbutton (such as OK or Done) to close the About... dialog box. The code attached to the `OnClick` event of the pushbutton should contain the following statement:

```
form.Close()
```

5

6

WEEK 1

Menus

In Chapter 1, “Writing Your First dBASE Program,” you designed a simple menu with only one item and attached this menu to a form. In this chapter, you'll learn other important menu features: You'll learn how to design a cascading menu (a submenu), how to assign shortcut keys to menu items, how to include a separator bar in a menu, how to write code that disables and enables menu items, and how to write code that places a checkmark next to a menu item.

The COLORS Program

In the following sections you will write a dBASE program called COLORS that has a menu attached to its main window. The COLORS program illustrates how to write code that disables and enables menu items and places checkmarks next to menu items. Before you start writing the COLORS program, review what the program should look like and what it should do.

When you run the COLORS program, the main window should look like the one shown in Figure 6.1.

Figure 6.1.
The main window of the COLORS program.

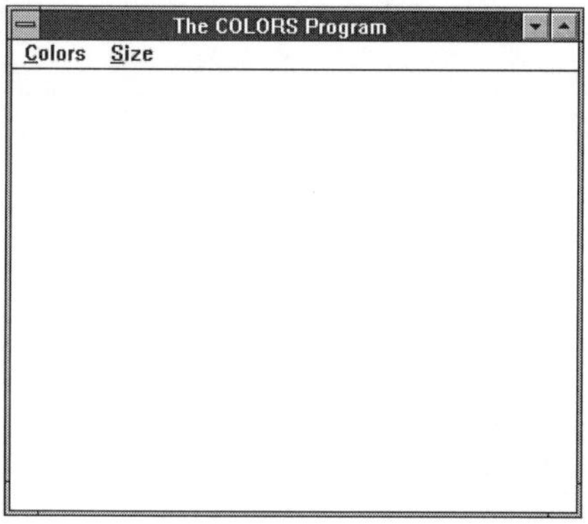

As shown in Figure 6.1, the COLORS program has two pop-up menus, Colors and Size, shown open in Figures 6.2 and 6.3.

Figure 6.2.
The Colors pop-up menu of the COLORS program.

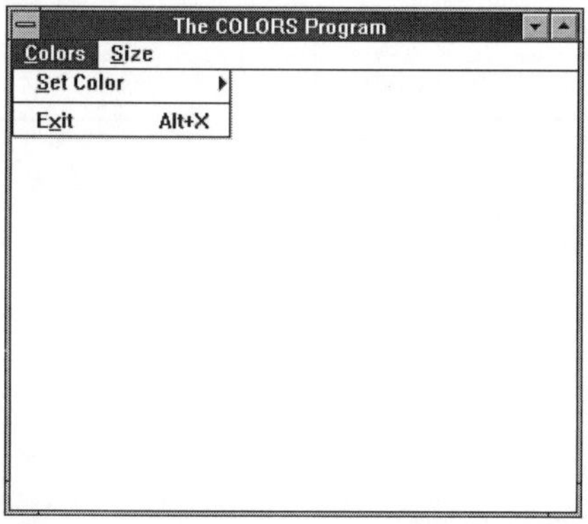

Figure 6.3.
The Size pop-up menu of the COLORS program.

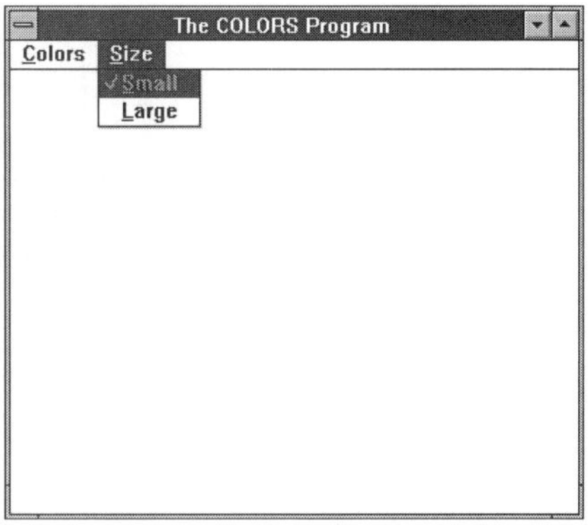

When you select Set Color from the Colors menu, a submenu (*cascading menu*) appears with three items: Red, Blue, and White. (See Figure 6.4.)

Figure 6.4.
The Set Color submenu.

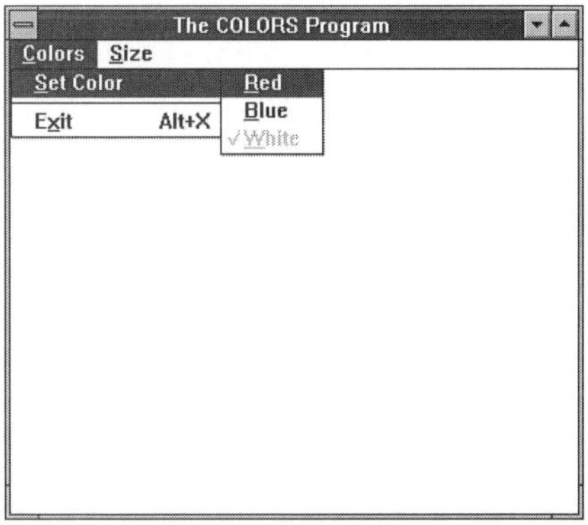

You can change the color of the main window of the COLORS program by selecting a color from the Set Color submenu. For example, if you select Red from the Set Color submenu, the main window will change its color to red.

Notice that in Figure 6.4 the White menu item is disabled (dimmed). Why? The color of the window is currently white and it makes no sense to change the color from white to white. Notice also that the White menu item has a checkmark next to it.

When you select another color from the Set Color submenu, the COLORS program paints the program's main window with the selected color and changes the disabled/enabled status and checked/unchecked status of the Set Color menu items accordingly. For example, in Figure 6.5, the Set Color submenu is shown after you select the Red menu item. The Red menu item is disabled and has a checkmark next to it. The other two menu items (Blue and White) are enabled and have no checkmarks next to them.

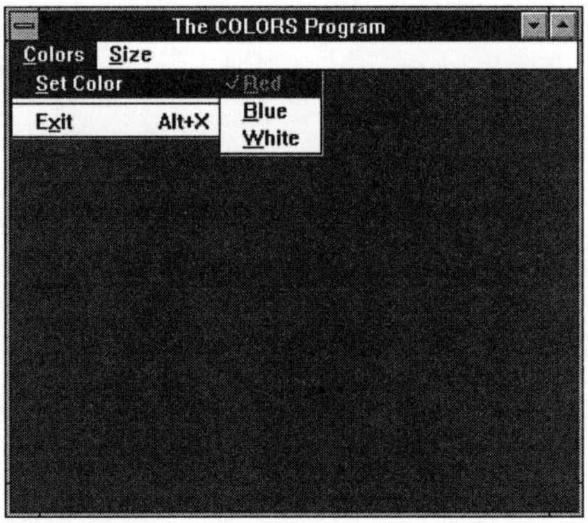

Figure 6.5.
The Set Color submenu after you select the Red menu item.

When you select Small or Large from the Size menu, the program's window changes to the selected size. Depending on which size you select, the appropriate menu item becomes disabled and a checkmark is placed next to it.

As shown in Figure 6.2, the Colors pop-up menu has a *separator bar* (a horizontal line) between the Set Color item and the Exit item. This separator bar is included just to visually separate menu items. You cannot select this item.

When you select Exit from the Colors menu, the program terminates.

Now that you know what the COLORS program is supposed to do, you can start writing the program.

The Visual Implementation of the COLORS Program

Create the COLORS.WFM form as follows:

☐ Type `MD C:\DBPROG\CH06` in the Command window, and then press Enter.

dBASE responds by creating the directory C:\DBPROG\CH06.

☐ Type `CREATE FORM C:\DBPROG\CH06\COLORS` in the Command window and press Enter.

dBASE responds by creating the COLORS.WFM form and displaying it in design mode.

☐ Customize the COLORS.WFM form according to the specifications in Table 6.1.

☐ Save your work by selecting Save from the File menu.

Table 6.1. The properties table of the COLORS.WFM form.

Object	Property	Setting
Form	**Text**	**The COLORS Program**
	MDI	.F.
	Height	18.00
	Left	1.00
	Top	0.00
	Width	63.00

Note: Table 6.1 instructs you to set the MDI property of the form to .F.. The MDI property of the form is listed in the Inspector window under the Windows Properties item.

Recall from Chapter 1 that by setting the MDI property to .F. you are disabling the MDI feature of the form. That is, you are specifying that the form won't conform to the MDI standard. Later when you attach a menu to the COLORS.WFM form, it will be displayed on the form's window (not on the dBASE window).

To see your visual design in action do the following:

☐ Press F2 on your keyboard.

dBASE responds by running the COLORS.WFM form. (See Figure 6.6.)

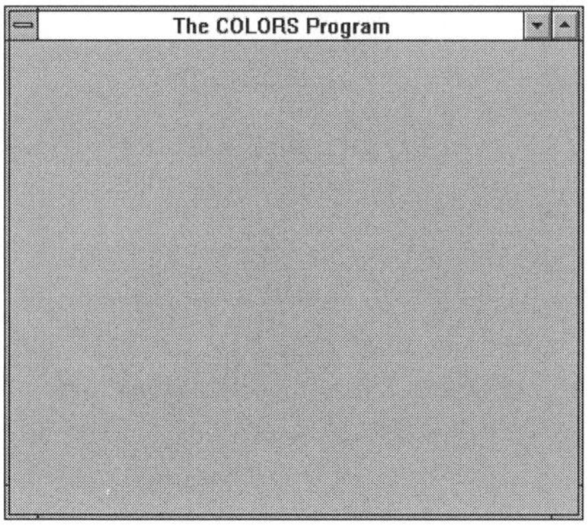

Figure 6.6.
The COLORS.WFM form in runtime mode.

- ☐ Change the COLORS.WFM back to design mode by pressing Shift+F2.
- ☐ Close the COLORS.WFM form by selecting Close from the File menu.

The visual implementation of the COLORS.WFM form isn't finished yet. You still have to attach a menu to the form, but you'll do that later in the chapter.

Designing the Menu of the COLORS Program

You'll now create and design a menu for the COLORS program called COLORS.MNU. Use the following steps to do this:

- ☐ Type `CREATE MENU C:\DBPROG\CH06\COLORS` and press Enter.

  dBASE responds by creating the COLORS.MNU menu and displaying it in design mode. (See Figure 6.7.)

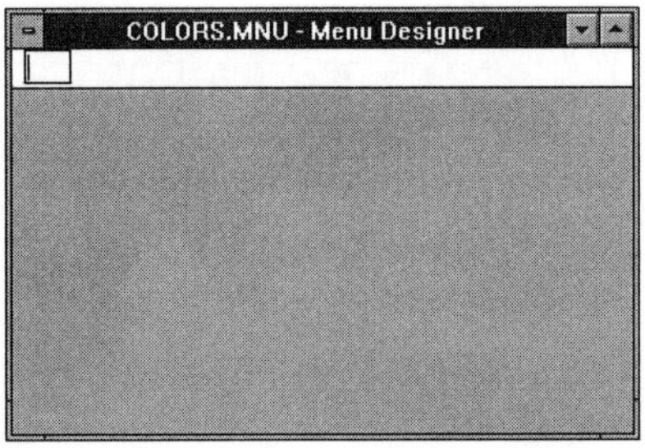

Figure 6.7.
The COLORS.MNU menu in design mode (before customization).

As you can see, the upper-left corner of the menu has a small, blank-outlined rectangle. This rectangle represents the menu title of the leftmost pop-up menu of the menu bar. Because you want its title to be Colors, you have to set the title to &Colors:

- ☐ Type `&Colors` in the small rectangle.

Your COLORS.MNU menu should now look like the one shown in Figure 6.8.

> **Note:** Recall from Chapter 1 that the & character before the *C* in &Colors underlines the character *C*. Therefore, when the COLORS.MNU menu is displayed, pressing Alt+C will produce the same results as clicking the Colors menu title—the Colors pop-up menu will open.

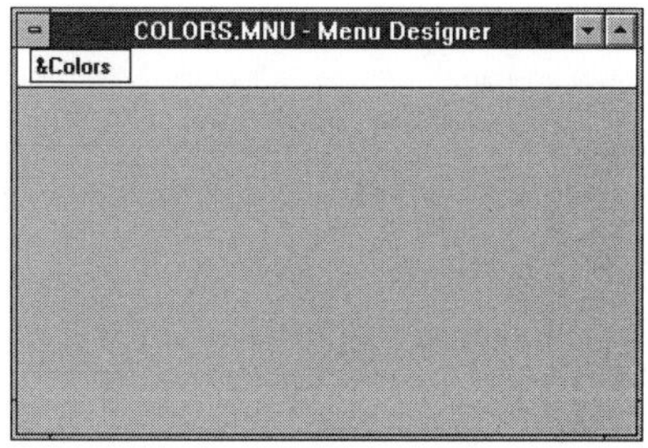

Figure 6.8.
Setting the title of the first pop-up menu.

Now add the Set Color menu item to the Colors pop-up menu:

☐ Press the down-arrow key on your keyboard.

dBASE responds by adding a menu item to the Colors pop-up menu. (See Figure 6.9.)

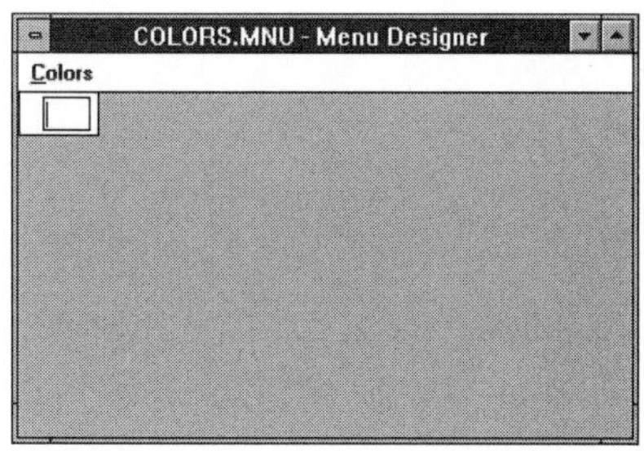

Figure 6.9.
Adding a menu item to the Colors pop-up menu.

☐ Type `&Set Color` in the new menu item.

Your COLORS.MNU menu should now look like the one shown in Figure 6.10.

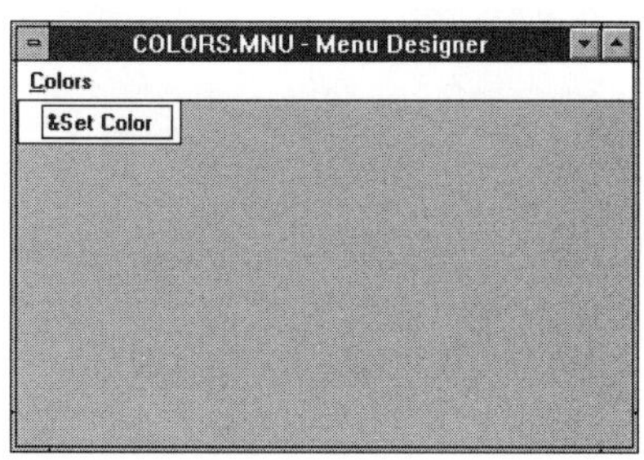

Figure 6.10.
Adding the Set Color menu item.

The Set Color menu item should have a submenu (a cascading menu) attached to it. Follow these steps to add a submenu to the Set Color menu item:

☐ Press Tab on your keyboard.

dBASE responds by adding a submenu to the Set Color menu item. (See Figure 6.11.)

Figure 6.11.
Adding a submenu to the Set Color menu item.

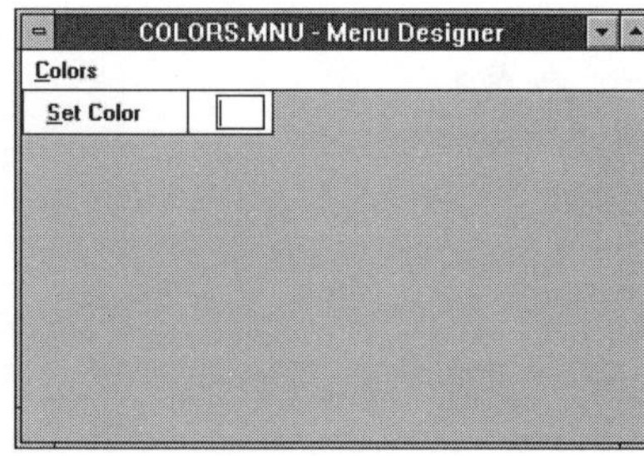

☐ Type `&Red` in the first menu item of the Set Color submenu.

Your COLORS.MNU menu should now look like the one shown in Figure 6.12.

Figure 6.12.
Adding the Red menu item to the Set Color submenu.

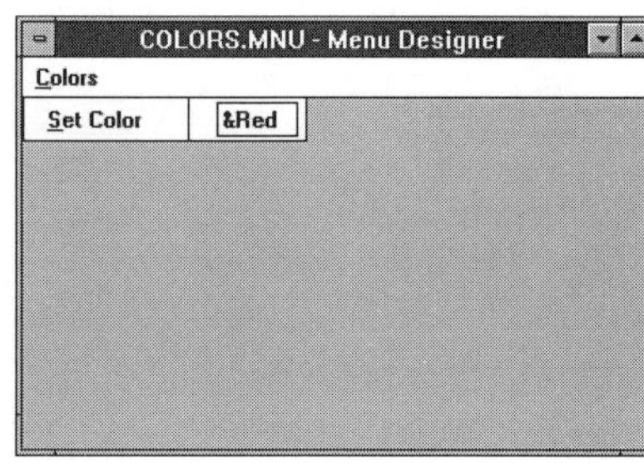

☐ Press the down-arrow key on your keyboard.

dBASE responds by adding a second menu item to the Set Color submenu.

☐ Type `&Blue` in the second menu item of the Set Color submenu.

☐ Press the down-arrow key on your keyboard again.

dBASE responds by adding a third menu item to the Set Color submenu.

☐ Type `&White` in the third menu item of the Set Color submenu.

Your COLORS.MNU menu should now look like the one shown in Figure 6.13.

You have finished the Set Color submenu!

Continue adding menu items to the Colors pop-up menu:

☐ Click the mouse on the Set Color menu item.

dBASE responds by moving the selection rectangle to the Set Color menu item.

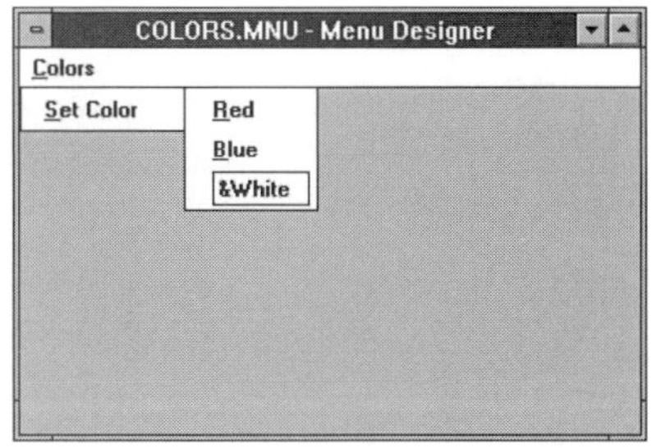

Figure 6.13.
Adding three menu items (Red, Blue, and White) to the Set Color submenu.

- ☐ Press the down-arrow key.

  dBASE responds by adding a new menu item under the Set Color menu item. (See Figure 6.14.)

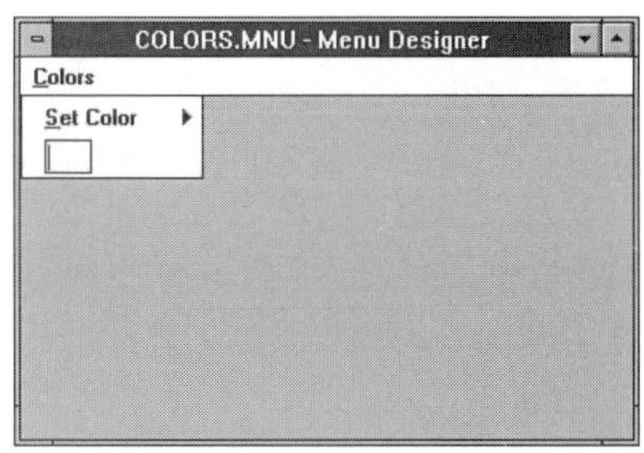

Figure 6.14.
Adding another menu item under the Set Color menu item.

The menu item under the Set Color menu item should be a separator bar. (Refer to Figure 6.2.) To make this menu item a separator bar, you have to set its Separator property to .T.:

- ☐ Select the Inspector window by selecting Inspector from the View menu.

  dBASE responds by making the Inspector window the active window.

- ☐ Set the Separator property to .T..
- ☐ Select the COLORS.MNU window.

Your COLORS.MNU menu should now look like the one shown in Figure 6.15—the menu item under the Set Color menu item is a separator bar!

The last item you have to add to the Colors pop-up menu is the Exit menu item:

- ☐ Press the down-arrow key.

  dBASE responds by adding a new menu item under the separator bar.

Figure 6.15.
Adding a separator bar under the Set Color menu item.

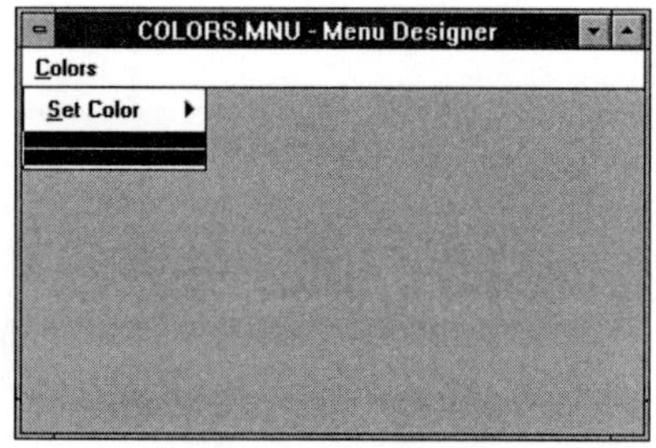

☐ Type `E&xit` in the new menu item.

Your COLORS.MNU menu should now look like the one shown in Figure 6.16.

Figure 6.16.
Adding the Exit menu item to the Colors pop-up menu.

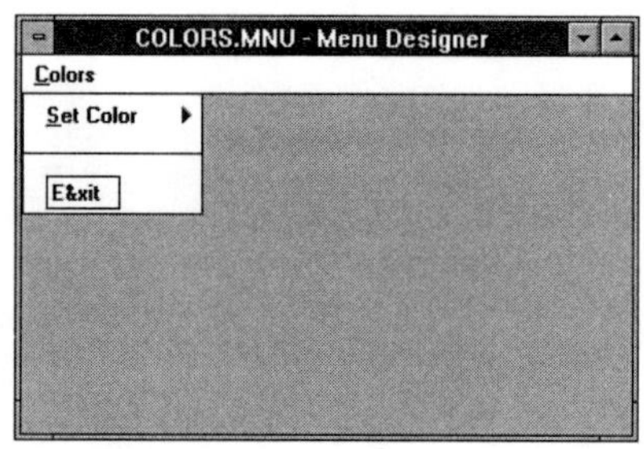

The COLORS.MNU menu is almost complete. The last thing you have to do is add a second pop-up menu. Here's how you do that:

☐ Click on the title of the Colors pop-up menu (or press the up-arrow key three times).

dBASE responds by moving the selection rectangle to the title of the Colors pop-up menu. (See Figure 6.17.)

Figure 6.17.
Selecting the title of the Colors pop-up menu.

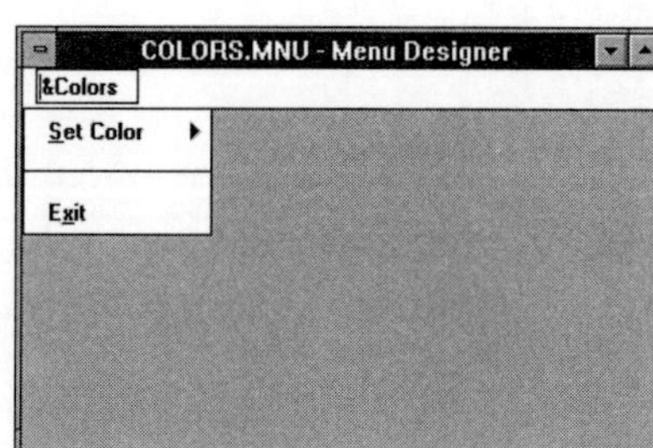

☐ Press Tab on your keyboard.

dBASE responds by adding a new pop-up menu to the COLORS.MNU menu. (See Figure 6.18.)

Figure 6.18.
Adding a new pop-up menu.

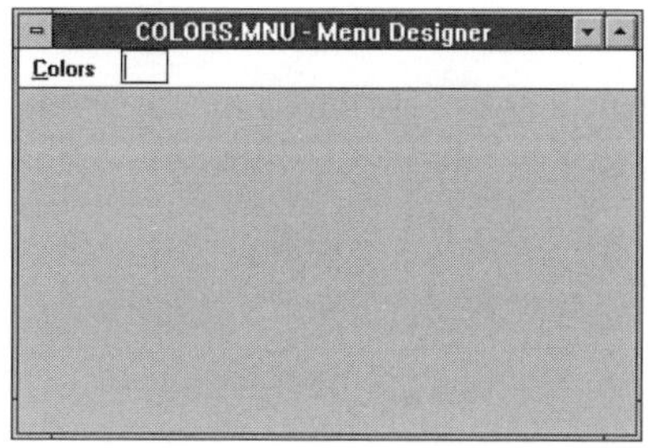

☐ Type `&Size` in the title of the new pop-up menu.

☐ Press the down-arrow key on your keyboard.

dBASE responds by adding a menu item to the Size pop-up menu.

☐ Type `&Small` in the menu item of the Size pop-up menu.

☐ Press the down-arrow key on your keyboard again.

dBASE responds by adding a second menu item to the Size pop-up menu.

☐ Type `&Large` in the second menu item of the Size pop-up menu.

Your COLORS.MNU menu should now look like the one shown in Figure 6.19.

Figure 6.19.
Adding two menu items to the Size pop-up menu.

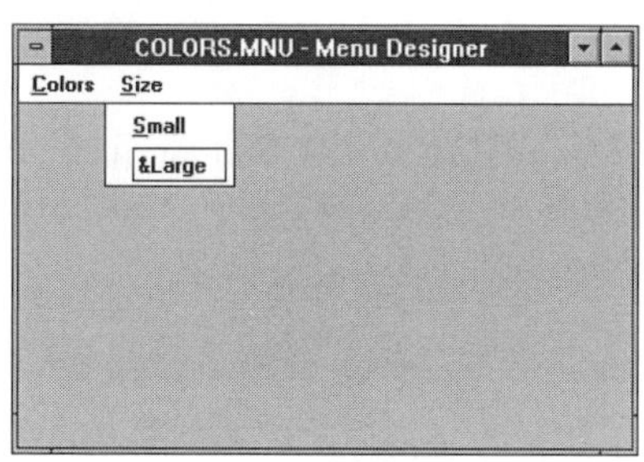

You have finished the design of the COLORS.MNU menu!

☐ Save your work by selecting Save from the File menu.

☐ Close the COLORS.MNU menu by selecting Close from the File menu.

Attaching the COLORS.MNU Menu to the COLORS.WFM Form

To attach the COLORS.MNU menu to the COLORS.WFM form, set the MenuFile property of the COLORS.WFM form to the name of the COLORS.MNU menu by following these steps:

☐ Type `MODIFY FORM ?` in the Command window, press the Enter key, then select the file C:\DBPROG\CH06\COLORS.WFM from the Open Form dialog box that dBASE displays.

dBASE responds by displaying the COLORS.WFM form in design mode.

☐ Locate the MenuFile property of the form in the Inspector window and select it by clicking it.

☐ Click the Tool button of the MenuFile property.

dBASE responds by displaying the MenuFile Property Builder dialog box. (See Figure 6.20.)

Figure 6.20.
The MenuFile Property Builder dialog box.

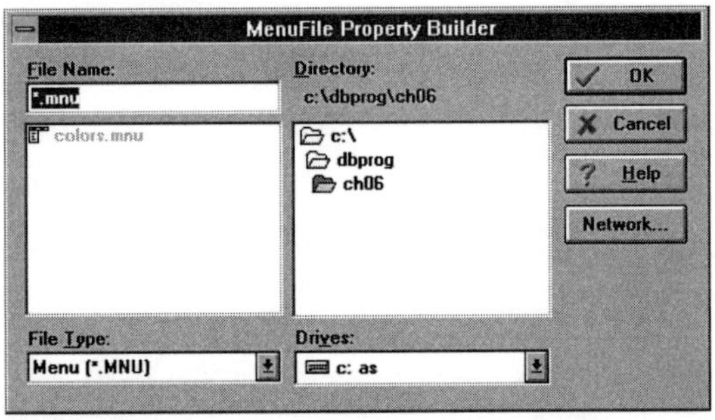

☐ Use the MenuFile Property Builder dialog box to select the menu file C:\DBPROG\CH06\COLORS.MNU and click the OK button.

The COLORS.MNU menu is now attached to the COLORS.WFM form!

☐ Save your work by selecting Save from the File menu.

To see your work in action follow these steps:

☐ Press the F2 key on your keyboard.

dBASE responds by running the COLORS.WFM form. (See Figure 6.21.)

As you can see, the COLORS.MNU menu you designed is attached to the COLORS.WFM form.

Figure 6.21.
The COLORS.WFM form with the COLORS.MNU menu attached.

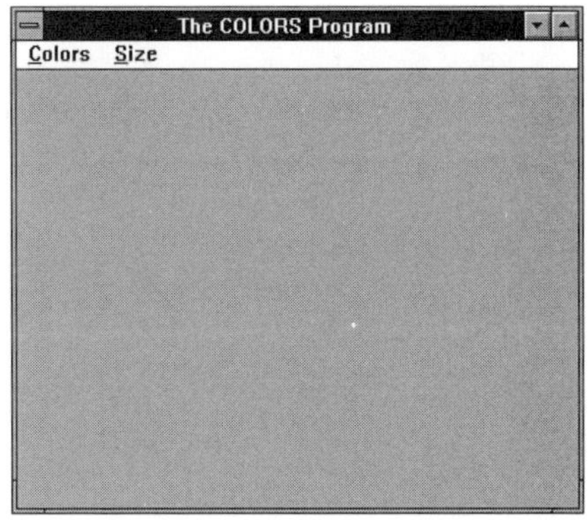

□ Experiment with the Colors pop-up menu, Set Color submenu, and Size pop-up menu.

Figure 6.22 shows the Colors pop-up menu, Figure 6.23 shows the Set Color submenu, and Figure 6.24 show the Size pop-up menu.

Figure 6.22.
The Colors pop-up menu.

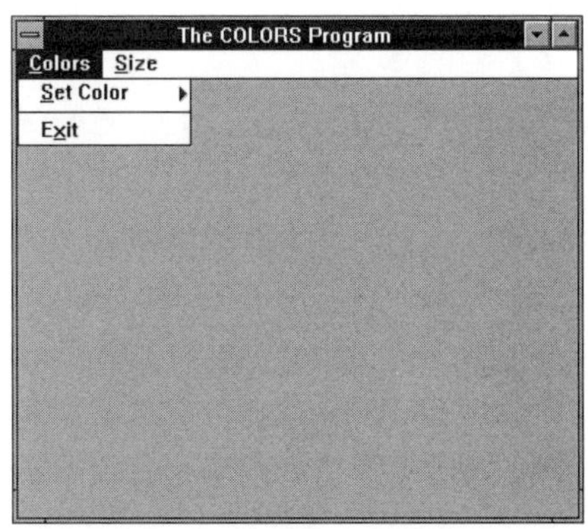

Figure 6.23.
The Set Color submenu.

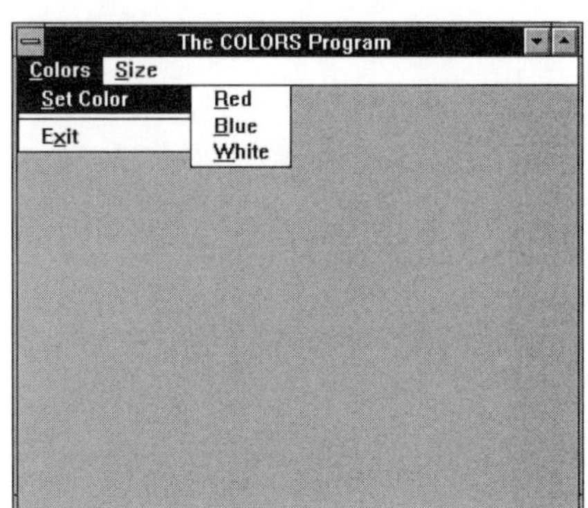

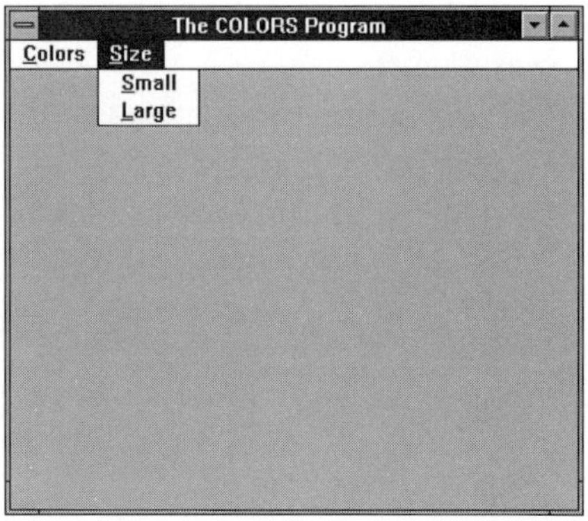

Figure 6.24.
The Size pop-up menu.

Of course, when you select these menu items, nothing happens. That's because you haven't attached any code to the menu items. You'll do that in the following sections.

- ☐ Change back to design mode by pressing Shift+F2 on your keyboard.
- ☐ Close the COLORS.WFM form by selecting Close from the File menu.

Attaching Code to the *OnClick* Event of the Exit Menu Item

Follow these steps to attach code to the `OnClick` event of the Exit menu item:

- ☐ Type `MODIFY MENU ?` in the Command window, press the Enter key, then select the menu file C:\DBPROG\CH06\COLORS.MNU from the Open Form dialog box that dBASE displays.

  dBASE responds by displaying the COLORS.MNU menu in design mode.

- ☐ Select the Exit menu item of the COLORS.MNU menu by clicking it.
- ☐ Make the Inspector window the active window by selecting Inspector from the View menu of dBASE.
- ☐ Make sure that the pull-down list box at the top of the Inspector window is set to form.root.colors.exit (because you are now going to attach code to an event associated with the Exit menu item of the Colors pop-up menu).
- ☐ Select the Events tab at the bottom of the Inspector window by clicking it.
- ☐ Select the `OnClick` event by clicking it.
- ☐ Click the Tool button of the `OnClick` event.

  dBASE responds by opening the Procedure Editor to let you write code in the `EXIT_OnClick` *procedure.*

Note: In the preceding steps you opened the procedure of a menu item's `OnClick` event by selecting the menu item, then selecting the `OnClick` event in the Inspector window, and finally clicking the Tool button of the `OnClick` event.

An easier way to open the procedure of a menu item's `OnClick` event is to select the menu item, and then double-click it.

☐ Write code in the `EXIT_OnClick` procedure so it looks like this:

```
Procedure EXIT_OnClick

  * Terminate the program by closing the form.
  form.Close()

Return
```

☐ Save your work by selecting Save from the File menu.

The statement you typed in the `EXIT_OnClick()` procedure:

```
form.Close()
```

closes the form you attached the menu to. Therefore, if you execute the COLORS.WFM form and select Exit from the Colors menu, the COLORS.WFM form will be closed.

To see in action the code you attached to the `OnClick` event of the Exit menu item, follow these steps:

☐ Close the COLORS.MNU menu by selecting Close from the File menu.

☐ Type `DO C:\DBPROG\CH06\COLORS.WFM` in the Command window and press Enter.

dBASE responds by executing the COLORS.WFM program. The window of the COLORS.WFM program appears, as shown back in Figure 6.21.

☐ Select Exit from the Colors menu of the COLORS.WFM program.

The COLORS.WFM program responds by terminating. The code you attached to the `OnClick` event of the Exit menu item is working!

Attaching Code to the *OnOpen* Event

As you know, the `OnOpen` event of a form occurs when the form is first opened. Therefore, the `OnOpen` event of the form is a good place to write initialization code for the form.

☐ Type `MODIFY FORM ?` in the Command window, press Enter, and then select the file C:\DBPROG\CH06\COLORS.WFM from the Open Form dialog box that dBASE displays.

dBASE responds by displaying the COLORS.WFM form in design mode.

☐ Attach the following code to the `OnOpen` event of the COLORS.WFM form. After you write this code, the `FORM_OnOpen` procedure should look like this:

```
Procedure Form_OnOpen

* Set the background color of the form to bright white.
form.ColorNormal = "N/W+"

* Place a checkmark next to the White menu item.
form.root.Colors.Set_Color.White.Checked = .T.

* Disable the White menu item.
form.root.Colors.Set_Color.White.Enabled = .F.

* Place a checkmark next to the Small menu item.
form.root.Size.Small.Checked = .T.

* Disable the Small menu item.
form.root.Size.Small.Enabled = .F.

Return
```

☐ Save your work by selecting Save from the File menu.

The first statement you typed in the `FORM_OnOpen` procedure:

```
form.ColorNormal = "N/W+"
```

sets the color of the form to `"N/W+"`. `"N/W+"` specifies that the foreground color is black (`"N"`) and the background color is bright white (`"W+"`). Therefore, when you start the program, the background color of the program's window will be bright white.

The next statement sets the Checked property of the White menu item to .T.:

```
form.root.Colors.Set_Color.White.Checked = .T.
```

Setting the Checked property of a menu item to .T. places a checkmark next to this menu item.

Note: This statement:

```
form.root.Colors.Set_Color.White.Checked = .T.
```

can be understood if you inspect it closely. If you translate this statement to English, it reads as follows:

Set the Checked property of the White menu item of the Set Color submenu of the Colors pop-up menu of the form to .T..

The next statement sets the Enabled property of the White menu item to .F.:

```
form.root.Colors.Set_Color.White.Enabled = .F.
```

Setting the Enabled property of a menu item to .F. disables it.

The next statement sets the Checked property of the Small menu item to .T.:

```
form.root.Size.Small.Checked = .T.
```

In other words, this statement places a checkmark next to the Small menu item of the Size pop-up menu.

Finally, the following statement sets the Enabled property of the Small menu item to .F.:

```
form.root.Size.Small.Enabled = .F.
```

In other words, this statement disables the Small menu item of the Size pop-up menu.

The initialization code you attached to the `OnOpen` event of the COLORS.WFM form performs five tasks:

- Sets the background color of the form to bright white.
- Places a checkmark next to the White menu item.
- Disables the White menu item.
- Places a checkmark next to the Small menu item.
- Disables the Small menu item.

To see in action the code you attached to the `OnOpen` event of the form:

☐ Execute the COLORS.WFM form by pressing the F2 key.

The COLORS.WFM form appears, as shown in Figure 6.25.

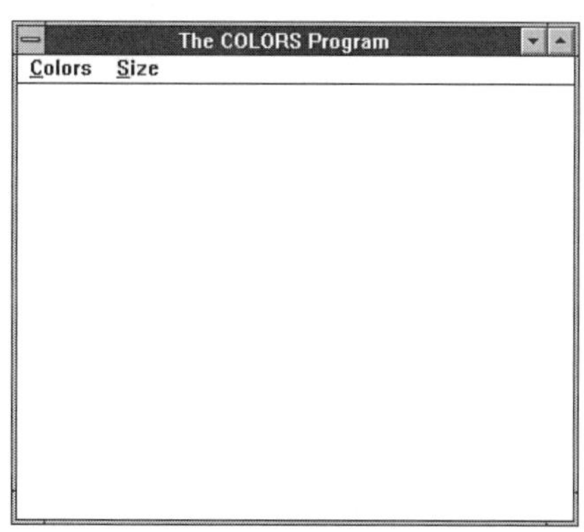

Figure 6.25.
The COLORS.WFM form in runtime mode with a bright white background.

As you can see from Figure 6.25, now the background of the COLORS.WFM form is bright white.

☐ Open the Colors pop-up menu, then open the Set Color submenu. (See Figure 6.26.)

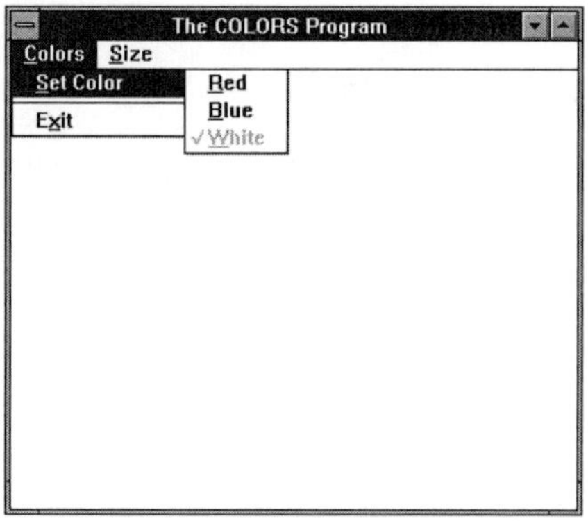

Figure 6.26.
The Set Color submenu (the White menu item is disabled and has a checkmark next to it).

As you can see, the White menu item of the Set Color submenu is disabled and has a checkmark next to it.

☐ Open the Size pop-up menu. (See Figure 6.27.)

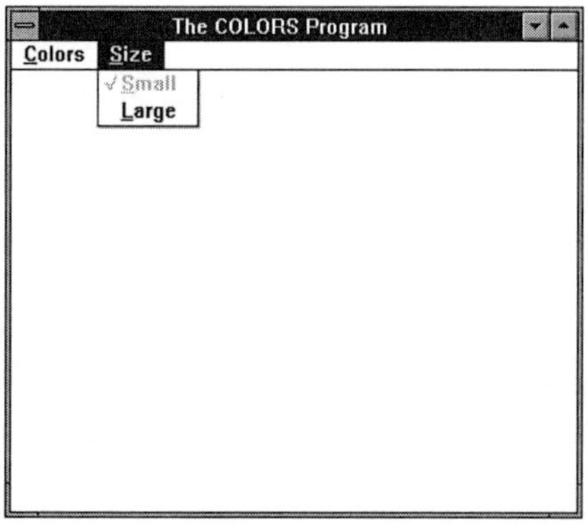

Figure 6.27.
The Size pop-up menu (the Small menu item is disabled and has a checkmark next to it).

As you can see, the Small menu item of Size pop-up menu is disabled and has a checkmark next to it.

☐ Terminate the COLORS.WFM form by selecting Exit from its Colors menu.

Attaching Code to the *OnClick* Event of the Red Menu Item

Follow these steps to attach code to the `OnClick` event of the Red menu item:

☐ Type `MODIFY MENU ?` in the Command window, press Enter, and then select the menu file C:\DBPROG\CH06\COLORS.MNU from the Open Form dialog box that dBASE displays.

dBASE responds by displaying the COLORS.MNU menu in design mode.

☐ Attach the following code to the `OnClick` event of the Red menu item. After you write this code, the `RED_OnClick` procedure should look like this:

```
Procedure RED_OnClick

* Set the background color of the form to red.
form.ColorNormal = "N/R"

* Place a checkmark next to the Red menu item.
form.root.Colors.Set_Color.Red.Checked = .T.

* Disable the Red menu item.
form.root.Colors.Set_Color.Red.Enabled = .F.

* Enable the Blue and White menu items.
form.root.Colors.Set_Color.Blue.Enabled = .T.
form.root.Colors.Set_Color.White.Enabled = .T.

* Un-check the Blue and White menu items.
form.root.Colors.Set_Color.Blue.Checked = .F.
form.root.Colors.Set_Color.White.Checked = .F.

Return
```

☐ Save your work by selecting Save from the File menu.

The first statement you typed in the `RED_OnClick` procedure sets the background color of the form to red: 6

```
form.ColorNormal = "N/R"
```

The next statement places a checkmark next to the Red menu item (by setting the Checked property of the Red menu item to .T.):

```
form.root.Colors.Set_Color.Red.Checked = .T.
```

The next statement disables the Red menu item by setting its Enabled property to .F.:

```
form.root.Colors.Set_Color.Red.Enabled = .F.
```

The next two statements enable the Blue and White menu items by setting the Enabled property of each of these menu items to .T.:

```
form.root.Colors.Set_Color.Blue.Enabled = .T.
form.root.Colors.Set_Color.White.Enabled = .T.
```

Finally, the following two statements uncheck (remove the checkmarks of) the Blue and White menu items by setting the Checked property of each of these menu items to .F.:

```
form.root.Colors.Set_Color.Blue.Checked = .F.
form.root.Colors.Set_Color.White.Checked = .F.
```

To see in action the code you attached to the `OnClick` event of the Red menu item, follow these steps:

☐ Close the COLORS.MNU menu by selecting Close from the File menu.

☐ Type `DO C:\DBPROG\CH06\COLORS.WFM` in the Command window and press Enter.

dBASE responds by executing the COLORS.WFM program.

☐ Open the Set Color submenu and select Red.

As expected, the COLORS.WFM program responds by changing the background color of its window to red.

☐ Open the Set Color submenu again and check that the Red item is disabled and has a checkmark next to it.

☐ Terminate the COLORS.WFM program by selecting Exit from its Colors menu.

Attaching Code to the *OnClick* Event of the Blue Menu Item

Follow these steps to attach code to the `OnClick` event of the Blue menu item:

☐ Type `MODIFY MENU ?` in the Command window, press Enter, and then select the menu file C:\DBPROG\CH06\COLORS.MNU from the Open Form dialog box that dBASE displays.

dBASE responds by displaying the COLORS.MNU menu in design mode.

☐ Attach the following code to the `OnClick` event of the Blue menu item. After you write this code, the `BLUE_OnClick` procedure should look like this:

```
Procedure BLUE_OnClick

 * Set the background color of the form to blue.
 form.ColorNormal = "N/B"

 * Place a checkmark next to the Blue menu item.
```

```
form.root.Colors.Set_Color.Blue.Checked = .T.

* Disable the Blue menu item.
form.root.Colors.Set_Color.Blue.Enabled = .F.

* Enable the Red and White menu items.
form.root.Colors.Set_Color.Red.Enabled = .T.
form.root.Colors.Set_Color.White.Enabled = .T.

* Un-check the Red and White menu items.
form.root.Colors.Set_Color.Red.Checked = .F.
form.root.Colors.Set_Color.White.Checked = .F.

Return
```

- [ ] Save your work by selecting Save from the File menu.

As you can see, the `BLUE_OnClick` procedure is very similar to the `RED_OnClick` procedure. To see in action the code you attached to the `OnClick` event of the Blue menu item, follow these steps:

- [ ] Close the COLORS.MNU menu by selecting Close from the File menu.
- [ ] Type `DO C:\DBPROG\CH06\COLORS.WFM` in the Command window and press Enter.

  dBASE responds by executing the COLORS.WFM program.

- [ ] Open the Set Color submenu and select Blue.

  As expected, the COLORS.WFM program responds by changing the background color of its window to blue.

- [ ] Open the Set Color submenu again and check that the Blue item is disabled and has a checkmark next to it.
- [ ] Terminate the COLORS.WFM program by selecting Exit from its Colors menu.

6

Attaching Code to the *OnClick* Event of the White Menu Item

Follow these steps to attach code to the `OnClick` event of the White menu item:

- [ ] Type `MODIFY MENU ?` in the Command window, press Enter, and then select the menu file C:\DBPROG\CH06\COLORS.MNU from the Open Form dialog box that dBASE displays.

  dBASE responds by displaying the COLORS.MNU menu in design mode.

- Attach the following code to the `OnClick` event of the White menu item. After you write this code, the `WHITE_OnClick` procedure should look like this:

```
Procedure WHITE_OnClick

* Set the background color of the form to bright white.
form.ColorNormal = "N/W+"

* Place a checkmark next to the White menu item.
form.root.Colors.Set_Color.White.Checked = .T.

* Disable the White menu item.
form.root.Colors.Set_Color.White.Enabled = .F.

* Enable the Red and Blue menu items.
form.root.Colors.Set_Color.Red.Enabled = .T.
form.root.Colors.Set_Color.Blue.Enabled = .T.

* Un-check the Red and Blue menu items.
form.root.Colors.Set_Color.Red.Checked = .F.
form.root.Colors.Set_Color.Blue.Checked = .F.

Return
```

- Save your work by selecting Save from the File menu.

As you can see, the `WHITE_OnClick` procedure is very similar to the `RED_OnClick` and `BLUE_OnClick` procedures. To see in action the code you attached to the `OnClick` event of the White menu item, follow these steps:

- Close the COLORS.MNU menu by selecting Close from the File menu.
- Type `DO C:\DBPROG\CH06\COLORS.WFM` in the Command window and press Enter.

  dBASE responds by executing the COLORS.WFM program.

- Open the Set Color submenu and select Red.

  The COLORS.WFM program responds by changing the background color of its window to red.

- Open the Set Color submenu again but this time select White.

  The COLORS.WFM program responds by changing the background color of its window to white.

- Open the Set Color submenu again and check that the White item is disabled and has a checkmark next to it.
- Terminate the COLORS.WFM program by selecting Exit from its Colors menu.

Attaching Code to the *OnClick* Event of the Large Menu Item

Follow these steps to attach code to the `OnClick` event of the Large menu item of the Size pop-up menu:

- ☐ Type `MODIFY MENU ?` in the Command window, press Enter, and then select the menu file C:\DBPROG\CH06\COLORS.MNU from the Open Form dialog box that dBASE displays.

  dBASE responds by displaying the COLORS.MNU menu in design mode.

- ☐ Attach the following code to the `OnClick` event of the Large menu item. After you write this code, the `LARGE_OnClick` procedure should look like this:

```
Procedure LARGE_OnClick

 * Set the size of the form to large.
 form.WindowState = 2

 * Place a checkmark next to the Large menu item.
 form.root.Size.Large.Checked = .T.

 * Disable the Large menu item.
 form.root.Size.Large.Enabled = .F.

 * Enable the Small menu item.
 form.root.Size.Small.Enabled = .T.

 * Un-check the Small menu item.
 form.root.Size.Small.Checked = .F.

Return
```

- ☐ Save your work by selecting Save from the File menu.

The first statement you typed in the `LARGE_OnClick` procedure sets the WindowState property of the form to 2:

```
form.WindowState = 2
```

When the WindowState property of a form is set to 2, the form is maximized (that is, displayed over the entire desktop of Windows).

The next statement places a checkmark next to the Large menu item (by setting the Checked property of the Large menu item to .T.):

```
form.root.Size.Large.Checked = .T.
```

The next statement disables the Large menu item by setting its Enabled property to .F.:

```
form.root.Size.Large.Enabled = .F.
```

The next statement enables the Small menu item by setting its Enabled property to .T.:

```
form.root.Size.Small.Enabled = .T.
```

Finally, the following statement unchecks (removes the checkmark of) the Small menu item by setting its Checked property to .F.:

```
form.root.Size.Small.Checked = .F.
```

To see the code you attached to the `OnClick` event of the Large menu item in action, follow these steps:

- ☐ Close the COLORS.MNU menu by selecting Close from the File menu.
- ☐ Type `DO C:\DBPROG\CH06\COLORS.WFM` in the Command window and press Enter.

  dBASE responds by executing the COLORS.WFM program.

- ☐ Open the Size pop-up menu and select Large.

  As expected, the COLORS.WFM program responds by maximizing its window.

- ☐ Open the Size menu again and check that the Large item is disabled and has a checkmark next to it.
- ☐ Terminate the COLORS.WFM program by selecting Exit from its Colors menu.

Attaching Code to the *OnClick* Event of the Small Menu Item

Follow these steps to attach code to the `OnClick` event of the Small menu item of the Size pop-up menu:

- ☐ Type `MODIFY MENU ?` in the Command window, press Enter, and then select the menu file C:\DBPROG\CH06\COLORS.MNU from the Open Form dialog box that dBASE displays.

  dBASE responds by displaying the COLORS.MNU menu in design mode.

- ☐ Attach the following code to the `OnClick` event of the Small menu item. After you write this code, the `SMALL_OnClick` procedure should look like this:

```
Procedure SMALL_OnClick

* Set the size of the form to small.
form.WindowState = 0

* Place a checkmark next to the Small menu item.
form.root.Size.Small.Checked = .T.

* Disable the Small menu item.
```

```
form.root.Size.Small.Enabled = .F.

* Enable the Large menu item.
form.root.Size.Large.Enabled = .T.

* Un-check the Large menu item.
form.root.Size.Large.Checked = .F.

Return
```

☐ Save your work by selecting Save from the File menu.

The first statement you typed in the `SMALL_OnClick` procedure sets the WindowState property of the form to 0:

```
form.WindowState = 0
```

When the WindowState property of a form is set to 0, the form is displayed at its normal size.

The remaining code in the `SMALL_OnClick` procedure is similar to the code of the `LARGE_OnClick` procedure. To see the code you attached to the `OnClick` event of the Small menu item in action, follow these steps:

☐ Close the COLORS.MNU menu by selecting Close from the File menu.

☐ Type `DO C:\DBPROG\CH06\COLORS.WFM` in the Command window and press Enter.

dBASE responds by executing the COLORS.WFM program.

☐ Open the Size pop-up menu and select Large.

The COLORS.WFM program responds by maximizing its window.

☐ Open the Size pop-up menu again, but this time select Small.

The COLORS.WFM program responds by restoring its window to the normal size.

☐ Open the Size menu again and check that the Small item is disabled and has a checkmark next to it.

☐ Terminate the COLORS.WFM program by selecting Exit from its Colors menu.

Shortcut Keys

You can enhance the menu of the COLORS program by adding shortcut keys. A *shortcut key* enables you to execute a menu item quickly by pressing a combination of keys on the keyboard. For example, in the COLORS program you can assign the shortcut key Alt+X to the Exit menu item. By doing so, when you press Alt+X, the program will terminate.

Follow these steps to assign the shortcut key Alt+X to the Exit menu item:

- Type `MODIFY MENU ?` in the Command window, press the Enter key, then select the menu file C:\DBPROG\CH06\COLORS.MNU from the Open Form dialog box that dBASE displays.

    dBASE responds by displaying the COLORS.MNU menu in design mode.

- Select the Exit menu item of the COLORS.MNU menu by clicking it.
- Make the Inspector window the active window by selecting Inspector from the View menu of dBASE.
- Make sure that the pull-down list box at the top of the Inspector window is set to form.root.colors.exit (because you're now going to set a property of the Exit menu item of the Colors pop-up menu).
- Select the Properties tab at the bottom of the Inspector window by clicking it.
- Select the Shortcut property by clicking it.
- Type Alt+X in the entry field of the Shortcut property and press Enter.

To see in action the Alt+X shortcut that you assigned to the Exit menu item, follow these steps:

- Close the COLORS.MNU menu by selecting Close from the File menu.
- Type `DO C:\DBPROG\CH06\COLORS.WFM` in the Command window and press Enter.

    dBASE responds by executing the COLORS.WFM program.

- Open the Colors pop-up menu. (See Figure 6.28.)

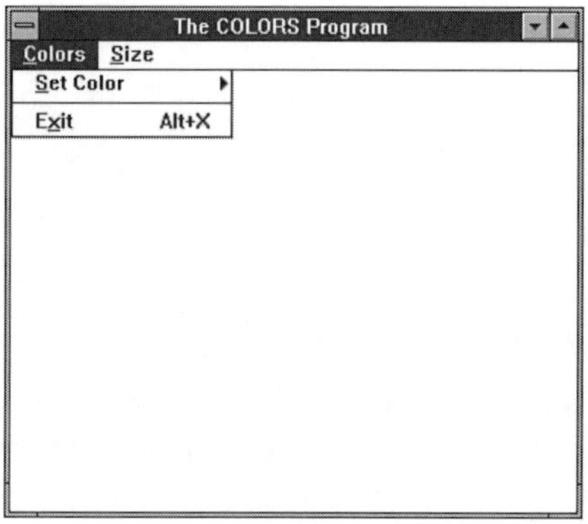

Figure 6.28.
Adding a shortcut key to the Exit menu item.

As shown in Figure 6.28, now the Exit menu item includes the text Alt+X to indicate that the Alt+X shortcut is assigned to the Exit menu item.

☐ Close the Colors pop-up menu.

☐ Press Alt+X on your keyboard.

The COLORS program responds by terminating.

Summary

In this chapter you have written a dBASE program that uses a menu. You have learned how to use the following techniques:

- How to write code that disables/enables a menu item.
- How to write code that checks/unchecks a menu item.
- How to incorporate a submenu.
- How to include a separator bar in a menu.
- How to assign a shortcut key to a menu item.

Q&A

Q In this chapter I have learned how to write code that disables menu items. How can I disable an entire pop-up menu?

A To disable an entire pop-up menu, you need to set the Enabled property of the pop-up title to .F.. For example, in the COLORS program, the following statement would disable the entire Size pop-up menu:

```
form.root.Size.Enabled=.F.
```

Q How many levels of submenus can a menu include?

A dBASE for Windows doesn't impose a limit on the number of submenu levels. Figure 6.29 shows four levels of submenus.

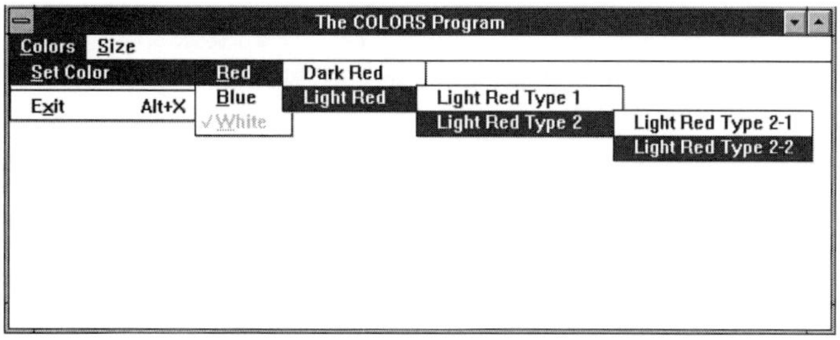

Figure 6.29.
Four levels of submenus.

Quiz

1. Suppose you design a menu file called MyMenu.MNU that includes a pop-up menu called Edit. The Edit pop-up menu includes a menu item called Find. What does the following statement do?

   ```
   form.root.Edit.Find.Enabled=.F.
   ```

2. Suppose you design a menu file called MyMenu.MNU that includes a pop-up menu called View. The View pop-up menu includes a menu item called Full Screen. What does the following statement do?

   ```
   form.root.View.Full_Screen.Checked=.T.
   ```

3. What is a separator bar and how do you create it?
4. What are shortcut keys and how do you create them?

Exercise

In the COLORS program of this chapter you assigned the Alt+X shortcut key to the Exit menu item. Enhance the COLORS program as follows:

- Assign the Ctrl+R shortcut key to the Red menu item of the Set Color submenu.
- Assign the Ctrl+B shortcut key to the Blue menu item of the Set Color submenu.
- Assign the Ctrl+W shortcut key to the White menu item of the Set Color submenu.

Quiz Answers

1. This statement disables the Find menu item of the Edit pop-up:

   ```
   form.root.Edit.Find.Enabled=.F.
   ```

2. This statement places a checkmark next to the Full Screen menu item of the View pop-up menu:

   ```
   form.root.View.Full_Screen.Checked=.T.
   ```

3. A separator bar is a horizontal line used to separate menu items. To make a menu item a separator bar, set the Separator property of the menu item to .T..
4. A shortcut key enables you to execute a menu item by pressing a combination of keys on the keyboard (for example, Alt+X, Ctrl+C, Ctrl+A). You assign a shortcut key to a menu item during design time by setting the Shortcut property of the menu item to the desired key combination.

Exercise Answer

Assign the following shortcut key combinations to menu items in the Set Color submenu:

- Set the Shortcut property of the Red menu item to Ctrl+R.
- Set the Shortcut property of the Blue menu item to Ctrl+B.
- Set the Shortcut property of the White menu item to Ctrl+W.

6

7

Controls

As you have seen in previous chapters, a major component of dBASE programming is using controls (for example, the pushbutton control, the text control, the browse control). In this chapter you'll write a program that uses three common Windows controls: a scroll bar, radio buttons, and check boxes.

The SPEED Program

In the following sections you will write a dBASE program called SPEED that illustrates how to use a scroll bar, check boxes, and radio buttons. But before you start writing the SPEED program, review what the program should look like and what it should do. When you run the SPEED program, the main window of the SPEED program should look like the one shown in Figure 7.1.

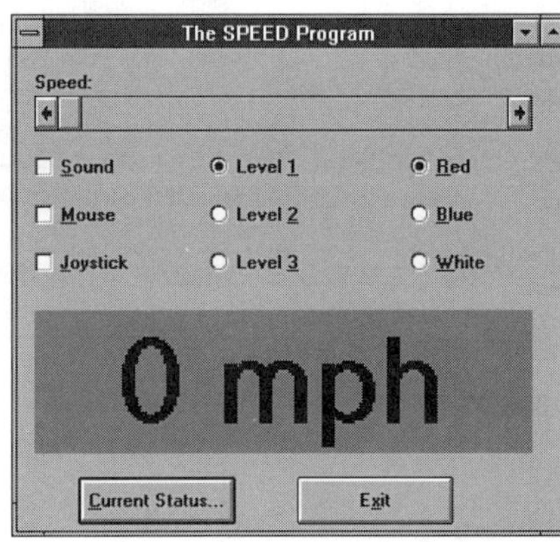

Figure 7.1.
The main window of the SPEED program.

As shown in Figure 7.1, the main window of the SPEED program contains several controls: a horizontal scroll bar, three check boxes (Sound, Mouse, and Joystick), one group of three radio buttons (Level 1, Level 2, and Level 3), another group of three radio buttons (Red, Blue, and White), a text control (displaying the text `0 mph`), and two pushbuttons (Current Status... and Exit).

You can use the horizontal scroll bar of the SPEED program to select an integer from 0 through 100. When you change the horizontal scroll bar (by moving the scroll bar's thumb), the program updates the text control accordingly. In Figure 7.1 the text control displays the text `0 mph` because the scroll bar's thumb is at the leftmost position, but in Figure 7.2 the scroll bar's thumb is at the midpoint position, so the text control displays the text `50 mph`. In Figure 7.3 the scroll bar's thumb is at the rightmost position, so the text control displays the text `100 mph`.

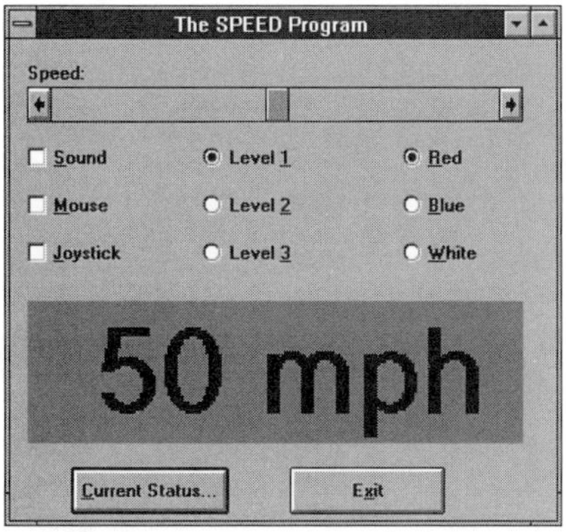

Figure 7.2.
The window of the SPEED program when the scroll bar's thumb is at the midpoint position.

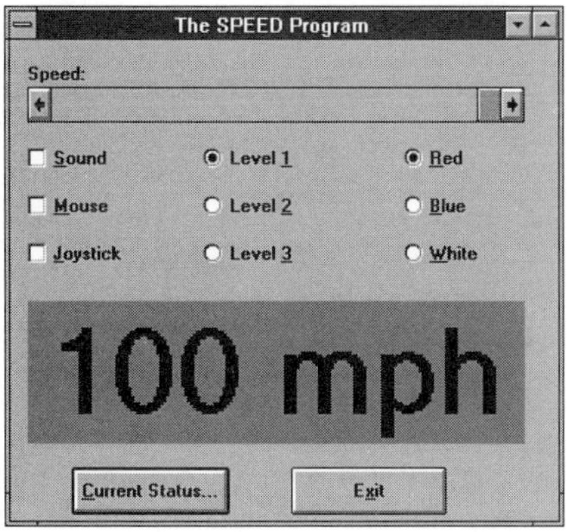

Figure 7.3.
The window of the SPEED program when the scroll bar's thumb is at the rightmost position.

You can place or remove an × in any of the three check boxes (Sound, Mouse, and Joystick) by clicking them. In Figure 7.3 all three check boxes are unchecked, and in Figure 7.4 the Sound and Mouse check boxes are checked and the Joystick check box is unchecked.

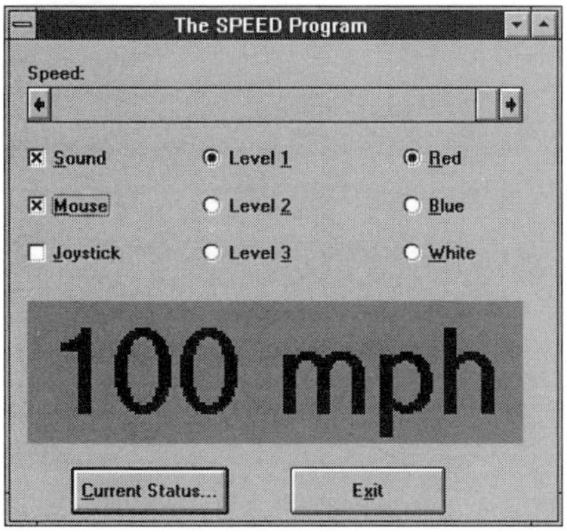

Figure 7.4.
The window of the SPEED program after you check the Sound and Mouse check boxes.

At any given time, you can select only one radio button from the group of Level radio buttons (Level 1, Level 2, and Level 3) and only one radio button from the group of Color radio buttons (Red, Blue, and White). For example, in Figure 7.4 the Level 1 radio button is selected in the Level group, and the Red radio button is selected in the Color group. In Figure 7.5 the Level 2 radio button is selected in the Level group, and the White radio button is selected in the Color group.

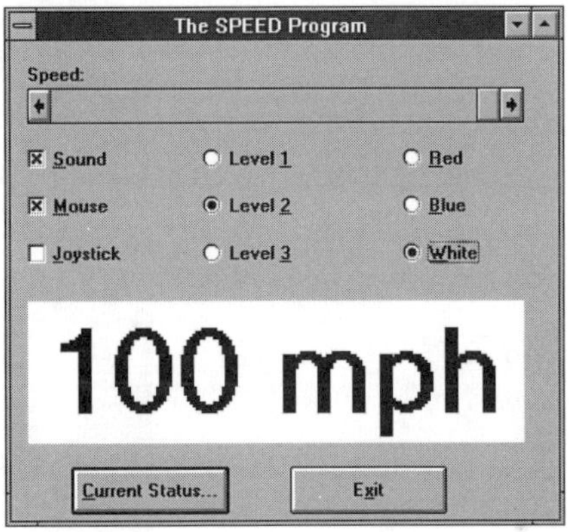

Figure 7.5.
The window of the SPEED program with the Level 2 and White radio buttons selected.

When you select a color from the Color group of radio buttons, the SPEED program changes the color of the text control to the selected color. For example, if you select the Red radio button, the text control changes its color to red.

When you click the Current Status... pushbutton, the SPEED program displays a message box that lists the current status of each of the controls. (See Figure 7.6.)

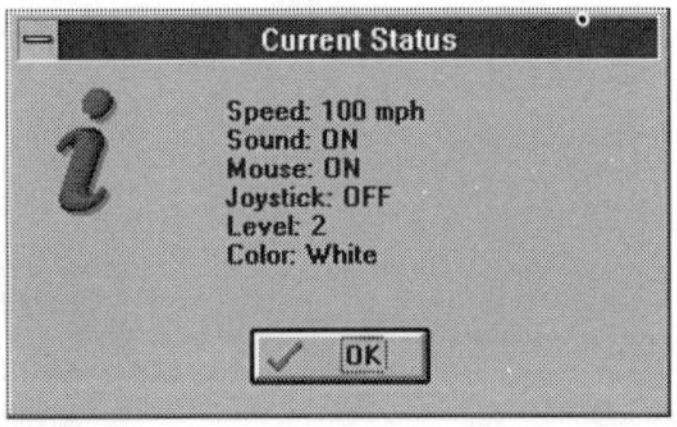

Figure 7.6.
The Current Status message box.

When you click the Exit pushbutton, the program terminates.

Now that you know what the SPEED program is supposed to do, you can start writing this program.

The Visual Implementation of the SPEED Program

Create the SPEED.WFM form as follows:

☐ Type `MD C:\DBPROG\CH07` in the Command window, and then press Enter.

dBASE responds by creating the directory C:\DBPROG\CH07.

☐ Type `CREATE FORM C:\DBPROG\CH07\SPEED` in the Command window and press Enter.

dBASE responds by creating the SPEED.WFM form and displaying it in design mode.

☐ Customize the SPEED.WFM form according to the specifications in Table 7.1. When you finish customizing the form, it should look like the one shown in Figure 7.7.

Note: If you have trouble locating any of the icons for the controls mentioned in Table 7.1, see Figure 7.8 for the icons of all the standard controls in the Control Palette window.

☐ Save your work by selecting Save from the File menu.

Table 7.1. The properties table of the SPEED.WFM form.

Object	Property	Setting
Form	**Text**	**The SPEED Program**
	Height	20.23
	Left	1.00
	Top	0.00
	Width	63.00
Text	**Name**	**Text1**
	Text	Speed
	Height	1.00
	Left	2.00
	Top	1.00
	Width	7.00

continues

Table 7.1. continued

Object	Property	Setting
Horizontal Scroll Bar	**Name**	**SpeedScrollbar**
	RangeMin	0
	RangeMax	100
	Value	0
	Height	1.53
	Left	2.00
	Top	2.00
	Width	57.00
Check Box	**Name**	**SoundCheck**
	Text	&Sound
	Height	2.00
	Left	2.00
	Top	4.00
	Width	15.00
Check Box	**Name**	**MouseCheck**
	Text	&Mouse
	Height	2.00
	Left	2.00
	Top	6.00
	Width	15.00
Check Box	**Name**	**JoystickCheck**
	Text	&Joystick
	Height	2.00
	Left	2.00
	Top	8.00
	Width	15.00
Radio Button	**Name**	**Level1Radio**
	Text	Level &1
	Group	.T.
	Value	.T.

Object	Property	Setting
	Height	2.00
	Left	22.00
	Top	4.00
	Width	16.00
Radio Button	**Name**	**Level2Radio**
	Text	Level &2
	Group	.F.
	Value	.F.
	Height	2.00
	Left	22.00
	Top	6.00
	Width	16.00
Radio Button	**Name**	**Level3Radio**
	Text	Level &3
	Group	.F.
	Value	.F.
	Height	2.00
	Left	22.00
	Top	8.00
	Width	16.00
Text	**Name**	**SpeedText**
	Text	0 mph
	ColorNormal	N/R+
	Alignment	4-Center
	FontName	MS Sans Serif
	FontSize	60
	Height	6.00
	Left	2.00
	Top	11.00
	Width	57.00

continues

Table 7.1. continued

Object	Property	Setting
Radio Button	**Name**	**RedRadio**
	Text	&Red
	Group	.T.
	Value	.T.
	Height	2.00
	Left	45.00
	Top	4.00
	Width	16.00
Radio Button	**Name**	**BlueRadio**
	Text	&Blue
	Group	.F.
	Value	.F.
	Height	2.00
	Left	45.00
	Top	6.00
	Width	16.00
Radio Button	**Name**	**WhiteRadio**
	Text	&White
	Group	.F.
	Value	.F.
	Height	2.00
	Left	45.00
	Top	8.00
	Width	16.00
PushButton	**Name**	**CurrentStatusButton**
	Text	&Current Status...
	Height	2.00
	Left	7.00
	Top	18.00
	Width	18.00

Object	Property	Setting
PushButton	**Name**	**ExitButton**
	Text	E&xit
	Height	2.00
	Left	32.00
	Top	18.00
	Width	18.00

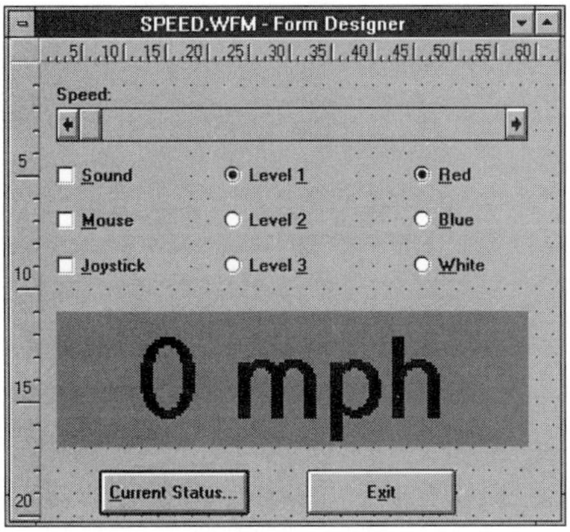

Figure 7.7.
The SPEED.WFM form in design mode (after customization).

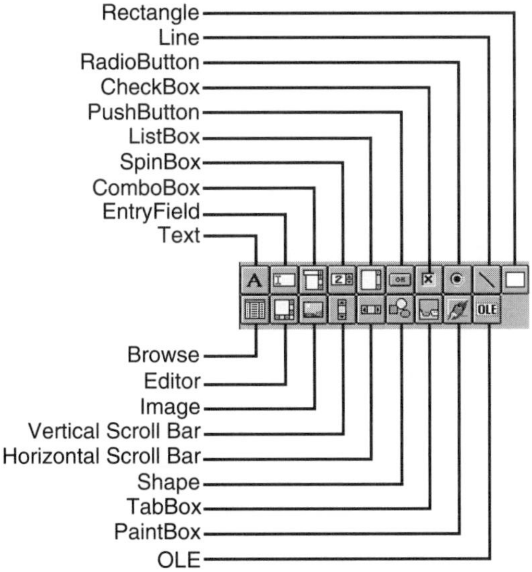

Figure 7.8.
The icons of the standard controls in the Control Palette.

Note: Table 7.1 instructs you to set the RangeMin property of the SpeedScrollbar scroll bar to 0 and the RangeMax property to 100. The RangeMin and RangeMax properties are listed under the Edit Properties item in the Inspector window.

The RangeMin property of a horizontal scroll bar specifies the value of the scroll bar when the scroll bar's thumb is at the leftmost position (the minimum value); the RangeMax property specifies the value of the scroll bar when the scroll bar's thumb is at the rightmost position (the maximum value).

Note: Table 7.1 instructs you to set the Group property of the Level1Radio radio button to .T.. The Group property is listed under the Access Properties item in the Inspector window.

You make the Level1Radio, Level2Radio, and Level3Radio radio buttons members of one group as follows: Set the Group property of the Level1Radio radio button to .T., then place two additional radio buttons in the form, and finally set the Group property of the two additional radio buttons to .F..

The RedRadio, BlueRadio, and WhiteRadio radio buttons are also members of one group because you set the Group property of the RedRadio radio button to .T., place two additional radio buttons, and set their Group property to .F..

When several radio buttons belong to the same group, you can select only one of these radio buttons at a time.

So to make several radio buttons belong to one group, do the following:

- ☐ Place the first radio button of the group in the form and set its Group property to .T..
- ☐ Place the other radio buttons in the form and set the Group property of each to .F..

To see your program's design in action do the following:

☐ Press F2 on your keyboard.

dBASE responds by running the SPEED.WFM form.

☐ Experiment with the three check boxes (Sound, Mouse, and Joystick) and notice that you can check several check boxes at a time.

☐ Experiment with the three Level radio buttons (Level 1, Level 2, and Level 3) and notice that you can select only one level at a time.

- Experiment with the three Color radio buttons (Red, Blue, and White) and notice that you can select only one color at a time.
- Change back to design mode by pressing Shift+F2 on your keyboard.

The visual implementation of the SPEED.WFM form is complete.

Entering the Code of the SPEED Program

In the following sections you'll attach code to the SPEED.WFM form's controls.

Attaching Code to the *OnClick* Event of the Exit Pushbutton

When you click the Exit button, the SPEED program should terminate. You'll now write the code that accomplishes this task.

- Attach the following code to the `OnClick` event of the Exit pushbutton. After you write this code, the `EXITBUTTON_OnClick` procedure should look like this:

```
Procedure EXITBUTTON_OnClick

   form.close()

Return
```

- Save your work by selecting Save from the File menu.

The following statement terminates the program by closing the form:

```
form.Close()
```

To see in action the code you attached to the `OnClick` event of the Exit button, follow these steps:

- Press F2 on your keyboard.

  dBASE responds by running the SPEED.WFM form.

- Click the Exit button.

  The SPEED program responds by terminating.

7

Attaching Code to the *OnChange* Event of the SpeedScroll Scroll Bar

When you change the value of the SpeedScroll scroll bar, the SPEED program should update the SpeedText text control with the appropriate value. For example, if you change the value of the SpeedScroll scroll bar to 10, the SPEED program should display the text `10 mph`. You'll now write the code that accomplishes this task.

☐ Type `MODIFY FORM ?` in the Command window, press the Enter key, then select the file C:\DBPROG\CH07\SPEED.WFM from the Open Form dialog box that dBASE displays.

dBASE responds by displaying the SPEED.WFM form in design mode.

☐ Attach the following code to the `OnChange` event of the SpeedScrollbar scroll bar. After you write this code, the `SPEEDSCROLLBAR_OnChange` procedure should look like this:

```
Procedure SPEEDSCROLLBAR_OnChange

* Update the SpeedText text control with the current
* value of the SpeedScrollbar scroll bar.
form.SpeedText.Text=STR(form.SpeedScrollbar.Value,3)+" mph"

Return
```

☐ Save your work by selecting Save from the File menu.

As its name implies, the `OnChange` event of a scroll bar occurs when the scroll bar changes its value.

The code you entered in the `SPEEDSCROLLBAR_OnChange` procedure has a single statement:

```
form.SpeedText.Text=STR(form.SpeedScrollbar.Value,3)+" mph"
```

This statement changes the Text property of the SpeedText text control according to the current value of the SpeedScrollbar scroll bar. For example, if the current value of the SpeedScrollbar scroll bar is 15, then the preceding statement sets the Text property of the SpeedText text control to the string `15 mph`.

To see in action the code you attached to the `OnChange` event of the SpeedScrollbar scroll bar, follow these steps:

☐ Press F2 on your keyboard.

dBASE responds by running the SPEED.WFM form.

☐ Change the value of the SpeedScrollbar scroll bar to any value (by dragging the scroll bar's thumb).

The SPEED program responds by displaying the value you selected in the SpeedText text control.

☐ Change back to design mode by pressing Shift+F2 on your keyboard.

Attaching Code to the *OnChange* Event of the Blue Radio Button

When you select the Blue radio button, the SPEED program should change the background color of the SpeedText text control to blue. You'll now write the code that accomplishes this task.

☐ Attach the following code to the OnChange event of the Blue radio button. After you write this code, the BLUERADIO_OnChange procedure should look like this:

```
Procedure BLUERADIO_OnChange

 * If the Blue radio button is selected, change the
 * color of the SpeedText text control to W/B
 * (W/B = White over blue).
 IF form.BlueRadio.Value = .T.
    form.SpeedText.ColorNormal = "W/B"
 ENDIF

Return
```

☐ Save your work by selecting Save from the File menu.

As its name implies, the OnChange event of a radio button occurs when the radio button changes its status.

The code you entered in the BLUERADIO_OnChange procedure is made of an IF statement:

```
IF form.BlueRadio.Value = .T.
   form.SpeedText.ColorNormal = "W/B"
ENDIF
```

If the Value property of the Blue radio button is equal to .T., the Blue radio button is selected, the IF condition of the preceding IF statement is satisfied, and this statement under the IF condition is executed:

```
form.SpeedText.ColorNormal = "W/B"
```

This statement changes the color of the SpeedText text control to W/B. W/B means white foreground over blue background.

When you change the status of the Blue radio button, the BLUERADIO_OnChange procedure is automatically executed and the code you wrote in this procedure changes the color of the SpeedText text control to W/B, provided that the Blue radio button is selected.

Note that the BLUERADIO_OnChange procedure is executed whenever the value of the Blue radio button is changed. That is, it is executed when the user selects the Blue radio button as well as when the user deselects the Blue radio button. This is the reason you used the IF statement in the preceding code. That is, you want to change the color of the SpeedText box to W/B only if the user selected the Blue radio button. If the user deselected the Blue radio button, you don't want the BLUERADIO_OnChange procedure to do anything.

To see in action the code you attached to the OnChange event of the Blue radio button, follow these steps:

☐ Press F2 on your keyboard.

dBASE responds by running the SPEED.WFM form.

☐ Click the Blue radio button.

The SPEED program responds by changing the color of the SpeedText text control to white text over blue background.

☐ Change back to design mode by pressing Shift+F2 on your keyboard.

Attaching Code to the *OnChange* Event of the Red Radio Button

When you select the Red radio button, the SPEED program should change the background color of the SpeedText text control to red. You'll now write the code that accomplishes this task.

☐ Attach the following code to the `OnChange` event of the Red radio button. After you write this code, the `REDRADIO_OnChange` procedure should look like this:

```
Procedure REDRADIO_OnChange

 * If the Red radio button is selected, change the
 * color of the SpeedText text control to N/R+.
 * (N/R+ = Black over bright red).
 IF form.RedRadio.Value = .T.
    form.SpeedText.ColorNormal = "N/R+"
 ENDIF

Return
```

☐ Save your work by selecting Save from the File menu.

As you can see, the code you attached to the `OnChange` event of the Red radio button is similar to the code for the Blue radio button. When you change the status of the Red radio button, the `REDRADIO_OnChange` procedure is automatically executed, and the code you wrote in this procedure changes the color of the SpeedText text control to N/R+ (black over bright red), if the Red radio button is selected.

To see in action the code you attached to the `OnChange` event of the Red radio button, follow these steps:

☐ Press F2 on your keyboard.

dBASE responds by running the SPEED.WFM form.

☐ Click the Blue radio button.

The SPEED program responds by changing the color of the SpeedText text control to white over blue.

☐ Click the Red radio button.

The SPEED program responds by changing the color of the SpeedText text control to black over bright red.

☐ Change back to design mode by pressing Shift+F2 on your keyboard.

Attaching Code to the *OnChange* Event of the White Radio Button

When you select the White radio button, the SPEED program should change the background color of the SpeedText text control to white. You'll now write the code that accomplishes this task.

☐ Attach the following code to the `OnChange` event of the White radio button. After you write this code, the `WHITERADIO_OnChange` procedure should look like this:

```
Procedure WHITERADIO_OnChange

 * If the White radio button is selected, change the
 * color of the SpeedText text control to N/W+.
 * (N/W+ = Black over bright white).
 IF form.WhiteRadio.Value = .T.
    form.SpeedText.ColorNormal = "N/W+"
 ENDIF

Return
```

☐ Save your work by selecting Save from the File menu.

As you can see, the code you attached to the `OnChange` event of the White radio button is similar to the code for the Blue and Red radio buttons.

When you change the status of the White radio button, the `WHITERADIO_OnChange` procedure is automatically executed, and the code you wrote in this procedure changes the color of the SpeedText text control to N/W+ (black over bright white) if the White radio button is selected.

To see in action the code you attached to the `OnChange` event of the White radio button, follow these steps:

☐ Press F2 on your keyboard.

dBASE responds by running the SPEED.WFM form.

☐ Click the White radio button.

The SPEED program responds by changing the color of the SpeedText text control to black over bright white.

☐ Change back to design mode by pressing Shift+F2 on your keyboard.

7

Attaching Code to the *OnClick* Event of the Current Status... Pushbutton

When you click the Current Status... pushbutton, the SPEED program should display a message box listing the current status of each of the controls. You'll now write the code that accomplishes this task.

☐ Attach the following code to the `OnClick` event of the Current Status... pushbutton. After you write this code, the `CURRENTSTATUS_OnClick` procedure should look like this:

```
Procedure CURRENTSTATUSBUTTON_OnClick

* Get the speed.
Speed = "Speed: "+form.SpeedText.Text

* Get the Sound check box status.
IF form.SoundCheck.Value = .T.
   Sound = "Sound: ON"
ELSE
   Sound = "Sound: OFF"
ENDIF

* Get the Mouse check box status.
IF form.MouseCheck.Value = .T.
   Mouse = "Mouse: ON"
ELSE
   Mouse = "Mouse: OFF"
ENDIF

* Get the Joystick check box status.
IF form.JoystickCheck.Value = .T.
   Joystick = "Joystick: ON"
ELSE
   Joystick = "Joystick: OFF"
ENDIF

* Get the Level radio buttons status.
DO CASE
   CASE form.Level1Radio.Value = .T.
        Level = "Level: 1"
   CASE form.Level2Radio.Value = .T.
        Level = "Level: 2"
   CASE form.Level3Radio.Value = .T.
        Level = "Level: 3"
ENDCASE

* Get the Color radio buttons status.
DO CASE
   CASE form.RedRadio.Value = .T.
        Color = "Color: Red"
   CASE form.BlueRadio.Value = .T.
        Color = "Color: Blue"
   CASE form.WhiteRadio.Value = .T.
        Color = "Color: White"
ENDCASE

* Display the current status.
CR = CHR(13)
Status=Speed+CR+Sound+CR+Mouse+CR+Joystick+CR+Level+CR+Color
MsgBox(Status,"Current Status",64)

Return
```

☐ Save your work by selecting Save from the File menu.

The first statement you entered in the `CURRENTSTATUS_OnClick` procedure updates the variable `Speed` with the current speed displayed in the SpeedText text control:

```
Speed = "Speed: "+form.SpeedText.Text
```

The next statement is an `IF...ELSE` statement:

```
IF form.SoundCheck.Value = .T.
   Sound = "Sound: ON"
ELSE
   Sound = "Sound: OFF"
ENDIF
```

If the SoundCheck check box is currently checked, the `IF` condition of the preceding `IF` statement is satisfied, and the variable `Sound` is filled with the string `"Sound: ON"`. If, however, the `IF` condition is not satisfied, the `Sound` variable is filled with the string `"Sound: OFF"`.

The next statement is another `IF...ELSE` statement:

```
IF form.MouseCheck.Value = .T.
   Mouse = "Mouse: ON"
ELSE
   Mouse = "Mouse: OFF"
ENDIF
```

If the MouseCheck check box is currently checked, the `IF` condition of the preceding `IF` statement is satisfied, and the variable `Mouse` is filled with the string `"Mouse: ON"`. If, however, the `IF` condition is not satisfied, the `Mouse` variable is filled with the string `"Mouse: OFF"`.

The next statement is yet another `IF...ELSE` statement:

```
IF form.JoystickCheck.Value = .T.
   Joystick = "Joystick: ON"
ELSE
   Joystick = "Joystick: OFF"
ENDIF
```

If the JoystickCheck check box is currently checked, the `IF` condition of the preceding `IF` statement is satisfied, and the variable `Joystick` is filled with the string `"Joystick: ON"`. If, however, the `IF` condition is not satisfied, the `Joystick` variable is filled with the string `"Joystick: OFF"`.

The next group of statements uses a `DO CASE` to determine which of the three Level radio buttons is currently selected:

```
DO CASE
   CASE form.Level1Radio.Value = .T.
        Level = "Level: 1"
   CASE form.Level2Radio.Value = .T.
        Level = "Level: 2"
   CASE form.Level3Radio.Value = .T.
```

```
      Level = "Level: 3"
ENDCASE
```

For example, if the Level2Radio radio button is currently selected, then the second `CASE` condition will be satisfied, and the variable `Level` will be filled with the string `"Level: 2"`.

The next group of statements uses another `DO CASE` to determine which of the three color radio buttons is currently selected:

```
DO CASE
   CASE form.RedRadio.Value = .T.
        Color = "Color: Red"
   CASE form.BlueRadio.Value = .T.
        Color = "Color: Blue"
   CASE form.WhiteRadio.Value = .T.
        Color = "Color: White"
ENDCASE
```

If, for example, the BlueRadio radio button is currently selected, then the second `CASE` condition will be satisfied, and the variable `Color` will be filled with the string `"Color: Blue"`.

Finally, the contents of the variables `Speed`, `Sound`, `Mouse`, `Joystick`, `Level`, and `Color` are displayed by using the `MsgBox()` function:

```
CR = CHR(13)
Status=Speed+CR+Sound+CR+Mouse+CR+Joystick+CR+Level+CR+Color
MsgBox(Status,"Current Status",64)
```

Notice that the carriage return character, `CHR(13)`, is used so the `MsgBox()` function will display the contents of each variable on a separate line.

To see in action the code you attached to the `OnClick` event of the Current Status… button, follow these steps:

- ☐ Press F2 on your keyboard.

  dBASE responds by running the SPEED.WFM form.

- ☐ Set the scroll bar, check boxes, and radio buttons to any desired settings.

- ☐ Click the Current Status… button.

  The SPEED program responds by displaying a message box listing the status of the controls.

- ☐ Terminate the SPEED program by clicking its Exit button.

Summary

In this chapter you have written a dBASE program that uses three types of controls: a scroll bar, check boxes, and radio buttons. As you have seen, knowing how to use a control amounts to knowing how to set and read the control's properties and knowing how to attach code to the control's events.

Q&A

Q In this chapter I attached code to the `OnChange` event of a scroll bar control and the `OnChange` event of radio button controls. Does the check box control also have an `OnChange` event?

A Yes. You can easily see whether the check box control has an `OnChange` event by selecting any check box in a form and inspecting the Events tab of the Inspector window. You will see that the check box control has an `OnChange` event. Just like the `OnChange` event of scroll bars and radio buttons, the `OnChange` event of a check box control occurs when the value of the check box is changed.

Q In the previous chapter I learned that to disable a menu item I have to set the Enabled property of the menu item to .F.. How can I disable a scroll bar, a check box, or a radio button?

A You disable a scroll bar, a check box, or a radio button the same way you disable a menu item—set the Enabled property of the control to .F.. For example, in the SPEED program the following statement would disable the SpeedScrollbar scroll bar:

```
form.SpeedScrollbar.Enabled = .F.
```

After you execute this statement, the SpeedScrollbar scroll bar control becomes disabled.

To enable a control, set its Enabled property to .T..

Q Is it possible to completely hide a control from view?

A Yes. To hide a control, set the Visible property of the control to .F.. For example, in the SPEED program, the following statement would make the SpeedScrollbar scroll bar invisible:

```
form.SpeedScrollbar.Visible = .F.
```

After you execute this statement, the Speed scroll bar control becomes invisible.

To make a control visible, set its Visible property to .T..

Q I've noticed that the Controls window of dBASE also includes a vertical scroll bar. How is a vertical scroll bar different from a horizontal scroll bar?

A The vertical scroll bar has the same properties and events as the horizontal scroll bar. The only difference between the two is visual—the horizontal scroll bar is aligned horizontally and the vertical scroll bar is aligned vertically.

Quiz

1. How do you set the minimum and maximum values of a scroll bar control?
2. What does the Value property of a scroll bar control report?

3. What does the Value property of a radio button control report?
4. What does the Value property of a check box control report?
5. What is the Group property of a radio button control used for?

Exercise

The SPEED program has two groups of radio buttons. One group includes the Level 1, Level 2, and Level 3 radio buttons, and the second group includes the Red, Blue, and White radio buttons.

Add a third group to the SPEED program that includes three radio buttons: Small, Medium, and Large.

Note that the Small-Medium-Large group of radio buttons has no functionality. That is, you don't have to attach any code to these radio buttons. The only reason for implementing this group of radio buttons is to enable you to practice creating a group of radio buttons.

If you want to make the Small, Medium, and Large radio buttons functional, you have to attach code to the `OnChange` events of these radio buttons (like you attached code to the `OnChange` events of the Red, Blue, and White radio buttons). For example, you can attach code to the `OnChange` events of the Small, Medium, and Large radio buttons that changes the size of the form depending on which radio button is selected. Recall from the previous chapter that you can set the size of the form by using the WindowState property of the form.

Quiz Answers

1. To specify the minimum value of a scroll bar control, set the RangeMin property of the scroll bar. To specify the maximum value of a scroll bar control, set the RangeMax property of the scroll bar.
2. The Value property of a scroll bar control specifies the current value of the scroll bar.
3. The Value property of a radio button control can be either .T. or .F.. When the Value property of a radio button control is .T., the radio button is selected.
4. The Value property of a check box control can be either .T. or .F.. When the Value property of a check box control is .T., the check box is checked.
5. You use the Group property of a radio button control to make several radio buttons belong to the same group.

   To make several radio buttons belong to one group, do the following:

   Place the first radio button of the group in the form and set the Group property of this radio button to .T..

   Place the other radio buttons in the form and set the Group property of each of these radio buttons to .F..

Exercise Answer

To add the Small, Medium, and Large radio buttons to the form and make them a group, follow these steps:

- Type `MODIFY FORM ?` in the Command window, press the Enter key, and then select the file C:\DBPROG\CH07\SPEED.WFM from the Open Form dialog box that dBASE displays.

  dBASE responds by displaying the SPEED.WFM form in design mode.

- Add a new radio button to the form and set its properties as follows:

Object	*Property*	*Setting*
Radio Button	**Name**	**SmallRadio**
	Group	.T.
	Text	Small

- Add two additional radio buttons to the form and set their properties as follows:

Object	*Property*	*Setting*
Radio Button	**Name**	**MediumRadio**
	Group	.F.
	Text	Medium
Radio Button	**Name**	**LargeRadio**
	Group	.F.
	Text	Large

WEEK 2 AT A GLANCE

8

9

10

11

12

13

14

In Chapter 8 you will learn how to write dBASE code that creates a table. Other topics covered on this day include writing code to rename tables, writing code to copy tables, and writing code to delete tables.

In Chapter 9 you'll learn how to detect and make use of mouse events. You'll learn how to attach code to mouse events and how to use the parameters of the mouse event procedures.

In Chapter 10 you'll learn how to access files from within your dBASE programs. In particular, you'll learn how to read the contents of text files and you'll learn how to use the Editor control of dBASE.

In Chapter 11 you'll learn how to use the dBASE tools to join and link tables. As you'll see, joining and linking tables with dBASE amounts to clicking the mouse on various items, but the resultant joined table enables you to perform some powerful tasks without writing any code.

Week 2 at a Glance

In Chapter 12 you'll write a dBASE program that uses the joined table that you created in Chapter 11. You will learn how to utilize the query (QBE file) that you created in Chapter 11, and you'll learn how to design a form that makes use of a query file. During the implementation of the program, you'll learn other important topics such as appending records and deleting records.

In Chapter 13 you'll implement the SearchIt program, a program that demonstrates how to implement a search mechanism from within your dBASE programs. In this chapter you'll learn how to use the `Seek()` and `Locate()` functions of dBASE for searching data in tables.

In Chapter 14 you'll learn how to create a filter for your tables, where only certain records of the table (those records that comply with your filter statements) are displayed. In this chapter you'll also learn how to perform various common calculations on the fields of your tables.

WEEK 2

8

Creating a Table from Within Your Program

In this chapter you will learn how to write dBASE code that creates a table. Other topics covered in this chapter include writing code to rename tables, writing code to copy tables, and writing code to delete tables.

The CREATE Program

In the following sections you will write a dBASE program called CREATE that creates a table. The CREATE program also includes code that renames a table, copies a table, and deletes a table.

Before you start writing the CREATE program, you need to know how the program should look and what it should do.

When the CREATE program is run, the main window of the CREATE program should look like the one shown in Figure 8.1.

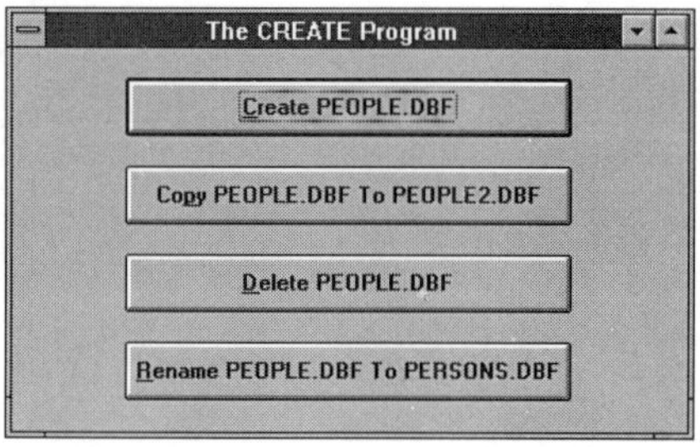

Figure 8.1.
The main window of the CREATE program.

The main window of the CREATE program has four buttons: Create PEOPLE.DBF, Copy PEOPLE.DBF To PEOPLE2.DBF, Delete PEOPLE.DBF, and Rename PEOPLE.DBF To PERSONS.DBF.

When the user clicks the Create PEOPLE.DBF button, the CREATE program creates a table called PEOPLE.DBF in the directory from which the CREATE program is being executed. The CREATE program also adds an index to the PEOPLE.DBF table.

When the user clicks the Copy PEOPLE.DBF To PEOPLE2.DBF button, the CREATE program copies the PEOPLE.DBF table into a new table called PEOPLE2.DBF. The PEOPLE2.DBF table is created in the directory from which the CREATE program is being executed.

When the user clicks the Delete PEOPLE.DBF button, the CREATE program deletes the PEOPLE.DBF table.

When the user clicks the Rename PEOPLE.DBF To PERSONS.DBF button, the CREATE program renames the PEOPLE.DBF table to PERSONS.DBF.

Now that you know what the CREATE program is supposed to do, it's time to start writing it.

The Visual Implementation of the CREATE Program

Create the CREATE.WFM form as explained here:

☐ Type `MD C:\DBPROG` in the Command window, and then press Enter.

dBASE responds by creating the directory C:\DBPROG. (If this directory already exists, dBASE displays a message box telling you that the directory cannot be created.)

☐ Type `MD C:\DBPROG\CH08` in the Command window, and then press Enter.

dBASE responds by creating the directory C:\DBPROG\CH08.

☐ Type `CREATE FORM C:\DBPROG\CH08\CREATE` in the Command window, and press Enter.

dBASE responds by creating the CREATE.WFM form and displaying it in design mode.

☐ Customize the CREATE.WFM form according to the specifications in Table 8.1. When you finish customizing the form, it should look like the one shown in Figure 8.2.

Table 8.1. The properties table of the CREATE.WFM form.

Object	Property	Setting
Form	**Text**	**The CREATE Program**
	Height	2.00
	Left	1.00
	Top	0.00
	Width	41.50
PushButton	**Name**	**CreateButton**
	Height	2.00
	Left	10.66
	Top	1.00
	Width	41.50
	Text	&Create PEOPLE.DBF
PushButton	**Name**	**CopyButton**
	Height	2.00
	Left	10.66
	Top	4.00

continues

Table 8.1. continued

Object	Property	Setting
	Width	41.50
	Text	Co&py PEOPLE.DBF To PEOPLE2.DBF
PushButton	**Name**	**DeleteButton**
	Height	2.00
	Left	10.66
	Top	7.00
	Width	41.50
	Text	&Delete PEOPLE.DBF
PushButton	**Name**	**RenameButton**
	Height	2.00
	Left	10.66
	Top	10.00
	Width	41.50
	Text	&Rename PEOPLE.DBF To PERSONS.DBF

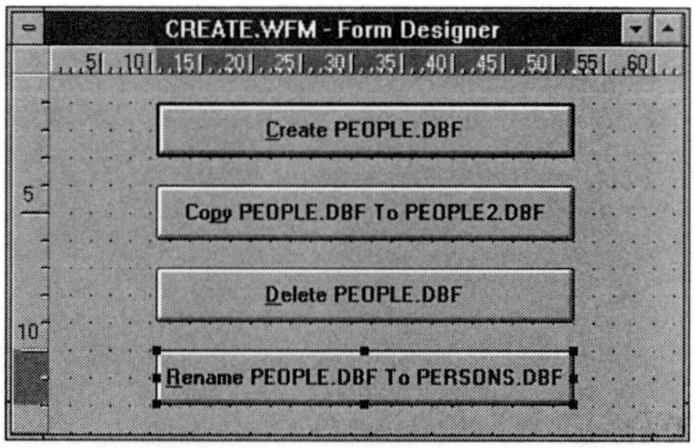

Figure 8.2.
The CREATE.WFM form in design mode (after customization).

To see your visual implementation in action, follow these steps:

- ☐ Execute the CREATE.WFM form by clicking the Run tool on the toolbar of dBASE (or by pressing F2 on the keyboard).

  dBASE responds by executing the CREATE.WFM form. (Refer to Figure 8.1.)

- ☐ Try clicking the pushbuttons of the form.

Of course, nothing happens when you click these buttons because you have not yet attached any code to the `OnClick` events of these buttons.

☐ Change the mode of the CREATE.WFM back to design mode by clicking the Design tool on the toolbar of dBASE (or by pressing Shift+F2 on the keyboard).

Entering the Code of the CREATE Program

In the following section you'll attach code to the CREATE program so that it will do what it's supposed to do.

Attaching Code to the *OnOpen* Event of the CREATE.WFM Form

As you know, the `OnOpen` event of a form occurs when the form is first opened. The `OnOpen` event of the form is therefore a good place to write initialization code for the form.

☐ Attach the following code to the `OnOpen` event of the CREATE.WFM form. After you write this code, the `Form_OnOpen` procedure should look as follows:

```
Procedure Form_OnOpen

 * Declare a public (global) variable to hold the name
 * of the directory where the program resides.
 PUBLIC gProgDir

 * Get the directory name where the program resides.
 gProgDir = LEFT(PROGRAM(0),RAT("\",PROGRAM(0)))

 * Set safety off.
 SET SAFETY OFF

Return
```

☐ Save your work by selecting Save from the File menu.

The first statement you typed in the `Form_OnOpen` procedure:

```
PUBLIC gProgDir
```

declares a public (global) variable called `gProgDir`.

The next statement:

```
gProgDir = LEFT(PROGRAM(0),RAT("\",PROGRAM(0)))
```

extracts the directory name from which the program is executed and stores this name in the global variable `gProgDir`. For example, if the CREATE.WFM program resides in the directory C:\DBPROG\CH08, the global variable `gProgDir` is filled with the string `"C:\DBPROG\CH08"`.

The next statement disables the safety feature of dBASE:

```
SET SAFETY OFF
```

This means that from now on, when the CREATE.WFM program is going to overwrite a file or delete a file, dBASE will not prompt the user with a confirmation message. You don't want dBASE to display confirmation messages to the user because you want your own code to control which messages (if any) to display to the user.

So the initialization code you attached to the `OnOpen` event of the CREATE.WFM form performs two tasks:

- It fills a global variable, called `gProgDir`, with the name of the directory from which the CREATE.WFM program is executed.
- It disables the safety feature of dBASE so that dBASE will not prompt the user with confirmation messages when the program is going to delete or overwrite files.

Attaching Code to the *OnClick* Event of the Create PEOPLE.DBF Pushbutton

When the user clicks the Create PEOPLE.DBF button, the CREATE.WFM program should create a table called PEOPLE.DBF.

This PEOPLE.DBF table will have the following specifications:

- The PEOPLE.DBF table will have three fields: FIRSTNAME, LASTNAME, and PHONE.
- The PEOPLE.DBF table will also have an index, called PHONE, that indexes the table on the PHONE field.

☐ Attach the following code to the `OnClick` event of the Create PEOPLE.DBF pushbutton. After you write this code, the `CREATEBUTTON_OnClick` procedure should look as follows:

```
Procedure CREATEBUTTON_OnClick

 * Create a structure table (called Struct.DBF).
 StructDB = gProgDir + "Struct.DBF"
 CREATE &StructDB STRUCTURE EXTENDED

 * The following statements fill the Struct.DBF
 * table with data that specifies the structure
 * of the PEOPLE.DBF table that we want to create.
```

```
    * Specify the characteristics of the first field
    * of PEOPLE.DBF.
    APPEND BLANK
    REPLACE Field_Name WITH "FIRSTNAME"
    REPLACE Field_Type WITH "C"
    REPLACE Field_Len  WITH 20
    REPLACE Field_Dec  WITH 0

    * Specify the characteristics of the second field
    * of PEOPLE.DBF.
    APPEND BLANK
    REPLACE Field_Name WITH "LASTNAME"
    REPLACE Field_Type WITH "C"
    REPLACE Field_Len  WITH 20
    REPLACE Field_Dec  WITH 0

    * Specify the characteristics of the third field
    * of PEOPLE.DBF.
    APPEND BLANK
    REPLACE Field_Name WITH "PHONE"
    REPLACE Field_Type WITH "C"
    REPLACE Field_Len  WITH 13
    REPLACE Field_Dec  WITH 0

    * Create the PEOPLE.DBF table as specified by Struct.DBF
    PeopleDB = gProgDir + "PEOPLE.DBF"
    CREATE &PeopleDB FROM &StructDB TYPE DBASE

    * Delete the StructDB.DBF table.
    DELETE TABLE &StructDB

    * Add an index to the PEOPLE.DBF table.
    INDEX ON PHONE TAG PHONE

    * Close all tables.
    CLOSE DATABASES

    * Display a message box.
    MsgBox("The table " + PeopleDB + " was created!","MESSAGE")

Return
```

☐ Save your work by selecting Save from the File menu.

The first two statements you typed in the `CREATEBUTTON_OnClick` procedure use the `CREATE STRUCTURE EXTENDED` statement to create a structure table:

```
StructDB = gProgDir + "Struct.DBF"
CREATE &StructDB STRUCTURE EXTENDED
```

These statements create a structure table called Struct.DBF.

What is a structure table? To create a table, you must first create a structure table. After creating the structure table, you fill the structure table with the specifications of the table you want to create. Finally, you tell dBASE to create a table as specified by the structure table.

Note: In the preceding code, you created a structure table using two statements:

```
StructDB = gProgDir + "Struct.DBF"
CREATE &StructDB STRUCTURE EXTENDED
```

The first statement fills the `StructDB` variable with the full pathname of the structure table you want to create:

```
StructDB = gProgDir + "Struct.DBF"
```

Recall that you filled the `gProgDir` variable (in the `Form_OnOpen` procedure) with the name of the directory where the program resides. If, for example, the CREATE.WFM program resides in the D:\DBPROG\CH08 directory, the preceding statement fills `StructDB` with the string `"D:\DBPROG\CH08\Struct.DBF"`.

The second statement actually creates the structure table:

```
CREATE &StructDB STRUCTURE EXTENDED
```

As you can see, this statement specifies the name of the structure table to be created by using the `StructDB` variable.

At this point, you have an empty structure table called Struct.DBF. The Struct.DBF table is currently open (because it was just created).

This is the next block of statements:

```
APPEND BLANK
REPLACE Field_Name WITH "FIRSTNAME"
REPLACE Field_Type WITH "C"
REPLACE Field_Len  WITH 20
REPLACE Field_Dec  WITH 0
```

These statements add a record to the Struct.DBF table and fill this record with the specifications of the first field of the PEOPLE.DBF table. As you can see, these statements specify that the name of the field will be FIRSTNAME, the field type will be C (Character type), and the field length will be 20. Note that `Field_Dec` specifies the number of decimal places for numeric fields. Because the FIRSTNAME field is of type Character, the value you assign to `Field_Dec` is not important.

This is the next block of statements:

```
APPEND BLANK
REPLACE Field_Name WITH "LASTNAME"
REPLACE Field_Type WITH "C"
REPLACE Field_Len  WITH 20
REPLACE Field_Dec  WITH 0
```

These statements add a new record to the Struct.DBF table and fill this record with the specifications of the second field of the PEOPLE.DBF table. As you can see, these statements specify that the name of the field will be LASTNAME, the field type will be C (Character type), and the field length will be 20.

This is the next block of statements:

```
APPEND BLANK
REPLACE Field_Name WITH "PHONE"
REPLACE Field_Type WITH "C"
REPLACE Field_Len  WITH 13
REPLACE Field_Dec  WITH 0
```

These statements add a new record to the Struct.DBF table and fill this record with the specifications of the third field of the PEOPLE.DBF table. As you can see, these statements specify that the name of the field will be PHONE, the field type will be C (Character type), and the field length will be 13.

At this point, the Struct.DBF table is filled with the specifications of the PEOPLE.DBF table you want to create.

These are the next two statements:

```
PeopleDB = gProgDir + "PEOPLE.DBF"
CREATE &PeopleDB FROM &StructDB TYPE DBASE
```

These statements use the `CREATE FROM` command to create the PEOPLE.DBF table as specified by the Struct.DBF table.

Note that the preceding statements create the PEOPLE.DBF table in the directory where the program resides (`gProgDir`). Recall that you updated the global variable `gProgDir` in the `Form_OnOpen` procedure.

This is the next statement:

```
DELETE TABLE &StructDB
```

This statement uses the `DELETE TABLE` command to delete the Struct.DBF table. You delete this table because you don't need it anymore.

The next statement uses the `INDEX ON` statement to add an index to the PEOPLE.DBF table:

```
* Add an index to the PEOPLE.DBF table.
INDEX ON PHONE TAG PHONE
```

This index indexes the table on the PHONE field (`ON PHONE`), and the name of the index is PHONE (`TAG PHONE`).

Note that the preceding statement adds an index to the PEOPLE.DBF table because currently the PEOPLE.DBF table is open. When you created the PEOPLE.DBF table with the `CREATE FROM` command, the PEOPLE.DBF table was automatically opened.

The next statement closes the PEOPLE.DBF table:

```
CLOSE DATABASES
```

Finally, this statement displays a message box informing the user that the PEOPLE.DBF table has been created:

```
MsgBox("The table "+PeopleDB+" was created!","MESSAGE")
```

Writing Code That Creates a Table

To write code that creates a table, you follow these steps:

1. Use the `CREATE STRUCTURE EXTENDED` statement to create a structure table.
2. Fill the structure table with data that specifies the structure of the table you want to create.
3. Use the `CREATE FROM` statement to create a table as specified by the structure table you filled.
4. If you want to add an index to the table you created, use the `INDEX ON` command. (If you want to add several indexes, use the `INDEX ON` command several times.)

To see in action the code you attached to the `OnClick` event of the Create PEOPLE.DBF button, follow these steps:

☐ Execute the CREATE.WFM form by clicking the Run tool on the toolbar of dBASE.

☐ Click the Create PEOPLE.DBF button.

The CREATE.WFM program responds by creating the PEOPLE.DBF table in the directory where the CREATE.WFM program resides (that is, in the C:\DBPROG\CH08 directory). When the program finishes creating the table, a message box is displayed. (See Figure 8.3.)

Figure 8.3.
The message box that the CREATE.WFM program displays after it creates the PEOPLE.DBF table.

☐ Close the message box by clicking its OK button.

☐ You can now verify that the PEOPLE.DBF table has been created by going to the File Manager (or DOS shell) and viewing the files in the C:\DBPROG\CH08 directory.

You will see that the C:\DBPROG\CH08 directory has two new files in it: PEOPLE.DBF and PEOPLE.MDX.

The file PEOPLE.MDX is the index file of the PEOPLE.DBF table. It was created because you added an index to the PEOPLE.DBF table.

☐ Change the mode of the CREATE.WFM form back to design mode by clicking the Design tool on the toolbar of dBASE.

Attaching Code to the *OnClick* Event of the Copy PEOPLE.DBF To PEOPLE2.DBF Pushbutton

You'll next attach code to the `OnClick` event of the Copy PEOPLE.DBF To PEOPLE2.DBF pushbutton. This code uses the `COPY TABLE` command to copy the source table (PEOPLE.DBF) into a new target table (PEOPLE2.DBF).

☐ Attach the following code to the `OnClick` event of the Copy PEOPLE.DBF To PEOPLE2.DBF pushbutton. After you write this code, the `COPYBUTTON_OnClick` procedure should look as follows:

```
Procedure COPYBUTTON_OnClick

 * Close all tables.
 CLOSE DATABASES

 * The name of the source table.
 SourceDB = gProgDir + "PEOPLE.DBF"

 * The name of the target table.
 TargetDB = gProgDir + "PEOPLE2.DBF"

 * If source table exists, copy source to target.
 IF FILE(SourceDB)
    COPY TABLE &SourceDB TO &TargetDB
    MsgBox(SourceDB+" was copied to "+TargetDB, "MESSAGE")
 ELSE
    MsgBox(SourceDB+" does not exist!", "MESSAGE")
 ENDIF

Return
```

☐ Save your work by selecting Save from the File menu.

The first statement you typed in the `COPYBUTTON_OnClick` procedure closes all the open tables (if there are any):

```
CLOSE DATABASES
```

This action ensures that the target table (PEOPLE2.DBF) is not open. (If the target table is open while you issue the `COPY TABLE` command, dBASE generates an error.)

The next statement fills the variable `SourceDB` with the full pathname of the source table (PEOPLE.DBF):

```
SourceDB = gProgDir + "PEOPLE.DBF"
```

The next statement fills the variable `TargetDB` with the full pathname of the target table (PEOPLE2.DBF):

```
TargetDB = gProgDir + "PEOPLE2.DBF"
```

Finally, an `IF...ELSE` statement is used:

```
IF FILE(SourceDB)
   COPY TABLE &SourceDB TO &TargetDB
   MsgBox(SourceDB+" was copied to "+TargetDB, "MESSAGE")
ELSE
  MsgBox(SourceDB+" does not exist!", "MESSAGE")
ENDIF
```

If the source file (PEOPLE.DBF) exists, the `IF` condition is satisfied:

```
IF FILE(SourceDB)
```

and the two statements under the `IF` are executed:

```
COPY TABLE &SourceDB TO &TargetDB
MsgBox(SourceDB+" was copied to "+TargetDB, "MESSAGE")
```

The first of these statements copies the source table (PEOPLE.DBF) into the target table (PEOPLE2.DBF):

```
COPY TABLE &SourceDB TO &TargetDB
```

The second statement under the `IF` displays a message box informing the user that the source table has been copied to the target table:

```
MsgBox(SourceDB+" was copied to "+TargetDB, "MESSAGE")
```

If the source file (PEOPLE.DBF) does not exist, the `IF` condition is not satisfied, and the statement under the `ELSE` is executed:

```
MsgBox(SourceDB+" does not exist!", "MESSAGE")
```

This statement displays a message box informing the user that the source table does not exist.

To see the code you attached to the `OnClick` event of the Copy PEOPLE.DBF To PEOPLE2.DBF button in action, follow these steps:

- ☐ Execute the CREATE.WFM form by clicking the Run tool on the toolbar of dBASE.
- ☐ Click the Copy PEOPLE.DBF To PEOPLE2.DBF button.

The CREATE.WFM program responds by copying the PEOPLE.DBF table to the PEOPLE2.DBF table. When the program finishes copying the table, a message box is displayed. (See Figure 8.4.)

Figure 8.4.
The message box that the CREATE.WFM program displays after it copies the PEOPLE.DBF table to the PEOPLE2.DBF table.

- ☐ Close the message box by clicking its OK button.
- ☐ You can now verify that the PEOPLE2.DBF table has been created by running the File Manager (or DOS shell) and viewing the files in the C:\DBPROG\CH08 directory.

You will see that the C:\DBPROG\CH08 directory has two new files in it: PEOPLE2.DBF and PEOPLE2.MDX.

The file PEOPLE2.MDX is the index file of the PEOPLE2.DBF table. It was created because the source table (PEOPLE.DBF) also had an index file (PEOPLE.MDX). That is, the `COPY TABLE` command copies the DBF file and the index file that is associated with the DBF file.

- ☐ Change the mode of the CREATE.WFM form back to design mode by clicking the Design tool on the toolbar of dBASE.

Attaching Code to the *OnClick* Event of the Delete PEOPLE.DBF Pushbutton

You'll next attach code to the `OnClick` event of the Delete PEOPLE.DBF pushbutton. This code deletes the PEOPLE.DBF table.

- ☐ Attach the following code to the `OnClick` event of the Delete PEOPLE.DBF pushbutton. After you write this code, the `DELETEBUTTON_OnClick` procedure should look as follows:

```
Procedure DELETEBUTTON_OnClick

 * Close all tables.
 CLOSE DATABASES

 * The full pathname of the file to be deleted.
 FileName = gProgDir + "PEOPLE.DBF"

 * If the file to be deleted exists, delete it.
 IF FILE(FileName)
    DELETE TABLE &FileName
    MsgBox(FileName+" was deleted!", "MESSAGE")
```

```
    ELSE
       MsgBox(FileName+" does not exist!", "MESSAGE")
    ENDIF

 Return
```

- Save your work by selecting Save from the File menu.

The first statement you typed in the `DELETEBUTTON_OnClick` procedure closes all the open tables (if there are any):

```
CLOSE DATABASES
```

This action is necessary because dBASE generates an error if you attempt to delete an open table.

The next statement fills the variable `FileName` with the full pathname of the table to be deleted (PEOPLE.DBF):

```
FileName = gProgDir + "PEOPLE.DBF"
```

Then, an `IF...ELSE` statement is used:

```
IF FILE(FileName)
   DELETE TABLE &FileName
   MsgBox(FileName+" was deleted!", "MESSAGE")
ELSE
   MsgBox(FileName+" does not exist!", "MESSAGE")
ENDIF
```

If the file to be deleted (PEOPLE.DBF) exists, the `IF` condition is satisfied:

```
IF FILE(FileName)
```

and the two statements under the `IF` are executed:

```
DELETE TABLE &FileName
MsgBox(FileName+" was deleted!", "MESSAGE")
```

The first of these statements deletes the PEOPLE.DBF table:

```
DELETE TABLE &FileName
```

The second statement under the `IF` displays a message box informing the user that the PEOPLE.DBF table has been deleted:

```
MsgBox(FileName+" was deleted!", "MESSAGE")
```

If the PEOPLE.DBF table does not exist, the `IF` condition is not satisfied, and the statement under the `ELSE` is executed:

```
MsgBox(FileName+" does not exist!", "MESSAGE")
```

This statement displays a message box informing the user that the PEOPLE.DBF table does not exist.

To see in action the code you attached to the `OnClick` event of the Delete PEOPLE.DBF button, follow these steps:

- ☐ Execute the CREATE.WFM form by clicking the Run tool on the toolbar of dBASE.
- ☐ Click the Delete PEOPLE.DBF button.

  The CREATE.WFM program responds by deleting the PEOPLE.DBF table. When the program finishes deleting the table, a message box is displayed. (See Figure 8.5.)

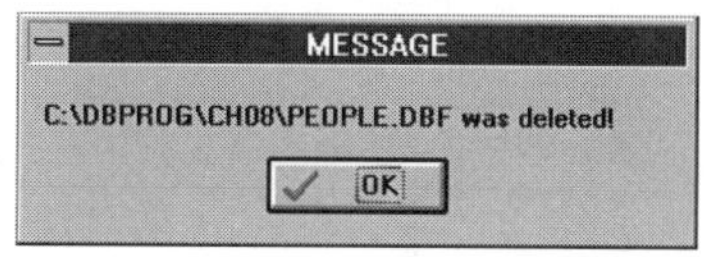

Figure 8.5.
The message box that the CREATE.WFM program displays after it deletes the PEOPLE.DBF table.

- ☐ Close the message box by clicking its OK button.
- ☐ You can now verify that the PEOPLE.DBF table has been deleted by going to the File Manager (or DOS shell) and viewing the files in the C:\DBPROG\CH08 directory.

You will see that the C:\DBPROG\CH08 directory does not have the PEOPLE.DBF and PEOPLE.MDX files.

- ☐ Change the mode of the CREATE.WFM form back to design mode by clicking the Design tool on the toolbar of dBASE.

Attaching Code to the *OnClick* Event of the Rename PEOPLE.DBF To PEOPLE2.DBF Pushbutton

You'll now attach code to the `OnClick` event of the Rename PEOPLE.DBF To PERSONS.DBF pushbutton. This code uses the `RENAME TABLE` command to rename the source table (PEOPLE.DBF) into a new target table (PERSONS.DBF).

- ☐ Attach the following code to the `OnClick` event of the Rename PEOPLE.DBF To PERSONS.DBF pushbutton. After you write this code, the `RENAMEBUTTON_OnClick` procedure should look as follows:

```
Procedure RENAMEBUTTON_OnClick

 * Close all tables.
 CLOSE DATABASES

 * The name of the source table.
 SourceDB = gProgDir + "PEOPLE.DBF"
```

```
* The name of the target table.
TargetDB = gProgDir + "PERSONS.DBF"

* If source table does not exist, terminate this procedure.
IF .NOT. FILE(SourceDB)
   MsgBox(SourceDB+" does not exist!", "MESSAGE")
   RETURN
ENDIF

* If target table exists, delete it.
IF FILE(TargetDB)
   DELETE TABLE &TargetDB
ENDIF

* Rename the source to the target.
RENAME TABLE &SourceDB TO &TargetDB

* Inform the user that the table was renamed.
MsgBox(SourceDB+" was renamed to "+TargetDB, "MESSAGE")

Return
```

☐ Save your work by selecting Save from the File menu.

The first statement you typed in the `RENAMEBUTTON_OnClick` procedure closes all the open tables (if there are any):

```
CLOSE DATABASES
```

The next statement fills the variable `SourceDB` with the full pathname of the source table (PEOPLE.DBF):

```
SourceDB = gProgDir + "PEOPLE.DBF"
```

The next statement fills the variable `TargetDB` with the full pathname of the target table (PERSONS.DBF):

```
TargetDB = gProgDir + "PERSONS.DBF"
```

The next statement is an `IF` statement:

```
* If source table does not exist, terminate this procedure.
 IF .NOT. FILE(SourceDB)
    MsgBox(SourceDB+" does not exist!", "MESSAGE")
    RETURN
 ENDIF
```

This `IF` statement determines whether the source table exists. If the source table does not exist, the two statements under the `IF` are executed:

```
MsgBox(SourceDB+" does not exist!", "MESSAGE")
RETURN
```

These statements display a message box and terminate the procedure.

The next statement is another `IF` statement:

```
IF FILE(TargetDB)
   DELETE TABLE &TargetDB
ENDIF
```

This `IF` statement checks whether the target table exists. If it exists, the statement under the `IF` deletes the target table. It is necessary to delete the target table before issuing the `RENAME TABLE` command because dBASE generates an error if you try to rename a table to a target filename of a file that exists.

This is the next statement:

```
RENAME TABLE &SourceDB TO &TargetDB
```

This statement uses the `RENAME TABLE` command to rename the source table into the target table.

Finally, a message box is displayed, informing the user that the table has been renamed:

```
MsgBox(SourceDB+" was renamed to "+TargetDB, "MESSAGE")
```

To see in action the code you attached to the `OnClick` event of the Rename PEOPLE.DBF To PERSONS.DBF button, follow these steps:

- ☐ Execute the CREATE.WFM form by clicking the Run tool on the toolbar of dBASE.
- ☐ Click the Create PEOPLE.DBF button.

  The CREATE.WFM program responds by creating the PEOPLE.DBF table. When the program finishes creating the table, a message box is displayed. (Refer to Figure 8.3.)

- ☐ Close the message box by clicking its OK button.
- ☐ Click the Rename PEOPLE.DBF To PERSONS.DBF button.

  The CREATE.WFM program responds by renaming PEOPLE.DBF to PERSONS.DBF. When the program finishes renaming the table, a message box is displayed. (See Figure 8.6.)

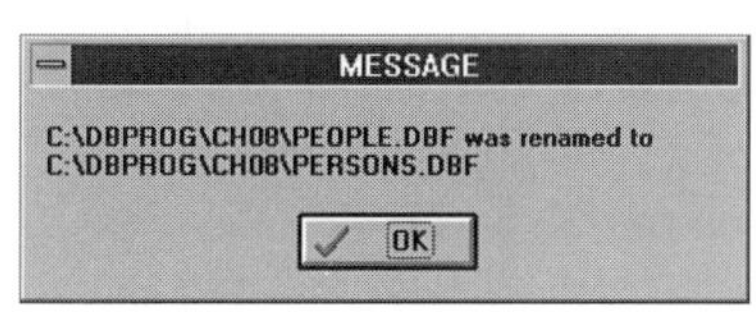

Figure 8.6.
The message box that the CREATE.WFM program displays after it finishes renaming the PEOPLE.DBF table.

- ☐ Close the message box by clicking its OK button.
- ☐ You can now verify that the PEOPLE.DBF table has been renamed to PERSONS.DBF by going to the File Manager (or DOS shell) and viewing the files in the C:\DBPROG\CH08 directory.

You will see that the C:\DBPROG\CH08 directory has two new files in it: PERSONS.DBF and PERSONS.MDX. You will also see that the files PEOPLE.DBF and PEOPLE.MDX do not exist.

Summary

In this chapter you have written a dBASE program that creates a table. You have learned the following:

- How to write code that creates a table
- How to write code that copies a table
- How to write code that deletes a table
- How to write code that renames a table

Q&A

Q Why is it important to know how to write code that creates a table?

A Knowing how to write code that creates a table is important because in many cases you will want to write a dBASE program that uses a table that might not exist yet. When the user runs the program, your code detects whether the table exists, and if the table does not exist, your program creates the table.

Quiz

1. What does the statement `SET SAFETY OFF` do?
2. Describe what the following code does:

```
StructDB = "C:\TRY\Struct.DBF"
CREATE &StructDB STRUCTURE EXTENDED

APPEND BLANK
REPLACE Field_Name WITH "FIRSTNAME"
REPLACE Field_Type WITH "C"
REPLACE Field_Len  WITH 20
REPLACE Field_Dec  WITH 0

APPEND BLANK
REPLACE Field_Name WITH "LASTNAME"
REPLACE Field_Type WITH "C"
REPLACE Field_Len  WITH 20
REPLACE Field_Dec  WITH 0

MyTableDB = "C:\TRY\MyTable.DBF"
CREATE &MyTable FROM &StructDB TYPE DBASE
```

3. What does the following code do?

```
SourceDB = "C:\TRY\MyTable1.DBF"
TargetDB = "C:\TRY\MyTable2.DBF"
IF FILE(SourceDB)
   COPY TABLE &SourceDB TO &TargetDB
ENDIF
```

4. What does the following code do?

```
FileName = "C:\TRY\MyTable.DBF"
IF FILE(FileName)
   DELETE TABLE &FileName
   MsgBox(FileName+" was deleted!", "MESSAGE")
ENDIF
```

Exercise

Enhance the CREATE.WFM program as detailed here:

- Add another pushbutton control to the CREATE.WFM form, and set its properties as shown here:

Property	*Setting*
Name	StatesButton
Text	Create STATES.DBF

- Attach code to the `OnClick` event of the Create STATES.DBF button so that when the user clicks this button, the program will create a table called STATES.DBF. The table should be created in the directory where the CREATE.WFM program resides.
- The structure of the STATES.DBF table should be as shown here:

Field Name	*Type*	*Width*	*Decimal*
STATE	Character	2	0
POPULATION	Numeric	9	0

Quiz Answers

1. The statement `SET SAFETY OFF` disables the safety feature of dBASE. After this statement has been executed, dBASE will not prompt the user with a confirmation message before executing commands that overwrite or delete a file. Typically, when you write a program, you don't want dBASE to display confirmation messages to the user because you want your own code to control which messages (if any) to display to the user.
2. This code creates a table called MyTable.DBF in the directory C:\TRY. The MyTable.DBF table is created with two fields: FIRSTNAME and LASTNAME. Here is the same code with comments that explain it:

```
* Create a structure table (called Struct.DBF).
StructDB = "C:\TRY\Struct.DBF"
CREATE &StructDB STRUCTURE EXTENDED

* Specify the characteristics of the first field
* of MyTable.DBF.
APPEND BLANK
REPLACE Field_Name WITH "FIRSTNAME"
REPLACE Field_Type WITH "C"
REPLACE Field_Len  WITH 20
REPLACE Field_Dec  WITH 0

* Specify the characteristics of the second field
* of MyTable.DBF.
APPEND BLANK
REPLACE Field_Name WITH "LASTNAME"
REPLACE Field_Type WITH "C"
REPLACE Field_Len  WITH 20
REPLACE Field_Dec  WITH 0

* Create the MyTable.DBF table as specified by Struct.DBF
MyTableDB = "C:\TRY\MyTable.DBF"
CREATE &MyTable FROM &StructDB TYPE DBASE
```

3. The code

```
SourceDB = "C:\TRY\MyTable1.DBF"
TargetDB = "C:\TRY\MyTable2.DBF"
IF FILE(SourceDB)
   COPY TABLE &SourceDB TO &TargetDB
ENDIF
```

copies the source table C:\TRY\MyTable1.DBF into the target table C:\TRY\MyTable2.DBF. The copying is performed only if the source table exists.

4. The code

```
FileName = "C:\TRY\MyTable.DBF"
IF FILE(FileName)
   DELETE TABLE &FileName
   MsgBox(FileName+" was deleted!", "MESSAGE")
ENDIF
```

deletes the table C:\TRY\MyTable.DBF. The deletion is performed only if the C:\TRY\MyTable.DBF table exists.

Exercise Answer

The following code creates the STATES.DBF table:

```
Procedure STATESBUTTON_OnClick

 * Create a structure table (called Struct.DBF).
 StructDB = gProgDir + "Struct.DBF"
 CREATE &StructDB STRUCTURE EXTENDED
```

```
* The following statements fill the Struct.DBF
* table with data that specifies the structure
* of the STATES.DBF table that we want to create.

* Specify the characteristics of the first field
* of STATES.DBF.
APPEND BLANK
REPLACE Field_Name WITH "STATE"
REPLACE Field_Type WITH "C"
REPLACE Field_Len  WITH 2
REPLACE Field_Dec  WITH 0

* Specify the characteristics of the second field
* of STATES.DBF.
APPEND BLANK
REPLACE Field_Name WITH "POPULATION"
REPLACE Field_Type WITH "N"
REPLACE Field_Len  WITH 9
REPLACE Field_Dec  WITH 0

* Create the STATES.DBF table as specified by Struct.DBF
StatesDB = gProgDir + "STATES.DBF"
CREATE &StatesDB FROM &StructDB TYPE DBASE

* Delete the StructDB.DBF table.
DELETE TABLE &StructDB

* Close all tables.
CLOSE DATABASES

* Display a message box.
MsgBox("The table "+StatesDB+" was created!","MESSAGE")

Return
```

9

WEEK 2

The Mouse

Many Windows programs make heavy use of the mouse device. In this chapter you'll learn how to detect and use various mouse events.

The DRAW Program

In the following sections you will write a dBASE program called DRAW that illustrates how to attach code to mouse events.

Before you start writing the DRAW program, you need to know how the program should look and what it should do.

When you run the DRAW program, the main window of the DRAW program should look like the one shown in Figure 9.1.

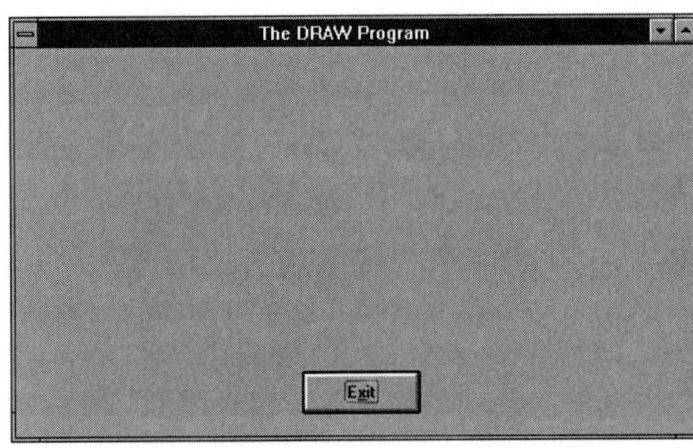

Figure 9.1.
The main window of the DRAW program.

The main window of the DRAW program contains one control: an Exit pushbutton.

The DRAW program enables the user to use the mouse for drawing lines. When the user presses the left button of the mouse and moves the mouse, the DRAW program draws lines in accordance with the mouse movements. Figure 9.2 shows an example of a drawing performed with the DRAW program.

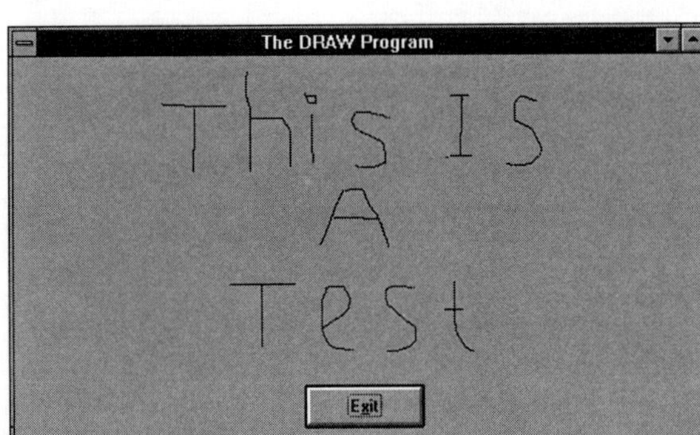

Figure 9.2.
An example of a drawing performed with the DRAW program.

When the user clicks the Exit pushbutton, the DRAW program terminates itself.

Now that you know what the DRAW program is supposed to do, it's time to start writing it.

The Visual Implementation of the DRAW Program

Create the DRAW.WFM form as explained here:

☐ Type `MD C:\DBPROG` in the Command window, and then press Enter.

dBASE responds by creating the directory C:\DBPROG. (If this directory already exists, dBASE displays a message box telling you that the directory cannot be created.)

☐ Type `MD C:\DBPROG\CH09` in the Command window, and then press Enter.

dBASE responds by creating the directory C:\DBPROG\CH09.

☐ Type `CREATE FORM C:\DBPROG\CH09\DRAW` in the Command window and press Enter.

dBASE responds by creating the DRAW.WFM form and displaying it in design mode.

☐ Customize the DRAW.WFM form according to the specifications in Table 9.1. When you finish customizing the form, it should look like the one shown in Figure 9.3.

Table 9.1. The properties table of the DRAW.WFM form.

Object	Property	Setting
Form	**Text**	**The DRAW Program**
	Height	18
	Left	1.00
	Top	0.00
	Width	86.00
PushButton	**Name**	**ExitButton**
	Text	E&xit
	Height	2
	Left	36
	Top	15
	Width	15

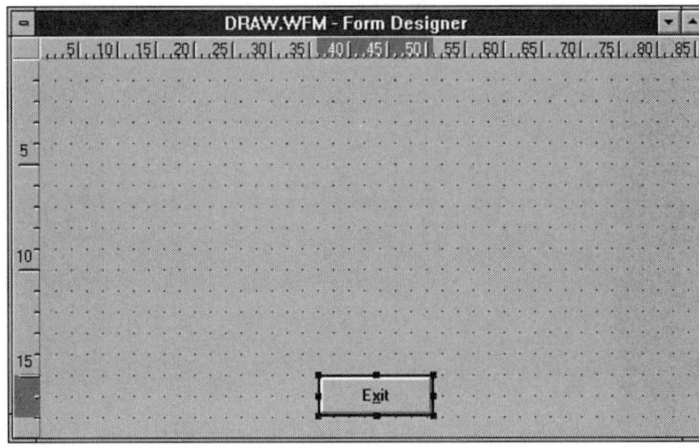

Figure 9.3.
The DRAW.WFM form in design mode (after customization).

☐ Save your work by selecting Save from the File menu.

The visual implementation of the DRAW.WFM form is complete.

Entering the Code of the DRAW Program

In the following sections you'll enter the code of the DRAW program.

Attaching Code to the *OnClick* Event of the Exit Pushbutton

When the user clicks the Exit button, the DRAW program should terminate itself. You'll now write the code that accomplishes this task.

☐ Attach the following code to the `OnClick` event of the Exit pushbutton. After you write this code, the `EXITBUTTON_OnClick` procedure should look as follows:

```
Procedure EXITBUTTON_OnClick

 form.close()

Return
```

☐ Save your work by selecting Save from the File menu.

The statement you typed in the `EXITBUTTON_OnClick` procedure terminates the program by closing the form:

```
form.Close()
```

To see in action the code you attached to the `OnClick` event of the Exit button, follow these steps:

- [ ] Press F2 on your keyboard.

  dBASE responds by running the DRAW.WFM form.

- [ ] Click the Exit button.

  The DRAW program responds by terminating itself.

9

Attaching Code to the *OnOpen* Event of the DRAW.WFM Form

As you know, the `OnOpen` event of a form occurs when the form is first opened. The `OnOpen` event of the form is therefore a good place to write initialization code for the form.

- [ ] Type `MODIFY FORM ?` in the Command window, press Enter, and then select the file C:\DBPROG\CH09\DRAW.WFM from the Open Form dialog box that dBASE displays.

  dBASE responds by displaying the DRAW.WFM form in design mode.

- [ ] Attach the following code to the `OnOpen` event of the DRAW.WFM form. After you write this code, the `Form_OnOpen` procedure should look as follows:

```
Procedure Form_OnOpen

* Declare gX and gY as public variables.
PUBLIC gX, gY

* Initialize gX and gY
gX = 0
gY = 0

Return
```

- [ ] Save your work by selecting Save from the File menu.

The first statement you typed in the `Form_OnOpen` procedure, declares two public (global) variables called `gX` and `gY`:

```
PUBLIC gX, gY
```

As you'll see later, the DRAW program uses these variables to store the X and Y coordinates of the current location of the mouse.

The next two statements initialize the `gX` and `gY` global variables to 0:

```
gX = 0
gY = 0
```

Note: The DRAW program uses two global (public) variables called `gX` and `gY`. Because these variables are declared as public, they will be visible in all the procedures of the form.

An alternate way to make variables visible in all the procedures of the form is to make these variables custom form properties.

To make `gX` and `gY` custom form properties, all you have to do is to change the code of the `OnOpen` procedure so that it looks as follows:

```
Procedure Form_OnOpen

* Initialize form.gX and forn.gY
form.gX = 0
form.gY = 0

Return
```

From now on, all the procedures of the form can refer to these variables as `form.gX` and `form.gY`.

Attaching Code to the *OnLeftMouseDown* Event of the DRAW.WFM Form

As implied by its name, the `OnLeftMouseDown` event of the form occurs when the user presses the left button of the mouse over the form.

- ☐ Attach the following code to the `OnLeftMouseDown` event of the DRAW.WFM form. After you write this code, the `Form_OnLeftMouseDown` procedure should look as follows:

```
Procedure Form_OnLeftMouseDown(flags, col, row)

* Update gX and gY with the current position of the mouse.
gX = col
gY = row

Return
```

- ☐ Save your work by selecting Save from the File menu.

As you can see, the `Form_OnLeftMouseDown` procedure has three parameters: `flags`, `col`, and `row`. The `col` parameter specifies the X coordinate of the mouse at the moment the user pressed the left mouse button. The `row` parameter specifies the Y coordinate of the mouse at the moment the user pressed the left mouse button. The `flags` parameter specifies which (if any) key was pressed with the left mouse button. The details of the `flags` parameter will be discussed later in this chapter.

The statements you typed in the `Form_OnLeftMouseDown` procedure update the `gX` and `gY` global variables with the current position of the mouse:

```
gX = col
gY = row
```

Therefore, when the user presses the left mouse button, the `gX` and `gY` variables are updated with the X and Y coordinates of the current position of the mouse.

9

Attaching Code to the *OnMouseMove* Event of the DRAW.WFM Form

As implied by its name, the `OnMouseMove` event of the form occurs when the user moves the mouse over the form.

- ☐ Attach the following code to the `OnMouseMove` event of the DRAW.WFM form. After you write this code, the `Form_OnMouseMove` procedure should look as follows:

```
Procedure Form_OnMouseMove(flags, col, row)

* If the left button of the mouse is down, draw a line.
IF BITSET(flags,0)=.T.

   * Draw a line from the previous position of the mouse
   * to the new position of the mouse.
   Ln=NEW LINE(form)
   Ln.Left=gX
   Ln.Top=gY
   Ln.Bottom=row
   Ln.Right=col

   * Update gX and gY with the new position of the mouse.
   gX=col
   gY=row

ENDIF

Return
```

- ☐ Save your work by selecting Save from the File menu.

As you can see, the `Form_OnMouseMove` procedure has the same three parameters as the `Form_OnLeftMouseDown` procedure: `flags`, `col`, and `row`. The `col` parameter specifies the current X coordinate of the mouse, and the `row` parameter specifies the current Y coordinate of the mouse.

You can use the `flags` parameter to determine whether any of the mouse buttons is currently pressed. Depending on which mouse button is currently pressed, a different bit in the `flags` parameter will be set. To determine which bit is set in the `flags` parameter, you can use the `BITSET()` function.

For example, if the left mouse button is currently pressed, bit number 0 of `flags` will be set, and the expression `BITSET(flags,0)` will return .T.. (The details of the `flags` parameter are discussed later in this chapter.)

The code you typed in the `Form_OnMouseMove` procedure is composed of an `IF` statement:

```
IF BITSET(flags,0)=.T.

   * Draw a line from the previous position of the mouse
   * to the new position of the mouse.
   Ln=NEW LINE(form)
   Ln.Left=gX
   Ln.Top=gY
   Ln.Bottom=row
   Ln.Right=col

   * Update gX and gY with the new position of the mouse.
   gX=col
   gY=row

ENDIF
```

The condition of this `IF` statement is satisfied only if the left mouse button is currently pressed (that is, the user moved the mouse while holding the left mouse button down).

The first five statements under the `IF` draw a line from the previous position of the mouse to the current position of the mouse:

```
Ln=NEW LINE(form)
Ln.Left=gX
Ln.Top=gY
Ln.Bottom=row
Ln.Right=col
```

The statement

```
Ln=NEW LINE(this)
```

creates a new line object in the form and names this new line object `Ln`. This statement has the same effect as placing a Line control in the form (by double-clicking the Line control in the Control Palette window) and setting the Name property of the new line control to `Ln`.

After the preceding statement is executed, the form has a new line object in it, and the name of this line object is `Ln`.

These are the next four statements:

```
Ln.Left=gX
Ln.Top=gY
Ln.Bottom=row
Ln.Right=col
```

These statements set the Left, Top, Bottom, and Right properties of the `Ln` line so that the line would be drawn from the previous position of the mouse (`X=gX`, `Y=gY`) to the new position of the mouse (`X=col`, `Y=row`). That is, the line is drawn from the point where the mouse was before the user moved it to the point where the user moved the mouse.

These are the last two statements under the `IF`:

```
gX=col
gY=row
```

These statements update `gX` and `gY` with the new position of the mouse. This is done so that the next time the user moves the mouse, a line will be drawn from the current position of the mouse.

To see in action the code you attached to the `OnLeftMouseDown` and `OnMouseMove` events of the DRAW.WFM form, follow these steps:

☐ Press F2 on your keyboard.

dBASE responds by running the DRAW.WFM form.

☐ Hold the left button of the mouse down, and move the mouse.

As you can see, the DRAW program draws in accordance with the way you move the mouse. That is, for every slight movement of the mouse, an `OnMouseMove` event occurs, and the code that you attached to the `OnMouseMove` event draws a line from the previous location of the mouse to the new location of the mouse.

☐ Terminate the DRAW program by clicking its Exit button.

The *flags* Parameter of the Mouse Event Procedures

In the `Form_OnMouseMove()` procedure, you used the `flags` parameter to determine whether the left mouse button is down:

```
* Is the left mouse button down?
IF BITSET(flags,0)=.T.
   .............
   .............
   .............
ENDIF
```

That is, if `BITSET(flags,0)` returns .T., the left mouse button is currently down.

To determine whether the right mouse button is currently down, use `BITSET(flags,1)`:

```
* Is the right mouse button down?
IF BITSET(flags,1)=.T.
   .............
   .............
   .............
ENDIF
```

That is, if `BITSET(flags,1)` returns .T., the right mouse button is currently down.

To determine whether the Shift key of the keyboard is currently pressed, use `BITSET(flags,2)`:

```
* Is the Shift key pressed?
IF BITSET(flags,2)=.T.
   .............
   .............
   .............
ENDIF
```

That is, if `BITSET(flags,2)` returns .T., the Shift key is currently pressed.

To determine whether the Ctrl key of the keyboard is currently pressed, use `BITSET(flags,3)`:

```
* Is the Ctrl key pressed?
IF BITSET(flags,3)=.T.
   .............
   .............
   .............
ENDIF
```

That is, if `BITSET(flags,3)` returns .T., the Ctrl key is currently pressed.

To determine whether the middle mouse button is currently down, use `BITSET(flags,4)`:

```
* Is the middle mouse button down?
IF BITSET(flags,4)=.T.
   .............
   .............
   .............
ENDIF
```

That is, if `BITSET(flags,4)` returns .T., the middle mouse button is currently down.

To determine whether a combination of two keys is currently pressed, you must use two `BITSET()` expressions. For example, to determine whether both the left mouse button and the Ctrl key are currently pressed, use the following `IF` statement:

```
* Are the left mouse button and Ctrl key both down?
IF BITSET(flags,0)=.T. .AND. BITSET(flags,3)=.T.
   .............
   .............
   .............
ENDIF
```

That is, if both `BITSET(flags,0)` and `BITSET(flags,3)` return .T., both the left mouse button and the Ctrl key are currently down.

Other Mouse Events

In the DRAW.WFM program, you attached code to the `OnLeftMouseDown` and `OnMouseMove` events of the form. A form has eight additional mouse events: `OnLeftDblClick`, `OnLeftMouseUp`, `OnMiddleDblClick`, `OnMiddleMouseDown`, `OnMiddleMouseUp`, `OnRightDblClick`, `OnRightMouseDown`, and `OnRightMouseUp`.

The name of each of these events describes when the event occurs. For example, the `OnLeftDblClick` event of a form occurs when the user double-clicks the left mouse button while the mouse is over the form.

Note: Just as a form has mouse events, so do other controls. For example, when the user moves the mouse over a pushbutton control, the `OnMouseMove` event of the pushbutton control occurs.

Summary

In this chapter you have learned about mouse events. As you have seen, the parameters of the mouse event procedures provide you with information regarding the state of the mouse at the time of the event. The `col` and `row` parameters tell you the location of the mouse at the time of the event, and the `flags` parameter tells you the state of the Shift and Ctrl keys and the state of the mouse buttons.

Q&A

Q While I was experimenting with the DRAW program, I noticed that when I draw over the Exit pushbutton, the DRAW program does not draw. How come?

A You attached the code that is responsible for the drawing to the `OnMouseMove` event of the form. This event occurs only when the mouse is moved over a free area of the form. When the mouse is moved over a control that is in the form (for example, over a pushbutton or an entry field), the `OnMouseMove` event of the form does not occur. (When you move the mouse over a control, the `OnMouseMove` event of the control occurs.)

Quiz

1. When does the `OnMouseMove` event of a form occur?
2. When does the `OnMouseMove` event of a browse control occur?

3. What do the `row` and `col` parameters of the `Form_OnMouseMove` procedure report?
4. What does the `flags` parameter of the `Form_OnMouseMove` procedure report?

Exercise

Currently, the user of the DRAW program draws by using the left button of the mouse. Enhance the DRAW program so that the user can draw by using either the left mouse button or the right mouse button.

Quiz Answers

1. The `OnMouseMove` event of a form occurs when the user moves the mouse over a free area of the form.
2. The `OnMouseMove` event of a browse control occurs when the user moves the mouse over the browse control.
3. The `row` and `col` parameters of the `Form_OnMouseMove` procedure report the current X,Y coordinate of the mouse position.
4. The `flags` parameter reports the current state of the Shift and Ctrl keyboard keys and the current state of the mouse buttons.

Exercise Answer

To enable the user to draw by using either the left mouse button or the right mouse button, you must change the `IF` statement in the `Form_OnMouseMove()` procedure from

```
IF BITSET(flags,0)=.T.
```

to

```
IF BITSET(flags,0)=.T. .OR. BITSET(flags,1)=.T.
```

After you make this change, the `Form_OnMouseMove()` procedure should look as follows:

```
Procedure Form_OnMouseMove(flags, col, row)

* If the left button of the mouse is down or the
* right mouse button is down, draw a line.
IF BITSET(flags,0)=.T. .OR. BITSET(flags,1)=.T.

   * Draw a line from the previous position of the mouse
   * to the new position of the mouse.
   Ln=NEW LINE(form)
   Ln.Left=gX
   Ln.Top=gY
   Ln.Bottom=row
   Ln.Right=col
```

```
   * Update gX and gY with the new position of the mouse.
   gX=col
   gY=row

ENDIF

Return
```

In the preceding code, the `IF` condition

```
IF BITSET(flags,0)=.T. .OR. BITSET(flags,1)=.T.
```

will be satisfied if the left mouse button is currently down *or* the right mouse button is currently down. `BITSET(flags,0)` returns .T. when the left mouse button is down, and `BITSET(flags,1)` returns .T. when the right mouse button is down.

You also must attach to the `OnRightMouseDown` event of the form the same code you attached to the `OnLeftMouseDown` event of the form. That is, the `Form_OnRightMouseDown` procedure should look as follows:

```
Procedure Form_OnRightMouseDown(flags, col, row)

* Update gX and gY with the current position of the mouse.
gX = col
gY = row

Return
```

WEEK 2

10

Accessing Text Files

In this chapter you'll learn how to access files from within your dBASE programs. In particular, you'll learn how to read the contents of text files and you'll learn how to use the Editor control of dBASE.

The Read Text Program

In the following sections you'll design and implement the Read Text program. As implied by its name, the Read Text program reads the contents of text files.

Before you implement the Read Text program by yourself, here's a review of its specifications:

- When you execute the Read Text program, the window shown in Figure 10.1 appears.

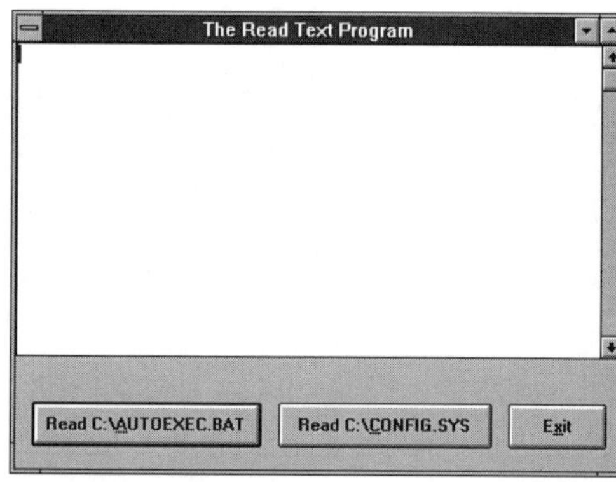

Figure 10.1.
The window of the Read Text program.

- The user can click the Read C:\AUTOEXEC.BAT button to display the contents of the AUTOEXEC.BAT file. (See Figure 10.2.) The user also can click the Read C:\CONFIG.SYS button to display the contents of the CONFIG.SYS file. (See Figure 10.3.)

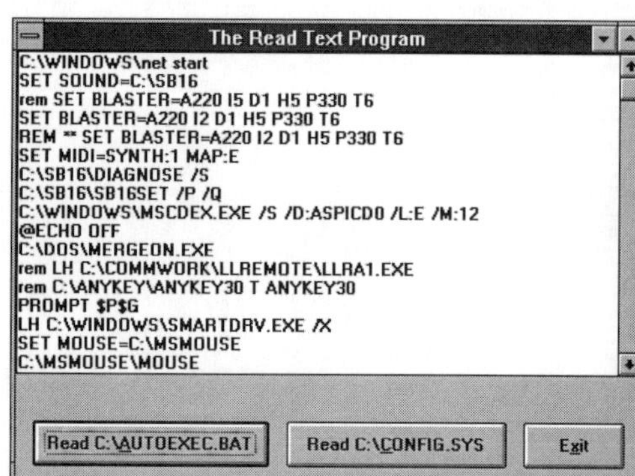

Figure 10.2.
Reading and displaying the contents of the AUTOEXEC.BAT file.

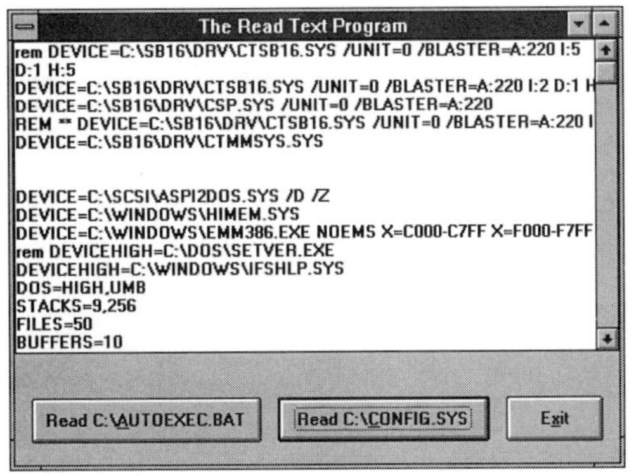

Figure 10.3.
Reading and displaying the contents of the CONFIG.SYS file.

Now that you know what the Read Text program should do, it's time to implement it.

The Visual Implementation of the Read Text Program

You'll now visually implement the Read Text program.

☐ Create the C:\DBPROG\CH10 directory.

☐ In the Command window, type `Create Form C:\DBPROG\CH10\ReadText`, and then press Enter.

☐ Implement the form of the Read Text program according to the specifications in Table 10.1. When you finish implementing the form, it should look like the one shown in Figure 10.4.

> **Note:** Table 10.1 instructs you to place an Editor control in the form. The icon of the Editor control in the Control Palette of dBASE is shown in Figure 10.5.

Table 10.1. The properties table of the Read Text form.

Object	Property	Setting
Form	**Text**	**The Read Text Program**
	Height	19
	Width	74
	Left	13
	MDI	.F.
	Top	1
Editor	**Name**	**Editor1**
	Height	14
	Width	74
	Left	0
	Top	0
	Modify	.F.
	Value	(make it empty)
PushButton	**Name**	**AutoexecButton**
	Height	2
	Width	28
	Text	Read C:\&AUTOEXEC.BAT
	Left	2
	Top	16
PushButton	**Name**	**ConfigButton**
	Height	2
	Width	26
	Text	Read C:\&CONFIG.SYS
	Left	32
	Top	16
PushButton	**Name**	**ExitButton**
	Height	2
	Width	12
	Text	E&xit
	Left	60
	Top	16

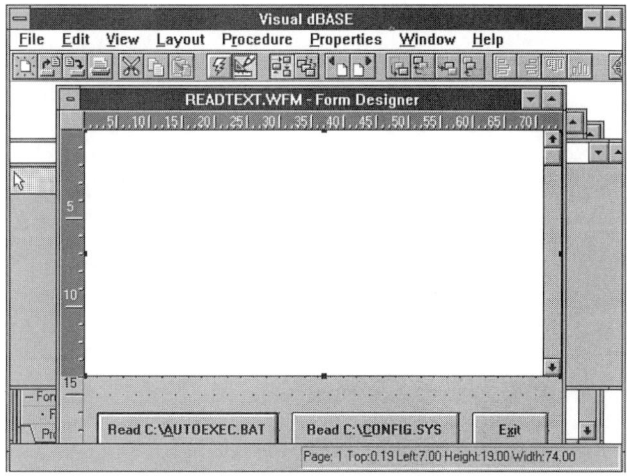

Figure 10.4.
The form of the Read Text program (in design mode).

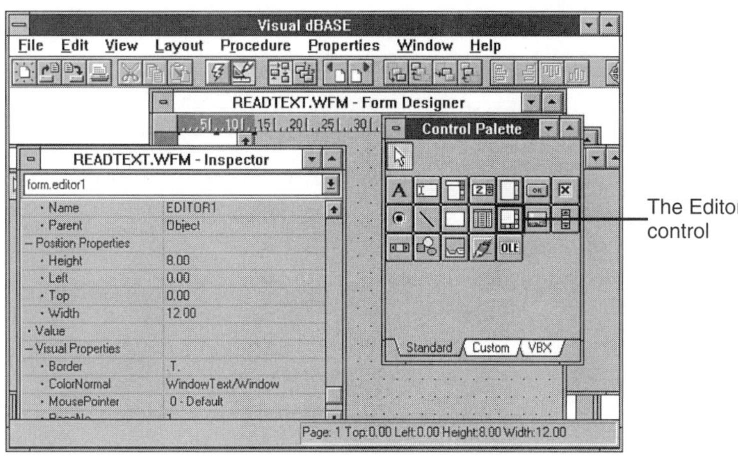

Figure 10.5.
The icon of the Editor control in the Control Palette window.

Entering the Code of the Read Text Program

In the following sections you'll enter the code of the Read Text program.

Attaching Code to the *OnClick* Event of the Exit Button

You'll now attach code to the `OnClick` event of the Exit button.

☐ Attach code to the `OnClick` event of the Exit button so that the `ExitButton_OnClick` procedure looks as follows:

```
Procedure EXITBUTTON_OnClick

   form.Close()

Return
```

Attaching Code to the *OnClick* Event of the Read C:\AUTOEXEC.BAT Button

You'll now attach code to the `OnClick` event of the Read C:\AUTOEXEC.BAT button.

- ☐ Attach code to the `OnClick` event of the Read C:\AUTOEXEC.BAT button. After you attach the code, the `AUTOEXECBUTTON_OnClick` procedure should look as follows:

```
Procedure AUTOEXECBUTTON_OnClick

IF .NOT. FILE("C:\AUTOEXEC.BAT")

MsgBox("The file C:\AUTOEXEC.BAT does not exist","MESSAGE")
RETURN

ENDIF

   * Get the size of the file.
   FileSize = FSIZE("C:\AUTOEXEC.BAT")

   * Open the AUTOEXEC.BAT file for reading.
   FileHandle=FOPEN("C:\AUTOEXEC.BAT","R")

IF FileHandle=-1

MsgBox("The file C:\AUTOEXEC.BAT cannot be opened.", "MESSAGE")
RETURN

ENDIF

   FileContents = FREAD(FileHandle, FileSize)

   form.Editor1.Value=FileContents

   * Close the file.
   FCLOSE(FileHandle)

Return
```

- ☐ Select Save from the File menu to save your work.

The code you typed executes an `IF` statement:

```
IF .NOT. FILE("C:\AUTOEXEC.BAT")
MsgBox("The file C:\AUTOEXEC.BAT does not exist","MESSAGE")
RETURN

ENDIF
```

The preceding IF statement checks for the existence of the C:\AUTOEXEC.BAT file by using the FILE() function. If the C:\AUTOEXEC.BAT file is not found, a message box is displayed, and then the RETURN statement is executed to terminate the procedure.

> **Note:** The FILE() function returns .T. if the file that is mentioned in the parameter of the FILE() function exists. Otherwise, the FILE() function returns .F.

Next, the file size of C:\AUTOEXEC.BAT is assigned to the FileSize variable as shown here:

```
* Get the size of the file.

FileSize = FSIZE("C:\AUTOEXEC.BAT")
```

The FOPEN() function is then executed to open the C:\AUTOEXEC.BAT file:

```
* Open the AUTOEXEC.BAT file for reading.
FileHandle=FOPEN("C:\AUTOEXEC.BAT","R")
```

> **Note:** The second parameter of the FOPEN() function indicates how the file should be opened. When you supply R as the second parameter of the FOPEN() function, the file that is mentioned as the first parameter of the FOPEN() function is opened for reading only. (You cannot modify the contents of the file.)

Note that the FOPEN() function returns a value. The return value of FOPEN() is –1 if the file could not be opened. An IF statement is then executed to examine the returned value of the FOPEN() function:

```
IF FileHandle=-1

MsgBox("The file C:\AUTOEXEC.BAT cannot be opened.", "MESSAGE")
RETURN

ENDIF
```

So if for some reason the file could not be opened, a message box is displayed, and the procedure is terminated.

The FREAD() function is then executed to read the contents of the opened file, and the FileContents variable is assigned the entire contents of the opened file:

```
FileContents = FREAD(FileHandle, FileSize)
```

So at this point, the `FileContents` variable holds the contents of the C:\AUTOEXEC.BAT file.

The Value property of the Editor control is then assigned the contents of the C:\AUTOEXEC.BAT file:

```
form.Editor1.Value=FileContents
```

Now the Editor control displays the contents of the C:\AUTOEXEC.BAT file.

Finally, the file is closed:

```
* Close the file.
FCLOSE(FileHandle)
```

The `FCLOSE()` function closes the file whose handler is specified in the parameter of the `FCLOSE()` function. Recall that when you opened the C:\AUTOEXEC.BAT file (with the `FOPEN()` function), the returned value of `FOPEN()` was assigned to the `FileHandle` variable. So when you execute the `FCLOSE()` function, you supply `FileHandle` as the parameter of `FCLOSE()`. This closes the C:\AUTOEXEC.BAT file.

Attaching Code to the *OnClick* Event of the Read C:\CONFIG.SYS Button

You'll now attach code to the `OnClick` event of the Read C:\CONFIG.SYS button.

- ☐ Attach code to the `OnClick` event of the Read C:\CONFIG.SYS button. After you attach the code, the `CONFIGBUTTON_OnClick` procedure should look as follows:

```
Procedure CONFIGBUTTON_OnClick

IF .NOT. FILE("C:\CONFIG.SYS")

MsgBox("The file C:\CONFIG.SYS does not exist", "MESSAGE")
RETURN

ENDIF

   * Get the size of the file.
   FileSize = FSIZE("C:\CONFIG.SYS")

   * Open the CONFIG.SYS file for reading.
   FileHandle=FOPEN("C:\CONFIG.SYS","R")

IF FileHandle=-1
MsgBox("The file C:\CONFIG.SYS cannot be opened.","MESSAGE")
RETURN
ENDIF

   FileContents = FREAD(FileHandle, FileSize)

   form.Editor1.Value=FileContents
```

```
    * Close the file.
    FCLOSE(FileHandle)

Return
```

The code you typed is very similar to the code you attached to the Read C:\AUTOEXEC.BAT button. Now, however, you are opening and displaying the contents of the C:\CONFIG.SYS file.

☐ Select Save from the File menu to save your work.

☐ Execute the Read Text program and check its proper operation.

Summary

In this chapter you have learned that dBASE is equipped with "regular" file manipulation statements that enable you to open and read text files. You have learned about the `FOPEN()`, `FREAD()`, `FSIZE()`, and `FCLOSE()` statements.

Q&A

Q Can I write into a file with dBASE?

A Yes. Use the `FWRITE()` function to write into a file as shown here:

```
FWRITE(FileHandle, MyString)
```

This statement assumes that the file handle of the file is `FileHandle`. Also, it is assumed that the file was opened with the `FOPEN()` function and that the second parameter of the `FOPEN()` function was `RW`. That is, the file was opened for reading and writing.

Q How do I create a new file?

A Use the `FCREATE()` function as shown here:

```
FileHandler = FCREATE ( "MyFile.TXT", "RW")
```

This statement creates a new file called MyFile.TXT. The file is opened for reading and writing. You can write into the file by using the `FWRITE()` function.

Quiz

1. The `FILE()` function is used for ____________________.
2. The `FSIZE()` function is used for ____________________.
3. The `FOPEN()` function is used for ____________________.
4. The returned value of `FOPEN()` is used for ____________________.
5. The `FREAD()` function is used for ____________________.

Exercise

Use a text editor (such as Notepad) to create a text file. Then write a program that displays the contents of the text file.

Quiz Answers

1. The FILE() function is used for determining whether a file exists. The file that is being examined is supplied as the parameter of the FILE() function, as in the following statement:

   ```
   FileExists =  FILE("C:\CONFIG.SYS")
   ```

   If FileExists is equal to .T., the C:\CONFIG.SYS file exists. If FileExists is equal to .F., the C:\CONFIG.SYS file does not exist.

2. The FSIZE() function is used for determining the size of a file. For example, the statement

   ```
   FileSize = FSIZE("C:\AUTOEXEC.BAT")
   ```

   assigns the FileSize variable a number that represents the size of the C:\AUTOEXEC.BAT file.

3. The FOPEN() function is used for opening a file. The name of the file to be opened is supplied as the first parameter of the FOPEN() function, as in the following statement:

   ```
   * Open the AUTOEXEC.BAT file for reading.
   FileHandle=FOPEN("C:\AUTOEXEC.BAT","R")
   ```

   The second parameter of the FOPEN() function in the preceding statement is R. This means that the file is opened for reading only.

4. The returned value of FOPEN() is used for determining whether the file was opened successfully. If the returned value is equal to –1, the file was not opened successfully.

   Also, if the file was opened successfully, then from now on, your code refers to the file by the returned value of the FOPEN() function (which is the handle of the opened file).

   For example, if the returned value of FOPEN() is assigned to FileHandle, later in the procedure you can close the file by executing the following statement:

   ```
   FCLOSE(FileHandle)
   ```

5. The FREAD() function is used for reading the contents of the file. For example, the following statement assigns the contents of the file to a variable called FileContents:

   ```
   FileContents = FREAD(FileHandle, FileSize)
   ```

Exercise Answer

Follow the same steps you used to implement the Read Text program.

Here are the main statements that are required to open a text file:

- ☐ Determine whether the file exists with the `FILE()` statement.
- ☐ Open the file with the `FOPEN()` function.
- ☐ Read the file's contents with the `FREAD()` function.

Don't forget to close the file with the `FCLOSE()` function.

11

WEEK 2

Joining Tables

In this chapter you will use the dBASE tools to join two tables. The resulting joined table enables you to view and edit the records of both tables.

What does it mean to join two tables? As you will soon see, after you join two tables, the two tables become one entity. That is, you can simultaneously view the data of both tables as if the two tables were a single table.

The JOBS Program

In this chapter you will write a dBASE program called JOBS that uses a table composed of two tables: CUSTOMER.DBF and JOBS.DBF. The CUSTOMER.DBF table is used for storing information about customers, and the JOBS.DBF table is used for storing information about jobs that were performed for the customers.

Before you begin joining the CUSTOMER.DBF and JOBS.DBF tables, you should know how the JOBS program should look and what it should do.

When you run the JOBS program, the main window of the JOBS program should look like the one shown in Figure 11.1.

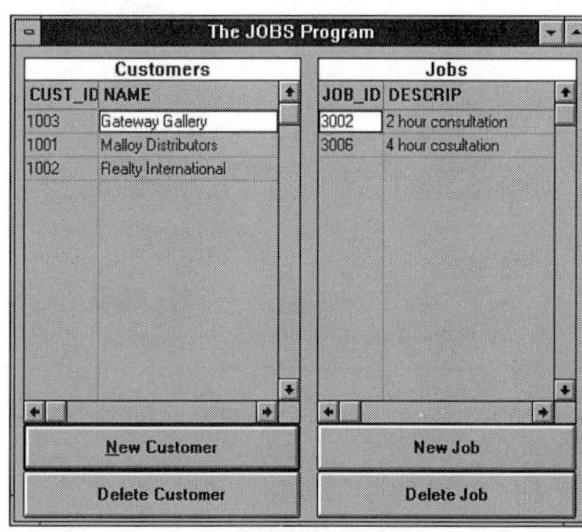

Figure 11.1.
The main window of the JOBS program.

The JOBS program enables the user to view and edit information about customers and about jobs that were performed for these customers.

As shown in Figure 11.1, the main window of the JOBS program has two browse controls: Customers and Jobs.

The user can select a customer by highlighting the desired customer in the Customers browse control. When the user selects a customer, the Jobs browse control is automatically filled with all the jobs that were performed for that customer. For example, in Figure 11.1, the Jobs browse control lists all the jobs that were performed for the customer Gateway Gallery. In Figure 11.2 the Jobs browse control lists all the jobs that were performed for the customer Malloy Distributors.

Figure 11.2.
Listing the jobs of the customer Malloy Distributors.

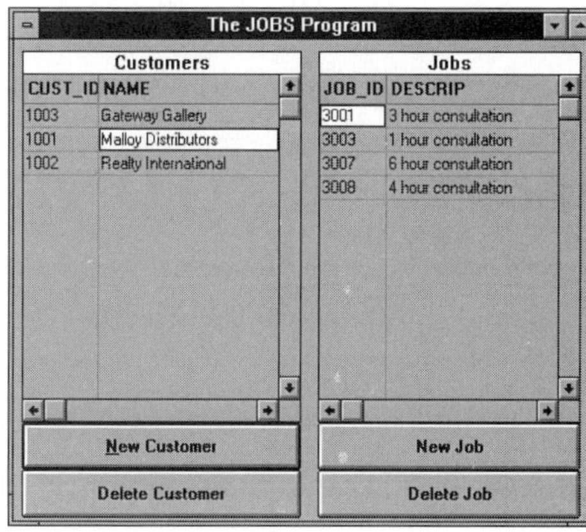

As you might have guessed, the Customers browse control displays the records of the CUSTOMER.DBF table, and the Jobs browse control displays the records of the JOBS.DBF table. However, because the JOBS.WFM program joins the CUSTOMER.DBF and JOBS.DBF tables, from the user's point of view, the CUSTOMER.DBF and JOBS.DBF tables are one entity. That is, as the user moves from one record to another in the Customers browse control, the Jobs browse control automatically displays only the jobs that belong to the current customer in the Customers browse control.

As shown in Figures 11.1 and 11.2, the main window of the JOBS program also includes four pushbuttons: New Customer, Delete Customer, New Job, and Delete Job.

When the user clicks the New Customer button, the JOBS program adds a new customer to the CUSTOMER.DBF table. The JOBS program also automatically assigns a unique customer ID to the new customer. As shown in Figures 11.1 and 11.2, each customer has a unique customer ID (CUST_ID). The user cannot change the value of this field.

When the user clicks the Delete Customer button, the JOBS program deletes the currently selected customer and all the jobs of this customer.

When the user clicks the New Job button, the JOBS program adds a new job for the currently selected customer. The JOBS program also automatically assigns a unique job ID to the new job. As shown in Figures 11.1 and 11.2, each listed job has a unique job ID (JOB_ID). The user cannot change the value of this field.

When the user clicks the Delete Job button, the JOBS program deletes the currently selected job.

You might think that writing a program with the features of the JOBS program requires a lot of code writing. As you will soon see, however, writing the JOBS program is easy! Very little code writing is required to implement a program such as the JOBS program. Why? Joined tables automatically perform the major tasks that are needed by the JOBS program.

Now that you know what the JOBS program is supposed to do, it's time to start writing the program and joining the tables.

Creating the CUSTOMER.DBF and JOBS.DBF Tables

The JOBS program will use two tables: CUSTOMER.DBF and JOBS.DBF. In the following steps you'll create these tables.

Follow these steps to create the CUSTOMER.DBF table:

☐ Start Visual dBASE.

☐ Type `MD C:\DBPROG` in the Command window, and then press Enter.

dBASE responds by creating the directory C:\DBPROG. (If this directory already exists, dBASE displays a message box telling you that the directory cannot be created.)

☐ Type `MD C:\DBPROG\CH11` in the Command window, and then press Enter.

dBASE responds by creating the directory C:\DBPROG\CH11.

☐ Type `CREATE C:\DBPROG\CH11\CUSTOMER` in the Command window and press Enter.

dBASE responds by displaying the Table Structure window for the CUSTOMER.DBF table.

☐ Set the structure of the CUSTOMER.DBF table as specified in Table 11.1.

Table 11.1. The structure of the CUSTOMER.DBF table.

Field Name	Type	Width	Decimal	Index
CUST_ID	Character	4	0	Ascend
NAME	Character	20	0	Ascend

☐ Save your work by selecting Save from the File menu.

☐ Close the Table Structure window by selecting Close from the File menu.

As you can see, the CUSTOMER.DBF table has two fields: CUST_ID and NAME.

The CUST_ID field is a Character field that will be used for storing the customer IDs. Each customer will have a unique customer ID. Table 11.1 instructs you to add an ascending index to the CUST_ID field. This way, when you write the code of the JOBS program, you can order the records of the table by the CUST_ID field.

The NAME field is a character field that will be used for storing the name of the customer. Table 11.1 instructs you to add an ascending index to the NAME field. This way, when you write the code of the JOBS program, you can order the records of the table by the NAME field.

> **Note:** In the preceding steps you were instructed to create the CUSTOMER.DBF table with only two fields (CUST_ID and NAME).
>
> Usually, a table that stores information about customers requires additional fields (for example, street, city, state, ZIP, phone, fax). For the purpose of illustrating the topic of joining tables, however, two fields are sufficient.

Next create the JOBS.DBF table:

- ☐ Type `CREATE C:\DBPROG\CH11\JOBS` in the Command window, and press Enter.

  dBASE responds by displaying the Table Structure window for the JOBS.DBF table.

- ☐ Set the structure of the JOBS.DBF table according to the specifications in Table 11.2.
- ☐ Save your work by selecting Save from the File menu.
- ☐ Close the Table Structure window by selecting Close from the File menu.

Table 11.2. The structure of the JOBS.DBF table.

Field Name	Type	Width	Decimal	Index
JOB_ID	Character	4	0	Ascend
CUST_ID	Character	4	0	Ascend
DESCRIP	Character	20	0	None

As you can see, the JOBS.DBF table has three fields: JOB_ID, CUST_ID, and DESCRIP.

The JOB_ID field is a Character field that will be used for storing the job IDs. Each job will have a unique job ID. Table 11.2 instructs you to add an ascending index to the JOB_ID field. This way, when you write the code of the JOBS program, you can order the records of the table by the JOB_ID field.

The CUST_ID field is a Character field that will be used for storing the customer ID of the customer for whom the job is performed. That is, every job is performed for a certain customer, and the CUST_ID field specifies who the customer is. Table 11.2 instructs you to add an ascending index to the CUST_ID field. The reason for adding an index for this field is discussed later in the chapter.

The DESCRIP field is a character field that will be used for storing the description of the job.

Note: In the preceding steps you were instructed to create the JOBS.DBF table with only three fields (JOB_ID, CUST_ID, and DESCRIP).

Usually, a table that stores information about jobs requires additional fields (for example, JOB_DATE, JOB_COST). For the purpose of illustrating the topic of joining tables, however, three fields are sufficient.

Filling the CUSTOMER.DBF and JOBS.DBF Tables with Test Data

Later in this chapter, you'll write the code of the JOBS program. This code will enable the user to view and edit the records of the CUSTOMER.DBF and JOBS.DBF tables.

Before you write the code of the JOBS program, you should first add some test data to the CUSTOMER.DBF and JOBS.DBF tables. This way, you'll be able to test your code immediately.

☐ Type `USE C:\DBPROG\CH11\CUSTOMER` in the Command window, and then press Enter.

dBASE responds by opening the CUSTOMER.DBF table.

☐ Type `BROWSE` in the Command window, and then press Enter.

☐ Make sure that the CUSTOMER.DBF window is the active window, select Add Records from the Table menu, and add three records to CUSTOMER.DBF. Fill in the data of the three records as shown here:

```
Record Number 1
CUST_ID = 1001
NAME    = Malloy Distributors

Record Number 2
CUST_ID = 1002
NAME    = Realty International
```

```
Record Number 3
CUST_ID = 1003
NAME    = Gateway Gallery
```

☐ Close the Browse window by selecting Close from the File menu.

Next add five test records to the JOBS.DBF table:

☐ Type `USE C:\DBPROG\CH11\JOBS` in the Command window, and then press Enter.

dBASE responds by opening the JOBS.DBF table.

☐ Type `BROWSE` in the Command window, and then press Enter.

☐ Make sure that the JOBS.DBF window is the active window, select Add Records from the Table menu, and add five records to JOBS.DBF. Fill in the data of the three records as shown here:

```
Record Number 1
JOB_ID   = 3001
CUST_ID  = 1001
DESCRIP  = 3 hour consultation

Record Number 2
JOB_ID   = 3002
CUST_ID  = 1003
DESCRIP  = 2 hour consultation

Record Number 3
JOB_ID   = 3003
CUST_ID  = 1001
DESCRIP  = 1 hour consultation

Record Number 4
JOB_ID   = 3004
CUST_ID  = 1002
DESCRIP  = 2 hour consultation

Record Number 5
JOB_ID   = 3005
CUST_ID  = 1002
DESCRIP  = 1 hour consultation
```

☐ Close the Browse window by selecting Close from the File menu.

> **Note:** When you add the records to the CUSTOMER.DBF and JOBS.DBF tables, be sure to exactly type the data you were instructed to type.
>
> Entering the exact data is necessary so that later you'll be able to follow the steps that test the program's code.

Joining the CUSTOMER.DBF and JOBS.DBF Tables

Although CUSTOMER.DBF and JOBS.DBF are two different tables, when the user executes the JOBS program, you want the user to feel as if the CUSTOMER.DBF and JOBS.DBF are one entity. Therefore, you must join the CUSTOMER.DBF and JOBS.DBF tables.

The easiest way to join two tables is by creating a QBE file (a query file). QBE stands for *query by example.* In the following steps you'll create a QBE file called CUST_JOB.QBE. As implied by its name, the CUST_JOB.QBE query file will join the two tables CUSTOMER.DBF and JOBS.DBF.

Before following the steps to join the CUSTOMER.DBF and JOBS.DBF tables (by creating the CUST_JOB.QBE file), you should consider several overhead tasks. These tasks are discussed in the following section.

Before You Join Two Tables...

Before joining two tables, you must determine two items of information:

- Which field will be used as the linking field (that is, which field will be used for joining the two tables)?
- Which table of the two tables will be the parent table, and which table will be the child table?

Determining which is the linking field is easy. The linking field is a common field that both tables have. In the case of the CUSTOMER.DBF and JOBS.DBF tables, the linking field is the CUST_ID field. Both the CUSTOMER.DBF table and the JOBS.DBF table have this field.

After you know which is the linking field, you can determine which is the parent table and which is the child table. The parent table is the table that has unique values in the linking field. That is, no two records in the parent table can have the same value in the linking field.

In the case of the CUSTOMER.DBF and JOBS.DBF tables, the parent table is the CUSTOMER.DBF table. Why? Each record in the CUSTOMER.DBF table has a unique value in the CUST_ID field. That is, no two records in the CUSTOMER.DBF table will have the same value in the CUST_ID field.

On the other hand, each record in the JOBS.DBF table does *not* have a unique value in the CUST_ID field. That is, several records in the JOBS.DBF table might have the same value in the CUST_ID field (because you can have several jobs for the same customer). Therefore, in the case of the CUSTOMER.DBF and JOBS.DBF tables, the JOBS.DBF table is the child table.

After you determine which is the linking field, which is the parent table, and which is the child table, you must ensure that the child table is indexed on the linking field. For example, in the case of the CUSTOMER.DBF and JOBS.DBF tables, the child table, JOBS.DBF, must be indexed on the CUST_ID field. This is why when you created the JOBS.DBF table you were instructed to add an index to the CUST_ID field of the JOBS.DBF table.

To summarize, before you join two tables, you must follow these steps:

1. Determine which is the linking field (the common field of the two tables).
2. Determine which is the parent table and which is the child table.
3. Make sure that the linking field of the child table has an index.

Creating the CUST_JOB.QBE Query File

In the preceding section, you determined that in the case of the CUSTOMER.DBF and JOBS.DBF tables, the linking field is the CUST_ID field, the parent table is CUSTOMER.DBF, and the child table is JOBS.DBF.

In the following steps you'll create a QBE file called CUST_JOB.QBE. The CUST_JOB.QBE query file will join the two tables CUSTOMER.DBF and JOBS.DBF.

☐ Type `CLOSE DATABASES` in the Command window, and then press Enter.

☐ Type `USE C:\DBPROG\CH11\CUSTOMER` in the Command window and press Enter.

dBASE responds by opening the CUSTOMER.DBF table.

☐ Type `CREATE QUERY C:\DBPROG\CH11\CUST_JOB` in the Command window, and then press Enter.

dBASE responds by displaying the Query Designer dialog box for the CUST_JOB.QBE file. (See Figure 11.3.) In the following steps you'll use this dialog box to design the CUST_JOB.QBE file in a way that will join the CUSTOMER.DBF table with the JOBS.DBF table.

As shown in Figure 11.3, the Query Designer dialog box displays the fields of the CUSTOMER.DBF table in a row.

The Query Designer dialog box displays the fields of the CUSTOMER.DBF table because before issuing the `CREATE QUERY` command, you opened the CUSTOMER.DBF table.

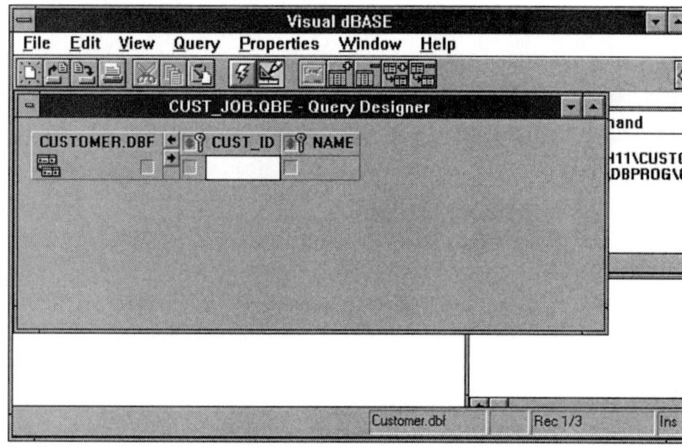

Figure 11.3.
The Query Designer dialog box.

> **Note:** You were instructed to open the CUSTOMER.DBF table before issuing the `CREATE QUERY` command so that the Query Designer dialog box would display the fields of the CUSTOMER.DBF table.
>
> You need to open the CUSTOMER.DBF table (and not the JOBS.DBF table) because the CUSTOMER.DBF table is the parent table.

To add the JOBS.DBF table to the CUST_JOB.QBE query, follow these steps:

☐ Select Add Table from the Query menu of dBASE.

dBASE responds by displaying the Open Table Required dialog box. (See Figure 11.4.)

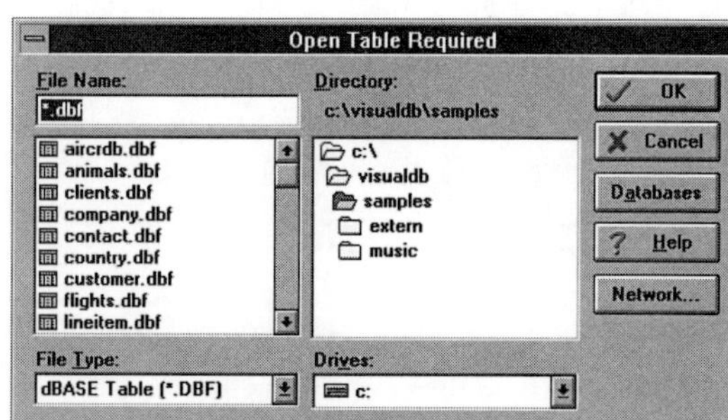

Figure 11.4.
The Open Table Required dialog box that dBASE displays after you select Add Table from the Query menu.

☐ Use the Open Table Required dialog box to select the C:\DBPROG\CH11\JOBS.DBF table, and then click the OK button of the dialog box.

dBASE responds by adding a second row to the Query Designer dialog box. This new row displays the fields of the JOBS.DBF table. (See Figure 11.5.)

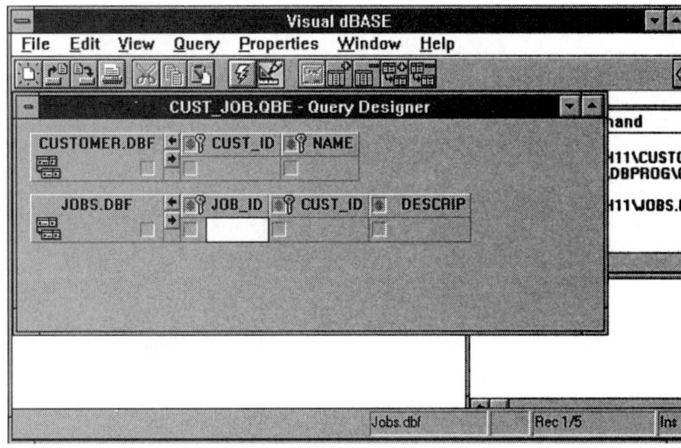

Figure 11.5.
The Query Designer dialog box after you add the JOBS.DBF table to it.

> **Note:** At this point, the CUST_JOBS.QBE query includes the CUSTOMER.DBF table and the JOBS.DBF table. The CUSTOMER.DBF table is the parent table, and the JOBS.DBF table is the child table.
>
> Because the first table you added to the CUST_JOB.QBE query is the CUSTOMER.DBF table, dBASE knows that you want the parent table to be the CUSTOMER.DBF table. You added the CUSTOMER.DBF table to the query by opening the CUSTOMER.DBF table before issuing the `CREATE QUERY` command.

You are almost done with the design of the CUST_JOBS.QBE query. The last thing you must do is set a relation between the CUSTOMER.DBF table and the JOBS.DBF table. Here is how you do that:

☐ Select Set Relation from the Query menu of dBASE.

dBASE responds by displaying the Define Relation dialog box. (See Figure 11.6.)

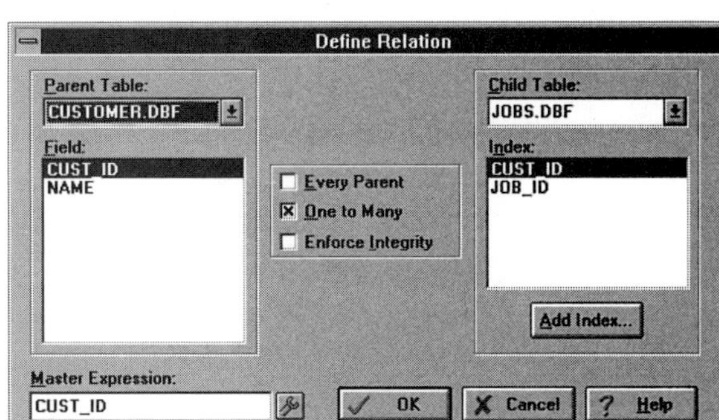

Figure 11.6.
The Define Relation dialog box.

You'll now use the Define Relation dialog box to set a relation between the CUSTOMER.DBF and JOBS.DBF tables.

☐ Click the Tool icon that appears to the right of the Master Expression box.

dBASE responds by displaying the Master Expression dialog box.

☐ Set the Master Expression dialog box as shown in Figure 11.7. That is, set the Category to Field, select the CUSTOMER table, and select CUST_ID from the Paste list.

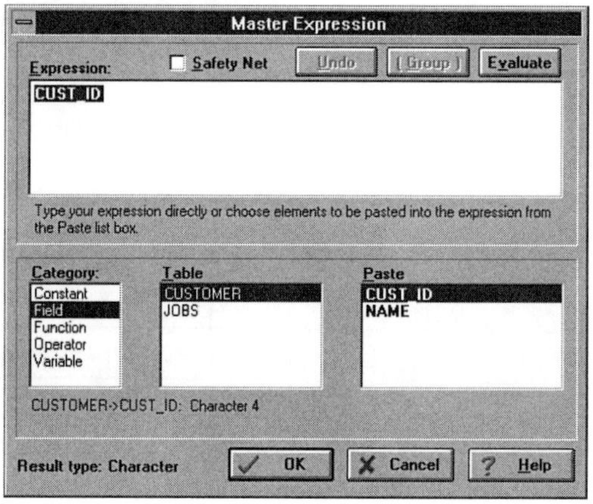

Figure 11.7.
Setting the Master Expression dialog box.

☐ Click the OK button of the Master Expression dialog box.

dBASE responds by displaying the Define Relation dialog box.

The last thing you must do is set the three check boxes in the middle of the Define Relation dialog box:

☐ Place an × in the Every Parent check box.

☐ Ensure that the One To Many check box has an × in it.

☐ Place an × in the Enforce Integrity check box.

☐ Ensure that the CUST_ID item in the Index list is selected, as shown in Figure 11.8 (because CUST_ID is the joining field).

The Define Relation dialog box should now look like the one shown in Figure 11.8.

Figure 11.8.
Defining the relation between CUSTOMER.DBF and JOBS.DBF.

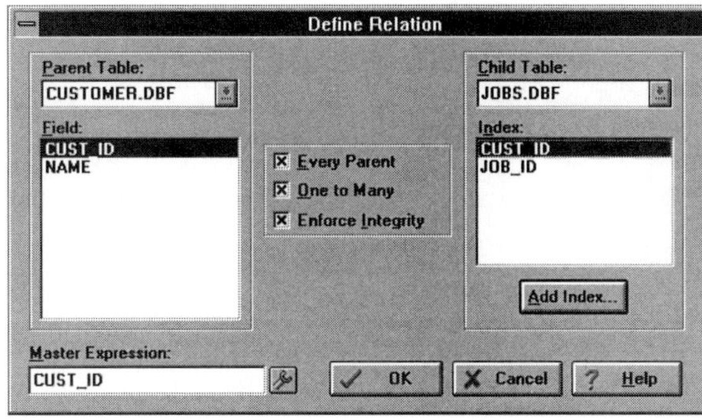

☐ Click the OK button of the Define Relation dialog box.

> *dBASE responds by setting a relation between the CUSTOMER.DBF table and the JOBS.DBF table.*

You have finished the design of the CUST_JOB.QBE query!

The Query Designer window now has an arrow that points from the parent table (CUSTOMER.DBF) to the child table (JOBS.DBF), as shown in Figure 11.9.

Figure 11.9.
The Query Designer window now has an arrow that points from the parent table (CUSTOMER.DBF) to the child table (JOBS.DBF).

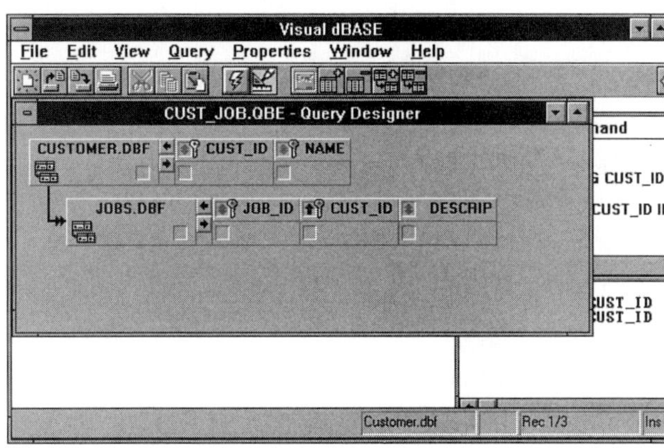

By setting CUST_ID in the Master Expression entry field, you are specifying that the joining field of the relation is the CUST_ID field. (As stated earlier, the joining field is the common field of the two tables.)

> **Note:** The purpose of the three check boxes—Every Parent, One to Many, and Enforce Integrity—is discussed later.
>
> For now, just ensure that these check boxes are set as shown in Figure 11.8. That is, each of these three check boxes should have an × in it.

- ☐ Save your work by selecting Save from the File menu.
- ☐ Select Close from the File menu of dBASE.

  dBASE responds by closing the Query Designer dialog box.

Testing the CUST_JOB.QBE Query

To see the CUST_JOB.QBE query in action, follow these steps:

- ☐ Type `CLOSE DATABASES` in the Command window, and press Enter.

  dBASE responds by closing all the open tables.

- ☐ Type `SET VIEW TO C:\DBPROG\CH11\CUST_JOB.QBE` in the Command window, and press Enter.

  dBASE responds by opening the CUST_JOB.QBE query.

By opening the CUST_JOB.QBE query, you actually opened both the CUSTOMER.DBF table and the JOBS.DBF table. That is, because the CUST_JOB.QBE query joins the CUSTOMER.DBF table with the JOBS.DBF table, when you issued the `SET VIEW` command to open the CUST_JOB.QBE query, dBASE opened both tables and joined them.

Each of the two tables is open in its own work area. To switch to a work area, you must use the `SELECT` command:

- ☐ Type `SELECT JOBS` in the Command window, and press Enter.

  dBASE responds by switching to the work area of the JOBS.DBF table.

To verify that you are currently in the work area of the JOBS.DBF table, carry out the following actions:

- ☐ Type `?DBF()` in the Command window, and press Enter.

  As expected, dBASE responds by displaying the name of the JOBS.DBF table in the results pane of the Command window.

Next switch to the work area of the CUSTOMER.DBF table:

☐ Type `SELECT CUSTOMER` in the Command window, and press Enter.

dBASE responds by switching to the work area of the CUSTOMER.DBF table.

To verify that you are currently in the work area of the CUSTOMER.DBF table, do this:

☐ Type `?DBF()` in the Command window, and press Enter.

As expected, dBASE responds by displaying the name of the CUSTOMER.DBF table in the results pane of the Command window.

So as you have just verified, both the CUSTOMER.DBF and the JOBS.DBF tables are currently open. Each of them is open in its own work area.

Next verify that the CUSTOMER.DBF and JOBS.DBF tables are joined:

☐ Type `BROWSE` in the Command window, and press Enter.

dBASE responds by displaying the browse window of the CUSTOMER.DBF table. (See Figure 11.10.)

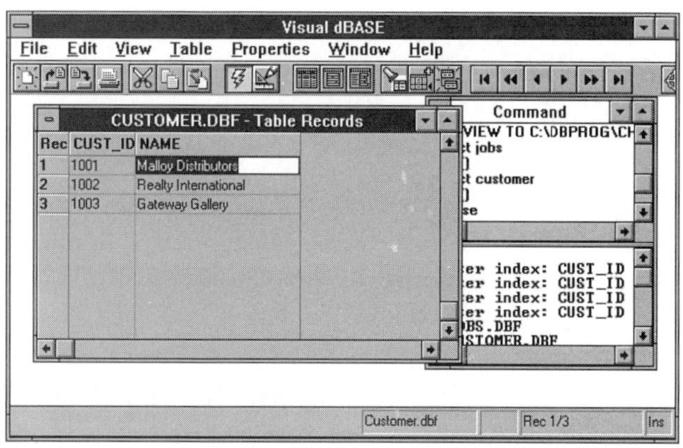

Figure 11.10.
The browse window of the CUSTOMER.DBF table.

Note that in the preceding step dBASE displayed the browse window of the CUSTOMER.DBF table because you are currently in the work area of the CUSTOMER.DBF table.

☐ Type `SELECT JOBS` in the Command window, and press Enter.

dBASE responds by switching to the work area of the JOBS.DBF table.

☐ Type `BROWSE` in the Command window, and press Enter.

dBASE responds by displaying the browse window of the JOBS.DBF.

☐ Move the window of the JOBS.DBF browse window so that it does not overlap the window of the CUSTOMER.DBF table. (See Figure 11.11.)

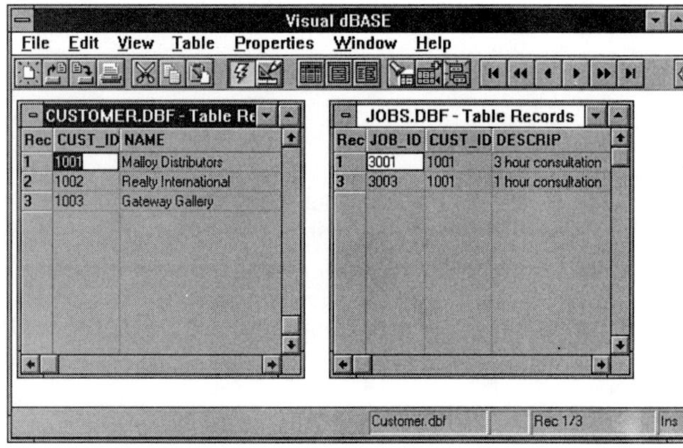

Figure 11.11.
Viewing the browse windows of the CUSTOMER.DBF and JOBS.DBF tables.

You can verify that the CUSTOMER.DBF and JOBS.DBF tables are joined as explained here:

Notice that in Figure 11.11, the currently selected record in the browse window of CUSTOMER.DBF table is the record whose CUST_ID field contains 1001. As a result, the browse window of the JOBS.DBF table displays only the records whose CUST_ID fields contain 1001.

☐ Make the browse window of the CUSTOMER.DBF table the active window and use the down- and up-arrow keys to move from one record to another.

As you can see, as you move from one record to another in the browse window of the CUSTOMER.DBF table, the JOBS.DBF table automatically displays only the records whose CUST_ID field is equal to the value of the CUST_ID field of the current record in the CUSTOMER.DBF table. (See Figures 11.12 and 11.13.)

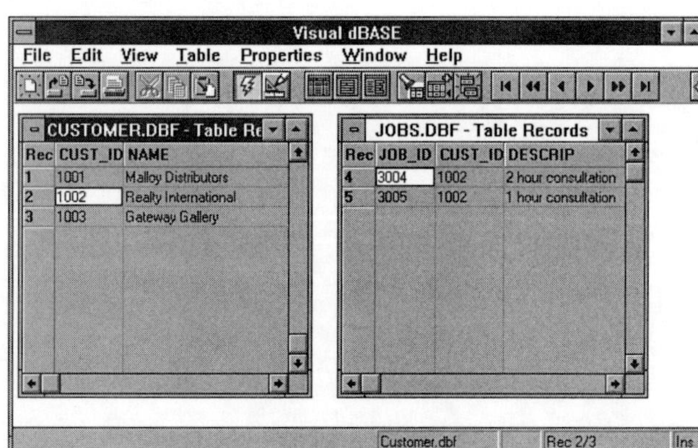

Figure 11.12.
The two browse windows when the current record of the CUSTOMER.DBF table is the record whose CUST_ID field contains 1002.

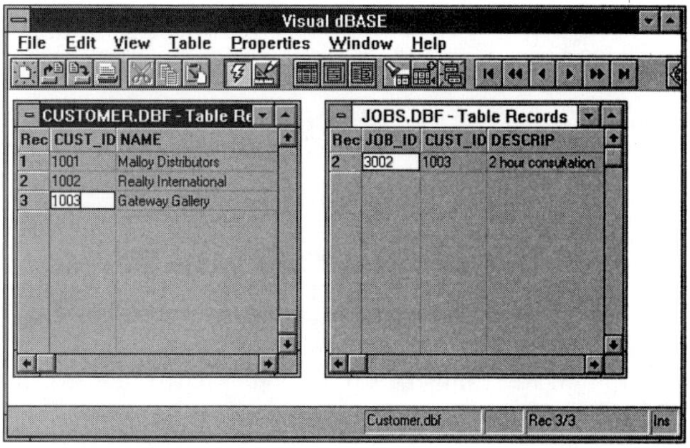

Figure 11.13.
The two browse windows when the current record of the CUSTOMER.DBF table is the record whose CUST_ID field contains 1003.

In the preceding steps you verified that when you open the CUST_JOB.QBE query (by using the `SET VIEW TO` command), the following things happen:

- The CUSTOMER.DBF and JOBS.DBF tables are both opened (each in its own work area).
- The CUSTOMER.DBF and JOBS.DBF tables are joined on the CUST_ID field. That is, when you move the record pointer of the CUSTOMER.DBF table to any record, the JOBS.DBF table is automatically updated so that it includes only records with the same CUST_ID value as that of the current record in the CUSTOMER.DBF table.

Note: Do not close the browse windows of the CUSTOMER.DBF and JOBS.DBF tables yet. In the following section you'll continue experimenting with them.

Opening the Same Table Again in a New Work Area

As a result of opening the CUST_JOB.QBE query, both the CUSTOMER.DBF table and the JOBS.DBF table are currently open (each in its own work area).

Suppose that you want to open the JOBS.DBF table in another work area without disturbing the work area where the JOBS.DBF table is currently open.

To open the JOBS.DBF table in a new work area, follow these steps:

☐ Type `SELECT SELECT()` in the Command window, and then press Enter.

dBASE responds by switching to the next available work area.

Note: The `SELECT()` function returns the next available work area. Therefore, by executing the statement

```
SELECT SELECT()
```

you are telling dBASE to switch to the next available work area (that is, a work area not yet used by any table).

Now that you have switched to a work area that is not used by any table, you can open any table in this new work area.

Your next objective is to open the JOBS.DBF table:

☐ Type `USE C:\DBPROG\CH11\JOBS.DBF AGAIN ALIAS Temp`, and then press Enter.

dBASE responds by opening the JOBS.DBF table in the new work area.

At this point, the JOBS.DBF table is open two times, in two different work areas.

In the preceding statement, you used the `USE` statement with the keyword `AGAIN`. You had to use the `AGAIN` keyword because you want the JOBS.DBF table that is open in the other work area to remain open. In other words, when you use the `AGAIN` keyword, you are telling dBASE to leave the table open in the other work area.

In the preceding statement, you used the `USE` statement also with the `ALIAS` keyword:

```
USE C:\DBPROG\CH11\JOBS.DBF AGAIN ALIAS Temp
```

By specifying `ALIAS Temp`, you are telling dBASE that the name of the current work area is Temp.

So at this point you have three work areas: Jobs, Customer, and Temp.

You can now switch from one work area to another by using the `SELECT` command:

☐ Type `SELECT CUSTOMER` in the Command window, and then press Enter.

dBASE responds by switching to the work area of the CUSTOMER.DBF table.

To verify that you are currently in the work area of the CUSTOMER.DBF table, take the following action:

- ☐ Type `?DBF()` in the Command window, and then press Enter.

  dBASE responds by displaying the name of the CUSTOMER.DBF table in the results pane of the Command window.

Similarly, you can switch to the Jobs work area by executing the statement `SELECT JOBS`, and you can switch to the Temp work area by executing the statement `SELECT TEMP`.

The JOBS.DBF table that you opened in the Temp work area is not joined to the CUSTOMER.DBF table. You can verify this in the following way:

- ☐ Type `SELECT TEMP` in the Command window, and then press Enter.

  dBASE responds by switching to the Temp work area.

- ☐ Type `BROWSE` in the Command window, and then press Enter.

  dBASE responds by displaying another browse window for the JOBS.DBF table.

- ☐ Move the new browse window of the JOBS.DBF browse window so that it does not overlap the other two browse windows.

You can now verify that the JOBS.DBF table in the Temp work area is not joined to the CUSTOMER.DBF table as explained here:

- ☐ Make the browse window of the CUSTOMER.DBF table the active window, and use the down- and up-arrow keys to move from one record to another.

As you move from one record to another in the browse window of the CUSTOMER.DBF table, the browse window of the JOBS.DBF table of the Temp work area is not changed.

The One to Many Check Box of the Define Relation Dialog Box

The relation that the CUST_JOB.QBE query establishes between the CUSTOMER.DBF table and the JOBS.DBF table is called a *one-to-many* relation. This means that for every *one* record in the parent table, the child table can include *many* (that is, several) records with a matching value in the joining field.

For example, in Figure 11.12, the JOBS.DBF table includes two records whose CUST_ID field matches the value of the CUST_ID field of the CUSTOMER.DBF table.

The reason the CUST_JOB.QBE query establishes a one-to-many relation is that you specified as much when you created the CUST_JOB.QBE query. That is, when you set the Define Relation of the CUST_JOB.QBE query, you made sure that the One-to-Many check box had an × in it. (Refer to Figure 11.8.)

The Every Parent Check Box of the Define Relation Dialog Box

As shown in Figure 11.8, when you set the Define Relation dialog box of the CUST_JOB.QBE query, you placed an × in the Every Parent check box. By placing an × in this check box, you are ensuring that while the CUST_JOB.QBE query is open, every record of the CUSTOMER.DBF table will be included even if this record has a CUST_ID that is not in the JOBS.DBF table. For example, suppose that one of the records of the CUSTOMER.DBF table has a record with a CUST_ID of 1234. When you open the CUST_JOB.QBE query, the browse window of the CUSTOMER.DBF table will display the record whose CUST_ID is 1234, even if the JOBS.DBF table does not have any record with a CUST_ID of 1234.

The Enforce Integrity Check Box of the Define Relation Dialog Box

As shown in Figure 11.8, when you set the Define Relation dialog box of the CUST_JOB.QBE query, you placed an × in the Enforce Integrity check box. By placing an × in this check box, you are specifying that while the CUST_JOB.QBE query is open, dBASE will do the following things for you:

- When you try to delete a record in the parent table (CUSTOMER.DBF), dBASE checks whether the child table (JOBS.DBF) has records with the same CUST_ID as the CUST_ID of the record you are trying to delete. If such records exist in the child table, dBASE displays a message box that enables you to delete these records. In other words, when you delete a record in the parent table, dBASE automatically deletes the related records in the child table. This automatic delete is called a *cascaded delete.*
- When you add a new record to the JOBS.DBF table (the child table), the CUST_ID field (the joining field) of the new record is automatically filled with the value of the CUST_ID field of the current record of the CUSTOMER.DBF table, and this value is read-only. For example, if the CUST_ID field of the current record in CUSTOMER.DBF has a value of 1234, then when you add a new record to the JOBS.DBF table, the CUST_ID field of the new record is automatically set to a value of 1234, and this value is read-only (that is, you cannot change this value).

☐ Type `CLOSE DATABASES` in the Command window, and then press Enter.

dBASE responds by closing all the open tables.

Summary

In this chapter you have learned how to join tables. In particular, you have learned how to design a query (QBE file) that uses and joins two tables.

In the next chapter you'll learn how to write a program (the JOBS program) that uses the joined table.

Q&A

Q Why is it necessary to use and join two tables? Why not simply use one table with many fields?

A Using and joining two tables is much more efficient than using one table with many fields. To appreciate the efficiency of using and joining two tables, consider the following example:

Suppose that you have two tables: CUSTOMER.DBF and JOBS.DBF.

The CUSTOMER.DBF table has the fields CUST_ID, NAME, STREET, CITY, STATE, ZIP, and PHONE.

The JOBS.DBF table has the fields JOB_ID, CUST_ID, JOB_DATE, and JOB_COST.

Now, suppose that the JOBS.DBF table is filled with 10,000 records, and 1,000 of these records belong to one particular customer whose name is John Smith.

If John Smith ever changes his address or phone number, all you'll have to do is update one record—that of John Smith in the CUSTOMER.DBF table.

If, however, instead of having two tables, you have only one table with many fields (NAME, STREET, CITY, STATE, ZIP, PHONE, JOB_DATE, and JOB_COST), when Mr. Smith changes his address or phone number, you will have to update 1,000 records!

And, of course, the address of John Smith is stored on the hard drive only once (in the CUSTOMER.DBF table). If you had the address stored in 1,000 records of the JOBS.DBF table, the address would appear 1,000 times on the hard drive. As you can see, you save a lot of hard-drive space by designing your tables properly.

Also, suppose that the tables are located on a remote computer and the data is sent to your PC via network cables. Because the address is not stored in the JOBS.DBF table, less data will have to be sent, and your PC will receive the data more quickly.

Quiz

1. What does the following code do?

```
SELECT SELECT()
USE C:\TRY\TABLE1.DBF

SELECT SELECT()
USE C:\TRY\TABLE2.DBF
```

2. What is a one-to-many relation?

Exercise

Design two tables—CLIENTS.DBF and INVOICES.DBF—and create a query called CLNT_INV.QBE that joins these two tables.

Create the CLIENTS.DBF table so that it has the fields CLIENT_ID, NAME, and PHONE. Create the INVOICES.DBF table so that it has the fields INVOICE_NO, CLIENT_ID, DESCRIP, and COST.

Quiz Answers

1. This code opens the two tables TABLE1.DBF and TABLE2.DBF. Each table is opened in its own work area.
2. A one-to-many relation is a relation in which for every *one* record in the parent table, the child table can include *many* records with a matching value in the joining field.

   For example, in the example used in this chapter, the JOBS.DBF table (the child table) may include several records whose CUST_ID field matches the value of the CUST_ID field of the CUSTOMER.DBF table (the parent table). That is, *one* customer may have *many* jobs associated with it.

Exercise Answer

To create the CLIENTS.DBF and INVOICES.DBF tables, and the CLNT_INV.QBE query, you must take steps similar to those you took when you created the CUSTOMER.DBF table, the JOBS.DBF table, and the CUST_JOB.QBE query:

- The joining field will be the CLIENT_ID field.
- The parent table will be the CLIENTS.DBF table.
- The child table will be the INVOICES.DBF table.
- The CLIENT_ID field of the child table (INVOICES.DBF) must have an index.

12

WEEK 2

Using Joined Tables from Within Your Programs

In this chapter you will write a dBASE program that uses the joined table you created in the preceding chapter. The program enables the user to view and edit the records of both tables.

The Visual Implementation of the JOBS Program

In the preceding chapter you finished designing and testing the CUST_JOB.QBE query. Now you can design a form that uses this query. In the following steps you'll create the JOBS.WFM form. This form will use the CUST_JOB.QBE query.

Create the JOBS.WFM form as explained here:

☐ Type `CREATE FORM C:\DBPROG\CH11\JOBS` in the Command window, and press Enter. Note that you are creating the JOBS program in the C:\DBPROG\CH11 directory. (You created the C:\DBPROG\CH11 directory in the previous chapter.)

dBASE responds by creating the JOBS.WFM form and displaying it in design mode.

☐ Customize the JOBS.WFM form according to the specifications in Table 12.1. When you finish customizing the form, it should look like the one shown in Figure 12.1.

☐ Save your work by selecting Save from the File menu.

Table 12.1. The properties table of the JOBS.WFM form.

Object	Property	Setting
Form	**Text**	**The JOBS Program**
	View	C:\DBPROG\CH11\CUST_JOB.QBE
	Height	20
	Left	1
	MDI	.F.
	Top	0
	Width	70
Browse Control	**Name**	**CustomerBrowse**
	Text	Customers
	Height	16
	Left	1
	Top	1
	Width	34

Object	Property	Setting
Browse Control	**Name**	**JobsBrowse**
	Text	Jobs
	Height	16
	Left	37
	Top	1
	Width	32
PushButton	**Name**	**NewCustomerButton**
	Text	New Customer
	Height	2
	Left	1
	Top	16
	Width	34
PushButton	**Name**	**DeleteCustomerButton**
	Text	Delete Customer
	Height	2
	Left	1
	Top	18
	Width	34
PushButton	**Name**	**NewJobButton**
	Text	New Job
	Height	2
	Left	37
	Top	16
	Width	32
PushButton	**Name**	**DeleteJobButton**
	Text	Delete Job
	Height	2
	Left	37
	Top	18
	Width	32

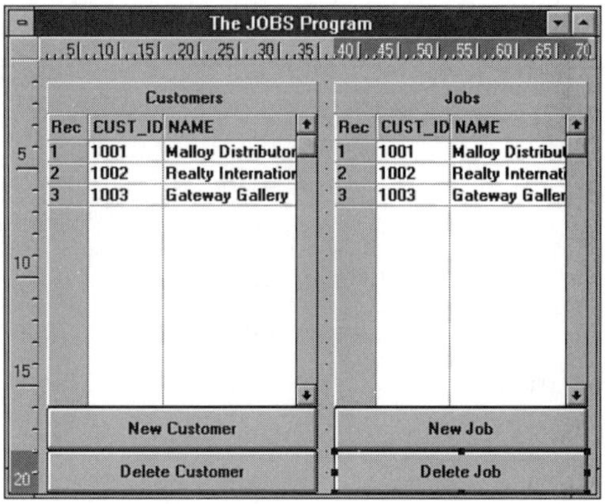

Figure 12.1.
The JOBS.WFM form (in design mode).

Note that Table 12.1 instructs you to set the View property of the JOBS.WFM form to the filename of the CUST_JOB.QBE query. By doing this, you are associating the JOBS.WFM form with the CUST_JOB.QBE query. This means that when the JOBS.WFM is opened, the CUST_JOB.QBE query will be automatically opened. As you know, when the CUST_JOB.QBE query is open, the CUSTOMER.DBF and JOBS.DBF tables are both open (each table in its own work area).

The visual implementation of the JOBS.WFM form is not complete yet. You still must set several properties of the CustomerBrowse and JobsBrowse browse controls. You'll do that in the following two sections.

Setting Additional Properties of the CustomerBrowse Browse Control

You still must set several properties for the CustomerBrowse and JobsBrowse browse controls. In this section you'll set the properties of the CustomerBrowse browse control, and in the next section you'll set the properties of the JobsBrowse browse control.

The Alias property of a browse control determines which table the browse control will access. Follow these steps to set the Alias property of the CustomerBrowse browse control:

- ☐ Make sure that the CustomerBrowse browse control is selected (by clicking on it).
- ☐ Select the Alias property in the Properties window, and then click the tool icon of the Alias property. (The Alias property of the browse control is listed under the Data Linkage Properties item in the Properties window.)

dBASE responds by displaying the Alias Property Builder dialog box. (See Figure 12.2.)

Figure 12.2.
The Alias Property Builder dialog box.

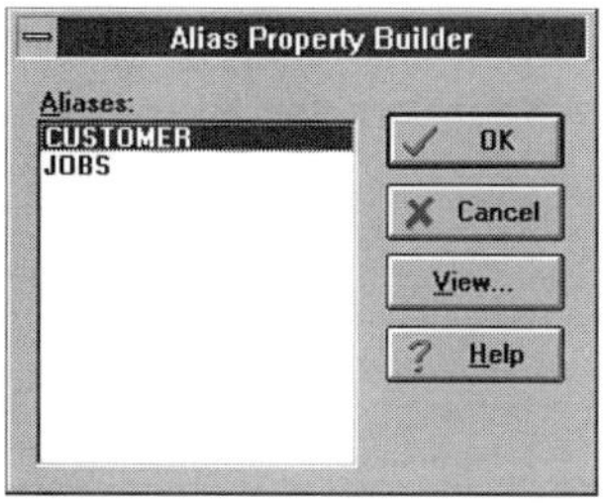

☐ Select CUSTOMER in the Alias Property Builder dialog box, and click the OK button.

By setting the Alias property of the CustomerBrowse browse control to CUSTOMER, you are specifying that the CustomerBrowse browse control will access the CUSTOMER.DBF table.

Next, you must set the Fields property of the CustomerBrowse browse control. As implied by its name, the Fields property of a browse control determines which fields the browse control will display.

Follow these steps to set the Fields property of the CustomerBrowse browse control:

☐ Make sure that the CustomerBrowse browse control is selected (by clicking on it).

☐ Select the Fields property in the Properties window, and then click the Tool icon of the Fields property. (The Fields property of the browse control is listed under the Data Linkage Properties item in the Properties window.)

dBASE responds by displaying the Choose Fields dialog box. (See Figure 12.3.)

Figure 12.3.
The Choose Fields dialog box.

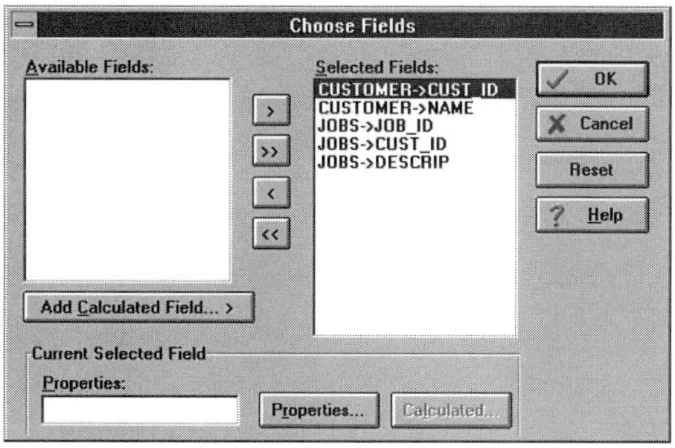

As you can see, the Choose Fields dialog box has two list boxes: Available Fields and Selected Fields.

The Selected Fields list box determines which fields will be included in the browse control. Currently, the Selected Fields list box lists five fields:

```
CUSTOMER->CUST_ID
CUSTOMER->NAME
JOBS->JOB_ID
JOBS->CUST_ID
JOBS->DESCRIP
```

Note: Notice the notation used for the field names:

CUSTOMER->CUST_ID is the CUST_ID field of the CUSTOMER.DBF table, CUSTOMER->NAME is the NAME field of the CUSTOMER.DBF table, JOBS->JOB_ID is the JOB_ID field of the JOBS.DBF table, and so on.

You want the CustomerBrowse browse control to include only the CUSTOMER->CUST_ID and CUSTOMER->NAME fields, so you must change the Selected Fields list to include only these fields. Here is how you do that:

☐ Click the << button in the Choose Fields dialog box.

dBASE responds by moving all the fields listed in the Selected Fields list into the Available Fields list. (See Figure 12.4.)

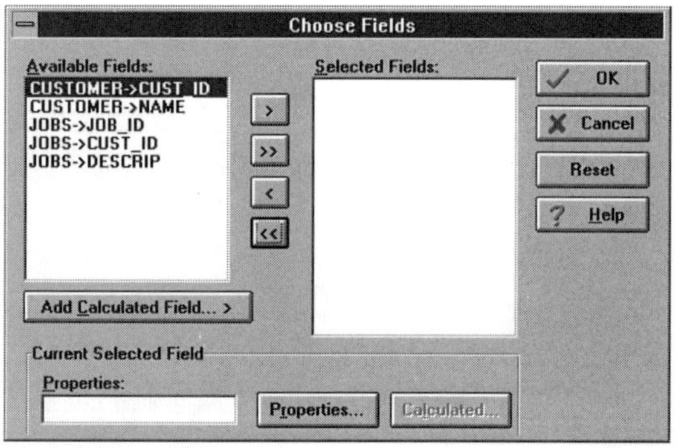

Figure 12.4.
The Choose Fields dialog box after you click the << button.

☐ Select the CUSTOMER->CUST_ID field in the Available Fields list, and click the > button.

dBASE responds by moving the CUSTOMER->CUST_ID field from the Available Fields list into the Selected Fields list.

- [ ] Select the CUSTOMER->NAME field in the Available Fields list, and click the > button.

dBASE responds by moving the CUSTOMER->NAME field from the Available Fields list into the Selected Fields list.

Your Choose Fields dialog box should now look like the one shown in Figure 12.5.

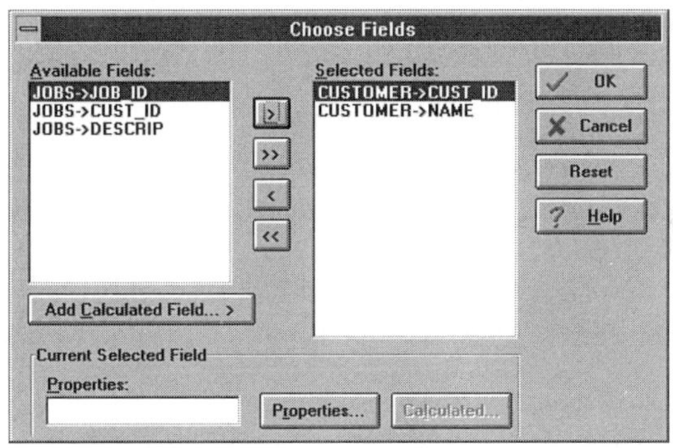

Figure 12.5.
The Choose Fields dialog box after you fill the Selected Fields list with only the CUSTOMER->CUST_ID and CUSTOMER->NAME fields.

Before you close the Choose Fields dialog box, you must do one more thing: You must specify that the CUSTOMER->CUST_ID field will be a read-only field. This step is necessary because you don't want the user to be able to change the value of the CUST_ID field.

To make the CUSTOMER->CUST_ID field read-only, follow these steps:

- [ ] Make sure that the CUSTOMER->CUST_ID field is highlighted in the Selected Fields list, and then click the Properties button.

dBASE responds by displaying the Field Properties dialog box for the CUSTOMER->CUST_ID field. (See Figure 12.6.)

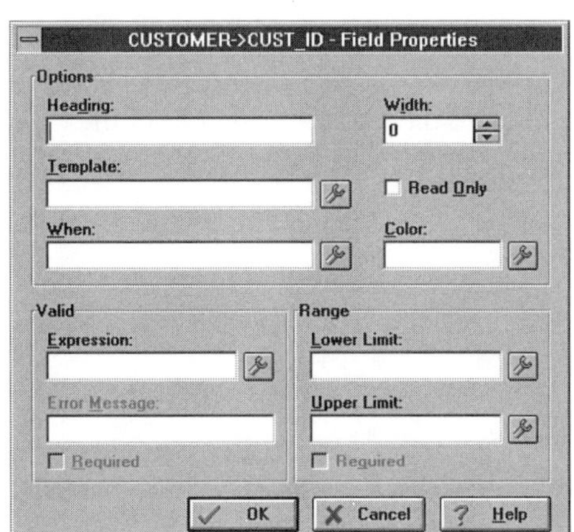

Figure 12.6.
The Field Properties dialog box for the CUSTOMER->CUST_ID field.

As shown in Figure 12.6, the Field Properties dialog box has a Read Only check box. Currently the Read Only check box is empty.

☐ Place an × in the Read Only check box by clicking it.

☐ Close the Field Properties dialog box by clicking its OK button.

☐ Close the Choose Fields dialog box by clicking its OK button.

You've finished setting the Fields property of the CustomerBrowse browse control. You specified that the browse control will include the two fields, CUST_ID and NAME, and that the CUST_ID field is read-only.

Next, you must set the Append and Delete properties of the CustomerBrowse browse control. These properties are listed under the Edit Properties entry of the Properties window.

☐ Set the Append property of the CustomerBrowse browse control to .F..

By setting the Append property of the CustomerBrowse browse control to .F., you are specifying that the user will not be able to append new records to the table by using the browse control. That is, when the user selects the last record in the browse control and then clicks the down-arrow key, nothing will happen. (As you'll see later, the user will be able to add records to the table by clicking the Add Customer button.)

☐ Set the Delete property of the CustomerBrowse browse control to .F..

By setting the Delete property of the CustomerBrowse browse control to .F., you are specifying that the user will not be able to delete a record by using the browse control. (As you'll see later, the user will be able to delete records from the table by clicking the Delete Customer button.)

The last property you must set for the CustomerBrowse browse control is the ShowRecNo property. This property is listed under the Visual Properties entry of the Properties window.

☐ Set the ShowRecNo property of the CustomerBrowse browse control to .F..

By setting the ShowRecNo property of the CustomerBrowse browse control to .F., you are specifying that the browse control will not include the Rec column.

You've finished setting the properties of the CustomerBrowse browse control.

☐ Save your work by selecting Save from the File menu.

Setting Properties of the JobsBrowse Browse Control

Just as you set the Alias, Fields, Append, Delete, and ShowRecNo properties of the CustomerBrowse browse control, you must similarly set the same properties of the JobsBrowse browse control:

- ☐ Set the Alias property of the JobsBrowse browse control to JOBS.
- ☐ Set the Fields property of the JobsBrowse browse control to the two fields JOBS->JOB_ID and JOBS->DESCRIP.
- ☐ Make the JOBS->JOB_ID field a read-only field (just as you made the CUST_ID field of the CustomerBrowse browse control read-only).
- ☐ Set the Append property of the JobsBrowse browse control to .F..
- ☐ Set the Delete property of the JobsBrowse browse control to .F..
- ☐ Set the ShowRecNo property of the JobsBrowse browse control to .F..

You've completed the Visual design of the JOBS.WFM form. Your JOBS.WFM form should now look like the one shown in Figure 12.7.

Figure 12.7.
The completed JOBS.WFM form (in design mode).

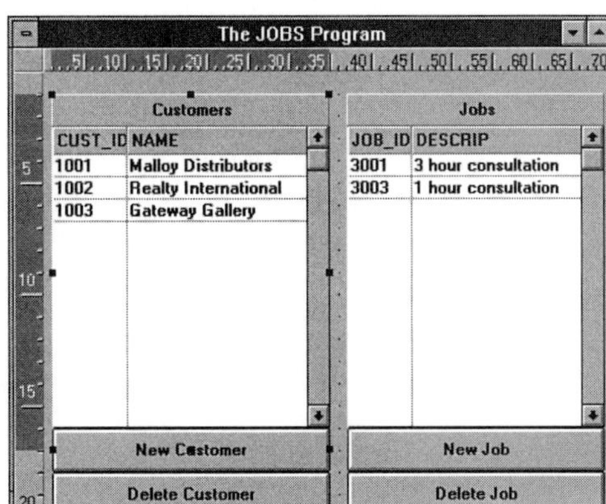

To see your visual implementation in action, follow these steps:

- ☐ Execute the form by clicking the Run tool on the toolbar of dBASE.

    dBASE responds by executing the JOBS.WFM form. (See Figure 12.8.)

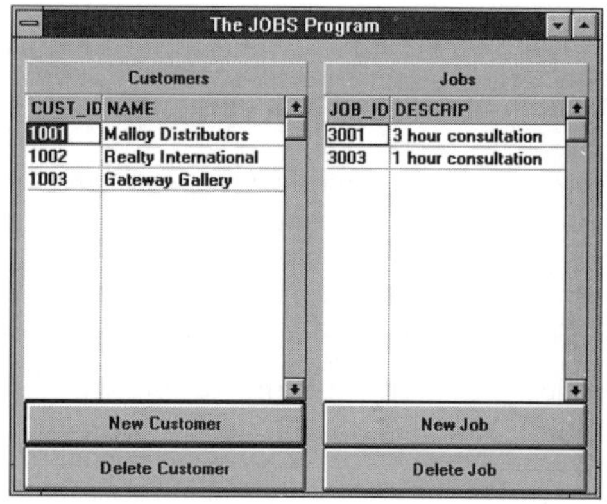

Figure 12.8.
The JOBS.WFM form in run mode.

Experiment with the JOBS.WFM form as instructed next:

- Move from one record to another in the browse control of the CUSTOMER.DBF table.

As you move from one record to another, the browse control of the JOBS.DBF table displays the jobs of the currently selected customer.

- Try to type something in the CUST_ID field of any record of the CUSTOMER.DBF table.

As expected, nothing happens when you type in the CUST_ID field of the CUSTOMER.DBF browse control. That's because you made the CUST_ID field of the CUSTOMER.DBF browse control read-only.

- Try to type something in the JOB_ID field of any record of the JOBS.DBF table.

Again, as expected, nothing happens when you type in the JOB_ID field of the JOBS.DBF browse control. That's because you made the JOB_ID field of the JOBS.DBF browse control read-only.

- Click the minus icon of the JOBS program to display the system menu, and then select Close from the System menu that pops up.

Note: As you develop your Visual dBASE program, you might find the following shortcuts useful:

- To execute a program, press F2.
- To terminate the program and place the form in design mode, press Shift+F2.

Do not, however, press Shift+F2 while a browse control has the focus. That is, press Tab until a pushbutton has the focus, and then press Shift+F2 to terminate the program. (If you press Shift+F2 while the browse control has the focus, the program will not terminate; rather the browse control will changes its display mode.)

As you have just verified, although you have not yet written a single line of code, the JOBS.WFM form already has a lot of functionality. For one thing, the CUSTOMER.DBF and JOBS.DBF tables are joined on the CUST_ID field. As you move from one record to another in the CUSTOMER.DBF table, the browse control of the JOBS.DBF table displays the appropriate records.

The CUSTOMER.DBF and JOBS.DBF tables are joined thanks to the CUST_JOB.QBE query you designed. That is, because you set the View property of the JOBS.WFM form to the CUST_JOB.QBE query, when the form is opened, the CUST_JOB.QBE query is automatically opened. The CUST_JOB.QBE query opens both the CUSTOMER.DBF table and the JOBS.DBF table (each table in its own work area) and joins these tables on the CUST_ID field.

Entering the Code of the JOBS Program

In the following sections you'll attach code to the JOBS.WFM form. This code will enable the user to delete records from and add records to the CUSTOMER.DBF and JOBS.DBF tables.

Attaching Code to the *OnOpen* Event of the JOBS.WFM Form

As you know, the `OnOpen` event of a form occurs when the form is first opened. The `OnOpen` event of the form is therefore a good place to write initialization code for the form.

☐ Attach the following code to the `OnOpen` event of the JOBS.WFM form. After you write this code, the `Form_OnOpen` procedure should look as follows:

```
Procedure Form_OnOpen

 * Declare a public (global) variable to hold the name
 * of the directory where the program resides.
 PUBLIC gProgDir
 * Get the name of the directory where the program resides.
 gProgDir = LEFT(PROGRAM(0),RAT("\",PROGRAM(0)))

 * Deleted records should be ignored.
 SET DELETED ON
```

```
    * Order the records by the NAME field.
    SET ORDER TO NAME

    * Move the record pointer to the first record.
    GOTO TOP

  Return
```

☐ Save your work by selecting Save from the File menu.

The first statement you typed in the `Form_OnOpen` procedure declares a public (global) variable called `gProgDir`:

```
PUBLIC gProgDir
```

The next statement extracts the directory name from which the program is executed and stores this name in the global variable `gProgDir`:

```
gProgDir = LEFT(PROGRAM(0),RAT("\",PROGRAM(0)))
```

For example, if the JOBS.WFM program resides in the directory C:\DBPROG\CH11, the global variable `gProgDir` is filled with the string `"C:\DBPROG\CH11\"`.

The next statement tells dBASE not to process records that are marked for deletion.

```
SET DELETED ON
```

Later in the chapter you'll write the code that enables the user to delete records. By setting `SET DELETED` to `ON`, you are specifying that all the records that the user deletes will not be seen by the user.

The next statement orders the records of the CUSTOMER.DBF table by the NAME field:

```
SET ORDER TO NAME
```

Recall that when you created the CUSTOMER.DBF table, you added an index to the NAME field.

Finally, the record pointer of the CUSTOMER.DBF table is moved to the first record in the table by issuing the `GOTO TOP` command:

```
GOTO TOP
```

> **Note:** Because you set the View property of the JOBS.WFM form to the name of the CUST_JOB.QBE query, when the JOBS.WFM is opened, both tables, CUSTOMER.DBF and JOBS.DBF, are automatically opened (each table in its own work area).

> The two statements you typed in the `OnOpen` procedure, work on the CUSTOMER.DBF table (*not* on the JOBS.DBF table):
>
> ```
> SET ORDER TO NAME
> GOTO TOP
> ```
>
> That's because on startup of the JOBS.WFM program, the current work area is set by default to the work area of the parent table (CUSTOMER.DBF).

So the initialization code you attached to the `OnOpen` event of the JOBS.WFM form performs four tasks:

- It fills a global variable, called `gProgDir`, with the name of the directory from which the JOBS.WFM program is executed.
- It sets the `DELETED` setting `ON` so that all deleted records will be invisible.
- It orders the CUSTOMER.DBF table by the NAME field.
- It moves the record pointer of CUSTOMER.DBF to the first record of the table.

To see the code you attached to the `OnOpen` event in action, do the following:

☐ Execute the JOBS.WFM form (press F2).

The JOBS.WFM form appears, as shown in Figure 12.9.

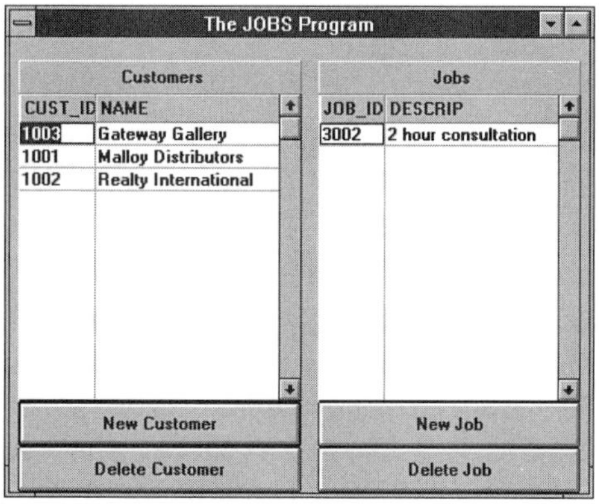

Figure 12.9.
The JOBS.WFM form in run mode (now the records of the CUSTOMER.DBF table are ordered by the NAME field).

As you can see in Figure 12.9, the records of the CUSTOMER.DBF table are now ordered by the NAME field.

☐ Change the mode of the JOBS.WFM form back to design mode by moving the focus to any of the pushbuttons and pressing Shift+F2.

Attaching Code to the *OnClick* Event of the New Customer Pushbutton

When the user clicks the New Customer button, the JOBS.WFM program should add a new record to the CUSTOMER.DBF table and fill the CUST_ID field of the new record with a unique customer ID. You'll next write the code that accomplishes this task.

☐ Attach the following code to the `OnClick` event of the New Customer pushbutton. After you write this code, the `NEWCUSTOMER_OnClick` procedure should look as follows:

```
Procedure NEWCUSTOMERBUTTON_OnClick

 * Switch to the work area of the CUSTOMER.DBF table.
 SELECT CUSTOMER

 * Get the next unique Customer ID number.
 SET ORDER TO CUST_ID
 GOTO BOTTOM
 CustID = VAL(CUSTOMER->CUST_ID)+1

 * Convert CustID to a string.
 strCustID = STR(CustID,4,0,"0")

 * Add a new record to the CUSTOMER.DBF table.
 APPEND BLANK

 * Set the CUST_ID field of the new record.
 REPLACE CUSTOMER->CUST_ID WITH strCustID
 * Order the records by the NAME field.
 SET ORDER TO NAME

 * Give the keyboard focus to the CustomerBrowse
 * browse control.
 form.CustomerBrowse.SetFocus()

Return
```

☐ Save your work by selecting Save from the File menu.

The first statement you typed in the `NEWCUSTOMER_OnClick` procedure sets the current work area to the work area of the CUSTOMER.DBF table:

```
SELECT CUSTOMER
```

All subsequent commands in the procedure will therefore be performed on the CUSTOMER.DBF table.

The next three statements find a unique customer ID for the new record:

```
SET ORDER TO CUST_ID
GOTO BOTTOM
CustID = VAL(CUSTOMER->CUST_ID)+1
```

The statement

```
SET ORDER TO CUST_ID
```

orders the records of the CUSTOMER.DBF table by the CUST_ID field. So at this point the last record in the CUSTOMER.DBF table has the largest customer ID. The record pointer is moved to the last record in the table by the statement

```
GOTO BOTTOM
```

And finally a unique customer ID is calculated by incrementing the value of the CUST_ID field of the last record by 1:

```
CustID = VAL(CUSTOMER->CUST_ID) + 1
```

So at this point the variable `CustID` holds a numeric value of a unique customer ID.

The next statement converts the numeric value of the `CustID` variable to a string, and this string is assigned to the variable `strCustID`:

```
strCustID = STR(CustID,4,0,"0")
```

So at this point the string variable `strCustID` holds a unique customer ID.

The next statement adds a new, blank record to the CUSTOMER.DBF table:

```
APPEND BLANK
```

Then the CUST_ID field of the new record is filled with the value of the `strCustID` variable:

```
REPLACE CUSTOMER->CUST_ID WITH strCustID
```

So now the CUST_ID field is filled with a unique customer ID.

The next statement orders the records of the CUSTOMER.DBF table by the NAME field:

```
SET ORDER TO NAME
```

And finally, the statement

```
form.CustomerBrowse.SetFocus()
```

gives the keyboard focus to the CustomerBrowse browse control (so that the user will be able to type data into the new added record).

To see in action the code you attached to the `OnClick` event of the NewCustomer pushbutton, follow these steps:

☐ Execute the JOBS.WFM form.

☐ Click the New Customer button.

The JOBS.WFM program responds by adding a new record to the CUSTOMER.DBF table and assigning a unique customer ID to this new record. (See Figure 12.10.)

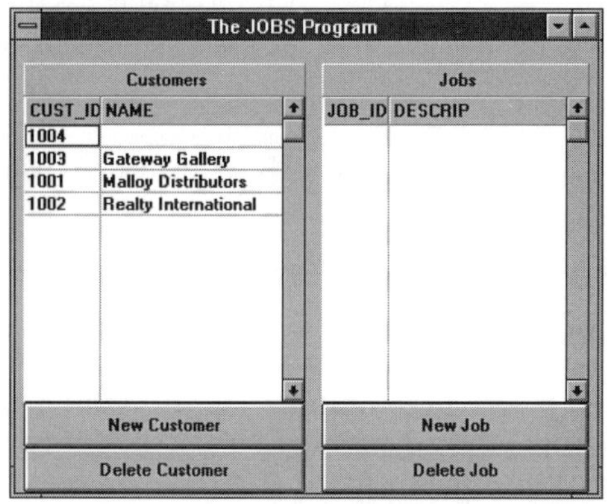

Figure 12.10.
The JOBS.WFM form after you click the New Customer button. A new record with a unique customer ID has been added to the CUSTOMER.DBF table.

☐ Type the name `Golden Studios` in the NAME field of the new customer.

☐ Move the record pointer of the CUSTOMER.DBF table (by pressing the Page Up key), and notice how the browse control reorders the records of the CUSTOMER.DBF table so that the records (including the record you've just added) are ordered by the NAME field.

☐ Change the mode of the JOBS.WFM form back to design mode.

Attaching Code to the *OnClick* Event of the Delete Customer Pushbutton

When the user clicks the Delete Customer pushbutton, the JOBS.WFM program should delete the currently selected record in the CUSTOMER.DBF table. The program should also delete all the jobs of this customer (if any) in the JOBS.DBF table. You'll now write the code that accomplishes these tasks.

☐ Attach the following code to the `OnClick` event of the Delete Customer pushbutton. After you write this code, the `DELETECUSTOMER_OnClick` procedure should look as follows:

```
Procedure DELETECUSTOMERBUTTON_OnClick

* Select the work area of the CUSTOMER.DBF table.
SELECT CUSTOMER

* If the CUSTOMER.DBF table is empty, terminate
* this procedure.
```

```
IF EOF()
   RETURN
ENDIF

* Get a confirmation from the user.
Question = "Are you sure you want to delete this customer?"
Response = MsgBox (Question, "QUESTION", 4+32)

* If user's response is Yes, issue a DELETE command.
IF Response = 6


   * Delete the record in the CUSTOMER.DBF table.
   ON ERROR MsgBox("Record was not deleted!","MESSAGE",48)
   DELETE
   ON ERROR

   * Move the record pointer to the first record.
   GOTO TOP

ENDIF

Return
```

☐ Save your work by selecting Save from the File menu.

The first statement you typed in the `DELETECUSTOMER_OnClick` procedure sets the current work area to the work area of the CUSTOMER.DBF table:

```
SELECT CUSTOMER
```

All subsequent commands in the procedure will therefore be performed on the CUSTOMER.DBF table.

12

The next statement is an `IF` statement:

```
IF EOF()
   RETURN
ENDIF
```

This `IF` statement checks whether the record pointer is at the end of file. If the record pointer is at the end of file, the CUSTOMER.DBF table is currently empty, in which case the `RETURN` statement is executed to terminate the procedure.

If, however, the CUSTOMER.DBF table has at least one record, the remaining statements in the procedure are executed.

The two statements

```
Question = "Are you sure you want to delete this customer?"
Response = MsgBox (Question, "QUESTION", 4+32)
```

display a message box asking the user to confirm the deletion.

An `IF` statement is then used to evaluate the user's answer:

```
IF Response = 6

   * Delete the record in the CUSTOMER.DBF table.
   ON ERROR MsgBox("Record was not deleted!","MESSAGE",48)
   DELETE
   ON ERROR

   * Move the record pointer to the first record.
   GOTO TOP

ENDIF
```

If the user clicked the Yes button of the message box, the preceding `IF` statement is satisfied, and the three statements under the `IF` are executed:

```
ON ERROR MsgBox("Record was not deleted!","MESSAGE",48)
DELETE
ON ERROR
```

These statements issue a `DELETE` command. As a result, the current record in the CUSTOMER.DBF table is deleted. Note that before the `DELETE` command is issued, an error trap is set with the statement

```
ON ERROR MsgBox("Record was not deleted!","MESSAGE",48)
```

Therefore, if the `DELETE` command fails, the program displays a message box with the `Record was not deleted!` message.

After the `DELETE` command is issued, the error trap is removed:

```
ON ERROR
```

That is, using the `ON ERROR` statement without specifying a command removes the error trap.

Finally, the following statement is executed:

```
GOTO TOP
```

After the user deletes a customer, the record pointer of the CUSTOMER.DBF table will move to the first record.

As you'll soon see, when the user deletes a record of a certain customer in the CUSTOMER.DBF table, dBASE automatically deletes all the records with the same CUST_ID in the JOBS.DBF table. dBASE takes this action because when you specified the relation of the CUSTOMER.DBF and JOBS.DBF tables (refer to Figure 11.8 in Chapter 11), you placed an × in the Enforce Integrity check box.

To see in action the code you attached to the `OnClick` event of the Delete Customer pushbutton, follow these steps:

☐ Execute the JOBS.WFM form.

☐ Select the customer `Malloy Distributors` in the CUSTOMER.DBF browse control.

☐ Click the Delete Customer button.

The JOBS.WFM program responds by displaying a message box asking you to confirm that you want to perform the deletion. (See Figure 12.11.)

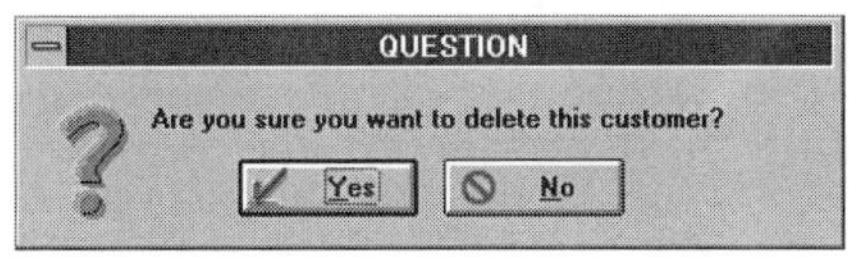

Figure 12.11.
The message box that the JOBS.WFM program displays after you click the Delete Customer button.

☐ Click the Yes button of the message box. (That is, yes you want to perform the deletion.)

Another message box appears. (See Figure 12.12.) This message box is telling you that the customer you are trying to delete has related records in the JOBS.DBF table.

Figure 12.12.
The Alert message box that appears when the user tries to delete a customer that has related records in the JOBS.DBF table.

☐ Click the No button of the Alert message box. (That is, you don't want to perform the deletion.)

Another message box appears, telling you that the deletion has not been performed. (See Figure 12.13.)

Figure 12.13.
The message box that the JOBS.WFM program displays after you cancel the deletion by clicking the No button of the Alert message box.

Now, repeat the previous steps, but this time do not cancel the deletion:

☐ Make sure that the customer `Malloy Distributors` is currently selected in the CUSTOMER.DBF browse control.

☐ Click the Delete Customer button.

The JOBS.WFM program responds by displaying a message box asking you to confirm that you want to perform the deletion.

☐ Click the Yes button of the message box.

An Alert message box appears.

☐ Click the Yes button of the Alert message box.

The JOBS.WFM program responds by deleting the record of the customer you selected as well as all the related records in the JOBS.DBF table. That is, all the jobs of the customer you deleted are also deleted.

☐ Change the mode of the JOBS.WFM form back to design mode.

Note that you did not have to write the code that displays the Alert message (see Figure 12.13), and you did not have to write the code that automatically deletes all the related records in the JOBS.DBF table. These tasks were performed for you by dBASE because when you defined the relation of the CUSTOMER.DBF and JOBS.DBF tables (refer to Figure 11.8 in Chapter 11), you placed an × in the Enforce Integrity check box.

Attaching Code to the *OnClick* Event of the New Job Pushbutton

When the user clicks the New Job button, the JOBS.WFM program should perform the following three tasks:

- Add a new record to the JOBS.DBF table.
- Fill the JOB_ID field of the new record with a unique job ID.
- Fill the CUST_ID field of the new record with the same value of the CUST_ID field of the current record in the CUSTOMER.DBF table (because the user is adding a job for the currently selected customer).

You'll now write the code that performs these tasks.

☐ Attach the following code to the `OnClick` event of the New Job pushbutton. After you write this code, the `NEWJOB_OnClick` procedure should look as follows:

```
Procedure NEWJOBBUTTON_OnClick

 * If the CUSTOMERS.DBF table is empty, terminate
 * this procedure.
 SELECT CUSTOMER
```

```
IF EOF()
   RETURN
ENDIF

* Get the next unique Job ID number.
SELECT SELECT()
JobsDBF = gProgDir+"JOBS.DBF"
USE &JobsDBF AGAIN ALIAS Temp
SET ORDER TO JOB_ID
GOTO BOTTOM
JobID = VAL(TEMP->JOB_ID)+1
USE

* Convert JobID to a string.
strJobID = STR(JobID,4,0,"0")

* Select the work area of the JOBS.DBF table.
SELECT JOBS

* Add a new record to the JOBS.DBF table.
APPEND BLANK

* Set the CUST_ID field of the new record.
REPLACE JOBS->JOB_ID WITH strJobID

* Give the keyboard focus to the JobsBrowse
* browse control.
form.JobsBrowse.SetFocus()

Return
```

☐ Save your work by selecting Save from the File menu.

The first statement you typed in the `NEWJOB_OnClick` procedure sets the current work area to the work area of the CUSTOMER.DBF table:

```
SELECT CUSTOMER
```

The next statement is an `IF` statement:

```
IF EOF()
   RETURN
ENDIF
```

This `IF` statement checks whether the record pointer of the CUSTOMER.DBF table is at the end of file. If the record pointer is at the end of file, the CUSTOMER.DBF table is currently empty, in which case the `RETURN` statement is executed to terminate the procedure.

The reason for terminating the procedure when the CUSTOMER.DBF table is empty is that you always want the user to add a job that relates to a customer. In other words, the user is not allowed to add a job that is not performed for a certain customer.

If the CUSTOMER.DBF table has at least one record, the remaining statements in the procedure are executed.

12

The next block of statements finds a unique job ID for the new record:

```
SELECT SELECT()
JobsDBF = gProgDir+"JOBS.DBF"
USE &JobsDBF AGAIN ALIAS Temp
SET ORDER TO JOB_ID
GOTO BOTTOM
JobID = VAL(TEMP->JOB_ID)+1
USE
```

The statement

```
SELECT SELECT()
```

selects a new work area.

Then, the statements

```
JobsDBF = gProgDir+"JOBS.DBF"
USE &JobsDBF AGAIN ALIAS Temp
```

open the JOBS.DBF table in the new work area. (Note that by specifying `ALIAS Temp`, you are telling dBASE that the name of the current work area is Temp.)

Then the statement

```
SET ORDER TO JOB_ID
```

orders the records of the JOBS.DBF table by the JOB_ID field. At this point, the last record in the JOBS.DBF table (in the Temp work area) has the largest job ID. The record pointer is then moved to the last record in the table by the statement

```
GOTO BOTTOM
```

And a unique job ID is calculated by incrementing the value of the JOB_ID field of the last record by 1:

```
JobID = VAL(TEMP->JOB_ID)+1
```

So now the variable `JobID` holds a numeric value of a unique job ID.

The next statement closes the JOBS.DBF table in the current work area (the Temp work area):

```
USE
```

That is, when you use the `USE` command without specifying a table name, the table in the current work area is closed.

The next statement converts the numeric value of the `JobID` variable to a string, and this string is assigned to the variable `strJobID`:

```
strJobID = STR(JobID,4,0,"0")
```

At this point, the string variable `strJobID` holds a unique job ID.

The next statement sets the current work area to the work area of the JOBS.DBF table:

```
SELECT JOBS
```

All subsequent commands in the procedure will therefore be performed on the JOBS.DBF table.

The next statement adds a new, blank record to the JOBS.DBF table:

```
APPEND BLANK
```

Then the JOB_ID field of the new record is filled with the value of the `strJobID` variable:

```
REPLACE JOBS->JOB_ID WITH strJobID
```

So now the JOB_ID field is filled with a unique job ID.

Finally, the statement

```
form.JobsBrowse.SetFocus()
```

gives the keyboard focus to the JobsBrowse browse control (so that the user will be able to type data into the new added record).

Note that in the preceding code you did not have to write the code that updates the CUST_ID field of the new record you added to JOBS.DBF. dBASE automatically filled the CUST_ID field of the new record of JOBS.DBF with the value of the CUST_ID field of the current record in the CUSTOMER.DBF table. dBASE performs this task for you automatically because when you defined the relation of the CUSTOMER.DBF and JOBS.DBF tables (refer to Figure 11.8 in Chapter 11), you placed an × in the Enforce Integrity check box.

12

To see in action the code you attached to the `OnClick` event of the New Job pushbutton, follow these steps:

- ☐ Execute the JOBS.WFM form.
- ☐ Select any of the customers in the browse control of the CUSTOMER.DBF table.
- ☐ Click the New Job push button.

  The JOBS.WFM program responds by adding a new record to the JOBS.DBF table (for the currently selected customer) and assigning a unique job ID to this new record.

- ☐ Change the mode of the JOBS.WFM form back to design mode.

Attaching Code to the *OnClick* Event of the Delete Job Pushbutton

When the user clicks the Delete Job button, the JOBS.WFM program should delete the currently selected job in the JOBS.DBF table. You'll next write the code that accomplishes this task.

- Attach the following code to the OnClick event of the Delete Job pushbutton. After you write this code, the DELETEJOB_OnClick procedure should look as follows:

```
Procedure DELETEJOBBUTTON_OnClick

* Select the work area of the JOBS.DBF table.
SELECT JOBS

* If the JOBS.DBF table is empty, terminate this procedure.
IF EOF()
   RETURN
 ENDIF

* Get a confirmation from the user.
Question = "Are you sure you want to delete this job?"
Response = MsgBox (Question, "QUESTION", 4+32)
* If user's response is Yes, delete this job.
IF Response = 6

   * Delete the current record in the JOBS.DBF table.
   DELETE

ENDIF

Return
```

- Save your work by selecting Save from the File menu.

The first statement you typed in the DELETEJOB_OnClick procedure sets the current work area to the work area of the JOBS.DBF table:

```
SELECT JOBS
```

Therefore, all subsequent commands in the procedure will be performed on the JOBS.DBF table.

The next statement is an IF statement:

```
IF EOF()
   RETURN
ENDIF
```

This IF statement checks whether the record pointer is at the end of file. If the record pointer is at the end of file, the JOBS.DBF table is currently empty, in which case the RETURN statement is executed to terminate the procedure.

If, however, the JOBS.DBF table has at least one record, the remaining statements in the procedure are executed.

The two statements

```
Question = "Are you sure you want to delete this job?"
Response = MsgBox (Question, "QUESTION", 4+32)
```

display a message box asking the user to confirm the deletion.

An `IF` statement is then used to evaluate the user's answer:

```
IF Response = 6

   * Delete the current record in the JOBS.DBF table.
   DELETE

ENDIF
```

If the user clicked the Yes button of the message box, the preceding `IF` statement is satisfied, and the statement under the `IF` is executed:

```
DELETE
```

This statement issues a `DELETE` command. As a result, the current record in the JOBS.DBF table is deleted.

To see in action the code you attached to the `OnClick` event of the Delete Job pushbutton, follow these steps:

- ☐ Execute the JOBS.WFM form.
- ☐ Select any customer that has related jobs.
- ☐ Select any job in the JOBS.DBF browse control.
- ☐ Click the Delete Job button.

  The JOBS.WFM program responds by displaying a message box asking you to confirm that you want to perform the deletion. (See Figure 12.14.)

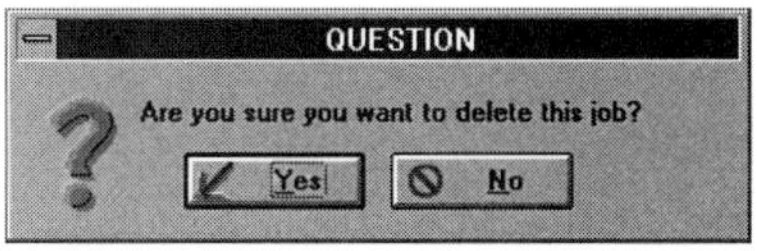

Figure 12.14.
The message box that the JOBS.WFM program displays after you click the Delete Job button.

- ☐ Click the Yes button of the message box. (That is, yes you want to perform the deletion.)

  The JOBS.WFM program responds by deleting the record you selected.

- ☐ Change the mode of the JOBS.WFM form back to design mode.

Summary

In this chapter you have written a dBASE program (the JOBS program) that uses a joined table. Before writing the program, you had to join two tables (prepare a query). The program you wrote used the query. In this chapter you also implemented a mechanism for appending and deleting records.

Q&A

Q In Chapter 11 I learned that to open a query file I must use the `SET VIEW` command. Yet in this chapter I wrote a program that uses a query, and the `SET VIEW` command was not used. Why not?

A The reason you did not have to use the `SET VIEW` command when you wrote the code of the JOBS.WFM program is that during the visual implementation of the JOBS.WFM form, you set the View property of the form to the name of the query file you want to use (the CUST_JOB.QBE query). This means that when JOBS.WFM is opened, the CUST_JOB.QBE query will be automatically opened. That is, the form executes the `SET VIEW` command for you.

Quiz

1. Suppose that you have a form called MyForm.WFM and a query file called MyQuery.QBE. How would you associate the MyQuery.QBE query with the MyForm.WFM form?
2. Suppose that you created a query file, called TB1_TB2.QBE, that joins the two tables TABLE1.DBF and TABLE2.DBF. What happens after you execute the following statement:

   ```
   SET VIEW TO TB1_TB2.QBE
   ```
3. Which property of a browse control do you have to set in order to specify which table is accessed by the browse control?
4. Which property of a browse control do you have to set in order to specify which fields will be included in the browse control?

Exercise

In the exercise of the preceding chapter, you designed two tables, CLIENTS.DBF and INVOICES.DBF, and created a query called CLNT_INV.QBE that joins these two tables.

Write a dBASE program that uses the CLNT_INV.QBE query.

Quiz Answers

1. To associate the MyForm.WFM form with the MyQuery.QBE query, you must set the View property of the MyForm.WFM form to the name of the MyQuery.QBE file.
2. After you execute the statement

   ```
   SET VIEW TO TB1_TB2.QBE
   ```

   the two tables TABLE1.DBF and TABLE2.DBF will be opened (each table in its own work area). The two tables will also be joined as specified by the TB1_TB2.QBE query.
3. To specify which table the browse control will access, you must set the Alias property of the browse control.
4. To specify which fields the browse control will include, you must set the Fields property of the browse control.

Exercise Answer

Use the same steps you used for creating the JOBS program. When the user browses through the records of the CLIENTS.DBF table, the corresponding records of the INVOICES.DBF table are displayed.

WEEK 2

13

Searching

In this chapter you'll learn how to write code that searches for particular data in a database. After all, this is the main reason people use PCs for storing data. That is, a huge amount of information is stored electronically on the hard drive (instead of being stored on hard copies). The program you'll write in this chapter enables the user to search for any particular record in the database by just clicking a button (a process that is of course quicker and easier than searching for data among thousands of sheets of paper).

In the next chapter you'll enhance the program. In particular, you will learn how to perform various field calculations and how to create a filter for your tables.

Creating the CUSTOMER.DBF Table

The SearchIt program you'll write in this chapter uses the CUSTOMER.DBF table. Here is how you create the CUSTOMER.DBF table:

☐ Type `MD C:\DBPROG\CH13` in the Command window, and then press Enter.

dBASE responds by creating the directory C:\DBPROG\CH13.

☐ In the Command window type `Create C:\DBPROG\CH13\CUSTOMER`, and then press Enter.

dBASE responds by displaying the Table Structure window. (See Figure 13.1.)

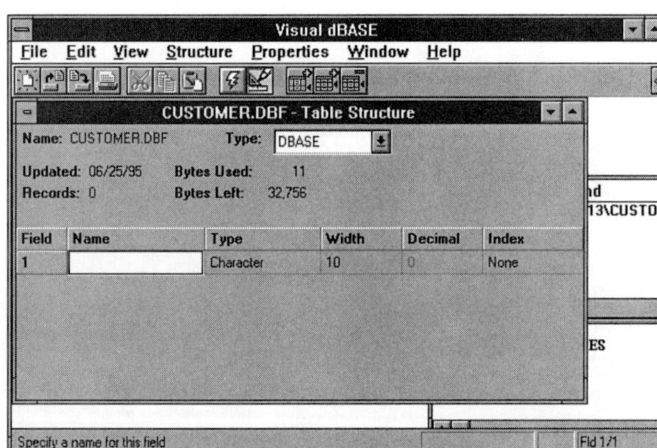

Figure 13.1.
The empty Table Structure of the CUSTOMER.DBF table.

☐ Fill in the Table Structure of the CUSTOMER.DBF table as shown here:

Field	*Name*	*Type*	*Width*	*Index*
1	NAME	Character	20	Ascend
2	STREET	Character	20	None
3	CITY	Character	20	None

4	STATE	Character	5	None
5	ZIPCODE	Character	5	None

The completed Table Structure window is shown in Figure 13.2.

☐ Select Save from the File menu to save the structure of the CUSTOMER.DBF table.

☐ Select Close from the File menu to close the Table Structure of the CUSTOMER.DBF table.

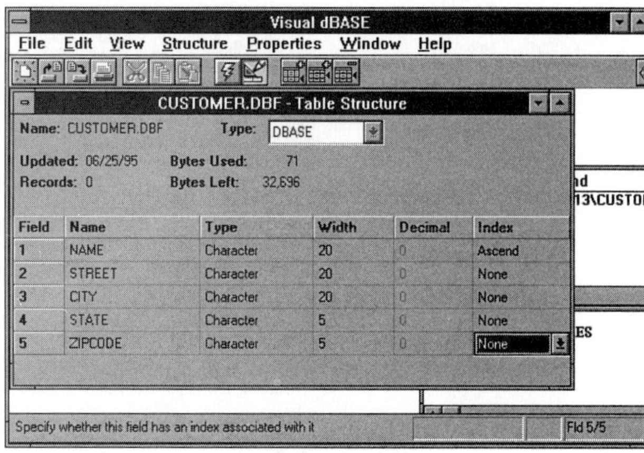

Figure 13.2.
The Table Structure of the CUSTOMER.DBF table.

Filling the CUSTOMER.DBF Table with Data

The SearchIt program you'll write in this chapter demonstrates how you can locate records in the CUSTOMER.DBF table. As you'll soon see, there are various ways of searching records, and each method has its advantages and disadvantages. Basically, a "good" search is a search that is being performed quickly. You'll be able to evaluate how fast or slow the search is if the table has many records in it. Your next step, therefore, is to fill the CUSTOMER.DBF table with a lot of records. You'll fill the CUSTOMER.DBF table with 10,000 records.

☐ In the Command window type `GENERATE 10000`, and then press Enter.

dBASE responds by filling 10,000 records with random data. Depending on how fast your PC is, the process of generating 10,000 records might take some time. If you don't have enough hard-drive space, generate only 1,000 records by typing

```
GENERATE 1000
```

To browse through the records of the CUSTOMER.DBF table, take the following action:

- ☐ In the Command window type `BROWSE`, and then press Enter.

  dBASE responds by displaying the CUSTOMER.DBF window, ready for you to browse. (See Figure 13.3.) You can now press the arrow keys to browse through the CUSTOMER.DBF table.

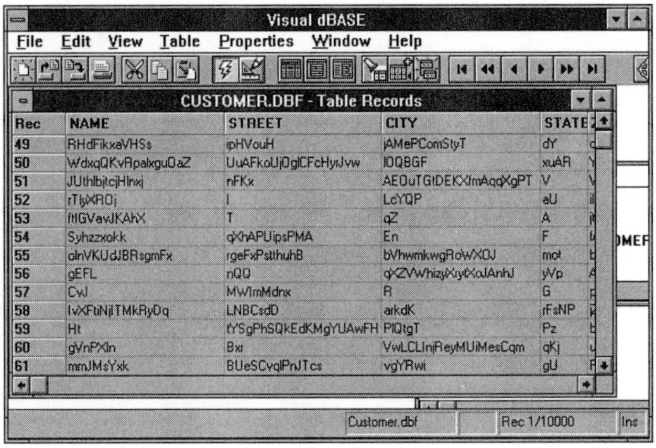

Figure 13.3.
The CUSTOMER.DBF table with random data in it.

The SearchIt Program

The SearchIt program demonstrates how to write a dBASE program that searches for a record. Before you start writing the SearchIt program, you need to know what the program should do.

When you start the SearchIt program, the main window should look like the one shown in Figure 13.4.

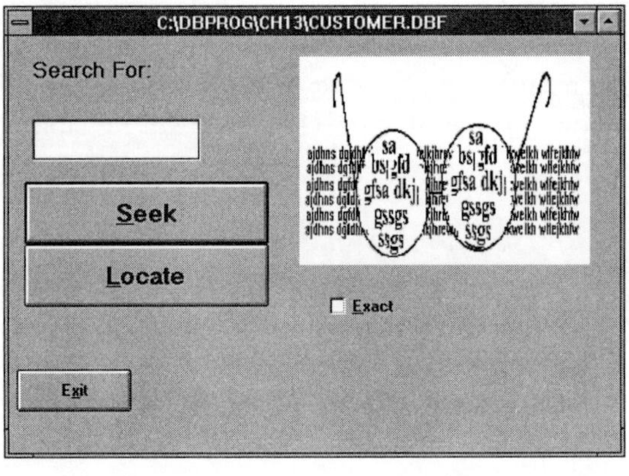

Figure 13.4.
The main window of the SearchIt program.

The main window of the SearchIt program contains a picture of magnifying glasses (an appropriate picture for searching). Of course, the image is placed in the window for cosmetic purposes only.

Note: dBASE for Windows is a serious programming package used for performing serious database manipulations. Nevertheless, your user expects your program to behave like other Windows programs. This means that your user expects your program to include attractive-looking windows that contain some graphics in them (such as the glasses picture shown in Figure 13.4).

The user can type a name in the Search For entry field. Then the user clicks a button to search for a record whose NAME field is equal to the name typed in the entry field. As you can see, there are two buttons: Seek and Locate.

When you click the Seek button, the SearchIt program searches for the record using the dBASE `Seek()` function.

When you click the Locate button, the SearchIt program searches for the record using the dBASE `Locate` command.

Note: In the Q&A section at the end of the chapter you will learn how to further enhance the SearchIt program so that when a search is successful, the SearchIt program prompts the user with a human voice audio prompt.

The SearchIt program will play the audio prompt (human voice) whether the user has a sound card or not. That is, if the user has a sound card, the voice will be played through the sound card. If, however, the user does not have a sound card, the voice will be played through the internal built-in speaker that every PC has. (The SearchIt program will be able to play through the PC speaker without the need for any Windows drivers.)

The Visual Implementation of the SearchIt.WFM Form

You'll now visually implement the SearchIt.WFM form.

☐ In the Command window type `CREATE FORM C:\DBPROG\CH13\SearchIt`, and then press Enter.

dBASE responds by creating the SearchIt.WFM form and displaying the empty SearchIt.WFM form.

☐ Implement the SearchIt.WFM form according to the specifications in Table 13.1. When you finish implementing the form, it should look like the one shown in Figure 13.5.

Table 13.1. The properties table of the SearchIt.WFM form.

Object	Property	Setting
Form	**Text**	**Form**
	Top	0
	Width	80
	MDI	.F.
	View	C:\DBPROG\CH13\CUSTOMER.DBF
	Height	20
	Left	1
Entry Field	**Name**	**NameEntry**
	Top	2
	Width	22
	Value	(make it empty)
	Height	2
	Left	3
Text	**Name**	**Text1**
	Top	4
	Width	30
	Text	Search For:
	FontSize	12
	ColorNormal	N/W
	Height	2
	Left	3
PushButton	**Name**	**SeekButton**
	Top	7
	Width	32
	Text	&Seek
	FontSize	14

Object	Property	Setting
	ColorNormal	N/W
	Height	3
	Left	2
PushButton	**Name**	**LocateButton**
	Top	10
	Width	32
	Text	&Locate
	FontSize	14
	ColorNormal	N/W
	Height	3
	Left	2
Browse	**Name**	**CustomerBrowse**
	Top	11
	Width	58
	FontBold	.F.
	ColorNormal	N/W
	Height	6
	Left	4
PushButton	**Name**	**ExitButton**
	Top	16
	Width	15
	Text	E&xit
	Height	2
	Left	1
Image	**Name**	**Image1**
	Alignment	0 - Stretch
	Top	1
	Width	38
	DataSource	(load a bitmap)
	Height	10
	Left	38

continues

Table 13.1. continued

Object	Property	Setting
Check Box	**Name**	**ExactCheck**
	Top	12
	Width	13
	Text	&Exact
	Value	.F.
	ColorNormal	N/W
	Height	2
	Left	42

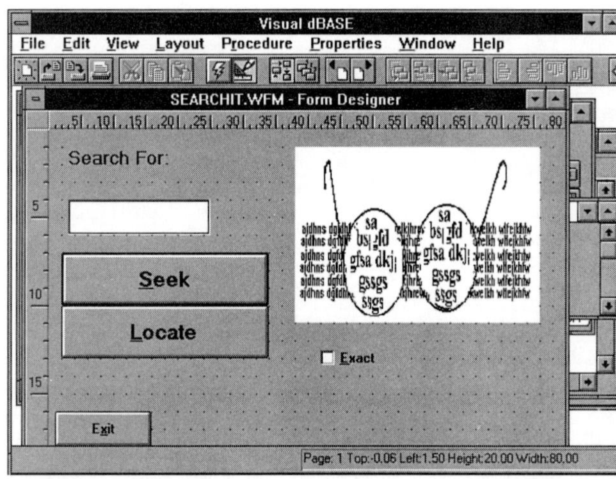

Figure 13.5.
The SearchIt.WFM form (in design mode).

When you're implementing Table 13.1 note the following comments:

- The Text property of the form is Form (which is the default value of the Text property of the form). The Text property will be updated during runtime with the name of the DBF table (CUSTOMER.DBF) that the program uses.
- Table 13.1 instructs you to place an image control in the form and to set its DataSource property to a BMP file. You can draw a small BMP file with Paintbrush and then set the DataSource property of the image control to the BMP file you prepared. As previously discussed, a picture of a magnifying glass is appropriate for the SearchIt program.

Entering the Code of the SearchIt.WFM Program

In the following sections you'll enter the code of the SearchIt program.

Attaching Code to the *OnOpen* Event of the SearchIt.WFM Form

You'll now attach code to the `OnOpen` event of the SearchIt.WFM form.

☐ Attach the following code to the `OnOpen` event of the SearchIt.WFM form. After you attach the code, the `Form_OnOpen` procedure of the SearchIt.WFM form should look as follows:

```
Procedure Form_OnOpen

* Set the path to the directory where the
* program resides.
ProgramPath = Left (Program(0),Rat("\",Program(0)))
Set Path to &ProgramPath

* Set the Text property of the form.
Set FullPath ON
form.Text=dbf()

Return
```

☐ Save your work by selecting Save from the File menu.

The code you typed assigns to the `ProgramPath` variable the name of the directory from which the SearchIt program is executed:

```
ProgramPath = Left (Program(0),Rat("\",Program(0)))
```

For example, if the SearchIt program is executed from the C:\DBPROG\CH13 directory, `ProgramPath` is equal to C:\DBPROG\CH13.

The dBASE `Path` is then set to the directory from which the SearchIt program is executed:

```
Set Path to &ProgramPath
```

The next statement sets `FullPath` to `ON`:

```
Set FullPath ON
```

The next statement sets the Text property of the form to `dbf()`:

```
form.Text=dbf()
```

`dbf()` returns the name of the DBF table currently in use. The Text property of the form therefore indicates the name of the table. You set `FullPath` to `ON`, because when it's `ON`, the `dbf()` function also returns the drive and directory of the currently used DBF table.

Attaching Code to the *OnClick* Event of the Exit Button

You'll now attach code to the `OnClick` event of the Exit button.

☐ Attach code to the `OnClick` event of the Exit button. After you type the code, the `ExitButton_OnClick` procedure should look as follows:

```
Procedure EXITBUTTON_OnClick

          form.Close()

Return
```

☐ Select Save from the File menu to save your work.

The code you typed executes the `Close()` method on the form (which causes the termination of the SearchIt program).

Attaching Code to the *OnClick* Event of the Seek Button

You'll now attach code to the `OnClick` event of the Seek button.

☐ Attach the following code to the `OnClick` event of the Seek button. After you type the code, the `SeekButton_OnClick` procedure should look as follows:

```
Procedure SEEKBUTTON_OnClick

* Make sure the user typed something in the
* NameEntry entry field.
if len(LTRIM(TRIM(form.NameEntry.Value)))=0
   MSGBOX("Please type the name to be searched")
   return
endif

* Change the settings of the text control
* so that the user will be able to see that a
* search is in progress.
form.Text1.ColorNormal="R/W"
form.Text1.Text="<<<< Searching >>>>"

* Set exact ON (or OFF) depending on the
* ExactCheck check box.
If form.ExactCheck.Value = .T.
   SET EXACT ON
else
   SET EXACT OFF
endif

* Set the index to NAME.
SET ORDER TO NAME
```

```
****************************
*** Perform the search
****************************
SEEK(LTRIM(TRIM(form.NameEntry.Value)))

* Examine the search result and act accordingly.
if NAME=LTRIM(TRIM(form.NameEntry.Value))

   MsgBox("I found a match")
else
   MSGBOX("No Match")
endif

form.Text1.ColorNormal="N/W"
form.Text1.Text="Search For:"

Return
```

☐ Select Save from the File menu to save your work.

The code you typed uses an `if` statement to examine whether the NameEntry field has text in it:

```
if len(LTRIM(TRIM(form.NameEntry.Value)))=0
   MSGBOX("Please type the name to be searched")
   return
endif
```

If the user clicked the Seek button without first typing a name in the NameEntry field, the `if` condition is satisfied, and a message box is displayed. This message box tells the user to type the name to be searched. The `return` statement is then executed to terminate the `SeekButton_OnClick` procedure.

If the `if` condition is not satisfied, the procedure continues with the next statement. The color of the text that appears above the name entry field is changed to read

```
form.Text1.ColorNormal="R/W"
```

and the Text property is changed to `<<<< Searching >>>>`:

```
form.Text1.Text="<<<< Searching >>>>"
```

This action is necessary because during the search, you want your user to know that a search is in progress.

The next block of statements is an `if...else` block of statements that checks the Value property of the Exact check box:

```
If form.ExactCheck.Value = .T.
   SET EXACT ON
else
   SET EXACT OFF
endif
```

If the Value property of the ExactCheck check box is .T. (the check box has an × in it), the `SET EXACT ON` statement is executed. If the check box does not have an × in it, the `SET EXACT OFF` statement is executed.

`SET EXACT` determines how the search is performed. For example, suppose that one of the records in the CUSTOMER.DBF table has its NAME field equal to Smith. When searching, you can search for `Smi`. If `SET EXACT` is set `ON`, the search will not be successful, because `Smi` is not exactly equal to `Smith`. If, however, `SET EXACT` is `OFF`, the search will be successful. In other words, when `SET EXACT` is `OFF`, the search will be successful if the first characters of the searched field are matched with the text being searched.

Note: Here are some examples that demonstrate the result of the search when `SET EXACT` is `ON`:

Field	Text Being Searched	Search Result
Smith	Smith	Found
Smith	Smi	Not found
locksmith	Smith	Not found
SmithLock	Smith	Not found

Here are some examples that demonstrate the result of the search when `SET EXACT` is `OFF`:

Field	Text Being Searched	Search Result
Smith	Smith	Found
Smith	Smi	Found
locksmith	Smith	Not found
SmithLock	Smith	Found
Smith	S	Found

The next statement sets the `ORDER` to `NAME`:

```
SET ORDER TO NAME
```

Recall (from Figure 13.2) that the CUSTOMER.DBF table has its NAME field indexed. The `SET ORDER` statement causes the data in the Browse control to be ordered by the indexed NAME field. That is, if you browse through the table, you'll see that the NAME field is arranged in alphabetical order.

You must have the CUSTOMER.DBF table ordered according to an indexed field, because in the next statement, you'll use the `Seek()` function to seek a record. The `Seek()` function works if the field you are searching is indexed.

The next statement seeks the record whose NAME field equals `LTRIM(TRIM(form.NameEntry.Value))`:

```
Seek(LTRIM(TRIM(form.NameEntry.Value)))
```

The `TRIM()` function removes trailing spaces (the spaces that appear to the right of the text). For example, if `x` represents a space, `TRIM("My Spacexxxx")` returns the string `"My Space"`. In other words, the four rightmost spaces are removed by the `TRIM()` function.

Similarly, the `LTRIM()` function removes the spaces that appear at the beginning of the string. If `x` represents a space, `LTRIM("xxxMy Space")` returns the string `"My Space"`.

So `LTRIM(TRIM())` removes both the trailing spaces and the leading spaces. For example, if `x` represents a space, `LTRIM(TRIM("xxxMy Spacexxxx"))` returns the string `"My Space"`.

Note that you supplied the text that was typed in NameEntry as the parameter of the `Seek()` function:

```
Seek(LTRIM(TRIM(form.NameEntry.Value)))
```

So what will the `Seek()` function search for? It will search for a record in the CUSTOMER.DBF table that has a NAME field equal to the text that was typed in the NameEntry control. The `Seek()` function will try to match the NAME field (not, for example, the STREET field) because the CUSTOMER.DBF table is currently indexed by the NAME field.

An `if` statement is then executed to examine the result of the search:

```
if NAME=LTRIM(TRIM(form.NameEntry.Value))
   MsgBox("I found a match")
else
   MSGBOX("No Match")
endif
```

The `if` statement is satisfied if the search was successful:

```
if NAME=LTRIM(TRIM(form.NameEntry.Value))
   ..................................
   .... The Seek() found a match ....
   ..................................
else
   .........................................
   .... The Seek() did not find a match ....
   .........................................
endif
```

That is, the `if` statement checks whether the NAME field of the current record is equal to `LTRIM(TRIM(form.NameEntry.Value))`.

Note that the `if` statement complies with the `SET EXACT` setting. For example, if NameEntry.Text is equal to `Smi` and the NAME field of the current record is equal to `Smith`, then if `SET EXACT` is currently `OFF`, the `if` condition is satisfied.

13

If the `if` condition is satisfied, a message box is displayed, telling the user that a match was found:

```
MsgBox("I found a match")
```

If a record was not found, the code under the `else` statement is executed:

```
MSGBOX("No Match")
```

This code tells the user that a match was not found.

The last two statements you typed set the Text1 control to its original settings:

```
form.Text1.ColorNormal="N/W"
form.Text1.Text="Search For:"
```

This gives the user the indication that the search is over, and a new search can be requested.

Attaching Code to the *OnClick* Event of the Locate Button

You'll now attach code to the `OnClick` event of the Locate button.

☐ Attach the following code to the `OnClick` event of the Locate button. After you type the code, the `LocateButton_OnClick` procedure should look as follows:

```
Procedure LOCATEBUTTON_OnClick

* Make sure that the NameEntry entry field is not blank.
if len(LTRIM(TRIM(form.NameEntry.Value)))=0
   MSGBOX("Please type the name to be searched")
   return
endif

* Change the settings of the text so that the
* user will be able to notice that a search
* is in progress.
form.Text1.ColorNormal="R/W"
form.Text1.Text="<<<< Searching >>>>"

* Set the EXACT setting according to the
* setting of the ExactCheck check box.
if form.ExactCheck.Value = .T.
   SET EXACT ON
else
   SET EXACT OFF
endif

* Remove the index setting
SET ORDER TO && No Index (natural order)

**************************
*** Perform the search
**************************
```

```
SearchFor = LTRIM(TRIM(form.NameEntry.Value))
LOCATE FOR NAME = SearchFor

IF NAME = LTRIM(TRIM(form.NameEntry.Value))

   MSGBOX("A match was found!")

   Do While .T.
      Answer=MSGBOX("Continue Searching?", ;
                    "Question", ;
                     4+32)
      If Answer= 6 && Yes
         Continue
         IF NAME = LTRIM(TRIM(form.NameEntry.Value))

            MSGBOX("A match was found!")
         ELSE
            MSGBOX("No Match")
            exit
         ENDIF
      Else
         Exit
      Endif
   EndDo
ELSE
   MSGBOX("No Match")
ENDIF

form.Text1.ColorNormal="N/W"
form.Text1.Text="Search For:"

Return
```

☐ Select Save from the File menu to save your work.

The code you typed uses an `if` statement to ensure that the user typed text in the NameEntry control:

```
if len(LTRIM(TRIM(form.NameEntry.Value)))=0
   MSGBOX("Please type the name to be searched")
   return
endif
```

The preceding `if` statement is identical to the `if` statement used in the `SeekButton_OnClick` procedure.

Then the color and text of the Text1 control are changed:

```
form.Text1.ColorNormal="R/W"
form.Text1.Text="<<<< Searching >>>>"
```

The preceding two statements are identical to the statements of the `SeekButton_OnClick` procedure. Again, the settings of the Text1 control were changed to give the user a visual indication that a search is in progress.

An `if...else` statement is then executed to determine whether `SET EXACT` should be `ON` or `OFF`:

```
if form.ExactCheck.Value = .T.
   SET EXACT ON
else
   SET EXACT OFF
endif
```

The preceding `if...else` block of code is identical to the code that exists in the `SeekButton_OnClick` procedure. This code sets `SET EXACT` to `ON` or `OFF` according to the current setting of the Exact check box.

Then the CUSTOMER.DBF table is arranged according to its natural order:

```
SET ORDER TO && No Index (natural order)
```

That is, if you want to arrange the records of the DBF table according to the index NAME field, you must use the following statement:

```
SET ORDER TO NAME
```

When you don't supply an index name, you are arranging the records of the DBF table in the order in which the records were originally entered.

The reason you are arranging the records of the CUSTOMER.DBF table according to their natural order is that in the next statement you will use the `LOCATE` statement to search for a record. The `LOCATE` statement does not need to use an indexed table. The preceding code arranges the records of the CUSTOMER.DBF table according to their natural order to emphasize that no index is required for the execution of the `LOCATE` statement.

The `LOCATE` statement is then executed:

```
SearchFor = LTRIM(TRIM(form.NameEntry.Value))
LOCATE FOR NAME = SearchFor
```

As you can see, the syntax of the `LOCATE` statement is different from the syntax of the `Seek()` function. When you are using the `Seek()` function, there is no need to specify which field should be compared, because the `Seek()` function will try to match the text that is supplied as the parameter of the `Seek()` function with the indexed field as it appears on the `SET ORDER TO` statement. For example, if you set both the NAME field and the STREET field as index fields when you are constructing the CUSTOMER.DBF table, you can later use the following statement:

```
SET ORDER TO NAME
```

The `Seek()` function will perform the search according to the indexed NAME field (because this is how the table is arranged). On the other hand, if you set the `ORDER` as

```
SET ORDER TO STREET
```

the `Seek()` function will perform the search according to the indexed STREET field (because this is how the table is now arranged).

On the other hand, when using the LOCATE statement, you must specify which field should be compared:

```
SearchFor = LTRIM(TRIM(form.NameEntry.Value))
LOCATE FOR NAME = SearchFor
```

An IF...ELSE statement is then executed to determine whether a record was found:

```
IF NAME = LTRIM(TRIM(form.NameEntry.Value))
   ...........................
   ... Yes, a record was found.
   ...........................
ELSE
   MSGBOX("No Match")
ENDIF
```

Note that the IF statement complies with the setting of the SET EXACT setting. For example, if the text to be searched is Smi and the NAME field contains Smith, then if SET EXACT is OFF, the IF condition is satisfied.

Note: The preceding code determines whether the search was successful by using the following IF...ELSE statement:

```
IF NAME = LTRIM(TRIM(form.NameEntry.Value))
   ...........................
   ... Yes, a record was found.
   ...........................
ELSE
   ................................
   ... No, a record was not found.
   ................................
ENDIF
```

An alternate and easier way to determine whether the search was successful is to utilize the FOUND() dBASE function as follows:

```
IF FOUND()
   ...........................
   ... Yes, a record was found.
   ...........................
ELSE
   ................................
   ... No, a record was not found.
   ................................
ENDIF
```

That is, if the search was successful, the FOUND() function will return .T., and the code under the IF will be executed. However, if the search failed (that is, the desired record was not found), then the code under the ELSE will be executed.

Note that the FOUND() function also works for determining whether a search that was performed with the SEEK() function was successful.

If a record was found, a message box is displayed:

```
MSGBOX("A match was found!")
```

It is important to realize that the LOCATE statement is much slower than the Seek() function. If you are working with a CUSTOMER.DBF table that has many records in it, you will actually see the differences in performance. The LOCATE statement, however, has the advantage that it does not require the DBF table to be indexed.

When the table is indexed, all the records are arranged in alphabetical order. For example, these are the records in the vicinity of the Smith record:

NAME	*STREET*
Smith	123 Pine Street
Smith	33 7th Street
SmithLock	771 First Avenue

There is no reason to use another search for seeking the next Smith, because all the Smith records are arranged one after another.

When the table is not indexed, all the Smith records are not one after the other. For example, the first Smith record could be record number 1003, and the next Smith record could be record number 4444. This means that to find the next Smith record, you must use the LOCATE statement again. The LOCATE statement, however, always starts searching from the first record of the table. So if you execute the LOCATE statement again, the LOCATE statement will again find record 1003 (the first record that matches Smith).

To locate the next record that matches Smith, you must use the CONTINUE statement. The CONTINUE statement performs a search identical to the one performed with the preceding LOCATE statement. The only difference is that the CONTINUE statement does not start searching from the first record of the table.

A Do While .T. loop is then executed to keep executing the CONTINUE statement:

```
Do While .T.
   Answer=MSGBOX("Continue Searching?", ;
                 "Question", ;
                  4+32)
   If Answer= 6 && Yes
      CONTINUE
      IF NAME = LTRIM(TRIM(form.NameEntry.Value))

         MSGBOX("A match was found!")
      ELSE
         MSGBOX("No Match")
         exit
      ENDIF
```

```
    Else
       Exit
    Endif
 EndDo
```

The first statement in the `Do While` loop displays a message to the user, asking the user whether to continue the search:

```
Answer=MSGBOX("Continue Searching?", ;
                    "Question", ;
                     4+32)
```

If the user clicks the Yes button in the message box, the `CONTINUE` statement is executed to search for the next record:

```
If Answer= 6 && Yes
   CONTINUE
   IF NAME = LTRIM(TRIM(form.NameEntry.Value))

      MSGBOX("A match was found!")
   ELSE
      MSGBOX("No Match")
      exit
   ENDIF
Else
   Exit
Endif
```

If a match was found, a message box is displayed:

```
MSGBOX("A match was found!")
```

If no match was found, the code under the `ELSE` statement is executed:

```
MSGBOX("No Match")
exit
```

The preceding two statements display a message box that tells the user that no match was found and then exit the `While Do .T.` loop.

If a match was found with the `CONTINUE` statement, the program returns to the beginning of the `Do While .T.` loop, executing the loop all over again.

Eventually, all the matched records are found (unless the user chooses not to continue with the search), and the last two statements of the `LocateButton_OnClick` procedure are executed:

```
form.Text1.ColorNormal="N/W"
form.Text1.Text="Search For:"
```

The preceding two statements set the settings of the Text1 control to its original settings so that your user gets a visual indication that a new search can be performed.

- ☐ Execute the SearchIt program, and check its proper operation. For example, type `fs` in the NameEntry control, make sure that the Exact check box is *not* checked, and then click the Seek button to seek a record whose NAME field starts with the characters `fs`.

- Place an × in the Exact check box, and search for a record that has its NAME field equal to `fs`.
- Repeat the previous experiments by clicking the Locate button.

As you can see, after a record is located, the SearchIt program displays a message box asking whether you want to continue the search. If you click the Yes button, the `CONTINUE` statement is executed to locate the next match. This process continues until there are no more matched records, or until you click the No button to stop continuing the search.

Note: `Seek()`, `Locate`, and `CONTINUE` are vital concepts in dBASE. It is important that you fully understand these topics.

It is recommended that you practice with `Seek()`, `LOCATE`, and `CONTINUE` until you feel comfortable with these important topics.

You can practice with `Seek()`, `LOCATE`, and `CONTINUE` as detailed here:

- Terminate the SearchIt program.
- Remove the SearchIt.WFM form from the desktop of dBASE.
- In the Command window type `Close Databases`.

  dBASE responds by closing all the tables (if there are any).

- To open CUSTOMER.DBF, in the Command window type `USE C:\DBPROG\CH12\CUSTOMER.DBF`, and then press Enter.

  dBASE responds by opening the CUSTOMER.DBF table.

- To set the `ORDER` of the table, type `SET ORDER TO NAME` in the Command window, and then press Enter.

  dBASE responds by arranging the CUSTOMER.DBF table according to the NAME field. You can check this as shown in the next step:

- In the Command window type `Browse`, and then press Enter.

  dBASE responds by displaying a window that has the CUSTOMER.DBF table arranged according to the NAME field and ready to be browsed by you. As you can see, the CUSTOMER.DBF table is indeed arranged according to its NAME field.

- In the Command window type `SET EXACT OFF`, and then press Enter.

  dBASE responds by setting the `SET EXACT` *setting to* `OFF`.

- [ ] Type the statement `Seek("fs")` in the Command window, and then press Enter.

  dBASE responds by searching for a record whose NAME field starts with the `fs` *characters.*

You can view the result of the search in the browse window and in the Result window (the Result window is the window below the Command window).

In a similar way, you can experiment with the `LOCATE` and `CONTINUE` statements.

Summary

In this chapter you have learned how to search records by using `Seek()`, `LOCATE`, and `CONTINUE`.

In the next chapter you'll continue to work with the SearchIt program. In particular, you'll learn about calculated fields and filtering.

Q&A

Q I realize that `Seek()` works much faster than `LOCATE` and `CONTINUE`. Why would anybody want to use `LOCATE` and `CONTINUE`?

A `LOCATE` and `CONTINUE` do not require that the DBF file be indexed. So `LOCATE` and `CONTINUE` work more slowly than `Seek()`, but `LOCATE` and `CONTINUE` have the advantage of not forcing you to index any of the fields of the table.

Q In the SearchIt program that I wrote in this chapter, the code of the program informs the user about the search results by using a message box. Is it possible to enhance the SearchIt program so that the search results will be spoken to the user with human voice through the built-in PC speaker?

A Yes. You can incorporate real human voice (for example, your own voice) into your programs and play this voice through the built-in PC speaker that every PC has. You can do that by utilizing a VBX control called TegoMM.VBX.

As you'll learn in Chapter 16, "Using VBX Controls," a VBX control enables you to extend the capabilities of the off-the-shelf Visual dBASE package.

The TegoMM.VBX VBX control enables you to play sound (voice and music) through the internal PC speaker that every PC has or through a sound card if the user has one. That is, you can use the TegoMM.VBX control to play voice and music through the best device in the system. If the user has a sound card, the sound is played through the sound card. If, however, the user does not have a sound card, the sound is played through the internal PC speaker that every PC has. The playback through the PC speaker is accomplished without the need for any drivers.

The TegoMM.VBX control is included with the disk you can purchase to accompany this book. (See the disk offer at the end of this book.)

Quiz

1. If you need to evaluate search performance, you should use a large table. To obtain a table with many records in it, you should:
   a. Purchase a CD that contains a database with many records in it.
   b. Fill the fields of the records by actually typing data.
   c. Use the `GENERATE` command to fill the records of the table with random data.
2. The `LOCATE` statement can be used to locate records in a table that has an index field.
   a. True
   b. False
   c. It does not matter whether the table is indexed
3. If you search for the string `ABC` and `SET EXACT` is `ON`, `ABCD` is a match.
   a. True
   b. False
4. If you search for the string `ABC` and `SET EXACT` is `OFF`, `ABCD` is a match.
   a. True
   b. False
5. If you search for the string `ABCD` and `SET EXACT` is `OFF`, `ABC` is a match.
   a. True
   b. False
6. If you search for the string `ABCD` and `SET EXACT` is `ON`, `ABC` is a match.
   a. True
   b. False

Exercise

Enhance the SearchIt program so that it will also enable the user to locate a ZIP code.

Quiz Answers

1. c. For example, to fill 1,000 records, type `Generate 1000` in the Command window. Don't go wild with the `Generate` statement! It is very easy to just type `Generate 1000000` in the Command window, but do you have enough disk space to store a million records?
2. c. That is, `LOCATE` can be used to locate a record in a database that happens to have one or more of its fields indexed. The fact that the table is indexed, however, does not improve the performance of the search.
3. b
4. a
5. b
6. b

Exercise Answer

Of course, there are many ways to implement this activity. Here is one way:

☐ Add the following option button to the SearchIt.WFM form:

Property	*Setting*
Name	ZIPCODEOPTION
Text	ZIP code
Value	.F.

☐ Add the following option button to the SearchIt.WFM form:

Property	*Setting*
Name	NAMEOPTION
Text	Name
Value	.T.

So the user sees two option buttons. If the Name option button is selected, the LOCATE button will search for a record that has a NAME field equal to the text in the entry field.

If the ZIP code option button is selected, the LOCATE button will search for a record that has a ZIPCODE field equal to the text in the entry field.

The code in the `LocateButton_OnClick` procedure must use the `LOCATE` function for locating a NAME or for locating a ZIPCODE. The code will make the decision as to which `LOCATE` statement to use based on the Value properties of the option buttons.

Here is the code in the LocateButton_OnClick procedure that determines which LOCATE statement to execute:

```
If form.NameOption.Value = .T.
   SearchFor = LTRIM(TRIM(form.NameEntry.Value))
   LOCATE FOR NAME = SearchFor
Else
   SearchFor = LTRIM(TRIM(form.NameEntry.Value))
   LOCATE FOR ZIPCODE = SearchFor
EndIf
```

14

WEEK 2

Field Calculations and Filtering

dBASE responds by summing the contents of all the QUANTITY fields. The sum is stored in a variable called `mAllQuantities`.

To examine the value of `mAllQuantities`, carry out these steps:

- In the Command window type `? mAllQuantities`, and then press Enter.

  dBASE responds by displaying the value of `mAllQuantities` *in the Result window.*

- Just to ensure that the `CALCULATE SUM()` statement is working properly, type `Browse` in the Command window and then press Enter to display the CUSTOMER.DBF table in a browse window.

- Change the QUANTITY field of one record to 1, change the QUANTITY field of another record to 2, and change the QUANTITY field of a third record to 3.

- In the Command window type `CALCULATE SUM(QUANTITY) To mAllQuantities`, and then press Enter.

  dBASE responds by summing the contents of all the QUANTITY fields. The sum is stored in a variable called `mAllQuantities`.

To examine the value of `mAllQuantities` take the following action:

- In the Command window type `? mAllQuantities`, and then press Enter.

  dBASE responds by displaying the value of `mAllQuantities` *in the Result window. The result should be 1+2+3=6.*

You can use `CALCULATE` to calculate the average of the fields' contents as shown here:

- In the Command window type `CALCULATE AVG(QUANTITY) TO mAvg`, and then press Enter.

Of course, CUSTOMER.DBF currently has three records, with QUANTITY fields equal to 1, 2, and 3. The rest of the 9,997 records of the CUSTOMER.DBF table are all 0s. The average is therefore a very small number (almost 0).

To calculate the standard deviation, use `CALCULATE` as shown here:

- In the Command window type `CALCULATE STD(QUANTITY) TO mStd`, and then press Enter.

To calculate the record which has the largest number in the QUANTITY field use `CALCULATE` as shown here:

- In the Command window type `CALCULATE MAX(QUANTITY) TO mMax`, and then press Enter.

After the preceding statement is executed, `mMax` is equal to 3, because among all the records of the CUSTOMER.DBF table, the largest value that the QUANTITY field has is 3.

To calculate the record that has the smallest number in the QUANTITY field, use `CALCULATE` as shown here:

☐ In the Command window type `CALCULATE MIN(QUANTITY) TO mMin`, and then press Enter.

After the preceding command is executed, `mMin` is equal to 0, because among all the records of the CUSTOMER.DBF table, the smallest value that the QUANTITY field has is 0.

☐ In the Command window type `? mMax`, and then press Enter.

dBASE responds by displaying the value of `mMax` *(which is 3).*

☐ In the Command window type `? mMin`, and then press Enter.

dBASE responds by displaying the value of `mMin` *(which is 0).*

> **Note:** The preceding discussion demonstrates how to use `CALCULATE`, `MIN()`, and `MAX()` when the field under investigation is a numeric field.
>
> You can, however, apply `MIN()` and `MAX()` to fields of type Date. For example, if you add the field DUE_DATE of type Date to the CUSTOMER.DBF table, you can use the statement `CALCULATE MIN(DUE_DATE) TO mMinDueDate`, and then press Enter to find the earliest date among all the records. You also can use the statement `CALCULATE MAX(DUE_DATE) TO mMaxDueDate`, and then press Enter to find the latest date.

Filtering Records

Sometimes, you will want to work with only a certain number of records. For example, your table might include 100,000 records, but you want to browse through only the records whose STATE field is equal to `CA`. To be able to do that, you will have to write code that filters out all the records whose STATE fields are not equal to `CA`.

You can write such code by yourself using dBASE statements.

☐ Type the following code in the Command window:

```
SET EXACT OFF  {Enter}
SET FILTER TO STATE="ca"  {Enter}
GOTO TOP {Enter}
```

Note that in the preceding code, after you execute the `SET FILTER` command you execute the `GOTO TOP` command. This is necessary because the `SET FILTER` command does not go into effect until after you move the record pointer. That is, after using the `SET FILTER` command you have to move the record pointer in order for the filter to be active.

☐ Now browse through the CUSTOMER.DBF table.

If the `GENERATE` statement you used (when you randomly filled the 10,000 records of the CUSTOMER.DBF table) filled some records with STATE equal to `ca`, then after executing the preceding `SET FILTER` statement, you'll see only those records whose STATE field is equal to `ca`. Again, you can use the Command window for practicing with the dBASE statements, and after you are satisfied that you fully understand how the statements work, you can incorporate the statements into your dBASE program.

Note that to cancel the `FILTER`, you have to use this statement:

```
SET FILTER TO  {Enter}
```

Summary

In this chapter you have learned how to use the `CALCULATE` statement. The `CALCULATE` statement enables you to perform various calculations on the fields of the currently open table.

In this chapter you have also learned how to implement a filter (with the `SET FILTER TO` statement) that filters out records.

Q&A

Q After I set the QUANTITY fields of the first records of the CUSTOMER.DBF table to 1, 2, and 3, the calculated average of the QUANTITY field was a small number. Why?

A The average is calculated in the following manner:

(1+2+3+0+0+0+...+0)/10000

So the resultant average is a small number.

Q Some statements in dBASE can only be performed if I first issue the statement

```
USE C:\DBPROG\CH13\CUSTOMER.DBF Exclusive
```

How can I tell which are the statements that require the table to be opened exclusively?

A dBASE tables can be used across a network, which means that many users can use the dBASE tables. dBASE will not enable you to modify the tables in any way that will affect other users who are currently using the tables. For example, suppose that you are trying to modify the structure of a table. If you opened the table exclusively, dBASE would enable you to modify the structure of the table. However, dBASE refuses to modify the structure of a table that was not opened exclusively. Similarly, dBASE refuses to perform other operations on a table that will affect the work of other people who are currently working with the tables. Note that even if you are not running dBASE on a network, the same table can be shared by several programs that are currently running.

Quiz

1. The statement

   ```
   CALCULATE CNT() TO mNumberOfRecords
   ```

   performs the following action: ______________________________

2. The statement

   ```
   CALCULATE SUM(QUANTITY) To mAllQuantities
   ```

   performs the following action: ______________________________

3. The statement

   ```
   CALCULATE AVG(QUANTITY) TO mAvg
   ```

   performs the following action: ______________________________

4. The statement

   ```
   CALCULATE MAX(QUANTITY) TO mMax
   ```

   performs the following action: ______________________________

Exercises

1. Enhance the SearchIt program, which you started to develop in the preceding chapter, as shown here:

   - Add a pushbutton to the form. This pushbutton serves as the "a" button.
   - Add a pushbutton to the form. This pushbutton serves as the "b" button.
   - Add a pushbutton to the form. This pushbutton serves as the "c" button.

   When the user clicks the "a" button, the browse control should display only the records whose CITY fields start with the letter *a*. When the user clicks the "b" button, the browse control should display only the records whose CITY fields start with the letter *b*, and so on.

14

2. Design a dBASE program that makes good use of the `SET FILTER TO` statement.
3. You have practiced enough with the CUSTOMER.DBF table. If you look at your hard drive, you'll see that the CUSTOMER.DBF file is a very large file (because it contains 10,000 random records). Delete the records from the CUSTOMER.DBF table.

Quiz Answers

1. The statement

   ```
   CALCULATE CNT() TO mNumberOfRecords
   ```

   assigns `mNumberOfRecords` the number of records that the currently open table has.
2. The statement

   ```
   CALCULATE SUM(QUANTITY) To mAllQuantities
   ```

   assigns `mAllQuantities` the sum of all the QUANTITIES fields of the currently open table.
3. The statement

   ```
   CALCULATE AVG(QUANTITY) TO mAvg
   ```

   assigns `mAvg` a number that is the average of all the QUANTITIES fields of the currently open table.
4. The statement

   ```
   CALCULATE MAX(QUANTITY) TO mMax
   ```

   assigns `mMax` the largest number that exists in any of the QUANTITY fields of the currently opened table.

Exercise Answers

1. Place the "a" pushbutton in the form of the SearchIt program.

   Place the "b" pushbutton in the form of the SearchIt program.

   Place the "c" pushbutton in the form of the SearchIt program.

   Attach code to the `OnClick` event of the "a" button. Here is the code you should attach:

   ```
   SET EXACT OFF
   SET FILTER TO CITY = "a"
   ```

   You set `EXACT` to `OFF`.

Then you set the FILTER as shown here:

```
SET FILTER TO CITY = "a"
```

Now the browse control displays only the records whose CITY fields start with the character *a*.

Similarly, you should attach code to the OnClick events of the "b" and "c" buttons. For example, this is the SET FILTER statement you should attach to the "b" button:

```
SET FILTER TO CITY = "b"
```

And this is the SET FILTER statement you should attach to the "c" button:

```
SET FILTER TO CITY = "c"
```

Typically, you will also place another pushbutton in the form, the No Filter pushbutton. The code that is attached to the OnClick event of the No Filter pushbutton should remove the filter as shown here:

```
SET FILTER TO
```

It is important to understand that the statement

```
SET FILTER TO CITY = "a"
```

causes the browse control to display only the records whose CITY fields start with the character *a*. The statement

```
SET FILTER TO CITY = "A"
```

causes the browse control to display only the records whose CITY fields start with the character *A*.

If you want to create a filter that causes the browse control to display the records whose CITY fields start with the character *a* or *A*, use the following statement:

```
SET FILTER TO UPPER(CITY)="U"
```

Can you guess what SET FILTER statement you should type for causing the browse control to display only the records whose CITY fields start with the characters *B*, *b*, *C*, and *c*? Here is the required statement:

```
SET FILTER TO UPPER(CITY)>"A" .AND. UPPER(CITY)<"D"
```

2. You can design a form that includes a StateEntry entry field control in which the user must type the name of the state.

   The form should also include a browse control (so that the user can browse through the CUSTOMER.DBF table).

   The form should also include a ShowRecordButton pushbutton.

After the user types the name of the state, the user will have to click the Show Records button. This action causes the browse control to include only the records whose STATE field equals the state that the user typed.

The `ShowRecordsButton_OnClick` procedure should include the following statements:

```
StateVar = LTRIM(TRIM(form.StateEntry.Value))
SET FILTER TO STATE = "&StateVar"
goto top
Return
```

The preceding code causes the browse control to display only the records whose STATE field equals the name of the state typed in the entry field control.

3. In the Command window type `Close Databases`, and then press Enter.

   dBASE responds by closing all open tables.

   In the Command window open the CUSTOMER.DBF table exclusively by typing `USE C:\DBPROG\CH13\Customer.DBF Exclusive`, and then press Enter.

   dBASE responds by opening the CUSTOMER.DBF table exclusively.

   In the Command window type `Zap` and then press Enter.

   dBASE responds by displaying the Zap Records dialog box shown in Figure 14.2.

Figure 14.2.
The Zap Records dialog box.

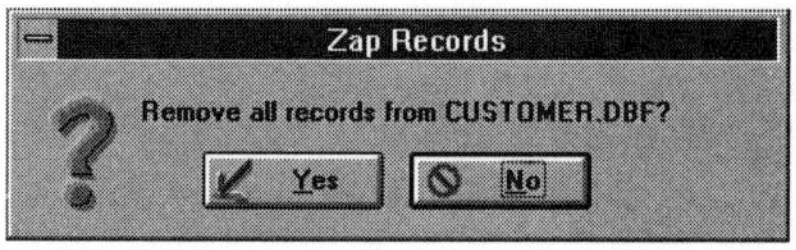

Click the Yes button of the Zap Records dialog box.

dBASE responds by removing all the records from the CUSTOMER.DBF table.

Obviously, the Zap command is very dangerous. It removes all the records from a table. There is no real loss, however, in zapping the CUSTOMER.DBF table, because the "data" of CUSTOMER.DBF is just random data you generated in the preceding chapter with the GENERATE command. You can regenerate the 10,000 records as easily as you can zap them.

WEEK 3 AT A GLANCE

In Chapter 15 you'll learn how to prepare your dBASE programs for distribution. Visual dBASE includes a Deploy Application tool that lets you create distribution disks and a sophisticated professional Setup.EXE program with great ease. The Setup.EXE program copies files from the distribution disks to your user's hard drive and also creates a program group for the installed program. Note that the Deploy Application tool is included only with the Visual dBASE Compiler product or with the Client/Server version of Visual dBASE.

In Chapter 16 you'll learn about VBX technology. In particular, you'll write a program using the Switch VBX control that comes with your Visual dBASE package.

In Chapter 17 you'll learn about the important topics of dynamic link libraries (DLL). In this chapter you'll write a program that uses several API functions.

Week 3 at a Glance

In Chapter 18 you'll learn how to incorporate multimedia technology into your dBASE programs. You'll learn how to play WAV files, MIDI files, movie AVI files, and CD audio. In this chapter you'll also learn how to perform animation. You'll learn how to design nonsynchronized animation as well as synchronized animation.

In Chapter 19 you'll learn how to use the timer control of dBASE for performing periodical tasks.

In Chapter 20 you'll learn how to write a dBASE 3D virtual reality program that enables the user to travel inside a three-dimensional picture. As the user moves inside the 3D picture (by using the mouse or the keyboard) the 3D picture changes accordingly.

In Chapter 21 you'll learn more about writing a dBASE 3D virtual reality program. In particular, you'll learn how to add sprites (stationary sprites as well as moving sprites) to the three-dimensional picture. Therefore, as the user travels inside the 3D picture, the user encounters other objects inside the 3D picture.

15

WEEK
3

Installing Your dBASE Programs

You have designed a dBASE program, and now it is time to distribute your program to your users. In this chapter you'll learn how to create a distribution disk and an install program that installs your dBASE program on your user's PC. When you purchase a professional program package such as Visual dBASE, you expect the package to include a professional install program. Likewise, your user expects your program to include a professional install program. As it turns out, one of the tools that comes with Visual dBASE enables you to create distribution disks and a professional install program with great ease.

The MyProg Program

In the next section you'll create a program called MyProg.EXE. Later in this chapter you'll create a distribution disk for the MyProg program. The distribution disk will contain the MyProg program and the Setup program. Setup.EXE is a program that performs the installation.

As you'll see, the Setup program that you'll include with your distribution disk will copy the MyProg.EXE file from the distribution disk to your user's hard drive, enable the user to select a drive and a directory to which the installed program should be copied, and create a program group for the installed program.

Before you implement the MyProg program, here's a review of its specifications:

- When you execute the MyProg program, the window shown in Figure 15.1 appears.

Figure 15.1.
The window of the MyProg program.

- The user can click the Click Me button to display a message box.
- The user can click the Exit button to terminate the program.

The Visual Implementation of the MyProg Program

You'll now visually design the form of the MyProg program.

- ☐ Create the directory C:\DBPROG\CH15.
- ☐ In the Command window type `Create Form C:\DBPROG\CH15\MyProg`, and then press Enter.

  dBASE responds by creating the MyProg.WFM form.

- ☐ Implement the MyProg.WFM form according to the specifications in Table 15.1. When you finish implementing the form, it should look like the one shown in Figure 15.2.

Table 15.1. The properties table of the MyProg.WFM form.

Object	Property	Setting
Form	**Text**	**The MyProg program**
	MDI	.F.
PushButton	**Name**	**ExitButton**
	Text	E&xit
PushButton	**Name**	**ClickMeButton**
	Text	&Click Me

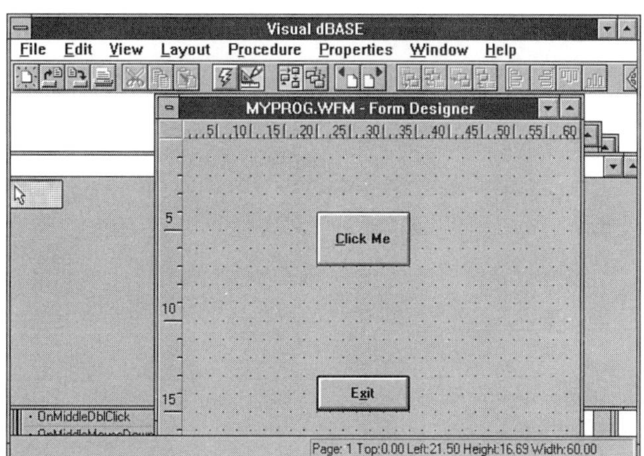

Figure 15.2.
The form of the MyProg program in design mode.

Entering the Code of the MyProg Program

In the following sections you'll enter the code of the MyProg program.

Attaching Code to the *OnClick* Event of the Exit Button

You'll now attach code to the `OnClick` event of the Exit button.

☐ Attach code to the `OnClick` event of the Exit button. After you attach the code, the `EXITBUTTON_OnClick` procedure should look as follows:

```
Procedure EXITBUTTON_OnClick

form.Close()

Return
```

Attaching Code to the *OnClick* Event of the Click Me Button

You'll now attach code to the `OnClick` event of the Click Me button.

☐ Attach code to the `OnClick` event of the Click Me button. After you attach the code, the `CLICKMEBUTTON_OnClick` procedure should look as follows:

```
Procedure CLICKMEBUTTON_OnClick

MSGBOX("I was Installed properly!", "Message")

Return
```

The code you typed displays a message box when the user clicks the Click Me button.

☐ Select Save from the File menu to save your work.

Before going on with the preparation of the Setup program, you should make sure that the MyProg program is working properly.

☐ Press F2 to execute the MyProg program.

☐ Click the Click Me button.

MyProg responds by displaying a message box.

☐ Click the Exit button to terminate the MyProg program.

Creating an EXE File for the MyProg Program

You'll now create the MyProg program.

☐ In the Command window type `Modify Form ?` and then press Enter.

dBASE responds by displaying a dialog box that enables you to select the WFM form.

☐ Select the C:\DBPROG\CH15\MyProg.WFM file.

dBASE responds by displaying the MyProg.WFM form in design mode.

If you installed the compiler of Visual dBASE, the program menu (while the Command window is the active window) contains the Build Executable menu item, as shown in Figure 15.3.

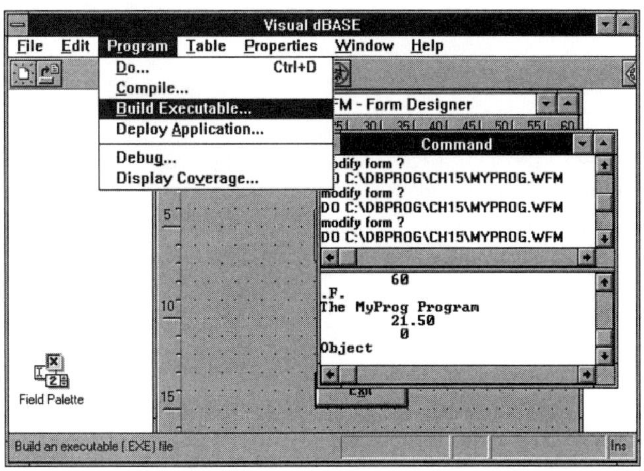

Figure 15.3.
The Build Executable item of the Program menu. This Program menu appears when the Command window is the active window. The Build Executable menu item appears if you installed the compiler of dBASE.

☐ Select the Build Executable item from the Program menu.

dBASE responds by displaying the Build Executable window, shown in Figure 15.4. You use the Build Executable window to specify how and where the EXE program should be created.

☐ Click the Tool icon that appears to the right of the Directory box.

dBASE responds by displaying the Choose Directory window, shown in Figure 15.5. You use the Choose Directory window to select the directory where the source files reside. An EXE file will be generated from the source files that you'll specify.

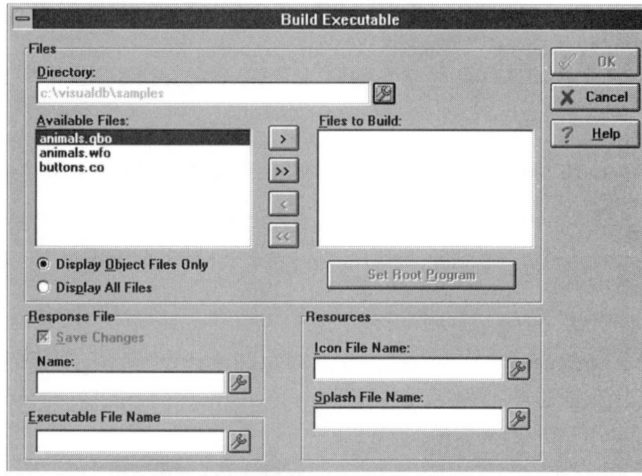

Figure 15.4.
The Build Executable window.

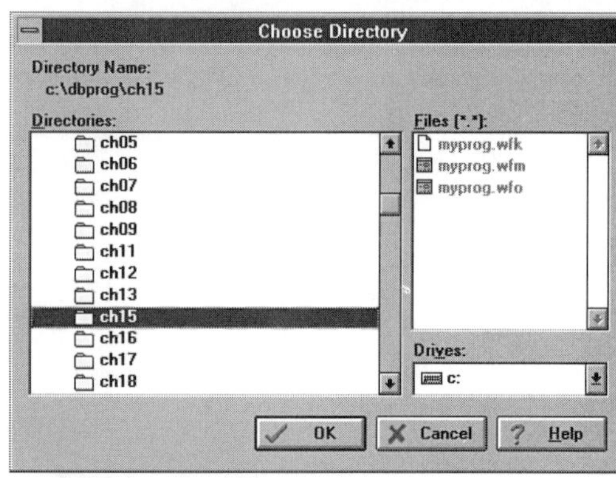

Figure 15.5.
The Choose Directory window enables you to choose the directory where the source files reside.

- ☐ Select the C:\DBPROG\CH15 directory, and then click the OK button of the Choose Directory window.

  dBASE responds by again displaying the Build Executable window, shown in Figure 15.6. As you can see from the figure, the MyProg.WFO file appears in the Available Files list.

- ☐ Click the > button.

  dBASE responds by moving the MyProg.WFO item to the Files to Build list, as shown in Figure 15.7.

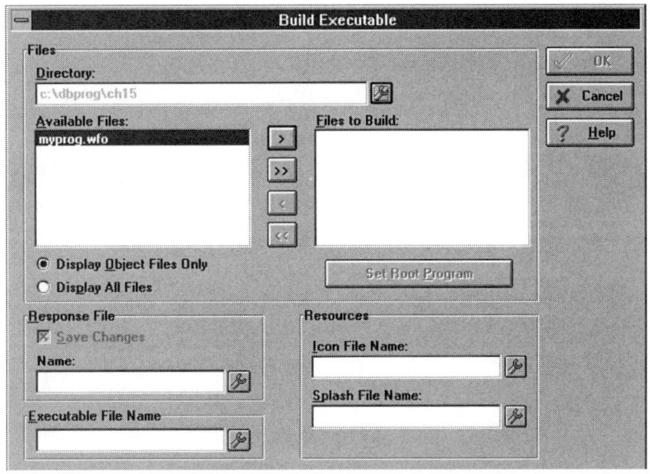

Figure 15.6.
The MyProg.WFO file appears in the Available Files list of the Build Executable window.

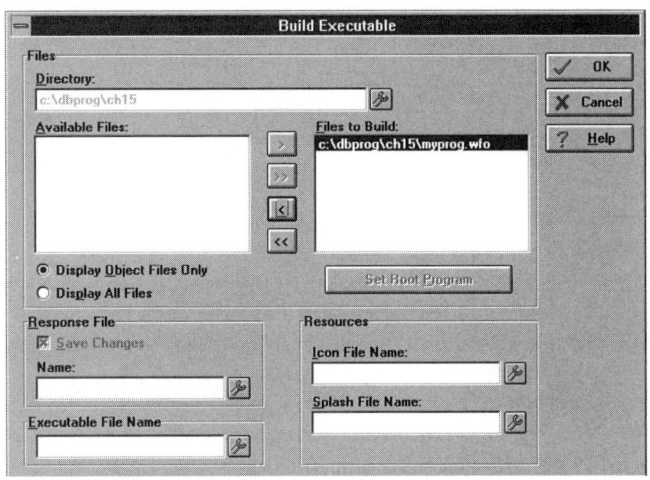

Figure 15.7.
The MyProg.WFO file is used as the source file from which the MyProg program will be generated.

Note: If you don't specify an icon for the EXE file, a default program icon will be used.

You can, however, click the Tool icon that appears to the right of the Icon File Name box of the Build Executable window and then select an icon for the EXE file you are preparing.

- Click the Tool icon that appears to the right of the Executable File Name box.

  dBASE responds by displaying the Save File dialog box, shown in Figure 15.8. This dialog box enables you to specify the name of the EXE file you are creating.

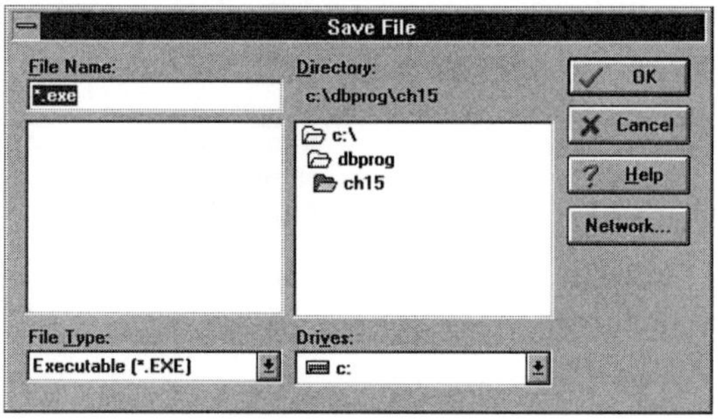

Figure 15.8.
The dialog box that enables you to specify the name of the EXE file you are creating.

- Set the Save File dialog box as shown in Figure 15.9. That is, the EXE file you are now creating will be MyProg.EXE, and it will be saved in the C:\DBPROG\CH15 directory.

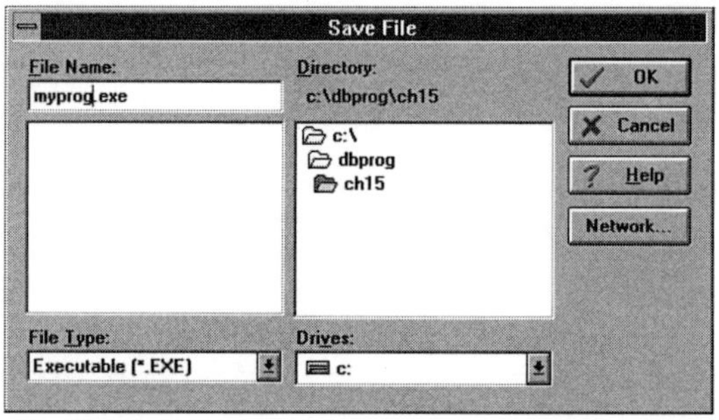

Figure 15.9.
The EXE file will be saved as MyProg.EXE in the C:\DBPROG\CH15 directory.

- Click the OK button of the Save File dialog box, and then click the OK button of the Build Executable window.

  dBASE responds by building the MyProg.EXE file according to your specifications. When the building is finished, the Build Completed dialog box is displayed, as shown in Figure 15.10.

Figure 15.10.
The Build Completed dialog box that is displayed when dBASE finishes building the EXE file.

Testing the EXE File You Created

In the previous steps, you created the MyProg program. Before proceeding with the implementation of the Setup program, you should check whether the MyProg.EXE file is working properly.

☐ Use File Manager to double-click the MyProg.EXE file that resides in the C:\DBPROG\CH15 directory.

Windows responds by executing the MyProg program.

☐ Experiment with the MyProg program, and then click its Exit button to terminate the program.

Preparing the Setup Program and the Distribution Disks

So far, you have designed and implemented the MyProg program, and you have created an executable file, MyProg.EXE. Next, you'll copy the MyProg.EXE file to a disk, and copy an install program (the Setup program) to the disk. Your user will execute the Setup program, which copies the MyProg.EXE file to the user's PC and creates a program group for the MyProg program.

☐ Make the Command window the active window.

The Program menu has an item menu called Deploy Application. (See Figure 15.11.)

☐ Create a new directory on your hard drive. Name the new directory C:\TRY. The C:\TRY directory will be used to store all the files you'll have to copy to your distribution disk.

☐ Create a new directory on your hard drive. Name the new directory C:\MYPROG.

☐ Copy the MyProg.EXE file from the C:\DBPROG\CH15 directory into the C:\MYPROG directory.

Figure 15.11.
The Deploy Application menu item.

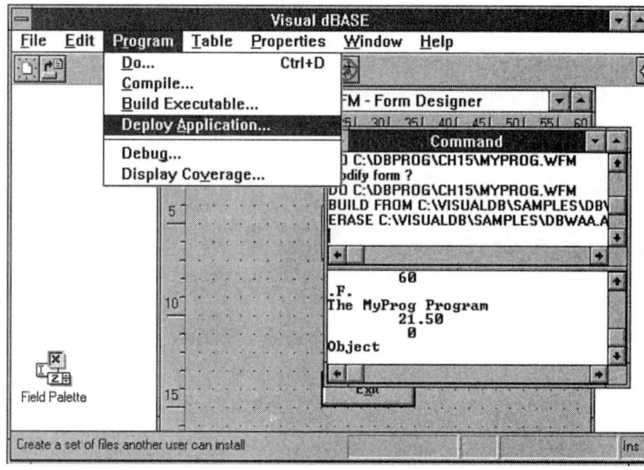

Note: The distribution disk you'll prepare in the following steps will include all the files you copied into the C:\MYPROG directory. In this example, you need to copy only one file (MyProg.EXE) into the C:\MYPROG directory. In other applications, however, you might need to copy other files, such as report files, WAV files, and BMP files, to the C:\MYPROG directory.

☐ Select the Deploy Application menu item from the Program menu.

dBASE responds by displaying the Deploy Application window, shown in Figure 15.12.

Figure 15.12.
The Deploy Application window.

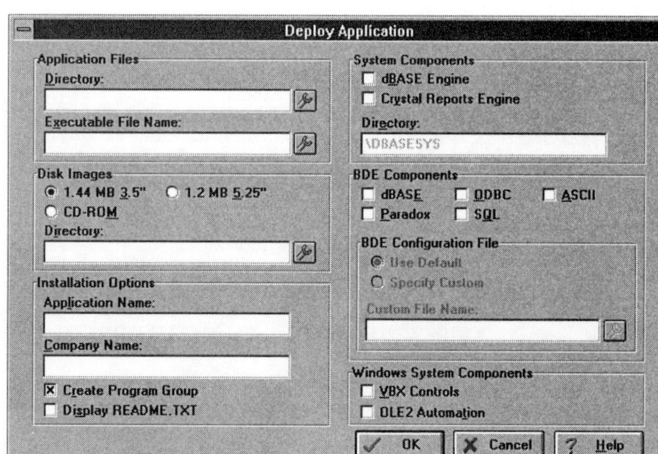

You'll next set the Deploy Application window so that a distribution disk will be generated for installing the MyProg program.

☐ Click the Tool icon that appears to the right of the Directory box of the Disk Images section, and select the C:\TRY directory.

The Disk Images section of the Deploy Application window has several option buttons. If you intend to distribute the MyProg program on a 1.44 MB 3.5" disk, select the 1.44 MB 3.5" option button. If you intend to distribute the program on a 1.2 MB 5.25" disk, select the 1.2 MB 5.25" option button. If you intend to distribute the program on a CD, select the CD-ROM option button.

dBASE needs to know the type of media on which your application is distributed, because if the files are large and need to be distributed on more than one disk, the number of disks depends on the disk media you selected.

☐ Select the 1.44 MB 3.5" option button.

☐ In the Directory box of the Application Files section of the Deploy Application window, type `C:\MYPROG`.

This means that during the installation, the user will see C:\MYPROG as the default directory in which the MyProg program will be installed. Also, when dBASE prepares your distribution disks, all the files that are in the C:\MYPROG directory will be copied to the distribution disks.

☐ In the Executable File Name box of the Application Files section of the Deploy Application window, type `C:\MYPROG\MyProg.EXE`.

This means that the Setup program will install the MyProg.EXE file.

☐ In the Company Name box of the Installation Options, type `The My Company Inc.`

This means that during the installation, the user will see The My Company Inc. as the name of the company.

☐ Make sure that the Create program Group check box has an × in it (so that the Setup program will generate a program group).

Your Deploy Application window should now look like the one shown in Figure 15.13.

☐ Click the OK button of the Deploy Application window.

dBASE responds by copying all the necessary files into the C:\TRY directory, and then the Deploy Application Status window appears, as shown in Figure 15.14.

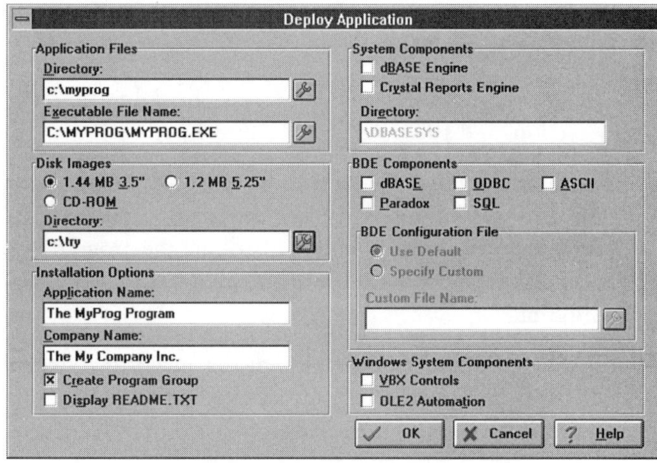

Figure 15.13.
The Deploy Application window, ready to generate the files.

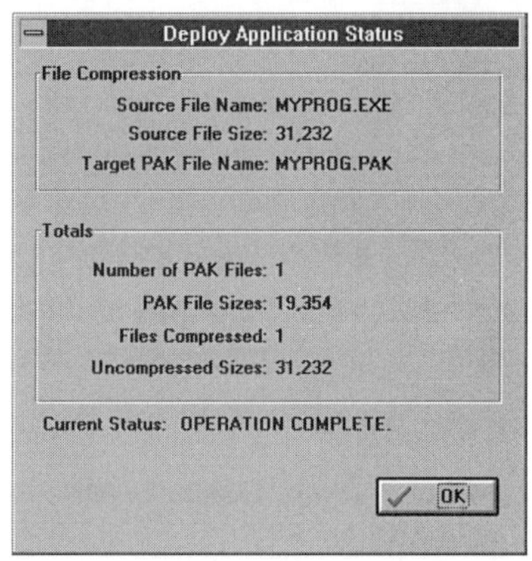

Figure 15.14
The Deploy Application Status dialog box.

☐ Click the OK button of the Deploy Application Status dialog box.

That's it! Your application is ready in the C:\TRY directory.

☐ Use File Manager to inspect the C:\TRY directory.

In the C:\TRY directory you'll see the DISK1 directory. To distribute your application, you must copy the contents of C:\TRY\DISK1 to a 1.44MB 3.5" disk.

Note: If your application is large, C:\TRY will contain additional subdirectories. For example, C:\TRY will include the DISK1 subdirectory and the DISK2 subdirectory. In this case you'll copy the entire C:\TRY\DISK1 directory to a 1.44MB 3.5" disk and mark the disk as Disk 1 of 2. You'll then copy the entire C:\TRY\DISK2 directory to another 1.44MB 3.5" disk and mark the disk as Disk 2 of 2.

Installing the MyProg Program

You'll now test the Setup program. As stated, the Setup program should create a directory called C:\MYPROG, and it will copy the MyProg program from the distribution disk to the C:\MYPROG directory. Also, it should create a program group for the MyProg program.

Typically, you will copy the contents of the C:\TRY\DISK1 directory to a disk, and you will execute the Setup program from the disk. To test your work, however, you can also execute the Setup program from the C:\TRY\DISK1 directory.

☐ Use File Manager to delete the C:\MYPROG directory.

Recall that you created the C:\MYPROG directory so that dBASE would know which files should be included on the distribution disks. You now want to delete this directory, because you want to test the Setup program. Setup.EXE should create the C:\MYPROG directory and will copy files from the C:\TRY\DISK1 directory to the C:\MYPROG directory.

The following steps are also the steps your user will perform to install your program. (Your user, however, will execute the Setup program from the Disk 1 you'll provide, whereas the following steps instruct you to execute the Setup program from the C:\TRY\DISK1 directory.)

☐ Use File Manager to execute the C:\TRY\DISK1\Setup program.

Setup.EXE responds by starting to install the MyProg program. Eventually you'll see the Install Destination Drive dialog box. (See Figure 15.15.)

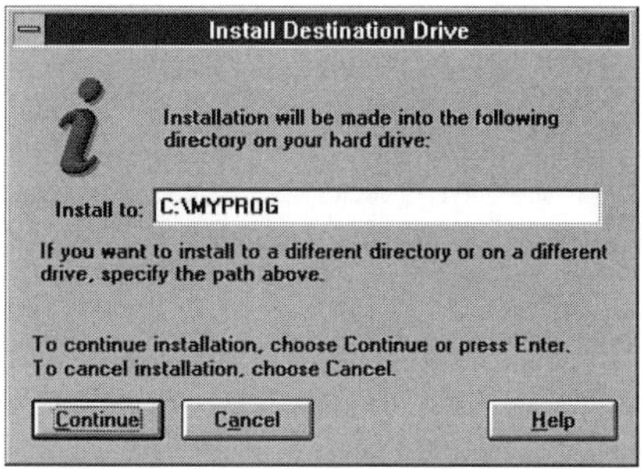

Figure 15.15.
The Install Destination Drive dialog box.

As you can see in Figure 15.15, the Setup program suggests to install the program in the C:\MYPROG directory.

☐ Click the Continue button.

Setup.EXE responds by displaying the Setup Alert dialog box, shown in Figure 15.16.

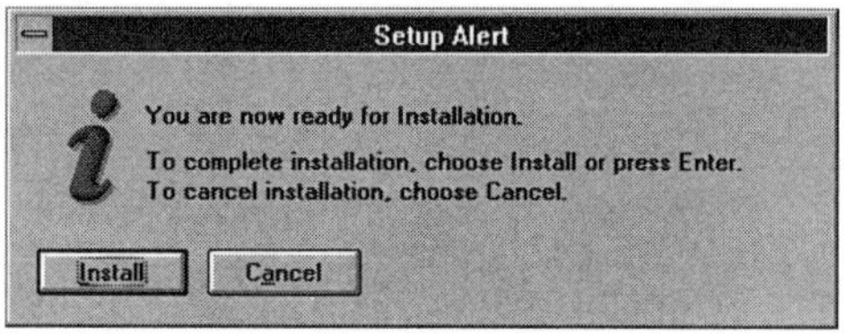

Figure 15.16.
The Setup Alert dialog box.

☐ Click the Install button of the Setup Alert dialog box.

Setup.EXE responds by installing the MyProg.EXE file into the C:\MYPROG directory. During the installation, the picture shown in Figure 15.17 is displayed.

Figure 15.17.
The picture that Setup.EXE displays during the installation.

Note: During the installation, a picture of a road and gauges of a car is displayed, as shown in Figure 15.17. This picture is also displayed when a Borland product, such as Delphi, Visual dBASE, and Borland C++, is installed.

When the installation is finished, the Setup Notification dialog box is displayed, as shown in Figure 15.18.

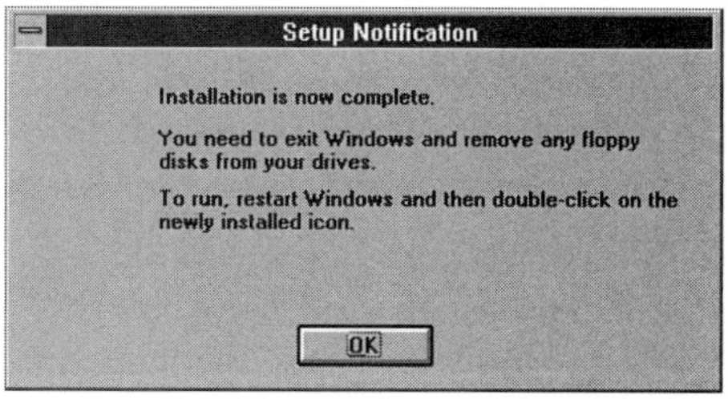

Figure 15.18.
The Setup Notification dialog box.

- Click the OK button of the Setup Notification dialog box to terminate the Setup program.
- Take a look at your Program Manager window.

Your Program Manager window should now contain the MyProg program group with a program icon in it. (See Figure 15.19.)

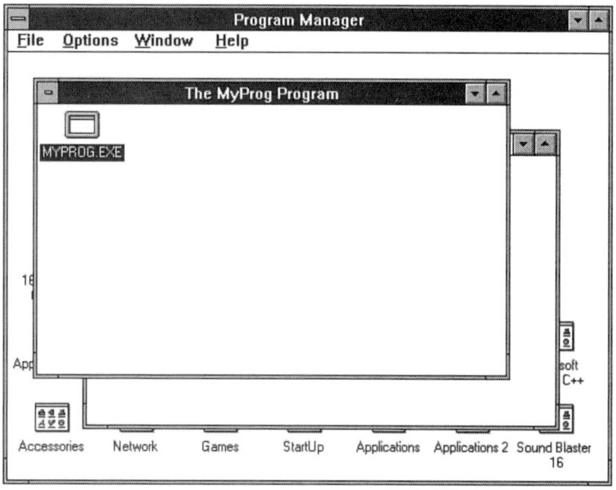

Figure 15.19.
The MyProg program group.

- Double-click the icon in the MyProg program group to execute the MyProg program.
- Experiment with the MyProg program and verify its proper operation.
- Terminate the MyProg program.
- Use File Manager to examine the C:\MYPROG directory.

As you can see, the MyProg.EXE file resides in the C:\MYPROG directory.

Summary

In this chapter you have created a simple program called MyProg. You have also created the MyProg.EXE file, which is the executable MyProg program.

You have used the Deploy Application tool of dBASE to create the distribution files that will be copied to the distribution disk.

Q&A

Q In this chapter, I used the Deploy Application feature of dBASE to create a Setup program and the files that should be copied to the distribution disks. The files are stored in the C:\TRY\DISK1 directory. I don't recognize some of these files. What are they?

A These files are the ones needed by the Setup program. Note that some of the files have the underscore character (_) in the filename extension. These are compressed files. The Setup program automatically uncompresses the compressed files and copies these files to the user's hard drive. By placing compressed files in the distribution disks, you'll be able to send your users fewer disks.

Q Looking at Figure 15.13, I see that there are other options in the Deploy Application window that I can choose. What are these options?

A You can learn about these other options by clicking the Help button of the Deploy Application window. As you can see from the Help window, the Display README.TXT check box, for example, enables you to attach a readme.txt file. That is, after the installation is finished, the reader will be able to read your readme.txt file. If you place an × in the Display README.TXT check box, you'll have to include a readme.txt file in the directory from which the files are copied to the distribution disk. (In this chapter's example, you'll have to place the readme.txt file in the C:\MYPROG directory.)

Similarly, if your application uses VBX files, the Setup program can copy the VBX files to the \WINDOWS\SYSTEM directory of your user. All you must do is place an × in the VBX Controls check box of the Deploy Application window.

Q My main job is to create in-house dBASE programs for my company (I'm not involved in designing commercial applications). This means that I will not use the Deploy Application feature of dBASE. Right?

A On the contrary. When you distribute your program to other people in your company, it makes sense to provide them with a professional install program such as the one you can generate with the Deploy Application feature of dBASE.

Quiz

1. To create a professional Setup program, which of the following do you do?

   a. Use the Deploy Application menu item of the program menu.
   b. Write a Setup program by yourself.

2. Suppose you used the Deploy Application menu item of the Program menu to create distribution disks for your program. What instructions do you have to give your users so that they'll be able to install your program?

Exercise

Design a program. Then create a Setup program with a distribution disk your user can use to install the program.

Quiz Answer

1. a. and b. That is, you can write your own Setup program that performs the installation. The easy way, however, is to use the Deploy Application tool as discussed in this chapter. In most cases, the Deploy Application tool is sufficient to perform professional installation of your software.
2. To install your program your users need to simply execute the Setup program that resides on Disk 1 of the distribution disks.

Exercise Answer

Follow the steps outlined in this chapter to perform this exercise.

Here are the basic steps:

- ☐ Design a program, and then test it.
- ☐ Make an EXE file for the program you designed, and then test the EXE program.
- ☐ Select Deploy Application from the Program menu, and set the various options and settings of the Deploy Application window to create your Setup program and the corresponding distribution files.

16

WEEK 3

Using VBX Controls

VBX controls are files that enable you to enhance the off-the-shelf capabilities of Visual dBASE. After you install a VBX control into your Visual dBASE for Windows, the Controls Palette window of dBASE has a new control you can incorporate into your dBASE programs.

What Is a VBX Control?

After you install a VBX file into dBASE, the Controls Palette window of dBASE will have a new control in it. The new control will have its own properties and events just like the standard dBASE controls (for example, scroll bar and pushbutton). VBX files have a .VBX file extension (for example, BUTTON.VBX).

In this chapter you will write a dBASE program that uses the SWITCH.VBX file. This VBX file is included with your Visual dBASE. It was copied to your \VISUALDB\SAMPLES directory when you installed Visual dBASE.

Note: In this chapter you'll use a VBX control that came with your Visual dBASE package.

The SWITCH Program

In the following sections you will write a dBASE program called SWITCH that illustrates how to install and use a VBX control.

Before you start writing the SWITCH program, you need to know how the program should look and what it should do.

When you run the SWITCH program, the main window of the SWITCH program should look like the one shown in Figure 16.1.

Figure 16.1.
The main window of the SWITCH program.

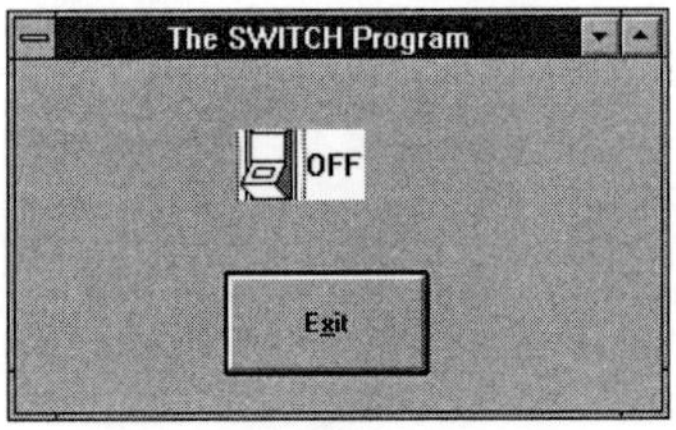

As shown in Figure 16.1, the main window of the SWITCH program contains two controls: an ON/OFF switch control and an Exit button (a regular pushbutton control).

The user can turn the switch control ON and OFF by clicking it. In Figure 16.1, the ON/OFF switch is shown in its OFF state. In Figure 16.2, the ON/OFF switch is shown in its ON state.

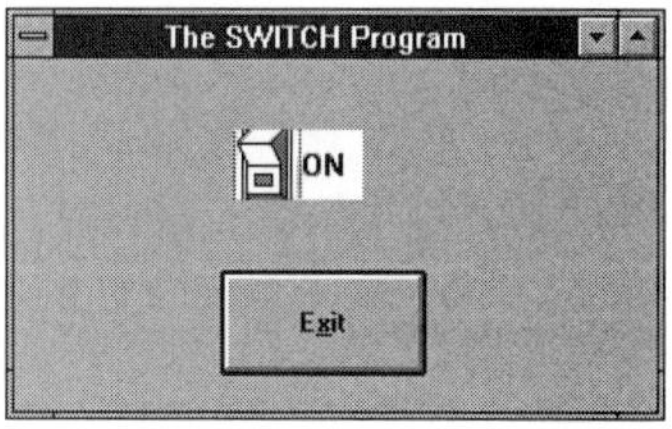

Figure 16.2.
The main window of the SWITCH program when the switch is in its ON state.

When the user turns the switch ON, a message box with the text `You turned the switch ON` is displayed. (See Figure 16.3.)

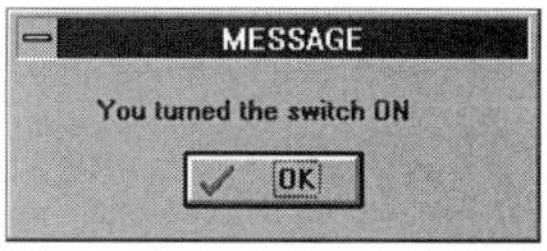

Figure 16.3.
The message box that the SWITCH program displays when the user turns the switch ON.

When the user turns the switch OFF, a message box with the text `You turned the switch OFF` is displayed. (See Figure 16.4.)

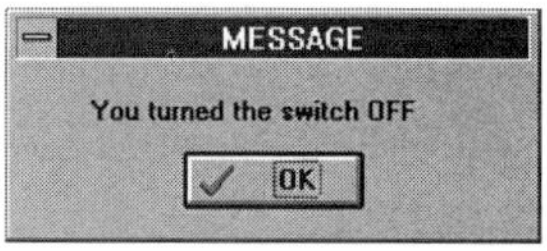

Figure 16.4.
The message box that the SWITCH program displays when the user turns the switch OFF.

When the user clicks the Exit pushbutton, the SWITCH program terminates itself.

Now that you know what the SWITCH program is supposed to do, it's time to start writing the program.

The Visual Implementation of the SWITCH Program

Create the SWITCH.WFM form as instructed here:

☐ Type `MD C:\DBPROG` in the Command window, and then press Enter.

dBASE responds by creating the directory C:\DBPROG. (If this directory already exists, dBASE displays a message box telling you that the directory cannot be created.)

- Type `MD C:\DBPROG\CH16` in the Command window, and then press Enter.

  dBASE responds by creating the directory C:\DBPROG\CH16.

- Type `CREATE FORM C:\DBPROG\CH16\SWITCH` in the Command Window, and press Enter.

  dBASE responds by creating the SWITCH.WFM form and displaying it in design mode.

Before you start customizing the SWITCH.WFM form, first add the SWITCH.VBX control to the Controls window of dBASE. Here is how you do that:

- Select Set Up Custom Controls from the File menu of dBASE.

  dBASE responds by displaying the Set Up Custom Controls dialog box. (See Figure 16.5.)

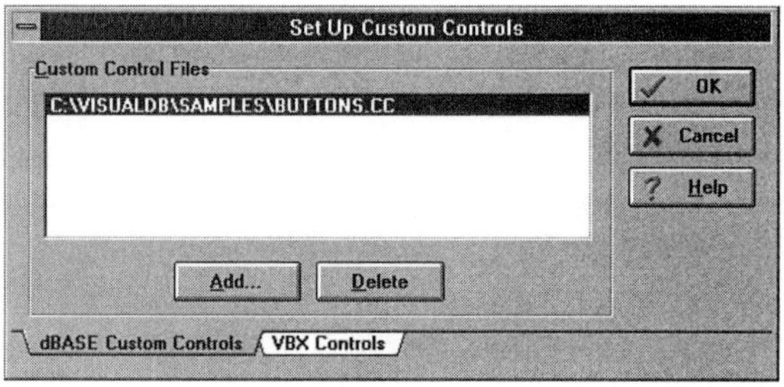

Figure 16.5.
The Set Up Custom Controls dialog box.

- Click the VBX Controls tab of the Set Up Custom Controls dialog box (because you want to add a VBX control to the Controls Palette of dBASE).

- Click the Add button, select the \VISUALDB\SAMPLES\SWITCH.VBX file, and then click the OK button of the Set Up Custom Controls dialog box.

  dBASE responds by adding the SWITCH.VBX control to the Controls Palette window of dBASE.

To verify that the SWITCH.VBX control now appears in the Controls Palette window of dBASE, follow these steps:

- Select the Control Palette window of dBASE.

- Click the VBX tab of the Control Palette window.

As shown in Figure 16.6, the SWITCH.VBX control is in the VBX page of the Control Palette.

Now that you've verified that the SWITCH.VBX control appears in the Controls window of dBASE, you can design a form that uses this control.

- Customize the SWITCH.WFM form according to the specifications in Table 16.1. When you finish customizing the form, it should look like the one shown in Figure 16.7.

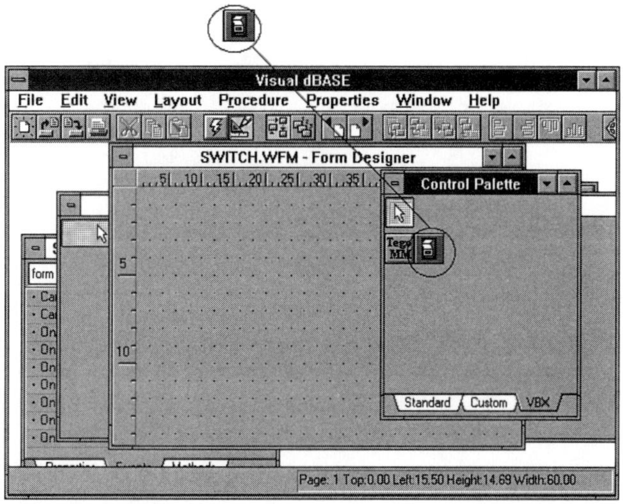

Figure 16.6.
The icon of the SWITCH.VBX control in the Control Palette window of dBASE.

> **Note:** Table 16.1 instructs you to place one BISWITCH (SWITCH.VBX) control in the form and one PushButton control in the form.
>
> To place the BISWITCH (SWITCH.VBX) control in the form, select the VBX tab of the Control Palette window, and then double-click the icon of the BISWITCH control.
>
> To place the PushButton control in the form, select the Standard tab of the Control Palette window, and then double-click the icon of the PushButton control.

☐ Save your work by selecting Save from the File menu.

Table 16.1. The properties table of the SWITCH.WFM form.

Object	Property	Setting
Form	**Text**	**The SWITCH Program**
	Height	10
	Left	1
	MDI	.F.
	Top	0
	Width	50

continues

Table 16.1. continued

Object	Property	Setting
BISWITCH (SWITCH.VBX)	**Name**	**Switch**
	Caption	OFF
	Height	2
	Left	19
	Top	2
	Width	10
PushButton	**Name**	**ExitButton**
	Text	E&xit
	Height	3
	Left	16
	Top	6
	Width	16

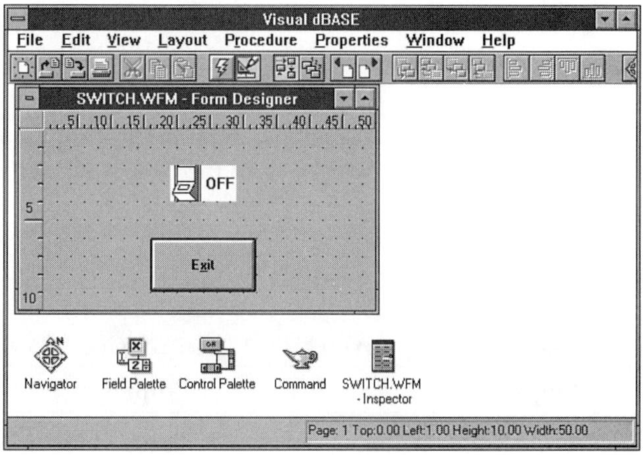

Figure 16.7.
The SWITCH.WFM form in design mode.

The visual implementation of the SWITCH.WFM form is finished. To see your visual design in action, follow these steps:

- ☐ Press F2 on your keyboard.

    dBASE responds by running the SWITCH.WFM form.

☐ Experiment with the switch control. That is, click the switch control several times.

As you can see, when you click the switch, the state of the switch toggles. The caption of the switch, however, remains OFF all the time (even when the switch is ON). You'll write the code that changes the caption of the switch, depending on the state of the switch, later in this chapter.

☐ Change the mode of the SWITCH.WFM form back to design mode by pressing Shift+F2.

16

Entering the Code of the SWITCH Program

In the following sections you'll enter the code of the SWITCH program.

Attaching Code to the *OnClick* Event of the Exit Pushbutton

When the user clicks the Exit button, the SWITCH program should terminate itself. You'll now write the code that accomplishes this task.

☐ Attach code to the `OnClick` event of the Exit pushbutton. After you write this code, the `EXITBUTTON_OnClick` procedure should look as follows:

```
Procedure EXITBUTTON_OnClick

 form.close()

Return
```

☐ Save your work by selecting Save from the File menu.

The statement you typed in the `EXITBUTTON_OnClick` procedure:

```
form.Close()
```

terminates the program by closing the form.

To see the code you attached to the `OnClick` event of the Exit button in action, follow these steps:

☐ Press F2 on your keyboard.

dBASE responds by running the SWITCH.WFM form.

☐ Click the Exit button.

The SWITCH program responds by terminating itself.

Attaching Code to the *OnOn* Event of the Switch Control

When the user changes the state of the switch control to ON, the program should change the caption of the switch control to ON, and the program should display a message box with the text `You turned the switch ON`. You'll now write the code that accomplishes these tasks.

- ☐ Type `MODIFY FORM ?` in the Command window, press Enter, and then select the file C:\DBPROG\CH16\SWITCH.WFM from the Open Form dialog box that dBASE displays.

  dBASE responds by displaying the SWITCH.WFM form in design mode.

- ☐ Attach the following code to the `OnOn` event of the switch control. After you write this code, the `SWITCH_OnOn` procedure should look as follows:

```
Procedure SWITCH_OnOn

* Change the Caption of the switch to ON.
form.Switch.Caption="ON"

* Display a message box.
MsgBox("You turned the switch ON", "MESSAGE")

Return
```

- ☐ Save your work by selecting Save from the File menu.

As implied by its name, the `OnOn` event of the switch control occurs when the switch control is switched ON.

The first statement you typed in the `SWITCH_OnOn` procedure is this:

```
form.Switch.Caption="ON"
```

This statement changes the Caption property of the switch control to ON.

The second statement:

```
MsgBox("You turned the switch ON", "MESSAGE")
```

displays a message box with the message `You turned the switch ON`.

So when the user switches the switch control ON, the `SWITCH_OnOn` procedure will be automatically executed, and the code you wrote in this procedure will change the caption of the switch control to ON and display the message `You turned the switch ON`.

To see in action the code you attached to the `OnOn` event of the switch control, follow these steps:

- ☐ Press F2 on your keyboard.

  dBASE responds by running the SWITCH.WFM form.

☐ Click the switch control.

The SWITCH program responds by turning the switch control ON, changing the caption of the switch control to ON, and displaying a message box with the text `You turned the switch ON.`

☐ Click the OK button of the message box.

☐ Change the mode of the SWITCH.WFM form back to design mode by pressing Shift+F2.

16

Attaching Code to the *OnOff* Event of the Switch Control

When the user changes the state of the switch control to OFF, the program should change the caption of the switch control to OFF and display a message box with the text `You turned the switch OFF`. You'll now write the code that accomplishes these tasks.

☐ Attach the following code to the `OnOff` event of the switch control. After you write this code, the `SWITCH_OnOff` procedure should look as follows:

```
Procedure SWITCH_OnOff

* Change the Caption of the switch to OFF.
form.Switch.Caption="OFF"

* Display a message box.
MsgBox("You turned the switch OFF", "MESSAGE")

Return
```

☐ Save your work by selecting Save from the File menu.

As implied by its name, the `OnOff` event of the switch control occurs when the switch control is switched OFF.

The first statement you typed in the `SWITCH_OnOff` procedure is this:

```
form.Switch.Caption="OFF"
```

This statement changes the Caption of the switch control to OFF.

The second statement:

```
MsgBox("You turned the switch OFF", "MESSAGE")
```

displays a message box with the text `You turned the switch OFF`.

So when the user switches the switch control OFF, the `SWITCH_OnOff` procedure will be automatically executed, and the code you wrote in this procedure will change the caption of the switch control to OFF and display the message `You turned the switch OFF`.

To see in action the code you attached to the `OnOff` event of the switch control, follow these steps:

- ☐ Press F2 on your keyboard.

  dBASE responds by running the SWITCH.WFM form.

- ☐ Click the switch control.

  The SWITCH program responds by turning the switch control ON, changing the caption of the switch control to ON, and displaying a message box with the text `You turned the switch ON.`

- ☐ Click the OK button of the message box.
- ☐ Click the switch control again.

  The SWITCH program responds by turning the switch control OFF, changing the caption of the switch control to OFF, and displaying a message box with the text `You turned the switch OFF.`

- ☐ Terminate the SWITCH program by clicking its Exit button.

Using Other VBX Controls

The SWITCH.VBX control you used in the preceding sections is a very simple VBX control. Many powerful VBX controls are available from various vendors. For example, Borland International sells a product called Borland Visual Solutions Pack. This product contains various useful VBX controls you can incorporate into your Visual dBASE for Windows programs.

An example of a VBX control that you can incorporate into your dBASE programs is the TegoMM.VBX advanced multimedia control. The TegoMM.VBX multimedia control enables you to include multimedia features in your dBASE programs. These features include playback, recording, and editing of WAV sound files; playback of MIDI sound files; playback of AVI movie files; and playback of CD audio. The TegoMM.VBX control also enables you to write dBASE programs that play WAV files through the internal PC speaker (for users who do not have a sound card). You will learn how to write programs that use the TegoMM.VBX multimedia control in Chapter 18, "Multimedia and Animation."

Another example of a VBX control that you can incorporate into your dBASE programs is the Tego3DVR.VBX 3D virtual reality control. This control enables you to write 3D virtual reality dBASE programs where your user moves inside a three-dimensional picture. The control also enables you to incorporate stationary and moving objects (sprites) that interact with the user. You will learn how to write programs that use the Tego3DVR.VBX 3D virtual reality control in Chapter 20, "3D Virtual Reality: Part I," and Chapter 21, "3D Virtual Reality: Part II."

> **Note:** The TegoMM.VBX advanced multimedia control and the Tego3DVR.VBX 3D virtual reality control are included with the disk you can order to accompany this book. (See the disk offer at the end of this book.)

dBASE is just one of many programming languages that can use VBX controls. Other programming languages that support VBX controls include Visual Basic, Visual C++, Delphi, Borland C++, and others.

Typically, as a programmer you want to finish a project in the shortest possible time. One way to achieve this objective is by utilizing VBX controls. For example, suppose that you are implementing a project with dBASE, and you need a certain feature in your program. The particular feature you are trying to implement, however, is not included in the off-the-shelf dBASE package. You are faced with the following options:

- Implement the feature you need using the dBASE programming language.
- Use an off-the-shelf VBX control that is readily available from a third-party vendor, and the control is available at a reasonable price.
- Implement the required VBX yourself.

If you decide to implement the VBX yourself, you can use a programming package such as Visual C++, which enables you to design your own VBX controls using the C++ programming languages.

Depending on the feature involved, implementing the feature with pure dBASE code might prove to be time-consuming.

So before you invest time in trying to implement the feature by using the dBASE programming language, or in implementing the VBX control yourself, it might be worthwhile for you to research the availability of off-the-shelf VBX controls. You just might find that the VBX control you are looking for is available. This is a popular trend followed by many programmers when they are using a modern modular programming language, such as dBASE, Delphi, Visual Basic, and other object-oriented programming languages.

As stated, VBX controls can save you a tremendous amount of developing time. Another important advantage of using VBX controls is that you must learn the VBX control only once. That is, suppose that you used dBASE and a certain VBX control in one of your projects. The fact that you already used the VBX control in your dBASE program means that you studied the control and you understand its properties and events. If you then are involved in another project using a different programming language (for example, Delphi or Visual Basic), you can use the same VBX control you used in your dBASE programs. Therefore, you also save development time because you do not have to again study the properties and events of the VBX control (because you are using the same VBX control).

It is important to understand that several programs can use the same VBX control simultaneously. For example, you can develop several dBASE programs that all use the same VBX control, and you can also develop several Delphi or Visual Basic programs that use that same VBX control. The PC on which all these programs are executed needs only one copy of the VBX control. Typically, the VBX controls reside in the \WINDOWS\SYSTEM directory. Every program that uses VBX controls first looks for the VBX control in the \WINDOWS\SYSTEM directory.

Summary

In this chapter you have learned that your dBASE for Windows programs can use VBX controls. As you have seen, after you add a VBX control to the Controls window of dBASE, you can use this control as if it were a regular dBASE control. That is, you can place it in a form, set its properties, and attach code to its events.

In this chapter you have implemented the SWITCH program, which uses the SWITCH.VBX control. The SWITCH.VBX control comes with your Visual dBASE package.

Q&A

Q Can I create VBX controls with Visual dBASE?

A No. You can use VBX controls from within your dBASE for Windows programs, but you can't create them using dBASE for Windows.

Q How can I create my own VBX controls?

A Most programmers create VBX controls using the C/C++ programming language. The book *Master Visual C++ 2*, by Gurewich & Gurewich, Sams Publishing, includes a detailed step-by-step tutorial that shows how to create a VBX control using Visual C++ 2.

Quiz

1. When does the `OnOn` event of the switch control occur?
2. When does the `OnOff` event of the switch control occur?

Exercise

Add code to the SWITCH.WFM form so that when the user turns the switch ON, the program beeps two times, and when the user turns the switch OFF, the program beeps one time.

Quiz Answers

1. The `OnOn` event of the switch control occurs when the switch control is switched ON.
2. The `OnOff` event of the switch control occurs when the switch control is switched OFF.

16

Exercise Answer

To make the program beep two times when the switch control is switched ON, add the following two statements to the `SWITCH_OnOn` procedure:

```
?CHR(7)
?CHR(7)
```

To make the program beep one time when the switch control is switched OFF, add the following statement to the `SWITCH_OnOff` procedure:

```
?CHR(7)
```

17

WEEK 3

Using Dynamic Link Libraries

DLL is the abbreviation for *dynamic link library.* DLLs are files that contain powerful functions and procedures that can be used by your program. This chapter shows you how to incorporate DLL functions into your programs. As you'll soon see, incorporating DLLs into your Visual dBASE programs enables you to extend the off-the-shelf capabilities of Visual dBASE.

What Is a DLL?

DLLs are files that contain functions that can be used by your program. Typically DLL files have either the .DLL file extension or the .EXE file extension (for example, MyDLL.DLL, MyDLL.EXE).

There are two types of DLL files:

- Windows API DLLs
- Third-party DLLs

Windows API DLLs are shipped with the Windows package, and therefore your program can safely assume that your user has these DLLs installed on the PC.

The Windows API DLLs contain powerful functions that extend the capabilities of the Visual dBASE package.

In addition to the standard Windows API DLLs, your program can use third-party DLLs (DLLs distributed by companies other than Microsoft). These DLLs contain functions that further extend the capabilities of Visual dBASE. You cannot, however, assume that your user has the third-party DLLs installed on the PC. Therefore, if your program makes use of third-party DLLs, your distribution disk must include these DLLs, and your installation program must copy these DLL files from the distribution disk onto the user's hard drive. Of course, you must comply with the software licensing agreement of the third-party vendor.

You can also create DLL files yourself. Usually, DLL files are created using the C/C++ programming language.

This chapter shows you how to use several functions from the Windows API DLLs. Because there are so many API DLLs, they can't all be covered in this chapter. After you practice and use the DLLs that are presented in this chapter, however, you'll get the idea of how to use DLLs.

The API Program

In the following sections you will write a dBASE program called API that illustrates how to use Windows API DLL functions. As you'll soon see, using Windows API functions enables you to perform tasks that are not available in Visual dBASE.

Before you start writing the API program, you need to know how the program should look and what it should do.

When you run the API program, the main window of the API program should look like the one shown in Figure 17.1.

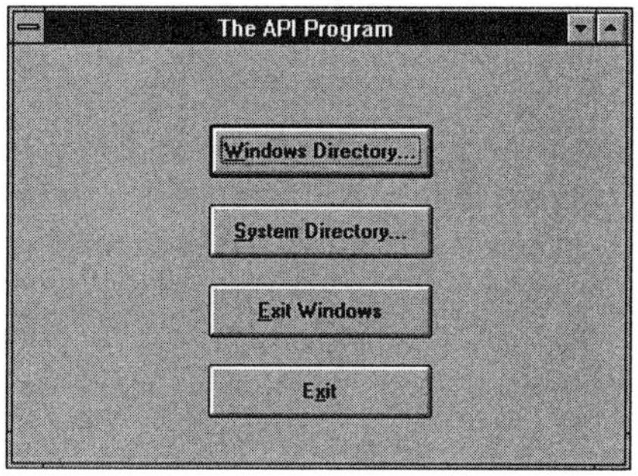

Figure 17.1.
The main window of the API program.

As shown in Figure 17.1, the main window of the API program contains four pushbuttons: Windows Directory, System Directory, Exit Windows, and Exit.

When the user clicks the Windows Directory button, the API program opens a message box that displays the name of the directory where Windows resides. For example, if the user's Windows directory is C:\WINDOWS, then after the user clicks the Windows Directory button, the message box shown in Figure 17.2 will be displayed.

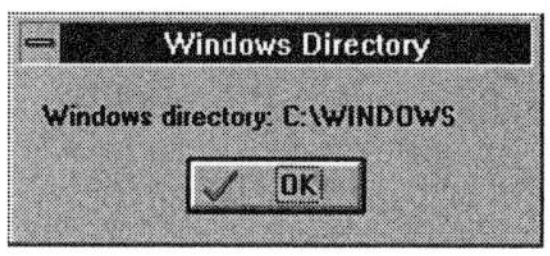

Figure 17.2.
The Windows Directory message box.

When the user clicks the System Directory button, the API program opens a message box that displays the name of the user's Windows system directory. For example, if the user's Windows system directory is C:\WINDOWS\SYSTEM, then after the user clicks the System Directory button, the message box shown in Figure 17.3 will be displayed.

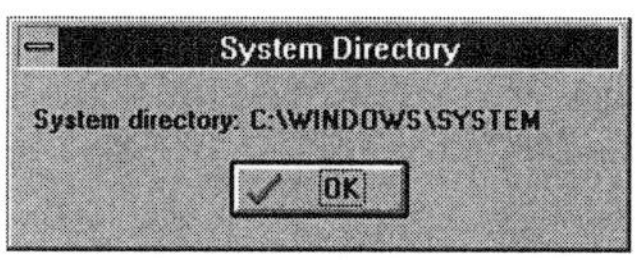

Figure 17.3.
The System Directory message box.

The Exit Windows button of the API program enables the user to exit Windows. When the user clicks the Exit Windows button, the API program displays a Yes/No confirmation message box. (See Figure 17.4.) If the user clicks the Yes button of the confirmation message box, the API program causes Windows to terminate.

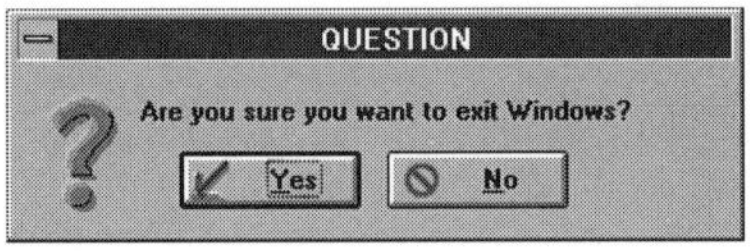

Figure 17.4.
The confirmation message box the API program displays after the user clicks the Exit Windows button.

When the user clicks the Exit pushbutton, the API program terminates itself.

Now that you know what the API program is supposed to do, it's time to start writing it.

The Visual Implementation of the API Program

Create the API.WFM form as instructed here:

☐ Type `MD C:\DBPROG` in the Command window, and then press Enter.

dBASE responds by creating the directory C:\DBPROG. (If this directory already exists, dBASE displays a message box telling you that the directory cannot be created.)

☐ Type `MD C:\DBPROG\CH17` in the Command window, and then press Enter.

dBASE responds by creating the directory C:\DBPROG\CH17.

☐ Type `CREATE FORM C:\DBPROG\CH17\API` in the Command window and press Enter.

dBASE responds by creating the API.WFM form and displaying it in design mode.

☐ Customize the API.WFM form according to the specifications in Table 17.1. When you finish customizing the form, it should look like the one shown in Figure 17.5.

☐ Save your work by selecting Save from the File menu.

Table 17.1. The properties table of the API.WFM form.

Object	Property	Setting
Form	**Text**	**The API Program**
	Height	18
	Left	1

Object	Property	Setting
	Top	0
	Width	63
	MDI	.F.
PushButton	**Name**	**WindowsDirectoryButton**
	Text	&Windows Directory
	Height	2
	Left	20
	Top	3
	Width	23
PushButton	**Name**	**SystemDirectoryButton**
	Text	&System Directory
	Height	2
	Left	20
	Top	6
	Width	23
PushButton	**Name**	**ExitWindowsButton**
	Text	&Exit Windows
	Height	2
	Left	20
	Top	9
	Width	23
PushButton	**Name**	**ExitButton**
	Text	E&xit
	Height	2
	Left	20
	Top	12
	Width	23

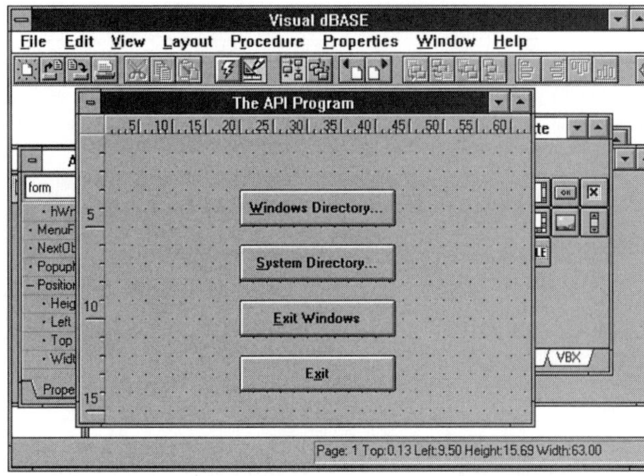

Figure 17.5.
The API.WFM form in design mode (after customization).

The visual implementation of the API.WFM form is complete.

Entering the Code of the API Program

In the following sections you'll attach code to the four pushbuttons of the form.

Attaching Code to the *OnClick* Event of the Exit Pushbutton

When the user clicks the Exit button, the API program should terminate itself. You'll now write the code that accomplishes this task.

☐ Attach the following code to the `OnClick` event of the Exit pushbutton. After you write this code, the `EXITBUTTON_OnClick` procedure should look as follows:

```
Procedure EXITBUTTON_OnClick

 form.Close()

Return
```

☐ Save your work by selecting Save from the File menu.

The statement you typed in the `EXITBUTTON_OnClick()` procedure:

```
form.Close()
```

terminates the program by closing the form.

To see in action the code you attached to the `OnClick` event of the Exit button, follow these steps:

☐ Press F2 on your keyboard.

dBASE responds by running the API.WFM form.

☐ Click the Exit button.

The API program responds by terminating itself.

Attaching Code to the *OnClick* Event of the Windows Directory Pushbutton

When the user clicks the Windows Directory button, the API program should open a message box that displays the name of the user's Windows directory. You'll now write the code that accomplishes this task.

17

☐ Type `MODIFY FORM ?` in the Command window, press Enter, and then select the file C:\DBPROG\CH17\API.WFM from the Open Form dialog box that dBASE displays.

dBASE responds by displaying the API.WFM form in design mode.

☐ Attach the following code to the `OnClick` event of the Windows Directory button. After you write this code, the `WINDOWSDIRECTORYBUTTON_OnClick` procedure should look as follows:

```
Procedure WINDOWSDIRECTORYBUTTON_OnClick

* Declare the GetWindowsDirectory() API function.
EXTERN CINT GetWindowsDirectory (CSTRING,CINT) KRNL386.EXE

* Fill the string variable WinDir with 144 spaces.
WinDir = SPACE(144)

* Fill the WinDir variable with the Windows directory name.
GetWindowsDirectory(WinDir,144)

* Display the Windows directory name.
MsgBox("Windows directory: "+WinDir, "Windows Directory")

Return
```

☐ Save your work by selecting Save from the File menu.

The first statement you typed in the `WINDOWSDIRECTORYBUTTON_OnClick` procedure is this:

```
EXTERN CINT GetWindowsDirectory (CSTRING,CINT) KRNL386.EXE
```

This statement uses the `EXTERN` command to declare the `GetWindowsDirectory()` API function.

Where did this declaration come from? You can find the dBASE declarations of the Windows API functions in the file \VISUALDB\INCLUDE\WINAPI.H.

Note: To find the dBASE declaration of an API function, look for the declaration of the desired function in the file \VISUALDB\INCLUDE\WINAPI.H.

For example, to find the declaration of the `GetWindowsDirectory()` API function, take the following steps:

- ☐ Use your favorite text editor or word processor to open the file \VISUALDB\INCLUDE\WINAPI.H.
- ☐ Use the Search (or Find) feature of your word processor to look for the string `GetWindowsDirectory`.

You will find that the `GetWindowsDirectory()` function is declared as shown here:

```
extern CINT GetWindowsDirectory (CSTRING,CINT) KRNL386.EXE
```

Notice how the declaration of the `GetWindowsDirectory()` API function is constructed:

```
EXTERN CINT GetWindowsDirectory (CSTRING,CINT) KRNL386.EXE
```

The first keyword, `EXTERN`, begins the declaration.

The second word, `CINT`, represents the returned value of the function. That is, the `GetWindowsDirectory()` function returns a `CINT` data type. `CINT` is a numeric data type.

The third keyword, `GetWindowsDirectory`, is the name of the DLL function that is being declared.

The name of the function is followed by parentheses that contain the types of parameters of the function:

```
(CSTRING,CINT)
```

This means that the first parameter of the `GetWindowsDirectory()` function is of type CSTRING (a character type) and the second parameter is of type CINT (a numeric type).

The last keyword of the declaration, `KRNL386.EXE`, specifies the name of the DLL file in which the function is stored. This means that the `GetWindowsDirectory()` function is in the DLL file KRNL386.EXE.

This is the next statement in the `WINDOWSDIRECTORYBUTTON_OnClick` procedure:

```
WinDir = SPACE(144)
```

This statement initializes the `WinDir` variable as a character type and fills the variable `WinDir` with 144 spaces.

This is the next statement:

```
GetWindowsDirectory(WinDir,144)
```

This statement calls the `GetWindowsDirectory()` API function. As you can see, the first parameter passed to the `GetWindowsDirectory()` function is the `WinDir` variable. The second parameter is the length of the `WinDir` variable.

What does the `GetWindowsDirectory()` function do? It fills the character variable that is passed to it (`WinDir`) with the full pathname of the Windows directory.

So at this point, `WinDir` is filled with the full pathname of the Windows directory. For example, if the user's Windows directory is C:\WINDOWS, then `WinDir` is filled with the string `"C:\WINDOWS"`.

17

Finally, the value of the `WinDir` variable is displayed by using the `MsgBox()` function:

```
MsgBox("Windows directory: "+WinDir, "Windows Directory")
```

To see in action the code you attached to the `OnClick` event of the Windows Directory pushbutton, follow these steps:

☐ Press F2 on your keyboard.

dBASE responds by running the API.WFM form.

☐ Click the Windows Directory button.

The API program responds by opening a message box that displays the name of your Windows directory.

☐ Click the OK button of the message box.

☐ Change the mode of the API.WFM form back to design mode by pressing Shift+F2.

Attaching Code to the *OnClick* Event of the System Directory Pushbutton

When the user clicks the System Directory button, the API program should open a message box that displays the name of the user's Windows system directory. You'll now write the code that accomplishes this task.

☐ Attach the following code to the `OnClick` event of the System Directory button. After you write this code, the `SYSTEMDIRECTORYBUTTON_OnClick` procedure should look as follows:

```
Procedure SYSTEMDIRECTORYBUTTON_OnClick

* Declare the GetSystemDirectory() API function.
EXTERN CINT GetSystemDirectory (CSTRING, CINT) KRNL386.EXE
```

```
* Fill the string variable SysDir with 144 spaces.
SysDir = SPACE(144)

* Fill the SysDir variable with the System directory name.
GetSystemDirectory(SysDir,144)

* Display the System directory name.
MsgBox("System directory: "+SysDir, "System Directory")

Return
```

☐ Save your work by selecting Save from the File menu.

The first statement you typed in the `SYSTEMDIRECTORYBUTTON_OnClick` procedure is this:

```
EXTERN CINT GetSystemDirectory(CSTRING, CINT) KRNL386.EXE
```

This statement uses the `EXTERN` command to declare the `GetSystemDirectory()` API function. This declaration was taken from the file \VISUALDB\INCLUDE\WINAPI.H.

This is the next statement:

```
SysDir = SPACE(144)
```

This statement fills the variable `SysDir` with 144 spaces.

This is the next statement:

```
GetSystemDirectory(SysDir,144)
```

This statement calls the `GetSystemDirectory()` API function. As you can see, the first parameter passed to the `GetSystemDirectory()` function is the `SysDir` variable. The second parameter is the length of the `SysDir` variable.

The `GetSystemDirectory()` function fills the character variable that is passed to it (`SysDir`) with the full pathname of the Windows system directory.

So at this point, `SysDir` is filled with the full pathname of the Windows system directory. For example, if the user's Windows system directory is C:\WINDOWS\SYSTEM, then `SysDir` is filled with the string `"C:\WINDOWS\SYSTEM"`.

Finally, the value of the `SysDir` variable is displayed by using the `MsgBox()` function:

```
MsgBox("System directory: "+SysDir, "System Directory")
```

To see in action the code you attached to the `OnClick` event of the System Directory pushbutton, follow these steps:

☐ Press F2 on your keyboard.

dBASE responds by running the API.WFM form.

☐ Click the System Directory button.

The API program responds by opening a message box that displays the name of your Windows system directory.

☐ Click the OK button of the message box.

☐ Change the mode of the API.WFM form back to design mode by pressing Shift+F2.

Attaching Code to the *OnClick* Event of the Exit Windows Pushbutton

When the user clicks the Exit Windows button, the API program should enable the user to exit Windows. You'll now write the code that accomplishes this task.

17

☐ Attach the following code to the `OnClick` event of the Exit Windows button. After you write this code, the `EXITWINDOWS_OnClick` procedure should look as follows:

```
Procedure EXITWINDOWSBUTTON_OnClick

* Declare the ExitWindows() API function.
EXTERN CLOGICAL ExitWindows (CLONG, CINT)  USER.EXE

* Get a confirmation from the user.
Question = "Are you sure you want to exit Windows?"
Response = MsgBox (Question, "QUESTION", 4+32)

* If user's response is Yes, exit Windows.
IF Response = 6
   ExitWindows(0,0)
ENDIF

Return
```

☐ Save your work by selecting Save from the File menu.

The first statement you typed in the `EXITWINDOWS_OnClick` procedure is this:

```
EXTERN CLOGICAL ExitWindows(CLONG, CINT) USER.EXE
```

This statement uses the `EXTERN` command to declare the `ExitWindows()` API function. This declaration was taken from the file \VISUALDB\INCLUDE\WINAPI.H. Notice that the last keyword in the declaration of the `ExitWindows()` function is `USER.EXE`. This means that the `ExitWindows()` function is in the DLL file USER.EXE.

These are the next two statements:

```
Question = "Are you sure you want to exit Windows?"
Response = MsgBox (Question, "QUESTION", 4+32)
```

These statements display a Yes/No message box to confirm that the user really wants to exit Windows.

An `IF` statement is then used to evaluate the user's answer:

```
IF Response = 6
   ExitWindows(0,0)
ENDIF
```

If the user clicks the Yes button of the message box, the preceding `IF` statement is satisfied, and the statement under the `IF` is executed:

```
ExitWindows(0,0)
```

This statement terminates Windows by calling the `ExitWindows()` API function.

To see in action the code you attached to the `OnClick` event of the Exit Windows pushbutton, follow these steps:

☐ Press F2 on your keyboard.

dBASE responds by running the API.WFM form.

☐ Click the Exit Windows button.

The API program responds by displaying a message box asking you whether you are sure you want to exit Windows.

☐ Click the Yes button of the message box.

The API program responds by terminating Windows.

Declaring and Using Third-Party DLLs

The API.WFM program you wrote in the previous sections uses the functions `GetWindowsDirectory()` and `GetSystemDirectory()` of the KRNL386.EXE API DLL, and the `ExitWindows()` function of the USER.EXE API DLL. If you want to distribute the API.WFM program to your users, you can safely assume that the KRNL386.EXE and USER.EXE files reside on your user's hard drive. You can make this assumption because the KRNL386.EXE and USER.EXE files are part of the Windows operating system.

When, however, your program uses functions of DLL files of third-party vendors, you cannot assume that your user will have the third-party DLL files installed on the hard drive. Therefore, if your program uses third-party DLLs, your distribution disk must include these DLLs, and your installation program must copy these DLL files from the distribution disk into the user's hard drive. Of course, you must comply with the software licensing agreement of the third-party vendor.

The best way to install a third-party DLL file into the hard drive is to copy the DLL file to the Windows system directory (for example, C:\WINDOWS\SYSTEM). This way, your program will be able to use the DLL file, and other programs that use the same DLL file will also be able to use this DLL file.

You declare a function from a third-party DLL file the same way you declare an API DLL function. That is, you use the `EXTERN` command.

The following example illustrates how to install and use a third-party DLL file:

Suppose you purchased a third-party DLL file called MyDLL.DLL and you want to use the functions of this DLL. To install the MyDLL.DLL file, you must copy the MyDLL.DLL file to your Windows system directory. For example, if your Windows system directory is C:\WINDOWS\SYSTEM, you must copy the MyDLL.DLL file to your C:\WINDOWS\SYSTEM directory. After the MyDLL.DLL file is in your Windows system directory, you can use the functions of this DLL just as you used the API DLL functions. That is, first declare the DLL functions by using the `EXTERN` statement, and then use the DLL functions. The syntax of the function declaration (that is, the parameters and returned value of the function) should be provided with the documentation of the DLL.

17

Using Other API Functions

In this chapter you have used three API functions: `GetWindowsDirectory()`, `GetSystemDirectory()`, and `ExitWindows()`. There are many other API functions you can use.

To be able to use these API functions, you must know the Windows API. That is, you must know what each API function accomplishes, what parameters it takes, and what value it returns.

You can find complete descriptions of all the Windows API DLL functions in the book *Microsoft's Programmer's Reference, Volume 2: Functions.* This book is part of the Microsoft Windows Software Development Kit (SDK).

As stated earlier, to find the dBASE declaration of an API function, you can open the \VISUALDB\INCLUDE\WINAPI.H file with your favorite text editor or word processor and locate the declaration of the desired function by using the Search or Find feature of the word processor. Be careful not to modify the WINAPI.H file.

Summary

In this chapter you have learned that your Visual dBASE programs can use DLL functions. The DLLs can be any of the standard DLLs included in every PC that runs Windows (API DLLs), or they can be custom DLLs written by third-party vendors.

Q&A

Q Can I write DLLs with Visual dBASE?

A No. You can use DLLs from within your Visual dBASE programs, but you can't write them using Visual dBASE.

Q How can I write DLLs?

A Most programmers write DLLs by using the C/C++ programming language. You can use the C/C++ compiler by Microsoft, the C/C++ compiler by Borland, or other C compilers from other vendors.

Quiz

1. What does the following statement do?

   ```
   EXTERN CLONG MyFunction (CINT, CINT) MyDLL.DLL
   ```

2. Use the \VISUALDB\INCLUDE\WINAPI.H file to find the dBASE declaration of the API function `GetWinFlags()`.
3. Suppose that you have purchased a DLL file called MyDLL.DLL. To which directory in your hard drive should you copy this DLL file so that your dBASE programs, as well as other programs, can use this DLL file?

Exercise

The API function `GetFreeSpace()` has one parameter. When you call the `GetFreeSpace()` API function with its parameter set to 0, the `GetFreeSpace()` function returns the amount of free memory (in bytes) available in the system.

The dBASE declaration of the `GetFreeSpace()` function is as follows:

```
EXTERN CLONG GetFreeSpace (CINT) KRNL386.EXE
```

Add a pushbutton to the API.WFM form you designed in this chapter, and set the properties of this pushbutton as shown here:

Object	*Property*	*Setting*
PushButton	**Name**	**FreeSpaceButton**
	Text	&Free Space

Attach code to the `OnClick` event of the Free Space pushbutton that uses the `GetFreeSpace()` function to display the amount of free memory (in bytes) available in the system.

Quiz Answers

1. The statement

   ```
   EXTERN CLONG MyFunction (CINT, CINT) MyDLL.DLL
   ```

   declares a function called `MyFunction()` from a DLL called MyDLL.DLL.

2. By opening the \VISUALDB\INCLUDE\WINAPI.H file with any text editor or word processor and searching for the text `GetWinFlags`, you'll find that the dBASE declaration of the `GetWinFlags()` API function is as follows:

   ```
   EXTERN CLONG GetWinFlags (CVOID) KRNL386.EXE
   ```

3. You must copy the MyDLL.DLL file to your Windows system directory. After the MyDLL.DLL file is in your Windows system directory, you can use the functions of this DLL. That is, first declare the DLL functions using the `EXTERN` statement, and then use the functions. The syntax of the function declaration (that is, the parameters and returned value of the function) should be provided with the DLL's documentation.

17

Exercise Answer

The following code uses the API function `GetFreeSpace()` to get the amount of free memory (in bytes) available in the system:

```
Procedure FREESPACEBUTTON_OnClick

* Declare the GetFreeSpace() API function.
EXTERN CLONG GetFreeSpace (CINT) KRNL386.EXE

* Fill the variable FreeSpace with the amount of
* free memory (in bytes) available in the system.
FreeSpace = GetFreeSpace(0)

* Convert FreeSpace to a string.
strFreeSpace = STR(FreeSpace)

* Trim strFreeSpace.
strFreeSpace = LTRIM(TRIM(strFreeSpace))

* Display strFreeSpace.
MsgBox ("Free space: "+strFreeSpace, "Free Space")

Return
```

18

WEEK 3

Multimedia and Animation

In this chapter you'll learn how to incorporate multimedia technology into your dBASE programs.

What Is Multimedia?

Multimedia is becoming very popular, and as you'll soon see, it is easy to incorporate multimedia technology into your dBASE programs. Basically, multimedia technology consists of utilizing your PC for playing sound files (WAV and MIDI files), performing animation, playing movie AVI files, and playing CD audio. Incorporating multimedia into your dBASE programs enables you to write some very sophisticated applications. For example, you can write an encyclopedia-type application, in which dBASE is used for the purpose of searching and extracting information from a database, and multimedia is used for outputting the information in the form of sound, graphics, movie, and animation.

> **Note:** Multimedia is a very popular and desired feature, and your users expect to see this fancy technology incorporated into your dBASE applications. When you incorporate multimedia into your programs, your programs become more fun to use.

Hardware Needed to Perform Animation Tasks

One of the major components of multimedia is the capability to play sound files. There are two types of sound files:

- WAV files
- MIDI files

Generating WAV files is very similar to generating a recording with a regular tape recorder. That is, when you use a tape recorder, you speak into the microphone, and your recording is saved on a cassette. When recording WAV files with the PC, you also use a microphone, the recording mechanism is in the form of a sound card you install into your PC, and the recording is saved in a WAV file on your hard drive (for example, MySong.WAV). Figure 18.1 is a schematic drawing that shows a sound card installed inside a PC. As shown in the figure, a microphone and two speakers are connected to the sound card. The WAV file is played through these external speakers. Unlike a tape recorder's mechanical buttons (Play, Rewind, Forward, Stop), the sound card's "buttons" are displayed as Windows buttons on your screen.

MIDI files are also sound files. However, unlike the WAV files, which are actual recordings and therefore contain bytes that represent the actual samples of the recording, MIDI files are more like music notes. MIDI files contain instructions to the sound card, telling the sound card the music note to be played, the instrument to be played (piano, drums, and so on), the tempo, and other instructions regarding the playback. Whereas a WAV file can contain the recording of whatever was received by the microphone at the time of the recording (human voice, music), MIDI files can only play music. MIDI files typically are used for playing background music.

Figure 18.1.
The sound card.

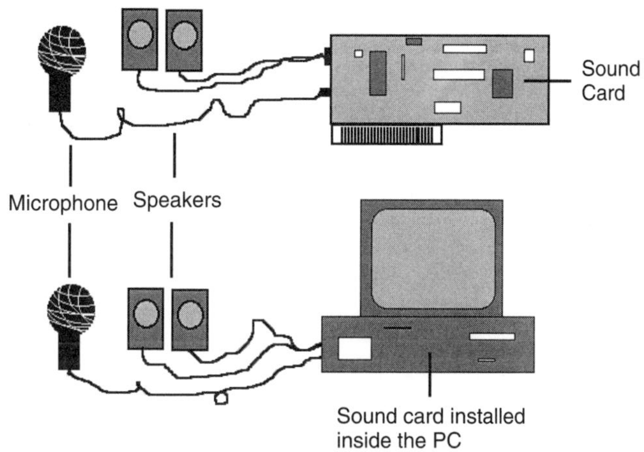

Another type of multimedia file is the movie AVI file (for example, MyMovie.AVI). A movie AVI file contains both video and sound. To play movie AVI files on your PC, you don't need any special hardware. That is, as long as your PC is 80386 or better, and your PC has a VGA monitor or better, you'll be able to view movie AVI files on your PC. To record a movie AVI file yourself, you need a video capture card and a camcorder. Note that the movie AVI file also has audio in it. For you to be able to see the movie simultaneously with the playback of the audio of the movie, your PC must have a sound card installed in it.

In addition to playing WAV files, MIDI files, and AVI files, your PC can play CD audio. CD audio is regular CDs you typically purchase in a music store. The CD is inserted into your CD drive, and typically the music of the CD is played through the sound card. In many cases, the CD-ROM drive your PC uses for reading data CDs is also capable of playing CD audio. (Check the owner's manual of your CD-ROM drive to see whether your CD-ROM drive is capable of playing CD audio.)

Testing the Multimedia Capabilities of Your PC

When you install the multimedia hardware, you also must install the software that comes with the hardware. The sound card comes with various drivers for playing WAV files, MIDI files, and CD audio.

To play movie AVI files, you must install special drivers that enable your PC to play the movie AVI files.

Here is how you can test the multimedia capabilities of your PC:

- Start the Media Player program of Windows. The Media Player program icon usually is in the Accessories group. (See Figure 18.2.)

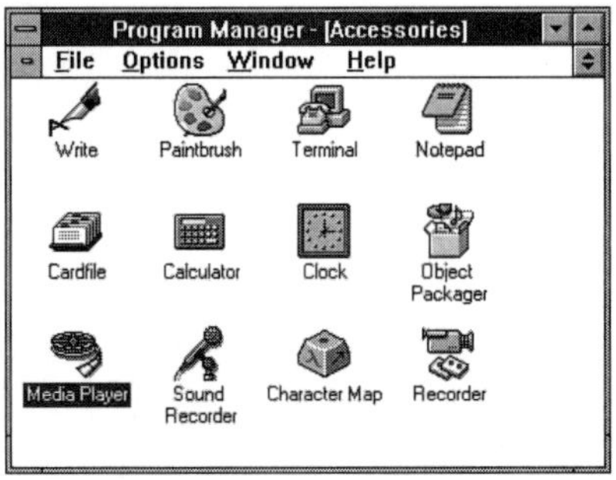

Figure 18.2.
The Media Player program icon in the Accessories group.

Windows responds by displaying the Media Player window. (See Figure 18.3.)

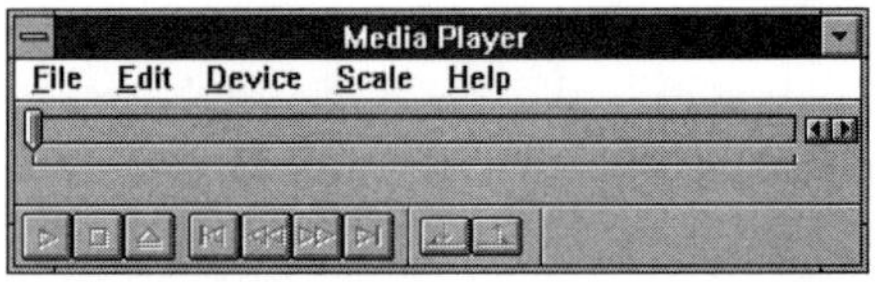

Figure 18.3.
The Media Player window.

- Select the Device menu.

Media Player responds by displaying the Device menu, shown in Figure 18.4.

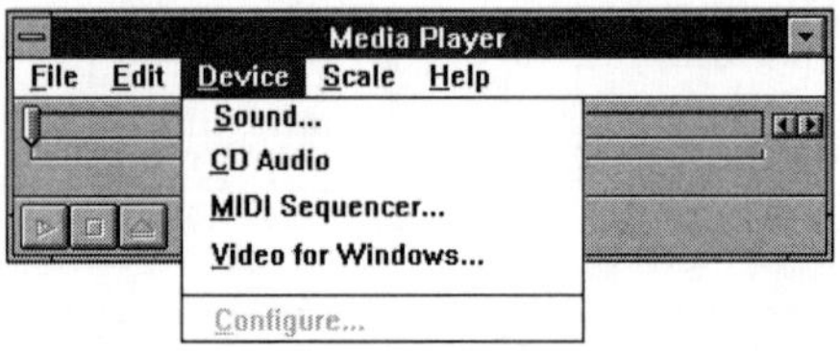

Figure 18.4.
The Device menu of the Media Player program.

In Figure 18.4, the Device menu includes the items Sound (for playing WAV files), CD Audio (for playing CD audio), MIDI Sequencer (for playing MIDI files), and Video for Windows (for playing AVI files). This means that the PC on which the Media Player program shown in Figure 18.4 was executed is capable of using all of these multimedia devices. If your Media Player program does not have one of these items in its Device menu, your PC is not capable of using the media device that is missing from the Device menu.

> **Note:** If your PC has a certain multimedia device installed in it and that multimedia device does not appear in the Device menu of Media Player, you are missing a driver or the multimedia device is not installed properly. In this case, install the appropriate drivers. Remember, the ultimate test for determining whether your PC has multimedia capabilities is the Device menu of Media Player.
>
> For example, it is possible that you are using some software that uses a certain multimedia device successfully, yet you don't see that multimedia device in the Device menu of Media Player. This means that you are still missing a driver for this multimedia device. If the Device Menu of Media Player contains the device, *any* Windows application that uses this multimedia device will be able to use this device successfully.

Using the dBASE *PLAY SOUND* Command

You can use the dBASE `PLAY SOUND` command to play a WAV file or WAV sound that is stored inside a binary field of a table.

To see the `PLAY SOUND` command of dBASE in action, follow these steps:

☐ Start Visual dBASE.

☐ Type `PLAY SOUND FILENAME C:\WINDOWS\CHIMES.WAV` in the Command window.

dBASE responds by playing the WAV file C:\WINDOWS\CHIMES.WAV.

In the preceding statement you used the `PLAY SOUND` command with the keyword `FILENAME` followed by the name of the WAV file that you want to play. You can also use the `PLAY SOUND` command with the keyword `BINARY`, as in:

```
PLAY SOUND BINARY MyBinField
```

When you use the `BINARY` keyword, dBASE will play the WAV sound that is stored in the specified binary field of the currently selected table. For example, in the preceding statement, the sound that is stored in the binary field MyBinField of the current record inside the currently selected table will be played.

As you can see, the dBASE `PLAY SOUND` command enables you to play a WAV file or WAV sound that is stored in a binary field. But what if you want to play sound with more flexibility? For example, suppose you want to write a program that can change sound characteristics such as tempo or volume and play a particular section of the sound. Or suppose you want to write a dBASE program that detects whether the user has a sound card, and accordingly direct the playback of sound to the sound card (if the user has one) or to the internal PC speaker that every PC has (without the need for a sound card and without the need for Windows drivers). If you want to perform such multimedia tasks, you can use a VBX control. As you learned in Chapter 16, "Using VBX Controls," Visual dBASE supports VBX controls. This means that you can extend the off-the-shelf capabilities of dBASE by using a VBX control. In the remainder of this chapter, you'll learn how to incorporate a multimedia VBX control into your Visual dABSE programs.

VBX Controls for Playing Multimedia

In this chapter, the TegoMM.VBX control is used for playing multimedia devices. This control is capable of playing and recording WAV files, as well as playing MIDI files, CD audio, and movie AVI files. This control is also capable of determining whether the PC is equipped with a sound card. If the PC is not equipped with a sound card, you can still play WAV files through the PC speaker (without a need for any drivers).

The TegoMM.VBX is capable of performing synchronized and nonsynchronized animation, as will be demonstrated in this chapter. With the multimedia control, you can also perform almost any conceivable sound manipulation, such as increasing and decreasing volume; adding echo; cutting, copying, and pasting sections of sound; merging sound files; and mixing sound files.

Note: It is recommended that you read this chapter even if you don't have a copy of the multimedia control. By reading the chapter, you'll learn how to incorporate multimedia into your dBASE programs, and you'll learn about other aspects of multimedia technology.

The TegoMM.VBX control is included with the disk you can purchase to accompany this book. (See the disk offer at the end of this book.) This disk also includes the source code for all the book's programs and another powerful VBX control—a 3D virtual reality control.

To be able to use the TegoMM.VBX advanced multimedia controls from within your dBASE program, you must copy the TegoMM.VBX file to your \WINDOWS\SYSTEM directory. If you don't own the TegoMM.VBX file, you can purchase it directly from TegoSoft, Inc. (See the disk offer at the end of this book.)

After you copy the TegoMM.VBX control into your \WINDOWS\SYSTEM directory, you must add the TegoMM.VBX control to the Control Palette window of dBASE. Later in this chapter you'll be instructed to add the multimedia control to the Control Palette window.

The PlayWAV Program

The PlayWAV program demonstrates how to play WAV files from within your dBASE programs.

Before you write the PlayWAV program, here's a review of its specifications.

When you start the PlayWAV program, the window shown in Figure 18.5 appears.

Figure 18.5.
The PlayWAV program.

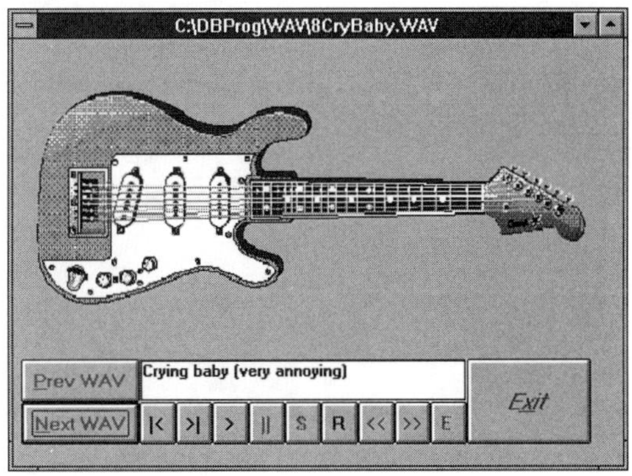

Your user can click the Play button (the button with the single arrow pointing to the right) to play the WAV file. The name of the WAV file that will be played appears in the title of the PlayWAV window.

The user can click the Prev WAV button and the Next WAV button to view and listen to other WAV files.

Note that the window shown in Figure 18.5 also displays a short description of the WAV file. For example, in Figure 18.5, the description of the WAV file is `Crying baby (very annoying)`.

Creating the WAVList.DBF Table

The PlayWAV program uses a DBF table called WAVList.DBF. You'll now create the WAVList.DBF table.

☐ In the Command window type `Create C:\DBPROG\CH18\WAVList`, and then press Enter.

dBASE responds by creating the WAVList.DBF table and displaying the Table Structure window, ready to be edited by you.

☐ Create the table structure shown in Figure 18.6. That is, the WAVList.DBF table has these two fields in it:

Name	*Type*	*Width*	*Index*
WAV_NAME	Character	100	None
DESCRIP	Character	250	None

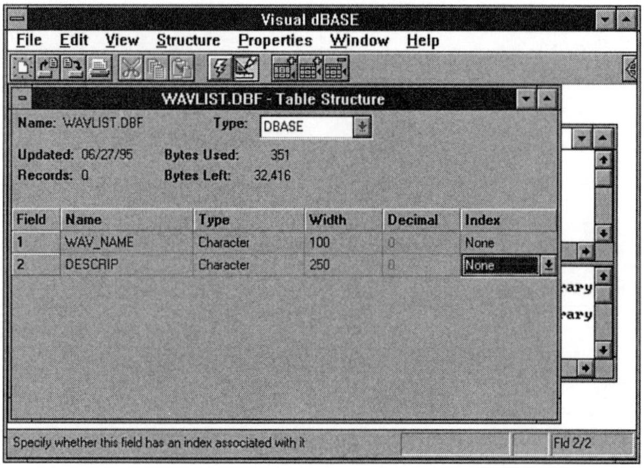

Figure 18.6.
The Table Structure window of the WAVList.DBF table.

☐ Save your work by selecting Save from the File menu.

☐ Close the Table Structure window by selecting Close from the File menu.

☐ In the Command window type `BROWSE`, and then press Enter.

dBASE responds by displaying the WAVList.DBF table, ready to be browsed by you.

☐ Select Add Records from the Table menu.

dBASE responds by enabling you to add records to the WAVList.DBF table.

☐ In the WAV_NAME fields, type the path and filenames of the WAV files you have on the hard drive of your PC.

For example, Figure 18.7 shows the WAVList.DBF table with five records in it. Each record contains the path and filename of a WAV file in the WAV_NAME field and a short description of the WAV file in the DESCRIP field.

Here are the five records of the WAVList.DBF table:

WAV_NAME	*DESCRIP*
C:\DBProg\WAV\8CryBaby.WAV	Crying baby (very annoying)
C:\DBProg\WAV\8Kenned3.WAV	A speech by president Kennedy

C:\DBProg\WAV\Bourb1m1.WAV	Nice relaxing music
C:\DBProg\WAV\Holid1m1.WAV	Holiday music
C:\DBProg\WAV\LastC1m0.WAV	Better than TADA.WAV!!!

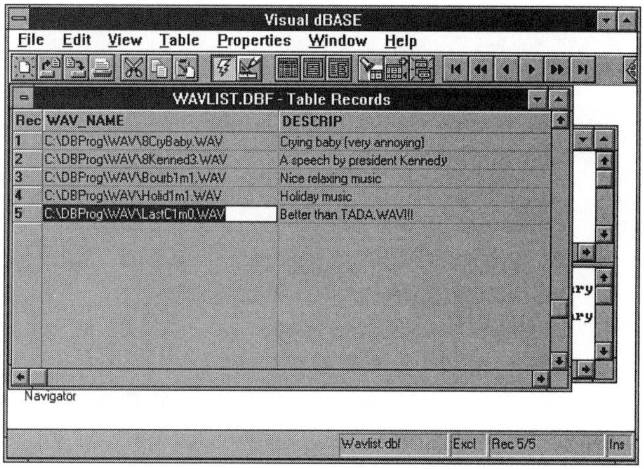

Figure 18.7.
The WAVList.DBF table with five records in it.

The Visual Implementation of the PlayWAV Program

You'll now visually implement the PlayWAV.WFM form.

☐ Create and implement the C:\DBPROG\CH18\PlayWAV.WFM form according to the specifications in Table 18.1. That is, in the Command window type `Create Form C:\DBPROG\CH18\PlayWAV`, and then press Enter. When you finish implementing the form, it should look like the one shown in Figure 18.8.

Table 18.1. The properties table of the PlayWAV.WFM form.

Object	Property	Setting
Form	**Text**	**The PlayWAV Program**
	Height	20
	Left	1
	Top	0
	Width	78
	View	C:\DBPROG\CH18\WAVLIST.DBF
	MDI	.F.

continues

Table 18.1. continued

Object	Property	Setting
PushButton	**Name**	**NextButton**
	Text	&Next WAV
	Height	2
	FontName	MS Serif
	Left	1
	FontSize	10
	Top	17
	Width	15
	ColorNormal	B+/W
PushButton	**Name**	**PrevButton**
	Text	&Prev WAV
	Height	2
	FontName	MS Serif
	Left	1
	FontSize	10
	Top	15
	Width	15
	ColorNormal	B+/W
Image	**Name**	**Image1**
	Height	14
	Left	1
	Top	0
	Width	74
	DataSource	(Load a BMP file that is appropriate for the subject of this program)
	Alignment	2
TegoMM.VBX	**Name**	**Tegomm1**
	Height	2
	Left	16
	Top	17
	Width	42

Object	Property	Setting
PushButton	**Name**	**ExitButton**
	Text	E&xit
	Height	4
	FontItalic	.T.
	FontName	MS San Serif
	Left	58
	FontSize	12
	Top	15
	Width	16
	ColorNormal	R/W
Entry Field	**Name**	**InfoEntry**
	Border	.T.
	Enabled	.F.
	Height	2
	Left	16
	Top	15
	Width	42
	DataLink	WAVLIST->DESCRIP

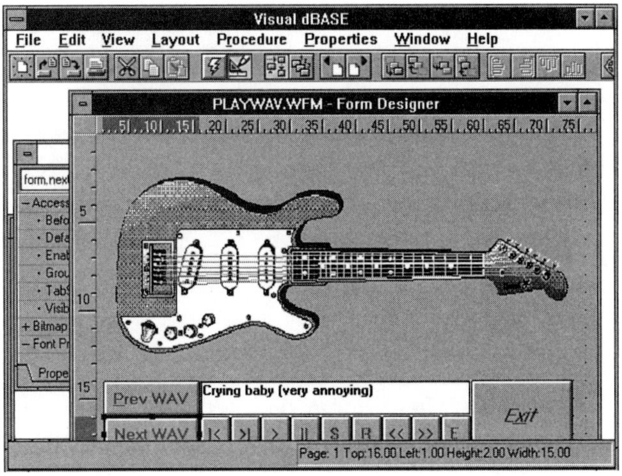

Figure 18.8.
The PlayWAV.WFM form (in design mode).

Table 18.1 instructs you to set the DataLink property of the InfoEntry entry field to WAVLIST ->DESCRIP. This means that you must set the DataLink property to the DESCRIP field of the WAVLIST.DBF table.

Table 18.1 also instructs you to place the TegoMM.VBX control in the form. You'll be able to place this control in the PlayWAV.WFM form if you first install this control in the Control Palette window of dBASE. Here is how you install the TegoMM.VBX control in the Control Palette window:

- ☐ Make sure that the TegoMM.VBX control does not already appear in the Control Palette window. You do that by making the Control Palette window the active window and then clicking the VBX tab that appears at the bottom of the Control Palette window.

  dBASE responds by displaying all the currently installed VBX controls.

- ☐ Look for the TegoMM.VBX control. If this control appears in the Control Palette window, you do not have to proceed to the next steps (because the control is already installed). Figure 18.9 shows the Control Palette window with the TegoMM.VBX multimedia control installed in it.

Figure 18.9.
The Control Palette window with the TegoMM multimedia control in it. Note that the control is installed in the VBX page of the Control Palette window.

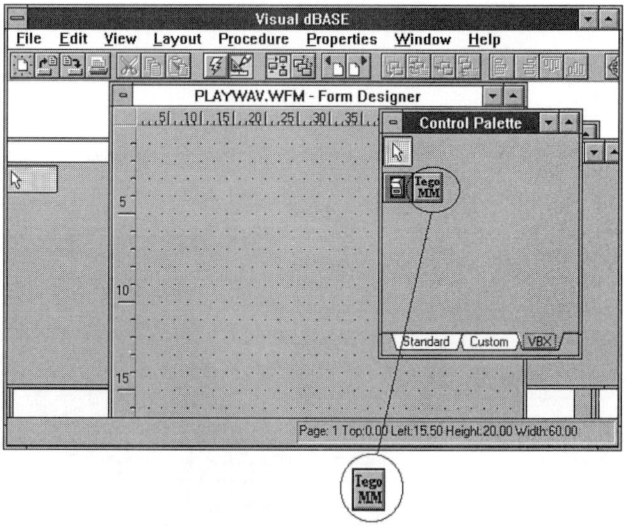

- ☐ Copy the TegoMM.VBX file into your \WINDOWS\SYSTEM directory.

- ☐ Select Set Up Custom Controls from the File menu.

  dBASE responds by displaying the Set Up Custom Controls dialog box.

- [ ] Select the VBX Controls page, click the Add button, and select the \WINDOWS\SYSTEM\TegoMM.VBX file. Then click the OK button.

  dBASE responds by installing the TegoMM multimedia control in the VBX page of the Control Palette window.

Entering the Code of the PlayWAV Program

In the following sections you'll enter the code of the PlayWAV program.

Attaching Code to the *OnClick* Event of the Exit Button

You'll now attach code to the `OnClick` event of the Exit button.

- [ ] Attach code to the `OnClick` event of the Exit button. When you finish adding the code, the `ExitButton_OnClick` procedure should look as follows:

```
Procedure EXITBUTTON_OnClick

    form.Close()

Return
```

- [ ] Select Save from the File menu to save your work.

Attaching Code to the *OnOpen* Event of the PlayWAV.WFM Form

You'll now attach code to the `OnOpen` event of the PlayWAV.WFM form.

- [ ] Attach the following code to the `OnOpen` event of the PlayWAV form. When you finish adding the code, the `Form_OnOpen` procedure should look as follows:

```
Procedure Form_OnOpen

* Go to the first record of the table.
GOTO TOP

IF EOF()
   MSGBOX ("There are no WAV files listed in the table!", ;
           "No WAV Files", 0+16)
   form.Close()
ENDIF

form.Text=LTRIM(TRIM(WAV_NAME))
form.Tegomm1.DeviceType="WaveAudio"
form.Tegomm1.FileName= LTRIM(TRIM(WAV_NAME))
form.Tegomm1.Command="Open"

Return
```

18

☐ Save your work by selecting Save from the File menu.

Recall that you set the View property of the form to C:\DBPROG\CH18\WAVLIST.DBF. This means that when the PlayWAV program starts, the WavList.DBF table is automatically opened.

The first statement you typed in the `Form_OnOpen` procedure moves the record pointer to the first record of the WAVList.DBF table:

```
GOTO TOP
```

An `IF` statement is then executed to determine whether the table has any records in it:

```
IF EOF()
   MSGBOX ("There are no WAV files listed in the table!", ;
           "No WAV Files", 0+16)
   form.Close()
ENDIF
```

If the table has no records in it, a message box is displayed, telling the user that the table does not contain any records, and then the program terminates.

The next statement sets the Text property of the form to the contents of the WAV_NAME field of the WAVList.DBF table:

```
form.Text=LTRIM(TRIM(WAV_NAME))
```

The title of the PlayWAV.WFM form will display the name of the WAV file.

Then, the DeviceType property of the multimedia control is set to play WAV files through the sound card:

```
form.Tegomm1.DeviceType="WaveAudio"
```

The FileName property of the multimedia control is set to the contents of the WAV_NAME field:

```
form.Tegomm1.FileName= LTRIM(TRIM(WAV_NAME))
```

Finally, the `Open` command is issued:

```
form.Tegomm1.Command="Open"
```

Attaching Code to the *OnDone* Event of the Multimedia Control

You'll now attach code to the `OnDone` event of the Tegomm1 multimedia control.

☐ Attach code to the `OnDone` event of the Tegomm1 control. When you finish adding the code, your `Tegomm1_OnDone` procedure should look as follows:

```
Procedure TEGOMM1_OnDone

IF form.Tegomm1.Position = form.Tegomm1.Length

   form.Tegomm1.Command="Prev"

ENDIF

Return
```

☐ Select Save from the File menu to save your work.

The `OnDone` event occurs automatically when the multimedia control finishes executing a command. For example, during the course of the program, you'll issue the `Play` command to play the WAV file. After the multimedia control finishes the playback, the `OnDone` event occurs. Of course, there could be numerous other reasons for the execution of the `OnDone` event, so an `IF` statement is used to examine the reason for the occurrence of the `OnDone` event:

```
IF form.Tegomm1.Position = form.Tegomm1.Length

   form.Tegomm1.Command="Prev"

ENDIF
```

That is, an `IF` statement checks whether the Position property of the multimedia control is equal to the Length property of the multimedia control. If this `IF` condition is satisfied, the WAV file was played in its entirety. The code under the `IF` statement rewinds the WAV file:

```
form.Tegomm1.Command="Prev"
```

Why do you need to rewind the WAV file? After the WAV file has been played in its entirety, the current position of the WAV file is at the end of the WAV file. This means that if you don't rewind the WAV file from within the code of the program as you do in the `Tegomm1_OnDone` procedure, after playing the WAV file, the user will have to click the Rewind button of the multimedia control and then click the Play button. This situation creates a little inconvenience for your user; therefore, it is better to do the rewinding automatically.

Attaching Code to the *OnClick* Event of the NextButton Button

You'll now attach code to the `OnClick` event of the NextButton button.

☐ Attach code to the `OnClick` event of the NextButton pushbutton. When you finish adding the code, the `NextButton_OnClick` procedure should look as follows:

```
Procedure NEXTBUTTON_OnClick

      SKIP 1

      IF EOF()
         GOTO BOTTOM
```

```
        ??CHR(7)
    ENDIF

     form.Text=LTRIM(TRIM(WAV_NAME))
     form.Tegomm1.FileName= LTRIM(TRIM(WAV_NAME))
     form.Tegomm1.Command="Open"

Return
```

☐ Save your work by selecting Save from the File menu.

The code you typed moves the record pointer one record forward:

```
SKIP 1
```

Then an `IF` statement is executed to examine whether the record pointer points to the end of file (EOF):

```
IF EOF()
   GOTO BOTTOM
   ??CHR(7)
ENDIF
```

If, before executing the `SKIP 1` statement, the record pointer was pointing to the last record of the table, the `SKIP 1 statement` places the record pointer at the EOF (end of file). The code under the `IF` statement places the record pointer at the last record of the table:

```
GOTO BOTTOM
```

And a beep is played:

```
??CHR(7)
```

The title of the form is filled with the name of the new WAV file:

```
form.Text=LTRIM(TRIM(WAV_NAME))
```

Finally, the WAV file is opened:

```
form.Tegomm1.FileName= LTRIM(TRIM(WAV_NAME))
form.Tegomm1.Command="Open"
```

Attaching Code to the *OnClick* Event of the Prev Button

You'll now attach code to the `OnClick` event of the Prev button.

☐ Attach code to the `OnClick` event of the Prev button. After attaching the code, the `PrevButton_OnClick` procedure should look as follows:

```
Procedure PREVBUTTON_OnClick

        SKIP -1

        IF BOF()
           GOTO TOP
           ??CHR(7)
        ENDIF

         form.Text=LTRIM(TRIM(WAV_NAME))
         form.Tegomm1.FileName= LTRIM(TRIM(WAV_NAME))
         form.Tegomm1.Command="Open"

Return
```

☐ Save your work by selecting Save from the File menu.

The code you typed is very similar to the code you typed in the `NextButton_OnClick` procedure. The only difference is that now the `SKIP -1` statement is used to set the record pointer one record backward:

```
SKIP -1
```

If, before executing the `SKIP -1` statement, the record pointer was pointing to the first record of the table, then the `SKIP -1` statement places the record pointer at the BOF (bottom of file). The code under the `IF` statement places the record pointer at the first record of the table:

```
GOTO BOTTOM
```

And a beep is played:

```
??CHR(7)
```

☐ Execute the PlayWAV program and check its proper operation. That is, click the Next WAV button and the Prev WAV button to move from one WAV file to another, and then click the Play button of the multimedia control to play the WAV file.

☐ Experiment with the PlayWAV program, and then click its Exit button to terminate the program.

Recording

The multimedia control is capable of recording WAV files as well as playing them.

Take a look at Figure 18.5. The fourth button from the right on the multimedia control (the button with the R on it) is the Record button.

To record, click the R button, and then speak into the microphone. (You can try this with the PlayWAV program.)

To stop the recording, click the S (Stop) button. To hear your recording, click the Rewind button, and then click the Play button.

Alternatively, you can issue the `Record` command from within your code. For example, you can set the Visible property of the multimedia control to .F. in the `Form_OnOpen` procedure (so that during runtime the multimedia control is invisible). During design time, you can place a Record button in the form and attach code to the Record button that causes the multimedia control to record, as shown here:

```
RecordButton_OnClick()

form.Tegomm1.Command = "Record"

Return
```

During design time, you also can place the Stop button in the form. This is the code you need to provide in the `StopButton_OnClick()` procedure:

```
StopButton_OnClick()

form.Tegomm1.Command = "Stop"

Return
```

During design time, you also can place the Play button in the form. This is the code you need to provide in the `PlayButton_OnClick()` procedure:

```
PlayButton_OnClick()

form.Tegomm1.Command = "Prev"
form.Tegomm1.Command = "Play"

Return
```

Why would you provide your own buttons instead of using the buttons of the multimedia control? This way, you can enable and disable the buttons according to the logic of your program. For example, if the logic of your program is such that the user can record only at certain points in the program, you can enable and disable the Record button by setting its Enabled properties to .T. or .F. as shown here:

```
form.RecordButton.Enabled=.F.
```

or

```
form.RecordButton.Enabled=.T.
```

Also, by providing your own multimedia buttons, you can make the buttons as fancy as you like. For example, you can attach pictures to your buttons—a microphone to the Record button, a stop sign to the Stop button, a person playing a piano to the Play button, and so on.

Playing MIDI Files

Playing MIDI files is similar to playing WAV files.

In this chapter you'll write the PlayMIDI program. The PlayMIDI program is much like the PlayWAV program. In fact, the only difference between the programs is that the PlayMIDI program plays MIDI files.

Playing Movie AVI Files

Playing movie AVI files is similar to playing WAV and MIDI files. Figure 18.10 shows the main window of the PlayAVI program.

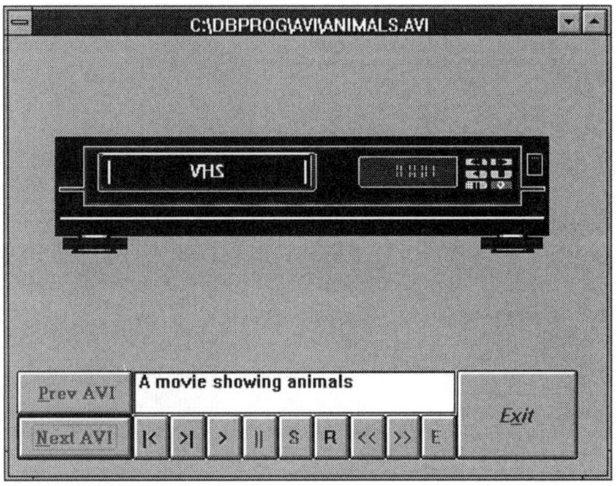

Figure 18.10.
The PlayAVI program.

In the Exercises section at the end of this chapter you'll write the PlayAVI program.

Playing CD Audio

Playing CD audio is similar to playing WAV, MIDI, and movie AVI files. Figure 18.11 shows the main window of the PlayCD program.

Figure 18.11.
The PlayCD program.

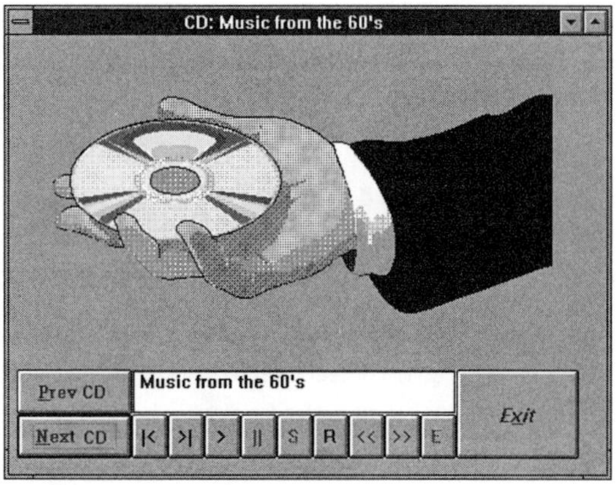

In this chapter's exercises you'll write the PlayCD program.

Playing Through the PC Speaker

Playing WAV files through the PC speaker is similar to playing WAV, MIDI, movie AVI, and CD audio. Figure 18.12 shows the main window of the PlayPC program.

Figure 18.12.
The PlayPC program.

In the Exercises section at the end of this chapter you'll write the PlayPC program.

Nonsynchronized Animation

The Anim program you'll next write demonstrates how you can design an impressive animation program with dBASE. As you'll soon see, this Anim program performs an animation with nonsynchronized sound. Later in this chapter, you'll write the Kennedy program, which is a synchronized animation program.

A nonsynchronized animation program plays sound simultaneously with a display of pictures. The sound played, however, has no relationship to the animation. A synchronized animation program, on the other hand, displays animation simultaneously with a playback of sound, but the sound is played in synchronization with the displayed picture.

The Anim Program

Before you write the Anim program, here's a review of its specifications. Initially, the Anim program shows a couple standing. Figure 18.13 shows the Dance1.BMP file in which the couple standing.

Figure 18.13.
The Dance1.BMP picture. A couple standing, waiting for the music to start.

When the user clicks the Start Dance button of the Anim program, the Anim program displays the couple dancing to music. Figures 18.14 through 18.16 show the pictures (BMP files) used during the dance.

Figure 18.14.
The Dance2.BMP picture.

Figure 18.15.
The Dance3.BMP picture.

Figure 18.16.
The Dance4.BMP picture.

At the end of the dance, the couple thanks the audience, and the woman dancer bows to the crowd. (See Figure 18.17.)

Figure 18.17.
The Dance5.BMP picture. The woman thanking the crowd.

Then a credit frame appears (see Figure 18.18), and the couple is again shown in a standing position, ready for their next dance.

Figure 18.18.
The Dance6.BMP picture. The credit frame.

Creating the Bitmap Table

From the specifications of the Anim program, it is obvious that you need to somehow load and display various BMP files during runtime. The Anim program uses a dBASE table called Anim.DBF that contains the various BMP files used in the program. Here is how you create the Anim.DBF table:

- ☐ Close any form that appears on the desktop of dBASE (if any) by making the form you want to close the active form and then selecting Close from the File menu.
- ☐ In the Command window type `Close Databases`, and then press Enter.

  dBASE responds by closing all open tables.
- ☐ In the Command window type `Create C:\DBPROG\CH18\Anim`, and then press Enter.

  dBASE responds by creating the Anim.DBF table, and the empty new structure of Anim.DBF appears.
- ☐ Create two fields in the Anim.DBF table as shown here:

Field	*Type*	*Width*	*Decimal*	*Index*
FRAMENUM	Numeric	3	0	Ascend
BMP	Binary	N/A	N/A	N/A

The table structure of Anim.DBF is shown in Figure 18.19.

Figure 18.19.
The table structure of the Anim.DBF table.

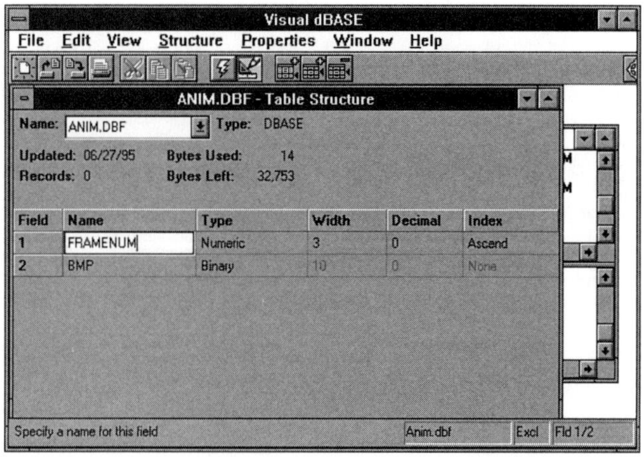

- ☐ Select Save from the File menu to save the structure of the Anim.DBF table.
- ☐ Close the Table Structure window of Anim.DBF by selecting Close from the File menu.

Because the Anim program uses six BMP files, you first need to create the BMP pictures that will be used by the program. Here is how you can create the six BMP pictures of the Anim program:

- ☐ Start Paintbrush.
- ☐ Select Image Attributes from the Options menu of Paintbrush.

  Paintbrush responds by displaying the Image Attributes dialog box.

- ☐ Select the pels option (so that the units of the image will be in pixels).
- ☐ Set the Width of the image to 124.
- ☐ Set the Height of the image to 124.

The Image Attribute dialog box should now look like the one shown in Figure 18.20.

Figure 18.20.
The Image Attributes dialog box of Paintbrush.

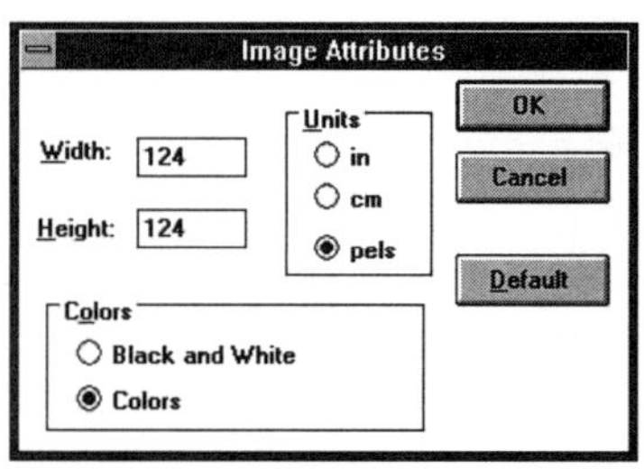

☐ Click the OK button of the Image Attributes dialog box.

Paintbrush responds by displaying an empty image ready to be painted by you. The size of the image is 124 pixels by 124 pixels. (See Figure 18.21.)

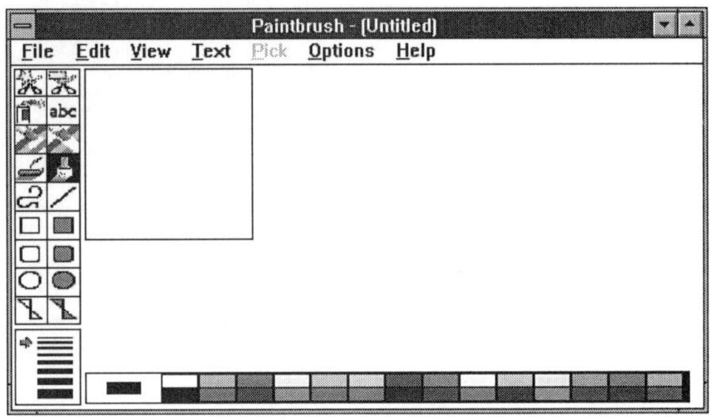

Figure 18.21.
The new empty image with a size of 124 pixels by 124 pixels.

☐ Draw a picture of a couple standing up (something like Figure 18.13).

☐ Save the image as a BMP file in the C:\DBPROG\BMP directory. Name the file Dance1.BMP.

☐ Repeat the previous steps to create the Dance2.BMP, Dance3.BMP, Dance4.BMP, Dance5.BMP, and Dance6.BMP files. Save these files in the C:\DBPROG\BMP directory. Try to make the six BMP files similar to the BMP files shown in Figures 18.13 through 18.18.

Filling the Records of the Anim.DBF Table

You'll next fill the records of the Anim.DBF table.

☐ In the Command window type `BROWSE`, and then press Enter. (If the Anim.DBF table is currently not in use, you first must type `USE C:\DBPROG\CH18\Anim.DBF` in the Command window, and then press Enter. You can then type the `BROWSE` command.)

☐ Select Add Records from the Table menu.

dBASE responds by displaying the Anim.DBF table, ready for you to edit.

The FRAMENUM field contains a number that represents the frame number in the dance show. As previously stated, the Anim program is composed of six frames. You therefore could fill the FRAMENUM fields with the numbers 1, 2, 3, 4, 5, and 6. It is better, however, to set the values of the fields to the numbers 10, 20, 30, 40, 50, and 60. Why? In the future you might want to insert additional frames between these six frames.

☐ Fill the FILENUM fields with the following values:

Record Number	*FRAMENUM*
1	10
2	20
3	30
4	40
5	50
6	60

You'll now fill the BMP fields with the contents of the BMP files you created with Paintbrush. After you fill the BMP fields, the Anim.DBF table should look as follows:

Record Number	*FRAMENUM*	*BMP*
1	10	The contents of the Dance1.BMP file
2	20	The contents of the Dance2.BMP file
3	30	The contents of the Dance3.BMP file
4	40	The contents of the Dance4.BMP file
5	50	The contents of the Dance5.BMP file
6	60	The contents of the Dance6.BMP file

The following steps show you how to fill the BMP field:

☐ Double-click the BMP field of record number 1 in the Browse window.

dBASE responds by displaying the Empty Binary Field dialog box. (See Figure 18.22.)

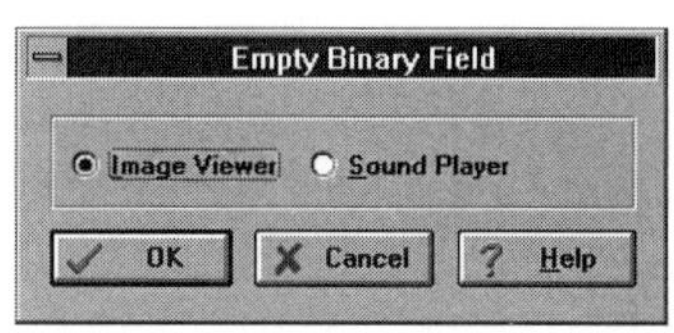

Figure 18.22.
The Empty Binary Field dialog box.

☐ Make sure that the Image Viewer option button is selected, and then click the OK button.

dBASE responds by displaying the Image Viewer window. (See Figure 18.23.)

As you can see in Figure 18.23, the Image Viewer window is empty. That is, the BMP field of record number 1 of the Anim.DBF table currently has no BMP file in it.

The dBASE desktop conforms to MDI (multiple document interface) standards. This means that certain menus appear on the menu bar of the dBASE desktop, depending on the currently active window. When the Image Viewer window is the active window, the File menu contains the Insert from File item. (See Figure 18.24.)

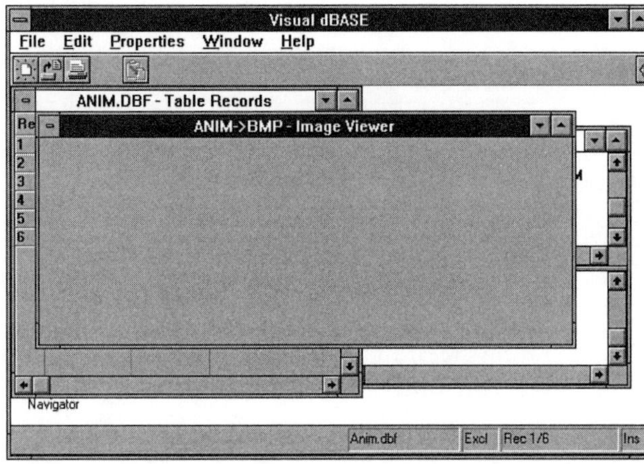

Figure 18.23.
The Image Viewer window.

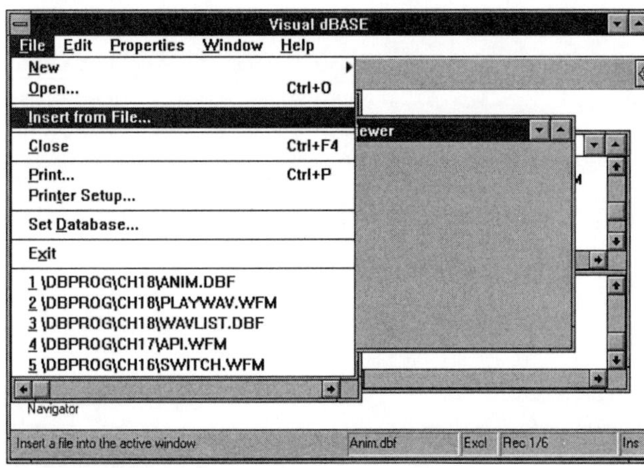

Figure 18.24.
The Insert from File item of the File menu (when the Image Viewer window is the active window).

☐ Select the Insert from File item from the File menu.

dBASE responds by displaying the Choose Image dialog box. (See Figure 18.25.)

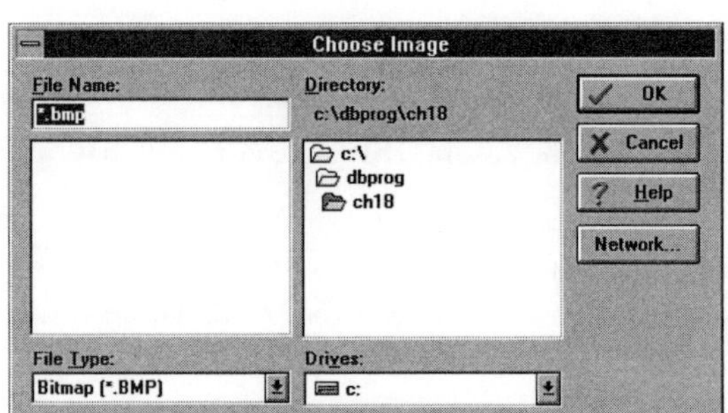

Figure 18.25.
The Choose Image dialog box.

☐ Select the C:\DBPROG\BMP\Dance1.BMP file, and then click the OK button.

dBASE responds by inserting the contents of the Dance1.BMP file into the Image Viewer window. (See Figure 18.26.)

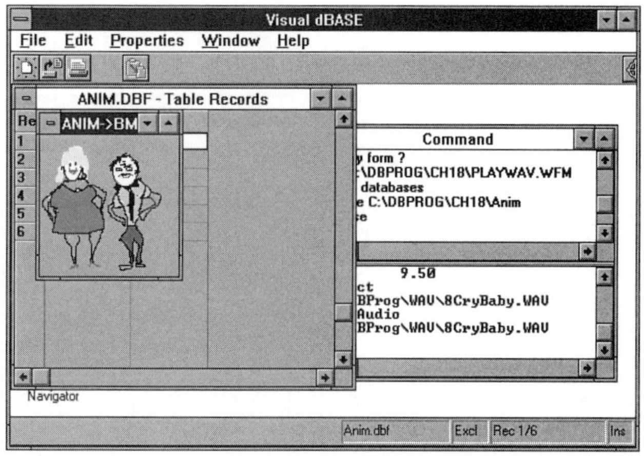

Figure 18.26.
The Image Viewer window with the contents of the Dance1.BMP file embedded in it.

☐ Repeat the previous steps to fill the rest of the BMP fields with the contents of the Dance?.BMP files. That is, double-click the BMP field of the record you want to fill, select the Insert from File item from the File menu, and choose the BMP file.

When you finish filling the Anim.DBF table, it should look like the one shown in Figure 18.27. Note that the BMP fields are filled with picture icons. These icons are indications that the BMP fields are filled with the contents of BMP files.

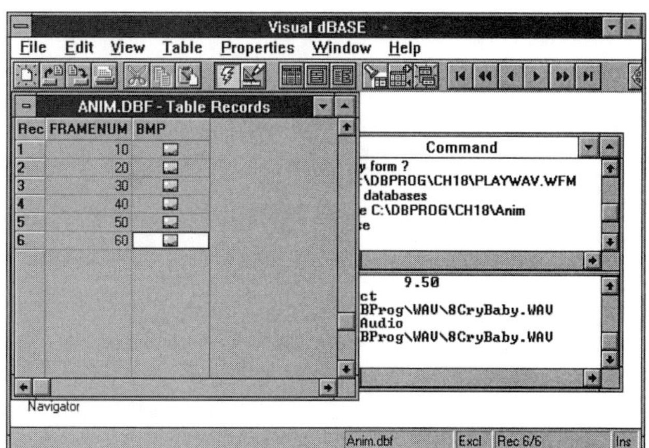

Figure 18.27.
The Anim.DBF table with six records in it. The BMP fields are filled with picture icons, indicating that the fields are filled with the contents of BMP files.

The Visual Implementation of the Anim Form

You'll now visually implement the Anim form.

☐ In the Command window type `CREATE FORM C:\DBPROG\CH18\Anim`, and then press Enter.

dBASE responds by creating the Anim.WFM form, and the new empty form is displayed.

☐ Implement the Anim.WFM form according to the specifications in Table 18.2. When you finish implementing the form, it should look like the one shown in Figure 18.28.

Table 18.2. The properties table of the Anim.WFM form.

Object	Property	Setting
Form	**Text**	**The Anim Program**
	MDI	.F.
	Height	19
	Left	18
	Top	1
	Width	63
	View	C:\DBPROG\CH18\ANIM.DBF
PushButton	**Name**	**ExitButton**
	Height	2
	Text	E&xit
	Left	2
	Top	17
	Width	15
PushButton	**Name**	**StartButton**
	Height	5
	Text	&Start Dance
	Left	31
	Top	14
	FontSize	18
	Width	31

Object	Property	Setting
Image	**Name**	**Image1**
	Alignment	2
	DataSource	BINARY ANIM->BMP
	Height	10
	Left	14
	Top	2
	Width	34
TegoMM.VBX	**Name**	**Tegomm1**
	Height	2
	Left	2
	Top	13
	Width	39

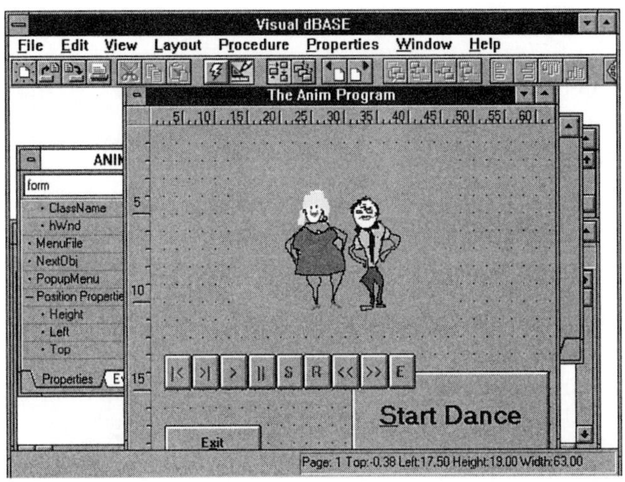

Figure 18.28.
The Anim.WFM form (in design mode).

Table 18.2 instructs you to set the DataSource property of the Image1 image control to the BMP field of the Anim.DBF table. Here is how you set this property:

☐ Make the Image1 control the active control, and then click the DataSource property in the Properties window.

dBASE responds by displaying the tool icon in the DataSource property item of the Control window.

☐ Click the tool icon.

dBASE responds by displaying the DataSource Property Builder dialog box. (See Figure 18.29.)

Figure 18.29.
The DataSource Property Builder dialog box.

☐ Set the Location to Binary (as shown in Figure 18.29), and then click the tool icon of the Bitmap entry field.

☐ Select the BMP field of the Anim.DBF table (see Figure 18.30) and then click the OK button.

dBASE responds by displaying the DataSource Property Builder dialog box again. (See Figure 18.31.) As shown in Figure 18.31, the bitmap is set to the BMP file of the Anim.DBF table.

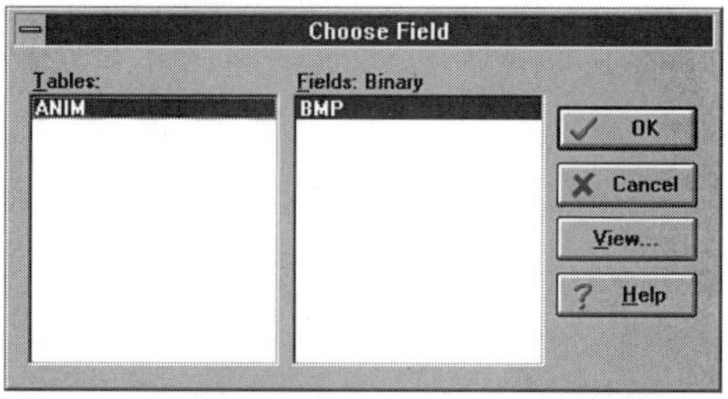

Figure 18.30.
The Choose Field dialog box.

Figure 18.31.
The DataSource Property Builder dialog box, set to the BMP field of the Anim.DBF table.

☐ Click the OK button of the DataSource Property Builder dialog box.

Entering the Code of the Anim Program

In the following sections you'll enter the code of the Anim program.

Attaching Code to the *OnClick* Event of the Exit Button

You'll now attach code to the `OnClick` event of the Exit button of the Anim.WFM form.

- [ ] Attach code to the `OnClick` event of the Exit button. When you finish typing the code, the `ExitButton_OnClick` procedure should look as follows:

```
Procedure EXITBUTTON_OnClick

   form.Close()

Return
```

- [ ] Save your work by selecting Save from the File menu.

18

Attaching Code to the *OnOpen* Event of the Anim Form

You'll now attach code to the `OnOpen` event of the Anim.WFM form.

- [ ] Attach code to the `OnOpen` event of the Anim.WFM form. When you finish typing the code, the `Form_OnOpen` procedure should look as follows:

```
Procedure Form_OnOpen

   Public gDanceInProgress

   * Order the table by the FRAMENUM field.
   SET ORDER TO FRAMENUM


   * There is no show in progress.
   gDanceInProgress=.F.

   form.Tegomm1.Visible=.F.
   form.Tegomm1.UpdateInterval=250
   form.Tegomm1.DeviceType = "WaveAudio"
   form.Tegomm1.FileName="C:\DBPROG\WAV\BOURB1M1.WAV"
   form.Tegomm1.Command="Open"

Return
```

- [ ] Save your work by selecting Save from the File menu.

The code you typed declares a public variable:

```
Public gDanceInProgress
```

Because you declared the variable as public, this variable is accessible by every procedure in the program.

The Anim.WFM form uses a global (public) variable called `gDanceInProgress`. Because this variable is declared as public, it will be visible in all the procedures of the form.

An alternate way to make a variable visible in all the procedures of the form is to make the variable a custom form property.

You can make `gDanceInProgress` a custom form property by modifying the `Form_OnOpen` procedure as follows:

- Remove the statement `PUBLIC gDanceInProgress`.
- Change the statement `gDanceInProgress=.F.` to `Form.gDanceInProgress=.F.`.

From now on, all the procedures of the form can refer to this variable as `Form.gDanceInProgress`.

The next statement sets the order of the Anim.DBF table by the FRAMENUM field:

```
SET ORDER TO FRAMENUM
```

Note: If the table is not indexed, then when you use the `SKIP` statement, the record pointer advances to the next "natural ordered" record. For example, suppose that you entered data to the Anim.DBF table in the following order:

Record Number	FRAMENUM
1	10
2	20
3	30
4	50
5	40
6	60

If the current record is record number 1 and you use the `SKIP` statement five times, the record pointer will point to the following sequence of records:

Record Number	FRAMENUM
2	20
3	30
4	50
5	40
6	60

Note that in the preceding sequence, the record with FRAMENUM 50 appears before the record with FRAMENUM 40.

On the other hand, because you set the order to FRAMENUM, if the current record is record number 1 and you execute the `SKIP` statement five times, the record pointer will point to the following sequence of records:

Record Number	FRAMENUM
1	10
2	20
3	30
5	40
4	50
6	60

That is, no matter in which order you entered the data into the Anim.DBF table, the `SKIP` statement will cause the record pointer to go to the next record according to the value of the FRAMENUM field.

The next statement sets the `gDanceInProgress` variable to .F.:

```
gDanceInProgress=.F.
```

The `gDanceInProgress` variable serves as a flag that indicates whether a dance is in progress. Initially, there is no dance in progress, and therefore the `gDanceInProgress` variable is set to .F..

The multimedia control is then made invisible:

```
form.Tegomm1.Visible=.F.
```

The UpdateInterval property of the multimedia control is set to 250 milliseconds:

```
form.Tegomm1.UpdateInterval=250
```

This means that the `Tegomm1_StatusUpdate` procedure will automatically be executed every 250 milliseconds. You will write the code of the `Tegomm1_StatusUpdate` procedure later in this chapter.

The multimedia control is set to play through the sound card:

```
form.Tegomm1.DeviceType = "WaveAudio"
```

The FileName property of the multimedia control is set:

```
form.Tegomm1.FileName="C:\DBPROG\WAV\BOURB1M1.WAV"
```

Finally, the `Open` command is issued:

```
form.Tegomm1.Command="Open"
```

Attaching Code to the *OnClick* Event of the Start Dance Button

You'll now attach code to the `OnClick` event of the Start Dance button.

☐ Attach code to the `OnClick` event of the Start Dance button. After you attach the code, the `StartButton_OnClick` procedure should look as follows:

```
Procedure STARTBUTTON_OnClick


   IF form.StartButton.Text="&Start Dance"
      gDanceInProgress=.T.
      form.StartButton.Text="&Stop Dance"
      form.Tegomm1.Command="Prev"
      form.Tegomm1.Command="Play"
   ELSE

      form.Tegomm1.Command="Stop"

      * Bow
      Seek(50)
      SLEEP 1

      Seek(10)
      SLEEP 2

      Seek(50)
      SLEEP 1

      Seek(10)
      SLEEP 1

      Seek(50)
      SLEEP 1
```

```
        Seek(60)
        SLEEP 2

        Seek(10)

        gDanceInProgress=.F.
        form.StartButton.Text="&Start Dance"

    ENDIF

  Return
```

☐ Save your work by selecting Save from the File menu.

The Text property of the StartButton button was set during design time to &Start Dance. During runtime, the Text property of this button is changed. That is, initially, the text property of the button is &Start Dance. After the user clicks this button, the Text property is changed to &Stop Dance.

After clicking the Start Dance button, the user sees a Stop Dance button, which enables the user to stop the dance. The user can click the button to stop the dance (in which case the Text property of the button changes back to Start Dance). If the user does not click the Stop Dance button, the WAV file is played in its entirety. At the end of the playback, the Text property of the button changes back to &Start Dance, enabling the user to start the dance all over again. So, then, the StartButton button is used for both starting the dance and stopping the dance.

An `IF...ELSE` statement is used to determine the current value of the Text property of the StartButton button:

```
IF form.StartButton.Text="&Start Dance"
   ...............................................
   ... Currently, there is no dance in progress
   ... so start the show.
   ...............................................
ELSE
   ...........................................
   ... Currently, there is a dance in progress
   ... so stop the show.
   ...............................................
ENDIF
```

If currently there is no dance is progress, the code under the `IF` is executed. This code sets the value of the `gDanceInProgress` variable to .T.:

```
gDanceInProgress=.T.
```

The Text property of the button is set to &Stop Dance:

```
form.StartButton.Text="&Stop Dance"
```

And the multimedia is instructed to start the playback of the WAV file:

```
form.Tegomm1.Command="Prev"
form.Tegomm1.Command="Play"
```

If there is a dance in progress, the code under the `ELSE` is executed. This code causes the multimedia to stop the playback:

```
form.Tegomm1.Command="Stop"
```

Then the record pointer is pointed to the record with FRAMENUM equal to 50:

```
Seek(50)
```

Recall that the BMP field of the record that has its FRAMENUM equal to 50 contains the BMP file that shows the woman bowing. So the Anim program now displays the woman bowing. Use of the `SLEEP` statement with `1` as its parameter causes this picture to remain for one second:

```
SLEEP 1
```

The picture is then changed to the BMP that contains the picture of the man and the woman standing up:

```
Seek(10)
```

This picture remains on the screen for two seconds:

```
SLEEP 2
```

This process repeats itself several times:

```
Seek(50)
SLEEP 1

Seek(10)
SLEEP 1

Seek(50)
SLEEP 1
```

The preceding statements shows the woman standing and then bowing several times.

Then the Credit frame is displayed:

```
Seek(60)
SLEEP 2
```

Then the final image is displayed (the image that shows the couple standing up):

```
Seek(10)
```

The last two statements under the `ELSE` statement set the `gDanceInProgress` variable to .F. and set the Text property of the StartButton button to &Start Dance:

```
gDanceInProgress=.F.
form.StartButton.Text="&Start Dance"
```

Attaching Code to the *OnStatusUpdate* Event of the Multimedia Control

You'll now attach code to the `OnStatusUpdate` event of the multimedia control. Recall that in the `Form_OnOpen` procedure you set the UpdateInterval property of the multimedia control to 250. This means that the `Tegomm1_OnStatusUpdate` procedure is automatically executed every 250 milliseconds.

- ☐ Attach code to the `Tegomm1_OnStatusUpdate` procedure. After you type the code, the `Tegomm1_OnStatusUpdate` procedure should look as follows:

```
Procedure TEGOMM1_OnStatusUpdate

   IF gDanceInProgress = .F.

      Return

   ENDIF


   SKIP 1
   IF FRAMENUM = 50

      Seek(20)

   ENDIF

Return
```

- ☐ Save your work by selecting Save from the File menu.

The code you typed is the code that performs the animation! Remember that this procedure will be executed every 250 milliseconds no matter what the current value of the `gDanceInProgress` variable is. An `IF` statement is executed to verify that a dance is in progress, and if this is not the case, the procedure terminates:

```
IF gDanceInProgress = .F.

      Return

ENDIF
```

If a dance is in progress, the record pointer is advanced to the next record:

```
SKIP 1
```

During design time, you associated the image control with the BMP field of the Anim.DBF table, so the `SKIP` statement causes the image control to display a new picture, the picture of the BMP field of the record pointed to by the record pointer.

The animation during the dance should display the following sequence of pictures:

```
Dance2.BMP
Dance3.BMP
Dance4.BMP
Dance2.BMP
Dance3.BMP
Dance4.BMP
...
...
...
```

The contents of the BMP field of the record with FRAMENUM equal to 20 is Dance2.BMP.

The contents of the BMP field of the record with FRAMENUM equal to 30 is Dance3.BMP.

The contents of the BMP field of the record with FRAMENUM equal to 40 is Dance4.BMP.

An `IF` statement causes the preceding sequence of pictures to be displayed:

```
IF FRAMENUM = 50

      Seek(20)

ENDIF
```

In other words, the `SKIP` statement advances the record pointer to the next record until the record pointer points to the record with FRAMENUM equal to 50, and then the record pointer is set back to the record with FRAMENUM equal to 20.

Attaching Code to the *OnDone* Event of the Multimedia Control

You'll now attach code to the `OnDone` event of the multimedia control. The `OnDone` event occurs automatically when the multimedia control finishes the execution of a command.

☐ Attach code to the `OnDone` event of the multimedia control. After you type the code, the `Tegomm1_OnDone` procedure should look as follows:

```
Procedure TEGOMM1_OnDone

   IF form.Tegomm1.Position = form.Tegomm1.Length

      form.StartButton_OnClick()

   ENDIF

Return
```

☐ Save your work by selecting Save from the File menu.

As stated earlier, the `OnDone` event occurs when the multimedia control finishes an operation. The code you typed verifies that the `OnDone` events occurred because the WAV file was played in its entirety. That is, previously, the Anim program issued the `Play` command. If the user did not click the Stop Dance button during the playback, the `OnDone` event occurred when the WAV file was played in its entirety.

The `IF` statement compares the Position property of the multimedia control (which is the current position of the WAV file) with the Length property (which is the size of the WAV file). If the two are equal, the WAV file was played in its entirety. The code under the `IF` statement executes the `StartButton_OnClick` procedure:

```
IF form.Tegomm1.Position = form.Tegomm1.Length

      form.StartButton_OnClick()

ENDIF
```

So when the multimedia control finishes playing the entire WAV file, the `Tegomm1_OnDone` procedure emulates a clicking on the Stop Dance button.

You have finished writing the Anim program.

☐ Execute the Anim program.

☐ Click the Start Dance program.

Anim responds by starting the dance. You see the couple dancing, and simultaneously, you hear the music through the sound card. Figure 18.32 shows one of the frames during the dance show.

Figure 18.32.
The Anim program in action.

☐ You can let the Anim program finish the show (by letting the program play the entire WAV file), or you can stop the show by clicking the Stop Dance button.

Note that when you stop the show (or when the show is stopped because the entire WAV file was played), the Anim program shows the woman bowing several times, then the credit frame appears, and finally the couple is shown standing up, waiting for you to start the next show.

The Kennedy Program

The Anim program illustrated how to write a nonsynchronized animation program. That is, during the dance, there is no correlation between the playback of the WAV file and the images being displayed. The Kennedy program, which you'll write next, demonstrates how to write a synchronized animation show.

Before you write the Kennedy program, here's a review of its specifications:

When you start the Kennedy program, the window shown in Figure 18.33 is displayed.

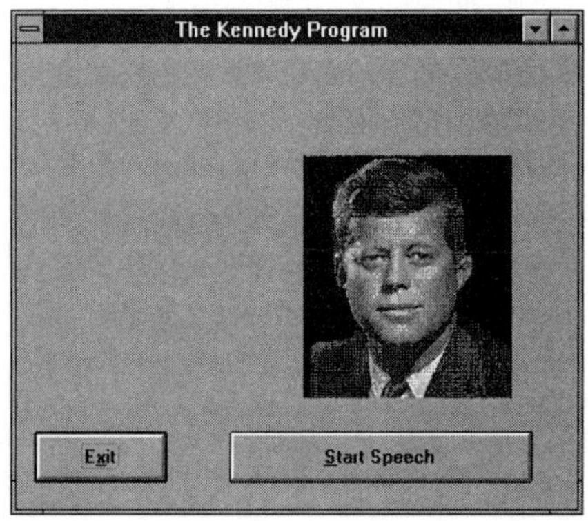

Figure 18.33.
The window of the Kennedy program.

To start playing a famous speech of Kennedy's, the user must click the Start Speech button.

During the speech, the sound card plays the speech simultaneously and in synchronization with the display of BMP pictures. Figure 18.34 shows the window that is displayed while the phrase "So my fellow Americans" is being played by the sound card.

Figure 18.34.
Playing and displaying the phrase "So my fellow Americans."

Figure 18.35 shows the window that is displayed while the phrase "Ask not what your country can do for you" is being played by the sound card.

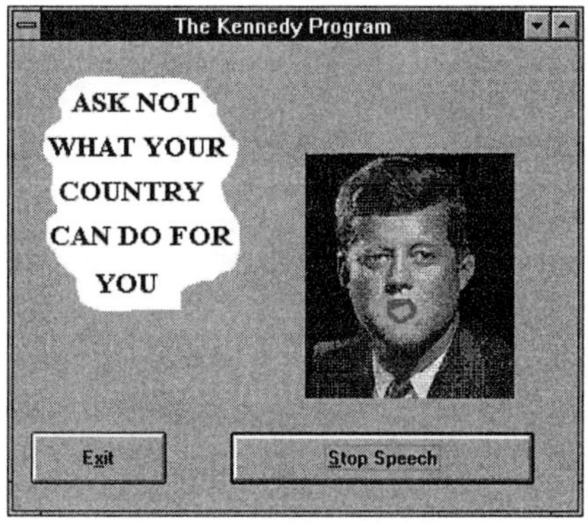

Figure 18.35.
Playing and displaying the phrase "Ask not what your country can do for you."

Figure 18.36 shows the window that is displayed while the phrase "Ask what you can do for your country" is being played by the sound card.

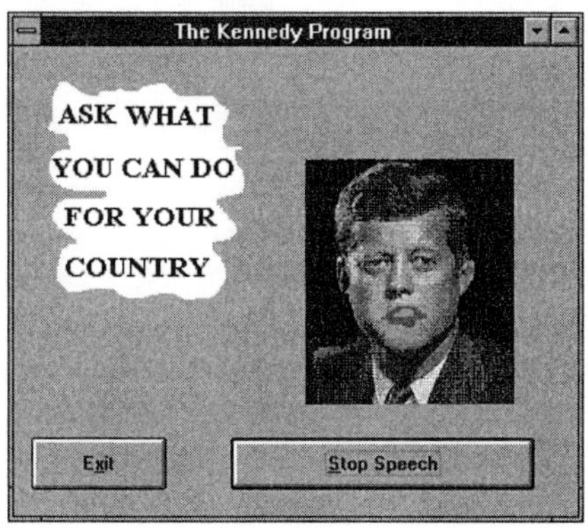

Figure 18.36.
Playing and displaying the phrase "Ask what you can do for your country."

During the playback, the text of the Start Speech button changes to Stop Speech. If the user clicks the Stop Speech button, the speech stops.

During the speech, the mouth of the Kennedy picture displayed in the window changes to give the impression that the mouth moves during the speech.

Creating the Kennedy.DBF Table

You'll now create the Kennedy.DBF table.

☐ In the Command window type `Create C:\DBPROG\CH18\Kennedy`, and then press Enter.

dBASE responds by creating the Kennedy.DBF table, and the new empty table structure appears.

☐ Create the fields of the Kennedy.DBF table as shown in Figure 18.37. That is, the table structure of the Kennedy.DBF table should have the following structure:

Field	*Name*	*Type*	*Width*	*Decimal*	*Index*
1	FRAMENUM	Numeric	3	0	Ascend
2	BMP	Binary	N/A	N/A	N/A
3	FROM	Numeric	10	0	None
4	TO	Numeric	10	0	None

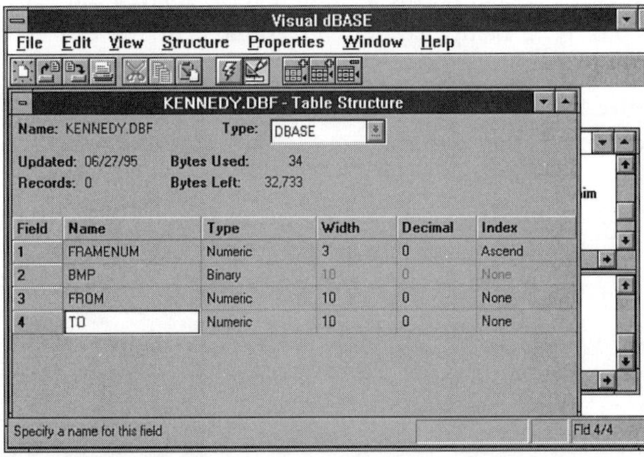

Figure 18.37.
The table structure of the Kennedy.DBF table.

☐ Select Save from the File menu to save the table structure of the Kennedy.DBF table.

Filling the Records of the Kennedy.DBF Table

You'll now fill the records of the Kennedy.DBF table.

☐ In the Command window type `BROWSE`, and then press Enter.

dBASE responds by displaying the Kennedy.DBF table, ready for you to browse.

☐ Select Add Records from the Table menu.

dBASE responds by placing the Kennedy.DBF table in edit mode (so that you can enter records into the table).

☐ Fill in the data of the Kennedy.DBF table as shown here (see Figure 18.38):

Rec	*FRAMENUM*	*BMP*	*FROM*	*TO*
1	10	C:\DBPROG\BMP\Ken1.BMP	0	3000
2	20	C:\DBPROG\BMP\Ken2.BMP	3001	7000
3	30	C:\DBPROG\BMP\Ken3.BMP	7001	11900

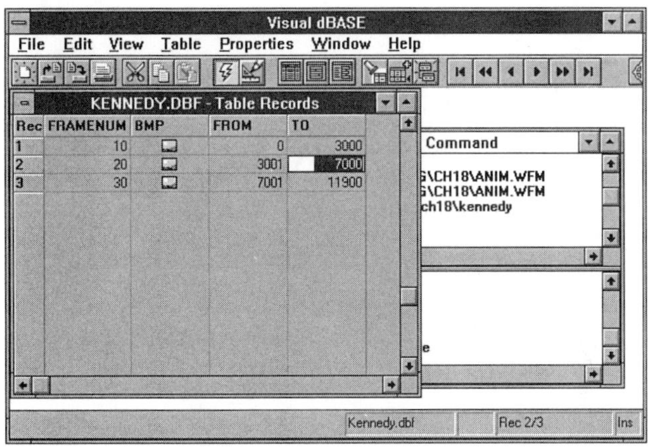

Figure 18.38.
The table records of the Kennedy.DBF table.

You were instructed to fill the BMP field of the Kennedy.DBF table with three BMP files. You can create these three BMP pictures using Paintbrush. When creating these pictures with Paintbrush, don't forget to set the Image Attributes (from the Options menu of Paintbrush) to a smaller BMP size, and save the BMP pictures as Ken1.BMP, Ken2.BMP, and Ken3.BMP. The three BMP files used in the Kennedy program are shown in Figures 18.39, 18.40, and 18.41. Remember that to insert the BMP contents of the BMP file into the BMP field of the Kennedy.DBF table, you must double-click the BMP field, make the Image Viewer window the active window, and then select the Insert from File item from the File menu.

Figure 18.39.
The Ken1.BMP picture.

Figure 18.40.
The Ken2.BMP picture.

Figure 18.41.
The Ken3.BMP picture.

The Visual Implementation of the Kennedy Form

You'll now visually implement the Kennedy form.

- ☐ In the Command window type `Create Form C:\DBPROG\CH18\Kennedy`, and then press Enter.
- ☐ Implement the Kennedy.WFM form according to the specifications in Table 18.3. When you finish implementing the form, it should look like the one shown in Figure 18.42.

Table 18.3. The properties table of the Kennedy.WFM form.

Object	Property	Setting
Form	**Text**	**The Kennedy Program**
	Top	0
	Width	63
	View	C:\DBPROG\CH18\KENNEDY.DBF
	MDI	.F.
	Height	18
	Left	1
PushButton	**Name**	**ExitButton**
	Text	E&xit
	Top	15
	Width	15
	Height	2
	Left	2

Object	Property	Setting
PushButton	**Name**	**StartButton**
	Text	&Start Speech
	Top	15
	Width	34
	Height	2
	Left	24
Image	**Name**	**SpeechImage**
	Visible	.F.
	Alignment	2
	DataSource	BINARY KENNEDY->BMP
	Top	1
	Width	25
	Height	11
	Left	2
Image	**Name**	**CurrentImage**
	Alignment	2
	DataSource	C:\DBPROG\BMP\KENNEDY.BMP
	Top	4
	Width	28
	Height	10
	Left	30
Image	**Name**	**KImage**
	Visible	.F.
	DataSource	C:\DBPROG\BMP\KENNEDY.BMP
	Top	1
	Width	7
	Height	3
	Left	27
Image	**Name**	**K1Image**
	Visible	.F.
	DataSource	C:\DBPROG\BMP\KENNEDY1.BMP

continues

Table 18.3. continued

Object	Property	Setting
	Top	1
	Width	7
	Height	3
	Left	34
Image	**Name**	**K2Image**
	Visible	.F.
	DataSource	C:\DBPROG\BMP\KENNEDY2.BMP
	Top	1
	Width	7
	Height	3
	Left	41
Image	**Name**	**K3Image**
	Visible	.F.
	DataSource	C:\DBPROG\BMP\KENNEDY3.BMP
	Top	1
	Width	7
	Height	3
	Left	48
TegoMM.VBX	**Name**	**Tegomm1**
	Top	12
	Width	39
	Height	2
	Left	0

Table 18.3 instructs you to place various image controls in the form. The SpeechImage image control is the image control that during runtime will contain the contents of the BMP field of the Kennedy.DBF table. This image control displays the Ken1.BMP, Ken2.BMP, and Ken3.BMP pictures in synchronization with the playback of the WAV file. Note that Table 18.3 instructs you to set the DataSource property of this image control to the BMP field of the Kennedy.DBF table. This means that during runtime, the contents of the BMP field of the current record are transferred automatically to the SpeechImage image control.

Figure 18.42.
The Kennedy.WFM form (design mode).

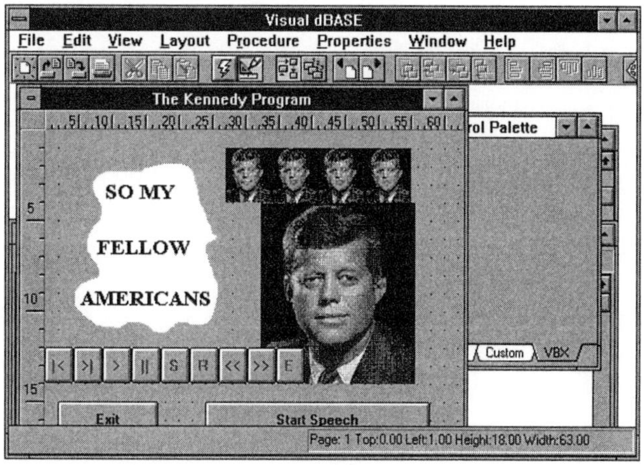

The CurrentImage image control contains the Kennedy.BMP picture. (See Figure 18.43.) You'll have to paste a picture of President Kennedy into Paintbrush, size the picture with the Image Attribute item of the Options menu of Paintbrush, and save the file as Kennedy.BMP.

Figure 18.43.
The Kennedy.BMP picture.

There are four more image controls in the Kennedy.WFM form: the KImage, K1Image, K2Image, and K3Image image controls. During design time, (that is, during the implementation of Table 18.3), you are instructed to place the Kennedy.BMP file (Figure 18.43) in the KImage control, the Kennedy1.BMP picture (Figure 18.44) in the K1Image image control, the Kennedy2.BMP picture (Figure 18.45) in the K2Image image control, and the Kennedy3.BMP picture (Figure 18.46) in the K3Image image control.

Figure 18.44.
The Kennedy1.BMP picture.

Figure 18.45.
The Kennedy2.BMP picture.

Figure 18.46.
The Kennedy3.BMP picture.

The Visible property of the CurrentImage control is set to .T.. The Visible properties of the KImage, K1Image, K2Image, and K3Image are set to .F..

During runtime, the images stored in the KImage, K1Image, K2Image, and K3Image image controls are copied to the CurrentImage image control. Because KImage, K1Image, K2Image, and K3Image contain pictures with different mouth expressions, the image in CurrentImage gives the impression that the mouth in the picture moves.

As previously stated, you generate the Kennedy.BMP picture by pasting a picture of President Kennedy into Paintbrush. You can generate the Kennedy1.BMP, Kennedy2.BMP, and Kennedy3.BMP pictures by using the Paintbrush tools to alter the mouth and then save the altered picture as a new BMP file. This way you can generate the Kennedy1.BMP, Kennedy2.BMP, and Kennedy3.BMP files from the Kennedy.BMP picture.

Entering the Code of the Kennedy Form

In the following sections you'll enter the code of the Kennedy form.

Attaching Code to the *OnClick* Event of the Exit Button

You'll now attach code to the `OnClick` event of the Exit button.

☐ Attach code to the `OnClick` event of the Exit button. After you attach the code, the `ExitButton_OnClick` procedure should look as follows:

```
Procedure EXITBUTTON_OnClick

   form.Close()

Return
```

☐ Select Save from the File menu to save your work.

The code you typed uses the `Close()` method to terminate the program.

Attaching Code to the *OnOpen* Event of the Kennedy Form

You'll now attach code to the `OnOpen` event of the form.

☐ Attach code to the `OnOpen` event of the form. After you attach the code, the `Form_OnOpen` procedure should look as follows:

```
Procedure Form_OnOpen

   PUBLIC gSpeechInProgress
   gSpeechInProgress=.F.


   form.Tegomm1.Visible=.F.
   form.Tegomm1.UpdateInterval=50
   form.Tegomm1.DeviceType="WaveAudio"
   form.Tegomm1.FileName="C:\DBPROG\WAV\8KENNED3.WAV"
   form.Tegomm1.Command="Open"

   SET ORDER TO FRAMENUM
   GOTO TOP

Return
```

☐ Select Save from the File menu to save your work.

The code you typed starts by declaring a public variable:

```
PUBLIC gSpeechInProgress
```

This means that the `gSpeechInProgress` variable is accessible by every procedure in the Kennedy.WFM form.

`gSpeechInProgress` serves as a flag that indicates whether the speech playback is in progress. Because initially the speech is not in progress, you set the value of this variable to .F.:

```
gSpeechInProgress=.F.
```

The multimedia control is made invisible:

```
form.Tegomm1.Visible=.F.
```

And the UpdateInterval property of the multimedia control is set to 50 milliseconds:

```
form.Tegomm1.UpdateInterval=50
```

This means that every 50 milliseconds, the `Tegomm1_StatusUpdate` procedure will be executed automatically.

The multimedia control is set so that it will play through the sound card:

```
form.Tegomm1.DeviceType="WaveAudio"
```

The FileName property of the multimedia control is then set:

```
form.Tegomm1.FileName="C:\DBPROG\WAV\8KENNED3.WAV"
```

Then the `Open` command is issued:

```
form.Tegomm1.Command="Open"
```

Finally, the Kennedy.DBF table is ordered by the FRAMENUM field, and the record pointer is set to point to the first record of the table:

```
SET ORDER TO FRAMENUM
GOTO TOP
```

Attaching Code to the *OnClick* Event of the Start Button

You'll now attach code to the `OnClick` event of the StartButton button.

☐ Attach code to the `OnClick` event. After you attach the code, the `StartButton_OnClick` procedure should look as follows:

```
Procedure STARTBUTTON_OnClick

   IF form.StartButton.Text = "&Start Speech"
      gSpeechInProgress = .T.
      form.StartButton.Text = "&Stop Speech"
      form.Tegomm1.Command="Prev"
      form.Tegomm1.Command="Play"
      form.SpeechImage.Visible=.T.
      GOTO TOP
   ELSE
      gSpeechInProgress = .F.
      form.StartButton.Text = "&Start Speech"
      form.CurrentImage.DataSource= form.KImage.DataSource
      form.Tegomm1.Command="Stop"
      form.SpeechImage.Visible=.F.
   ENDIF

Return
```

☐ Select Save from the File menu to save your work.

The code you typed uses an `IF...ELSE` statement to examine the status of the Start button. If the Text property of the Start button is currently set to &Start Speech, the user clicked the Start button to start the speech. The code under the `IF` statement therefore sets `gSpeechInProgress` to .T.:

```
gSpeechInProgress = .T.
```

The Text property of the button is set to &Stop Speech:

```
form.StartButton.Text = "&Stop Speech"
```

The multimedia control is rewound, and the `Play` command is issued to start the playback:

```
form.Tegomm1.Command="Prev"
form.Tegomm1.Command="Play"
```

The SpeechImage image control is made visible (because during the speech, this image control displays the contents of the BMP field of the Kennedy.DBF table):

```
form.SpeechImage.Visible=.T.
```

Finally, the record pointer is set to the first record of the Kennedy.DBF table:

```
GOTO TOP
```

If at the time the user clicked the Start button, the Text property of the button was not equal to &Start Speech, the user clicked the &Stop Speech button to stop the speech, and the code under the `Else` is executed.

The code under the `Else` sets `gSpeechInProgress` to .F.:

```
gSpeechInProgress = .F.
```

The Text property of the button is set to &Start Speech:

```
form.StartButton.Text = "&Start Speech"
```

The CurrentImage image control is set so that it displays the Kennedy.BMP picture:

```
form.CurrentImage.DataSource= form.KImage.DataSource
```

A `Stop` command is issued to the multimedia control to stop the playback of the WAV file:

```
form.Tegomm1.Command="Stop"
```

Finally, the SpeechImage image control is made invisible (because when no speech is in progress, the SpeechImage control should be invisible):

```
form.SpeechImage.Visible=.F.
```

Attaching Code to the *OnStatusUpdate* Event of the Multimedia Control

You'll now attach code to the `OnStatusUpdate` event of the multimedia control.

- ☐ Attach code to the `OnStatusUpdate` event of the multimedia control. After you type the code, the `Tegomm1_OnStatusUpdate` procedure should look as follows:

```
Procedure TEGOMM1_OnStatusUpdate
```

```
STATIC PictureNumber = 0

IF gSpeechInProgress = .F.
   Return
ENDIF

PictureNumber=PictureNumber+1
IF PictureNumber = 4
   PictureNumber = 0
ENDIF

DO CASE
   CASE PictureNumber = 0
     form.CurrentImage.DataSource= ;
           form.KImage.DataSource

   CASE PictureNumber = 1
        form.CurrentImage.DataSource= ;
           form.K1Image.DataSource

   CASE PictureNumber = 2
        form.CurrentImage.DataSource= ;
           form.K2Image.DataSource

   CASE PictureNumber = 3
        form.CurrentImage.DataSource=  ;
           form.K3Image.DataSource

ENDCASE


IF form.Tegomm1.Position > FROM .AND. ;
              form.Tegomm1.Position < TO
   Return
ELSE
   SKIP 1
   IF EOF()
      GOTO BOTTOM
   ENDIF
ENDIF

Return
```

- [ ] Select Save from the File menu to save your work.

The code you typed declares a static variable:

```
STATIC PictureNumber = 0
```

A static variable retains its value after the procedure terminates. For example, if during the execution of the `Tegomm1_OnStatusUpdate` procedure the value of `PictureNumber` changes to 3, then later, when the `Tegomm1_OnStatusUpdate` procedure is executed again, the value of `PictureNumber` is not set back to 0. The value of `PictureNumber` is 3, exactly as it was during the preceding execution of the `Tegomm1_OnStatusUpdate` procedure.

An `IF` statement checks the value of `gSpeechInProgress` to examine whether the speech is in progress:

```
IF gSpeechInProgress = .F.
   Return
ENDIF
```

If the speech is not in progress, the procedure terminates. If, however, the speech is in progress, the rest of the `Tegomm1_OnStatusUpdate` procedure is executed. The rest of the procedure is responsible for performing the animation.

`PictureNumber` is the static variable that was declared at the beginning of the procedure. This variable determines which picture will be displayed in the CurrentImage image control. Initially, the `PictureNumber` variable is 0. The following statement increases the value of this static variable:

```
PictureNumber=PictureNumber+1
If PictureNumber = 4
   PictureNumber = 0
Endif
```

That is, the static variable is set to 0+1=1. Recall that the `Tegomm1_OnStatusUpdate` procedure is executed every 50 milliseconds (because you set the UpdateInterval property of the Tegomm1 control to 50 in the `Form_OnOpen` procedure). So the next time the `Tegomm1_OnStatusUpdate` procedure is executed, `PictureNumber` is equal to 1, and its value is increased to 1+1=2. The `IF` statement makes sure that `PictureNumber` never exceeds 4. So if you look at the values of `PictureNumber` after the `IF` block of statements is executed, you see the following values for `PictureNumber`:

```
1,2,3,0,1,2,3,0,1,2,3,...
```

A `DO CASE` block of statements is then executed:

```
DO CASE
   CASE PictureNumber = 0
     form.CurrentImage.DataSource= ;
           form.KImage.DataSource

   CASE PictureNumber = 1
        form.CurrentImage.DataSource= ;
           form.K1Image.DataSource

   CASE PictureNumber = 2
        form.CurrentImage.DataSource= ;
           form.K2Image.DataSource

   CASE PictureNumber = 3
        form.CurrentImage.DataSource=  ;
           form.K3Image.DataSource

ENDCASE
```

In each case of the `DO CASE`, the value of `PictureNumber` is examined, and the corresponding picture is transferred to the CurrentImage control. For example, if `PictureNumber` is equal to 0, the DataSource property of the KImage image control (which contains the Kennedy.BMP picture) is transferred to the CurrentImage image control. Similarly, if `PictureNumber` is equal to 1, the DataSource property of the K1Image image control (which contains the Kennedy1.BMP picture) is transferred to the CurrentImage image control.

So the picture of the CurrentImage image control is changing every 50 milliseconds. The images that appear in CurrentImage are displayed in the following order:

```
Kennedy1.BMP
Kennedy2.BMP
Kennedy3.BMP
Kennedy.BMP
Kennedy1.BMP
Kennedy2.BMP
Kennedy3.BMP
Kennedy.BMP
Kennedy1.BMP
...
...
...
```

The preceding sequence of images gives the illusion that the mouth of the picture moves during the speech.

Note that the pictures of CurrentImage have no relation to the current position of the WAV file. That is, the animation shown in CurrentImage is nonsynchronized. On the other hand, the SpeechImage image control (which displays the contents of the BMP field of Kennedy.DBF) displays the images in synchronization with the current position of the WAV file. This task is accomplished with the following `IF…ELSE` statement:

```
IF form.Tegomm1.Position > FROM .AND. ;
              form.Tegomm1.Position < TO
   Return
ELSE
   SKIP 1
   IF EOF()
      GOTO BOTTOM
   ENDIF
ENDIF
```

If the current position of the WAV file (given by `form.Tegomm1.Position`) is greater than the value of the FROM field and less than the value of the TO field, the image in SpeechImage is the correct image for this range. If the current position of the WAV file is outside the (FROM, TO) range, it is time to change the picture in the SpeechImage control. This activity is accomplished under the `Else` by the use of the `SKIP` statement to place the record pointer at the next record.

Recall that the Kennedy.DBF table is a table with three records in it. The first record has the KEN1.BMP picture in the BMP field, the FROM field of the first record is 0, and the TO field of the second record is 3000. Indeed, the audio phrase "So my fellow Americans" is played within the first 3000 milliseconds of the WAV file. Similarly, the phrase "Ask not what you can do for your country" is played between the 3001 milliseconds position and the 7000 milliseconds position of the WAV file. The last phrase is played between the 7001 milliseconds position and the end of the WAV file.

Because during design time you set the DataSource of SpeechImage to the BMP field of the Kennedy.DBF table, the picture in the SpeechImage control changes automatically when the record pointer of the table changes. So to summarize, the `If` statement compares the current position of the WAV file with the values of the FROM and TO fields of the current record. If it is time to change pictures, the `SKIP` statement is executed.

Attaching Code to the *OnDone* Event of the Multimedia Control

You'll now attach code to the `OnDone` event of the multimedia control.

☐ Attach code to the `OnDone` event of the Tegomm1 control. When you finish typing the code, the `Tegomm1_OnDone` procedure should look as follows:

```
Procedure TEGOMM1_OnDone

   If form.Tegomm1.Position = form.Tegomm1.Length

      form.StartButton_OnClick()

   Endif

Return
```

☐ Select Save from the File menu to save your work.

The code you typed detects whether the WAV file was played in its entirety, and if so, the `StartButton_OnClick` procedure is executed. That is, during the playback, the Start button serves as the Stop button, and the preceding `If` statement emulates a click on the Stop button when the WAV file has been played in its entirety.

☐ Execute the Kennedy program and check its proper operation.

Summary

In this chapter you have learned how to play WAV files through a sound card. You have learned how to play WAV files through the PC speaker, how to play MIDI files, how to play movie AVI files, and how to play CD audio.

In this chapter you have also learned how to perform animation. The Anim program demonstrates how to design a nonsynchronized animation show and the Kennedy program demonstrates how to design a synchronized show.

Q&A

Q I want to impress my users by including multimedia in my programs. Should I use WAV files or MIDI files as the sound files?

A WAV files can contain human voice, music, or any other sound input into the microphone at the time of recording. On the other hand, MIDI files can contain only instructions that tell the sound card how to play music by using musical instruments (such as piano, guitar, and drums).

MIDI files are very short compared to WAV files. But if you want to include sound other than music played by instruments, you must use WAV files.

Q How do I generate WAV files?

A There are basically two ways to get WAV files:

You can record your own WAV files. To do so, you must install a sound card in your PC. As you can imagine, there are many types of sound cards. Due to the popularity of sound cards, the prices of sound cards have dropped significantly in the past few years; you now can purchase a sound card for less than $100. Of course, if you are really "into sound," you can purchase a more expensive sound card.

Typically, the sound-card package includes a set of two speakers. Some sound cards come with a microphone, and some do not. You can purchase a basic microphone for about $20.

Another way to obtain WAV files is to purchase a disk or CD that contains prerecorded WAV files. When purchasing prerecorded WAV files, be sure to read the software license agreement that comes with the product. Some packages allow you to use the WAV files on a single computer and forbid you to distribute the WAV files with your applications.

Q How do I generate MIDI files?

A You can generate MIDI files by purchasing the equipment that enables you to write your own music and then enables you to save your music as a MIDI file. Typically, the MIDI recording equipment consists of a music keyboard you can attach to the MIDI port (or to the game port) of your sound card. If you intend to write your own MIDI files using a keyboard and a sound card, make sure that the sound card you are purchasing is capable of interfacing with a MIDI keyboard.

As you can see, generating MIDI files is a little more complicated than generating WAV files. MIDI keyboards can cost anywhere from $80 to thousands of dollars. Of course, you'll also need the MIDI software that enables you to record the music. The MIDI software is typically included with the sound card and with the MIDI keyboard.

And probably the most important thing you'll need to have when recording MIDI files yourself is the knowledge of how to play a music keyboard, and a talent for writing your own music.

Alternatively, you can purchase MIDI files on disks and on CDs.

Quiz

The E button on the multimedia control is not available during the execution of the PlayWAV program. Why?

Exercises

1. In this chapter you wrote the PlayWAV program, which plays WAV files. Write the PlayMIDI program similar to the PlayWAV program, except make the PlayMIDI program play MIDI files rather than WAV files.
2. In this chapter you wrote the PlayWAV program, which plays WAV files. Write the PlayAVI program similar to the PlayWAV program, except make the PlayAVI program play movie AVI files rather than WAV files.
3. In this chapter you wrote the PlayWAV program, which plays WAV files. Write the PlayCD program similar to the PlayWAV program, except make the PlayCD program play CD audio rather than WAV files.
4. In this chapter you wrote the PlayWAV program, which plays WAV files. Write the PlayPC program similar to the PlayWAV program, except make the PlayPC program play WAV files through the PC speaker rather than through the sound card.

Quiz Answer

The E button is the Eject button. During the execution of the PlayWAV program, you opened a WAV file. It does not make sense to eject the WAV file.

On the other hand, while CD audio is being played, the E button is available, and pressing the E button causes the multimedia to eject the CD. That is, if your CD-ROM drive is equipped with the electromechanical feature that enables the software to open the door of the CD-ROM drive, the Eject button opens the door of the CD-ROM drive.

Exercise Answers

1. The main window of the PlayMIDI program is shown in Figure 18.47.

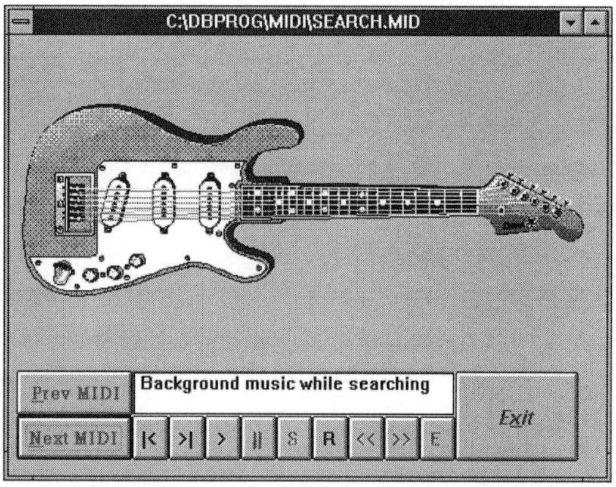

Figure 18.47.
The PlayMIDI program.

To play MIDI files, you must fill the DBF table with the path and names of MIDI files. The only other change you must make is to set the DeviceType property of the multimedia control to Sequencer. That is, the `Form_OnOpen` procedure of the PlayWAV program includes the following statement:

```
form.Tegomm1.DeviceType="WaveAudio"
```

You must set the DeviceType property to play MIDI files as shown here:

```
form.Tegomm1.DeviceType="Sequencer"
```

2. To play AVI movie files, you must fill the DBF table with the path and names of AVI files. The only other change you must make is to set the DeviceType property of the multimedia control to AVIVideo. That is, the `Form_OnOpen` procedure of the PlayWAV program includes the following statement:

```
form.Tegomm1.DeviceType="WaveAudio"
```

You must set the DeviceType property to play AVI files as shown here:

```
form.Tegomm1.DeviceType="AVIVideo"
```

3. The `Form_OnOpen` procedure of the PlayWAV program includes the following statement:

```
form.Tegomm1.DeviceType="WaveAudio"
```

You must set the DeviceType property to CDAudio, as shown here:

```
form.Tegomm1.DeviceType="CDAudio"
```

Unlike playing WAV, MIDI, and AVI files, when you are playing CD audio, there is no need to set the FileName property of the multimedia control.

4. The PlayWAV program plays WAV files through the sound card. The only change you must make is to set the DeviceType property of the multimedia control to PCSpeaker. That is, the `Form_OnOpen` procedure of the PlayWAV program includes the following statement:

   ```
   form.Tegomm1.DeviceType="WaveAudio"
   ```

   You must set the DeviceType property to play through the PC speaker as shown here:

   ```
   form.Tegomm1.DeviceType="PCSpeaker"
   ```

Note: The exercises illustrate how you can change the statement

```
form.Tegomm1.DeviceType="WaveAudio"
```

in the `Form_OnOpen` procedure of the form to play MIDI, AVI, CD audio, and PC speaker.

You can further enhance the programs by changing other cosmetic aspects. For example, you should set the Text properties of the buttons of the PlayMIDI program to Next MIDI and Prev MIDI (rather than Next WAV and Prev WAV). Similarly, you should change the Text properties of these buttons to Next Movie and Prev Movie in the PlayAVI program.

The image displayed in the form of the programs should reflect the subject of the programs. For example, the PlayMIDI program can display a picture of a guitar (as shown in Figure 18.47), the PlayAVI program can display a picture of VCR or camcorder, and so on.

You can also enhance the program by including option buttons that enable the user to select the multimedia device. The form therefore can contain the WAV, MIDI, AVI, and CD Audio option buttons. When the user selects the WAV option button, the following statements are executed:

```
form.Tegomm1.DeviceType="WaveAudio"
USE C:\DBPROG\CH18\WAVList
```

When the user selects the MIDI option button, the following statements are executed:

```
form.Tegomm1.DeviceType="Sequencer"
USE C:\DBPROG\CH18\MIDIList
```

When the user selects the AVI option button, the following statements are executed:

```
form.Tegomm1.DeviceType="AVIVideo"
USE C:\DBPROG\CH18\AVI
```

Of course, you'll have to prepare the WAVList.DBF, MIDIList.DBF, and AVIList.DBF tables.

Note: As discussed previously, you can write code that automatically detects whether the PC has a sound card installed in it. If the PC does not have a sound card, set the DeviceType to PCSpeaker so that the WAV file will be played through the PC speaker.

19

WEEK
3

The Timer Control

In Chapter 16, "Using VBX Controls," you learned what VBX controls are and how to incorporate a VBX control into a dBASE program. In this chapter you'll learn how to use a timer VBX control called DBTIMER.VBX. This VBX file is included with Visual dBASE. It was copied into your \VISUALDB\SAMPLES directory when you installed Visual dBASE.

The TIMER Program

In the following sections you will write a dBASE program called TIMER that illustrates how to use the DBTIMER.VBX VBX control.

Before you start writing the TIMER program, you need to know how the program should look and what it should do.

When you run the TIMER program, the main window of the TIMER program should look like the one shown in Figure 19.1.

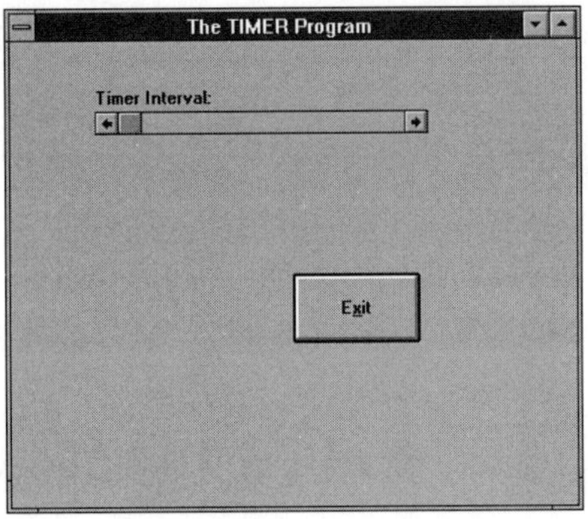

Figure 19.1.
The main window of the TIMER program.

As shown in Figure 19.1, the main window of the TIMER program contains two controls: a scroll bar and an Exit pushbutton.

Note that the TIMER program also uses a timer control. As you'll see later in this chapter, however, the timer control is visible only during design time. When the program is running, the timer control is invisible.

The TIMER program keeps automatically moving the Exit button to random locations in the main window of the program. For example, Figure 19.2 shows the Exit pushbutton in one such random location.

The user can change the rate at which the Exit pushbutton moves in the form by using the horizontal scroll bar.

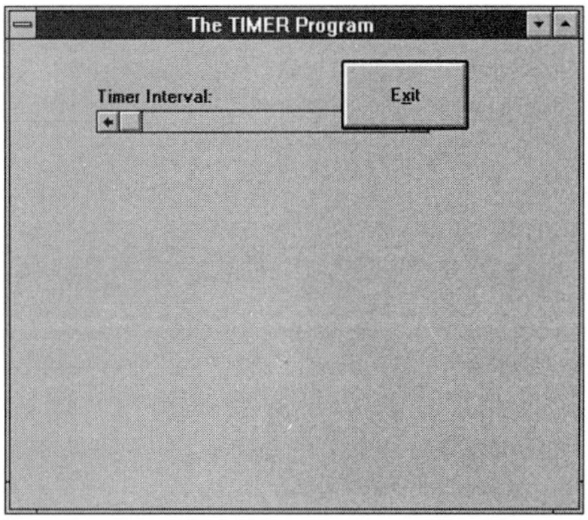

Figure 19.2.
While the TIMER program is running, the Exit button keeps moving to random locations within the program's window.

When the user clicks the Exit pushbutton, the TIMER program terminates.

Now that you know what the TIMER program is supposed to do, it's time to start writing it.

The Visual Implementation of the TIMER Program

Create the TIMER.WFM form as instructed here:

☐ Type `MD C:\DBPROG` in the Command window, and then press Enter.

dBASE responds by creating the directory C:\DBPROG. (If this directory already exists, dBASE displays a message box telling you that the directory cannot be created.)

☐ Type `MD C:\DBPROG\CH19` in the Command window, and then press Enter.

dBASE responds by creating the directory C:\DBPROG\CH19.

☐ Type `CREATE FORM C:\DBPROG\CH19\TIMER` in the Command window, and press Enter.

dBASE responds by creating the TIMER.WFM form and displaying it in design mode.

Before you start customizing the TIMER.WFM form, you need to add the DBTIMER.VBX control to the Control Palette window of dBASE. Here is how you do that:

☐ Select Set Up Custom Controls from the File menu of Visual dBASE.

dBASE responds by displaying the Set Up Custom Controls dialog box. (See Figure 19.3.)

☐ Click the VBX Controls tab, click the Add button, select the VBX file \VISUALDB\SAMPLES\DBTIMER.VBX, and then click the OK button.

dBASE responds by adding the DBTIMER.VBX control to the Control Palette window of dBASE.

19

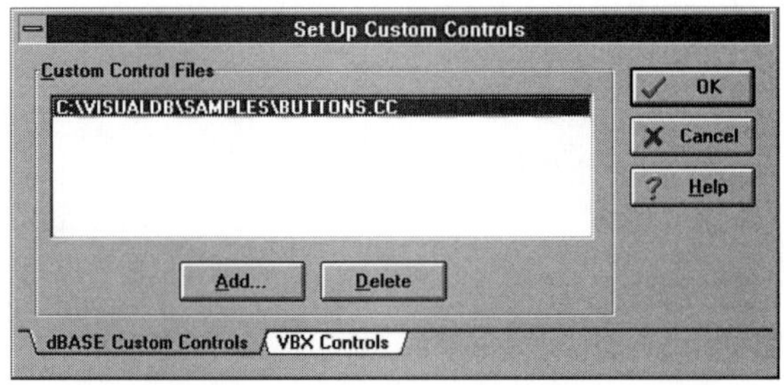

Figure 19.3.
The Set Up Custom Controls dialog box.

To verify that the DBTIMER.VBX control now appears in the Control Palette window of dBASE, follow these steps:

☐ Select the Control Palette window of dBASE.

☐ Click the VBX tab of the Control Palette window.

Figure 19.4 shows the Timer control icon in the VBX page of the Control Palette window.

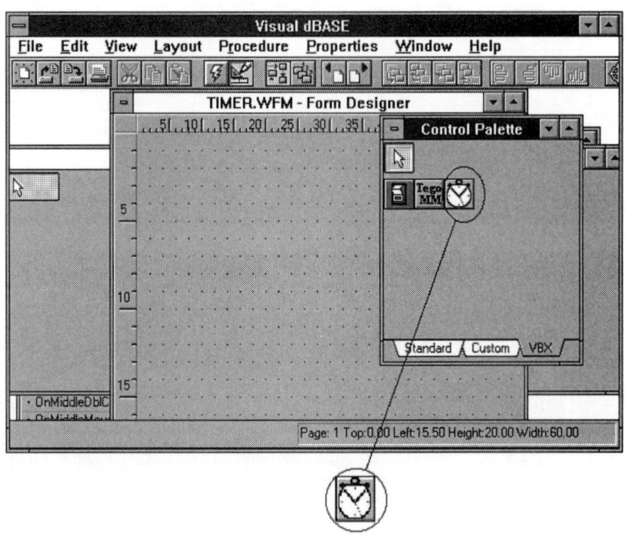

Figure 19.4.
The icon of the DBTIMER.VBX control in the Control Palette window of dBASE.

Now that you've verified that the DBTIMER.VBX control appears in the Control Palette window of dBASE, you can design a form that uses this control.

☐ Customize the TIMER.WFM form according to the specifications in Table 19.1. When you finish customizing the form, it should look like the one shown in Figure 19.5.

☐ Save your work by selecting Save from the File menu.

Table 19.1. The properties table of the TIMER.WFM form.

Object	Property	Setting
Form	**Text**	**The TIMER Program**
	Height	20
	Left	1
	MDI	.F.
	Top	0
	Width	80
Text	**Name**	**Text1**
	Text	Timer Interval:
	Height	1
	Left	10
	Top	2
	Width	15
Horizontal Scroll Bar	**Name**	**IntervalScrollbar**
	Rangemin	100
	Rangemax	200
	Value	100
	Height	1
	Left	10.00
	Top	3
	Width	39.00
dBTIMER (DBTIMER.VBX)	**Name**	**Timer**
	Enabled	.T.
	Seconds	1
	Height	2
	Left	0
	Top	0
	Width	5

continues

Table 19.1. continued

Object	Property	Setting
PushButton	**Name**	**ExitButton**
	Text	E&xit
	Height	3
	Left	33
	Top	10
	Width	15

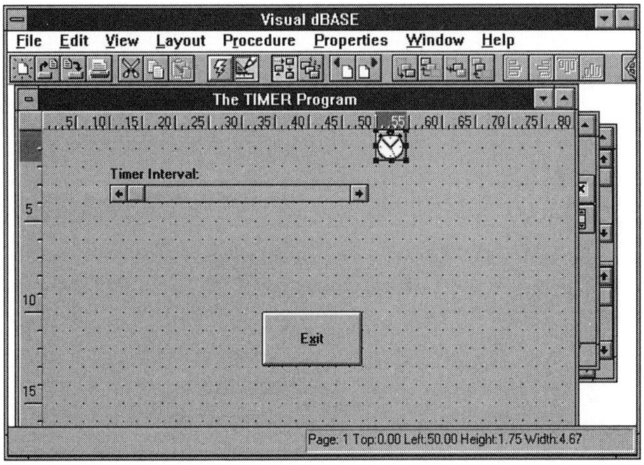

Figure 19.5.
The TIMER.WFM form in design mode (after customization).

Note: Table 19.1 instructs you to place a dBTIMER (DBTIMER.VBX) control, a text control, a horizontal scroll bar control, and a pushbutton control in the form.

To place the dBTIMER (DBTIMER.VBX) control in the form, select the VBX tab of the Control Palette window, and then double-click the icon of the dBTIMER control.

To place any of the other controls in the form, select the Standard tab of the Control Palette window, and then double-click the icon of the desired control.

The visual implementation of the TIMER.WFM form is finished. To see your visual design in action, follow these steps:

☐ Press the F2 key.

dBASE responds by running the TIMER.WFM form. (See Figure 19.6.)

Figure 19.6.
The TIMER.WFM form in run mode.

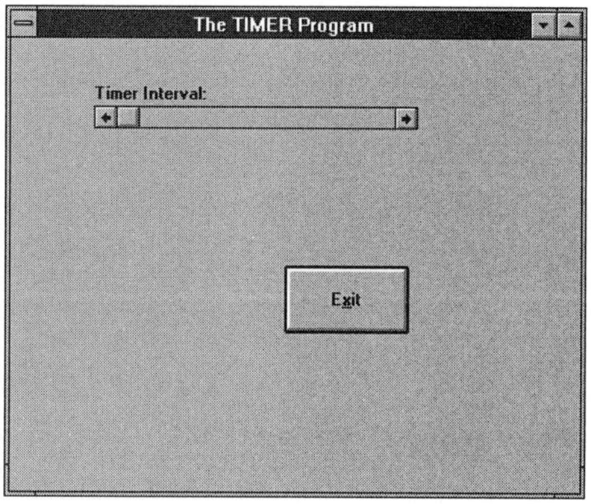

Notice that when the TIMER.WFM form is in design mode (as in Figure 19.5), the timer control is visible. But in run mode (as in Figure 19.6), the timer control is invisible.

☐ Change the mode of the TIMER.WFM form back to design mode.

Entering the Code of the TIMER Program

In the following sections you'll enter the code of the TIMER program.

Attaching Code to the *OnClick* Event of the Exit Pushbutton

When the user clicks the Exit button, the TIMER program should terminate. You'll now write the code that accomplishes this task.

☐ Attach the following code to the `OnClick` event of the Exit pushbutton. After you write this code, the `EXITBUTTON_OnClick` procedure should look as follows:

```
Procedure EXITBUTTON_OnClick

 form.close()

Return
```

☐ Save your work by selecting Save from the File menu.

The statement you typed in the `EXITBUTTON_OnClick` procedure:

```
form.Close()
```

terminates the program by closing the form.

To see in action the code you attached to the `OnClick` event of the Exit button, follow these steps:

☐ Press the F2 key.

dBASE responds by running the TIMER.WFM form.

☐ Click the Exit button.

The TIMER program responds by terminating itself.

Attaching Code to the *OnTimer* Event of the Timer Control

The timer control has an event called `OnTimer`. The `OnTimer` event occurs every *X* seconds, with *X* being the value of the Seconds property of the timer control.

Recall that during the visual design of the TIMER.WFM form, you were instructed to set the Seconds property of the timer control to 1 (refer to Table 19.1). The `OnTimer` event of the timer control therefore occurs every 1 second.

In the following steps you'll attach code to the `OnTimer` event of the timer control. Because you set the Seconds property of the timer control to 1, the code you'll attach to the `OnTimer` event will automatically be executed every second.

Recall that when you visually designed the TIMER.WFM form, you were also instructed to set the Enabled property of the timer control to .T. (refer to Table 19.1). This step was necessary because if you don't set the Enabled property of the timer control to .T., the `OnTimer` event does not occur.

☐ Type `MODIFY FORM ?` in the Command window, press Enter, and then select the file C:\DBPROG\CH19\TIMER.WFM from the Open Form dialog box that dBASE displays.

dBASE responds by displaying the TIMER.WFM form in design mode.

☐ Attach the following code to the `OnTimer` event of the Timer control. After you write this code, the `TIMER_OnTimer` procedure should look as follows:

```
Procedure TIMER_OnTimer

* Beep
?CHR(7)

* Move the Exit button to a random location.
Left=RANDOM()*(form.Width-form.ExitButton.Width)
Top=RANDOM()*(form.Height-form.ExitButton.Height)
form.ExitButton.Left=Left
form.ExitButton.Top=Top

Return
```

☐ Save your work by selecting Save from the File menu.

The first statement you typed in the `TIMER_OnTimer` procedure generates a beep:

```
??CHR(7)
```

These are the next four statements:

```
Left=RANDOM()*(form.Width-form.ExitButton.Width)
Top=RANDOM()*(form.Height-form.ExitButton.Height)
form.ExitButton.Left=Left
form.ExitButton.Top=Top
```

These statements move the Exit pushbutton to a random location in the form by setting the Left and Top properties of the Exit pushbutton to random numbers.

The Left property of the Exit button is set to the following expression:

```
RANDOM()*(form.Width - form.ExitButton.Width)
```

The `RANDOM()` function returns a random number in the range of 0 to 1 (for example, 0.5, 0.43, 0.99). The preceding expression therefore returns a random number that is within the range of `0` to `form.Width minus form.ExitButton.Width`. For example, if the form width is 100 and the Exit button width is 20, the preceding expression generates a number in the range of 0 to 80.

The Top property of the Exit button is set to the following expression:

```
RANDOM()*(form.Height - form.ExitButton.Height)
```

This expression returns a number that is within the range of `0` to `form.Height minus form.ExitButton.Height`. For example, if the form height is 100 and the Exit button height is 10, the preceding expression generates a random number in the range of 0 to 90. 19

So the code you wrote in the `TIMER_OnTimer` procedure performs two tasks:

- It generates a beep.
- It moves the Exit pushbutton to a random location within the form.

Because you set the Seconds property of the timer control to 1, these two tasks will be automatically performed every second. That is, every second, the program will generate a beep and move the Exit button to a random location within the form.

To see in action the code you attached to the `OnTimer` event of the timer control, follow these steps:

☐ Press the F2 key.

dBASE responds by running the TIMER.WFM form.

As you can see (and hear), every second the TIMER program beeps and moves the Exit button to a random location within the program's window.

☐ Change the mode of the TIMER.WFM form back to design mode.

Attaching Code to the *OnChange* Event of the IntervalScrollbar Scroll Bar

When the user changes the IntervalScrollbar scroll bar, the program should change the interval of the timer accordingly. You'll now write the code that accomplishes this task.

☐ Attach the following code to the `OnChange` event of the IntervalScrollbar scroll bar. After you write this code, the `INTERVALSCROLLBAR_OnChange` procedure should look as follows:

```
Procedure INTERVALSCROLLBAR_OnChange

* Change the timer interval per the scroll bar value.
form.Timer.Seconds = 100 / form.IntervalScrollbar.Value

Return
```

☐ Save your work by selecting Save from the File menu.

The code you typed in the `INTERVALSCROLLBAR_OnChange` procedure changes the Seconds property of the timer control according to the current value of the IntervalScrollbar scroll bar:

```
form.Timer.Seconds = 100 / form.IntervalScrollbar.Value
```

Recall that during design time you were instructed to set the Rangemin property of the IntervalScrollbar scroll bar to 100 and the Rangemax property of the IntervalScrollbar scroll bar to 200. Therefore, when the scroll bar thumb is at the far-left position (the minimum position), the preceding statement sets the Seconds property of the timer control to 100/100=1. This means that when the scroll bar thumb is set to the far-left position, the `OnTimer` event of the timer control occurs every second.

Similarly, when the scroll bar thumb is at the far-right position (the maximum position), the preceding statement sets the Seconds property of the timer control to 100/200=0.5. This means that when the scroll bar thumb is set to the far-right position, the `OnTimer` event of the timer control occurs every half second.

To see in action the code you attached to the `OnChange` event of the IntervalScrollbar scroll bar, follow these steps:

☐ Press the F2 key.

dBASE responds by running the TIMER.WFM form.

As you can see (and hear), every second, the TIMER program beeps and moves the Exit button to a random location within the program's window.

☐ Move the thumb of the scroll bar to the far-right position.

As you can see and hear, now the TIMER program beeps and moves the Exit button every half second.

☐ Terminate the TIMER program by clicking its Exit button. (If the Exit button moves too fast for you to click it, decrease the value of the scroll bar.)

Summary

In this chapter you have learned how to use the DBTIMER.VBX timer control. As you have seen, the timer control has an event called `OnTimer` that occurs every *X* milliseconds (with *X* being the value of the Seconds property of the timer control). For example, if you set the Seconds property of the timer control to 2, the code you attach to the `OnTimer` event of the timer control will automatically be executed every 2 seconds.

Q&A

Q When I visually implemented the TIMER.WFM form, I was instructed to set the Enabled property of the timer control to .T.. Why was this action necessary, and how can I use the Enabled property of the timer control from within my code?

A As implied by its name, the Enabled property of the timer control determines whether the timer control is enabled. When the Enabled property of the timer control is set to .T., the timer control is enabled, which means that the `OnTimer` event occurs every *X* seconds (*X* is the value of the Seconds property of the timer control). If, however, you set the Enabled property of the timer control to .F., the timer control is disabled, which means that the `OnTimer` event does not occur.

When you want to disable the timer control from within your code, simply set the Enabled property of the timer control to .F.. For example, in the TIMER.WFM program you wrote in this chapter, the following statement would disable the timer control:

```
form.Timer.Enabled = .F.
```

Quiz

1. What is the Seconds property of the timer control used for?
2. When does the `OnTimer` event of the timer control occur?

Exercise

Add to the TIMER program you wrote in this chapter a check box with the following specifications:

Object	*Property*	*Setting*
Check Box	**Name**	**EnableCheck**
	Value	.T.
	Text	&Enable Timer

Attach code to the `OnChange` event of the EnableCheck check box so that when the user places an × in this check box, the timer control is enabled, and when the user removes the × from the check box, the timer control is disabled.

Quiz Answers

1. The Seconds property of the timer control specifies the interval period of the timer.
2. The `OnTimer` event of the timer control occurs every *X* seconds, with *X* being the value of the Seconds property of the timer control. For example, if you set the Seconds property to 3, the `OnTimer` event will occur every 3 seconds.

Exercise Answer

To add the Enable Timer check box to the form, follow these steps:

☐ Type `MODIFY FORM ?` in the Command window, press Enter, and then select the file C:\DBPROG\CH19\TIMER.WFM from the Open Form dialog box that dBASE displays.

dBASE responds by displaying the TIMER.WFM form in design mode.

☐ Add a check box control to the form, and set its properties as shown here:

Object	*Property*	*Setting*
Check Box	**Name**	**EnableCheck**
	Value	.T.
	Text	Enable Timer

☐ Attach the following code to the `OnChange` event of the EnableCheck check box. After you write this code, the `ENABLECHECK_OnChange` procedure should look as follows:

```
Procedure ENABLECHECK_OnChange

IF form.EnableCheck.Value = .T.
   form.Timer.Enabled = .T.
ELSE
   form.Timer.Enabled = .F.
ENDIF

Return
```

WEEK 3

20

3D Virtual Reality: Part I

In this chapter and the next chapter you'll learn how to write 3D virtual reality programs by using a very powerful third-party VBX control—the 3D virtual reality VBX control. As you'll soon discover, writing a 3D virtual reality program by using the 3D virtual reality VBX control is easy.

> **Note:** To implement the virtual reality program discussed in this chapter and the next chapter, you need to have the 3D virtual reality VBX control—Tego3DVR.VBX. (See the disk offer at the end of this book.)
>
> Even if you do not have the 3D virtual reality VBX control (Tego3DVR.VBX), it is highly recommended that you read through this chapter and the next chapter so that you'll be able to see how you can extend the capabilities of Visual dBASE by incorporating powerful third-party VBX controls.
>
> As you'll see in this chapter and the next chapter, you can implement very sophisticated dBASE programs (with a very small amount of code writing) by incorporating VBX controls into your programs.

What Is a 3D Virtual Reality Program?

As implied by its name, a 3D virtual reality program is a program that simulates a 3D (three-dimensional) environment (a DOOM-like program). The user of the program feels as though he is moving in a 3D environment. The program enables the user to move in the 3D environment and interact with various objects (stationary objects as well as moving objects) in the 3D environment. Depending on the user's actions, the program displays the objects in a different way. For example, when the user moves toward a wall, the wall appears to be closer.

After you finish writing the graphics aspect of a virtual reality program, you can make the program feel more "real" by adding sound to the program. For example, when the user shoots a monster, the program plays the sound of a shooting gun, and if the user hits the monster, the program plays the sound of a screaming monster. You can add sound to the 3D virtual reality program by using the multimedia VBX control discussed in an earlier chapter.

You might think that writing a 3D virtual reality program takes a lot of code writing. As you'll soon see, however, writing a complete 3D virtual reality program by using the 3D virtual reality VBX control requires very little code writing.

What Is the 3D Virtual Reality VBX Control?

The 3D virtual reality VBX control (TEGO3DVR.VBX) enables you to write a 3D virtual reality program that displays a three-dimensional floor (with walls and rooms) and enables the user to move around in this floor. As the user moves around in the 3D floor, depending on the movements of the user, the 3D virtual reality VBX control displays the appropriate 3D views.

The control enables you to design a two-dimensional map of a floor by using any text editor (for example, the Notepad program that comes with Windows). The control then converts your two-dimensional map into a 3D picture of a floor, and the control enables the user to move around in this three-dimensional picture.

The TEGO3DVR.VBX VBX control also includes a sprites mechanism that enables you to add stationary objects (such as chairs and tables) as well as moving objects (such as dogs, cats, and monsters) to the 3D floor. Your program can enable the user to interact with the sprites. For example, if the user bumps into a chair, the program can move the chair.

Installing WinG

The TEGO3DVR.VBX control uses WinG technology. WinG (pronounced "win-gee") is a technology that enhances the standard graphics capabilities of Windows. It carries out graphics operations in a high-performance manner.

Because the TEGO3DVR.VBX control uses WinG technology, before you can execute and write programs that use the TEGO3DVR.VBX control, you must install WinG in your Windows system. To install WinG into your Windows system, take the following action:

- ☐ Install WinG into your Windows system as instructed by the README.TXT file on the disk you can order to accompany this book.

The 3D Floor Program

In the following sections, you'll write a program called 3D Floor that illustrates how to use the TEGO3DVR.VBX VBX control.

Before you start writing the 3D Floor program, you should execute the copy of this program that resides on the disk you can order to accompany this book. This way you'll know what the program is supposed to do.

- ☐ If you have not yet installed WinG into your Windows system, do so now. That is, follow the instructions for installing WinG as described in the README.TXT file on the disk you can order to accompany this book.

- ☐ Execute the 3D Floor program as described in the README.TXT file of the disk you can order to accompany this book.

  The main window of the 3D Floor program appears, as shown in Figure 20.1.

Figure 20.1.
The main window of the 3D Floor program.

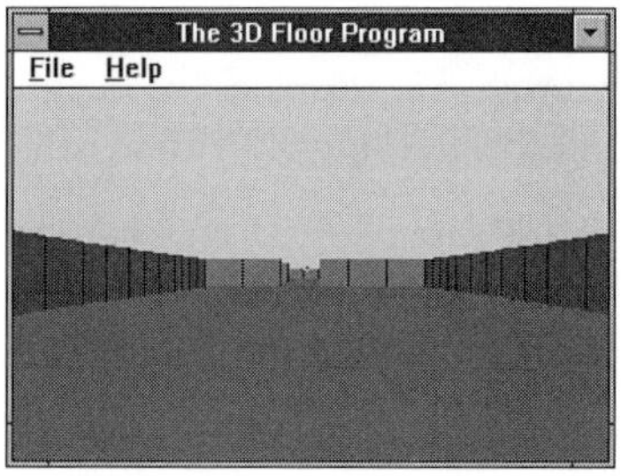

As you can see, the 3D Floor program placed you in a virtual 3D room. You are currently facing the exit door of the room.

You use the right-arrow key and the left-arrow key to rotate. When you press the right-arrow key, you rotate clockwise, and when you press the left-arrow key, you rotate counterclockwise. To see the right-arrow and left-arrow keys in action, take the following action:

- ☐ Press the left-arrow key several times.

Every time you press the left-arrow key, you rotate counterclockwise (about 6 degrees). Figures 20.2 through 20.5 show four snapshots of your 3D view as you rotate counterclockwise.

Figure 20.2.
Rotating counterclockwise (snapshot 1).

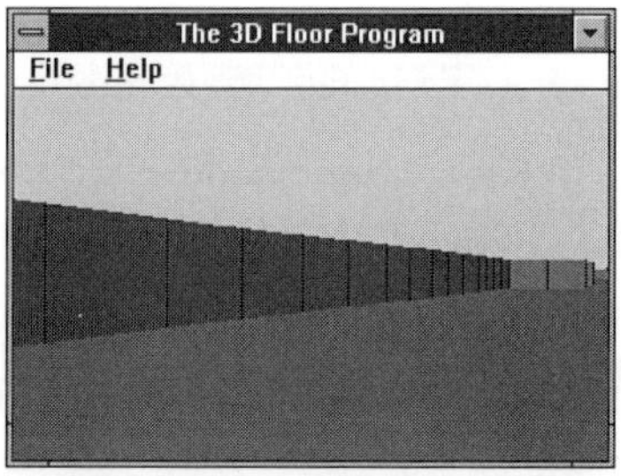

Figure 20.3.
Rotating counterclockwise (snapshot 2).

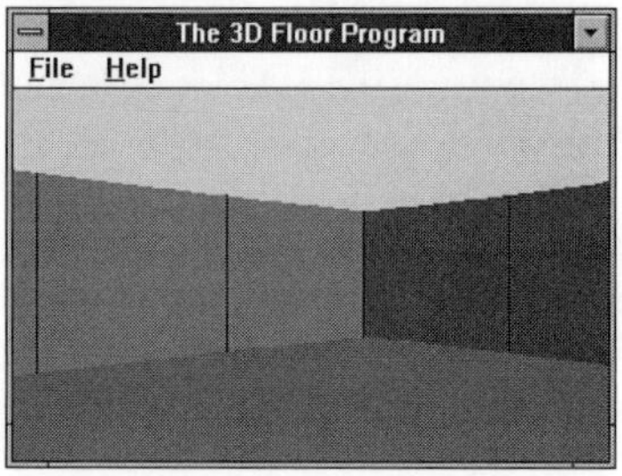

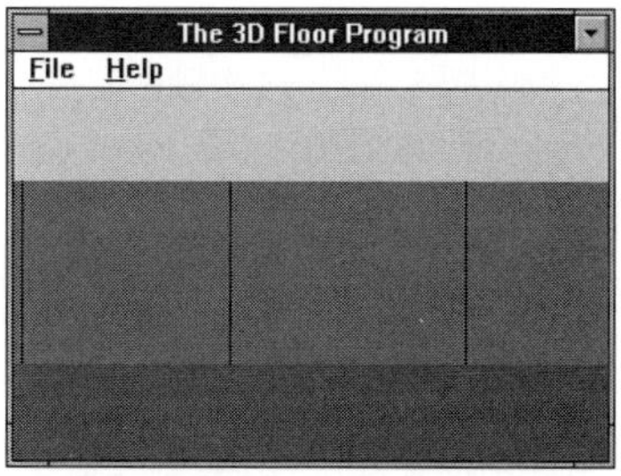

Figure 20.4.
Rotating counterclockwise (snapshot 3).

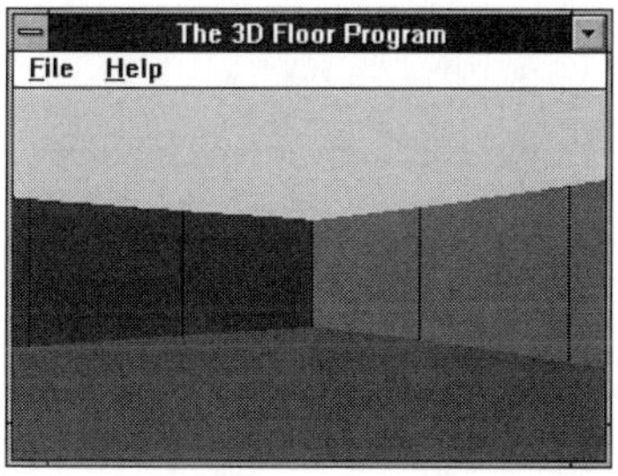

Figure 20.5.
Rotating counterclockwise (snapshot 4).

Note: The left- and right-arrow keys enable you to rotate around the point where you are currently standing. When you press the left- and right-arrow keys, you are not moving forward or backward. You are only rotating.

In snapshot 2 (Figure 20.3) you are facing one corner of the room, and in snapshot 4 (Figure 20.5) you are facing another corner of the room.

☐ Now press the left-arrow key and do not release it. That is, hold down the left-arrow key for several seconds.

As you can see, pressing the left-arrow key without releasing it makes you continuously rotate counterclockwise.

After continuously rotating in the counterclockwise direction, you might feel a little dizzy. So you'll next rotate in the clockwise direction.

☐ Press the right-arrow key several times (or press down the right-arrow key without releasing it).

Pressing the right-arrow key makes you rotate clockwise.

So far, you have only rotated around the point where you are standing. As you have seen, the right- and left-arrow keys enable you to change your viewing direction.

To move forward or backward in the direction you are currently facing (your viewing direction), you must use the up-arrow and down-arrow keys. The up-arrow key moves you forward in the current viewing direction. And the down-arrow key moves you backward in the current viewing direction.

To see the up- and down-arrow keys in action, take the following action:

☐ Use the left-arrow key to change your viewing direction until you are facing a corner of the room. (Refer to Figure 20.3.)

You can now get closer to the corner by pressing the up-arrow key.

☐ Press the up-arrow key several times.

Every time you press the up-arrow key, you are approaching the corner. Figures 20.6 through 20.8 show three snapshots of the 3D view as you are approaching the corner.

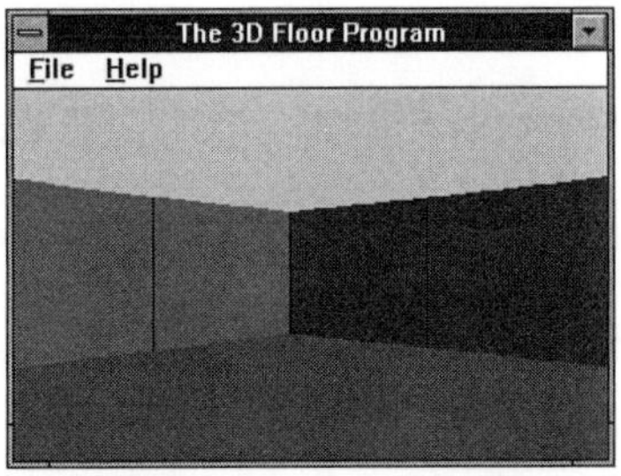

Figure 20.6.
Approaching the corner (snapshot 1).

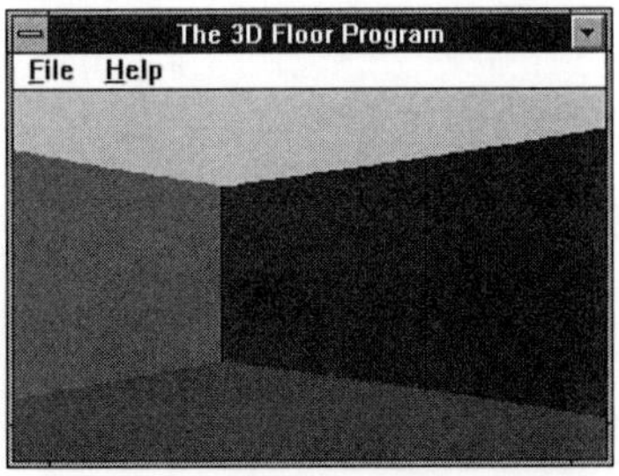

Figure 20.7.
Approaching the corner (snapshot 2).

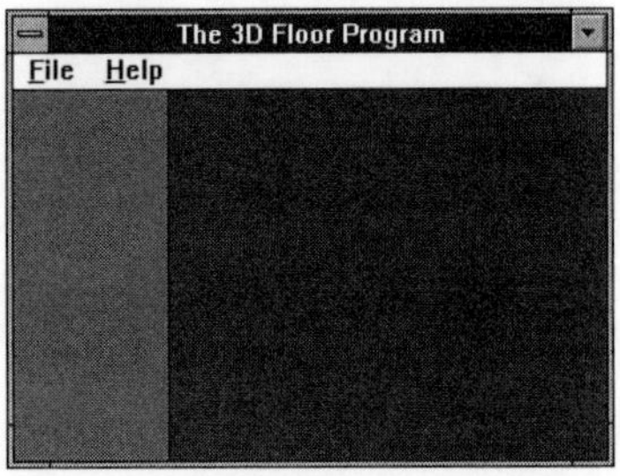

Figure 20.8.
Approaching the corner (snapshot 3).

In snapshot 3 (Figure 20.8), you are so close to the wall that you cannot see the ceiling.

In a similar manner, you can use the down-arrow key to move backward in the current viewing direction. That is, when you press the down-arrow key, you move in reverse.

> **Note:** To continuously move forward in the current viewing direction, you can continuously press the up-arrow key. That is, press the up-arrow key without releasing it.
>
> To continuously move backward in the current viewing direction, you can continuously press the down-arrow key. That is, press the down-arrow key without releasing it.

You should know that you are not alone on the floor. There are two more people on the floor. One person (a jogger) keeps running in the main hall of the floor, and another person (a woman) is exercising in another room on the floor. You'll soon have a chance to meet these people. But before you move to other rooms on the floor, look at Figure 20.9. This figure is a two-dimensional map of the floor you are moving around in.

Figure 20.9.
A two-dimensional map of the floor of the 3D Floor program.

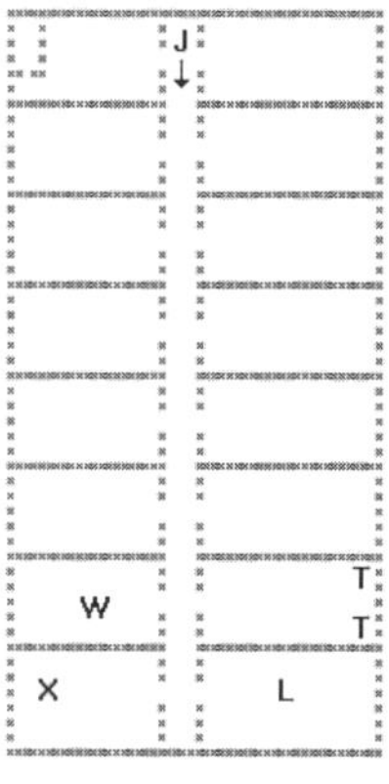

As shown in Figure 20.9, the floor of the 3D Floor program is made up of 16 rooms. The exit of each room connects to the main hall of the floor. As you can see from the figure, the room at the upper-left corner of the floor has a small subroom in it (at the upper-left corner of the room).

Figure 20.9 includes several uppercase letters on the floor. These letters represent various points on the floor where objects are (moving objects and stationary objects). Following is a description of each of these points.

Point X is the starting point of the program. This point is where you are when the program starts. Point W represents a woman who is exercising. Point J with the down arrow next to it represents a jogger who is running down the hall. The two T points represent two trees. Point L represents a light fixture (chandelier) that is attached to the ceiling.

Note: When you write your own 3D virtual reality program, the design of the floor (or floors) of the program is a very important part of the development. For example, you can develop a 3D virtual reality game in which the object of the game is to figure out the map of the floor. That is, the map of the floor is the secret of the game. After the user figures out the map of the floor (by traveling in it), the user can score more points.

As you'll see later in this chapter, designing a floor for the 3D virtual reality control is easy.

Now that you are familiar with the map of the floor of the 3D Floor program, it's time to travel on the floor.

☐ Use the arrow keys to move toward the room's exit.

Figures 20.10 through 20.14 show five snapshots of the 3D view as you get closer to the room's exit.

Figure 20.10.
Approaching the room's exit (snapshot 1).

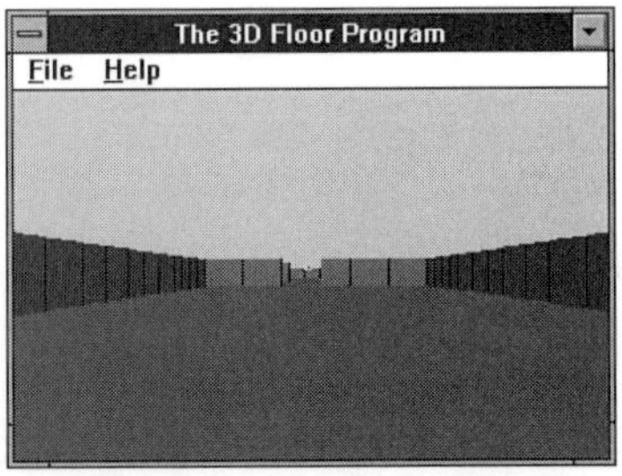

Figure 20.11.
Approaching the room's exit (snapshot 2).

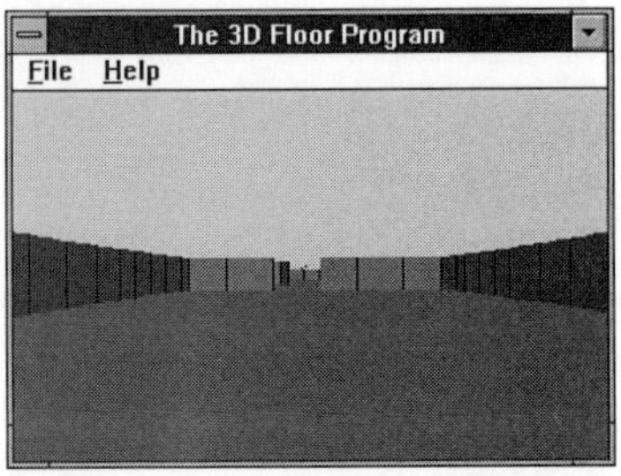

Figure 20.12.
Approaching the room's exit (snapshot 3).

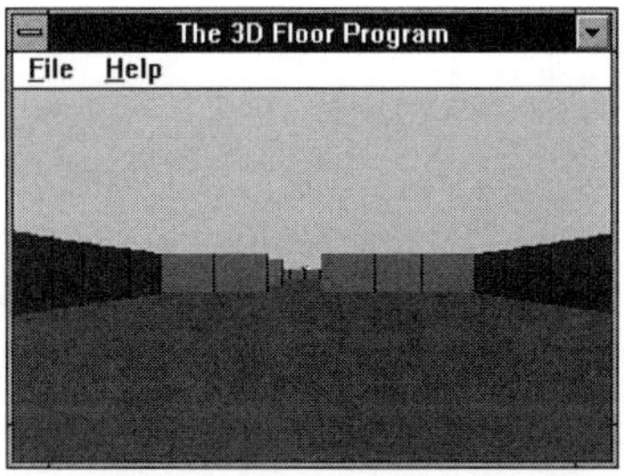

Figure 20.13.
Approaching the room's exit (snapshot 4).

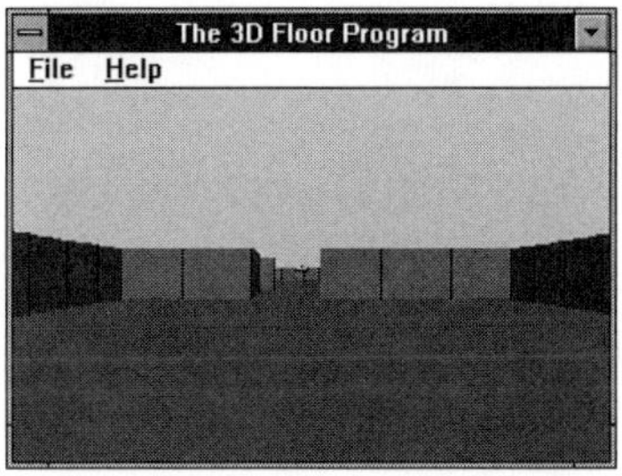

Figure 20.14.
Approaching the room's exit (snapshot 5).

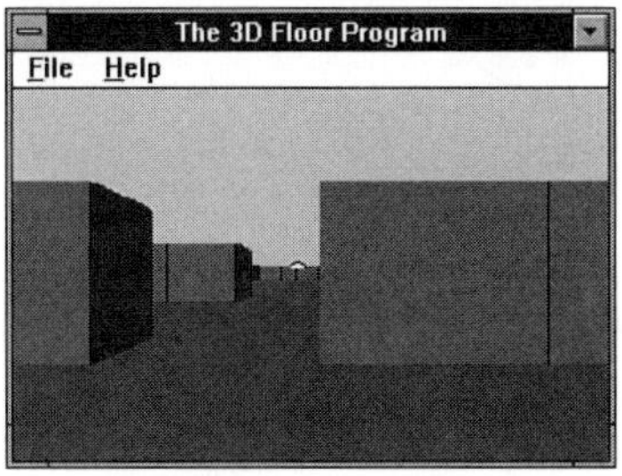

As you get closer to the exit, you start seeing more clearly the inside of the room on the other side of the hall. For example, in Figure 20.14, you can see that the room on the other side of the hall has a light fixture (chandelier) attached to the ceiling.

☐ Go out into the hall, and turn left so that you are facing the far end of the hall.

Figure 20.15 shows the 3D view when you are facing the far end of the hall.

As discussed earlier, a jogger is in the main hall. The jogger runs from the far end of the hall toward the point where you are now standing. After the jogger reaches the other side of the hall, the program places the jogger back at the far end of the hall, and the jogger runs in the same direction again.

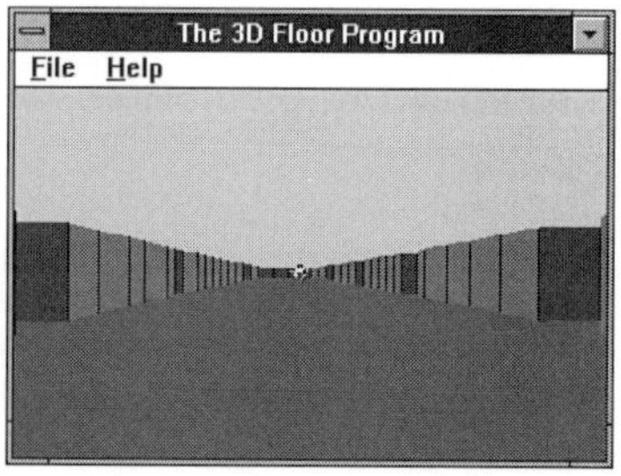

Figure 20.15.
Facing the far end of the hall.

In Figure 20.15, you can see a small image of the jogger coming in your direction. In Figure 20.15, the jogger appears small because he is still far away. Figures 20.16 through 20.20 show five snapshots of the jogger as he is approaching you.

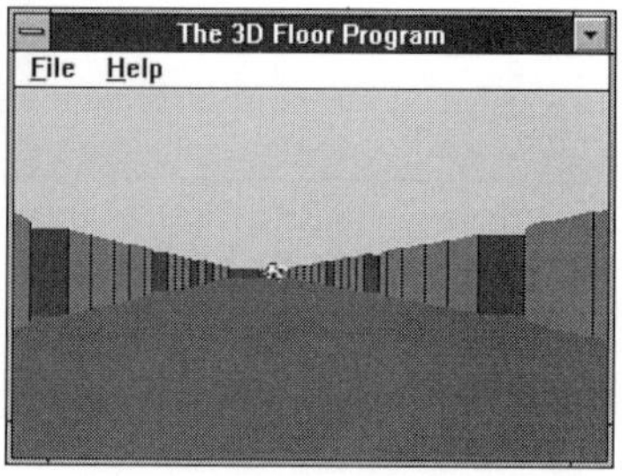

Figure 20.16.
The jogger running toward you (snapshot 1).

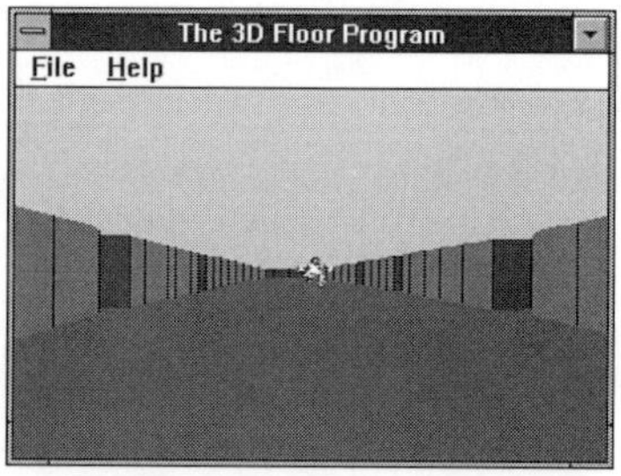

Figure 20.17.
The jogger running toward you (snapshot 2).

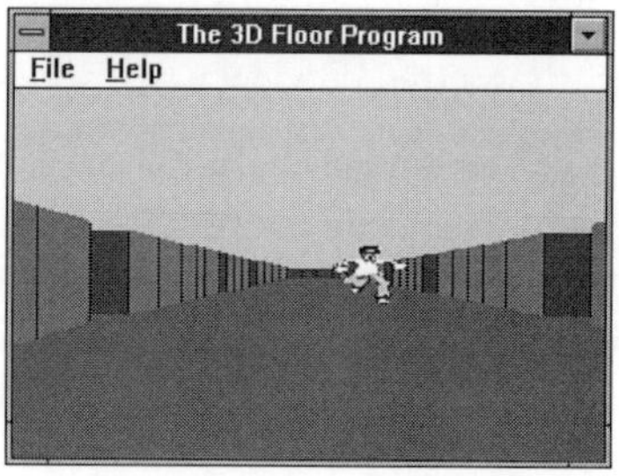

Figure 20.18.
The jogger running toward you (snapshot 3).

Figure 20.19.
The jogger running toward you (snapshot 4).

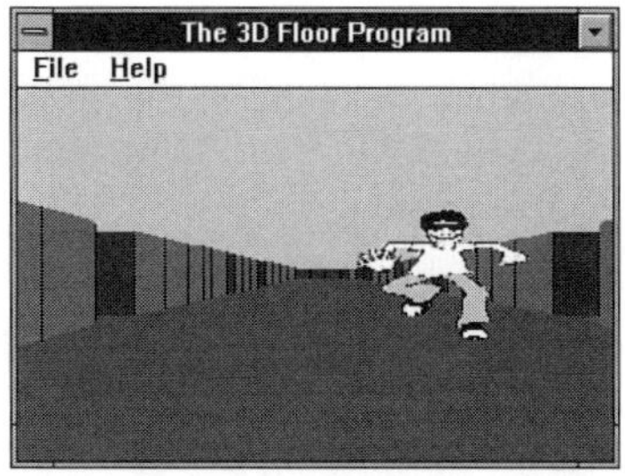

Figure 20.20.
The jogger running toward you (snapshot 5).

When the jogger is very close to you (Figure 20.20), you can see the details of his appearance. For example, you can see that he is wearing sunglasses, that he is in a good mood (he is smiling), and that he is wearing a short-sleeved shirt—you can even see the five fingers of his right hand.

Notice that the picture of the jogger is a sprite picture. That is, it has transparent regions. For example, the region between the legs of the jogger is a transparent region. Therefore, you can see through this area whatever is behind the jogger.

Notice also that the jogger's movement is an animation of two frames. In each movement, the jogger has a different foot and a different hand forward. That is, one time his left foot is forward on the floor while his right foot is in the air, and the next time his right foot is forward on the floor while his left foot is in the air. The two pictures (frames) that compose the animation of the jogger are shown in Figure 20.21.

Figure 20.21.
The two frames of the jogger's animation (when the jogger moves toward you).

After the jogger passes you, you can make a 180-degree turn (by pressing the left-arrow key or the right-arrow key for a while) so that you'll be able to see the back of the jogger as he is running away from you. Figures 20.22 through 20.24 show three snapshots of the jogger as he is running away from you.

Figure 20.22.
The jogger running away from you (snapshot 1).

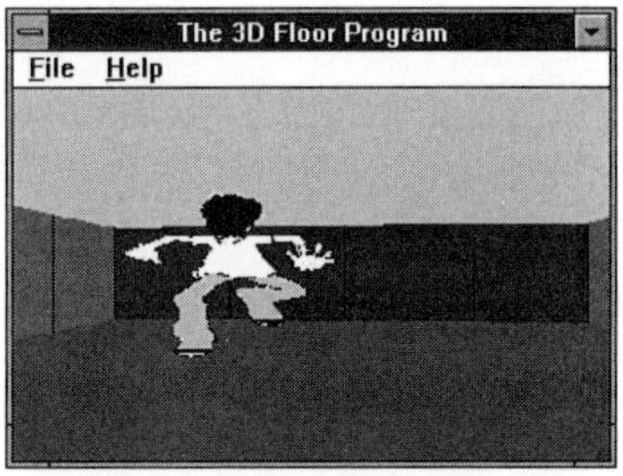

Figure 20.23.
The jogger running away from you (snapshot 2).

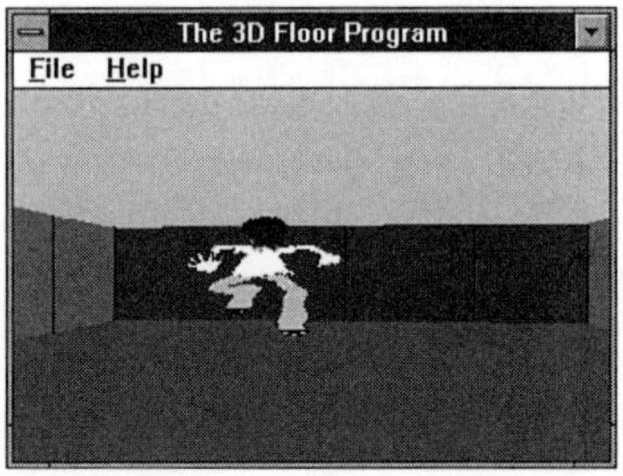

Figure 20.24.
The jogger running away from you (snapshot 3).

The animation of the jogger movement as he moves away from you is also composed of two frames. These two frames are shown in Figure 20.25.

Figure 20.25.
The two frames of the jogger's animation.

As shown back in Figure 20.9 (the two-dimensional map of the floor), the second room from the lower-left corner of the floor has a point marked with a W. As discussed earlier, this W represents the point where there is a woman exercising. Now go to the room where the woman is exercising:

☐ Move into the room where the woman is exercising.

Figures 20.26 through 20.30 show five snapshots of the exercising woman as you are approaching her.

Figure 20.26.
Moving toward the exercising woman (snapshot 1).

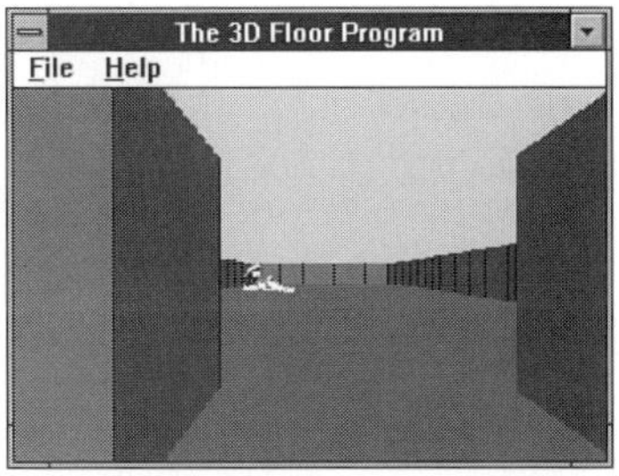

Figure 20.27.
Moving toward the exercising woman (snapshot 2).

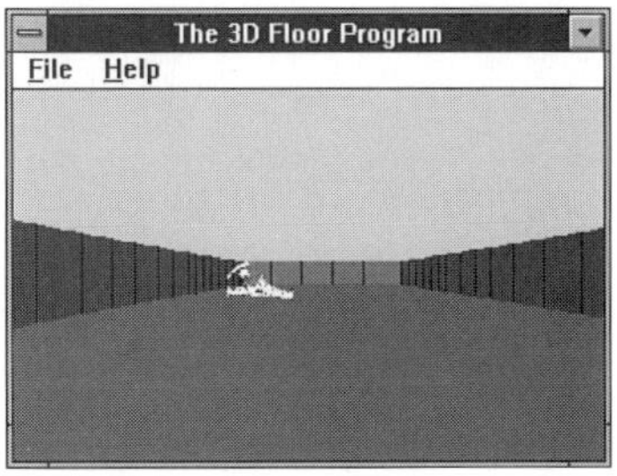

20

Figure 20.28.
Moving toward the exercising woman (snapshot 3).

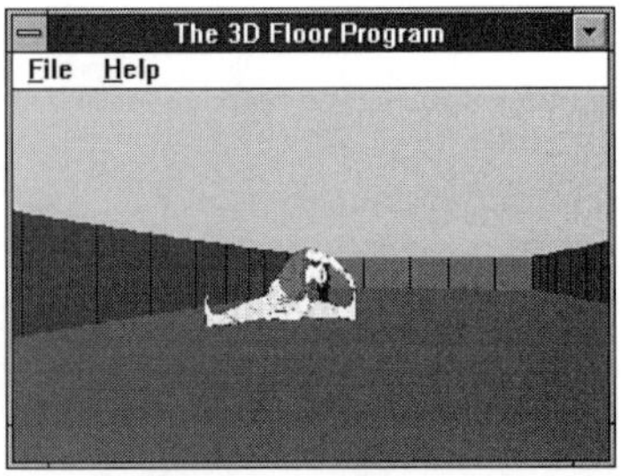

Figure 20.29.
Moving toward the exercising woman (snapshot 4).

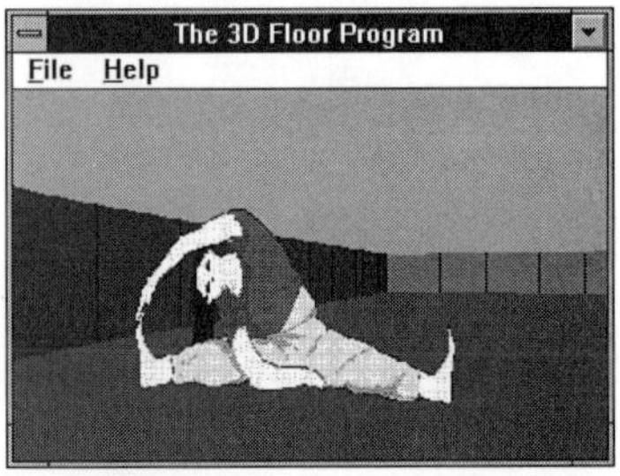

Figure 20.30.
Moving toward the exercising woman (snapshot 5).

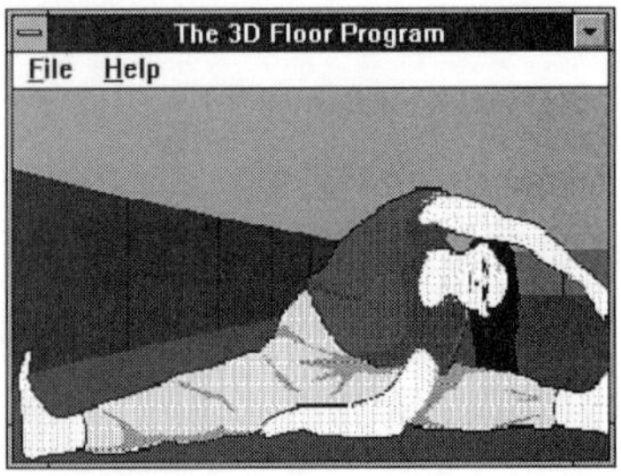

The movement of the exercising woman is an animation of two frames. These two frames are shown in Figure 20.31.

The 3D Floor program can be enhanced so that the woman's animation is composed of more frames. This way, the woman's movement will be smoother. For simplicity's sake, only two frames were included for the woman's animation.

So far, you've seen the jogger and the exercising woman. There are three more sprites you can inspect: two trees and a light fixture (a chandelier).

☐ Move into the room that contains the two trees. As shown back in Figure 20.9 (the two-dimensional map of the floor), the second room from the lower-right corner of the floor has two points marked with a T. As discussed earlier, the T represents a point where there is a tree.

Figure 20.31.
The two frames of the exercising woman animation.

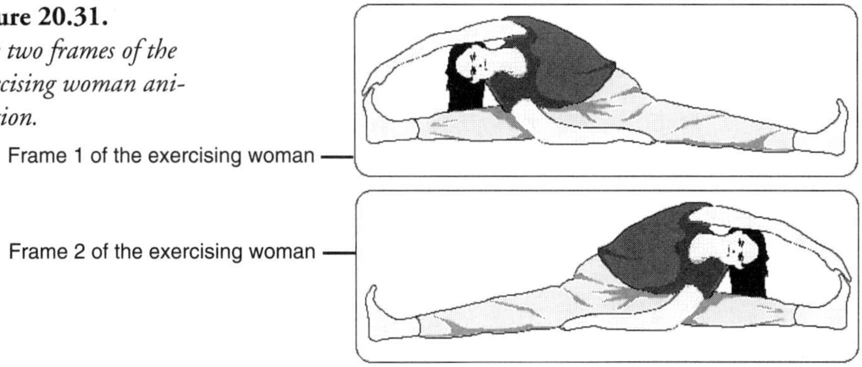

Figures 20.32 through 20.36 show five snapshots of the two trees as you move toward them.

Figure 20.32.
Moving toward the two trees (snapshot 1).

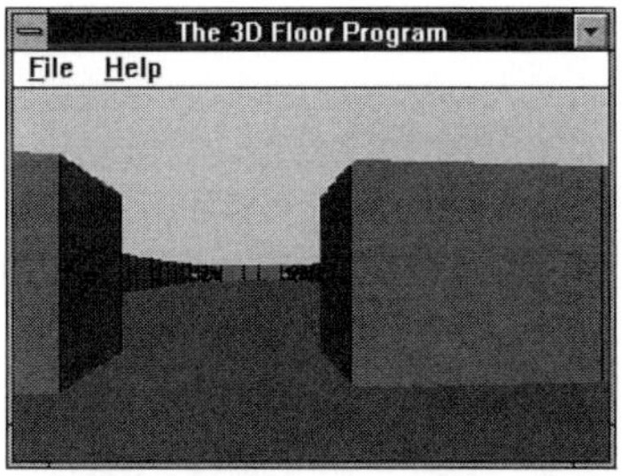

Figure 20.33.
Moving toward the two trees (snapshot 2).

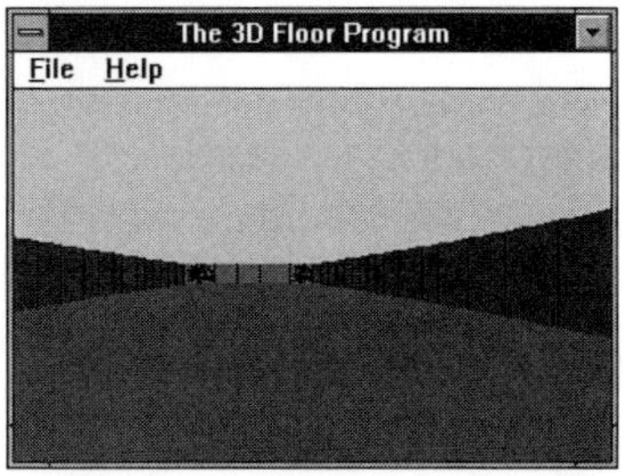

Figure 20.34.
Moving toward the two trees (snapshot 3).

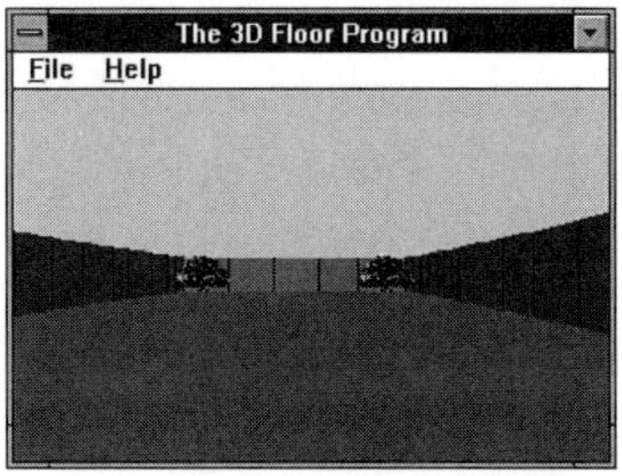

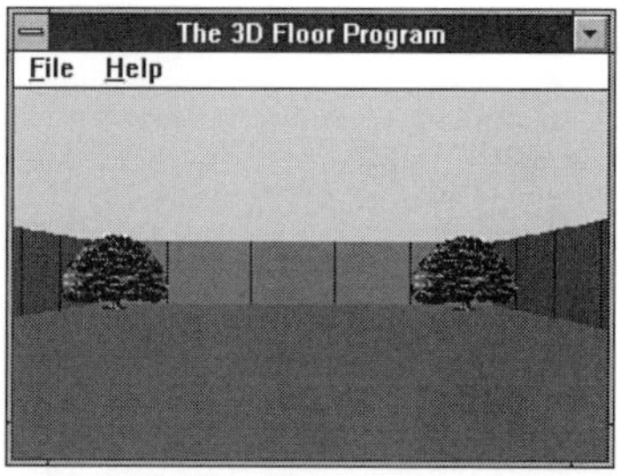

Figure 20.35.
Moving toward the two trees (snapshot 4).

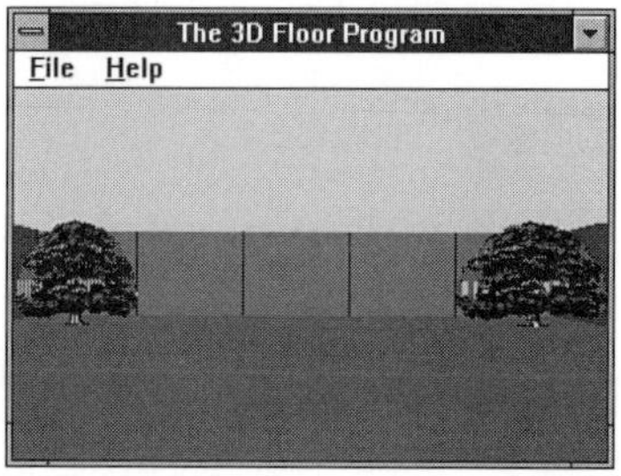

Figure 20.36.
Moving toward the two trees (snapshot 5).

Each tree is located in a different corner of the room. Figure 20.37 shows the 3D view when you get very close to one of the two trees.

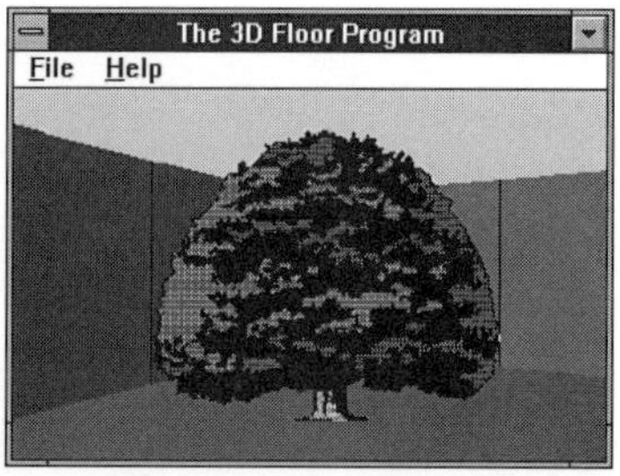

Figure 20.37.
Close to one of the two trees.

The last sprite you have not yet inspected closely is the light fixture (a chandelier). As shown back in Figure 20.9, the lower-right room of the floor has a point marked L. As discussed earlier, the L represents the point where the light fixture is located.

☐ Move into the room where the light fixture is located.

Figures 20.38 through 20.42 show five snapshots of the 3D view as you get closer to the light fixture.

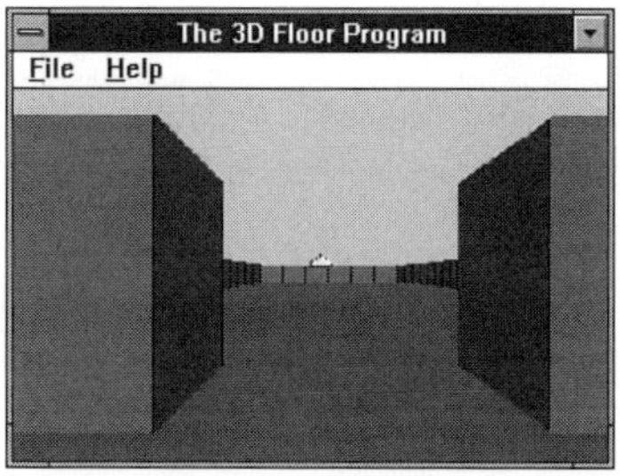

Figure 20.38.
Moving toward the light fixture (snapshot 1).

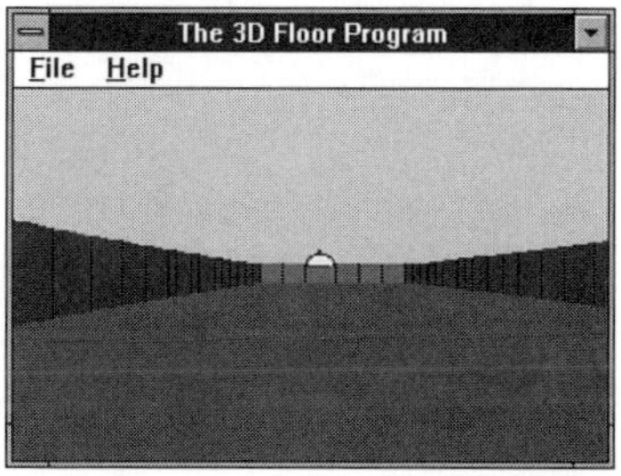

Figure 20.39.
Moving toward the light fixture (snapshot 2).

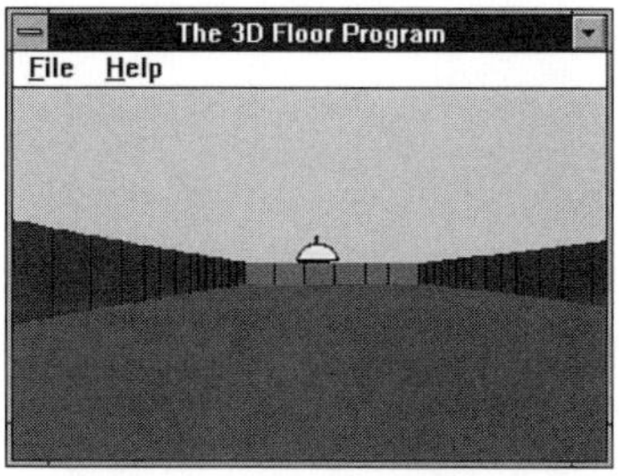

Figure 20.40.
Moving toward the light fixture (snapshot 3).

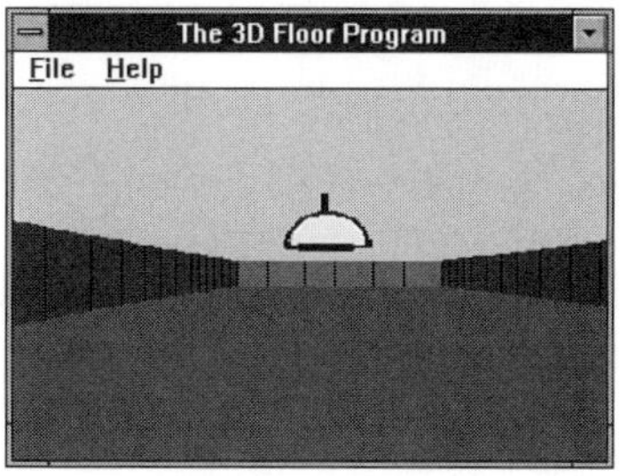

Figure 20.41.
Moving toward the light fixture (snapshot 4).

The light fixture is an example of a soft sprite. This means that you can walk through it. On the other hand, the jogger sprite, the exercising woman sprite, and the tree sprites are hard sprites. You cannot walk through the hard sprites. When you reach a hard sprite, you must walk around it.

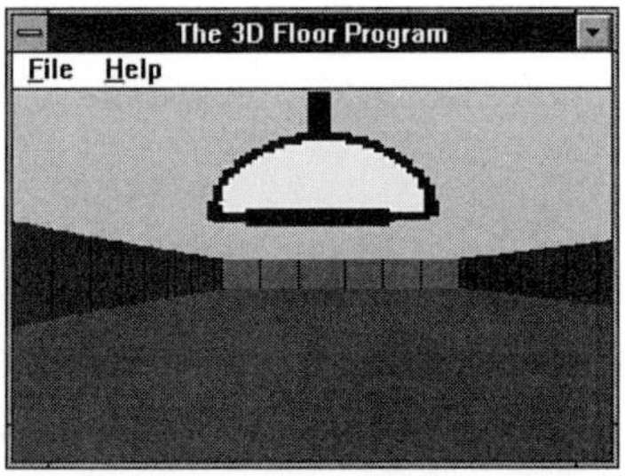

Figure 20.42.
Moving toward the light fixture (snapshot 5).

The light fixture sprite was made as a soft sprite because you should be able to walk through it. When you are exactly under the light fixture, you do not see it. Figure 20.43 shows the 3D view when you are standing under the light fixture.

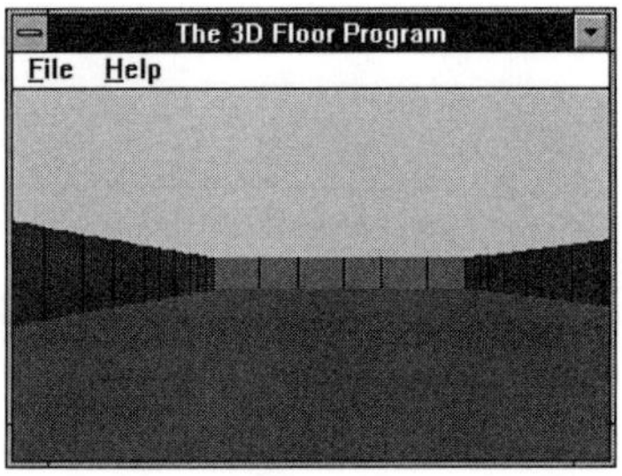

Figure 20.43.
The 3D view when you are standing under the light fixture.

As you'll see later when you write the code for the 3D Floor program, making a sprite either soft or hard is easy.

The 3D Floor program has a File menu and a Help menu. (See Figures 20.44 and 20.45.) When the user selects Exit from the File menu, the program is terminated. When the user selects About from the Help menu, the About message box shown in Figure 20.46 is displayed.

- ☐ Keep experimenting with the 3D Floor program by moving to various rooms.
- ☐ Terminate the 3D Floor program by selecting Exit from its File menu.

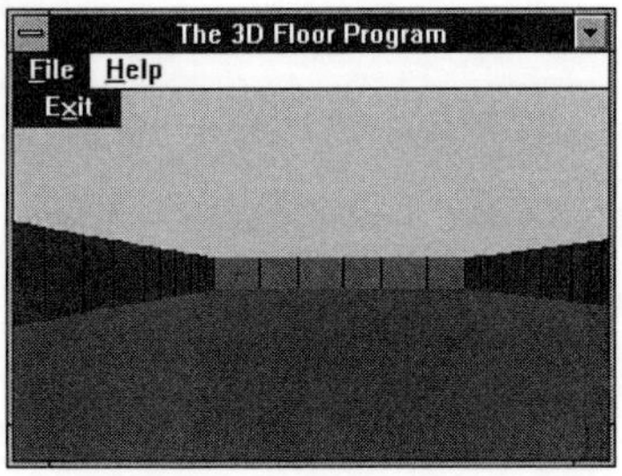

Figure 20.44.
The File menu of the 3D Floor program.

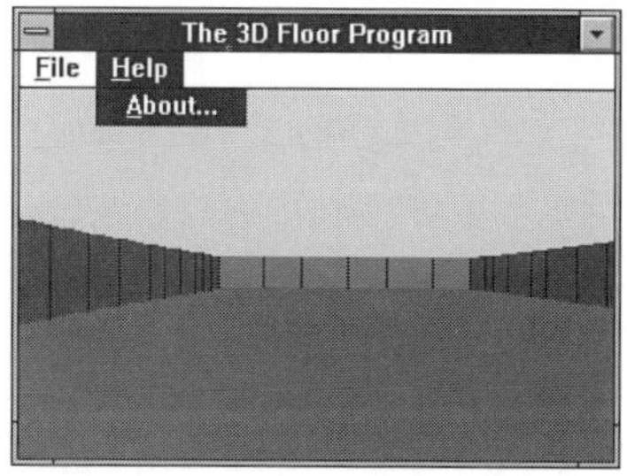

Figure 20.45.
The Help menu of the 3D Floor program.

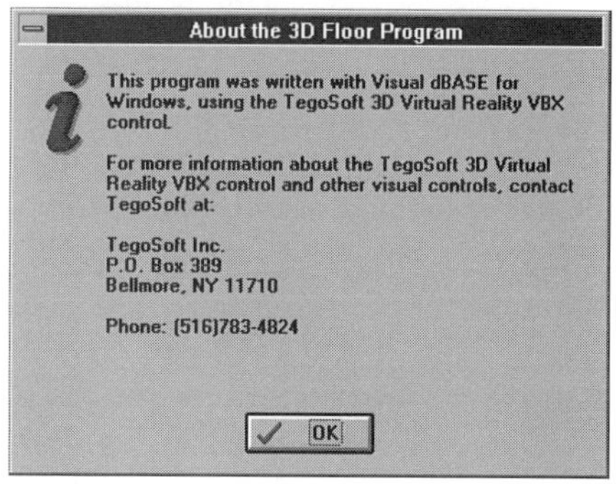

Figure 20.46.
The About message box of the 3D Floor program.

Now that you know what the 3D Floor program is supposed to do, it's time to start writing this program.

> **Note:** In the previous steps you were instructed to move around the floor by using the four arrow keys of the keyboard (the left-, right-, up-, and down-arrow keys). Another way to move around the floor is by dragging the mouse.
>
> Dragging the mouse to the left and right is equivalent to pressing the right- and left-arrow keys. It changes the viewing direction.
>
> Dragging the mouse up and down is equivalent to pressing the up- and down-arrow keys. It moves you forward or backward in the current viewing direction.
>
> Because the mouse is more sensitive than the keyboard, using the mouse for moving on the floor is not as easy as using the arrow keys. When you use the mouse, however, you can move faster.

The Visual Implementation of the 3D Floor Program

Create the 3DFloor.WFM form as instructed here:

☐ Type `MD C:\DBPROG` in the Command window, and then press Enter.

dBASE responds by creating the directory C:\DBPROG. (If this directory already exists, dBASE displays a message box telling you that the directory cannot be created.)

☐ Type `MD C:\DBPROG\CH20` in the Command window, and then press Enter.

dBASE responds by creating the directory C:\DBPROG\CH20.

☐ Type `CREATE FORM C:\DBPROG\CH20\3D Floor` in the Command window and press Enter.

dBASE responds by creating the 3DFloor.WFM form and displaying it in design mode.

The 3D Floor program uses two VBX controls:

- TEGO3DVR.VBX—A 3D virtual reality VBX control. As discussed earlier, this control is included on the disk you can order to accompany this book. (See the disk offer at the end of this book.)
- DBTIMER.VBX—A timer VBX control. This VBX control is included with Visual dBASE.

Before you can place these controls in the 3D Floor form, you must install these two VBX controls into the Control Palette of dBASE.

Follow these steps to install the TEGO3DVR.VBX control into the Control Palette of dBASE:

☐ Make sure that the file TEGO3DVR.VBX resides in your \WINDOWS\SYSTEM directory. (If the TEGO3DVR.VBX file is not in your \WINDOWS\SYSTEM directory, follow the instructions in the README.TXT file on the disk you can order to accompany this book to copy the file TEGO3DVR.VBX into your \WINDOWS\SYSTEM directory.)

☐ Select Set Up Custom Controls from the File menu of dBASE.

dBASE responds by displaying the Set Up Custom Controls dialog box. (See Figure 20.47.)

☐ Select the VBX Controls tab of the Set Up Custom Controls dialog box. (See Figure 20.48.)

☐ Click the Add button of the Set Up Custom Controls dialog box.

dBASE responds by displaying the Choose Custom Control dialog box.

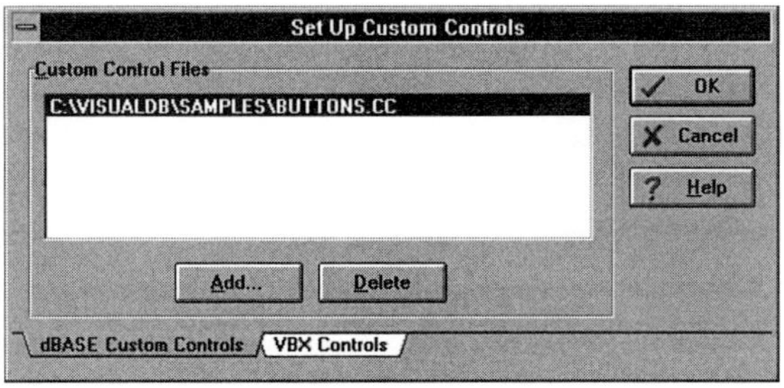

Figure 20.47.
The Set Up Custom Controls dialog box.

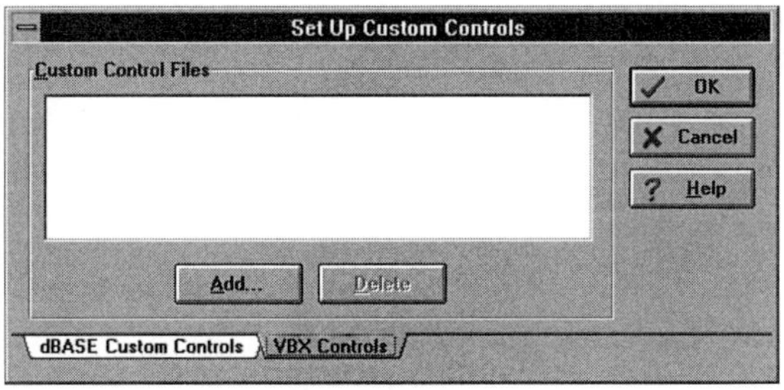

Figure 20.48.
Selecting the VBX Controls tab of the Set Up Custom Controls dialog box.

- ☐ Use the Choose Custom Control dialog box to select the VBX file C:\WINDOWS\SYSTEM\TEGO3DVR.VBX, and then click the OK button of the Choose Custom Control dialog box.
- ☐ Click the OK button of the Set Up Custom Control dialog box.

  dBASE responds by adding the TEGO3DVR.VBX control to the VBX tab of your Control Palette window.

The VBX tab of your Control Palette window should now include the icon of the TEGO3DVR.VBX control. (See Figure 20.49.)

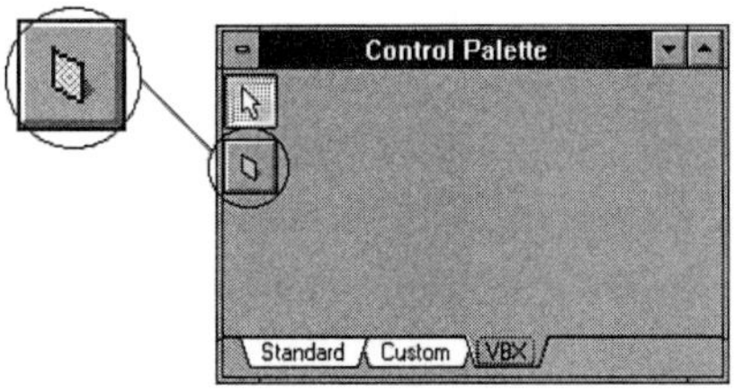

Figure 20.49.
The VBX tab of the Control Palette window with the icon of the TEGO3DVR.VBX control in it.

☐ Repeat the preceding steps to install the C:\VISUALDB\SAMPLES\DBTIMER.VBX control into the Control Palette window.

When you finish installing the DBTIMER.VBX control in the Control Palette window, the icon of the DBTIMER.VBX control should appear in the VBX tab of the Control Palette window, as shown in Figure 20.50.

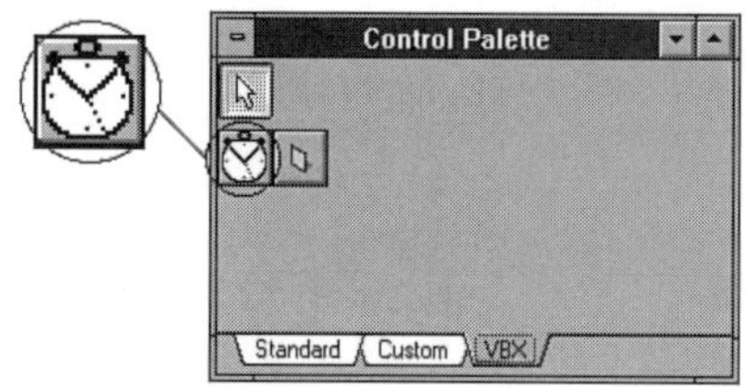

Figure 20.50.
The VBX tab of the Control Palette window with the icon of the DBTIMER.VBX control in it.

You can now visually implement the 3DFloor.WFM form:

☐ Customize the 3DFloor.WFM form according to the specifications in Table 20.1. When you finish customizing the form, it should look like the one shown in Figure 20.51.

Table 20.1. The properties table of the 3DFloor.WFM form.

Object	Property	Setting
Form	**Text**	**The 3D Floor Program**
	Height	7.44
	Left	15.17
	Top	7.69
	Width	59.50
	Maximize	.F.
	MDI	.F.
	Sizeable	.F.
Paint Box	**Name**	**PAINTBOX1**
	Height	5
	Left	0
	Top	0
	Width	8
3D Virtual Reality Control	**Name**	**TEGO3DVR1**
	Height	1.94

Object	Property	Setting
	Left	28.00
	Top	2.00
	Width	5.17
Timer Control	**Name**	**DBTIMER1**
	Enabled	.T.
	Seconds	0.4
	Height	1.75
	Left	54.00
	Top	2.00
	Width	4.67

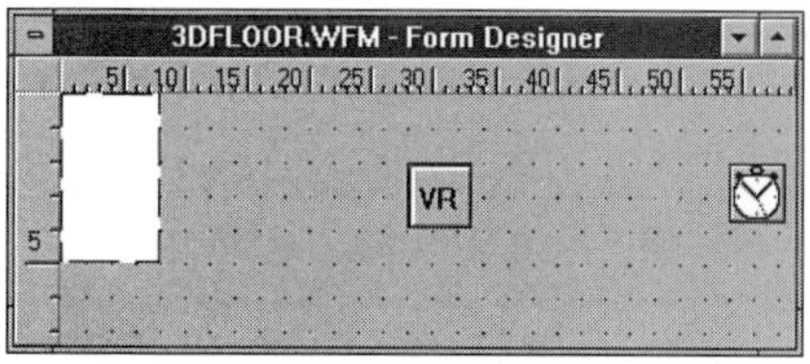

Figure 20.51.
The 3DFloor.WFM form in design mode (after customization).

☐ Save your work by selecting Save from the File menu.

Note: Table 20.1 instructs you to set the Maximize and Sizeable properties of the form to .F.. The Maximize and Sizable properties are listed under the Windows Properties item in the Inspector window. By setting the Maximize property to .F., you are specifying that the user will not be able to maximize the window. By setting the Sizable property to .F., you are specifying that the user will not be able to size the window.

Table 20.1 instructs you to place a paintbox control in the form. The icon of the paintbox control in the Control Palette window is shown in Figure 20.52.

Table 20.1 instructs you to place a 3D virtual reality control and a timer control in the form. The icons of these controls in the Control Palette window are shown back in Figures 20.49 and 20.50.

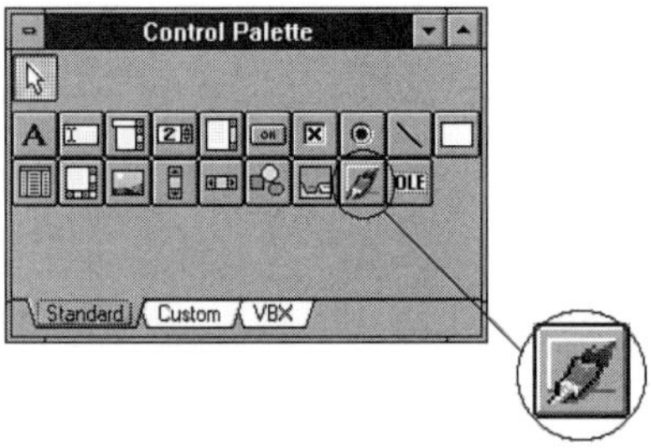

Figure 20.52.
The icon of the paintbox control in the Control Palette window.

The visual implementation of the 3DFloor.WFM form is finished.

Preparing a Floor File for the 3D Floor Program

Before you start writing the code for the 3D Floor program, you must prepare a floor file. A floor file is a text file that contains a 2D representation of a floor. After you finish preparing the floor file, you can use the 3D virtual reality VBX control to write a program that displays the floor file in 3D and enable the user to move within the 3D floor.

A floor file typically has the file extension .FLR (for example, MyFloor.FLR). Because a floor file is a regular text file, you can use any text editor to create and edit floor files.

To see how a floor file looks, carry out the following action:

☐ Use any text editor to open the floor file FLOOR50.FLR that is included on the disk you can order to accompany this book disk. (The FLOOR50.FLR floor file resides in the \DBPROG\CH20 directory of the disk.)

> **Note:** Because a floor file is a regular text file, you can use any text editor to create and edit floor files. For example, you can use the Notepad program or the Write program, both of which are shipped with Windows. The icons of Notepad and Write are usually in the Accessories program group.

Figures 20.53 and 20.54 show the Notepad program with the FLOOR50.FLR file open. The contents of the FLOOR50.FLR file are displayed in two figures because they do not fit on one Notepad screen. That is, to see the bottom section of the FLOOR50.FLR file with Notepad, you must scroll the file contents.

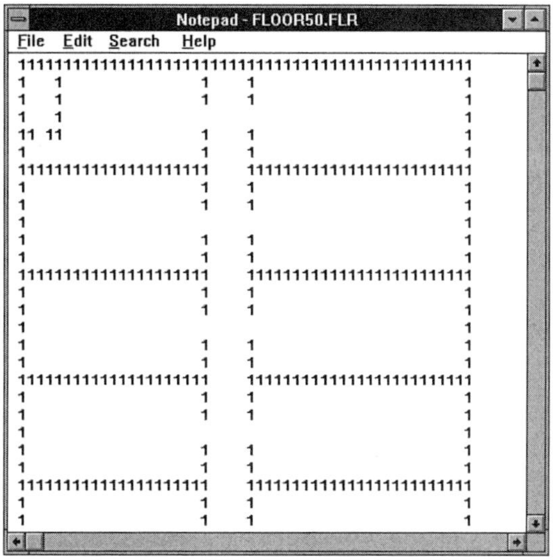

Figure 20.53.
Viewing the FLOOR50.FLR file with Notepad.

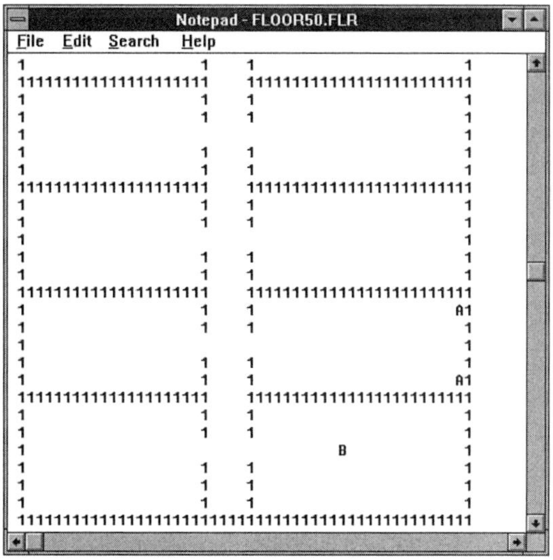

Figure 20.54.
Viewing the bottom section of the FLOOR50.FLR file with Notepad.

As you can see, a floor file is very simple. The 1 character represents a solid cell on the floor, and the space character (blank) represents an empty cell.

> **Note:** When you view a floor file with a word processor such as Word for Windows, you should set the font to Courier or Courier New. This step is necessary because you want all the characters of the FLR file (the 1s and the spaces) to be the same size.
>
> When you save the FLR file with a word processor such as Word for Windows, save it as a text file.

The following examples illustrate how to create floor files:

- To create a floor file that represents a floor with a width of 15 cells and a height of 10 cells and that contains only one room, type the following text in the floor file:

```
111111111111111
1             1
1             1
1             1
1             1
1             1
1             1
1             1
1             1
111111111111111
```

- The following text represents a floor that has a width of 20 cells and a height of 10 cells and that contains two rooms:

```
11111111111111111111
1                  1
1                  1
1                  1
1                  1
11111111  1111111111
1                  1
1                  1
1                  1
11111111111111111111
```

  As you can see, there is an opening between the two rooms. The opening is necessary because the user needs to be able to move from one room to the other. Of course, the preceding text is not the only way to create two rooms. You can rearrange the locations and sizes of the rooms in any way you want.

> **Note:** The 3D virtual reality VBX control enables you to place new cells or remove cells from the floor during runtime (from within your program). This feature of the 3D virtual reality control enables you to write game programs that have secret openings. When the user hits a secret cell, your program can remove the cell so that the user will be able to move into a secret room.

- The following text represents a floor that has a width of 20 cells and a height of 15 cells and that contains four rooms:

```
11111111111111111111
1        1         1
1        1         1
1        1         1
1        1         1
1111  11111111  1111
1        1         1
1                  1
1        1         1
11111111111111111111
```

  In addition to 1s and spaces, a floor file can also contain non-numeric characters (for example, A, B, C, a, b, c). These characters represent sprites. The pictures of these sprites are set during runtime from within your program. For example, your program might set the B sprite to a picture of a chair. Therefore, all cells in the FLR file that contain the letter B will display a chair.

Now that you know how a floor file is constructed, inspect the Floor50.FLR file with your text editor. (See Figures 20.53 and 20.54.) When you inspect the Floor50.FLR file, notice the following aspects:

- The width of the Floor50.FLR file is 50 cells, and the height of the file is also 50 cells.
- The floor file contains 16 rooms. Each of these rooms is connected to the main hall of the floor.
- The upper-left room contains a small subroom.
- The lower-right room contains the letter B in the middle of the room. (See Figure 20.54.) The B represents a sprite. When you write the code for the 3D Floor program, you will define sprite B as a picture of a light fixture (a chandelier). Therefore, when the user moves into the lower-right room, the user will see a light fixture in the middle of the room.
- The room above the lower-right room contains the letter A in two corners of the room. (See Figure 20.54.) The A represents a sprite. When you write the code for the 3D Floor program, you will define sprite A as a picture of a tree. Therefore, when the user moves into the room that contains the two A sprites, the user will see two trees.

Entering the Code of the 3D Floor Program

In the following sections you will write the code for the 3D Floor program. This code will use the FLOOR50.FLR floor file. Therefore, you need to copy the FLOOR50.FLR file from the disk you can order to accompany this book onto your hard drive:

☐ Copy the \DBPROG\CH20\FLOOR50.FLR file from the disk you can order to accompany this book into your C:\DBPROG\CH20 directory.

Attaching Code to the *OnOpen* Event of the 3DFloor.WFM Form

As you know, the `OnOpen` event of a form occurs when the form is first opened. The `OnOpen` event of the form is therefore a good place to write initialization code for the form.

The code you will next attach to the `OnOpen` event will open the FLOOR50.FLR floor file.

☐ Attach the following code to the `OnOpen` event of the 3DFloor.WFM form. After you write this code, the `Form_OnOpen` procedure should look as follows:

```
Procedure Form_OnOpen

* Declare and initialize global variables.
Public gPrevX, gPrevY
gPrevX = 0
gPrevY = 0

* Make the Tego3DVR1 control invisible.
form.Tego3DVR1.Visible = .F.

* Get the name of the directory where the
* program resides.
Path = LEFT(PROGRAM(0),RAT("\",PROGRAM(0)))

* Open the FLOOR50.FLR file.
form.Tego3DVR1.FileName = Path + "FLOOR50.FLR"
form.Tego3DVR1.hWndDisplay = form.Paintbox1.hWnd
form.Tego3DVR1.NumOfRows = 50
form.Tego3DVR1.NumOfCols = 50
form.Tego3DVR1.Command = "Open"

* If the FLR file could not be opened, terminate
* the program.
OpenResult = form.Tego3DVR1.ErrorCode
If OpenResult <> 0
   Message="Unable to open file: "+form.Tego3DVR1.FileName
   Message=Message + Chr(13) + Chr(10)
   Message=Message + "Error Code: " + Str(OpenResult)
   MsgBox (Message, "Error")
   form.Close()
EndIf
```

```
* Set the initial user's position and viewing angle.
form.Tego3DVR1.PixelPosX = 4 * form.Tego3DVR1.CellWidth
form.Tego3DVR1.PixelPosY = 4 * form.Tego3DVR1.CellWidth
form.Tego3DVR1.Angle = 0

* Set the StepSize property to 50.
form.Tego3DVR1.StepSize = 50

* Set the colors of the walls, ceiling, and floor.
form.Tego3DVR1.WallColorA = 7    && White
form.Tego3DVR1.WallColorB = 4    && Red
form.Tego3DVR1.CeilingColor = 11 && Light Cyan
form.Tego3DVR1.FloorColor = 2    && Green
form.Tego3DVR1.StripeColor = 0   && Black

Return
```

Note: The 3DFloor.WFM form uses two global (public) variables called `gPrevX` and `gPrevY`. Because these variables are declared as public, they will be visible in all the procedures of the form.

An alternate way to make variables visible in all the procedures of the form is to make the variables custom form properties.

Currently, `gPrevX` and `gPrevY` are declared and initialized in the `Form_OnOpen()` procedure as follows:

```
* Declare and initialize global variables.
Public gPrevX, gPrevY
gPrevX = 0
gPrevY = 0
```

You can make `gPrevX` and `gPrevY` custom form properties by modifying the `Form_OnOpen()` procedure as follows:

- ☐ Remove the statement

  ```
  Public gPrevX, gPrevY
  ```

- ☐ Change these statements:

  ```
  gPrevX = 0
  gPrevY = 0
  ```

  to this:

  ```
  Form.gPrevX = 0
  Form.gPrevY = 0
  ```

From now on, all the procedures of the form can refer to these variables as `Form.gPrevX` and `Form.gPrevY`.

20

☐ Save your work by selecting Save from the File menu.

The first three statements you typed in the `Form_OnOpen` procedure declare and initialize two public variables (`gPrevX` and `gPrevY`):

```
Public gPrevX, gPrevY
gPrevX = 0
gPrevY = 0
```

The purpose of these public variables is discussed later in this chapter.

The next statement:

```
form.Tego3DVR1.Visible = .F.
```

makes the Tego3DVR1 control (the 3D virtual reality control) invisible. You can make the 3D virtual reality control invisible because, as you'll soon see, the 3D pictures that the 3D virtual reality control displays are not displayed in the 3D virtual reality control.

The next statement:

```
Path = LEFT(PROGRAM(0),RAT("\",PROGRAM(0)))
```

fills the local variable `Path` with the name of the directory where the program resides. For example, if the program resides in the C:\DBPROG\CH20 directory, then after the preceding statement is executed, the variable `Path` will be filled with the string `"C:\DBPROG\CH20\"`. Subsequent statements in the procedure use the `Path` variable to determine in which directory the FLOOR50.FLR floor file resides. That is, the FLOOR50.FLR file is assumed to be in the same directory where the program resides.

The next five statements are responsible for opening the FLOOR50.FLR floor file:

```
* Open the FLOOR50.FLR file.
form.Tego3DVR1.FileName = Path + "FLOOR50.FLR"
form.Tego3DVR1.hWndDisplay = form.Paintbox1.hWnd
form.Tego3DVR1.NumOfRows = 50
form.Tego3DVR1.NumOfCols = 50
form.Tego3DVR1.Command = "Open"
```

The first statement:

```
form.Tego3DVR1.FileName = Path + "FLOOR50.FLR"
```

sets the FileName property of the 3D virtual reality control to the name of the FLOOR50.FLR floor file. The FileName property of the 3D virtual reality control specifies which floor file you want to open.

The second statement:

```
form.Tego3DVR1.hWndDisplay = form.Paintbox1.hWnd
```

sets the hWndDisplay property of the 3D virtual reality control to the window handle of the Paintbox1 paintbox control. The hWndDisplay property of the 3D virtual reality control specifies the handle of the window where the 3D graphics will be displayed. Because you want the 3D graphics to be displayed in the Paintbox1 paintbox control, you set the hWndDisplay property to the hWnd property of the Paintbox1 paintbox control.

Note: By setting the hWndDisplay property of the 3D virtual reality control to the hWnd property of the Paintbox1 paintbox control, you are specifying that the 3D graphics to be displayed by the 3D virtual reality control will be displayed in the Paintbox1 paintbox control.

You don't have to concern yourself with the width and height of the paintbox control. When the 3D virtual reality control displays the 3D graphics in the paintbox control, the 3D virtual reality control will automatically set the width and height of the paintbox control to the appropriate size.

These are the next two statements:

```
form.Tego3DVR1.NumOfRows = 50
form.Tego3DVR1.NumOfCols = 50
```

These statements set the NumOfRows and NumOfCols properties of the 3D virtual reality control to 50. The NumOfRows property specifies the height of the floor file in units of cells, and the NumOfCols property specifies the width of the floor file in units of cells. (Recall that when you inspected the FLOOR50.FLR file, you saw that both the width and the height of this floor file are 50 cells.)

Finally, an `Open` command is issued to the 3D virtual reality control to open the FLOOR50.FLR file:

```
form.Tego3DVR1.Command = "Open"
```

The `Open` command opens the floor file specified by the FileName property of the 3D virtual reality control.

The next block of statements evaluates the ErrorCode property of the 3D virtual reality control to see whether the floor file was opened successfully:

```
* If the FLR file could not be opened, terminate
* the program.
OpenResult = form.Tego3DVR1.ErrorCode
If OpenResult <> 0
   Message="Unable to open file: "+form.Tego3DVR1.FileName
   Message=Message + Chr(13) + Chr(10)
   Message=Message + "Error Code: " + Str(OpenResult)
   MsgBox (Message, "Error")
   form.Close()
EndIf
```

If the last issued command (that is, the `Open` command) failed, the condition of the preceding `If` statement will be satisfied, and the statements under the `If` will display an error message box and terminate the program.

> **Note:** To open a floor file, you first must set the FileName, hWndDisplay, NumOfRows, and NumOfCols properties of the 3D virtual reality control, and then issue an `Open` command to the 3D virtual reality control.
>
> The NumOfRows and NumOfCols properties of the 3D virtual reality control must be set to the correct height and width of the floor file. If you do not set the NumOfCols and NumOfRows properties to the correct values, the `Open` command will fail.
>
> After issuing an `Open` command, you can use the ErrorCode of the 3D virtual reality control to determine whether the `Open` command succeeded. If the ErrorCode property is 0, the `Open` command was issued successfully. If, however, the ErrorCode property is not 0, the `Open` command failed.

These are the next three statements:

```
* Set the initial user's position and viewing angle.
form.Tego3DVR1.PixelPosX = 4 * form.Tego3DVR1.CellWidth
form.Tego3DVR1.PixelPosY = 4 * form.Tego3DVR1.CellWidth
form.Tego3DVR1.Angle = 0
```

These statements set the initial position and viewing direction of the user.

You set the position of the user by setting the PixelPosX and PixelPosY properties of the 3D virtual reality control. The PixelPosX and PixelPosY properties determine the x,y coordinate of the user's position in units of pixels. The lower-left corner of the floor is at the x,y coordinate x=0, y=0. In the preceding code both the PixelPosX property and the PixelPosY property are set to this:

```
4 * form.Tego3DVR1.CellWidth
```

The CellWidth property of the 3D virtual reality control reports the width (in units of pixels) of one cell. The preceding code therefore places the user at the cell that is fourth from the bottom of the floor and fourth from the left side of the floor. If you inspect the bottom section of the FLOOR50.FLR file (see Figure 20.54), you'll see that the cell that is fourth from the bottom of the floor and fourth from the left of the floor is in the lower-left room of the floor. When starting the program, therefore, the user will be in the lower-left room of the floor.

The Angle property of the 3D virtual reality control specifies the viewing direction of the user in units of degrees. The Angle property can be set to an integer in the range of 0 through 359.

When you want the user to face the right side of the floor, you must set the Angle property to 0. In the preceding code you set the Angle property of the 3D virtual reality control to 0 because when the program starts, you want the user to face the exit of the lower-left room of the floor.

> **Note:** When the program starts, you must place the user somewhere on the floor by setting the PixelPosX and PixelPosY properties of the 3D virtual reality control. Be sure to place the user in an empty cell. That is, you don't want to place the user in a wall.

This is the next statement:

```
form.Tego3DVR1.StepSize = 50
```

This statement sets the StepSize property of the 3D virtual reality control to 50. As implied by its name, the StepSize property determines the step size of the user movements. By setting the StepSize property to 50 you are specifying that when the user moves forward (or backward) on the floor, the user will move 50 pixels in each step.

> **Note:** When you set the StepSize property, do not set it to a value greater than the value of the CellWidth Property. If you set the StepSize property to a value greater than the value of the CellWidth property, the user will be able to jump over walls. The default value of the CellWidth property is 65.

These are the last five statements you typed in the `Form_OnOpen` procedure:

```
* Set the colors of the walls, ceiling, and floor.
form.Tego3DVR1.WallColorA = 7    && White
form.Tego3DVR1.WallColorB = 4    && Red
form.Tego3DVR1.CeilingColor = 11 && Light Cyan
form.Tego3DVR1.FloorColor = 2    && Green
form.Tego3DVR1.StripeColor = 0   && Black
```

These statements set the colors of the walls, ceiling, and floor of the floor. The WallColorA property specifies the color of the vertical walls of the floor, the WallColorB property specifies the color of the horizontal walls, the CeilingColor property specifies the color of the ceiling, the FloorColor property specifies the color of the floor, and the StripeColor property specifies the color of the vertical stripes that separate cells. Table 20.2 lists all the possible values you can specify for the color properties of the 3D virtual reality control.

Table 20.2. The values you can assign to the Color properties of the 3D virtual reality control.

Value	Color
0	Black
1	Blue
2	Green
3	Cyan
4	Red
5	Magenta
6	Yellow
7	White
8	Gray
9	Light blue
10	Light green
11	Light cyan
12	Light red
13	Light magenta
14	Light yellow
15	Bright white

The code you typed in the `Form_OnOpen` procedure is responsible for opening the floor file. In the following section you'll write the code that actually displays the 3D floor.

Attaching Code to the *OnPaint* Event of the Paintbox Control

The `OnPaint` event of the paintbox control occurs when there is a need to redraw the paintbox control (for example, when the program is started). When there is a need to redraw the paintbox control, the program should draw the current 3D view of the floor. You'll next write the code that accomplishes this task.

☐ Attach the following code to the `OnPaint` event of the PAINTBOX1 paintbox control. After you write this code, the `PAINTBOX1_OnPaint` procedure should look as follows:

```
Procedure PAINTBOX1_OnPaint

* Set the width and height of the form to the same size as
* the paintbox control.
```

```
form.height = form.paintbox1.height
form.width  = form.paintbox1.width

* Display the 3D view.
form.Tego3DVR1.Command = "Display3D"

Return
```

☐ Save your work by selecting Save from the File menu.

These are the first two statements you typed in the `PAINTBOX1_OnPaint` procedure:

```
form.height = form.paintbox1.height
form.width  = form.paintbox1.width
```

These statements set the width and height of the form to the same size as the paintbox control. As stated earlier, the 3D virtual reality control will automatically size the paintbox control to the same size as the 3D picture. The preceding two statements therefore set the size of the form to the same size as the 3D picture.

The last statement you typed in the `PAINTBOX1_OnPaint` procedure is this:

```
form.Tego3DVR1.Command = "Display3D"
```

This statement displays the current 3D view of the floor by issuing a `Display3D` command to the 3D virtual reality control. The `Display3D` command displays the current 3D view of the floor based on the values of the PixelPosX, PixelPosY, and Angle properties of the 3D virtual reality control. (Recall that you initialized the PixelPosX, PixelPosY, and Angle properties of the 3D virtual reality control in the `Form_OnOpen` procedure.)

To see the code you have written so far in action, follow these steps:

☐ Execute the 3D Floor program by pressing the F2 key.

As you can see, the program displays a 3D view of the floor. (See Figure 20.55.) The program placed you in the lower-left room of the floor, and you are currently facing the room's exit.

20

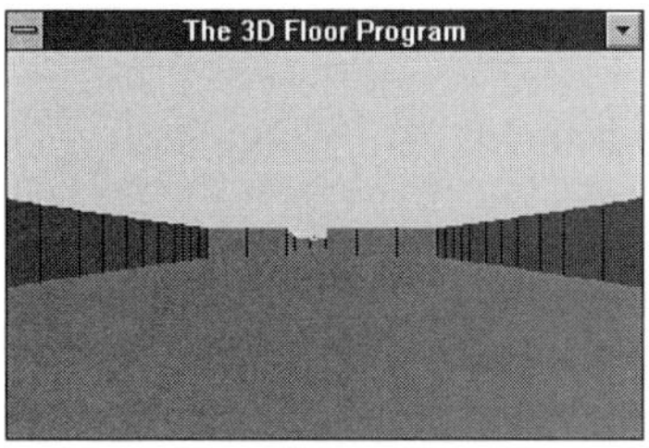

Figure 20.55.
The initial 3D view that the 3D Floor program displays.

Of course, if you try to move on the floor (by pressing the arrow keys), nothing will happen, because you have not yet written the code that accomplishes this task.

- ☐ Terminate the 3D Floor program by pressing Alt+F4 on your keyboard (or by double-clicking the minus icon at the upper-left corner of the program's window).

In the following section you'll write the code that enables the user to move on the floor.

Attaching Code to the *OnKeyDown* Event of the Paintbox Control

You'll next attach code to the `OnKeyDown` event of the PAINTBOX1 paintbox control. The `OnKeyDown` event of the paintbox control occurs when the user presses a key on the keyboard while the paintbox control has the keyboard focus. In the 3D Floor program the PAINTBOX1 paintbox control always has the keyboard focus because this is the only visible control in the program's window. (The other two controls, the 3D virtual reality control and the timer control, are invisible.)

The code you'll next attach to the `OnKeyDown` event of the PAINTBOX1 paintbox control will enable the user to move on the 3D floor by using the left-, right-, up-, and down-arrow keys.

- ☐ Type `MODIFY FORM ?` in the Command window, press Enter, and then select the file C:\DBPROG\CH20\3DFloor.WFM from the Open Form dialog box that dBASE displays.

  dBASE responds by displaying the 3DFloor.WFM form in design mode.

- ☐ Attach the following code to the `OnKeyDown` event of the PAINTBOX1 paintbox control. After you write this code, the `PAINTBOX1_OnKeyDown()` procedure should look as follows:

```
Procedure PAINTBOX1_OnKeyDown(nChar, nRepCnt, nFlags)

DO CASE

   CASE nChar=37 .OR. nChar= 100
        * Left key (37) or 4 key (100) was pressed.
        form.Tego3DVR1.Angle = form.Tego3DVR1.Angle + 6

   CASE nChar=39 .OR. nChar=102
        * Right key (39) or 6 key (102) was pressed.
        form.Tego3DVR1.Angle = form.Tego3DVR1.Angle - 6

   CASE nChar=38 .OR. nChar=104
        * Up key (38) or 8 key (104) was pressed.
        form.Tego3DVR1.Command = "Step"

   Case nChar=40 .OR. nChar=98
        * Down key (40) or 2 key (98) was pressed.
        form.Tego3DVR1.Command = "Back"

ENDCASE
```

```
* Display the 3D view.
form.Tego3DVR1.Command = "Display3D"

Return
```

☐ Save your work by selecting Save from the File menu.

The `nChar` parameter of the `PAINTBOX1_OnKeyDown()` procedure specifies which key the user pressed. The code you typed in the `PAINTBOX1_OnKeyDown()` procedure uses a `DO CASE` statement to evaluate the `nChar` parameter:

```
DO CASE

   CASE nChar=37 .OR. nChar= 100
        * Left key (37) or 4 key (100) was pressed.
        form.Tego3DVR1.Angle = form.Tego3DVR1.Angle + 6

   CASE nChar=39 .OR. nChar=102
        * Right key (39) or 6 key (102) was pressed.
        form.Tego3DVR1.Angle = form.Tego3DVR1.Angle - 6

   CASE nChar=38 .OR. nChar=104
        * Up key (38) or 8 key (104) was pressed.
        form.Tego3DVR1.Command = "Step"

   CASE nChar=40 .OR. nChar=98
        * Down key (40) or 2 key (98) was pressed.
        form.Tego3DVR1.Command = "Back"

ENDCASE
```

If the user pressed the left-arrow key (or the 4 key), the statement under the first `CASE` is executed:

```
form.Tego3DVR1.Angle = form.Tego3DVR1.Angle + 6
```

This statement increases the Angle property of the 3D virtual reality control by 6 degrees. If the Angle property is set to a value greater than 359, the 3D virtual reality control automatically adjusts the value of the Angle property to a value in the range of 0 through 359. For example, if the current value of the Angle property is 358, the preceding statement will set the Angle property to 4 (because 358+6 is 364, and 364 degrees is the same as 4 degrees).

If the user pressed the right-arrow key (or the 6 key), the statement under the second `CASE` is executed:

```
form.Tego3DVR1.Angle = form.Tego3DVR1.Angle - 6
```

This statement decreases the Angle property of the 3D virtual reality control by 6 degrees. If the Angle property is set to a value less than 0, the 3D virtual reality control automatically adjusts the value of the Angle property to a value in the range of 0 through 359. For example, if the current value of the Angle property is 5, the preceding statement will set the Angle property to 359 (because 5–6 is –1, and –1 degrees is the same as 359 degrees).

If the user pressed the up-arrow key (or the 8 key), the statement under the third `CASE` is executed:

```
form.Tego3DVR1.Command = "Step"
```

This statement issues a `Step` command to the 3D virtual reality control to advance the user's position forward in the current viewing direction. Because in the `Form_OnOpen` procedure you set the StepSize property of the 3D virtual reality control to 50, the preceding statement moves the user 50 pixels forward in the current viewing direction.

If the user pressed the down-arrow key (or the 2 key), the statement under the fourth `CASE` is executed:

```
form.Tego3DVR1.Command = "Back"
```

This statement issues a `Back` command to the 3D virtual reality control to move the user backward in the current viewing direction. Because in the `Form_OnOpen` procedure you set the StepSize property of the 3D virtual reality control to 50, the preceding statement moves the user 50 pixels backward in the current viewing direction.

The last statement you typed in the `PAINTBOX1_OnKeyDown()` procedure is this:

```
form.Tego3DVR1.Command = "Display3D"
```

This statement issues a `Display3D` command to the 3D virtual reality control to display the new 3D view that corresponds to the new position of the user.

To see the code you attached to the `OnKeyDown` event of the PAINTBOX1 paintbox control in action, follow these steps:

- ☐ Execute the 3D Floor program by pressing the F2 key.
- ☐ Use the left-, right-, up-, and down-arrow keys to move to various locations on the floor and verify that the arrow keys work properly.
- ☐ Terminate the 3D Floor program by pressing Alt+F4 on your keyboard (or by double-clicking the minus icon at the upper-left corner of the program's window).

Note: As you move on the floor, notice that at this point there aren't any sprites on the floor. In the next chapter you'll write the code that places sprites on the floor.

Attaching Code to the *OnMouseMove* Event of the Paintbox Control

At this point, the user can move on the 3D floor by using the arrow keys. You'll now add code to the program so that the user will also be able to use the mouse for moving on the 3D floor.

The code you'll now attach to the `PAINTBOX1_OnMouseMove()` procedure will enable the user to move on the floor by dragging the mouse over the form. Dragging the mouse to the left and right produces the same results as pressing the left- and right-arrow keys. That is, it changes the viewing direction. Dragging the mouse up and down produces the same results as pressing the up- and down-arrow keys. That is, it moves the user forward or backward in the current viewing direction.

☐ Display the 3DFloor.WFM form in design mode.

☐ Attach the following code to the `OnMouseMove` event of the PAINTBOX1 paintbox control. After you write this code, the `PAINTBOX1_OnMouseMove()` procedure should look as follows:

```
Procedure PAINTBOX1_OnMouseMove(flags, col, row)

* If none of the mouse buttons is pressed down,
* terminate this procedure.
IF flags = 0
   Return
ENDIF

* Change the user's position according to the
* mouse movement.
IF row < gPrevY
   form.Tego3DVR1.Command = "Step"
ENDIF
IF row > gPrevY
  form.Tego3DVR1.Command = "Back"
ENDIF
IF col < gPrevX
   form.Tego3DVR1.Angle = form.Tego3DVR1.Angle + 3
ENDIF
IF col > gPrevX
   form.Tego3DVR1.Angle = form.Tego3DVR1.Angle - 3
ENDIF

* Display the 3D view.
form.Tego3DVR1.Command = "Display3D"

* Update gPrevX and gPrevY for next time.
gPrevX = col
gPrevY = row

Return
```

☐ Save your work by selecting Save from the File menu.

The first statement you typed in the `PAINTBOX1_OnMouseMove()` procedure is an `IF` statement:

```
IF flags = 0
   Return
ENDIF
```

This `IF` statement evaluates the value of the parameter `flags` of the `PAINTBOX1_OnMouseMove()` procedure. If `flags` is equal to 0, none of the mouse buttons is currently pressed (that is, the user is not dragging the mouse). If this is the case, the preceding `IF` statement terminates the procedure. If, however, any of the mouse buttons is currently pressed down (that is, the user is dragging the mouse), the remaining statements in the procedure are executed.

The next block of code is a series of four `IF` statements:

```
IF row < gPrevY
   form.Tego3DVR1.Command = "Step"
ENDIF
IF row > gPrevY
  form.Tego3DVR1.Command = "Back"
ENDIF
IF col < gPrevX
   form.Tego3DVR1.Angle = form.Tego3DVR1.Angle + 3
ENDIF
IF col > gPrevX
   form.Tego3DVR1.Angle = form.Tego3DVR1.Angle - 3
ENDIF
```

These `IF` statements use the `gPrevX` and `gPrevY` global variables and the `col` and `row` parameters of the `PAINTBOX1_OnMouseMove()` procedure to determine in which direction the user moved the mouse. Recall that you declared and initialized `gPrevX` and `gPrevY` in the `Form_OnOpen` procedure. `gPrevX` and `gPrevY` hold the previous x,y position of the mouse. `col` and `row` (the second and third parameters of the `PAINTBOX1_OnMouseMove()` procedure) report the current x,y coordinate of the mouse position.

The preceding `If` statements change the user's position in the 3D floor based on the new position of the mouse. If the user moved the mouse upward, `row` (the current y position of the mouse) will be less than `gPrevY` (the previous y position of the mouse). If this is the case, the first `IF` condition will be satisfied, and the statement

```
form.Tego3DVR1.Command = "Step"
```

will be executed. This statement uses the `Step` command of the 3D virtual reality control to move the user forward in the current viewing direction.

If the user moved the mouse downward, `row` (the current y position of the mouse) will be greater than `gPrevY` (the previous y position of the mouse). If this is the case, the second `IF` condition will be satisfied, and the statement

```
form.Tego3DVR1.Command = "Back"
```

will be executed. This statement uses the `Back` command of the 3D virtual reality control to move the user backward in the current viewing direction.

If the user dragged the mouse to the left, `col` (the current x position of the mouse) will be less than `gPrevX` (the previous x position of the mouse). If this is the case, the third `If` condition will be satisfied, and the statement

```
form.Tego3DVR1.Angle = form.Tego3DVR1.Angle + 3
```

will be executed. This statement increases the Angle property of the 3D virtual reality control by 3 degrees.

If the user dragged the mouse to the right, `col` (the current x position of the mouse) will be greater than `gPrevX` (the previous x position of the mouse). If this is the case, the fourth `IF` condition will be satisfied, and the statement

```
form.Tego3DVR1.Angle = form.Tego3DVR1.Angle - 3
```

will be executed. This statement decreases the Angle property of the 3D virtual reality control by 3 degrees.

The next statement you typed in the `PAINTBOX1_OnMouseMove()` procedure is this:

```
form.Tego3DVR1.Command = "Display3D"
```

This statement uses the `Display3D` command of the 3D virtual reality control to display the 3D view that corresponds to the new position of the user.

Finally, the last two statements in the procedure update the `gPrevX` and `gPrevY` global variables:

```
gPrevX = col
gPrevY = row
```

On the next mouse movement, therefore, the `PAINTBOX1_OnMouseMove()` procedure will know the previous x and y positions of the mouse.

To see the code you attached to the `OnMouseMove` event of the PAINTBOX1 paintbox control in action, follow these steps:

- ☐ Execute the 3D Floor program by pressing the F2 key.
- ☐ Use the mouse (by dragging it forward, backward, to the left, and to the right) to move to various locations on the floor.
- ☐ Terminate the 3D Floor program by pressing Alt+F4 on your keyboard (or by double-clicking the minus icon at the upper-left corner of the program's window).

Summary

In this chapter you have written a 3D virtual reality program called 3D Floor that uses the 3D virtual reality VBX control. As you have seen, writing a program with the 3D virtual reality VBX control is easy. Basically, all you have to do is design a 2D floor file (FLR file). The 3D virtual reality control will convert your 2D FLR file to a 3D picture and will enable the user to move within this 3D picture.

In the next chapter you'll enhance the 3D Floor program—you'll add sprites (stationary sprites and moving sprites) to the 3D floor.

Q&A

Q The floor file (FLR file) that the 3D Floor file is using (the FLOOR50.FLR file) has in it several cells with the letters A and B. As was discussed in this chapter, these letters are supposed to represent sprites. So why didn't I see any sprites when I traveled on the floor?

A As was discussed in this chapter, in addition to 1s and spaces, a floor file can also contain non-numeric characters (for example, A, B, C, a, b, c). These characters represent sprites. The pictures of these sprites are set during runtime from within your program. For example, your program might set the B sprite to a picture of a chair. Therefore, all cells in the FLR file that contain the B letter will display a chair. The reason you do not see any sprites when you travel on the floor at this point is that you have not yet written the code that loads the pictures of the sprites. You will write this code in the next chapter.

Q In the visual implementation of the 3DFloor.WFM form, I was instructed to place a timer control in the form and to set the properties of this timer control. In this chapter, however, I was not instructed to attach any code to the timer control. Why?

A You'll be instructed to attach code to the timer control in the next chapter. As you'll see, the code you will attach to the timer control is responsible for animating the sprites.

Quiz

1. Assume that you have a form that contains a 3D virtual reality control whose name is Tego3DVR1 and a paintbox control whose name is PAINTBOX1. What do the following statements do?

```
form.Tego3DVR1.FileName = "C:\FLOORS\MyFloor.FLR"
form.Tego3DVR1.hWndDisplay = form.Paintbox1.hWnd
form.Tego3DVR1.NumOfRows = 10
form.Tego3DVR1.NumOfCols = 20
form.Tego3DVR1.Command = "Open"
```

2. Assume that you have a form that contains a 3D virtual reality control whose name is Tego3DVR1. What do the following statements do?

```
form.Tego3DVR1.PixelPosX = 4 * form.Tego3DVR1.CellWidth
form.Tego3DVR1.PixelPosY = 5 * form.Tego3DVR1.CellWidth
form.Tego3DVR1.Angle = 0
```

3. Assume that you have a form that contains a 3D virtual reality control whose name is Tego3DVR1. What does the following statement do?

```
form.Tego3DVR1.StepSize = 50
```

4. Assume that you have a form that contains a 3D virtual reality control whose name is Tego3DVR1. What does the following statement do?

```
form.Tego3DVR1.Command = "Display3D"
```

5. Assume that you have a form that contains a 3D virtual reality control whose name is Tego3DVR1. What do the following statements do?

```
form.Tego3DVR1.Command = "Step"
form.Tego3DVR1.Command = "Display3D"
```

6. Assume that you have a form that contains a 3D virtual reality control whose name is Tego3DVR1. What do the following statements do?

```
form.Tego3DVR1.Command = "Back"
form.Tego3DVR1.Command = "Display3D"
```

Exercise

Assume that you have a form that contains a 3D virtual reality control whose name is Tego3DVR1 and a paintbox control whose name is PAINTBOX1. Write the code that performs the following tasks:

- ☐ Opens the floor file C:\MYDIR\MyFloor.FLR. Assume that the width of the MyFloor.FLR file is 30 cells and the height of the MyFloor.FLR file is 40 cells.
- ☐ Places the user at the cell that is second from the bottom of the floor and third from the left side of the floor.
- ☐ Sets the viewing direction of the user to 0 degrees.

Quiz Answers

1. The statements

```
form.Tego3DVR1.FileName = "C:\FLOORS\MyFloor.FLR"
form.Tego3DVR1.hWndDisplay = form.Paintbox1.hWnd
form.Tego3DVR1.NumOfRows = 10
form.Tego3DVR1.NumOfCols = 20
form.Tego3DVR1.Command = "Open"
```

open the floor file C:\FLOORS\MyFloor.FLR. The height of this floor file is 10 cells, and the width of this floor file is 20 cells.

Because the second statement in the preceding code sets the hWndDisplay property of the 3D virtual reality control to the hWnd property of the PAINTBOX1 paintbox control, the 3D picture of the floor will be displayed in the PAINTBOX1 paintbox control.

2. The statements

   ```
   form.Tego3DVR1.PixelPosX = 4 * form.Tego3DVR1.CellWidth
   form.Tego3DVR1.PixelPosY = 5 * form.Tego3DVR1.CellWidth
   form.Tego3DVR1.Angle = 0
   ```

   set the position and viewing angle of the user on the floor. The first two statements place the user at the cell that is fourth from the left side of the floor and fifth from the bottom of the floor. And the third statement sets the viewing direction of the user to 0 degrees.

3. The statement

   ```
   form.Tego3DVR1.StepSize = 50
   ```

   sets the StepSize property of the 3D virtual reality control to 50. This means that subsequent `Step` and `Back` commands that will be issued to the 3D virtual reality control will move the user in steps of 50 pixels.

4. The statement

   ```
   form.Tego3DVR1.Command = "Display3D"
   ```

   displays the current 3D view of the floor.

5. The first statement:

   ```
   form.Tego3DVR1.Command = "Step"
   ```

   moves the user forward in the current viewing direction. The user is moved forward by the amount specified by the StepSize property.

   The second statement:

   ```
   form.Tego3DVR1.Command = "Display3D"
   ```

   displays the 3D view that corresponds to the new position of the user.

6. The first statement:

   ```
   form.Tego3DVR1.Command = "Back"
   ```

   moves the user backward in the current viewing direction. The user is moved backward by the amount specified by the StepSize property.

   The second statement:

   ```
   form.Tego3DVR1.Command = "Display3D"
   ```

   displays the 3D view that corresponds to the new position of the user.

Exercise Answer

The following code opens the C:\MYDIR\MyFloor.FLR floor file, sets the position of the user on the floor, and sets the viewing direction of the user. The width of the floor file is assumed to be 30 cells, and the height of the floor file is assumed to be 40 cells:

```
* Open the MyFloor.FLR file.
form.Tego3DVR1.FileName = "C:\MyDir\MyFloor.FLR"
form.Tego3DVR1.hWndDisplay = form.Paintbox1.hWnd
form.Tego3DVR1.NumOfRows = 40
form.Tego3DVR1.NumOfCols = 30
form.Tego3DVR1.Command = "Open"

* If the FLR file could not be opened, terminate
* the program.
OpenResult = form.Tego3DVR1.ErrorCode
If OpenResult <> 0
   Message="Unable to open file: "+form.Tego3DVR1.FileName
   Message=Message + Chr(13) + Chr(10)
   Message=Message + "Error Code: " + Str(OpenResult)
   MsgBox (Message, "Error")
   form.Close()
EndIf

* Set the initial user's position and viewing angle.
form.Tego3DVR1.PixelPosX = 3 * form.Tego3DVR1.CellWidth
form.Tego3DVR1.PixelPosY = 2 * form.Tego3DVR1.CellWidth
form.Tego3DVR1.Angle = 0
```

WEEK
3

21

3D Virtual Reality: Part II

In this chapter you'll enhance the 3D Floor program you wrote in the preceding chapter—you'll add sprites (stationary sprites as well as moving sprites) to the 3D floor.

What Is a Sprite?

Before you add sprites to the 3D Floor program, you need to know the answer to the question What is a sprite?

A sprite is similar to a regular picture. Unlike a regular picture, however, a sprite has a transparency feature that makes it superior to a regular picture. This means that the sprite has transparent sections. Whatever background is displayed behind the transparent sections of the sprite is not erased.

To illustrate the transparency feature of a sprite, consider the following example.

Suppose that you have two pictures: a picture of a bus (see Figure 21.1) and a picture of a road with trees next to it (see Figure 21.2).

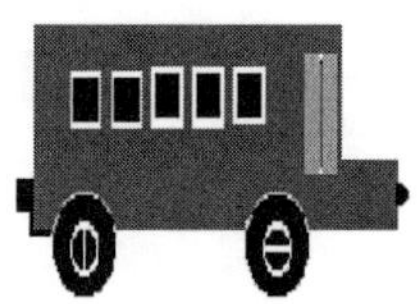

Figure 21.1.
A picture of a bus.

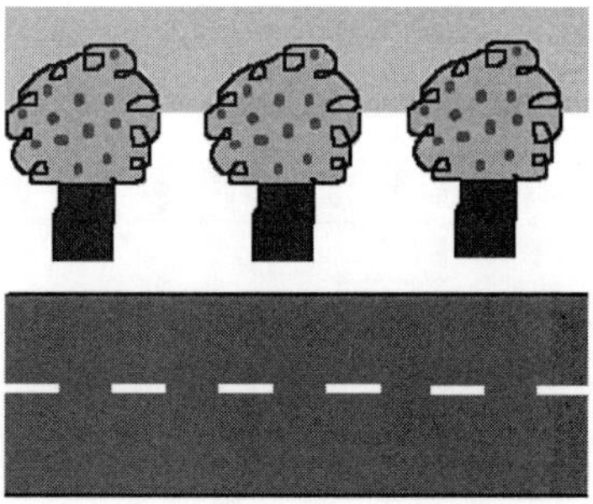

Figure 21.2.
A picture of a road with trees next to it.

Now say that you want to write a program that uses the two pictures. Your program will display the picture of the bus over the picture of the road and trees. That is, the picture of the road and trees will serve as the background picture for the picture of the bus. Your program can then move the picture of the bus to create the illusion that the bus is moving on the road.

If you try to implement such a program with standard pictures, you will have a problem: A regular picture does not have a transparency feature. So when you place the picture of the bus over the picture of the road, the parts of the bus that should be transparent will hide the background. This problem is shown in Figure 21.3.

Figure 21.3.
Displaying a picture of a bus over a picture of a road (using standard pictures).

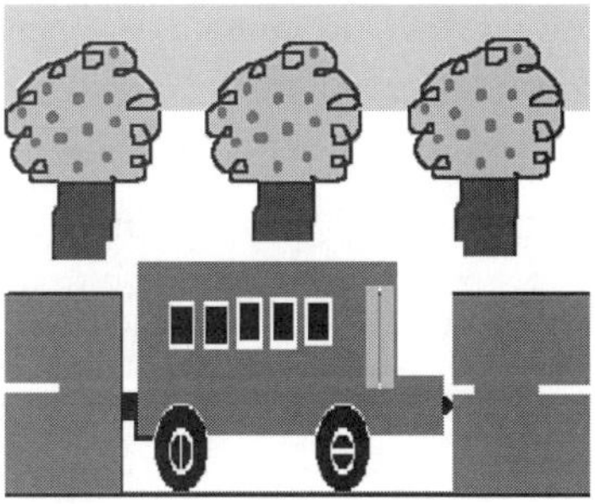

As shown in Figure 21.3, the bus picture does not have any transparent sections. As a result, the picture of the bus completely erases the section of the background picture (the picture of the road) that overlaps the picture of the bus.

If, however, instead of using two standard pictures you use two sprites, the picture that would result when you placed the bus sprite over the road picture would look like the one shown in Figure 21.4.

Figure 21.4.
Displaying a sprite picture of a bus over a picture of a road.

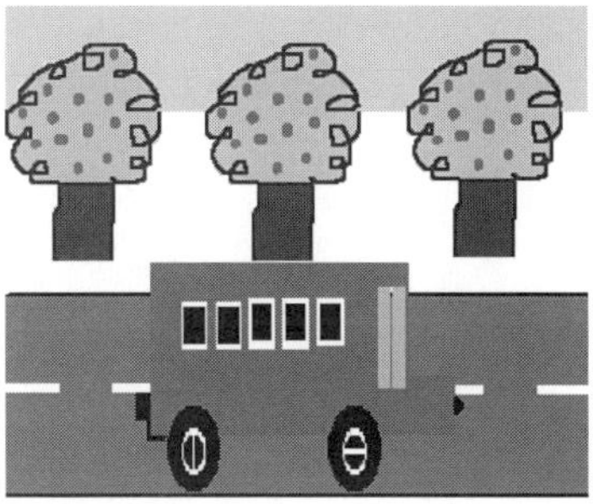

As shown in Figure 21.4, the problem is solved! Now the portion under the transparent parts of the bus sprite is not erased. Your program can now move the bus sprite over the road picture, and the illusion of a moving bus will be achieved.

To summarize, the sprite is similar to a regular picture. Unlike a regular picture, however, the sprite has a transparency feature.

Preparing BMP Files for a Sprite

A sprite has two BMP files associated with it:

- The bitmap file of the sprite
- The mask bitmap file of the sprite

The bitmap file of the sprite contains the picture of the sprite. This is the actual picture displayed onscreen.

The mask bitmap file of the sprite specifies which sections of the sprite picture are transparent and which sections are not transparent. The mask bitmap file has only two colors: white and black. The white sections of the mask bitmap are the nontransparent sections of the sprite, and the black sections of the mask bitmap are the transparent sections of the sprite.

For example, one of the sprites that the 3D Floor program uses is a Tree sprite. The two bitmap files of this Tree sprite are shown in Figures 21.5 and 21.6.

Figure 21.5.
The bitmap file of the Tree sprite used by the 3D Floor program.

Figure 21.6.
The mask bitmap file of the Tree sprite used by the 3D Floor program.

As you can see, the mask bitmap has only two colors: white and black. The white sections represent the nontransparent sections of the sprite, and the black sections represent the transparent sections of the sprite.

The sprite and mask BMP files you create for the 3D virtual reality VBX control must be 256-color BMP files. The name of the mask BMP file of a sprite you create for the 3D virtual reality VBX control must be the same as the filename of the sprite bitmap filename prefixed with the letter M. For example, if the sprite bitmap filename is MyPic.BMP, the mask bitmap filename must be MMyPic.BMP. The sprite BMP file and the mask BMP file must reside in the same directory.

Note: When you create the two BMP files for a sprite for the 3D virtual reality VBX control, follow these steps:

- ☐ Use any painting program that can create 256-color BMP files (for example, Paintbrush).
- ☐ Before drawing the picture of the sprite, set the width and height of the BMP file. Make the width and height of the bitmap so that your picture will fit inside it. (In Paintbrush you set the height and width of the BMP file by selecting Image Attributes from the Options menu.)
- ☐ Draw the picture.
- ☐ Select Save As from the File menu, and save the BMP file as a 256-color BMP file. Name the BMP file with any name you want (for example, MyPic.BMP), but do not use more than seven letters for the filename.

Next, you must create the mask BMP file:

- ☐ Select Save As from the File menu again, but this time name the BMP file as M*xxxx*.BMP (in which *xxxx* is the name of the first BMP file you created). For example, if the name of the first BMP file is MyPic.BMP, the name of the mask BMP file should be MMyPic.BMP.
- ☐ Use the tools of your painting program to fill all the areas of the picture you want to be transparent with the black color, and all the areas you want to be nontransparent with the white color.
- ☐ Save the bitmap as a 256-color BMP file.

Loading the Sprites of the 3D Floor Program

Recall from the preceding chapter that the 3D Floor program should contain several sprites (two trees, a light fixture, a jogger, and an exercising woman). In this section, you'll write the code that loads these sprites.

Before you write the code that loads these sprites, you must copy the BMP files of these sprites to your hard drive:

- ☐ Copy all the BMP files from the \DBPROG\CH20 directory of the disk you can order to accompany this book onto your hard drive C:\DBPROG\CH20 directory.

Your C:\DBPROG\CH20 directory should now contain the following BMP files:

- TREE.BMP—the bitmap file of the Tree sprite.
- MTREE.BMP—the mask bitmap file of the Tree sprite.
- LIGHT.BMP—the bitmap file of the Light Fixture sprite.
- MLIGHT.BMP—the mask bitmap file of the Light Fixture sprite.
- JOG1.BMP—the bitmap file of frame 1 of the Jogger sprite when the jogger is running toward the user.
- MJOG1.BMP—the mask bitmap file of frame 1 of the Jogger sprite when the jogger is running toward the user.
- JOG2.BMP—the bitmap file of frame 2 of the Jogger sprite when the jogger is running toward the user.
- MJOG2.BMP—the mask bitmap file of frame 2 of the Jogger sprite when the jogger is running toward the user.
- JOG3.BMP—the bitmap file of frame 1 of the Jogger sprite when the jogger is running away from the user.
- MJOG3.BMP—the mask bitmap file of frame 1 of the Jogger sprite when the jogger is running away from the user.
- JOG4.BMP—the bitmap file of frame 2 of the Jogger sprite when the jogger is running away from the user.
- MJOG4.BMP—the mask bitmap file of frame 2 of the Jogger sprite when the jogger is running away from the user.
- EX1.BMP—the bitmap file of frame 1 of the Exercising Woman sprite.
- MEX1.BMP—the mask bitmap file of frame 1 of the Exercising Woman sprite.
- EX2.BMP—the bitmap file of frame 2 of the Exercising Woman sprite.
- MEX2.BMP—the mask bitmap file of frame 2 of the Exercising Woman sprite.

Now that you have all the necessary BMP files for the sprites, it's time to write the code that loads these sprites. You'll write this code in the `Form_OnOpen` procedure of the 3D Floor.WFM form.

☐ Insert the following statements at the beginning of the `Form_OnOpen` procedure of the 3D Floor.WFM form:

```
* Declare and initialize global variables for the
* sprites animation.
Public gExerciseFrame, gJoggerY, gJoggerFrame
gExerciseFrame = 0
gJoggerY = 0
gJoggerFrame= 0
```

- [ ] Insert the following statements at the end of the `Form_OnOpen` procedure of the 3D Floor.WFM form:

```
* Load the sprites.
form.Tego3DVR1.SpritePath = Path
form.Tego3DVR1.SpriteNumber = 65
form.Tego3DVR1.SpriteFileName = "TREE.BMP"
form.Tego3DVR1.SpriteNumber = 66
form.Tego3DVR1.SpriteFileName = "LIGHT.BMP"
form.Tego3DVR1.SpriteNumber = 67
form.Tego3DVR1.SpriteFileName = "EX1.BMP"
form.Tego3DVR1.SpriteNumber = 68
form.Tego3DVR1.SpriteFileName = "EX2.BMP"
form.Tego3DVR1.SpriteNumber = 69
form.Tego3DVR1.SpriteFileName = "JOG1.BMP"
form.Tego3DVR1.SpriteNumber = 70
form.Tego3DVR1.SpriteFileName = "JOG2.BMP"
form.Tego3DVR1.SpriteNumber = 71
form.Tego3DVR1.SpriteFileName = "JOG3.BMP"
form.Tego3DVR1.SpriteNumber = 72
form.Tego3DVR1.SpriteFileName = "JOG4.BMP"

* Set sprite number 66 (the Light sprite)
* as a soft sprite
* (i.e., the user can walk through this sprite).
form.Tego3DVR1.SpriteNumber = 66
form.Tego3DVR1.Command = "SetSpriteSoft"
```

After you insert these statements into the `Form_OnOpen` procedure, the complete listing of the `Form_OnOpen` procedure should look as follows:

```
Procedure Form_OnOpen

* Declare and initialize global variables for the
* sprites animation.
Public gExerciseFrame, gJoggerY, gJoggerFrame
gExerciseFrame = 0
gJoggerY = 0
gJoggerFrame= 0

* Declare and initialize global variables.
Public gPrevX, gPrevY
gPrevX = 0
gPrevY = 0

* Make the Tego3DVR1 control invisible.
form.Tego3DVR1.Visible = .F.

* Get the name of the directory where the
* program resides.
Path = LEFT(PROGRAM(0),RAT("\",PROGRAM(0)))

* Open the FLOOR50.FLR file.
form.Tego3DVR1.FileName = Path + "FLOOR50.FLR"
form.Tego3DVR1.hWndDisplay = form.Paintbox1.hWnd
```

```
form.Tego3DVR1.NumOfRows = 50
form.Tego3DVR1.NumOfCols = 50
form.Tego3DVR1.Command = "Open"

* If the FLR file could not be opened, terminate
* the program.
OpenResult = form.Tego3DVR1.ErrorCode
If OpenResult <> 0
    Message = "Unable to open file: " + form.Tego3DVR1.FileName
    Message = Message + Chr(13) + Chr(10)
    Message = Message + "Error Code: " + Str(OpenResult)
    MsgBox (Message, "Error")
    form.Close()
EndIf

* Set the initial user's position and viewing angle.
form.Tego3DVR1.PixelPosX = 4 * form.Tego3DVR1.CellWidth
form.Tego3DVR1.PixelPosY = 4 * form.Tego3DVR1.CellWidth
form.Tego3DVR1.Angle = 0

* Set the StepSize property to 50.
form.Tego3DVR1.StepSize = 50

* Set the colors of the walls, ceiling, and floor.
form.Tego3DVR1.WallColorA = 7    && White
form.Tego3DVR1.WallColorB = 4    && Red
form.Tego3DVR1.CeilingColor = 11 && Light Cyan
form.Tego3DVR1.FloorColor = 2    && Green
form.Tego3DVR1.StripeColor = 0   && Black

* Load the sprites.
form.Tego3DVR1.SpritePath = Path
form.Tego3DVR1.SpriteNumber = 65
form.Tego3DVR1.SpriteFileName = "TREE.BMP"
form.Tego3DVR1.SpriteNumber = 66
form.Tego3DVR1.SpriteFileName = "LIGHT.BMP"
form.Tego3DVR1.SpriteNumber = 67
form.Tego3DVR1.SpriteFileName = "EX1.BMP"
form.Tego3DVR1.SpriteNumber = 68
form.Tego3DVR1.SpriteFileName = "EX2.BMP"
form.Tego3DVR1.SpriteNumber = 69
form.Tego3DVR1.SpriteFileName = "JOG1.BMP"
form.Tego3DVR1.SpriteNumber = 70
form.Tego3DVR1.SpriteFileName = "JOG2.BMP"
form.Tego3DVR1.SpriteNumber = 71
form.Tego3DVR1.SpriteFileName = "JOG3.BMP"
form.Tego3DVR1.SpriteNumber = 72
form.Tego3DVR1.SpriteFileName = "JOG4.BMP"

* Set sprite number 66 (the Light sprite)
* as a soft sprite
* (i.e., the user can walk through this sprite).
form.Tego3DVR1.SpriteNumber = 66
form.Tego3DVR1.Command = "SetSpriteSoft"

Return
```

The code you've just added to the Form_OnOpen procedure will be examined next.

The statements you inserted at the beginning of the Form_OnOpen procedure declare and initialize several global variables:

```
* Declare and initialize global variables for the
* sprites animation.
Public gExerciseFrame, gJoggerY, gJoggerFrame
gExerciseFrame = 0
gJoggerY = 0
gJoggerFrame= 0
```

These variables are used by the code that performs the sprite animation. You'll write the code that performs the sprite animation later in this chapter.

The statements you inserted at the end of the Form_OnOpen procedure are responsible for loading the sprites and setting the Light Fixture sprite as a soft sprite.

The first 17 statements are responsible for loading the sprites:

```
* Load the sprites.
form.Tego3DVR1.SpritePath = Path
form.Tego3DVR1.SpriteNumber = 65
form.Tego3DVR1.SpriteFileName = "TREE.BMP"
form.Tego3DVR1.SpriteNumber = 66
form.Tego3DVR1.SpriteFileName = "LIGHT.BMP"
form.Tego3DVR1.SpriteNumber = 67
form.Tego3DVR1.SpriteFileName = "EX1.BMP"
form.Tego3DVR1.SpriteNumber = 68
form.Tego3DVR1.SpriteFileName = "EX2.BMP"
form.Tego3DVR1.SpriteNumber = 69
form.Tego3DVR1.SpriteFileName = "JOG1.BMP"
form.Tego3DVR1.SpriteNumber = 70
form.Tego3DVR1.SpriteFileName = "JOG2.BMP"
form.Tego3DVR1.SpriteNumber = 71
form.Tego3DVR1.SpriteFileName = "JOG3.BMP"
form.Tego3DVR1.SpriteNumber = 72
form.Tego3DVR1.SpriteFileName = "JOG4.BMP"
```

The first statement:

```
form.Tego3DVR1.SpritePath = Path
```

sets the SpritePath property of the 3D virtual reality control to the value of the local variable Path. Recall that the Path variable is filled with the name of the directory where the program resides (see the code at the beginning of the Form_OnOpen procedure). So the preceding statement sets the SpritePath property of the 3D virtual reality control to the name of the directory where the program resides.

21

As implied by its name, the SpritePath property of the 3D virtual reality control specifies in which directory the Sprite control will look for the BMP files of the sprites.

These are the second and third statements:

```
form.Tego3DVR1.SpriteNumber = 65
form.Tego3DVR1.SpriteFileName = "TREE.BMP"
```

These two statements define sprite number 65 of the 3D virtual reality control as the sprite whose BMP file is TREE.BMP and whose mask BMP file is MTREE.BMP. Note that in the preceding statement the name MTREE.BMP was not specified. The 3D virtual reality control knows that the mask BMP file is MTREE.BMP by simply prefixing TREE.BMP with an M.

Note: When you define a sprite in the 3D virtual reality control, you have to specify only the bitmap file of the sprite. The mask bitmap filename of the sprite is always the bitmap filename of the sprite prefixed with an M. For example, the two statements

```
form.Tego3DVR1.SpriteNumber = 65
form.Tego3DVR1.SpriteFileName = "DOG.BMP"
```

define sprite number 65 of the 3D virtual reality control as the sprite whose BMP file is DOG.BMP and whose mask BMP file is MDOG.BMP.

The preceding statement defines sprite number 65 as the Tree sprite. Why was the number 65 used for the Tree sprite? The number 65 is the ASCII code for the letter A. Therefore, by defining sprite number 65 as the Tree sprite, you are telling the 3D virtual reality control to display the Tree sprite wherever the letter A appears in the floor file. For example, in the FLOOR50.FLR file one of the rooms contains the letter A in two of its corners (refer to Figure 20.54 in the preceding chapter). Therefore, when the user moves into this room, the user will see a tree in each of these corners.

Here are the next 14 statements:

```
form.Tego3DVR1.SpriteNumber = 66
form.Tego3DVR1.SpriteFileName = "LIGHT.BMP"
form.Tego3DVR1.SpriteNumber = 67
form.Tego3DVR1.SpriteFileName = "EX1.BMP"
form.Tego3DVR1.SpriteNumber = 68
form.Tego3DVR1.SpriteFileName = "EX2.BMP"
form.Tego3DVR1.SpriteNumber = 69
form.Tego3DVR1.SpriteFileName = "JOG1.BMP"
form.Tego3DVR1.SpriteNumber = 70
form.Tego3DVR1.SpriteFileName = "JOG2.BMP"
form.Tego3DVR1.SpriteNumber = 71
form.Tego3DVR1.SpriteFileName = "JOG3.BMP"
form.Tego3DVR1.SpriteNumber = 72
form.Tego3DVR1.SpriteFileName = "JOG4.BMP"
```

As you can see, these statements define the other sprites used by the program. For example, the two statements

```
form.Tego3DVR1.SpriteNumber = 66
form.Tego3DVR1.SpriteFileName = "LIGHT.BMP"
```

define sprite number 66 as the sprite whose BMP file is LIGHT.BMP and whose mask BMP file is MLIGHT.BMP. The number 66 is the ASCII code for the letter B. Therefore, when the 3D virtual reality control encounters the letter B in the FLOOR50.FLR floor file, the Light Fixture sprite will be displayed.

These are the last two statements you added to the `Form_OnOpen` procedure:

```
form.Tego3DVR1.SpriteNumber = 66
form.Tego3DVR1.Command = "SetSpriteSoft"
```

These statements use the `SetSpriteSoft` command of the 3D virtual reality control to set sprite number 66 (the Light Fixture sprite) as a soft sprite. As discussed in the preceding chapter, a soft sprite is a sprite that the user can walk through.

Note: By default, a sprite is a hard sprite (that is, the user cannot walk through it). To make a sprite soft, you must use the `SetSpriteSoft` command of the 3D virtual reality control. For example, the following two statements set sprite number 65 to a soft sprite:

```
form.Tego3DVR1.SpriteNumber = 65
form.Tego3DVR1.Command = "SetSpriteSoft"
```

In some programs you might find it useful to make a certain sprite sometimes soft and other times hard. To make a soft sprite hard, you must use the `SetSpriteHard` command. For example, the following statement sets sprite number 65 to a hard sprite:

```
form.Tego3DVR1.SpriteNumber = 65
form.Tego3DVR1.Command = "SetSpriteHard"
```

To see in action the code you added to the `Form_OnOpen` procedure, follow these steps:

- ☐ Execute the 3D Floor program.
- ☐ Move to the room where the Light Fixture sprite (sprite B) is located, and verify that the Light Fixture is there.
- ☐ Verify that the Light Fixture sprite is a soft sprite. That is, try to walk through the Light Fixture sprite.
- ☐ Move to the room where the two Tree sprites (sprite A) are located, and verify that the two trees are there.

- Terminate the 3D Floor program by pressing Alt+F4 on your keyboard (or by double-clicking the minus icon at the upper-left corner of the program's window).

Note that at this point, the Jogger sprite and the Exercising Woman sprite do not appear inside the floor. That's because the FLOOR50.FLR file does not contain cells with the letters that represent these sprites. In the following section you'll write the code that displays the Jogger and Exercising Woman sprites. This code will animate the Jogger and Exercising Woman sprites.

Animating the Jogger and Exercising Woman Sprites

Unlike the Tree and Light Fixture sprites, the Jogger and Exercising Woman sprites are moving sprites. That is, when the user looks at these sprites, the sprites appear to be moving.

The illusion of a moving sprite is accomplished by the animation of several frames. That is, the program displays several frames (one after the other). Each frame shows the character that is being animated (for example, the jogger) in a slightly different position. For example, the two frames used for the animation of the Jogger when the jogger moves toward the user are shown in Figure 21.7.

Figure 21.7.
The two frames used for the animation of the jogger when the jogger moves toward the user.

You'll now write the code that is responsible for the animation of the Jogger and Exercising Woman sprites. You'll attach the code that accomplishes these tasks to the `OnTimer` event of the timer control. Recall that during the visual implementation of the 3D Floor.WFM form, you set the Seconds property of the timer control to 0.4. The code you'll now attach to the `OnTimer` event of the timer control will therefore be executed every 0.4 second.

☐ Attach the following code to the OnTimer event of the DBTIMER1 timer control. After you write this code, the DBTIMER1_OnTimer procedure should look as follows:

```
Procedure DBTIMER1_OnTimer

* Display the next frame of the exercising woman
* (inside the cell at coordinate x=10, y=40).
* Frame 0 of the exercising woman is sprite
* number 67. And frame 1 of the exercising woman is
* sprite number 68.
IF gExerciseFrame = 0
   gExerciseFrame = 1
   form.SetCell(10, 40, 67)
ELSE
   gExerciseFrame = 0
   form.SetCell(10, 40, 68)
ENDIF

* Set the cell of the previous jogger position
* to an empty cell.
IF gJoggerY <> 0
   form.SetCell(23, gJoggerY, 0)
ENDIF

* If the jogger has reached the end of the hall,
* reset JoggerY to 0.
IF gJoggerY = 48
   gJoggerY = 0
ENDIF

* Increment JoggerY.
gJoggerY = gJoggerY + 1

* Set JoggerFrame to the next frame number.
IF gJoggerFrame = 0
   gJoggerFrame = 1
ELSE
   gJoggerFrame = 0
ENDIF

* If the user is facing the jogger, show the front
* of the jogger (sprites 69 and 70). Otherwise, show
* the back of the jogger (sprites 71 and 72).
If form.Tego3DVR1.CellPosY >= gJoggerY
   If gJoggerFrame = 0
      form.SetCell(23, gJoggerY, 69)
   Else
      form.SetCell(23, gJoggerY, 70)
   EndIf
Else
   If gJoggerFrame = 0
      form.SetCell(23, gJoggerY, 71)
   Else
      form.SetCell(23, gJoggerY, 72)
```

```
      EndIf
   EndIf

   * Display the 3D view.
   form.Tego3DVR1.Command = "Display3D"

   Return
```

- ☐ Save your work by selecting Save from the File menu.

The `DBTIMER1_OnTimer` procedure uses the global variables `gExerciseFrame`, `gJoggerY`, and `gJoggerFrame`. Recall that you declared and initialized these global variables in the `Form_OnOpen` procedure. As you'll soon see, `gExerciseFrame` stores the current frame number of the Exercising Woman animation. `gJoggerY` stores the current y position of the jogger as the jogger moves in the main hall of the floor. And `gJoggerFrame` stores the current frame number of the Jogger animation.

The first block of code you typed in the `DBTIMER1_OnTimer` procedure is an `If…Else` statement:

```
IF gExerciseFrame = 0
   gExerciseFrame = 1
   form.SetCell(10, 40, 67)
ELSE
   gExerciseFrame = 0
   form.SetCell(10, 40, 68)
ENDIF
```

This `If…Else` statement is responsible for animating the Exercising Woman sprite. In each iteration of the `DBTIMER1_OnTimer` procedure (that is, every 0.4 second) the preceding `If…Else` statement changes the value of the `gExerciseFrame` global variable. One time `gExerciseFrame` is set to 0, the next time (0.4 seconds later) `gExerciseFrame` is set to 1, the next time `gExerciseFrame` is set back to 0, and so on.

Depending on the current value of `gExerciseFrame`, the preceding `If…Else` statement displays a different sprite of the exercising woman. If `gExerciseFrame` is currently 0, the code under the `If` displays sprite number 67 in the cell whose x,y cell coordinate is x=10,y=40:

```
form.SetCell(10, 40, 67)
```

If, however, the current value of `gExerciseFrame` is 1, the code under the `Else` displays sprite number 68 in the cell whose x,y cell coordinate is x=10,y=40:

```
form.SetCell(10, 40, 68)
```

Therefore, in every execution of the `DBTIMER1_OnTimer` procedure (that is, every 0.4 second), a different frame of the exercising woman is displayed in the cell whose x,y cell coordinate is x=10,y=40. One time sprite number 67 is displayed, the next time sprite number 68 is displayed, the next time sprite number 67 is displayed again, and so on.

> **Note:** In the preceding statements, the `SetCell()` method of the 3D Floor.WFM form is being used. You have not yet written the code of the `SetCell()` method. You will write this code in the next section.

Following is the code responsible for animating the Jogger sprite:

```
* Set the cell of the previous jogger position
* to an empty cell.
IF gJoggerY <> 0
   form.SetCell(23, gJoggerY, 0)
ENDIF

* If the jogger has reached the end of the hall,
* reset JoggerY to 0.
IF gJoggerY = 48
   gJoggerY = 0
ENDIF

* Increment JoggerY.
gJoggerY = gJoggerY + 1

* Set JoggerFrame to the next frame number.
IF gJoggerFrame = 0
   gJoggerFrame = 1
ELSE
   gJoggerFrame = 0
ENDIF

* If the user is facing the jogger, show the front
* of the jogger (sprites 69 and 70). Otherwise, show
* the back of the jogger (sprites 71 and 72).
If form.Tego3DVR1.CellPosY >= gJoggerY
   If gJoggerFrame = 0
      form.SetCell(23, gJoggerY, 69)
   Else
      form.SetCell(23, gJoggerY, 70)
   EndIf
Else
   If gJoggerFrame = 0
      form.SetCell(23, gJoggerY, 71)
   Else
      form.SetCell(23, gJoggerY, 72)
   EndIf
EndIf
```

21

As you can see, the animation code of the Jogger sprite is more involved than the animation code of the Exercising Woman sprite. That's because the jogger does not remain in the same cell. Therefore, in addition to using a global variable that holds the current frame number of the Jogger animation (`gJoggerFrame`), the preceding code also uses the global variable `gJoggerY`. `gJoggerY` holds the current y cell position of the jogger.

In each iteration of the DBTIMER1_OnTimer procedure, the previous cell position of the jogger is set to an empty cell, then gJoggerY is incremented, and the Jogger sprite is displayed in the new y cell position. The x cell position of the jogger is always the same (23).

Depending on the new y position of the user, different sprites of the jogger are animated. If the y cell position of the user is greater than the y cell position of the jogger (that is, the user is facing the jogger), sprites 69 and 70 are animated (sprites 69 and 70 show the jogger facing the user). If, however, the y cell position of the user is less than the y cell position of the jogger (that is, the jogger is running away from the user), sprites 71 and 72 are animated (sprites 71 and 72 show the jogger with his back to the user).

The last statement you typed in the DBTIMER1_OnTimer procedure is this:

```
form.Tego3DVR1.Command = "Display3D"
```

This statement uses the Display3D command of the 3D virtual reality control to display the new 3D view that corresponds to the new status of the Exercising Woman and Jogger sprites.

Adding the *SetCell()* Method to the 3D Floor.WFM Form

The code you attached to the OnTimer event of the timer control uses the SetCell() method to set various cells inside the 3D floor with sprite pictures. You'll now add the SetCell() method to the 3D Floor.WFM form.

Follow these steps to add the SetCell() method to the 3D Floor.WFM form:

- ☐ Display the 3D Floor.WFM form in design mode (that is, type MODIFY FORM ? in the Command window, and then select the 3D Floor.WFM form).
- ☐ Select New Method from the Procedure menu of dBASE.

  dBASE responds by adding a new method to the 3D Floor.WFM form and by displaying the skeleton of the new method in the Procedure Editor window. (See Figure 21.8.)

dBASE named the new method Method. However, you want the name of the new method to be SetCell. You also want the SetCell() method to have three parameters: X, Y, and SpriteNumber. You therefore must change the first line of the new method as shown here:

- ☐ Change the first line of the new method so that it looks like this:

```
Procedure SetCell(X,Y,SpriteNumber)
```

Your Procedure Editor window should now look like the one shown in Figure 21.9.

Figure 21.8.
Adding a new method to the 3D Floor.WFM form.

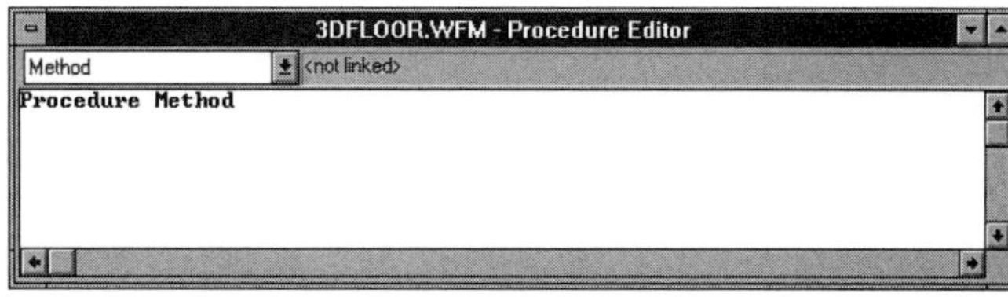

Figure 21.9.
The Procedure Editor window after you set the name and parameters of the new method.

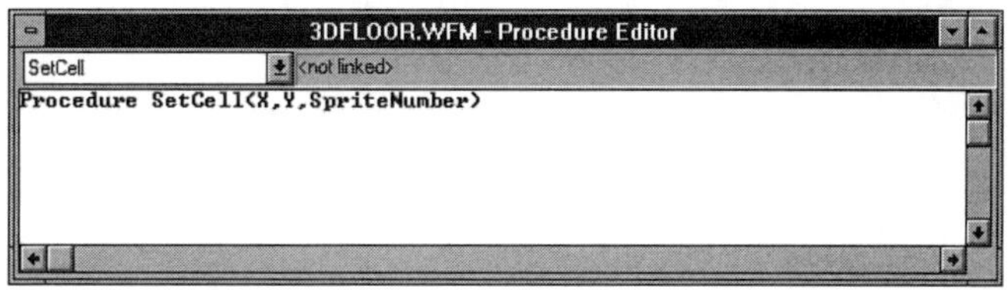

☐ Write code in the `SetCell()` method so that it looks like this:

```
Procedure SetCell(X,Y,SpriteNumber)

form.Tego3DVR1.CellX = X
form.Tego3DVR1.CellY = Y
form.Tego3DVR1.SpriteNumber = SpriteNumber
form.Tego3DVR1.Command = "SetCell"

Return
```

☐ Save your work by selecting Save from the File menu.

The code you wrote in the `SetCell()` method uses the `SetCell` command of the 3D virtual reality control to set the cell whose x,y position is specified by the `X` and `Y` parameters to the sprite whose number is specified by the `SpriteNumber` parameter:

```
form.Tego3DVR1.CellX = X
form.Tego3DVR1.CellY = Y
form.Tego3DVR1.SpriteNumber = SpriteNumber
form.Tego3DVR1.Command = "SetCell"
```

As you can see, before the `SetCell` command is issued, the CellX, CellY, and SpriteNumber properties of the 3D virtual reality control are set. The CellX and CellY properties specify the x,y cell coordinate of the cell you want to set, and the SpriteNumber property specifies the number of the sprite that will be placed in the cell. If the SpriteNumber property is set to 0, the cell will become an empty cell.

To see your sprite animation code in action, follow these steps:

☐ Execute the 3D Floor program.

☐ Move to the main hall of the floor, and verify that the jogger is running across the hall.

- ☐ Move to the room where the woman is exercising, and verify that the exercising woman is there.
- ☐ Terminate the 3D Floor program by pressing Alt+F4 on your keyboard (or by double-clicking the minus icon at the upper-left corner of the program's window).

Adding a Menu to the 3D Floor Program

The virtual reality aspect of the 3D Floor program is now finished. The last thing you must do is attach a menu to the 3D Floor.WFM form. This menu should include the Exit menu item (so that the user will be able to terminate the program easily) and an About menu item.

- ☐ Create a menu (MNU file) for the 3D Floor program that looks like the menu shown in Figures 20.44 and 20.45 in the preceding chapter.
- ☐ Attach the menu file you designed to the 3D Floor.WFM form.
- ☐ Attach code to the menu items of the menu.

If you have forgotten how to design a menu or how to attach a menu to a form, refer to Chapter 6, "Menus."

Summary

In this chapter you have added sprites to the 3D virtual reality program you started writing in the preceding chapter.

As has been demonstrated in this chapter, the 3D virtual reality VBX control enables you to add sprites (stationary sprites and moving sprites) to the 3D floor. A sprite can be hard or soft. A soft sprite (like the Light sprite of the 3D Floor program) is one that the user can walk through. A hard sprite (like the Tree sprites of the 3D Floor program) is one that the user cannot walk through.

You can further enhance the 3D Floor program by adding sound to it. For example, you can write code that plays a particular WAV file (or a particular section of a WAV file) when the user enters a particular room. You can add sound to the 3D Floor program by using the multimedia VBX control discussed in Chapter 18, "Multimedia and Animation."

Q&A

Q How can I write code that detects when the user moves into a particular room or onto a particular section of the floor?

A To write code that detects when the user moves into a particular room or onto a particular section of the floor, you can use the PixelPosX and PixelPosY properties of the 3D virtual reality control, or alternatively, you can use the CellPosX and CellPosY properties of the 3D virtual reality control. The PixelPosX and PixelPosY properties report the current x,y coordinate of the user's current position on the floor in units of pixels. The CellPosX and CellPosY properties report the current x,y coordinate of the user's current position on the floor in units of cells.

Quiz

1. Assume that you have a form that contains a 3D virtual reality control whose name is Tego3DVR1. What does the following statement do?

```
form.Tego3DVR1.SpritePath = "C:\SPRITES\"
```

2. Assume that you have a form that contains a 3D virtual reality control whose name is Tego3DVR1. What do the following statements do?

```
form.Tego3DVR1.SpriteNumber = 65
form.Tego3DVR1.SpriteFileName = "TREE.BMP"
```

3. Assume that you have a form that contains a 3D virtual reality control whose name is Tego3DVR1. What do the following statements do?

```
form.Tego3DVR1.CellX = 10
form.Tego3DVR1.CellY = 20
form.Tego3DVR1.SpriteNumber = 65
form.Tego3DVR1.Command = "SetCell"
```

Exercise

Enhance the 3D Floor program so that the lower-left room of the floor has a Tree sprite in its center.

Quiz Answers

1. The statement

```
form.Tego3DVR1.SpritePath = "C:\SPRITES\"
```

sets the SpritePath property of the Tego3DVR1 3D virtual reality control to the directory name C:\SPRITES\. The SpritePath property specifies in which directory the 3D virtual reality control will look for the BMP files of the sprites.

2. The two statements

```
form.Tego3DVR1.SpriteNumber = 65
form.Tego3DVR1.SpriteFileName = "TREE.BMP"
```

define sprite number 65 of the 3D virtual reality control as the sprite whose BMP file is TREE.BMP and whose mask BMP file is MTREE.BMP. Because the number 65 is the ASCII code for the letter A, by defining sprite number 65 as the Tree sprite, you are telling the 3D virtual reality control to display the Tree sprite wherever the letter A appears in the floor file.

3. The statements

```
form.Tego3DVR1.CellX = 10
form.Tego3DVR1.CellY = 20
form.Tego3DVR1.SpriteNumber = 65
form.Tego3DVR1.Command = "SetCell"
```

use the `SetCell` command of the 3D virtual reality control to fill the cell whose x,y cell coordinate is x=10,y=20 with sprite number 65.

Exercise Answer

To place the Tree sprite in the middle of the lower-left room of the floor, all you have to do is modify the FLOOR50.FLR floor file:

- ☐ Open the FLOOR50.FLR file with any text editor (for example, with the Notepad program of Windows).
- ☐ Delete the space character located in the center of the lower-left room of the floor, and replace it with the A character. (See Figure 21.10.)

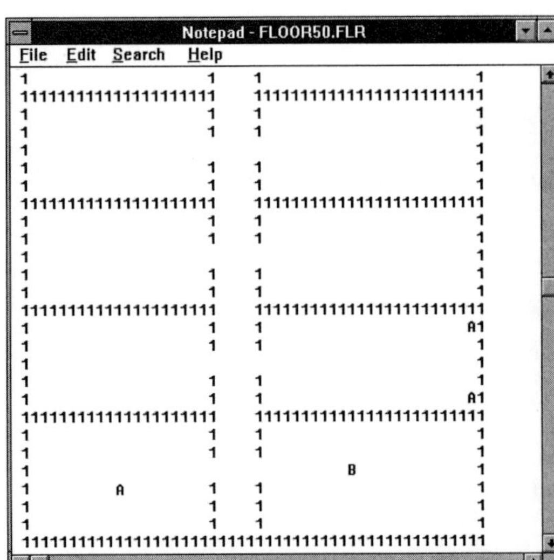

```
Notepad - FLOOR50.FLR
File  Edit  Search  Help
1                   1    1                      1
111111111111111111111    111111111111111111111111
1                   1    1                      1
1                   1    1                      1
1                                               1
1                   1    1                      1
1                   1    1                      1
111111111111111111111    111111111111111111111111
1                   1    1                      1
1                   1    1                      1
1                                               1
1                   1    1                      1
1                   1    1                      1
111111111111111111111    111111111111111111111111
1                   1    1                     A1
1                   1    1                      1
1                                               1
1                   1    1                      1
1                   1    1                     A1
111111111111111111111    111111111111111111111111
1                   1    1                      1
1                   1    1                      1
1                                 B             1
1         A         1    1                      1
1                   1    1                      1
1                   1    1                      1
1111111111111111111111111111111111111111111111111
```

Figure 21.10.
Viewing the bottom section of the FLOOR50.FLR file with Notepad (after you place the A character in the center of the lower-left room of the floor).

Index

Symbols

A

B

C

D

E

F

L

M

N

O

P

T

U

V

W–Z

Book ISBN 0-672-30673-5

Special Disk Offer for *Teach Yourself Visual dBASE 5.5 Programming in 21 Days*

You can order the companion disk of this book directly from TegoSoft, Inc. The companion disk includes

- The full version of the advanced multimedia VBX control
- The full version of the 3D Virtual Reality VBX Control
- The source code of this book's programs

These VBX controls can be incorporated into any programming language that supports VBX controls (for example, Visual dBASE, Delphi, Visual Basic, and Visual C++ 1.5*x*).

As discussed in this book, the TegoMM.VBX advanced multimedia control enables you to write dBASE programs that play WAV files through the PC speaker. If you have a sound card, you can play and record sound files through a sound card, play MIDI files, CD audio, and movie AVI files. You can use the control to detect whether your user has a sound card, and accordingly play the WAV files through a sound card, or through the PC speaker that every PC has. The multimedia control also lets you manipulate WAV files such as add echo, increase/decrease volume, mix and merge WAV files, and change the characteristics of your recording.

As discussed in this book, the virtual reality VBX control (Tego3DVR.VBX) lets you draw 2D drawings and then display the 2D drawings as 3D pictures. You can then let your user "travel" inside the 3D pictures, place static and dynamic sprites in the 3D pictures, and create amazing game programs.

The price of the companion disk is $29.95. Please add $5.00 for shipping and handling. New York State residents please add appropriate sales tax. When ordering from outside the U.S.A., checks or money orders must be in U.S. dollars drawn from a U.S. bank.

To order, send check or money order to:

TegoSoft, Inc.
Attn: TYdBASE 5.5 in 21 Days
Box 389
Bellmore, NY 11710
Phone: (516) 783-4824

Here's a look at just a few of the programs that you'll learn to write while reading *Teach Yourself Visual dBASE 5.5 Programming in 21 Days...*

Create 3D Virtual Reality programs where your user "travels" inside 3D pictures. Also, place animated sprites inside your 3D pictures.

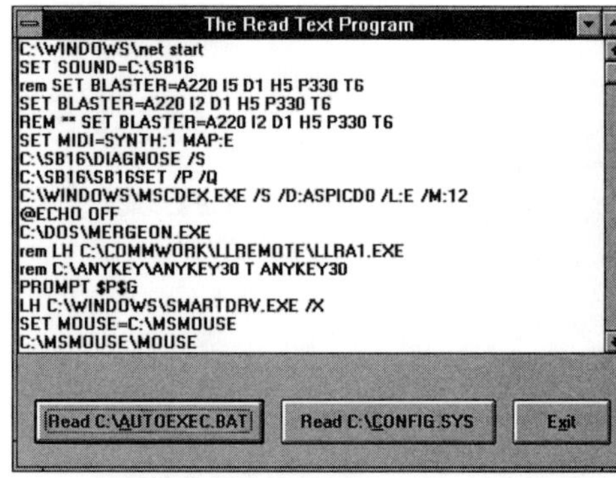

Learn how to access files from within your Visual dBASE programs.

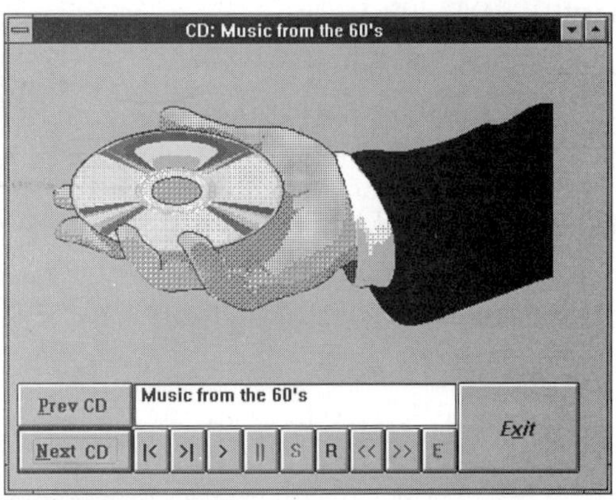

Learn how to play CD audio from within your Visual dBASE programs.

Learn how to write animation programs.

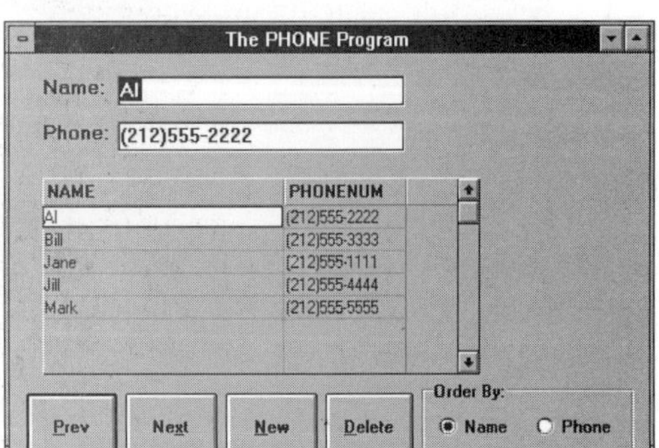

Create a phone book program.

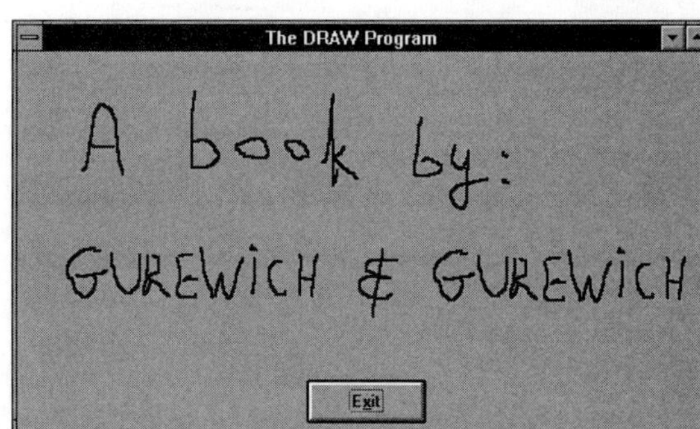

Learn how to create drawing programs.